Alpine Flowers

NORBERT GRIEBL

BLOOMSBURY WILDLIFE
LONDON · OXFORD · NEW YORK · NEW DELHI · SYDNEY

Contents

7	**Foreword**
8	**Introduction**
8	The appeal of alpine flora
9	Plant names
9	Descriptions
10	Similar species
10	Habitat
10	Distribution
10	Note
10	Distribution maps
10	Photographs
10	Plant identification
11	**Alpine regions**
12	**Botanical terms**
16	**How to use this book**

18 Ferns and relatives
('lower' plants/cryptogams/spore-bearing plants)

26 Conifers and relatives
(gymnosperms/naked-seeded plants)

30 Flowering plants, dicotyledons
('higher' plants with 2 cotyledons)

398 Flowering plants, monocotyledons
('higher' plants with 1 cotyledon)

442	Acknowledgements
442	Picture credits
443	Selected reading
446	Index of common names
454	Index of scientific names

Foreword

Rambling in the Alps is one the finest experiences for anyone interested in nature. The landscapes are second to none, the beauty of mountain flowers is hard to match, and this combination often creates an unforgettable picture.

Whoever loves nature and mountains will always return to the Alps to experience the splendour of its flowers. Certain mountains are often visited to find and photograph particular plants, and therefore it is necessary to learn how to recognise the species. For some it is enough just to see the mountain flowers and to enjoy their beauty, though if you photograph them it is satisfying to know what you have found. Naming the flowers you find can develop into a passion to search for and identify more species.

Knowledge of the plants is also important for nature conservation. If we don't know something, then we don't value it, and if we don't value it then we don't protect it. To be effective and enduring, the approach to nature conservation must appeal both to people's minds and hearts. As Norwegian ecologist Arne Naess writes: 'The necessary care flows naturally when the self becomes wider and deeper, so that protecting nature is felt and perceived as protecting ourselves.'

Wandering in the mountains is good for all our senses – healthy for our bodies and liberating for our souls. Alpine plants can never be boring – in their diversity and variety and with their marvellous colours and extraordinary vitality. Even if you have seen and photographed almost all of them, the variability of the individual species and hybrids that may be produced make alpine plants an almost endless playground for nature enthusiasts.

It is unfortunate for those who only see mountaineering as sport and cannot marvel at the abundant beauty in what are often seen as barren mountain landscapes.

I hope observant hikers in beautiful mountain country will enjoy this book.

Norbert Griebl, Stainz (Austria) 2018

Bavarian Gentian, *Gentiana bavarica* var. *subacaulis*, in the Hohe Tauern, Carinthia

Introduction

Roseroot, *Rhodiola rosea*, in the Adamello Group, Italy

THE APPEAL OF ALPINE FLORA

Around 4,500 wild vascular (higher) plants are currently recognised as growing in the alpine regions. Many of these however are found only in the lower sites, some as outliers from the Mediterranean region. In this book we concentrate mostly on plants that are typical of the Alps, that is, with plants growing mainly above the treeline, as well as characteristic species lower down. It should therefore be possible for a hiker to identify correctly all species found in the montane area and at higher altitudes. Grasses however, as the least conspicuous of alpine plants, are only covered superficially. Out of the 111 species of sedge and 67 species of fescue, only the most striking have been included. In total, more than 1,000 species are presented in words and pictures and more than 400 described.

In this book the plants are arranged alphabetically by botanical family, genus and species. This was preferred to a sequence reflecting relationships as these are subject to constant revision due to the many new findings of systematic research using molecular methods. Speedwell (*Veronica*) for example was for a long time placed in the Scrophulariaceae family, between Oleaceae and Globulariaceae, but at the start of this century was transferred to Antirrhinaceae, and then just a little later incorporated into Plantaginaceae, between Globulariaceae and Orobanchaceae. New knowledge makes such changes necessary, but we consider an alphabetical arrangement to be more reader-friendly.

The main groups – spore-bearing plants, naked-seeded plants, dicotyledons and monocotyledons – are treated in this order in separate sections.

PLANT NAMES

The English name (in **bold**) is followed by the scientific name (in *italics*) and the family, followed by any synonyms.

In the Alps there are 2 subspecies of Lilac Dusky Cranesbill, *Geranium phaeum*. This is subsp. *lividum*.

In the Alps there are 7 subspecies of Alpine Poppy. This is Kerner's Alpine Poppy, *Papaver alpinum* subsp. *kerneri*.

Scientific names are subject to revision and change which can be annoying for the plant enthusiast, and plant systematics is in a constant state of flux, with such necessary changes in nomenclature reflecting the use of modern techniques. These include investigation of chromosome number (karyology), phytochemistry, and the structure of pollen grains (palynology), as well as research into ultrastructure (mainly using the scanning electron microscope), isoenzyme research (enabling direct insight into the genome for the first time), and in the last 20 years, the amazing possibilities of DNA analysis (from fingerprint techniques to sequencing, i.e. analysing the sequence of the base pairs of DNA, the letters of the genetic code). All these have resulted in taxonomic changes.

A name may also change for technical reasons, usually because a traditional and therefore familiar name turns out not to comply with the rules of the International Code of Nomenclature.

Common synonyms are given in brackets (Syn.:). Many species have several synonyms, but including these would confuse rather than clarify. The 'authorities' of the Latin binomials have also not been included as these would be unhelpful and potentially confusing. The named authority refers only to the name, but not to the taxon and therefore has no bearing on the identity of the taxon.

Names of people are however mentioned if they are included in the scientific genus or species names, with a few words about the person honoured.

DESCRIPTION
The characteristics of each species that are useful for identification are described, including height, although deviations due to stunting or overgrowth for example, are not discussed. The descriptive paragraph ends with the usual flowering period. Abbreviations and technical terms have been avoided as far as possible.

SIMILAR SPECIES
Here similar species are mentioned with which the plant in question might be confused, with features that separate them noted. The similar species are usually in the same genus, though sometimes in different genera or even in another family.

HABITAT
The main habitats in which the species is predominantly found, followed by the usual altitudinal range, with any outliers mentioned.

Altitudes are given in metres above sea level. Although the use of more scientific terms such as montane and subalpine levels might be more informative, their altitude varies across the Alps. For example, the subalpine level in the northern Alps extends to around 1,900m, in the central Alps to about 2,400m, and in the southern Alps to roughly 2,000m. The demarcation of

Introduction

these regions is also more complex than can be seen on many simplified maps. Such parameters need not concern the amateur naturalist and are an unnecessary complication for those simply wishing to enjoy the beauty of alpine flowers, so we quote the usual altitudes as being more user-friendly.

DISTRIBUTION
This indicates the normal range of the species described, indicating whether it grows only in the Alps (endemic) or if it can be found on other mountains or elsewhere in the world.

NOTE
This section offers extra information about the species described, such as if it shows great variability within the Alps.

DISTRIBUTION MAPS
The small maps show the alpine area divided into regions and indicate the frequency of the species across the Alps.

The categories of *common*, *scattered*, *rare* and *very rare* are based both on personal experience and the literature. While reasonably accurate, they are naturally somewhat subjective.

If a particular species is found only in a small area but is rather common there, it may be classed as rare or very rare with respect to the entire Alps. At this scale we cannot indicate differences in frequency in the various regions.

An example: Shiny Rock-cress, *Arabis soyeri*, is scattered across the Alps but is rare in lower and upper Austria. Nevertheless, it is shown as blue in both these regions since the exact status in the individual regions is not usually known.

PHOTOGRAPHS
In the photographs care has been taken to ensure that features important for identification are clearly visible and typical habitat and typical flowers are portrayed. If this is not possible in a single image or if the species is variable (e.g. with several subspecies), there may be 2, or even 3 photographs.

IDENTIFICATION
On finding a plant, one often has an idea to which genus or family it might belong. Checking the pictures should help, enabling many species to be excluded. The description and reference to similar species will then help you to reach a final determination from the remaining possible candidates.

An example: you find a tall, yellow-flowered lousewort. This immediately excludes all the red- or pink-flowered louseworts. Its height also excludes *Pedicularis oederi*, *P. tuberosa*, *P. elongata*, *P. julica* and *P. ascendens*. The habitat is not wet and so *P. sceptrum-carolinum* is chosen. Three other possibilities remain: *P. foliosa*, *P. hoermanniana* and *P. hacquetii*. Under SIMILAR SPECIES you will find the characteristics to be considered in order to identify the species. The distribution map will also often help. If the lousewort was found in the Bavarian Alps, the only possibility then is *Pedicularis foliosa*.

Each species entry is accompanied by a distribution map, with the colour indicating whether it is common, scattered, rare or very rare:

green: common   blue: scattered   orange: rare   red: very rare   beige: non-native, status uncertain, or extinct – more information in the text.

ALPINE REGIONS

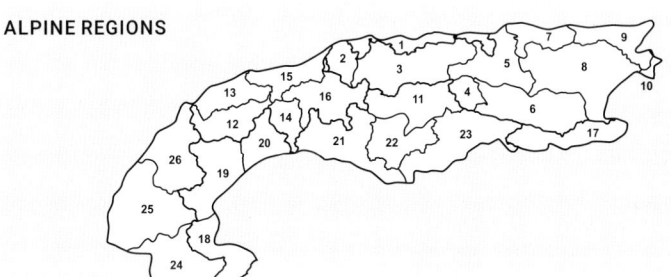

GERMANY
1 Germany (alpine parts of Upper Bavaria and Swabia)

AUSTRIA, LIECHTENSTEIN
2 Vorarlberg, Liechtenstein (alpine part)
3 North Tyrol
4 East Tyrol
5 Salzburg (alpine part)
6 Carinthia
7 Upper Austria (alpine part)
8 Styria (alpine part)
9 Lower Austria, Vienna (alpine part)
10 Burgenland (alpine part)

SOUTH TYROL
11 South Tyrol

SWITZERLAND
12 Valais
13 Bern, Waadt, Freiburg (alpine part)
14 Tessin
15 Lucerne, Unterwalden, Uri, Schwyz, Glarus, St. Gallen, Appenzell (alpine part)
16 Grisons (Graubünden)

SLOVENIA
17 Slovenia (alpine part, to the lower reaches of the Idrijca, the area south of this considered part of the Dinaric Alps)

ITALY
18 Savona, Imperia, Cuneo (alpine part)
19 Aosta, Turin (alpine part)
20 Novara, Verbania, Vercelli, Biella, Varese (alpine part)
21 Como, Lecco, Sondrio, Bergamo, Brescia, Verona (alpine part)
22 Trento
23 Vicenza, Treviso, Belluno, Pordenone, Udine (alpine part)

FRANCE
24 Maritime Alps (Alpes-Maritimes), Var, Alpes-de-Haute-Provence (alpine part)
25 High Alps, Drôme, Vaucluse, Isère (alpine part)
26 Savoy (Savoie), Haute-Savoie (alpine part)

Botanical terms

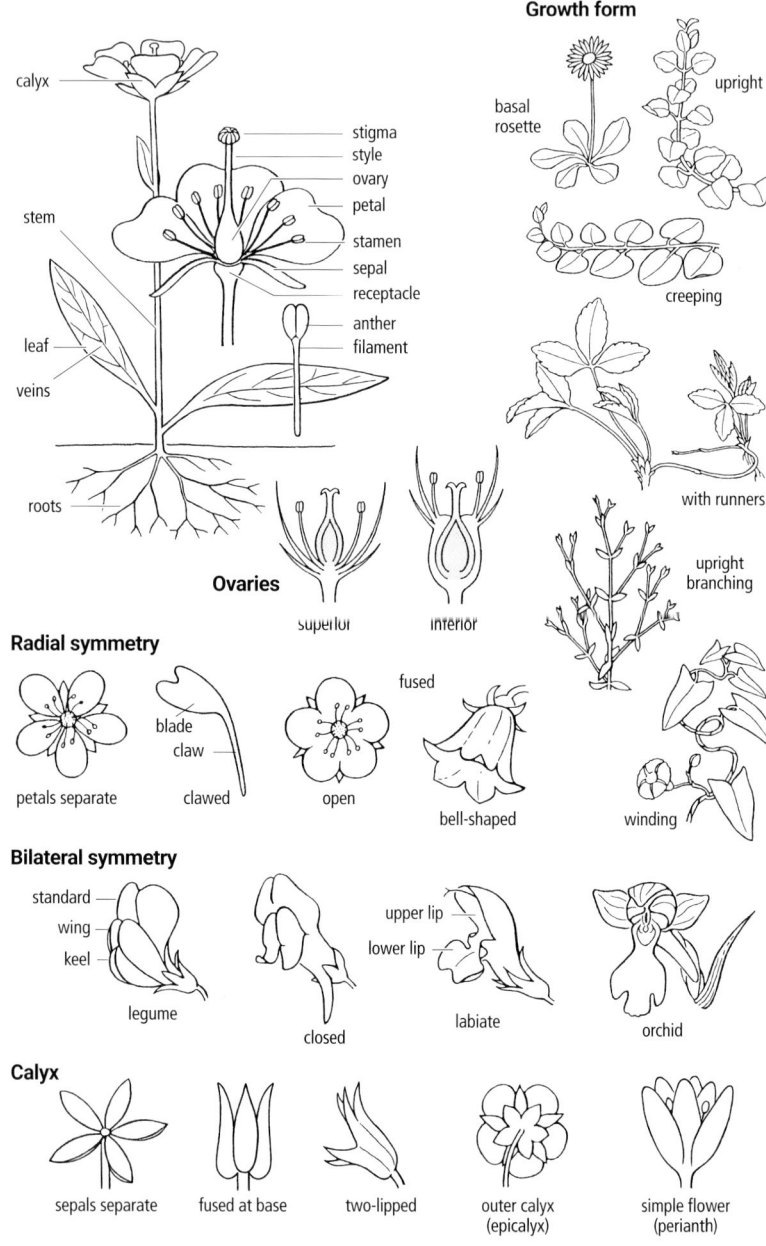

Inflorescences

spike | spadix | raceme | unilateral raceme | panicle | dichasium

umbel with bracts | compound umbel with bracts and bracteoles | racemose umbel | paniculate umbel | spikelet (grasses) (*P = palea* *L = lemma* *G = glume*)

Composite flowers

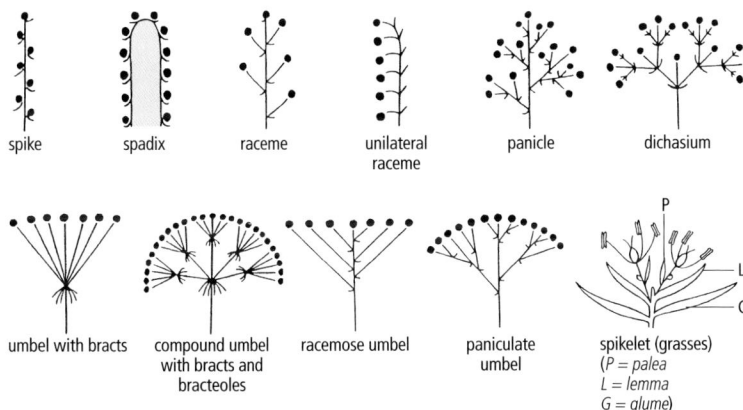

bracts | ray florets | disc (tube) florets | ray (outer) disc (inner) florets | receptacle with ray florets

Split fruit (schizocarp)

Indehiscent fruits

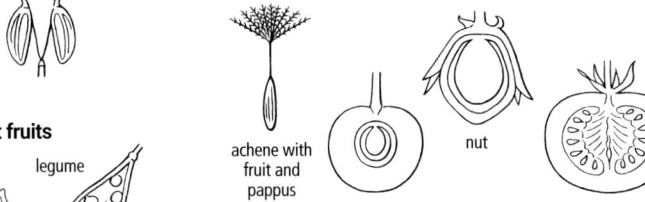

achene with fruit and pappus | drupe (stone fruit) | nut | berry

Dehiscent fruits

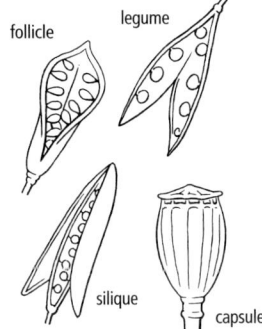

follicle | legume | silique | capsule

Fleshy fruits

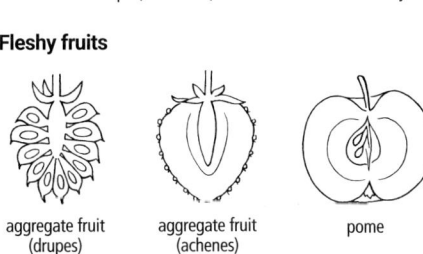

aggregate fruit (drupes) | aggregate fruit (achenes) | pome

Botanical terms

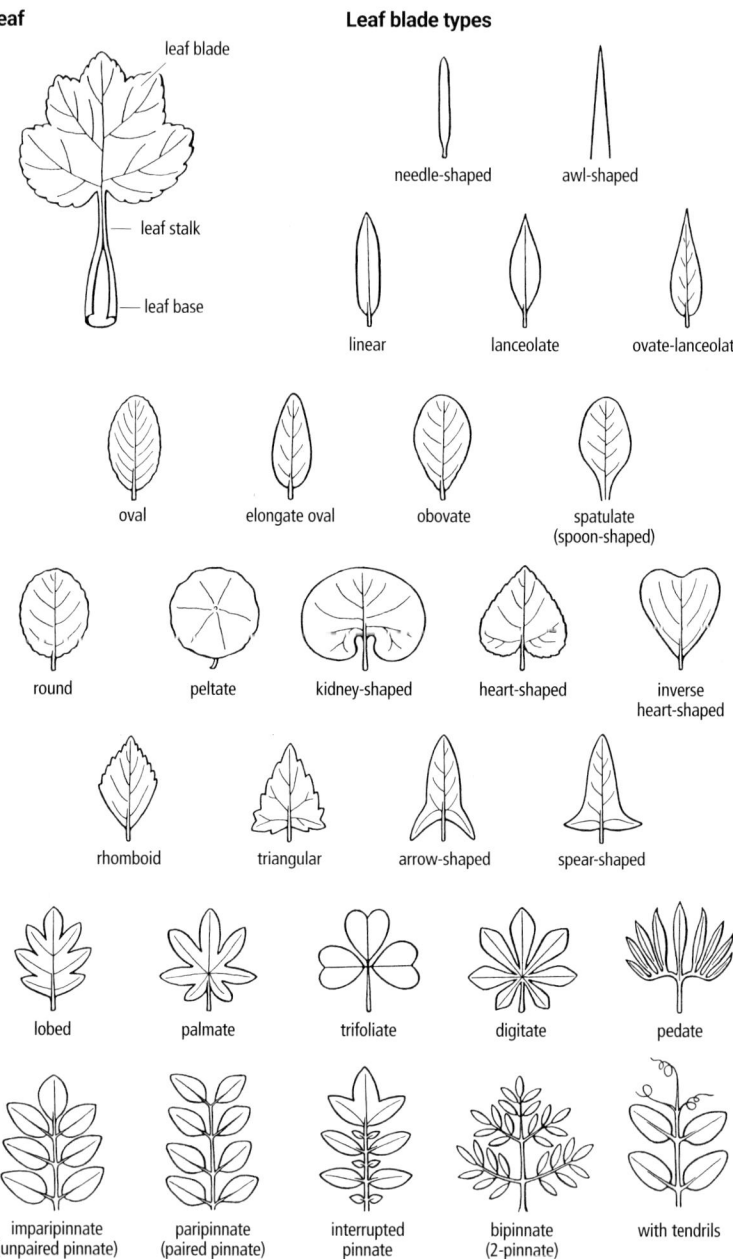

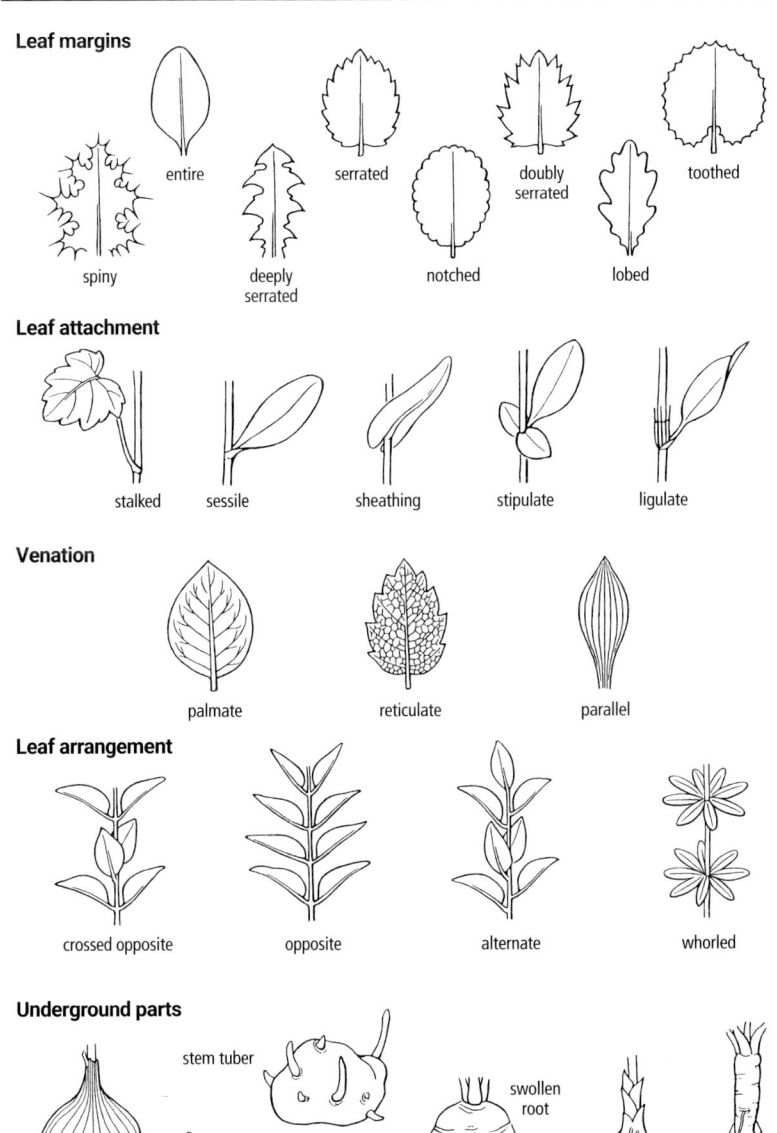

How to use this book

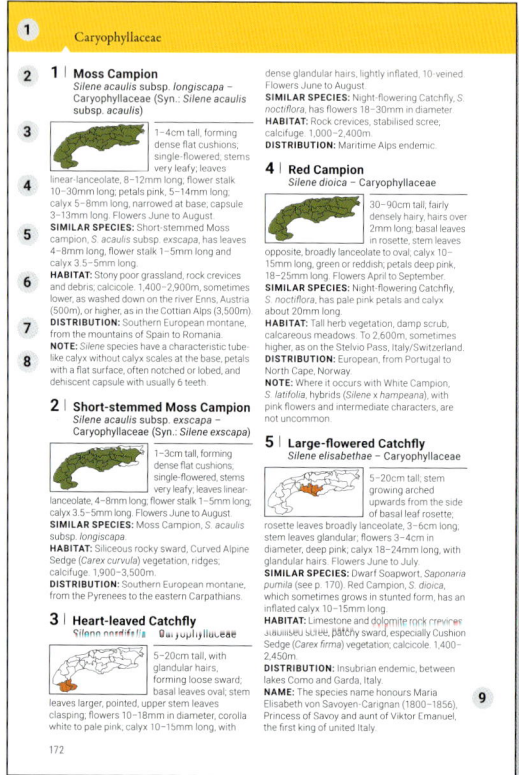

① **Colour bands** aid orientation. The plants are arranged in 4 large groups: ferns and relatives; conifers and relatives; flowering plants, dicotyledons; flowering plants, monocotyledons. Within these groups, the families and species are presented alphabetically, with the family name(s) also in the bar at the top of the page.

② The **common name** is in **bold**. This is followed by the scientific name of the species, the scientific family name and if appropriate, any synonyms.

③ The **distribution map** shows the regions in which the plant occurs, with the colour indicating its status, such as common or rare.

④ The **species descriptions** note characteristics that are important for identification.

⑤ **Similar species** are mentioned, along with the characteristics that separate them.

⑥ **Habitat** indicates the plant communities in which the species is usually to be found, and the typical altitude.

⑦ **Distribution**. In addition to the maps, notes on the distribution of the species indicate whether, for example, it is endemic to the Alps or is also native to other mountains.

⑧ **Note** gives any further relevant information about a species.

⑨ **Name**. Interesting information related to the origin or meaning of a name is also provided.

⑩ **Photographs**. The plates have at least one photograph of each species, with sometimes 2 used to show key features. If the species has different varieties these may also be illustrated. The number in each photograph corresponds to that of the species described.

FINDING YOUR WAY
To make it easier to find your way around the book, the flaps list all the plant families alphabetically within each of the 4 major groups. The English family names are also provided. A typical member of each family is illustrated, and keyed by number. The flaps can thus be used to help identification by leading quickly to the correct pages in the identification sections of the book.

17

Ferns and relatives

Aspleniaceae, Blechnaceae, Dennstaedtiaceae, Dryopteridaceae

1 | Hart's-tongue
Asplenium scolopendrium – Aspleniaceae (Syn.: *Phyllitis scolopendrium*)

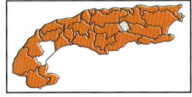

10–60cm tall; blade undivided, strap-shaped, shiny; young leaves mealy beneath, later smooth; sori (sporangia) linear, paired. Spores ripen July to September.
SIMILAR SPECIES: None.
HABITAT: Wooded gorges, damp rocks. To 2,000m.
DISTRIBUTION: European-Asiatic.

2 | Forked Spleenwort
Asplenium septentrionale – Aspleniaceae

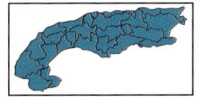

5–15cm tall; leaves bare, shiny, irregularly forked; segments long, linear, mostly with 1–2 pointed teeth; sori (sporangia) covering the whole lower leaf surface. Spores ripen July to October.
SIMILAR SPECIES: Dolomite Spleenwort, *A. seelosii*, has glandular hairs on both sides of 3-lobed leaves.
HABITAT: Rock crevices; calcifuge. To 2,500m.
DISTRIBUTION: European-Asiatic–North American.

3 | Green Spleenwort
Asplenium viride – Aspleniaceae

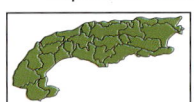

5–15cm tall; leaves simply pinnate, linear to lanceolate, with 10-30 leaflets on each side; petiole only brown at the base, otherwise green like the rachis; sori (sporangia) elongate towards midrib. Spores ripen July to August.
SIMILAR SPECIES: In Maidenhair Spleenwort, *A. trichomanes*, the whole petiole and rachis are dark brown.
HABITAT: Rock crevices, shady walls, rocky woods; calcicole. To 3,100m.
DISTRIBUTION: Eurosiberian–North American.

4 | Hard-fern
Blechnum spicant – Blechnaceae

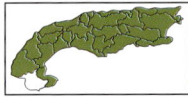

10–75cm tall; leaves lanceolate, narrowing towards tip, in a rosette, simply pinnate, with 30–60 pinnae, 3–5mm broad; sterile leaves spreading, overwintering; fertile leaves taller and erect, deciduous. Spores ripen July to September.
SIMILAR SPECIES: None.
HABITAT: Woods and dwarf shrub heath on moist, acid soils. To about 2,100m.
DISTRIBUTION: European-Asiatic–North American.

5 | Bracken
Pteridium aquilinum – Dennstaedtiaceae

30–250cm tall; leaves long-stalked, triangular in outline, 3-pinnate (sometimes 2-pinnate); petiole hairy; sori (sporangia) around margins of inrolled pinnules. Spores ripen July to September.
SIMILAR SPECIES: None.
HABITAT: Clearings, open woods, heaths, pasture margins. To 2,100m.
DISTRIBUTION: Cosmopolitan.

6 | Brittle Bladder-fern
Cystopteris fragilis – Dryopteridaceae

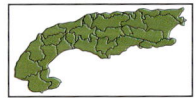

10–40cm tall; leaves lanceolate, 2–3 times as long as broad, 2–3-pinnate; lower pair of pinnae usually shorter than the next; veins ending in tips of pinnule teeth. Spores ripen July to September.
SIMILAR SPECIES: In Alpine Bladder-fern, *C. alpina*, the veins end in the pinnule notches.
HABITAT: Damp, shady rock crevices, walls, rocky woods, scree; calcicole. To 3,100m.
DISTRIBUTION: Cosmopolitan.

Dryopteridaceae, Equisetaceae, Lycopodiaceae

1 | Rigid (Villars') Buckler-fern
Dryopteris villarii – Dryopteridaceae

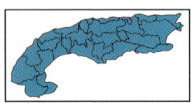

15–50cm tall; leaves lanceolate, 5–15cm broad, stiffly upright, 2-pinnate, in funnel-shaped tufts, densely glandular-hairy beneath, bitter smelling; lowest pinnae symmetrical; petiole ½–⅓ as long as blade; scales uniformly pale pinkish-brown. Spores ripen July to August.
SIMILAR SPECIES: There are several similar buckler-ferns in the Alps. Scaly Buckler-fern, *D. remota*, has 10–25cm broad leaves and asymmetric, triangular lowest main pinnae.
HABITAT: Coarse rubble, tall herb vegetation; calcicole. 1,100-2,500m.
DISTRIBUTION: Southern European montane.
NAME: In honour of the French botanist and doctor Dominique Villars (1745–1814), after whom the genus *Villarsia* in the Bogbean family is named.

2 | Oak Fern
Gymnocarpium dryopteris – Dryopteridaceae

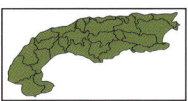

10–40cm tall; petiole and rachis lacking glands; leaves 2-pinnate, lowest pinnae almost as large as the rest of blade; pale green, thin, bare or sparsely glandular, blade broadly triangular; young leaves rolled. Spores ripen July to August.
SIMILAR SPECIES: Limestone Fern, *G. robertianum*, has dull green leaves, and petiole, rachis and blade covered with glandular hairs.
HABITAT: Acid, shady woods. To 2,800m.
DISTRIBUTION: Eurosiberian–North American.

3 | Holly Fern
Polystichum lonchitis – Dryopteridaceae

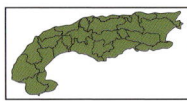

15–50cm tall; leaves lanceolate, 5–10x as long as broad, simply pinnate, coarse, overwintering, dark green; pinnae curving upwards, with stiff spines; sori (sporangia) in 2 rows coalescing towards tip. Spores ripen June to September.
SIMILAR SPECIES: The other shield-ferns, *Polystichum* spp., in the region are 2-pinnate.
HABITAT: Montane woods, rocky scree; calcicole. To 2,700m.
DISTRIBUTION: Eurosiberian–North American.

4 | Wood Horsetail
Equisetum sylvaticum – Equisetaceae

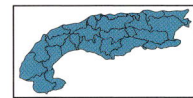

20–70cm tall; fertile and sterile fronds both with green branches, divided 1–2 times, fine, arching downwards; fertile stems at first pale and unbranched, later becoming green; stem sheath with 3–4 teeth. Spores ripen May.
SIMILAR SPECIES: The other horsetail species in the Alps are unbranched or with undivided branches. Variegated Horsetail, *E. variegatum* (**4B**) has stems that are unbranched or branched only at the base. It is found on flushes, sandy banks, and fens, up to the alpine level.
HABITAT: Damp, acid woods, pasture, mires. To about 1,900m.
DISTRIBUTION: Eurosiberian–North American.

5 | Alpine Clubmoss
Diphasiastrum alpinum – Lycopodiaceae

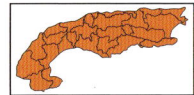

2–10cm tall; stems creeping above and below surface, branched in tufts above ground; shoots 4-angled, only slightly flattened, rectangular in cross section; leaves pointed and scale-like, slightly mealy, in 4 rows adpressed to stem; ventral leaves short-stalked; cones 1–2cm long, solitary and sessile, at ends of branches. Spores ripen July to September.
SIMILAR SPECIES: In Issler's Clubmoss, *D. complanatum* (**5B**), the stems are decidedly flattened, and the leaves small and ventral leaves unstalked.
HABITAT: Acid pasture, dwarf shrub heath, snowy rocky ground; calcifuge. 1,300–2,800m.
DISTRIBUTION: Arctic–alpine.

Lycopodiaceae, Ophioglossaceae, Pteridaceae, Selaginellaceae, Thelypteridaceae

1 | Fir Clubmoss
Huperzia selago – Lycopodiaceae

5–20cm tall; stems curving upwards, not creeping, forked; leaves 6–8mm long, in whorls or spirals of 4–5; sporangia in leaf axils. Spores ripen July to September.
SIMILAR SPECIES: Marsh Clubmoss, *Lycopodiella inundata*, has creeping stems, erect fertile branches, and leaves 4–6mm long.
HABITAT: Acid woods, dwarf shrub heath, siliceous soils; calcifuge. To 3,000m.
DISTRIBUTION: European-Asiatic–North American.
NAME: In honour of German botanist and doctor Johann Peter Huperz (1771–1816) who received his doctorate with dissertation on the dispersal of ferns.

2 | Interrupted Clubmoss
Lycopodium annotinum – Lycopodiaceae

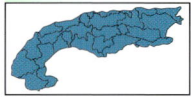

10–30cm tall; stems to 1m long, creeping with upright branches; leaves pointed, not ending in a hair, 5–9mm long, mostly finely serrated-toothed; cones sessile, solitary, 2–4cm long. Spores ripen July to September.
SIMILAR SPECIES: In Stag's-horn Clubmoss, *L. clavatum*, cones are in groups of 1–3 on long, leafy stems. Leaf tips end in a 1–3mm long hair.
HABITAT: Acid woods, especially coniferous woods, dwarf shrub heath, rocky sites. To 2,800m.
DISTRIBUTION: Eurosiberian–North American.

3 | Moonwort
Botrychium lunaria – Ophioglossaceae

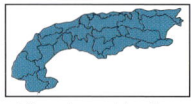

3–25cm tall; leaf unstalked or short-stalked, simply pinnate with 3–9 pairs of fan-shaped leaflets, entire or toothed; fertile blade branched, long-stalked. Spores ripen June to July.
SIMILAR SPECIES: In the very rare Least Moonwort, *B. simplex*, the leaf stalk is ⅓–1x as long as blade.
HABITAT: Pasture, poor grassland. To 3,100m.
DISTRIBUTION: Cosmopolitan.

4 | Parsley Fern
Cryptogramma crispa – Pteridaceae

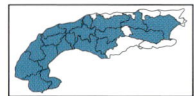

5–30cm tall; fertile and sterile leaves distinct, fertile with inrolled segments; sterile fronds oval to triangular in outline, coarsely notched to pinnate. Spores ripen June to August.
SIMILAR SPECIES: among others, the Cloak Fern, *Notholaena marantae*, which has similar-sized fertile and sterile leaves and is mainly found on serpentine substrates.
HABITAT: Siliceous rocks; scree, calcifuge. 1,000–3,000m, sometimes lower, as in Locarno in Tessin (250m).
DISTRIBUTION: European montane.

5 | Swiss Clubmoss
Selaginella helvetica – Selaginellaceae

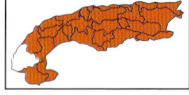

1–5cm tall; stem thread-like, creeping, leaves oval, with broad tips, opposite, in 4 rows; sporophyll 3–6cm long. Spores ripen June to August.
SIMILAR SPECIES: Lesser Clubmoss, *S. selaginoides* (**5B**) has lanceolate, pointed, toothed, alternate leaves.
HABITAT: Poor, sandy swards, shady rocks, damp banks. To 2,100m.
DISTRIBUTION: European-Asiatic.

6 | Beech Fern
Phegopteris connectilis – Thelypteridaceae

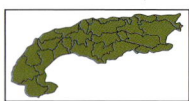

10–40cm tall; leaves triangular to arrowhead-shaped in outline, pale green, hairy, 1–2x as long as broad; 2-pinnate, 12–20 pinnae at each side, bending upwards toward tip; lowest pair flexed backwards; sori (sporangia) without indusium, close to margin. Spores ripen July to September.
SIMILAR SPECIES: In Lemon-scented Fern, *Thelypteris limbosperma* (= *Oreopteris limbosperma*), the leaf is 2–4x as long as broad, and the lower pinnae spread horizontally.
HABITAT: Woods, scrub. To 2,500m.
DISTRIBUTION: Eurosiberian–North American.

Conifers and relatives

Cupressaceae, Pinaceae

1 | Common Juniper
Juniperus communis – Cupressaceae

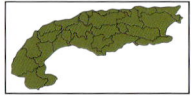

0.1–5m tall dioecious shrub; needle leaves, aromatic when crushed, bluish-white waxy stripes above; female cones fleshy and berry-like, spherical, with blue bloom, ripening in 2nd–3rd year, in leaf axils. Flowers March to August.
SIMILAR SPECIES: Savin Juniper, *J. sabina*, the leaves of older plants are scale-like, and the 'berries' terminal.
HABITAT: Pastures, dwarf shrub heath, rocky slopes, pine woods. To about 2,800m.
DISTRIBUTION: European-Asiatic–North American.
NOTE: Three subspecies in the Alps:
– *communis* (**1A**): 1–5m tall, leaves 10–18mm long, 1–1.5mm broad. Low levels.
– subsp. *nana* (**1B**): 0.2–0.6m tall, leaves 5–15mm long, 1–2mm broad. Montane.
– subsp. *hemisphaerica*: 0.2–0.6m tall, leaves 12–20mm long, 1.3–2mm broad. Southern French Alps.

2 | European Larch
Larix decidua – Pinaceae

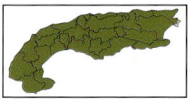

Up to 35m tall tree with grey-brown bark; needles flat, flexible, pale green, in bunches of 20–40 on short shoots, turning yellow and falling in autumn; male and female flowers on same branch; cones oval, falling after ripening. Flowers April to June.
SIMILAR SPECIES: None.
HABITAT: Montane forests. About 1,400–2,500m, often planted at lower levels.
DISTRIBUTION: Alpine–Carpathian.
NOTE: A light-requiring tree of upper montane to subalpine levels. With Arolla Pine it forms characteristic mixed forests. Pure Larch forests are mainly the result of centuries-old forestry practices. Without such human intervention, the more shade-tolerant Arolla Pine gradually displaces European Larch through natural forest succession. On many sites suitable for pasture, pine and larch have been cleared, and in some cases open larch woods are also grazed.

3 | Arolla Pine
Pinus cembra – Pinaceae

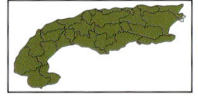

10–25m tall tree; needles in bunches of 5, triangular in section, 5–8cm long, 1–1.5mm broad; cones erect, with bluish to purplish sheen. Flowers June to July.
SIMILAR SPECIES: The other native alpine *Pinus* species have needles in bunches of 2–3.
HABITAT: Montane forests. 1,300–2,800m.
DISTRIBUTION: The Alps are the centre of its range – from the French Maritime Alps, east to Gamsstein in the Ybbstal Alps and to Monte Viso in the south. There are also small pockets in the High Tatra, and in the south and east Carpathians.
NOTE: Also known as 'Queen of the Alps'. It can grow to 1,000 years old. Its timber is considered the only hardwood amongst conifers, but its valuable wood has become rare in many areas. Closely associated with suggest the Northern Nutcracker (*Nucifraga caryocatactes*), for which its seeds are a major source of food, the bird also playing a key role in the natural regeneration of this tree.

4 | Dwarf Mountain Pine
Pinus mugo – Pinaceae

0.3–3m tall; shrub-like tree with low-lying to upwardly curving branches; needles in pairs, 3–5cm long, dark green; cones 2–5cm long, symmetrical. Flowers June to July.
SIMILAR SPECIES: Mountain Pine, *P. uncinata* (= *P. mugo* subsp. *uncinata*) has an upright, straight trunk, 3–10m tall. Cones 3–7cm long, asymmetrical at the base.
HABITAT: Rocky sites around the treeline, also in raised bogs at lower altitudes. Around 1,200–2,600m.
DISTRIBUTION: Southeast European montane.
NOTE: Dwarf Mountain Pine and Mountain Pine are not always easy to separate. Some authorities therefore regard them as subspecies. Both forms are connected by the hybrid named *Pinus* x *rotundata*.

Flowering plants: dicotyledons

Amaranthaceae, Apiaceae

1 | Good-King-Henry
Chenopodium bonus-henricus – Amaranthaceae (Syn.: *Blitum bonus-henricus*)

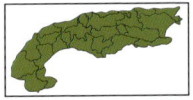

20–80cm tall; perennial; leaves pointed and triangular, 7–14cm long and 4–14cm broad, mealy surface; inflorescence green, panicule, with many short pseudo spikes. Flowers April to October.
SIMILAR SPECIES: Common Amaranth, *Amaranthus retroflexus*, which is an annual, has oval leaves, narrowing at either end.
HABITAT: Livestock-grazed fields, nitrate-rich tall herb vegetation, ruderal sites. To 2,600m, sometimes even to 3,100m (Gornergrat, Valais, Switzerland).
DISTRIBUTION: European species, from Spain to the Black Sea and southern Scandinavia.

2 | Leafy Goosefoot
Chenopodium foliosum – Amaranthaceae (Syn.: *Blitum virgatum*)

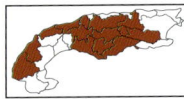

20–60cm tall; leafy to the tip, including around inflorescence; leaf lengthy triangular, irregularly shallowly-toothed; flowers inconspicuous, in spherical clusters in leaf axils; fruit bright red, fleshy, 4–12mm in diameter, bland-tasting. Flowers June to August.
SIMILAR SPECIES: Strawberry Spinach, *C. capitatum*, is not leafy to the tip.
HABITAT: Animal resting spots, nitrate-rich ruderal sites. About 900–2,100m, sometimes higher, as in the Tantermozza valley in Grisons (2,420m). Occasionally in lowland, but there mostly naturalised from cultivation.
DISTRIBUTION: European-Asiatic–North African, from the Atlas to the Himalaya.

3 | Wild Angelica
Angelica sylvestris – Apiaceae

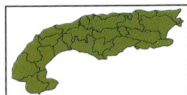

50–150cm tall; leaves to 60cm long, 2-pinnate, terminal leaflet broadly oval; leaflets toothed, oval (subsp. *sylvestris*) to lanceolate (subsp. *montana*); domed umbels, with 20–40 rays; bracts 0–3, many bracteoles. Flowers July to September.

SIMILAR SPECIES: *Conioselinum tataricum* is similar in habit and flowers, but its terminal leaflet is linear-lanceolate.
HABITAT: Damp, open woods, wooded gullies, fens, stream sides. To about 2,000m.
DISTRIBUTION: Eurosiberian, east to Lake Baikal.

4 | Shiny Chervil
Anthriscus nitidus – Apiaceae (Syn.: *A. nitida*)

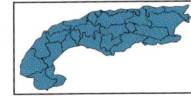

50–120cm tall; leaves shiny, 2–3-pinnate, lowest leaflets nearly as large as the rest of the leaf blade; edges of petal bare; fruit 5–7mm long, at most as long as its stalk. Flowers June to August.
SIMILAR SPECIES: In Cow Parsley, *A. sylvestris*, the lowest leaflets are much smaller than the rest of the leaf blade, and the fruit is at least as long as its stalk. In the similar Hairy Chervil, *Chaerophyllum hirsutum*, the edges of the petals are fringed.
HABITAT: Tall herb vegetation, wooded gullies, stream sides, rich meadows, moisture-loving. About 900–2,200m.
DISTRIBUTION: Central and southeast European.

5 | Bavarian Masterwort
Astrantia bavarica – Apiaceae

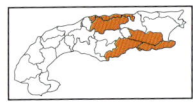

20–50cm tall; stem only branched in upper quarter; lower leaves with 5–7 lobes, the central lobe reaching almost to the leaf base; umbel and involucre 1–2cm in diameter; bracts 8–15mm long, 2–3mm broad, extending beyond umbel; umbels 1–5. Flowers June to August.
SIMILAR SPECIES: In Carniolan Masterwort, *A. carniolica* (**5B**), the central lobe of the lower leaves does not reach the leaf base, bracts 4–8mm long, 1–2mm broad, shorter or as long as the umbel. In Lesser Masterwort, *A. minor* (**5C**), the lower leaves are 7-lobed, the stem often branched from the middle.
HABITAT: Poor grassland, dwarf shrub heath, glacier scrub, stony woods, calcicole. 900–2,300m.
DISTRIBUTION: East alpine endemic.

Apiaceae

1 | Great Masterwort
Astrantia major – Apiaceae

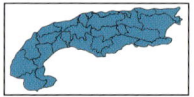

30–80cm tall; basal leaves 5–7 lobed, lobes broad, pointed and toothed; flowers greenish-white or pale pink, surrounded by whitish bracts with obvious side veins; sepals prickly; terminal umbel including bracts 2–5cm across. Flowers June to August.
SIMILAR SPECIES: The other masterwort species have terminal umbels and bracts of less than 2cm diameter and the bracts lack obvious side veins.
HABITAT: Deciduous woods, tall herb vegetation, Rusty Sedge (*Carex ferruginea*) grassland; calcicole. To 2,000m.
DISTRIBUTION: Southern European montane species, from the Spanish mountains to the Carpathians.
NOTE: There are 2 varieties in the region:
– var. *major* (**1A**): bracts as long or slightly longer than umbel, sepals about the same length as petals. Widespread in the Alps.
– var. *involucrata* (**1B**): bracts almost twice as long as umbel, sepals markedly longer than petals. So far known only from the eastern Alps.

2 | Candy Carrot
Athamanta cretensis – Apiaceae

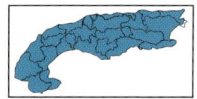

15–40cm tall; leaves grey-green, coarsely hairy, 3-pinnate, with linear lobes *c.* 1mm across; umbel 5–12-rayed; bracts 1–4, many bracteoles. Flowers June to August.
SIMILAR SPECIES: South-Tyrol Burr grass, *A. vestina* has umbel of 15–25 rays and shiny leaves. Fine-leaved Burr grass, *A. turbith*, has a 20–35-rayed umbel and hairless 0.3–0.5mm leaf lobes.
HABITAT: Rocks, rocky debris, stony sward; calcicole. To about 2,800m.
DISTRIBUTION: Southern European montane, from the French Massif Central to the eastern Alps.

3 | Fine-leaved Burr grass
Athamanta turbith – Apiaceae

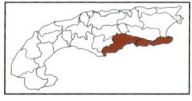

30–50cm tall; leaves hairless, leaf lobes 0.3–0.5mm, with thread-like hairs; umbel 20–35 rayed; bracts lacking or few; numerous bracteoles; fruit 7–8mm long. Flowers May to July.
SIMILAR SPECIES: Candy Carrot, *A. cretensis* (see **2**). *A. vestina* has umbel of 15–25 rays and 4–5mm long fruits.
HABITAT: Rocks, stony slopes; calcicole. To 1,600m.
DISTRIBUTION: Eastern alpine–Illyrian from Pordenone Province to Monte Maggiore (Učka).

4 | South-Tyrol Burr grass
Athamanta vestina – Apiaceae

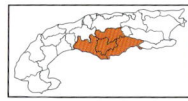

20–50cm tall; leaves hairless or sparsely hairy, leaf lobes 0.3–0.6mm broad, with thread-like hairs, shiny; umbels 15–25-rayed; bracts 1–2 or none; bracteoles 7–9; fruit 4–5mm long. Flowers May to July.
SIMILAR SPECIES: Candy Carrot, *A. cretensis* and Fine-leaved Burr grass, *A. turbith*. Spignel, *Meum athamanticum*, is also similar but has very fine leaf lobes 0.2–0.3mm and 3–15-rayed umbels.
HABITAT: Damp crevices on shady cliffs; calcicole. To 2,100m.
DISTRIBUTION: Southern alpine endemic from Brescia to Belluno.

5 | Rock Hare's-ear
Bupleurum petraeum – Apiaceae

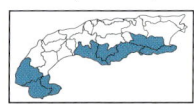

15–30cm tall; stem unbranched, leafless, with only bracts; Basal leaves grass-like, 3–5mm broad; umbel 5–15-rayed; bracts linear to lanceolate, pale green. Flowers June to August.
SIMILAR SPECIES: Three-veined Hare's-ear, *B. ranunculoides*, has a branched stem, with several leaves, and Starry Hare's-ear, *B. stellatum* (see p. 36).
HABITAT: Rock crevices, stony sward, Cushion Sedge (*Carex firma*) vegetation; calcicole. 1,300–2,200m, occasionally higher as on Montasch in the Julian Alps (2,300m).
DISTRIBUTION: Alpine endemic. Southern and western Alps, from the Maritime Alps to Kamnik Alps.

Apiaceae

1 | Three-veined Hare's-ear
Bupleurum ranunculoides – Apiaceae

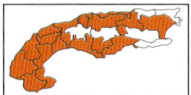

10–60cm tall, blue-green, hairless; stem branched and leafy; basal leaves narrowly lanceolate to linear; bracts and bracteoles usually 5, oval, fused at most at the base. Flowers July to August.
SIMILAR SPECIES: Rock Hare's-ear, *B. petraeum* (see p. 34).
HABITAT: Stony sward, dry poor meadows, rocks, scree; calcicole. To 2,800m.
DISTRIBUTION: Southern European montane.
NOTE: 2 subspecies in the Alps:
– subsp. *ranunculoides*: basal leaves 5–12mm broad.
– subsp. *caricinum*: basal leaves 2–4mm broad.

2 | Starry Hare's-ear
Bupleurum stellatum – Apiaceae

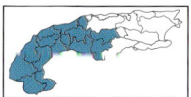

10–40cm tall; hairless, blue-green; stem mostly leafless or with only 1–2 leaves; leaves linear-lanceolate, entire, with 1 central vein beneath, otherwise with reticulate veins; bracts 2–4, bracteoles 8–12, mostly fused to above centre. Flowers July to August.
SIMILAR SPECIES: Rock Hare's-ear, *B. petraeum* (see p. 34) has leaves with several longitudinal veins and is scarcely reticulately veined. Long-leaved Hare's-ear, *B. longifolium*, is 30–80cm tall and has many stem leaves.
HABITAT: Rocky slopes, pasture, rock crevices, rubble; calcifuge. 1,200–2,600m, sometimes lower, as in Val Onsernone, Tessin (640m), or higher as on the southern slopes of Gornergrat, Zermatt, Switzerland (2,800m).
DISTRIBUTION: Alpine–Corsican.

3 | Hairy Chervil
Chaerophyllum hirsutum – Apiaceae

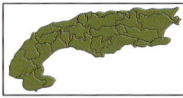

30–100cm tall, hairy, or almost hairless; leaves 2–3-pinnate, the lowest segments almost as large as the rest of the leaf; flowers white to pink. Flowers May to July.
SIMILAR SPECIES: In Villars' Chervil, *C. villarsii*, the lowest segments are much smaller than the rest of the leaf, and the plant is coarsely hairy.
HABITAT: Rich, damp meadows, tall herb vegetation, stream sides, shady damp woods. To 2,500m.
DISTRIBUTION: European montane.

4 | Villars' Chervil
Chaerophyllum villarsii – Apiaceae

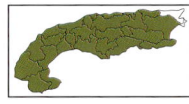

30–100cm tall, coarsely hairy; leaves 2–3-pinnate, lower segments much smaller than the rest of the leaf; leaf sheaths of the uppermost leaves 3–10mm long; flowers white, rarely pink. Flowers June to August.
SIMILAR SPECIES: Hairy Chervil, *C. hirsutum*. In the western alpine endemic Elegant Chervil, *C. elegans*, the sheaths of the uppermost leaves are 15–20mm long.
HABITAT: Tall herb vegetation, open woods, montane meadows, stream sides. 1,000–2,500m.
DISTRIBUTION: Southern European montane.
NAME: In honour of French botanist and doctor Dominique Villars (1745–1814), who studied the flora of Dauphiné, Provence, and Languedoc.

5 | Shining Lovage
Coristospermum lucidum subsp. *seguieri* – Apiaceae (Syn.: *Ligusticum lucidum*)

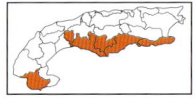

60–130cm tall, hairless; leaves 4-pinnate, lobes linear, with pale points; umbels 30–50-rayed; bracts 0–3, simple, bracteoles 5–8; flowers white. Flowers June to August.
SIMILAR SPECIES: Piedmont Lovage, *Ligusticum ferulaceum*, has pinnate bracts and 15–25-rayed umbels.
HABITAT: Stony slopes, scrub; calcicole. To 2,000m.
DISTRIBUTION: Southern European montane.
NAME: In honour of French Jesuit and naturalist Jean-François Séguier (1703–1784), who studied the flora of the South Tyrol.

Apiaceae

1 | Alpine Eryngo
Eryngium alpinum – Apiaceae

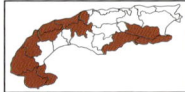

40–80cm tall; basal leaves long-stalked, undivided; upper leaves deeply lobed, toothed; flowers in dense clusters on long stalks, surrounded and overtopped by a ruff of spiny-toothed amethyst-blue bracts. Flowers July to August.
SIMILAR SPECIES: None.
HABITAT: Tall herb vegetation, rocky pasture; calcicole. 1,500–2,400m.
DISTRIBUTION: Alpine–Illyrian, from the French High Jura and mountains of northern Balkans, south to Montenegro.
NOTE: Inhabitants of the Alps used to hang a fan-like symmetrical bunch of this plant in the middle of a room. The rising heat caused the plant to move in a circular fashion, a botanical symbol representing changing fortune. Folk names such as 'Running Thistle' or 'Restless' refer to this custom.

2 | Silver Eryngo
Eryngium spinalba – Apiaceae

20–60cm tall; basal leaves long-stalked, irregularly lobed, with large, spiny teeth; flowers in oval heads, greenish, later blueish-white to silver-grey; bracts silvery-green. Flowers June to August.
SIMILAR SPECIES: Alpine Eryngo, *E. alpinum*, has amethyst-blue bracts and undivided basal leaves.
HABITAT: Rocky sward, scree; calcicole. 1,200–2,100m.
DISTRIBUTION: Western alpine endemic.

3 | Grafia
Grafia golaka – Apiaceae

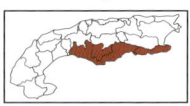

40–100cm tall, hairless, bluish-green; leaves shiny, to 30cm long, triangular to oval in outline; umbel ± 20-rayed; bracts numerous, entire or 2-lobed; bracteoles mostly only on outside of small umbels; petals notched. Flowers June to August.
SIMILAR SPECIES: Austrian Pleurospermum, *Pleurospermum austriacum*, has unnotched petals and divided bracts.
HABITAT: Rocky meadows, pasture, open scrub; calcicole. 600–1,500m.
DISTRIBUTION: Southeast European montane.
NAME: In honour of the Lower Styrian pharmacist and botanist Sigmund Graf (1801–1838) who researched the flora of western Slovenia.

4 | Broad-leaved Sanicle
Hacquetia epipactis – Apiaceae
(Syn.: *Sanicula epipactis*)

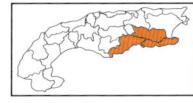

8–20cm tall; all leaves basal, 3–5-divided, long-stalked; flower stalk triangular; bracts conspicuous, 5–6, shiny green, blunt, serrated-toothed. Flowers March to May.
SIMILAR SPECIES: None.
HABITAT: Deciduous woods, woodland margins; calcicole. To about 1,700m.
DISTRIBUTION: Southeast European montane, from southeast Alps to the Carpathians.
NAME: The generic name honours Balthasar Hacquet (1739–1815) who studied the flora of Corinthia, Lower Styria and Istria, discovering several new species.
NOTE: Broad-leaved Sanicle is found in the southern Alps and adjacent Illyrian mountains, as well as the western Carpathians. A highly unusual monotypic species, it has an ancient evolutionary history.

5 | Dwarf Hogweed
Heracleum pumilum – Apiaceae
(Syn.: *Heracleum minimum*)

10–30cm tall; leaves shiny, dark green, 3-lobes, each lobe divided 3 times; umbel 3–6-rayed; bracts and bracteoles usually absent; outer petals of edge flowers only slightly enlarged. Flowers June to August.
SIMILAR SPECIES: Among others, Caraway Milk-parsley, *Peucedanum carvifolia* (Syn. *Dichoropetalum carvifolia*) which is 30–80cm tall with 6–18-rayed umbels.
HABITAT: Rock debris, sun-exposed rocks; calcicole. 1,500–2,200m.
DISTRIBUTION: Western alpine endemic.

Apiaceae

1 | White Austrian Hogweed
Heracleum austriacum subsp. *austriacum* – Apiaceae

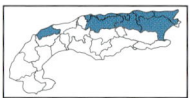

20–50cm tall; leaves simply pinnate, with 1–3 well separated pairs of lobes; leaflets oval, toothed, terminal leaflet rounded; umbel 7–13-rayed; petals white, outer petals much enlarged, 5–8mm long, deeply notched, each lobe 1–2.3mm broad. Flowers July to September.
SIMILAR SPECIES: Pink Austrian Hogweed, *H. austriacum* subsp. *siifolium*, has pink petals and the paired lobes of the outer petals are each 1.8–3.5mm broad.
HABITAT: Rocky sward, tall herb vegetation, open scrub; calcicole. 600–2,100m.
DISTRIBUTION: Alpine endemic.

2 | Pink Austrian Hogweed
Heracleum austriacum subsp. *siifolium* – Apiaceae

20–50cm tall, leaves simply pinnate, with 1–3 separated pairs of lobes; leaflets oval, toothed, terminal leaflet rounded; umbel 6–10-rayed; petals pink, the outer petals much enlarged, 6–10mm long, paired petal lobes each 1.8–3.5mm broad. Flowers July to September.
SIMILAR SPECIES: White Austrian Hogweed, *Heracleum austriacum* subsp. *austriacum*. Greater Burnet Saxifrage, *Pimpinella major*, also often has pink flowers, but the outer petals are not enlarged.
HABITAT: Rocky sward, tall herb vegetation, open scrub; calcicole. 1,100–2,000m.
DISTRIBUTION: Eastern alpine endemic.

3 | Mountain Hogweed
Heracleum sphondylium subsp. *elegans* – Apiaceae

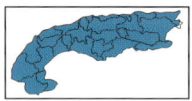

70–200cm tall; stem with bristly hairs; basal leaves not pinnate, rounded in outline, deeply 3–7-lobed, lobes pointed; umbels 15–30-rayed; bracts 0–3, bracteoles narrowly linear, numerous; petals mostly white, outer petals unilaterally enlarged. Flowers June to August.
SIMILAR SPECIES: Hogweed, *H. sphondylium* subsp. *sphondylium*, has pinnate basal leaves with 3–7 mostly stalked leaflets.
HABITAT: Tall herb vegetation, montane meadows, damp woods, glaciated herb habitats. 800–2,500m.
DISTRIBUTION: Southern European montane.
NOTE: In the Alps there are many forms of Hogweed, *Heracleum sphondylium* sens. lat., some with finely divided leaves, as well as hybrids with the introduced Giant Hogweed, *Heracleum mantegazzianum*.

4 | French Surmountain
Laserpitium gallicum – Apiaceae

30–150cm tall; leaves dark green, shiny above; leaves wedge-shaped to lanceolate; umbels 20–50-rayed; bracts and bracteoles present, with papery margins narrower than the green median stripe. Flowers June to July.
SIMILAR SPECIES: Narrow-leaved Surmountian, *L. siler*, has blue-green leaves that are not shiny.
HABITAT: Rocky debris, open scrub, stony poor sward; calcicole. To about 2,200m.
DISTRIBUTION: Southwest European montane.

5 | Haller's Surmountain
Laserpitium halleri – Apiaceae

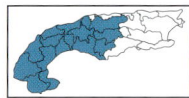

15–60cm tall; lower leaves 4–5-pinnate, leaf lobes 0.5–1.5mm across; umbels 15–40-rayed; bracts and bracteoles with ciliated papery margins. Flowers June to August.
SIMILAR SPECIES: Among others, Candy Carrot, *Athamanta cretensis* (see p. 34), which however has grey-green leaves, 5–12-rayed umbels and is calcicole.
HABITAT: Stony grassland, warm, dry slopes, open woods; calcifuge. 1,200–2,600m, sometimes lower, as in Schalderertal near Brixen (900m).
DISTRIBUTION: Alpine endemic.
NAME: In honour of the Swiss Albrecht von Haller (1708–1777), who studied the Swiss flora.

Apiaceae

1 | Gaudin's Surmountain
Laserpitium krapfii subsp. *gaudinii* – Apiaceae

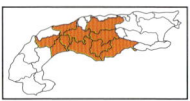

60–120cm tall; stem with blue bloom; leaves 1–2-pinnate; leaves repeatedly 3-lobed; umbel 7–15-rayed; bracts 0–5, falling; bracteoles numerous; flowers greenish-yellow. Flowers June to August.
SIMILAR SPECIES: Broad-leaved Surmountain, *L. latifolium*.
HABITAT: Stony slopes, scrub, open woods. To 2,400m.
DISTRIBUTION: Eastern alpine–Illyrian subspecies.
NAME: In honour of Swiss botanist Jean Gaudin (1766–1833), author of an early *Flora Helvetica*.

2 | Broad-leaved Surmountain
Laserpitium latifolium – Apiaceae

50–120cm tall; leaves 1–2-pinnate; leaflets oval, often asymmetric, blue-green, blunt-toothed; umbels 25–40-rayed; bracts and bracteoles numerous; petals white; fruit wavy-winged (**2B**). Flowers June to August.
SIMILAR SPECIES: Gaudin's Surmountain, *L. krapfii* subsp. *gaudinii*, has 7–15-rayed umbels and greenish-yellow flowers. Shiny Surmountain, *L. nitidum* (**2C**), endemic to the Insubrian (central southern) Alps, has green, spiny-toothed leaflets, and 12–25-rayed umbels.
HABITAT: Stony slopes, scrub, open woods; calcicole. To 2,400m.
DISTRIBUTION: European.

3 | Hog's Fennel Surmountain
Laserpitium peucedanoides – Apiaceae

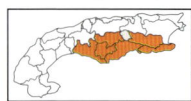

30–60cm tall, hairless; leaves 2–3 times trifoliate; leaflets narrowly lanceolate, entire, 15–100mm long, 2–12mm broad; umbels 5–15-rayed; bracts and bracteoles present; petals whitish to pale pink. Flowers June to August.
SIMILAR SPECIES: Narrow-leaved Surmountain, *L. siler*, has 20–50-rayed umbels.
HABITAT: Stony, dry slopes, scrub, montane meadows; calcicole. To 2,200m.
DISTRIBUTION: Eastern alpine–Illyrian.

4 | Narrow-leaved Surmountain
Laserpitium siler – Apiaceae

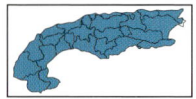

30–120cm tall; leaves blue-green, hairless, 2–4-pinnate; leaflets 15–70mm long and 3–25mm broad, with pale, narrow margins; umbels 20–50-rayed; bracts and bracteoles present. Flowers June to August.
SIMILAR SPECIES: Hog's Fennel Surmountain, *L. peucedanoides*, has 5–15-rayed umbels.
HABITAT: Dry, stony, sunny slopes, scrub, rocky debris, open woods; calcicole. To about 2,500m.
DISTRIBUTION: Southern European montane, from the Pyrenees to the Balkan mountains.

5 | Spignel
Meum athamanticum – Apiaceae

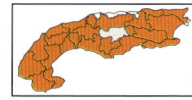

10–50cm tall, strongly aromatic; leaves 3–4-pinnate with dark green hair-fine segments, 0.2–0.3mm across; umbels 3–15-rayed; bracts 0–6, bracteoles numerous, lanceolate; petals white, sometimes suffused pink. Flowers May to August.
SIMILAR SPECIES: South-Tyrol Burr grass, *Athamanta vestina* (see p. 34).
HABITAT: Montane meadows, pasture, scree, dwarf woody scrub. 850–2,900m.
DISTRIBUTION: European mountain species, from Spain to Romania.

6 | Striped Hemlock
Molopospermum peloponnesiacum – Apiaceae

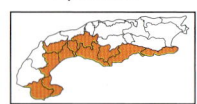

80–150cm tall, robust, hairless plant, aromatic when crushed; leaves shiny, large, 2–4-pinnate, to 100cm long; segments finely divided, extended, with forward-facing lobes; bracts numerous; terminal umbel 15–40-rayed, with several lateral umbels below, whorled. Flowers June to July.
SIMILAR SPECIES: Sweet Cicely, *Myrrhis odorata*, lacks bracts.
HABITAT: Rocky slopes. To 2,100m.
DISTRIBUTION: Southwest European montane.

Apiaceae

1 | Alpine Lovage
Mutellina adonidifolia – Apiaceae
(Syn.: *Ligusticum mutellina*)

10–50cm tall, with fibrous tuft at base of stem; leaves 2-pinnate, lobes about 1mm across; bracts 0–2, entire (when present), bracteoles usually 3, narrowly lanceolate, with membranous margins; flowers pink to white. Flowers June to August.
SIMILAR SPECIES: Unbranched Lovage, *Pachypleurum mutellinoides*. Candy Carrot, *Athamanta cretensis* (see p. 34) has many bracteoles.
HABITAT: Grazed sward, tall herb vegetation. 1,100–3,000m.
DISTRIBUTION: Southern European montane, from the French Massif Central to the mountains of Bulgaria.

2 | Sweet Cicely
Myrrhis odorata – Apiaceae

60–120cm tall, strongly aniseed-scented; stem and nodes hairy; leaves large, 2–4-pinnate; bracts usually absent, bracteoles almost entirely pale; umbel rays softly hairy; fruit 2–2.5cm long. Flowers June to July.
SIMILAR SPECIES: From the similar chervil species (*Chaerophyllum* and *Anthriscus*), it is distinguished by the typical aniseed smell and the almost completely pale bracteoles.
HABITAT: Tall herb vegetation, woodland clearings, Grey Alder woods; calcicole. To about 2,300m.
DISTRIBUTION: Southern European montane.
NOTE: Locally its status is unclear, whether native or introduced, because of the long history of its use as a herb or medicinally.

3 | Unbranched Lovage
Pachypleurum mutellinoides – Apiaceae (Syn.: *Ligusticum mutellinoides*)

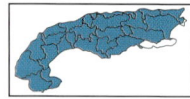

5–15cm tall, lacking fibrous tuft at stem base; leaves 1–2-pinnate, lobes c. 1mm across; umbels 12–20-rayed; bracts 5–10, divided, bracteoles numerous; flowers white to pink. Flowers July to August.
SIMILAR SPECIES: Alpine Lovage, *Mutellina adonidifolia*, has 0–2 bracts.
HABITAT: Grassy areas on deep, mostly calcium-poor soils, wind-exposed ridges. 1,600–3,350m.
DISTRIBUTION: Alpine-Carpathian.

4 | Masterwort
Peucedanum ostruthium – Apiaceae

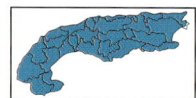

30–100cm tall; stem hollow, hairless (fluffy only beneath umbels), round and grooved; leaves trifoliate, leaflets 3-divided, to varying depth; umbels 15–50-rayed; bracts 0–1, bracteoles few. Flowers June to August.
SIMILAR SPECIES: Mountain Hogweed, *Heracleum sphondylium* subsp. *elegans*, which however has an angularly-furrowed, bristly-hairy stem.
HABITAT: Tall herb vegetation, livestock resting sites, damp meadows, stream sides. 1,200–2,800m, occasionally lower, as in Tessin near Magadino-Vira (210m).
DISTRIBUTION: Southern European montane.
NOTE: Masterwort was traditionally used as a medicinal plant, for herb-based schnapps and cheese, and as an aromatic at Christmas.

5 | Raibl Masterwort
Peucedanum rablense – Apiaceae
(Syn.: *P. austriacum* subsp. *rablense*)

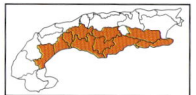

60–120cm tall, hairless; leaf lobes narrowly lanceolate, 10–20x as long as broad; umbels 10–20-rayed; bracts and bracteoles numerous, with membranous margins. Flowers July to August.
SIMILAR SPECIES: The closely-related Austrian Masterwort, *P. austriacum* (**5B**) has leaf lobes only 2–5x as long as broad. Schott's Masterwort, *P. schottii* (**5C**) has 6–10-rayed umbels, and usually lacks bracts and bracteoles.
HABITAT: Sunny, dry, rocky slopes, open woods, hedges. About 1,000–1,900m.
DISTRIBUTION: Alpine endemic.

Apiaceae

1 | Giant Hog Fennel
Peucedanum verticillare – Apiaceae

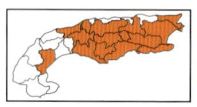

120–250cm tall; stem hollow, upper stem branching in whorls; leaves shiny, very large, 2–3-pinnate; leaflets 3–6cm long and 2–5cm broad; umbels in whorls; umbel rays numerous, of unequal length; bracts and bracteoles 0–2; flowers pale greenish-yellow. Flowers June to August.

SIMILAR SPECIES: Gaudin's Surmountain, *Laserpitium krapfii* subsp. *gaudinii* (see p. 42), is 50–120cm tall and has more than 3 bracteoles.
HABITAT: Bushy slopes, woodland margins, hedgerows, gullies. To about 1,800m.
DISTRIBUTION: Southern European montane.

2 | Greater Burnet Saxifrage
Pimpinella major – Apiaceae

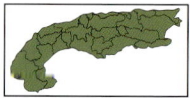

30–80cm tall, mostly hairless; stem deeply grooved, mostly hollow, leafy below and above; lower leaves simply pinnate, with 1–4 paired, oval, irregularly toothed leaflets; larger leaflets mostly stalked; umbel 10–15-rayed; flowers white (var. *major*) or pink (var. *rubra*, **2B**). Flowers June to September.

SIMILAR SPECIES: Alpine Burnet Saxifrage, *P. alpina* (**2C**), is leafy mainly towards the base, the stem mostly with leaf sheaths lacking blades; leaflets with pointed teeth, sessile; umbel 5–12-rayed.
HABITAT: Meadows, pasture, tall herb vegetation. To about 2,300m.
DISTRIBUTION: European, also in Caucasus.

3 | Austrian Pleurospermum
Pleurospermum austriacum – Apiaceae

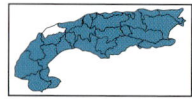

60–150cm tall, dark green, shiny, hairless; stem hollow, grooved; leaves 2–3-pinnate, to 50cm long, leaflets oval; umbels 15–40-rayed, large, 10–15cm across; bracts and bracteoles numerous. Flowers June to August.

SIMILAR SPECIES: Grafia, *Grafia golaka* (see p. 38), and Striped Hemlock, *Molopospermum peloponnesiacum* (see p. 42), from which it differs, among other aspects, in its longer leaves.
HABITAT: Tall herb vegetation, riverine woods, bushy slopes, montane meadows; calcicole. To about 2,100m.
DISTRIBUTION: Eastern European, from the western Alps to Sweden and southern Russia.

4 | Austrian Seseli
Seseli austriacum – Apiaceae

30–80cm tall, hairless; stem and leaves with blue bloom; lower leaves 3-pinnate with linear lobes scarcely 1mm across; stem leaves rapidly decreasing in size upwards; umbels 9–20-rayed, involucral bracts mostly absent, bracteoles numerous; petals about 0.75mm long. Flowers June to September.

SIMILAR SPECIES: There are a number of other *Seseli* species at lower altitudes, such as Koch's Seseli, *Seseli kochii* in the south-eastern Alps, which has 5–7-rayed umbels.
HABITAT: Stony steppe, rock crevices; calcicole. To about 1,600m.
DISTRIBUTION: Eastern alpine–Carpathian.

5 | Moon Carrot
Seseli libanotis – Apiaceae
(Syn.: *Libanotis montana*)

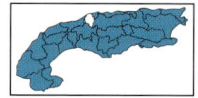

10–120cm tall, variable (**5A**, **5B**); stem solid and ridged; leaves 2-pinnate, lobes ± triangular; bracts and bracteoles numerous; umbels 20–40-rayed; sepals 0.5–1mm long; fruit hairy. Flowers July to September.

SIMILAR SPECIES: Among others, Alpine Burnet Saxifrage, *Pimpinella alpina* (**2C**) which lacks bracts and bracteoles. Hart's Wort, *Cervaria rivini*, has hairless fruits, and stem only slightly grooved.
HABITAT: Poor grassland, rocky slopes, scrub margins; calcicole. To 2,500m.
DISTRIBUTION: European.

Apiaceae, Asclepiadaceae, Asteraceae

1 | Trochiscanthes
Trochiscanthes nodiflora – Apiaceae

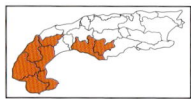

80–200cm tall, hairless: basal leaves very large, 3–4-pinnate; umbels small, in a loose panicle of secondary umbels; bracts 0–1, bracteoles 3–5; petals very pale green. Flowers June to August.
SIMILAR SPECIES: None.
HABITAT: Deciduous woods, bushy slopes. To about 1,900m.
DISTRIBUTION: Alpine–Apennine.

2 | Swallow-wort
Vincetoxicum hirundinaria – Asclepiadaceae

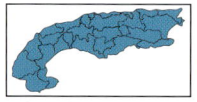

30–100cm tall; leaves entire, oval-heart-shaped, pointed; flowers white, yellowish-white or greenish-white, 5-lobed; fruit 3–5cm long, spindle-shaped, pointed; seeds plumed. Flowers May to July.
SIMILAR SPECIES: None.
HABITAT: Open woods, stony dry grassland, fine-soil rocky calcareous sward; calcicole. To 1,900m.
DISTRIBUTION: European-Asiatic, from Belgium across to the Altai.
NOTE: Swallow-wort was long considered the only native member of the milkweed family (Asclepiadaceae). However, the family is now often regarded as a subfamily of the dogbane family (Apocynaceae).

3 | Black Yarrow/Dark-stemmed Sneezewort
Achillea atrata – Asteraceae

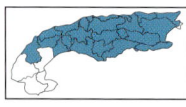

5–25cm tall; slightly aromatic; leaves 2-pinnate, lobes 0.6–1mm broad, basal segments of the middle stem leaves undivided; flower heads 11–19mm across; bracts edged black; ray florets 7–12, each 5–8mm long. Flowers June to September.
SIMILAR SPECIES: Clusius' Yarrow, *A. clusiana*, endemic to the north-eastern Alps, has leaf lobes 0.3–0.5mm broad and all segments of the middle stem leaves have 2–3 lobes.
HABITAT: Rocky sward, snow hollows, moraines; calcicole. 1,100–3,000m.
DISTRIBUTION: Alpine endemic.

4 | Silvery Yarrow/Silvery Milfoil
Achillea clavennae – Asteraceae

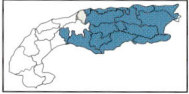

5–30cm tall, with silky hairs; middle stem leaves pinnately lobed to deeply split with 2–4 segments on each side; stem with 6–20 flower heads; involucre edged dark brown; ray florets 5–8, each 4–6mm long. Flowers June to August.
SIMILAR SPECIES: Few.
HABITAT: Rocky slopes, stony sward, rock crevices; on basic soils. 1,500–2,500m.
DISTRIBUTION: Eastern alpine–Illyrian.
NAME: In honour of the Italian botanist Nicolaus Clavena who included mention of this plant in a work of 1609.

5 | Large-leaved Yarrow/Sneezewort
Achillea macrophylla – Asteraceae

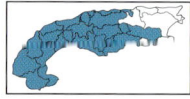

40–100cm tall; leaves pinnate, with 2–8 irregularly toothed segments on either side; stem with 5–40 flower heads; bracts edged brown; ray florets 5–7, each 4–7mm long. Flowers July to August.
SIMILAR SPECIES: Few.
HABITAT: Alder scrub, tall herb vegetation, wooded gullies. 1,000–2,100m.
DISTRIBUTION: Alpine–Apennine.

6 | Sudetan Yarrow
Achillea millefolium subsp. *sudetica* – Asteraceae

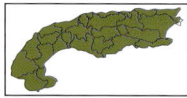

10–50cm tall; basal and lower stem leaves elongate, segments at most twice as long as broad; main inflorescence 4–12cm across; bracts mostly edged dark brown; ray florets mostly pink, about as broad as long; disc florets shorter than ray florets. Flowers July to October.
SIMILAR SPECIES: The various forms of Yarrow, *Achillea millefolium*, comprise a very difficult group, and have not yet been thoroughly investigated. In the Alps there are around a dozen species in the millefolium group, some of which also have pink ray florets.
HABITAT: Montane meadows, grassland. Around 1,000–2,900m.
DISTRIBUTION: European montane.

Asteraceae

1 | Musk Milfoil
Achillea moschata – Asteraceae

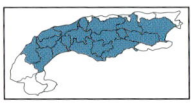

5–20cm tall, strongly aromatic; leaves hairless or nearly so, simply pinnate, lobes mostly entire; stem with 5–15 flower heads; bracts edged brown; ray florets 3.5–5mm long. Flowers June to September.
SIMILAR SPECIES: Simple-leaved Milfoil, *A. erba-rotta*, is similar, but the leaves are entire and toothed.
HABITAT: Patchy sward, stony fields; calcifuge. 1,400–3,400m.
DISTRIBUTION: Alpine endemic.

2 | Dwarf Milfoil
Achillea nana – Asteraceae

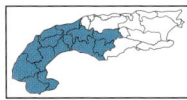

5–15cm tall, downy, strongly aromatic; leaves divided, with 6–12 lobes on each side; stem usually with 4–10 flower heads; bracts edged dark brown; ray florets 2–3.5mm long. Flowers July to August.
SIMILAR SPECIES: Few.
HABITAT: Scree, moraines, rocky sites; calcifuge. 1,800–3,300m.
DISTRIBUTION: Alpine endemic.

3 | Alpine Sneezewort
Achillea oxyloba – Asteraceae

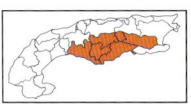

8–20cm tall; flower heads solitary; leaves pinnate, with linear lobes 0.5mm broad; flower head usually 2–30mm across; bracts with broad dark brown edges; ray florets mostly 13–18, 6–10mm long. Flowers July to September.
SIMILAR SPECIES: Black Yarrow/Dark-stemmed Sneezewort, *A. atrata*, is sometimes single-headed which can cause confusion, though this is usually found alongside the normal multi-headed form, and its ray florets are 4–8mm long.
HABITAT: Rocky debris and sward; calcicole. 1,500–3,200m.
DISTRIBUTION: Southeast alpine endemic.

4 | Hedge-leaved Adenostyles
Adenostyles alliariae – Asteraceae

60–160cm tall; leaves spidery-downy beneath, with irregularly toothed margins, upper leaves clasping stem; flower heads in densely branching clusters, each flower head with 3–5 florets; bracts hairy at tip. Flowers June to August.
SIMILAR SPECIES: Alpine Adenostyles, *A. alpina*, has regularly toothed leaves, below hairy only along veins, and 2–4 florets in each flower head.
HABITAT: Tall herb vegetation, wooded ravines, forest edges, stream sides. 1,100–2,700m, sometimes washed down to lower levels, as at Bruderholz near Basel (365m).
DISTRIBUTION: Southeast European montane.
NOTE: Hybrids within this genus are not uncommon.

5 | Alpine Adenostyles
Adenostyles alpina – Asteraceae
(Syn.: *A. glabra*)

30–80cm tall; all leaves stalked, upper leaves lacking clasping basal lobes, below hairy only along veins; leaf margins regularly toothed; each flower head with 2–4 florets, bracts hairless. Flowers June to August.
SIMILAR SPECIES: Hedge-leaved Adenostyles, *A. alliariae*.
HABITAT: Rocky sites, montane woods; calcicole. To 2,700m.
DISTRIBUTION: Southern European montane.

6 | White-leaved Adenostyles
Adenostyles leucophylla – Asteraceae

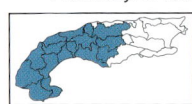

20–40cm tall; stem, leaf undersides and bracts covered in hairs; leaf margins coarsely toothed; each flower head with 12–25 florets; bracts 7–9. Flowers July to August.
SIMILAR SPECIES: Alpine Adenostyles, *A. alpina*, which however has only 2–4 florets in each flower head, and hairless bracts.
HABITAT: Rocky sites, mainly on acid substrates. 1,900–3,000m.
DISTRIBUTION: Alpine endemic.

Asteraceae

1 | Carpathian Cat's-foot
Antennaria carpatica – Asteraceae

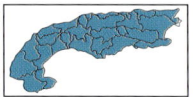

10–20cm tall, downy, lacking runners, few basal rosettes; basal leaves linear to oblong, ± pointed; inner bracts brownish-white, making the flower heads dark; flower heads 2–6 in a dense cluster. Flowers June to August.
SIMILAR SPECIES: Cat's-foot, *A. dioica*.
HABITAT: Grassland, stony pasture, exposed ridges. 1,400–3,100m.
DISTRIBUTION: Southern European montane.

2 | Cat's-foot
Antennaria dioica – Asteraceae

5–20cm tall, downy, with overground runners, rooting to form many basal rosettes; basal leaves spoon-shaped, pointed; dioecious, female flower heads with pink inner bracts, male flower heads white, on separate plants. Flowers May to July.
SIMILAR SPECIES: Carpathian Cat's-foot, *A. carpatica*, does not form runners and the basal leaves are linear to oblong and pointed, and the inner bracts brownish-white.
HABITAT: Poor grassland; calcifuge. To 3,100m.
DISTRIBUTION: Eurosiberian–North American.

3 | Carpathian Dog-daisy
Anthemis carpatica – Asteraceae

10–25cm tall, perennial; flower heads solitary; upper stem leafless, leaves 1–2-pinnate, somewhat coarse; flower head 3–4cm across; bracts edged dark brown; ray florets 12–16mm long. Flowers July to August.
SIMILAR SPECIES: Alpine Moon-daisy, *Leucanthemopsis alpina* (see p. 84), has ray florets 12–16mm long. The other alpine *Anthemis* species are ruderals, growing at lower altitudes, and their flower heads are not solitary.
HABITAT: Rocky sites; calcifuge. 1,800–2,300m.
DISTRIBUTION: Southern European montane. In the Alps, only in the Seckau Alps.

4 | Aposeris
Aposeris foetida – Asteraceae

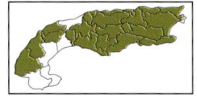

5–25cm tall, hairless; leaves basal, regularly pinnately lobed; flower heads solitary on leafless stem; flower head nodding before opening; milky sap with unpleasant smell. Flowers June to July.
SIMILAR SPECIES: In Perennial Hyoseris, *Hyoseris radiata*, a Mediterranean species, a ruderal, the flower head is upright before opening.
HABITAT: Woods, notably beech woods; calcicole. 800–2,000m, sometimes lower.
DISTRIBUTION: Southern European montane. Ranges from Spain and France across the Alps and the Balkans to Belarus and the Carpathians.
NOTE: Monotypic genus (this is the only species in the genus *Aposeris*).

5 | Arnica
Arnica montana – Asteraceae

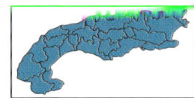

20–50cm tall, unbranched or with 2–4 lateral branches; basal leaves oval to broadly lanceolate, in a rosette; stem with 1–2 pairs of leaves; flowering stem and involucre with short glandular hairs and longer glandless hairs; flower head 4–7cm across; receptacle without paleae. Flowers June to August.
SIMILAR SPECIES: Yellow Ox-eye, *Buphthalmum salicifolium*, does not form rosettes and has alternate leaves. Species of the very similar Leopard's-banes, genus *Doronicum*, have involucral bracts on the receptacle.
HABITAT: Poor montane meadows, pasture, fens, dwarf shrub heath. To about 3,000m.
DISTRIBUTION: European.
NOTE: Arnica was once found in the lowlands as well as the mountains, but agricultural use of poor grassland and heath and afforestation have reduced it to a rarity there. It is now much commoner at higher altitudes where its habitats are not exploited so intensively.

It is commonly used as a medicinal plant, although it was not apparently known as such to ancient writers. The earliest mention of its use in this context is by Hildegard von Bingen in the 12th century.

Asteraceae

1 | Common Wormwood
Artemisia absinthium – Asteraceae

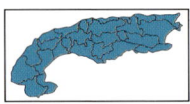

40–120cm tall, strongly aromatic when crushed; whole plant with silky hairs; leaves 2–3-pinnate, with mostly 2–4mm broad lobes; flower heads nodding, in dense panicle, 3–4mm in diameter. Flowers July to September.
SIMILAR SPECIES: Mugwort, *A. vulgaris*, has 1–2-pinnate leaves, dark green above.
HABITAT: Ruderal sites, pasture, ruins, roadsides. To 2,300m.
DISTRIBUTION: Ancient introduction, originally from western Asia.
NOTE: Wormwood is a constituent of absinthe, an alcoholic drink with extracts of Wormwood, Lemon Balm, Fennel and Anise. It became a fashionable drink and drug, in various forms, particularly during the 19th century, and was banned in many European countries due to its suspected damaging effects.

The genus *Artemisia* contains some 520 species, of which 54 are found in Europe. In the Alps there are 20 species, of which 5 (*A. atrata*, *A. genipi*, *A. glacialis*, *A. nivalis* and *A. vallesiaca*) are alpine endemics.

2 | Dark Alpine Wormwood
Artemisia atrata – Asteraceae

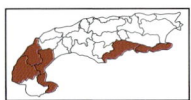

10–40cm tall, not aromatic; leaves 2-pinnate, with linear lobes about 1mm broad, bare, or slightly hairy; inflorescence with 20–40 flower heads, usually nodding, in a simple or short-branched raceme; flower heads mostly drooping; bracts 3.5–4mm long, with broad, brown margins. Flowers July to August.
SIMILAR SPECIES: Chamomile Wormwood, *A. chamaemelifolia*, in which the inflorescence has many short branches and bracts 2.5–3mm long.
HABITAT: Poor grassland, rocky debris; calcicole. 1,800–2,400m.
DISTRIBUTION: Alpine endemic.

3 | Chamomile Wormwood
Artemisia chamaemelifolia – Asteraceae

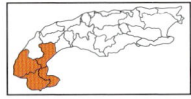

20–60cm tall; leaves 2–3-pinnate, with linear lobes about 1mm broad; inflorescence with many short branches; flower head 3–6mm across, broader than long, nodding; bracts 2.5–3mm long, edged brown. Flowers July to August.
SIMILAR SPECIES: Dark Alpine Wormwood, *A. atrata* and Valais Wormwood, *A. vallesiaca*, but in these the flower heads are 2–3mm broad and much longer than broad.
HABITAT: Rocky sites, stony grassland. To about 2,400m.
DISTRIBUTION: Western alpine–Pyrenean.

4 | Spiked Wormwood
Artemisia genipi – Asteraceae

5–20cm tall, mostly unbranched, with soft, grey hairs; lower leaves divided or 3–5-lobed, middle stem leaves pinnately split, short-stalked, or sessile; inflorescence spike-like, often nodding; flower heads upright, oval, 3–4mm across; receptacle and corolla hairless; inner bracts edged dark brown. Flowers July to September.
SIMILAR SPECIES: Alpine Wormwood, *A. mutellina* (see p. 56). Apennine Genepi, *A. eriantha*, from the south-western Alps has hairy corollas. Snow Wormwood, *A. nivalis*, endemic to the southern Valais Alps (Walliser Alpen), is completely hairless and has a reddish-brown stem.
HABITAT: Snowy damp stony sites, rocks, moraines. 2,100–3,800m.
DISTRIBUTION: Alpine endemic.

5 | Glacier Wormwood
Artemisia glacialis – Asteraceae

5–15cm tall, aromatic, with grey felty hairs; leaves 3-pinnate, lobes *c.* 1mm broad; flower heads hemispherical, 3–10, in terminal clusters, each 4–6mm in diameter; bracts edged dark brown; corolla golden yellow. Flowers July to August.
SIMILAR SPECIES: None.
HABITAT: Rocks, stony debris. 2,100–3,300m.
DISTRIBUTION: Western alpine endemic.

Asteraceae

1 | Alpine Wormwood
Artemisia mutellina – Asteraceae
(Syn.: *A. umbelliformis*)

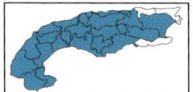

5–20cm tall, aromatic, mostly unbranched, with grey felty hairs; leaves with lobes about 1mm broad; middle stem leaves stalked, palmately divided; inflorescence bending to all sides; flower heads upright, oval, 3–4mm in diameter; bracts hairy; florets downy. Flowers July to August.
SIMILAR SPECIES: Shiny Wormwood, *A. nitida*, has flower heads 5–7mm in diameter, nodding at and after flowering. In Spiked Wormwood, *A. genipi*, the middle stem leaves are short-stalked or sessile and pinnately divided. Arctic Wormwood, *A. borealis*, has undivided stem leaves.
HABITAT: Stony debris, rock crevices. 1,900–3,700m.
DISTRIBUTION: Alpine–Apennine.

2 | Alpine Aster
Aster alpinus – Asteraceae

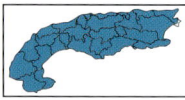

5–20cm tall; basal leaves lanceolate to elongate spoon-shaped, entire, blunt; stem leaves narrowly lanceolate; flower heads 3–4cm in diameter; ray florets pale violet. Flowers June to August.
SIMILAR SPECIES: None.
HABITAT: Poor grassland, stony sward. 1,100–3,100m, occasionally lower, as on Fläscherberg, Liechtenstein (500m).
DISTRIBUTION: Arctic–alpine.

3 | Star Aster
Bellidiastrum michelii – Asteraceae
(Syn.: *Aster bellidiastrum*)

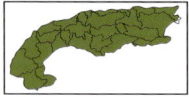

5–25cm tall: flower heads solitary, stems leafless; basal leaves elongate-obovate, mostly blunt-toothed; flower head 2–3cm in diameter; bracts pointed; disc florets yellow or white (white especially in the western Alps); base of flower head not hollow. Flowers May to July.
SIMILAR SPECIES: Daisy, *Bellis perennis*, has blunt bracts and a hollow base to flower head.
HABITAT: Rocks, slopes, open woods, flushes, stony grassland; calcicole. To 2,900m.
DISTRIBUTION: Southern European montane.

4 | Berardia
Berardia subacaulis – Asteraceae

5–15cm tall, with terminal flower head; leaves oval, with dense felty white hairs above and beneath; flower head 3.5–6cm in diameter; bracts long, pointed and lanceolate, with long, cottony hairs; disc florets pale yellow. Flowers July to August.
SIMILAR SPECIES: None.
HABITAT: Loose rocks, especially limestone. 1,500–2,900m.
DISTRIBUTION: Western alpine endemic.
NAME: In honour of the French botanist and apothecary Pierre Berard (1580–1662).

5 | Yellow Ox-eye
Buphthalmum salicifolium – Asteraceae

25–50cm tall; stem hairy, with one or few flower heads; leaves lanceolate, entire to distantly toothed; lowest leaves withering at flowering; flower head 3–6cm in diameter; bract-like leaves at base of flower head persist over the ripening fruiting head. Flowers June to September.
SIMILAR SPECIES: The genus *Inula* lacks bract-like leaves at flower head base. Arnica, *Arnica montana*, has a rosette of basal leaves.
HABITAT: Poor calcareous grassland, scrub, rocky sward; calcicole. To 2,200m.
DISTRIBUTION: Southern European montane.

6 | South-eastern Thistle
Carduus carduelis – Asteraceae

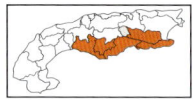

20–80cm tall; leaves white and cottony on underside; middle stem leaves with 6–8 lobes on each side, close to stem down to the next node; flower heads upright. Flowers June to August.
SIMILAR SPECIES: Alpine Thistle, *C. defloratus* (see p. 58).
HABITAT: Tall herb vegetation, stony pasture, open woods; calcicole. 800–2,000m.
DISTRIBUTION: Southeast European montane.

Asteraceae

1 | Alpine Thistle
Carduus defloratus – Asteraceae

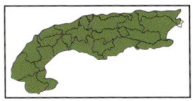

20–80cm tall; lower stem densely leafy, leaves with spiny wings, upper stem leafless; leaves not cottony beneath; flower heads solitary, 2.5–3cm in diameter. Flowers May to August.
SIMILAR SPECIES: South-eastern Thistle, *C. carduelis*, has at least the younger leaves cottony white beneath.
HABITAT: Rocky sward, poor meadows, livestock resting sites, tall herb vegetation, woodland clearings. To 3,000m.
DISTRIBUTION: Southern European montane.
NOTE: Very variable species, with 5 subspecies in the Alps, connected by intermediates. Hybrids with other *Carduus* species further complicates identification.
 – subsp. *defloratus* (= subsp. *viridis*) (**1A**): leaves green, pale green beneath, divided or entire, softly spiny; undersides of leaves hairy at least on the veins.
 – subsp. *carlinifolius* (**1B**): leaves divided, undulate, with 5mm long spines on all sides. South-western Alps.
 – subsp. *glaucus* (**1C**): leaves undivided, blue-green, scarcely spiny; central bracts 3–4x as long as broad. Outer eastern Alps.
 – subsp. *sumanus* (= subsp. *crassifolius*) (**1D**): leaves undivided, blue-green, central bracts 6–8x as long as broad.
 – subsp. *tridentinus* (**1E**): leaves divided to deeply cut, with sharp spines, with curled edges, blue-green.

2 | Italian Thistle
Carduus litigiosus – Asteraceae

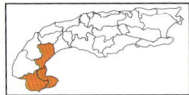

30–100cm tall, very spiny; stem cottony white; leaves broadly lanceolate, lobed, and cottony white above and below; flower heads usually 2–5, each 2–3cm in diameter. Flowers June to August.
SIMILAR SPECIES: Great Marsh Thistle, *C. personata*. The French alpine endemic, Aurouze Thistle, *C. aurosicus*, is 10–30cm tall and grows on subalpine to alpine calcareous scree.
HABITAT: Ruderal sites, pasture. To about 2,000m.
DISTRIBUTION: Mediterranean-montane.

3 | Musk Thistle
Carduus nutans – Asteraceae

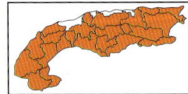

30–100cm tall; stem leafy almost up to flower head, with spiny wings; leaves irregularly pinnately lobed; flower heads nodding or upright, 3–6cm in diameter; bracts variably purplish, outer bracts bending outwards. Flowers June to August.
SIMILAR SPECIES: *Carduus* species have simple, undivided pappus hairs, while those of similar species of the genus *Cirsium* are divided.
HABITAT: Pasture, dry, rich ruderal sites, fallow land. To about 2,900m.
DISTRIBUTION: European.
NOTE: The alpine subspecies, subsp. *nutans*, subsp. *alpicola*, subsp. *macrolepis* and subsp. *platylepis* are probably the result of hybridisation with other *Carduus* species.

4 | Great Marsh Thistle
Carduus personata – Asteraceae

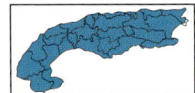

50–150cm tall, soft and short-spined, stems narrowly winged; lower leaves lobed, upper leaves oval, entire, green above, cottony beneath. Flowers June to August.
SIMILAR SPECIES: Welted Thistle, *C. crispus*, has divided upper leaves. The south-western alpine Italian Thistle, *C. litigiosus*, has very spiny stems and cottony leaves. Greimler's Thistle, *Cirsium greimleri*, has unwinged stems.
HABITAT: Tall herb vegetation, streamsides, alder woods. To 2,400m.
DISTRIBUTION: Southern European montane.

Asteraceae

1 | Plume Knapweed
Centaurea nervosa – Asteraceae

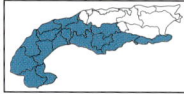

10–40cm tall; flower heads solitary; leaves broadly lanceolate, 10–20mm broad, toothed, green both sides and with curled hairs; involucre ± spherical, 18–25mm broad; many overlapping fibracts; bract appendages covering the green parts of bracts; flower head 4–6cm in diameter. Flowers June to August.
SIMILAR SPECIES: Singleflower Knapweed, *C. uniflora*. The south-western alpine endemic Jordan Knapweed, *C. jordaniana*, is low-growing to upright and has flower head 2–4cm across.
HABITAT: Poor grassland, montane meadows, dwarf montane scrub. 1,100–2,700m.
DISTRIBUTION: Southern European montane.
NOTE: Cornflower, formerly *Centaurea cyanus*, and the Mountain Cornflower group, formerly *Centaurea montana* agg. are now assigned their own genus *Cyanus*, following recent research.

2 | Short-fringed Knapweed
Centaurea nigrescens – Asteraceae
(Syn.: *C. dubia*)

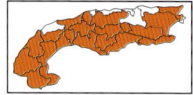

20–80cm tall; leaves entire, with at most a few of lower leaves divided; involucre chequered black and green, the dark bracts only partly obscuring the green; bract appendages less than 2.5mm long (not including fringes). Flowers June to September.
SIMILAR SPECIES: The south-west alpine Common/Black Knapweed, *C. nigra* (**2B**), lacks the spreading ray florets. The south-east alpine Julian Knapweed, *C. julica*, has large almost circular, light brown bract appendages, 5–9mm long.
HABITAT: Meadows, pasture, tall herb vegetation. To 2,200m.
DISTRIBUTION: Southeast European.

3 | Wig Knapweed
Centaurea pseudophrygia – Asteraceae

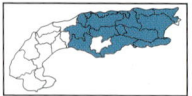

30–80 tall; multi-headed; leaves rough, but not cottony; middle stem leaves oval, 2–3x as long as broad; upper leaves sessile, rounded to heart-shaped at base; involucre ± spherical, 15–20mm across. Flowers July to September.
SIMILAR SPECIES: Narrow-scaled Knapweed, *C. stenolepis* (**3B**), restricted to the eastern fringes of the Alps has middle stem leaves 3–4x as long as broad. Plume Knapweed, *C. nervosa*, has solitary flower heads.
HABITAT: Meadows, woodland margins, usually on calcareous substrates. To about 2,300m.
DISTRIBUTION: European.

4 | Greater Knapweed
Centaurea scabiosa – Asteraceae

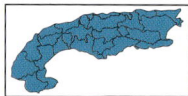

330–100cm tall; flower heads solitary; leaves 1–2-pinnate; involucre 15–30mm across; flowers purple, outer florets enlarged, with forked tips. Flowers June to August.
SIMILAR SPECIES: The rather variable Brown Knapweed, *C. jacea*, has undivided leaves.
HABITAT: Poor meadows, semi-dry grassland, rocky sward; calcicole. To 2,500m.
DISTRIBUTION: Eurasian.
NOTE: 5 subspecies in the Alps:
– subsp. *scabiosa*: entire Alps.
– subsp. *alpestris*: most of the Alps.
– subsp. *badensis*: lower Austria.
– subsp. *fritschii*: southeast Alps.
– subsp. *tenuifolia*: Aosta Valley to Trentin.

5 | Singleflower Knapweed
Centaurea uniflora – Asteraceae

10–40cm tall, with white hairs; flower heads solitary; leaves lanceolate, 5–12mm broad, 4–12x as long as broad, barely toothed; involucre ± spherical, 15–25mm across. Flowers July to August.
SIMILAR SPECIES: Plume Knapweed, *C. nervosa*, has markedly-toothed leaves, mostly broader than 10mm. Rhaetian Knapweed, *C. rhaetica* (**5B**), has involucre 8–15mm across, and dark green leaves.
HABITAT: Dry poor grassland, open scrub. 1,200–2,600m.
DISTRIBUTION: Western alpine–Apennine.

Asteraceae

1 | Acanthus-leaved Carline Thistle
Carlina acanthifolia – Asteraceae

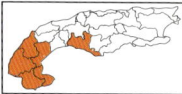

3–10cm tall; flower head solitary; leaves in rosette, divided to somewhat over the middle, softly hairy beneath; flower head 7–18cm in diameter, with spreading bracts; inner bracts straw yellow above. Flowers July to September.
SIMILAR SPECIES: None.
HABITAT: Dry grassland, pasture, scrub. To about 2,400m.
DISTRIBUTION: Southern European montane.

2 | Stemless Carline Thistle
Carlina acaulis – Asteraceae

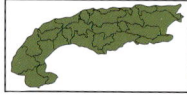

3–40cm tall; flower head solitary; leaves in rosette, pinnately divided; flower head 5–11cm in diameter, with spreading bracts; inner bracts silvery white above. Flowers June to September.
SIMILAR SPECIES: None.
HABITAT: Poor pasture and meadows, scrub. To 2,800m.
DISTRIBUTION: Southern European montane.
NOTE: 2 subspecies in the Alps:
– subsp. *acaulis*: leaves ± wavy, central lobes divided at most to middle; 3–10cm tall.
– subsp. *caulescens*: leaves curled, central lobes divided above middle; 10–40cm tall.

3 | Tolpis
Tolpis staticifolia – Asteraceae (Syn.: *Chlorocrepis staticifolia*, *Hieracium staticifolium*)

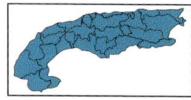

15–40cm tall, blueish-green, usually many-stemmed; flower heads 1–5; stem leafless or with 1–2 leaves and few scales; basal leaves linear, entire or with few teeth; flower head 25–35mm in diameter, yellow. Flowers June to August.
SIMILAR SPECIES: Torrent Nakedweed, *Chondrilla chondrilloides*, which has flower heads 15–25mm in diameter.
HABITAT: River gravel, rocky sites, quarries. To about 2,600m.
DISTRIBUTION: Southern European montane.

4 | Torrent Nakedweed
Chondrilla chondrilloides – Asteraceae

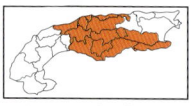

10–30cm tall, hairless, branched; stem leafless; basal leaves elongate-lanceolate, entire or with a few teeth; flower head terminal, stalked. Flowers June to August.
SIMILAR SPECIES: Tall Hawkweed, *Pilosella piloselloides*, with which it often occurs, is hairy and the stem has (few) leaves.
HABITAT: Gravel, sandy banks on alpine rivers; calcicole. To about 2,100m.
DISTRIBUTION: Eastern alpine–Apennine.

5 | Stemless/Dwarf Thistle
Cirsium acaule – Asteraceae

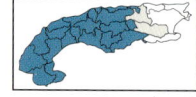

2–10cm tall; leaves in rosette, leaves pinnately lobed with spiny-toothed segments; flower heads solitary, on basal rosette or short-stalked. Flowers July to September.
SIMILAR SPECIES: None.
HABITAT: Poor meadows, pasture; calcicole. To about 2,500m.
DISTRIBUTION: European.
NOTE: Thistles of the genus *Cirsium* hybridise quite freely with each other, though not with those of the genus *Carduus*, as has occasionally been described.

6 | Carniolic Thistle
Cirsium carniolicum – Asteraceae

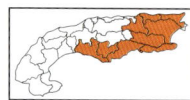

50–100cm tall; basal leaves stalked, elliptical, lobed; upper stem, flower head stalk, and upper and outer bracts covered with dense rust-brown hairs; flower head surrounded by bracts, dull yellow. Flowers June to July.
SIMILAR SPECIES: Yellow Melancholy Thistle, *C. eristhales* (see p. 64). Cabbage Thistle, *C. oleraceum*, lacks the rust-brown hairs.
HABITAT: Tall herb vegetation, pasture, morainic scrub; calcicole. To about 1,900m.
DISTRIBUTION: East alpine endemic.

1 | Woolly Thistle
Cirsium eriophorum – Asteraceae

60–120cm tall; stem not thorny-winged; leaves pinnately lobed, with strong yellowish spines; flower head 5–7cm in diameter; involucre densely cobweb-woolly. Flowers July to September.
SIMILAR SPECIES: Moris Thistle, *C. morisianum*, only found in the south-western Alps, has flower heads 3–5cm in diameter, and involucre only sparsely cobweb-woolly. Spear Thistle, *C. vulgare*, has a very spiny, winged stem and flower heads 3–5cm in diameter.
HABITAT: Pasture, dry slopes, woodland clearings. To 2,000m.
DISTRIBUTION: European montane.
NOTE: Thistles of the genus *Cirsium* often hybridise, even those as different as *Cirsium acaule* and *Cirsium spinosissimum*. The resultant hybrids may then hybridise further with the parent species, or with other species, leading to a fascinating range of forms and colours. Up to now, no definite hybrids have been found between *Cirsium arvense*, *C. eriophorum* and *C. vulgare*.

The genus contains about 250 species, of which 60 are European, with 19 in the Alps. Two species are originally restricted to the Alps: Spiniest Thistle, *Cirsium spinosissimum* (see p. 66), and Carniolic Thistle, *Cirsium carniolicum* (see p. 62). The *Cirsium* thistles are distinguished from *Carduus* thistles by their feathery pappus, which in *Carduus* is simple and not feathered.

2 | Yellow Melancholy Thistle
Cirsium erisithales – Asteraceae

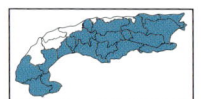

50–150cm tall, scarcely spiny; stem sticky, not winged; with few upper leaves; basal leaves pinnately lobed, upper leaves clasping stem at base; flower heads mostly solitary and terminal, not surrounded by bracts. Flowers June to August.
SIMILAR SPECIES: Carniolic Thistle, *C. carniolicum* (see p. 62), has flower heads surrounded by bracts.
HABITAT: Open woods, rocky sward, tall herb vegetation; calcicole. To about 2,100m.
DISTRIBUTION: Southern European montane.

3 | Melancholy Thistle
Cirsium heterophyllum – Asteraceae
(Syn.: *C. helenioides*)

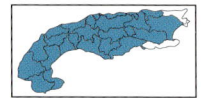

Flowers 50–100cm tall; stem simple or slightly branched, woolly-white, not spiny; leaves soft, entire or with some forward-facing segments, woolly-white beneath; flower heads solitary, long-stalked, 3–4cm in diameter. Flowers June to August.
SIMILAR SPECIES: In the west alpine Montpellier Thistle, *C. monspessulanum*, the leaves lack the white woolly undersides and the flower heads are 1–2.5cm in diameter.
HABITAT: Rich meadows, stream sides, tall herb vegetation. To about 2,200m.
DISTRIBUTION: Eurosiberian.

4 | Montpellier Thistle
Cirsium monspessulanum – Asteraceae

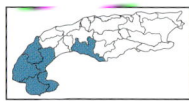

40–140cm tall; lower stem at least winged; leaves lanceolate to ovate-lanceolate, hairless, entire; leaf margins weakly spiny; flower heads 1–5, each 1–2.5cm in diameter; bracts 0.5–2mm broad. Flowers June to August.
SIMILAR SPECIES: Queen Anne's Thistle, *C. canum*, has bracts broader than 2mm.
HABITAT: Damp meadows, stream sides. To about 1,900m.
DISTRIBUTION: West Mediterranean.

5 | Mountain Thistle
Cirsium montanum – Asteraceae

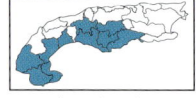

80–180cm tall, ± hairless; stem not spiny; lower leaves large, mostly over 10cm broad, with narrow lobes; flower heads in clusters of 2–8. Flowers June to August.
SIMILAR SPECIES: Brook Thistle, *C. rivulare*, has lower stem leaves less than 10cm broad. Tuberous Thistle, *C. tuberosum* (see p. 66), has solitary flower heads on long stalks, and cobweb-woolly leaves.
HABITAT: Meadows, stream sides. To about 2,000m.
DISTRIBUTION: Southern European montane.

Asteraceae

1 | Marsh Thistle
Cirsium palustre – Asteraceae

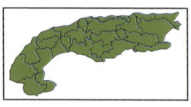

60–200cm tall; stems with spiny wings running the whole length; leaves wavy, deeply lobed; flower heads clustered, each 8–15mm in diameter. Flowers June to September.
SIMILAR SPECIES: Creeping Thistle, *C. arvense*, sometimes grows right up to subalpine regions. Its stem is neither winged nor spiny.
HABITAT: Wet meadows, ditches. To about 2,000m.
DISTRIBUTION: European-Asiatic.

2 | Spiniest Thistle
Cirsium spinosissimum – Asteraceae

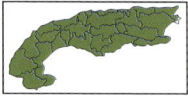

20–80cm tall, with long hairs; leaves and bracts spiny; leaves pinnately lobed to around the middle, spiny; flower heads pale yellow, in dense, terminal clusters, surrounded by spiny bracts. Flowers July to August.
SIMILAR SPECIES: Hardly any.
HABITAT: Pastures, tall herb vegetation, stream sides. 1,200–3,000m.
DISTRIBUTION: Alpine endemic.

3 | Tuberous Thistle
Cirsium tuberosum – Asteraceae

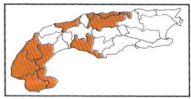

50–150cm tall; stem felty, upper stem leafless or with bracts; leaves deeply pinnate with 2–3-lobed segments, not clasping stem; flower heads solitary and terminal; flower head stalk much longer than involucre. Flowers June to August.
SIMILAR SPECIES: The only alpine *Cirsium* with tuberous roots. Brook Thistle, *C. rivulare*, has 2–4 flower heads at the end of the stem.
HABITAT: Damp meadows, ditches. To about 2,000m.
DISTRIBUTION: European.

4 | Greimler's Thistle
Cirsium greimleri – Asteraceae

70–200cm tall; stem not winged; leaves large, undivided, shallow-toothed; lower leaves long-stalked, 20–40cm long; upper stem leaves clasping stem at base; flower heads mostly 2–4, terminal, reddish-purple; involucre purplish-brown. Flowers June to July.
SIMILAR SPECIES: Great Marsh Thistle, *Carduus personata* (see p. 58) has a winged stem.
HABITAT: Tall herb vegetation, felled clearings, stream sides; mostly calcifuge, but also on calcareous substrates. 500–2,000m.
DISTRIBUTION: Eastern alpine–Balkan.
NAME: First separated in 2018 from the Carpathian Waldstein's Thistle, *Cirsium waldsteinii*, and in honour of contemporary Austrian botanist Josef Greimler.

5 | Pyrenean Hawk's-beard
Crepis albida – Asteraceae

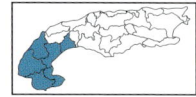

5–35cm tall; basal leaves lanceolate, 5–28cm long, 2–10mm broad, irregularly serrated to pinnately lobed; stem leaves few; bracts narrow and triangular, with broad pale green edges and purple tips; ray florets pale yellow. Flowers May to July.
SIMILAR SPECIES: Alpine Hawk's-beard, *C. alpestris*.
HABITAT: Rocks, stabilised scree; calcicole. To about 2,000m.
DISTRIBUTION: Southwest European.

6 | Alpine Hawk's-beard
Crepis alpestris – Asteraceae

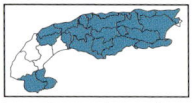

10–30cm tall; flower heads solitary; stem with pale, curly hairs, leafy mostly towards base; leaves lanceolate, lower leaves pinnately lobed; base of flower head not thickened, with whitish felty hairs; flower heads 2.5–4cm in diameter. Flowers May to July.
SIMILAR SPECIES: The western alpine Pyrenean Hawk's-beard, *C. albida*, has pale-edged bracts and pale yellow ray florets.
HABITAT: Stony sward, calcareous scree, poor meadows, open pine woods; calcicole. To about 2,400m.
DISTRIBUTION: Southern European montane.

Asteraceae

1 | Golden Hawk's-beard
Crepis aurea – Asteraceae

5–20cm tall, flower heads mostly solitary, long-stalked; stem leafless or with a few bracts; rosette leaves coarsely toothed or sharply pinnately lobed; involucre dark; ray florets orange. Flowers June to August.
SIMILAR SPECIES: None.
HABITAT: Meadows, pasture, low vegetation, snow-patches. 1,300–2,900m, occasionally lower.
DISTRIBUTION: Southern European montane.

2 | Frölich's Hawk's-beard
Crepis froelichiana – Asteraceae

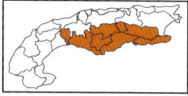

15–40cm tall; stem with 3–10 flower heads; rosette leaves 5–10cm long, narrowly oval, entire to weakly toothed. Flower cluster about as long as broad, opening from below upwards. Flowers May to June.
SIMILAR SPECIES: Pink Hawk's-beard, *C. praemorsa*, has 8–20 flower heads, opening from the top downwards.
HABITAT: Calcareous scree, pine woods, stony dry grassland; calcicole. To about 2,000m.
DISTRIBUTION: Eastern alpine–Illyrian.
NOTE: There are 2 subspecies in the Alps:
– subsp. *froelichiana*: ray florets pale yellow (**2A**).
– subsp. *dinarica*: ray florets pale purple to white (**2B**).
NAME: In honour of German medic, botanist, naturalist, and Chief Court Doctor Josef Alois von Frölich (1766–1841), the foster father of an illegitimate child of Napoleon's youngest brother, Jérôme Bonaparte, who was held prisoner in Ellwangen Castle with his second wife Princess Katharina of Württemberg after the Battle of Waterloo.

3 | Jacquin's Hawk's-beard
Crepis jacquinii – Asteraceae

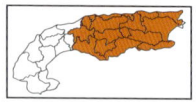

5–25cm tall; stem leaves divided, lateral lobes elongate to linear; basal leaves mostly entire or coarsely toothed; flower head 2–3cm in diameter; bracts with shaggy and stellate hairs. Flowers June to August.
SIMILAR SPECIES: Triglav Hawk's-beard, *C. terglouensis* (see p. 70), has flower heads 3.5–4.5cm across and divided basal leaves.
HABITAT: Rocky debris, stony grassland; calcicole. 1,300–3,000m, occasionally lower.
DISTRIBUTION: Southeast European montane.
NOTE: 2 subspecies in the Alps:
– subsp. *jacquinii*: flower heads 2–6, with 4–6 stem leaves.
– subsp. *kerneri*: flower heads 1–2, with 1–4 stem leaves (**3**).
NAME: In honour of Austrian botanist Nikolaus Joseph von Jacquin (1727–1817), Director of the Vienna Botanic Garden.

4 | Northern Hawk's-beard
Crepis mollis – Asteraceae

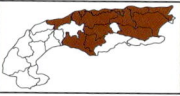

30–70cm tall; few flower heads together in loose cluster, hairless or with short hairs; upper leaves with rounded or weakly heart-shaped basal lobes, clasping stem; basal leaves often withering at flowering; involucre blackish-green, with hairs and glandular hairs. Flowers June to August.
SIMILAR SPECIES: Marsh Hawk's-beard, *C. paludosa* (**4B**), has arrow-shaped, pointed basal lobes clasping stem.
HABITAT: Meadows, fens, tall herb vegetation. To about 2,200m.
DISTRIBUTION: European montane.

5 | Mountain Hawk's-beard
Crepis pontana – Asteraceae
(Syn.: *Crepis bocconei*)

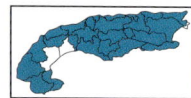

30–60cm tall, flower heads mostly solitary; basal leaves 4–12cm long, 1.5–3cm broad, with pointed teeth; stem leaves with lobes clasping stem; stem inflated beneath flower head; flower head 4–6cm in diameter. Flowers June to August.
SIMILAR SPECIES: Large-flowered Hawk's-beard, *C. conyzifolia*, has branching stems with several flower heads. Giant Catsear, *Hypocheris uniflora* (see p. 80).
HABITAT: Grassland, tall herb vegetation, scree; calcicole. 1,200–2,600m.
DISTRIBUTION: Southern European montane.

Asteraceae

1 | Pygmy Hawk's-beard
Crepis pygmaea – Asteraceae

3–12cm tall, curving upright; basal leaves oval, purplish beneath; involucre bell-shaped, with white felty hairs, 10–15mm long; ray florets yellow, often striped red; pappus pure white. Flowers July to August.
SIMILAR SPECIES: None.
HABITAT: Scree; calcicole. 1,500–2,800m.
DISTRIBUTION: Southwest European montane.

2 | Pyrenean Hawk's-beard
Crepis pyrenaica – Asteraceae

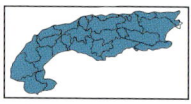

25–70cm tall; stem leafy, 1–6 flower heads, base of flower head not thickened: basal leaves withering; stem leaves 6–12, sessile, clasping; flower heads 3–4cm in diameter; involucral bracts with curled hairs. Flowers June to August.
SIMILAR SPECIES: Large-headed Hawk's-beard, *C. conyzifolia* (**2B**), has basal leaves persisting and stem thickened beneath flower head.
HABITAT: Tall herb vegetation, meadows. 800–2,300m.
DISTRIBUTION: Southern European montane.

3 | Triglav Hawk's-beard
Crepis terglouensis – Asteraceae

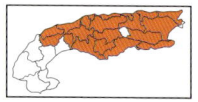

2–6cm tall, flower heads solitary; stem leafy, thickened below flower head; leaves irregularly pinnately lobed, with winged stalks; flower heads 3–5cm in diameter; bracts dark, hairy. Flowers June to August.
SIMILAR SPECIES: Rhetic Hawk's-beard, *C. rhaetica* (see p. 61, **5B**), has entire leaves and yellowish involucre. Mountain Scaly Hawkbit, *Scorzoneroides montana* (see p. 88), is also similar.
HABITAT: Rocky debris; calcicole. 1,800–2,800m.
DISTRIBUTION: Alpine endemic.

4 | Mountain Cornflower
Cyanus montanus – Asteraceae
(Syn.: *Centaurea montana*)

20–60cm tall; leaves dark green above, broadly lanceolate to elliptical, with short, erect hairs, 3–7x as long as broad, entire to slightly toothed; bracts with dark brown to black appendages, the fringes ± as long as the width of the black membranous margin. Flowers May to August.
SIMILAR SPECIES: The rather variable Squarrose Knapweed, *Cyanus triumfettii*, has lanceolate grey-green leaves, 5–20x as long as broad, and softly hairy on both sides.
HABITAT: Tall herb vegetation, montane meadows, open woods, dwarf scrub; calcicole. To about 2,200m.
DISTRIBUTION: European montane.

5 | Squarrose Knapweed
Cyanus triumfettii – Asteraceae
(Syn.: *Centaurea triumfettii*)

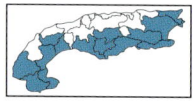

10–40cm tall; leaves with grey-green cobweb hairs on both sides, 5–20x as long as broad; bract appendages dark brown, the fringes longer than the width of the membranous margin. Flowers May to June.
SIMILAR SPECIES: Mountain Cornflower, *C. montanus*.
HABITAT: Dry slopes, semi-dry grassland, open woods. To about 2,200m.
DISTRIBUTION: Southern European–western Asiatic.
NAME: In honour of the Italian medic and botanist Giovanni Battista *Triumfetti* (1656–1708), after whom the genus Triumfetta in the mallow family (Malvaceae) is also named.

6 | Austrian Leopard's-bane
Doronicum austriacum – Asteraceae

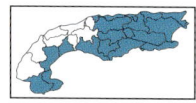

60–130cm tall, flower heads clustered, no runners; basal leaf stalks with deeply heart-shaped base, basal leaves withered by flowering time; middle leaves clasping stem; flower heads 4–7cm in diameter. Flowers June to July.
SIMILAR SPECIES: (Great) Leopard's-bane, *D. pardalianches* (see p. 74), has basal leaves present at flowering time.
HABITAT: Tall herb vegetation, forest clearings, stream sides, wooded ravines. To 2,100m.
DISTRIBUTION: Southern European montane.

Asteraceae

1 | Torrent Leopard's-bane
Doronicum cataractarum – Asteraceae

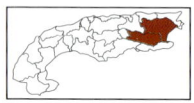

70–120cm tall; stem hairless; basal leaves large, blade 10–20cm long, rather like those of Marsh Marigold, hairless above, retained at flowering; upper flowering stalk branched, in 4–10 compact panicles; flower heads 4–8cm in diameter. Flowers June to July.
SIMILAR SPECIES: (Great) Leopard's-bane, *D. pardalianches* (see p.74), has a densely hairy stem. Austrian Leopard's-bane, *Doronicum austriacum* (see p.70), does not retain basal leaves at flowering.
HABITAT: Stream sides, wet flushes, especially on gneiss. 1,480–1,830m, even down to 1,270m in Rassinggraben, Austria.
DISTRIBUTION: Endemic to the Koralpe, Austria.

2 | Tufted (Clusius') Leopard's-bane
Doronicum clusii – Asteraceae

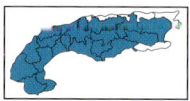

10–30cm tall; single-headed; basal and lower stem leaves elliptical to elongate-oval, 1.5–4cm as long as broad, wedge-shaped at base; leaf margins with soft hairs 1–1.5mm long, and curly hairs, not glandular. Flower heads 4.5–6.5cm in diameter. Flowers July to August.
SIMILAR SPECIES: Glacier Leopard's-bane, *D. glaciale*.
HABITAT: Rock debris, moraines; mostly on calcium-poor substrates. 1,600–3,300m.
DISTRIBUTION: Alpine–Carpathian.
NOTE: 2 subspecies in the Alps:
– subsp. *clusii*: leaf surfaces almost hairless on both sides.
– subsp. *villosum*: leaf surfaces densely hairy on both sides.
NAME: In honour of Carolus Clusius (1526–1609), who gave his name to many other plants as well as the Clusiusgasse in Vienna and the Clusius-Forschungsgesellschaft in Güssing.

3 | Heart-leaved Leopard's-bane
Doronicum columnae – Asteraceae

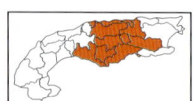

20–60cm tall, single-headed, lacking runners; lower stem hairless, upper stem with glandular hairs, few leaves; basal leaves in upright tufts, ovate to kidney-shaped, with hairless surfaces, margins regularly toothed; flower head 4–6cm in diameter. Flowers May to July.
SIMILAR SPECIES: Differs from the other alpine single-headed leopard's-banes in being sparsely hairy (only the upper stem, leaf margins, base of flower head and bracts hairy).
HABITAT: Rock debris, open woods, Dwarf Mountain Pine scrub; calcicole. 1,000–2,300m.
DISTRIBUTION: Southeast European montane.

4 | Glacier Leopard's-bane
Doronicum glaciale – Asteraceae

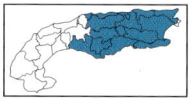

5–25cm tall, single-headed; basal and lower stem leaves elliptical to elongate-oval, 1.5–4 x as long as broad, wedge-shaped at base; leaf margins with long, stiff, multi-celled hairs, 0.5–1.2mm long, without curly hairs; flower head 4–7cm in diameter. Flowers June to August.
SIMILAR SPECIES: Tufted (Clusius') Leopard's-bane, *D. clusii*, has leaf margins with long and curly hairs.
HABITAT: Stony sward, snow-melt soils, scree, moraines, Dwarf Mountain Pine scrub; calcicole. 1,400–2,900m.
DISTRIBUTION: Eastern alpine endemic.
NOTE: 2 subspecies:
– subsp. *glaciale*: glandular hairs on leaf margins, flower stalk and bracts.
– subsp. *calcareum*: glandular hairs 1–2mm long on flower stalk and bracts but absent from leaf margins.

5 | Large-flowered Leopard's-bane
Doronicum grandiflorum – Asteraceae

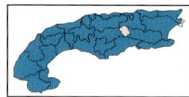

10–50cm tall, single-headed; stem and leaves with hairs and glandular hairs; basal and lower stem leaves rounded to oval, 3–7cm broad, lobed, or shallowly heart-shaped at base; bracts densely glandular-hairy; flower head 4–7cm in diameter. Flowers June to August.
SIMILAR SPECIES: Glacier Leopard's-bane, *D. glaciale*, and Tufted (Clusius') Leopard's-bane, *D. clusii*, have elliptical to elongate-oval lower stem leaves, 1.5–4 x as long as broad and wedge-shaped at base.
HABITAT: Rock debris, calcicole. 1,600–3,100m, occasionally lower.
DISTRIBUTION: Southern European montane.

Asteraceae

1 | Great Leopard's-bane
Doronicum pardalianches – Asteraceae

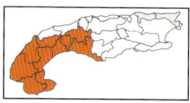

40–90cm tall, with knobbly-ended underground runners; stem with erect hairs, branched and multi-headed, usually 3–6 flower heads; blades of basal leaves heart-shaped, hairy on both sides; flower head 3–5cm in diameter. Flowers May to July.
SIMILAR SPECIES: Austrian Leopard's-bane, *D. austriacum* (see p. 70), does not produce runners and the basal leaves wither by flowering time.
HABITAT: Deciduous woods. To 1,400m.
DISTRIBUTION: Western European.

2 | Southern Globe Thistle
Echinops ritro – Asteraceae

30–80cm tall; stem with white felty hairs; leaves 1–2-pinnate, the lobes with rolled margins and 1–4mm long spines, white felty below; flower heads blue, 3.5–4.5cm in diameter, with many small individual flowers; bracts 12–17mm long. Flowers July to September.
SIMILAR SPECIES: Great Globe Thistle, *E. sphaerocephalus*, has silvery-white flower heads and bracts 18–30mm long.
HABITAT: Grazed sward, rock debris, dry slopes. To about 1,900m.
DISTRIBUTION: Southern European–western Asiatic.

3 | Hoppe's Cudweed
Gnaphalium hoppeanum – Asteraceae
(Syn.: *Omalotheca hoppeana*)

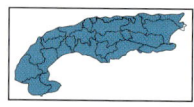

2–10cm tall; leaves linear-lanceolate, lower leaves 2–4mm broad, appressed and grey-white felty; flower heads in clusters of 3–10; bracts edged dark brown, ± upright at fruiting, outer bracts ⅓–½ as long as the inner. Flowers July to August.
SIMILAR SPECIES: Dwarf Cudweed, *G. supinum*, has bracts that open star-shaped at fruiting and outer bracts ± as long as the inner.
HABITAT: Snow hollows, damp pasture, scree, stony sward; calcicole. 1,600–2,900m.
DISTRIBUTION: Southern European montane.
NOTE: The cudweed genus contains about 80 species, of which nine are European and six found in the Alps. Some botanists divide it into several genera because of its being possibly polyphyletic (derived from two or more not closely-related ancestor species). According to this, most of the alpine species would be assigned to the genus *Omolotheca*.

4 | Norwegian Cudweed
Gnaphalium norvegicum – Asteraceae
(Syn.: *Omalotheca norvegica*)

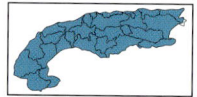

10–30cm tall; leaves 3-veined; central leaves 6–15mm broad, as long or longer than lower leaves; inflorescence at most ⅓ as long as the shoot, with 1–3 flower heads. Flowers July to September.
SIMILAR SPECIES: Heath Cudweed, *G. sylvaticum*, has 1-veined leaves, and central leaves 2–6mm broad, shorter than lower leaves.
HABITAT: Clearings, woodland margins, forest tracks, poor grassland, pasture; calcifuge. 1,300–2,800m.
DISTRIBUTION: Eurosiberian–North American.

5 | Dwarf Cudweed
Gnaphalium supinum – Asteraceae

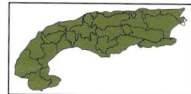

2–10cm tall, erect, or ascending, with white felty hairs; leaves narrowly lanceolate, to 3cm long and 3mm broad; flower heads 1–6, each 5–7mm long; bracts spreading star-shaped at fruiting, outer bracts ± as long as the inner. Flowers July to August.
SIMILAR SPECIES: Hoppe's Cudweed, *G. hoppeanum*.
HABITAT: Snow hollows, damp pasture, stony grassland; calcifuge. 1,300–3,300m.
DISTRIBUTION: Arctic–alpine.
NOTE: Once used to treat dysentery.

Asteraceae

1 | Alpine Fleabane
Erigeron alpinus – Asteraceae

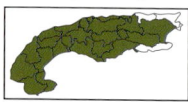

5–20cm tall, hairy, lacks glandular hairs; flower stems with 1–10 heads; leaves with erect hairs on both sides; bracts mostly green with purple tips; 1–2 rows of thread-like florets between the ray and disc florets; ray florets pinkish-purple to pale pink. Flowers July to September.
SIMILAR SPECIES: Neglected Fleabane, *E. neglectus*, has leaves hairless or only sparsely hairy, purple bracts, and white to pale pink ray florets, usually single-headed.
HABITAT: Stony grassland, pasture, bands of rock. 1,100–3,000m.
DISTRIBUTION: Southern European montane.
NOTE: The name fleabane comes from the folklore belief that it has the ability to ward off pests.

2 | Greek Fleabane
Erigeron atticus – Asteraceae

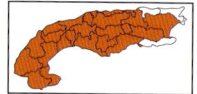

15–60cm tall, glandular; stem stiff and erect, usually only branched in upper third, lower stem 3–4mm in diameter; heads 20–30mm in diameter; ray florets purple to pink, mostly protruding horizontally. Flowers July to September.
SIMILAR SPECIES: Schleicher's Fleabane, *E. schleicheri*, and the variable Blue Fleabane, *E. acer*, which has flower heads 7–15mm diameter and mainly upright ray florets.
HABITAT: Stony grassland, rock crevices, moraines. 1,100–2,400m.
DISTRIBUTION: Southern European montane.

3 | Variable Fleabane
Erigeron glabratus – Asteraceae
(Syn.: *Erigeron polymorphus*)

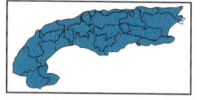

3–30cm tall, hairless or sparsely hairy; flowering stem with 1–6 heads; bracts with long hairs or almost hairless, hairs not twisted nor intertwined; no thread-like florets between the ray and disc florets; ray florets pinkish-purple to white. Flowers June to August.
SIMILAR SPECIES: Alpine Fleabane, *E. alpinus*, has thread-like florets between the ray and disc florets and leaves hairy on both sides. One-flowered Fleabane, *E. uniflorus*, is single-headed and has densely woolly bracts.
HABITAT: Stony grassland, rock crevices, rock debris; calcicole. 1,100–2,700m.
DISTRIBUTION: Southern European montane.
NOTE: 2 subspecies in the Alps:
– subsp. *glabratus*: ray florets pinkish-purple to pale pink; usually multi-headed (**3A**).
– subsp. *candidus*: ray florets white, stem always single-headed. Only in the Koralpe (**3B**).

4 | Schleicher's Fleabane
Erigeron schleicheri – Asteraceae
(Syn.: *Erigeron gaudinii*)

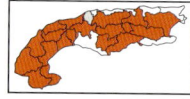

5–30cm tall, glandular; stem usually arched upwards, branching in lower half or unbranched, lower stem 1.5–2.5mm diameter; heads 15–25mm diameter; ray florets white or lilac. Flowers July to August.
SIMILAR SPECIES: Greek Fleabane, *E. atticus*, is 15–60cm tall, with stiff upright stem, lower stem 3–4mm diameter.
HABITAT: Rocks, moraines, stony ground. 1,000–3,100m.
DISTRIBUTION: Alps and Black Forest alpine.
NAME: In honour of Swiss botanist, bryologist, mycologist and algologist Johann Christoph Schleicher (1768–1834).

5 | One-flowered Fleabane
Erigeron uniflorus – Asteraceae

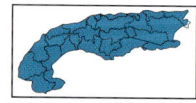

2–12cm tall; always single-headed; basal leaves sparsely hairy to almost hairless; bracts densely woolly, suffused greenish to purple; thread-like florets between ray and disc florets absent; ray florets white to purplish-pink. Flowers July to September.
SIMILAR SPECIES: Variable Fleabane, *E. glabratus*, and Neglected Fleabane, *E. neglectus*, the latter with 1–2 rows of thread-like florets between the ray and disc florets.
HABITAT: Exposed ridges, grassland. 1,500–3,700m.
DISTRIBUTION: Arctic–alpine.

Asteraceae

1 | Alpine Hawkweed
Hieracium alpinum – Asteraceae

5–20cm tall, usually single-headed, unbranched; stem leaves (0)1–2(4); leaves lanceolate, with long hairs and glandular hairs; involucre 12–18mm long, with glandular hairs. Flowers July to August.
SIMILAR SPECIES: Hairy Hawkweed, *H. glanduliferum* (Syn. *H. piliferum*), has a leafless stem covered with glandular hairs, and 0–2 scale-like bracts.
HABITAT: Rocky grassland, dwarf shrub heath, rock debris, exposed ridges; calcifuge. 1,100–3,300m.
DISTRIBUTION: Arctic–alpine.

2 | Glaucous Hawkweed
Hieracium glaucum – Asteraceae

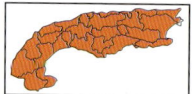

20–40cm tall, blue-green; flowering stems mostly 3–8-headed; basal leaves narrowly lanceolate, pointed, slightly toothed; stem leaves 2–6, narrowly lanceolate, toothed to entire; involucre 9–11mm long; bracts green, edged white. Flowers July to September.
SIMILAR SPECIES: Hare's-ear Hawkweed, *H. bupleuroides*, has mostly entire basal leaves, 5–10 stem leaves and 12–15mm long involucre. Leek-leaved Hawkweed, *H. porrifolium*, has linear leaves and 5–15-headed stems.
HABITAT: Stony debris, rocks, river gravel; calcicole. To 2,100m.
DISTRIBUTION: Southern European montane species, from the western Alps to the Dinaric Alps.

3 | Endive (Whitish) Hawkweed
Hieracium intybaceum – Asteraceae
(= *Schlagintweitia intybacea*)

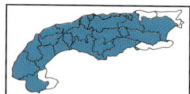

10–30cm tall; sticky glandular hairs, aromatic; leaves lanceolate, irregularly toothed; involucre 12–16mm long, hemispherical to inflated; ray florets pale yellow. Flowers July to August.
SIMILAR SPECIES: Rare hybrids with other hawkweeds, e.g. Huter's Hawkweed, *H. huteri* (**3B**).
HABITAT: Stony grassland, rock crevices, scree, dwarf shrub heath; calcifuge. 1,500–2,800m.
DISTRIBUTION: Alps, Pyrenees and Vosges.

4 | Moris's Hawkweed
Hieracium pilosum – Asteraceae
(Syn.: *Hieracium morisianum*)

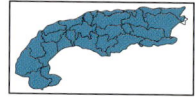

15–30cm tall, entire plant covered in long, soft woolly hairs; stem simple or forked, 2–4 flower heads, with 4–8 stem leaves; bracts similar, loosely appressed. Flowers June to August.
SIMILAR SPECIES: Shaggy Hawkweed, *H. villosum* (see p. 80).
HABITAT: Stony grassland, dwarf shrub heath; calcicole. 1,000–2,700m.
DISTRIBUTION: South-east European montane, from the western Alps and Jura to the Carpathians and Macedonia.

5 | Rough-leaved Hawkweed
Hieracium prenanthoides – Asteraceae

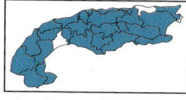

40–100cm tall; lower stem mostly hairless, upper stem dark and with glandular hairs; stem leaves 15–30, crowded, broadly lanceolate, with heart-shaped base encircling the stem; inflorescence branched, with 10–25 flower heads. Flowers July to September.
SIMILAR SPECIES: Few-headed Hawkweed, *H. sparsum*, has 6–10 stem leaves and 5–8 flower heads.
HABITAT: Woodland margins, tall herb vegetation, Green Alder scrub. 1,200–2,400m.
DISTRIBUTION: European–western Asiatic. Pyrenees, and from Iceland as far as the Hindu Kush and mountains of Tajikistan.

6 | Woolly Hawkweed
Hieracium tomentosum – Asteraceae
(Syn.: *Hieracium lanatum*)

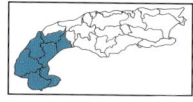

10–40cm tall, entire plant covered in white woolly hairs; upper stem usually branched, with 2–5 sessile leaves; 1–5 flower heads; basal leaves broadly lanceolate to ovate, entire or with sparse teeth. Flowers May to July.
SIMILAR SPECIES: None.
HABITAT: Dry slopes, rocky steppe, open pine woods; calcicole. To 2,200m.
DISTRIBUTION: West alpine, Jura and Apennines.

Asteraceae

1 | Shaggy Hawkweed
Hieracium villosum – Asteraceae

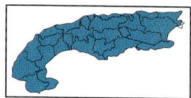

15–30cm tall, entire plant with long, soft, shaggy hairs; stem simple or branched, with 3–8 leaves; flower heads 1–4; stem leaves not narrowing, nor violin-shaped; outer bracts broad and protruding. Flowers June to August.
SIMILAR SPECIES: Hirsute Hawkweed, *H. valdepilosum*, is 30–50cm tall, and the central stem leaves violin-shaped and narrowing. Moris's Hawkweed, *H. pilosum*, has all bracts similar and loosely appressed.
HABITAT: Stony grassland, rocks, dwarf shrub heath; calcicole. 1,200–2,800m.
DISTRIBUTION: South-east European montane, from the Maritime Alps to the mountains of the Balkans and Calabria.
NOTE: Following recent research, *Pilosella*, formerly regarded as a subgenus of *Hieracium*, is now usually considered a separate genus.

2 | Purple (Alpine) Colt's-foot
Homogyne alpina – Asteraceae

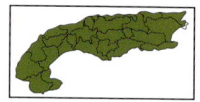

10–30cm tall, with leafy runners, single-headed; leaves kidney-shaped, leathery, 15–40mm in diameter, glossy above, green beneath; leaf margins shallowly toothed; stem with 2–3 bracts. Flower heads reddish-purple or violet, goblet-shaped (**2A**). Flowers June to August.
SIMILAR SPECIES: Felty Colt's-foot, *H. discolor* (**2C**), is felty white on the leaf undersides. Illyrian Colt's-foot, *H. sylvestris* (**2D**), restricted in the Alps to the south-eastern Alps, does not have leathery leaves, and the leaf margins are serrated.

When not flowering, the leaves of colt's-foots may resemble those of snowbells (*Soldanella*) (**2B**, *Homogyne alpina*), though they have hairless leaves.
HABITAT: Grassland, dwarf shrub heath, open woods, pasture; calcifuge. To about 2,900m.
DISTRIBUTION: Southern European montane.
NOTE: Three species are native to the Alps, and in the south-eastern Alps all 3 species may occur close together.

3 | Giant Cat's-ear
Hypochaeris uniflora – Asteraceae
(Syn.: *Hypochoeris uniflora*)

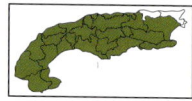

15–50cm tall; single-headed, on stout stems, swollen at the top; basal leaves ± upright, hairy on both sides; flower head 4–7cm across; outer bracts shaggy and hairy; pappus hairs feathery. Flowers June to August.
SIMILAR SPECIES: Facchini's Cat's-ear, *H. facchiniana*, has outer bracts with bare margins (hairy in the middle and at the base, ciliate on the edge), and flower head 2.5–4.5cm across. Mountain Hawk's-beard, *Crepis pontana* (see p. 68), has leaves almost hairless on both sides and pappus hairs not feathered.
HABITAT: Meadows, pasture, dwarf shrub heath; calcifuge. 1,200–2,800m.
DISTRIBUTION: Alpine–Carpathian.

4 | Alpine Sow-thistle
Lactuca alpina – Asteraceae
(Syn.: *Cicerbita alpina*)

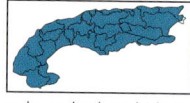

60–140cm tall, sturdy, with brown glandular hairs in upper stem; stem strong, hollow, unbranched, multi-headed, usually suffused violet; leaves deeply divided with large triangular terminal lobe; ray florets pale blue to lilac-blue. Flowers June to August.
SIMILAR SPECIES: Hairless Blue Sow-thistle, *L. plumieri* (Syn. *Cicerbita plumieri*), a western alpine species, is hairless.
HABITAT: Tall herb vegetation, montane forest, clearings. 900–2,200m.
DISTRIBUTION: European montane.

5 | Mountain (Blue) Lettuce
Lactuca perennis – Asteraceae

20–70cm tall, hairless, upper stem branched; leaves blue-green, pinnately lobed; lobes of middle stem leaves elongate to linear; lower leaves in rosette; flower heads 3–4cm in diameter, blue to pale lilac-blue. Flowers May to June.
SIMILAR SPECIES: Delicate Lettuce, *L. tenerrima*, has flower heads 1.5–2.5cm in diameter.
HABITAT: Rocky sites, dry grassland, walls. To 2,100m.
DISTRIBUTION: European.

Asteraceae

1 | Rough Hawkbit
Leontodon hispidus – Asteraceae

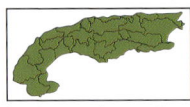

10–50cm tall, very variable species; single-headed, unbranched, hairy or hairless, with or without at most 2 bract-like scale leaves; flower head nodding before flowering; involucre narrowing at base. Flowers June to October.
SIMILAR SPECIES: Swiss Hawkbit, *Scorzoneroides helvetica* (see p. 88).
HABITAT: Meadows, pasture, open woods, rock debris. To about 3,000m.
DISTRIBUTION: European.

2 | Edelweiss
Leontopodium alpinum – Asteraceae

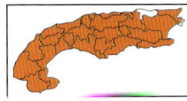

3–20cm tall, softly grey-white and woolly; leaves entire; flower heads yellowish, surrounded by star-shaped white woolly bracts. Flowers June to September.
SIMILAR SPECIES: None.
HABITAT: Stony sward, rocky ridges; calcicole. 1,500–3,100m, occasionally much lower, as on the banks of the Isonzo river, Slovenia (300m).
DISTRIBUTION: Southern European montane.

3 | Mountain Marguerite
Leucanthemum adustum – Asteraceae

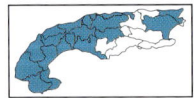

20–60cm tall; basal leaves round-toothed or almost entire; lower stem leaves mostly still present at flowering; middle stem leaves broadest near the centre, not lobed at base, regularly serrated-toothed; upper third of stem leafless; bracts edged dark brown. Flowers June to August.
SIMILAR SPECIES: Varied-leaved Marguerite, *L. heterophyllum*, has serrated basal leaves and mostly leafy stem.
HABITAT: Poor grassland, rocky ridges, pinewoods. To about 2,400m.
DISTRIBUTION: Southern European montane.
NOTE: 2 subspecies in the Alps:
– subsp. *adustum*: 20–40cm tall; lower stem at least hairy.
– subsp. *margaritae*: 40–60cm tall; stem leafless. Only on eastern outer Alps.

4 | Black-edged Marguerite (Saw-leaved Moon-daisy)
Leucanthemum atratum – Asteraceae

15–40cm tall, single-headed; leaves fleshy; basal leaves spoon-shaped, stem leaves sessile, lanceolate, 3–7mm broad; teeth of middle stem leaves almost triangular, ± 2x as long as broad, upright; bracts edged black; flower head 3–5cm in diameter. Flowers June to September.
SIMILAR SPECIES: Haller's Marguerite, *L. halleri*, has linear teeth to middle stem leaves more than 3x as long as broad. The south-eastern alpine endemic Kamnik Alp Marguerite, *L. lithopolitanicum*, has linear, ± 2mm broad middle stem leaves. The south-western alpine endemic Crow's-foot Marguerite, *L. coronopifolium*, has leaves divided to over the middle.
HABITAT: Stony sward, rock debris, snow-melt stony soils; calcicole. To about 2,300m
DISTRIBUTION: North-east alpine endemic.

5 | Varied-leaved Marguerite
Leucanthemum heterophyllum – Asteraceae

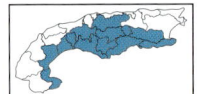

30–60cm tall; leaves often somewhat blue-green; basal leaves serrated; lower stem leaves withering at flowering; middle stem leaves 3–10mm broad, broadest near the middle, not lobed at base, regularly serrated-toothed; most of stem with leaves; bracts edged pale brown. Flowers June to September.
SIMILAR SPECIES: Mountain Marguerite, *L. adustum*. Wedge-leaved Marguerite, *L. cuneifolium*, restricted to the French Alps, has wedge-shaped leaves widest above the middle. Burnat's Marguerite, *L. burnatii*, endemic to the French Maritime and Provence Alps, is 10–25cm tall with linear leaves 1–2mm broad.
HABITAT: Poor stony grassland; calcicole. To about 2,200m.
DISTRIBUTION: Southern alpine–Apennine.
NOTE: All marguerite species are difficult to identify!

Asteraceae

1 | Alpine Moon-daisy
Leucanthemopsis alpina – Asteraceae

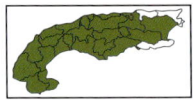

5–15cm tall, single-headed; usually only lower stem leafy; leaves pinnate with 2–4 entire lobes on each side; flower head 2–4cm in diameter; bracts edged dark brown, arranged like roof-tiles; ray florets 8–12mm long. Flowers June to August.
SIMILAR SPECIES: Carpathian Dog-daisy, *Anthemis carpatica* (see p. 52).
HABITAT: Grassland, rocky debris, snow-melt soil; especially on siliceous substrates. 1,600–3,800m, sometimes lower.
DISTRIBUTION: Southeast European montane.
NOTE: Variable species, especially with respect to hairiness.

2 | Glacier Mouse-ear-hawkweed
Pilosella angustifolia – Asteraceae
(Syn.: *Hieracium angustifolium, Hieracium glaciale*)

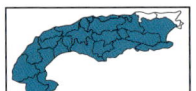

10–15cm tall; runners absent or very short; flowering stems 2–7-headed; leaves narrowly lanceolate, green, with long hairs; bracts not edged, with long hairs; flower head 1–2cm in diameter. Flowers July to August.
SIMILAR SPECIES: Glaucous Fox-and-cubs, *P. lactucella*. Tall Hawkweed, *P. piloselloides*, is at least 25cm tall and has an inflorescence with 10–40 flower heads.
HABITAT: Stony sward, rocky slopes, dwarf shrub heath; calcifuge. 1,800–2,900m.
DISTRIBUTION: Alpine endemic.
NOTE: The genus *Pilosella* is now usually separated from *Hieracium*, based on recent research.

3 | Fox-and-cubs
Pilosella aurantiaca – Asteraceae
(Syn.: *Hieracium aurantiacum*)

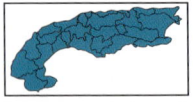

20–40cm tall, with or without surface or subterranean runners; stem with long hairs; leaves green, hairy on both sides; stem leaves 1–4; inflorescence with 4–10 flower heads; ray florets orange. Flowers June to August.
SIMILAR SPECIES: Several hybrid forms, mostly with yellow-orange ray florets.
HABITAT: Poor meadows, dwarf shrub heath; calcifuge. To about 2,300m.
DISTRIBUTION: European montane, from the Alps and Auvergne to the Carpathians, Scandinavia, and northwest Russia.

4 | Hoppe's Mouse-ear-hawkweed
Pilosella hoppeana – Asteraceae
(Syn.: *Hieracium hoppeanum*)

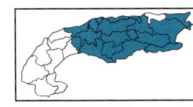

10–30cm tall, single-headed; runners 1–3cm long; stem leafless; basal leaves lanceolate, with glandular and normal hairs; bracts 2–4mm broad, with black hairs, broadest in the middle, pale-edged. Flowers May to August.
SIMILAR SPECIES: Mouse-ear-hawkweed, *P. officinarum* (Syn.: *Hieracium pilosella*), has bracts 0.5–2mm broad, and long runners. Shaggy Mouse-ear-hawkweed, *P. peleteriana*, has bracts broadest in lower third.
HABITAT: Pasture, grassland, dwarf shrub heath. To 2,800m.
DISTRIBUTION: Southeast European montane–southwest Asiatic.

5 | Glaucous Fox-and-cubs
Pilosella lactucella – Asteraceae
(Syn.: *Hieracium lactucella*)

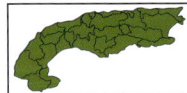

5–25cm tall; runners 5–8cm long, leafy; flowering stem 1–5(7)-headed, upper stem not glandular, usually with a bract-like leaf below the middle; basal leaves blue-green, broadly lanceolate, entire; ray florets pale yellow. Flowers May to August.
SIMILAR SPECIES: Glacier Mouse-ear-hawkweed, *Pilosella angustifolia*, has only very short runners or lacks runners, and narrowly lanceolate leaves with long hairs.
HABITAT: Poor grassland, fens, dwarf shrub heath. To 2,600m.
DISTRIBUTION: European, from Spain to the Arctic.

Asteraceae

1 | Alpine Butterbur
Petasites paradoxus – Asteraceae

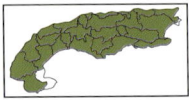

15–60cm tall; basal leaves 10–25cm broad, triangular-oval, felty white beneath, appearing towards the end of flowering; stem leaves dark pink to purplish-brown; Flower heads purplish-brown to dirty-white. Flowers April to May.
SIMILAR SPECIES: Butterbur, *P. hybridus*, mostly hairless leaves, 40–60cm broad. White Butterbur, *P. albus*, pale green stem leaves, white flower heads.
HABITAT: Seepage-moist rocky debris; calcicole. To 2,600m.
DISTRIBUTION: Southern European montane.

2 | Purple Lettuce
Prenanthes purpurea – Asteraceae

40–50cm tall, richly branching, multi-headed; leaves hairless, pointed, somewhat limp, blue-green beneath, with irregularly toothed margins to almost entire; upper leaves lobed at base, sessile; flower heads 2–5 florets; ray florets purple. Flowers July to September.
SIMILAR SPECIES: None.
HABITAT: Woods, forest clearings, tall herb vegetation. To 2,100m.
DISTRIBUTION: European.

3 | Giant Scabiosa
Rhaponticum scariosum – Asteraceae
(Syn.: *Stemmacantha rhapontica*)

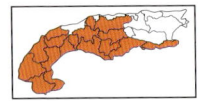

30–120cm tall; stem sturdy, single-headed, thickened and hollow towards flower head; lower leaves large, 25–60cm long, hairless above, felty white beneath, undivided to deeply cut; flower head 5–10cm in diameter. Flowers June to August.
SIMILAR SPECIES: None.
HABITAT: Tall herb vegetation, stony slopes. 1,300–2,500m.
DISTRIBUTION: Alpine endemic.
NOTE: At least 2 subspecies in the Alps.

4 | Alpine Saw-wort
Saussurea alpina – Asteraceae

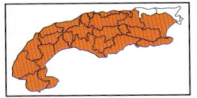

3–30cm tall; flowering stem with 3–10 heads; at least lower leaves stalked, with loose web-like hairs beneath or almost hairless; leaf stalks narrowly winged; blade lanceolate, entire or toothed. Flowers July to September.
SIMILAR SPECIES: Heart-leaved Saw-wort (Saussurea), *S. discolor*.
HABITAT: Grassland, stony debris, rock crevices. 1,800–3,100m.
DISTRIBUTION: Arctic–alpine.
NOTE: 3 subspecies in the Alps:
- subsp. *alpina*: 10–30cm tall, base of lower leaves wedge-shaped, gradually narrowing to petiole.
- subsp. *depressa*: 3–10cm tall.
- subsp. *macrophylla*: 10–30cm tall, base of lower leaves rounded to shallowly heart-shaped, narrowing abruptly to petiole.

NAME: Honours Swiss naturalist Horace-Benedict de Saussure (1740–1799).

5 | Heart-leaved Saw-wort (Saussurea)
Saussurea discolor – Asteraceae

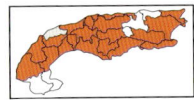

10–30cm tall; flowering stem 3–10 heads; at least lower leaves stalked, densely felty white beneath; leaf stalks unwinged; lower leaves mostly heart-shaped at base. Flowers July to September.
SIMILAR SPECIES: Alpine Saw-wort, *S. alpina*, lacks felty white undersides, and the leaf stalks narrowly winged.
HABITAT: Rock debris, stony sward, rock crevices; calcicole. 1,500–2,800m.
DISTRIBUTION: European-Asiatic.

6 | Dwarf Saw-wort (Saussurea)
Saussurea pygmaea – Asteraceae

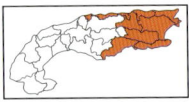

3–20cm tall; single-headed, hairy; leaves linear-lanceolate, 3–5mm broad, sessile, entire to indistinctly toothed, with rolled edges; flower head 2–3cm in diameter. Flowers June to July.
SIMILAR SPECIES: None.
HABITAT: Stony sward, rock debris, mat vegetation; calcicole. 1,600–2,600m.
DISTRIBUTION: Eastern alpine–Carpathian.

Asteraceae

1 | Bearded Viper's-grass
Scorzonera aristata – Asteraceae

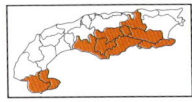

10–50cm tall; basal leaves linear, 1–5mm broad; stems mostly single-headed, leafless or with a single leaf and 0–4 scale-like bracts; involucre 20–25mm long, bracts 18–23, the outer bracts finely pointed; ray florets yellow, the outer florets sometimes striped red. Flowers June to July.
SIMILAR SPECIES: Austrian Viper's-grass, *S. austriaca*, has 2–6 leaves, and basal leaves mostly distinctly wavy. Low Viper's-grass, *S. humilis*, has leaves 10–30mm broad.
HABITAT: Meadows; calcicole. 1,200–2,400m.
DISTRIBUTION: Southern European montane.

2 | Rosy Viper's-grass
Scorzonera rosea – Asteraceae

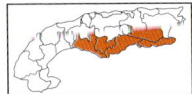

15–50cm tall; single-headed; leaves narrowly lanceolate, flat, 3–7mm broad; flower head 3–5cm in diameter; bracts 16–20; flowers pink. Flowers June to July.
SIMILAR SPECIES: Purple Viper's-grass, *S. purpurea*, has grooved leaves, 2–3mm broad, 12–16 bracts and lilac or purple-pink flowers.
HABITAT: Meadows, mat vegetation, pasture, stony slopes; calcicole. 1,200–2,100m.
DISTRIBUTION: Southeast European montane.

3 | Saffron Hawkbit
Scorzoneroides crocea – Asteraceae
(Syn.: *Leontodon croceus*)

10–35cm tall, basal leaves narrowly lanceolate with mostly backwardly-directed or almost entire teeth, beneath only hairy on veins; flower heads upright before opening; ray florets bright yellow-orange. Flowers June to August.
SIMILAR SPECIES: None. The yellow-orange flower heads distinguish it from all the other alpine *Scorzoneroides* species.
HABITAT: Meadows, damp hollows, dwarf shrub heath. 1,600–2,100m.
DISTRIBUTION: Eastern alpine–Carpathian.
NOTE: Species in the genus *Scorzoneroides* were previously assigned to *Leontodon*. Phenetic, karyological and phytochemical studies have necessitated their separation from the genus *Leontodon*.

4 | Swiss Hawkbit
Scorzoneroides helvetica – Asteraceae
(Syn.: *Leontodon helveticus*)

5–25cm tall, hairless or with simple hairs; basal leaves broadly lanceolate, lobe-toothed, or almost entire; stem single-headed, with several leaf scales; flower heads upright before opening; involucre gradually narrowing at the base. Flowers July to September.
SIMILAR SPECIES: Rough Hawkbit, *Leontodon hispidus* (see p. 82), which is very variable, has flower heads nodding before opening, involucre suddenly narrowing at the base, and stem without leaf scales or 2 at most.
HABITAT: Pasture, meadows, siliceous debris; calcifuge. 1,600–3,300m, occasionally descending to colline (hilly) levels.
DISTRIBUTION: Southern European montane.

5 Mountain Hawkbit
Scorzoneroides montana – Asteraceae
(Syn.: *Leontodon montanus*)

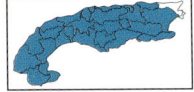

3–10cm tall; stem single-headed, only a little longer than the basal leaves, with 0–2 scale leaves; significantly thickened below flower head, with dark hairs; involucre with dark, erect hairs; pappus pure white, feathery. Flowers July to August.
SIMILAR SPECIES: Northeast Alpine Hawkbit, *S. montaniformis*, endemic to the north-eastern Alps, has a yellowish-white pappus and barely shows any thickening below the flower head. Triglav Hawk's-beard, *Crepis terglouensis* (see p. 70), has a leafy stem and an unfeathered pappus.
HABITAT: Rock debris; calcicole. 1,700–2,900m.
DISTRIBUTION: Southern European montane.
NOTE: The species has 4 subspecies, of which 2 are found in the Alps:
– subsp. *montana*: involucral hairs grey – western alpine, east to the East Tyrol.
– subsp. *melanotricha*: involucral hairs black – eastern alpine.

Asteraceae

1 | Pinnate-leaved Ragwort
Senecio abrotanifolius – Asteraceae

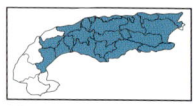

10–40cm tall, woody at base; stem upright, flower heads 2–6; leaves 1–3-pinnate, lobes 1–2mm broad, shiny dark green; flower heads bright yellow to deep orange (var. *tiroliensis*). Flowers June to August.
SIMILAR SPECIES: None.
HABITAT: Stony sward, Dwarf Mountain Pine scrub, mat vegetation, rocks, dwarf shrub heath. 1,300–2,800m, occasionally washed down to lower levels.
DISTRIBUTION: Alpine–Illyrian.

2 | Marjoram-leaved Ragwort
Senecio cacaliaster – Asteraceae

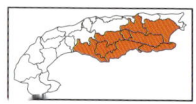

60–150cm tall; leaves somewhat curly-hairy, at least beneath, sharply toothed; blade of middle stem leaves 4–6x as long as broad; flower head stalk with glandular hairs; flower head without ray florets. Flowers July to August.
SIMILAR SPECIES: Differs from the other alpine species of the *Senecio nemorensis* group (*S. ovatus*, *S. hercynicus*, *S. nemorensis*) in its lack of ray florets.
HABITAT: Tall herb vegetation, forest clearings, Green Alder scrub, livestock resting spots. 1,000–2,000m.
DISTRIBUTION: Southern European montane.
NOTE: The hybrid between Marjoram-leaved Ragwort and Wood Ragwort (*S. ovatus*) is not uncommon. This, *Senecio* x *lamottei*, is easily distinguishable in the field by having few, sulphur yellow ray florets.

3 | Carniolan Ragwort
Senecio carniolicus – Asteraceae

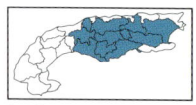

7–17cm tall; young leaves with felty hairs, later with grey felty hairs, or almost hairless; rosette leaves 5–11cm long, elongate-ovate, shallowly pinnately lobed, 2–5cm long, wedge-shaped at base; flower heads 6–14, with 3–6 yellow ray florets (**3A**). Flowers July to September.
SIMILAR SPECIES: Insubrian Ragwort, *S. insubricus*, is 4–9cm tall and has 2.6–6.5cm long rosette leaves with 1.5–2.5cm long blades. The leaves are densely covered in white felty hairs on both surfaces. Flower heads 2–5. Found in the Alps from Tessin to the East Tyrol, and (disjunct) also in the Carnic Alps and Karawanken.
Noric Ragwort, *S. norica* (**3B**), is 4–8cm tall and has 2.5–6cm long grey-green rosette leaves with 1.5–2.5cm long blades, deeply pinnately lobed, and ray florets 4–7mm long. Stony, open sites. Eastern alpine endemic, from East Tyrol to the Styrian Seckauer Tauern.
Disjunct Ragwort, *S. disjunctus*, is 5–16cm tall, with 3.5–8.5cm long, grey-green deeply cut rosette leaves. Disjunct distribution, from the Bergamask Alps to Graubünden, to the Ortler and Adamello group, but also in the Salzburg Tauern, Carinthia and Steiermark.
Grey Ragwort, *S. incanus* (**3C**), a western alpine species, has densely white-felted leaves, and divided almost to the central vein.
Persoon Ragwort, *S. persoonii*, endemic to the Italian Ligurian Alps, lacks ray florets.
HABITAT: Rocky sward, Curved Alpine Sedge (*Carex curvula*) vegetation; calcifuge. 1,700–3,200m.
DISTRIBUTION: Alpine–Carpathian. In the Alps, from the Rhaetian and Bergeller Alps to the Styrian Gleinalpe.
NOTE: The species *Senecio incanus* was formerly split into 3 subspecies: *incanus*, *carniolicus* and *insubricus*. More recent research has revealed 2 more taxa (*noricus*, *disjunctus*), and all these forms are now regarded as separate species.

4 | Alpine Ragwort
Senecio cordatus – Asteraceae (Syn.: *Senecio alpinus*)

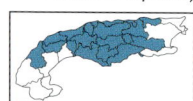

30–100cm tall; stem leaves evenly alternate; all leaves undivided; blades of basal and lower stem leaves heart-shaped; lower leaf blades ± 1.5x as long as broad; flower heads in flat-topped clusters; ray and disc florets bright yellow. Flowers July to August.
SIMILAR SPECIES: Mountain Ragwort, *Senecio subalpinus* (see p. 94), has at least the upper leaves ± pinnate.
HABITAT: Livestock resting sites, tall herb vegetation, stream sides; calcicole. To about 2,400m.
DISTRIBUTION: Alpine–Apennine.
NOTE: In the Alps there are often hybrids between Alpine Ragwort and Common Ragwort, *S. jacobaea*. In Vorarlberg, the hybrid *Senecio* x *eversii*, a characteristic plant between 800–900m.

Asteraceae

1 | Chamois Ragwort
Senecio doronicum – Asteraceae

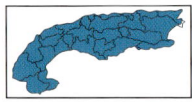

20–50cm tall, flaky-felty; leaves lanceolate to elongate-oval, toothed, alternate; flower heads usually 1–4, terminal, each 2–6cm in diameter; ray florets 10–25, dark yellow to orange-yellow. Flowers July to August.
SIMILAR SPECIES: The alpine leopard's-bane species, genus *Doronicum*, differ amongst other aspects, in having many more ray florets (mostly 20–40).
HABITAT: Rock debris, stony grassland. 1,300–3,100m.
DISTRIBUTION: Southern European montane.
NOTE: 2 subspecies in the Alps:
– subsp. *doronicum*: flower head 3–6cm in diameter, outer bracts as long as inner bracts.
– subsp. *gerardii*: flower head 2–3cm in diameter, outer bracts shorter than inner bracts.

2 | Spring Ragwort
Senecio fontanicola – Asteraceae

40–80cm tall; lower leaves obovate-lanceolate to elongate-lanceolate, 15–30cm long and 2–6cm broad; flower heads 15–20mm in diameter; ray florets usually 6–7. Flowers June.
SIMILAR SPECIES: Golden Ragwort, *S. doria*, usually has 5 ray florets, and flowers later, July to September.
HABITAT: Springs, fens. 450–850m.
DISTRIBUTION: Southeast alpine endemic.
NOTE: This species was only separated from *Senecio doria* in 1994 following a monographic reassessment of the Golden Ragwort group.

3 | Haller's Ragwort
Senecio halleri – Asteraceae

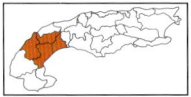

5–15cm tall, densely covered with white felty hairs, single-headed; lower leaves bluntly-toothed to pinnate, upper leaves ± entire; flower heads 2–3cm in diameter, with 7–20 ray florets. Flowers July to August.
SIMILAR SPECIES: Few.
HABITAT: Rocky sward, scree; calcifuge. 2,300–3,600m.
DISTRIBUTION: Western alpine endemic.
NAME: In honour of the Swiss Albrecht von Haller (1708–1777), a polymath with a wide range of skills and interests.

4 | Wood Ragwort
Senecio ovatus – Asteraceae

60–150cm tall; stem mostly hairless, usually suffused purple-brown, and evenly leafy; leaves lanceolate, finely toothed, hairless on both sides; blade of middle stem leaves 4–7x as long as broad; upper stem leaves narrowed at base, sessile or short-stalked; flower stalk and bracts not glandular. Flowers July to September.
SIMILAR SPECIES: Grove Ragwort, *S. nemorensis* (Syn.; *S. germanicus*), has upper stem at least hairy, leaves with curly hairs on underside, and blade of middle stem leaves usually 3–4x as long as broad.
Harz Ragwort, *S. hercynicus*, is glandular-hairy on flower stalk and bracts, and middle stem leaves 2.5–3x as long as broad.
HABITAT: Woods, woodland clearings. To about 2,000m.
DISTRIBUTION: European.

5 | Rock Ragwort
Senecio rupestris – Asteraceae

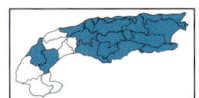

20–60cm tall, usually sparsely cobweb-hairy; leaves irregularly pinnate; middle stem leaves toothed around the centre; flower heads in irregular panicles, 18–25mm in diameter; bracts ± 21; ray florets 12–15. Flowers June to September.
SIMILAR SPECIES: Eastern Groundsel, *S. vernalis*, grows at lower altitudes and has shaggy woolly hairs when young.
HABITAT: Rock debris, ruderal sites. To 2,400m.
DISTRIBUTION: Southeast European montane.

Asteraceae

1 | Mountain Ragwort
Senecio subalpinus – Asteraceae

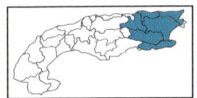

30–70cm tall; at least the upper leaves ± pinnate, narrowing towards the base and with lateral segments; lower stem leave blades about as long as broad; flower heads in flat panicles; ray and disc florets bright yellow. Flowers July to August.
SIMILAR SPECIES: Alpine Ragwort, *S. cordatus* (see p. 90), and also the hybrid between *S. cordatus* and *S. jacobaea*.
HABITAT: Tall herb vegetation, meadows, open woods, livestock resting sites. About 900–2,200m.
DISTRIBUTION: Southeast European montane.

2 | Large-headed Saw-wort
Serratula macrocephala – Asteraceae (Syn.: *Serratula tinctoria* subsp. *monticola*)

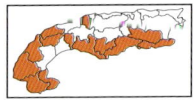

10–40cm tall; lower leaves pinnate; flower heads 2–5, terminal and closely clustered; involucre 8–10mm across; outer bracts 2–2.5mm broad. Flowers June to September.
SIMILAR SPECIES: (True) Saw-wort, *S. tinctoria*, is 30–100cm tall, with involucre 4–6mm across, and lower stem leaves undivided.
HABITAT: Pasture, sunny mountain slopes, Dwarf Mountain Pine scrub. 1,200–2,500m.
DISTRIBUTION: South European montane.

3 | Goldenrod
Solidago virgaurea – Asteraceae

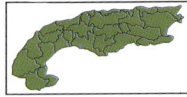

5–100cm tall; leaves alternate, lanceolate, coarsely toothed to almost entire; lower leaves elliptical, narrowing to a winged stalk; 6–12 ray florets, each 5–7mm long, notably longer than the disc florets. Flowers July to October.
SIMILAR SPECIES: Sticky Fleabane, *Dittrichia viscosa* (Syn.: *Inula viscosa*), a Mediterranean species, is glandular and sticky, and has 10–12mm long ray florets.
HABITAT: Open woods, pasture, poor grassland, dwarf shrub heath. To 2,800m.
DISTRIBUTION: Eurosiberian–North American.
NOTE: 2 subspecies in the Alps, with intermediates:
- subsp. *virgaurea*: 40–100cm tall; flower heads 40–200, each 10–15mm in diameter. Colline to montane.
- subsp. *minuta*: 5–30cm tall; flower heads 10–40, each 15–20mm in diameter. Upper montane to alpine levels.

4 | Scentless Feverfew
Tanacetum corymbosum subsp. *subcorymbosum* – Asteraceae (Syn.: *Tanacetum corymbosum* subsp. *clusii*)

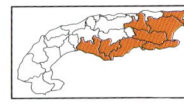

30–100cm tall; leaves pinnate, with sharply serrated segments; flower heads 30–50mm in diameter, in umbel-like raceme or panicle; bracts edged dark brown; ray florets 15–20mm long. Flowers June to July.
SIMILAR SPECIES: The nominate form, subsp. *corymbosum*, has bracts edged pale brown and 7–15mm long ray florets. Restricted to lower levels.
HABITAT: Herb-rich meadows, open woods; calcicole. About 1,000–2,100m.
DISTRIBUTION: Southeast European montane.

5 | Showy (Dwarf) Oxeye
Telekia speciosissima – Asteraceae

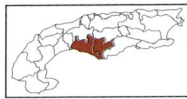

20–60cm tall; leaves broad and oval, 10–15cm long, 4–7cm broad, clasping stem or with heart-shaped base; flower heads 4–6cm in diameter; involucre multi-rowed. Flowers June to July.
SIMILAR SPECIES: The genera *Buphthalmum* and *Inula* have similar flower heads but lanceolate not broad oval leaves.
HABITAT: Stony slopes, rock crevices; carbonate substrates. To 2,000m.
DISTRIBUTION: Southern alpine endemic.
NAME: In honour of Hungarian count Samuel Teleki de Szek (1739–1822), Chancellor of the then Grand Duchy of Transylvania and an important patron of science and art.
NOTE: Showy (Dwarf) Oxeye is an Insubrian endemic. This region is especially rich in alpine plants and is home to a number of other endemics such as Two-lobed Buttercup, *Ranunculus bilobus* and Large-flowered Catchfly, *Silene elisabethae*.

Asteraceae

1 | Alpine Dandelion
Taraxacum sect. *Alpina* – Asteraceae

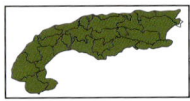

5–15cm tall; leaves narrowly obovate, deeply toothed, with large terminal lobes; leaf stalk not winged; flower heads 1.5–2cm in diameter; outer bracts oval, less than ½ as long as the involucre; ray florets striped below; fruit brownish-white. Flowers June to September.
SIMILAR SPECIES: The Mountain Dandelion group, *Taraxacum* sect. *Alpestria*, has winged leaf stalks.
HABITAT: Rich pasture, snow-melt hollows. 1,200–3,300m.
DISTRIBUTION: South European montane.
NOTE: Dandelions, genus *Taraxacum*, consist mainly of taxa that produce seeds asexually (agamospermy). This results in a wide range of subspecies that are the subject of much research and which can only be identified by specialists.

2 | Hooded Dandelion
Taraxacum sect. *Cucullata* – Asteraceae

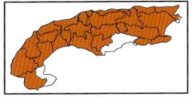

5–25cm tall; leaves toothed to somewhat divided, leaf stalk usually winged; ray florets straw yellow to ochre, rolled at the tip (hooded); flower head 3–4.5cm in diameter; bracts not horned, the outer bracts broadly ovate-lanceolate, dark green, often suffused purple. Flowers June to August.
SIMILAR SPECIES: The Horned Dandelion group, *Taraxacum* sect. *Ceratophora*, has bracts noticeably horned below the tip.
HABITAT: Rich pasture, snow-melt hollows. 1,500–2,800m.
DISTRIBUTION: Alpine–Corsican.

3 | Handel's Dandelion
Taraxacum handelii – Asteraceae

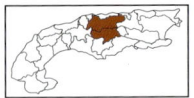

3–15cm tall; stem hairless, rather thick; leaves few, dark green, shiny, saw-like, with pointed, triangular, protruding or recurved segments; bracts dark green; ray florets yellow, often striped red on outside. Flowers July to August.

SIMILAR SPECIES: Reichenbach's Dandelion, *T. reichenbachii*, has undivided, entire to distantly toothed leaves. Pacher's Dandelion, *T. pacheri*, has orange ray florets.
HABITAT: Stony sites, rocky grassland, exposed ridges. 2,400–2,900m.
DISTRIBUTION: Eastern alpine endemic.
NAME: In honour of Austrian botanist Heinrich von Handel-Mazzetti (1882–1940), author of a monograph on the genus.

4 | Capitate Field Fleawort
Tephroseris integrifolia subsp. *capitata* – Asteraceae (Syn.: *Senecio capitatus*)

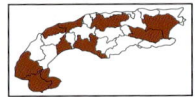

10–35cm tall, covered in dense white woolly hairs; lower leaves in rosette; flower head orange, with compact base, often purple in bud; bracts usually purple-brown. Flowers June to July.
SIMILAR SPECIES: Brook Fleawort, *T. crispa*, sometimes has orange flower heads (forma *croceus*) but lacks white woolly hair.
HABITAT: Stony grassland, pasture. 1,800–2,500m.
DISTRIBUTION: South European montane.
NOTE: One of the most beautiful and imposing of alpine flowers. In Carinthia it is known as 'Red Edelweiss' and honoured in a song.

5 | Brook Fleawort
Tephroseris crispa – Asteraceae (Syn.: *Senecio rivularis*)

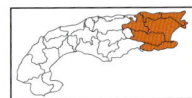

30–100cm tall; stem and leaves not glandular; basal leaf blades wavy, with winged stalk, ± heart-shaped at base; leaf margins serrated to toothed; flowering stems with 5–15 flower heads; ray florets egg-yolk yellow; fruit hairless. Flowers April to July.
SIMILAR SPECIES: Southern Alpine Fleawort, *T. pseudocrispa*, has ± flat basal leaf blades and densely hairy fruits. Long-leaved Fleawort, *T. longifolia*, is glandular-hairy and the basal leaves are not heart-shaped at base.
HABITAT: Tall herb vegetation, damp meadows, riverine woods. 400–2,000m.
DISTRIBUTION: European montane.

Asteraceae, Balsaminaceae

1 | Long-leaved Fleawort
Tephroseris longifolia – Asteraceae
(Syn.: *Senecio ovirensis*)

20–60cm tall, glandular-hairy, and usually cobweb-woolly; basal leaf blades ovate to elongate-elliptical, narrowing abruptly towards the wide-winged stalk; flowering stem with 3–10 flower heads; ray florets egg-yolk yellow; bracts usually 21; fruit hairless. Flowers May to July.
SIMILAR SPECIES: Brook Fleawort, *T. crispa* (see p. 96). Swiss Fleawort, *T. tenuifolia*, usually has 13 bracts. Steppe Fleawort, *T. integrifolia* subsp. *integrifolia*, has hairy fruits.
HABITAT: Meadows, tall herb vegetation, open woods. To about 2,200m.
DISTRIBUTION: Eastern alpine–Illyrian.
NOTE: The genus *Tephroseris* was long held to be part of the genus *Senecio*. Apart from the superficial similarity of their involucres, fleaworts and ragworts are not actually that closely related.

2 | Southern Alpine Fleawort
Tephroseris pseudocrispa – Asteraceae (Syn.: *Senecio pseudocrispus*)

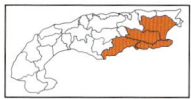

30–70cm tall; basal leaf blades ± flat, the stalk not or only slightly winged, stalk base ± heart-shaped; leaf margins serrated to toothed; flower heads 3–10; ray florets egg-yolk yellow; fruit densely hairy. Flowers May to July.
SIMILAR SPECIES: Brook Fleawort, *T. crispa* (see p. 96). Balbis Fleawort, *T. balbisiana*, a southwest alpine endemic, has hairless fruit.
HABITAT: Tall herb vegetation, stream sides, damp meadows, Dwarf Mountain Pine scrub. 700–2,100m.
DISTRIBUTION: Eastern alpine endemic.

3 | Swiss Fleawort
Tephroseris tenuifolia – Asteraceae
(Syn.: *Senecio gaudinii*)

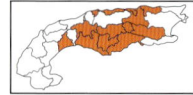

30–80cm tall, densely hairy to almost hairless; basal leaf blades gradually narrowing into the winged stalk; flower heads 5–15; ray florets pale to egg-yolk yellow; bracts usually 13; fruit densely hairy. Flowers May to July.
SIMILAR SPECIES: Spatulate Fleawort, *T. helenitis*, usually has 21 bracts, and basal leaf blades narrowing abruptly into the stalk.
HABITAT: Rich meadows, livestock resting sites, glaciated herbage. 900–2,500m.
DISTRIBUTION: Southeast European montane.
NAME: The synonym honours the Swiss botanist and clergyman Jean Gaudin (1766–1833), whose name is also given to the grass genus *Gaudinia*.

4 | Stalked Willemetia
Willemetia stipitata – Asteraceae
(Syn.: *Calycocorsus stipitatus*)

15–45cm tall; flower heads 1–5, stem with 0–2 leaves, upper leaves with erect black hairs; basal leaves hairless or sparsely hairy, blue-green beneath, lobed or entire; involucre blackish-green, with black glandular hairs. Flowers June to August.
SIMILAR SPECIES: Various hawk's-beard, *Crepis* species, such as Marsh Hawk's-beard, *Crepis paludosa*, which however has sessile upper leaves clasping the stem.
HABITAT: Mires, wet meadows. To about 2,500m.
DISTRIBUTION: South European montane.
NAME: In honour of French botanist and pharmacist Remi Willemet (1735–1807), Director of the Botanic Garden in Nancy.

5 | Touch-me-not Balsam
Impatiens noli-tangere – Balsaminaceae

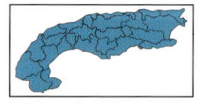

30–80cm tall, hairless; leaves elongate-oval, blunt-toothed, 3–12cm long, alternate; flowers bright yellow, solitary or few, drooping; petal-like sepals and spur 2.5–3cm long. Flowers July to August.
SIMILAR SPECIES: None. The Asian invasive Indian Balsam, *I. glandulifera* (**5B**), has purple-red, pink or white flowers and is increasingly spreading in the Alps.
HABITAT: Shady damp woods, ravine and valley woods, stream sides. To about 1,800m.
DISTRIBUTION: Eurosiberian.

Berberidaceae, Betulaceae, Boraginaceae

1 | Alpine Barrenwort
Epimedium alpinum – Berberidaceae

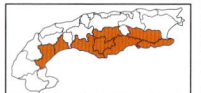

20–40cm tall; leaves 2-trifoliate, broadly lanceolate, with heart-shaped base, often edged red, spiny-toothed; flowers brownish-red, four-lobed, with yellow sac-like, spurred nectar petals. Flowers April.
SIMILAR SPECIES: None.
HABITAT: Deciduous woods, especially Sessile Oak woods, and scrub; calcicole. About 700–1,200m.
DISTRIBUTION: Eastern alpine–Illyrian, from Piedmont and parts of the Apennines to Albania and Bulgaria.

2 | Green Alder
Alnus alnobetula – Betulaceae (Syn.: *Alnus viridis*)

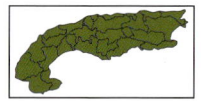

Shrub to 3m tall; bark smooth, grey-brown; leaves oval, pointed, green both sides, with 5–7 pairs of lateral veins; flowers opening with leaves. Flowers April to June.
SIMILAR SPECIES: Common Alder, *A. glutinosa*, which has more rounded leaves, and Grey Alder, *A. incana*, with 8–15 lateral leaf veins.
HABITAT: Forms scrub on rich, damp soils, such as near avalanches, and as understorey in acid woods. Mainly at 1,500–2,000m, sometimes down into valleys or as high as 2,900m.
DISTRIBUTION: Southern European montane, from the Pyrenees to the central German mountains and Rila Mountains of Bulgaria.

3 | Dwarf Birch
Betula nana – Betulaceae

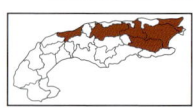

Dwarf shrub 20–100cm tall; young shoots with fluffy hairs, without resin glands; leaf blade 4–12mm long and 5–15mm broad, with 2–4 lateral veins on each surface, blunt-toothed; male and female catkins protruding or upright. Flowers April to May.
SIMILAR SPECIES: Shrubby Birch, *B. humilis*, which can grow to 2.5m, has resinous young shoots and sharply-toothed leaf margins.
HABITAT: Raised bogs. About 700–2,050m.
DISTRIBUTION: Eurosiberian–North American, from Iceland to the Yenisei region, and south to the mountains of central Europe. Widespread in the arctic tundra. In central Europe, only locally in the lowlands of north Germany, the Harz, Bohemian Forest, Ore Mountains and in the eastern Alps, as well as the alpine foothills, where it is critically endangered.

4 | Barrelier's Bugloss (False Alkanet)
Anchusa barrelieri – Boraginaceae (Syn.: *Cynoglottis barrelieri*)

30–60cm tall; leaves lanceolate, 3–10cm long, 1–2.5cm broad; corolla violet-blue; calyx 2–3mm long, 6mm in fruit. Flowers May to July.
SIMILAR SPECIES: Common Bugloss (Common Alkanet), *A. officinalis*, has dark violet corolla, calyx 5–7mm long, to 10mm in fruit.
HABITAT: Embankments, poor meadows, stony grassland; calcicole. To 1,500m.
DISTRIBUTION: Mediterranean-montane, from the south-western Alps to Ukraine.
NAME: In honour of French botanist and priest Jacques Barrelier (1606–1673).

5 | Smooth Honeywort
Cerinthe alpina – Boraginaceae (Syn.: *Cerinthe glabra*)

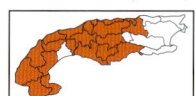

30–60cm tall, hairless, with bluish waxy coat; stem leaves oval, clasping; corolla tube-shaped, 10–15mm long, yellow with purple markings; corolla tip much shorter than corolla tube. Flowers May to July.
SIMILAR SPECIES: Lesser Honeywort, *C. minor*, has uniformly yellow corolla, with tip almost as long as corolla tube. Golden-drop species, genus *Onosma*, are very hairy.
HABITAT: Stony meadows, tall herb vegetation, livestock resting sites, Green Alder scrub; calcicole. 1,200–2,600m.
DISTRIBUTION: European–west Asiatic.

Boraginaceae

1 | Common Hound's-tongue
Cynoglossum officinale – Boraginaceae

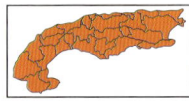

30–70cm tall, densely softly hairy, smells of mice; stem richly branched; leaves lanceolate, felty grey on both sides, to 25cm long; stem leaves 1.5–3cm broad; corolla purple-red to violet; fruits (nutlets) bristly, with thickened border. Flowers May to July.
SIMILAR SPECIES: Green Hound's-tongue, *C. germanicum*, has shiny, hairless or almost hairless leaves, and nutlets without thickened border. Dioscorides's Hound's-tongue, *C. dioscoridis*, has 0.6–1.5cm broad stem leaves.
HABITAT: Livestock resting spots, dry ruderal sites, forest clearings. To 2,500m.
DISTRIBUTION: European-Asiatic.

2 | King-of-the-Alps
Eritrichium nanum – Boraginaceae

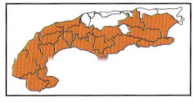

1–4cm tall; leaves mostly in rosettes, with shaggy hair; inflorescence 3–6-flowered, corolla bright pale blue, with yellow throat; bract under each flower; fruit with winged, comb-like, serrated edge. Flowers June to August.
SIMILAR SPECIES: Alpine Forget-me-not, *Myosotis alpestris* (see p. 104), in its low-growing form, lacks the flower bracts and the fruit is smooth-edged.
HABITAT: Rock crevices, stony sites, open grassy habitats. 2,200–3,300m, sometimes lower, as in the moraines of the Forno glacier (2,070m), or higher, as on the Weisstor (3,620m).
DISTRIBUTION: Alpine-Carpathian.

3 | Shrubby Moltkia
Moltkia suffruticosa – Boraginaceae

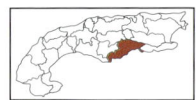

8–25cm tall; leaves linear, 5–15cm long, 1–3mm broad; corolla blue, 8–14mm long; calyx 5–6mm long. Flowers May to June.
SIMILAR SPECIES: None.
HABITAT: Rocks; calcicole. To 1,300m.
DISTRIBUTION: East alpine-Apennine.
NAME: In honour of Danish count and botanist Joachim Godske Moltke (1746–1818), founder of the Copenhagen Natural History Museum.

4 | Swiss Golden-drop
Onosma helvetica – Boraginaceae

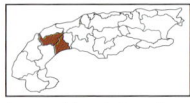

15–50cm tall, densely bristly-hairy; leaves linear-lanceolate; bristly hairs 1–4mm long, without star-shaped hairs; scattered hairs between bristles, but not downy; corolla pale yellow, 20–25mm long, tubular. Flowers May to July.
SIMILAR SPECIES: Halácsy's Golden-drop, *O. pseudoarenaria* has 0.1–0.3mm star-shaped hairs at the base of the 1–4mm long bristly hairs. Ligurian Golden-drop, *O. fastigiata*, restricted in the Alps to the south-west and Italy, is downy-hairy between the bristly hairs.
HABITAT: Dry slopes, open woods, sparse dry grassland. To 1,400m.
DISTRIBUTION: Western alpine endemic.
NOTE: Some botanists consider *O. pseudoarenaria*, and also *O. austriaca*, to belong to *O. helvetica*.

5 | Tuberous Comfrey
Symphytum tuberosum – Boraginaceae

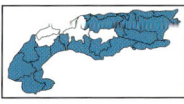

10–30cm tall; leaf blades elongate-oval, sheathing stem at base; corolla pale yellow, 14–19mm long, tubular; corolla scales not extending beyond the flower. Flowers April to June.
SIMILAR SPECIES: Bulbous Comfrey, *S. bulbosum*, has corolla only 8–11mm long, and the corolla scales extend beyond the flower.
HABITAT: Deciduous woods, tall herb vegetation. To 1,900m.
DISTRIBUTION: European.
NOTE: In the higher regions of the south-eastern Alps there are often populations with attractive apricot-orange flowers (**5B**). Valuable nectar plant for insects. Specialist species include Comfrey Mining Bee, *Andrena symphytii*, and Comfrey Lace Bug, *Dictyla humuli*. The abundant nectar is hidden so deep inside the flowers that it can only normally be reached by insects with long proboscies, such as bumblebees, and certain hoverflies and butterflies.

Boraginaceae

1 | Alpine Forget-me-not
Myosotis alpestris – Boraginaceae

5–30cm tall; leaves elliptical to lanceolate; rosette leaves mostly narrowing towards the stalk; fruits (nutlets) 2–2.5mm long, broadest in the middle. Flowers June to August.
SIMILAR SPECIES: Wood Forget-me-not, *M. sylvatica*.
HABITAT: Poor grassland, poor pasture, stabilised scree. 1,400–3,100m.
DISTRIBUTION: South European montane.
NOTE: The charming name 'forget-me-not' is very ancient, going back at least to the 14th century. The South Tyrolean poet Hans Vintler (died in 1419) referred to it by this name ('Vergissmeinnicht') several times in his poems.

2 | Lake Constance Forget-me-not
Myosotis rehsteineri – Boraginaceae

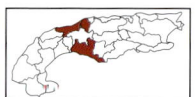

1–10cm tall, low-growing cushion plant producing rosettes at flowering; stem rounded, with forwardly-directed appressed hairs; corolla 4–9mm in diameter. Flowers April to June.
SIMILAR SPECIES: The other species from the *M. palustris* group (*M. scorpioides, M. nemorosa, M. laxa*) do not produce cushion rosettes.
HABITAT: Summer-flooded riverbanks and gravel beds that dry out in spring and autumn. To about 600m.
DISTRIBUTION: Possibly endemic to the Lake Constance region.
NOTE: This species has been reported from certain other alpine sites, such as Sondrio (Italy), Tessin (Switzerland), and Traunsee (Austria), but these have not been verified.
NAME: In honour of Swiss botanist and clergyman Johann Konrad Rehsteiner (1797–1858), who studied the flora of Appenzell and St Gallen.

3 | Water Forget-me-not
Myosotis scorpioides – Boraginaceae
(Syn.: *Myosotis palustris* p.p.)

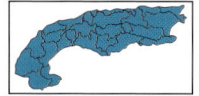

10–70cm tall; stem weakly ridged to almost round, either almost hairless or with upwardly-directed or horizontal hairs; corolla 6–11mm in diameter; fruiting stalk ± 2x as long as calyx. Flowers May to October.
SIMILAR SPECIES: Woodland Forget-me-not, *M. nemorosa*, usually has a stem that is clearly ridged and lower stem with downwardly-directed hairs or almost hairless. Corolla 3.5–7mm in diameter, and fruiting stalk at most 1.5x as long as calyx.
Tufted Forget-me-not, *M. laxa* (Syn.: *M. caespitosa*), has a round stem, corolla 3–6mm in diameter, and fruiting stalk more than 2x as long as calyx.
HABITAT: Wet meadows, banks, ditches, swampy woods. To 2,100m.
DISTRIBUTION: Eurosiberian.

4 | Wood Forget-me-not
Myosotis sylvatica – Boraginaceae

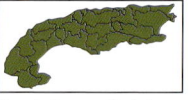

15–40cm tall, ± densely hairy; rosette leaves short-stalked, narrowing abruptly into the stalk; corolla tube as long as or somewhat shorter than the calyx, so not protruding beyond the calyx lobes; fruits (nutlets) 1.6–2mm long, broadest below the middle. Flowers May to July.
SIMILAR SPECIES: Lapland Forget-me-not, *M. decumbens*, has corolla tube longer than the calyx, and so extending beyond the calyx lobes. Alpine Forget-me-not, *M. alpestris*, has basal leaves narrowing gradually towards the stalk, and fruits (nutlets) 2–2.5mm long, broadest in the middle.
HABITAT: Moist meadows, forest clearings, tall herb vegetation. To about 2,800m.
DISTRIBUTION: European.

5 | Blue-eyed Mary
Omphalodes verna – Boraginaceae

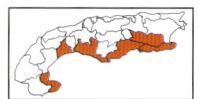

5–20cm tall; leaves broadly ovate, sometimes weakly heart-shaped at base; inflorescence of 10–20 flowers; corolla 10–12mm in diameter; corolla scales white. Flowers April to May.
SIMILAR SPECIES: Great Forget-me-not, *Brunnera macrophylla*, which is often cultivated and sometimes naturalised, has inflorescence with 50–100 flowers, and corolla 4–8mm in diameter. The alpine forget-me-not species, *Myosotis* spp., have yellow corolla scales.
HABITAT: Riverine woods, moist deciduous woods. To about 1,400m.
DISTRIBUTION: Southeast European.

Boraginaceae

1 | Southern Lungwort
Pulmonaria australis – Boraginaceae

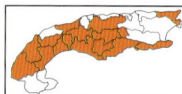

10–30cm tall; leaves soft, lanceolate, not spotted, or only slightly so; basal leaf blades narrowing into the stalk; leaf upper surface with bristles of clearly differing length; corolla deep blue to rich purple. Flowers March to June.
SIMILAR SPECIES: Kerner's Lungwort, *P. kerneri*, a north-east alpine endemic, has bristles of ± equal length on the leaf upper surface.
HABITAT: Open woods, dry meadows, dwarf shrub heath, Larch woods. 1,200–2,500m, sometimes lower, as in Gütenbach valley in the Vienna Forest (Wienerwald) at 320m, or higher, as in the Bernina region of Graubünden at 2,620m.
DISTRIBUTION: Alpine–Illyrian. Alps and mountains of the north-west Balkans.
NOTE: Many lungwort species are rather similar and require careful inspection of the basal leaves using a hand lens of at least 10x magnification to check on the type of hairs, which can be decisive for precise identification. The lungwort genus contains 18 species, all native to Europe. 14 are found in the Alps, 3 of which are restricted to the Alps: *P. carnica, P. kerneri,* and *P. vallarsae*.

2 | Carnic Lungwort
Pulmonaria carnica – Boraginaceae

10–25cm tall; basal leaf blades broadly elliptical to lanceolate, narrowing into the stalk; leaves unspotted or weakly spotted; corolla violet-blue. Flowers April to June.
SIMILAR SPECIES: Styrian Lungwort, *P. stiriaca.* Common Lungwort, *P. officinalis*, has heart-shaped or oval basal leaf blades, narrowing abruptly into the stalk. Vallarsa Lungwort, *P. villarsae*, has soft leaf blades with dense soft hairs as well as bristles and glandular hairs, and the margins of the summer leaves are wavy.
HABITAT: Tall herb vegetation, scrub, moist woods, meadows; calcicole. 800–1,900m.
DISTRIBUTION: South-east alpine endemic: Central and East Karawanks and Steiner Alps, and a somewhat isolated site further west near the Loibl Pass.

3 | Hairy Lungwort
Pulmonaria mollis – Boraginaceae

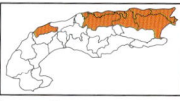

15–40cm tall; leaves unspotted, greyish; basal leaf blades 30–50cm long, ovate-lanceolate, narrowing quickly into the stalk; inflorescence sticky. Flowers April to June.
SIMILAR SPECIES: Mountain Lungwort, *P. montana*, leaves are not greyish and are very glandular above, although the inflorescence is not sticky.
HABITAT: Open woods, tall herb vegetation, scrub, clearings, meadows. To 1,800m (subsp. *alpigena*).
DISTRIBUTION: European.
NOTE: 2 subspecies in the Alps:
– subsp. *mollis*: basal leaves wavy and curly; leaves and calyx with soft hairs, and few bristles.
– subsp. *alpigena*: basal leaves hardly wavy or curly; leaves and calyx with many stiff bristles.

4 | Styrian Lungwort
Pulmonaria stiriaca – Boraginaceae

10–30cm tall; basal leaf blades lanceolate, mostly pointed, narrowing into the stalk; leaves mostly with white spots; stem and leaf stalks densely hairy with bristles and long-stalked glands; corolla intense azure blue. Flowers March to June.
SIMILAR SPECIES: Carnic Lungwort, *P. carnica*, has leaves that are unspotted or only faintly spotted, violet-blue corolla, and no obvious dense hair on stem and leaf stalks. Spotted Lungwort, *P. picta*, is usually heavily spotted and the basal leaves narrow abruptly into the stalk.
HABITAT: Moist woods, scrub, tall herb vegetation. To 1,800m.
DISTRIBUTION: Eastern alpine–Illyrian.

Brassicaceae

1 | Alpine Alison
Alyssum alpestre – Brassicaceae

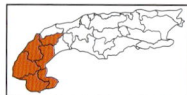

5–15cm tall; leaves spoon-shaped or inverse lanceolate, 5–10mm long, densely hairy; petals yellow, 2.5–3.5mm long; fruit almost circular, 4–5mm long, 3–4mm broad, hairy. Flowers June to August.
SIMILAR SPECIES: Silver Alison, *A. argenteum*, is 20–40cm tall with elliptical fruits 3–4mm long. Western alpine, on serpentine substrates.
HABITAT: Stony slopes, rock debris; calcicole. 2,400–3,100m.
DISTRIBUTION: Western alpine endemic.

2 | Ligurian Alison
Alyssum ligusticum – Brassicaceae

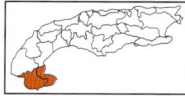

5–25cm tall, woody at base; leaves densely covered with grey felty hairs undivided, linear to spoon-shaped, narrowing towards base, 25–30mm long, 3–4mm broad, upper leaves smaller; petals 4, similar, white, 3–4mm long, with rounded tips; fruit round, hairless, 6–7mm long, 4–5mm broad, style 2–4mm long. Flowers April to June.
SIMILAR SPECIES: Candytuft species (genus *Iberis*), but these have unequal petals (2 long and 2 short).
HABITAT: Rock crevices; calcicole. 600–1,800m.
DISTRIBUTION: Western alpine endemic.

3 | Obir Alison
Alyssum ovirense – Brassicaceae
(Syn.: *Alyssum wulfenianum* subsp. *ovirense*)

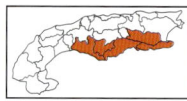

5–12cm tall; lower leaves rounded-elliptical, narrowing abruptly into the stalk, 4–7mm long, 2.5–5mm broad; undersides of middle leaves with 6–11 stellate hairs per mm²; petals yellow, 6–7mm long; fruit elliptical, 7–9mm long, 3.5–4.5mm broad, loosely hairy. Flowers June to July.
SIMILAR SPECIES: Wulfen's Alison, *A. wulfenianum*. Hochschwab Alison, *A. neglectum* (**3B**), has whitish leaves and leaf undersides with 15–20 stellate hairs per mm². Wedge-leaved Alison, *A. cuneifolium*, has densely hairy fruits and is restricted to the western Alps.
HABITAT: Rocks, rocky debris; calcicole. 1,700–2,400m.
DISTRIBUTION: Eastern alpine–Illyrian, southeast to Montenegro.

4 | Wulfen's Alison
Alyssum wulfenianum – Brassicaceae

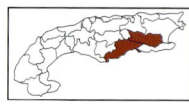

5–20cm tall; lower leaves elliptical-lanceolate, 6–14mm long, 1.5–4mm broad, narrowing gradually towards the stalk, with grey-white hairs; petals yellow, 5–6mm long; fruit elliptical, 6–8mm long, sparsely hairy, later almost hairless. Flowers May to July.
SIMILAR SPECIES: Mountain Alison, *A. montanum*, has a roughly circular, densely hairy fruit, 3–5mm long. Obir Alison, *A. ovirense*, has lower leaves rounded-elliptical, narrowing abruptly towards the stalk.
HABITAT: Rocky debris, sandy riverbanks; calcicole. 500–1,500m.
DISTRIBUTION: South-east alpine endemic.
NAME: In honour of Austrian botanist, mineralogist and clergyman Franz Xaver von Wulfen (1728–1805), who studied the flora of Carinthia.

5 | Allioni's Rock-cress
Arabis allionii – Brassicaceae

20–50cm tall; stem hairless; basal leaves hairless or sparsely hairy only on the veins and margins; stem leaves toothed, hairless, sessile, arrow-shaped at base, with ciliate margins; petals white, 6–7mm long; fruit 25–35mm long, 1.2–1.8mm broad. Flowers May to July.
SIMILAR SPECIES: Fringed Rock-cress, *A. ciliata*, is only 5–20cm tall, with broad-based sessile stem leaves. Hairy Rock-cress, *A. hirsuta*, has hairy lower stem and leaves.
HABITAT: Stable rock debris, stony sward; calcifuge. 1,600–2,500m.
DISTRIBUTION: Western alpine endemic.
NAME: In honour of Italian botanist and naturalist Carlo Ludovico Allioni (1728–1804), Director of the Turin Botanic Garden.

Brassicaceae

1 | Alpine Rock-cress
Arabis alpina – Brassicaceae

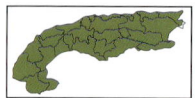

8–30cm tall, usually upright and branching, hairy, with many sterile rosettes; basal leaves oval, roughly toothed, short-stalked; stem leaves 3–10, stem-sheathing; petals white, 7–10mm long. Flowers April to October.
SIMILAR SPECIES: Rock Rock-cress, *A. nova*, has petals only 4–6mm long.
HABITAT: Rocky sward, rock crevices; calcicole. 400–3,200m.
DISTRIBUTION: 2 subspecies, from Iceland and the Sierra Nevada to the Pamir region.

2 | Blue Rock-cress
Arabis caerulea - Brassicaceae

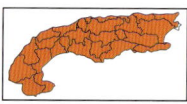

2–12cm tall; basal leaves oval, with 2–7 teeth towards the tip, mainly hairless; stem leaves 1–3, sessile; petals white, marked lilac, 4–5mm long; fruits 1–3cm long, 2.5–3mm broad, suffused blue before ripening. Flowers July to August.
SIMILAR SPECIES: Dwarf Rock-cress, *A. pumila*, has pure white petals.
HABITAT: Snow-melt hollows, damp rock debris; calcicole. 1,900–3,500m, sometimes lower, as in the Erschbaum Valley, East Tyrol (1,600m).
DISTRIBUTION: Alpine endemic.

3 | Dwarf Rock-cress
Arabis pumila – Brassicaceae (Syn.: *Arabis stellulata, A. bellidifolia*)

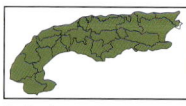

5–15cm tall; lower stem hairy; basal leaves oval, short-stalked; stem leaves 1–6, elongate-ovate, sessile; flowers 5–15, in a raceme; petals white; fruits 2–4cm long, 1.7–2.2mm broad. Flowers June to August.
SIMILAR SPECIES: Thyme-leaved Rock-cress, *A. serpillifolia* has fruits only 1mm broad.
HABITAT: Calcareous rock debris, limestone crevices; calcicole. 900–3,000m, sometimes lower, as in the Kundler Klamm gorge, Austria (550m).
DISTRIBUTION: Alpine–Apennine.

NOTE: 2 subspecies:
– subsp. *pumila*: lowest internode hairless or with 1–2-rayed hairs; mainly on calcareous rock debris.
– subsp. *stellulata*: lowest internode hairs 3–5-rayed; mainly on limestone rocks.

4 | Soyer's Rock-cress
Arabis soyeri – Brassicaceae

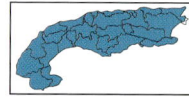

10–30cm tall, hairless, or with at most scattered hairs; basal leaves oval, shiny, entire or distantly toothed, short-stalked; stem leaves 4–12, sessile or somewhat clasping; petals white, 6–7mm long; fruits 2–4cm long, c. 2mm broad. Flowers May to August.
SIMILAR SPECIES: Bristol Rock-cress, *A. scabra*, has yellowish-white petals and 1–4 stem leaves. Piedmont Rock-cress, *Arabidopsis pedemontana*, Syn.: *Arabis pedemontana*, has round, long-stalked basal leaves.
HABITAT: Wet flushes, wet rocks; calcicole. 1,100–2,700m, often swept lower in streams and rivers.
DISTRIBUTION: South European montane, from the Pyrenees to the southern Carpathians
NOTE: Only subsp. *subcoriacea* is found in the Alps. The nominate form is native to the Pyrenees. Bristol Rock-cress, *A. scabra*, is so named in English because it is found as a very rare outlier in the Avon Gorge near Bristol, where it has been known since 1686.
NAME: In honour of French botanist and librarian Hubert Felix Soyer-Willemet (1791–1867), who researched the genus *Valerianella*, among others.

5 | Bohinj Rock-cress
Arabis vochinensis – Brassicaceae

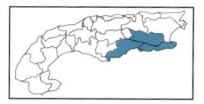

5–14cm tall; basal leaves 8–25mm long, obovate, blunt, narrowing gradually to a short stalk, hairless or almost so, with appressed, forked hairs on leaf margins; stem leaves 2–6; petals white, 5–7mm long. Flowers May to July.
SIMILAR SPECIES: Thyme-leaved Rock-cress, *A. serpillifolia*, is hairy also on the blades of the basal leaves, and is found in the western Alps.
HABITAT: Moist rocky soil, stony slopes, open grassland; calcicole. 500–2,200m.
DISTRIBUTION: Eastern alpine–Illyrian.
NOTE: The common and scientific names refer to the Lake Bohinj area of Slovenia.

Brassicaceae

1 | Pale-yellow Winter-cress
Barbarea bracteosa – Brassicaceae

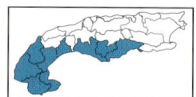

20–50cm tall; stem ridged; leaves shiny above, lower leaves with 4–8 lobes, upper leaves pinnate; bracts always present; petals pale yellow, 4–5mm long; sepals a similar colour, often with purple-brown tips; flowers often stay closed. Flowers April to June.
SIMILAR SPECIES: Distinguished from all the other alpine *Barbarea* species by the presence of bracts.
HABITAT: Livestock resting spots, pasture, nutrient-rich ruderal sites. About 800–2,000m.
DISTRIBUTION: Southern European montane.

2 | Smooth Buckler Mustard
Biscutella laevigata – Brassicaceae

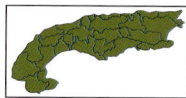

15–40cm tall, mostly branched; leaves lanceolate, entire, or toothed; basal leaves 25–90mm long; petals yellow, 4–8mm long; fruit flat with 2 round lobes, 5–8mm long, 9–13mm broad; style 3–5mm long. Flowers May to September.
SIMILAR SPECIES: Chicory-leaved Buckler Mustard, *B. cichoriifolia*, has 12–16mm long petals, and style 8–9mm long. Short-stemmed Buckler Mustard, *B. brevicaulis*, a western alpine species, is only 8–20cm tall, with 15–25mm long basal leaves.
HABITAT: Poor grassland, rock debris, pinewoods; calcicole. To 2,800m.
DISTRIBUTION: Southern European montane, from the Pyrenees to the Tatra Mountains.
NOTE: Four subspecies in the Alps:
– subsp. *laevigata*: widespread.
– subsp. *austriaca*: north-east alpine endemic.
– subsp. *lucida*: south-east Alps.
– subsp. *ossolana*: province of Novara, Italy.

3 | Alpine Braya
Braya alpina – Brassicaceae

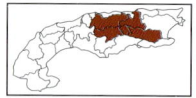

5–12cm tall; stem upright or ascending, hairy; basal leaves lanceolate to narrowly spoon-shaped, narrowing towards the stalk; leaves entire or indistinctly toothed; stem leaves linear, sessile; flowers in umbel-like racemes; petals white to pale lilac, 3–4mm long; fruit 5–7x as long as broad. Flowers July to August.
SIMILAR SPECIES: Whitlow-grass species, genus *Draba*, such as Tauern Whitlow-grass, *D. pacheri*, which has a fruit only 2–3x as long as broad.
HABITAT: Fine rock debris, sandy moraines, Cushion Sedge (*Carex firma*) sward, Mouse-tail Bog Sedge (*Carex myosuroides*) vegetation; especially on intermediate substrates. 2,000–3,100m, sometimes lower, as on the Solstein near Innsbruck (1,900m).
DISTRIBUTION: Eastern alpine endemic.
NAME: In honour of French naturalist and diplomat Franz Gabriel von Bray (1765–1832) who, among other things, was President of the Regensburg Botanical Society.

4 | Alpine Bitter-cress
Cardamine alpina – Brassicaceae

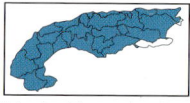

2–10cm tall; all leaves simple, undivided; stem leaves entire to shallowly toothed or lobed, without clasping auricles at the base; petals white, 3.5–5mm long, about twice as long as sepals. Flowers June to August.
SIMILAR SPECIES: Undivided, stunted forms of Mignonette-leaved Bitter-cress, *C. resedifolia* (see p. 116), which however has auricles at the base of leaf stalks.
HABITAT: Stony sites with soil, damp rocks, snow-melt hollows; calcifuge. 1,500–3,400m.
DISTRIBUTION: Alpine–Pyrenean.

5 | Large Bitter-cress
Cardamine amara – Brassicaceae

10–60cm tall, usually unbranched, with runners; stem pith-filled; leaves divided, with 2–9 pairs of lobes and large terminal lobe; petals white, 5–10mm long; anthers violet. Flowers April to June.
SIMILAR SPECIES: (True) Water-cress, *Nasturtium officinale*, has yellow anthers and a hollow stem.
HABITAT: Streams, ditches, wet flushes. To 2,400m, sometimes higher, as on the Grossvenediger, Austria (2,550m).
DISTRIBUTION: European–western Asiatic, from the Pyrenees and Ireland to the Altai region.
NOTE: Some authorities make a distinction between a montane form (subsp. *austriaca*) with 4–9 pairs of leaflets, and a lowland form (subsp. *amara*) with 2–4 leaflet pairs.

Brassicaceae

1 | Asarabacca-leaved Bitter-cress
Cardamine asarifolia – Brassicaceae

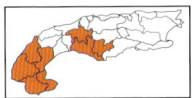

25–50cm tall, at most branching above, hairless to sparsely hairy; basal leaves large, round to kidney-shaped, shallow-notched, long-stalked; stem leaves similarly shaped, getting smaller towards the top; petals white, 8–12mm long; anthers violet; fruits linear-lanceolate, 20–30mm long. Flowers May to July.
SIMILAR SPECIES: Pyrenean Scurvygrass, *Cochlearia pyrenaica* (see p. 118), has round fruits, 4–6.5mm long.
HABITAT: Stream sides, wet flushes; calcifuge. 600–2,100m.
DISTRIBUTION: Alpine–Apennine.

2 | Coralroot Bitter-cress (Coral-root)
Cardamine bulbifera – Brassicaceae

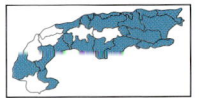

30–60cm tall, unbranched, ± hairless; lower stem leaves pinnate, whorled, with lanceolate, coarsely-toothed leaflets; upper leaves undivided, with dark bulbils in the axils; petals lilac to white, 12–18mm long. Flowers April to June.
SIMILAR SPECIES: Carpathian Bitter-cress, *C. glanduligera*, is 10–25cm tall and has no visible bulbils in the leaf axils. In the Alps, only known from near Ehrenhausen in Styria, Austria.
HABITAT: Deciduous woods, especially beech woods. To about 1,600m.
DISTRIBUTION: European, from Scotland to Armenia.

3 | Drooping Bitter-cress
Cardamine enneaphyllos – Brassicaceae

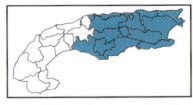

20–30cm tall, unbranched; stem ridged; stem leaves trifoliate, whorled, mostly in threes, fresh green to olive green, often sprouting purple, shiny; flowers drooping; petals pale yellow. Flowers March to May.
SIMILAR SPECIES: Kitaibel's Bitter-cress, *C. kitaibelii*.
HABITAT: Damp deciduous woods, tall herb vegetation and Dwarf Mountain Pine scrub. To about 2,000m, sometimes higher, as on the Gerlossteinwand, Austria (2,150m).
DISTRIBUTION: European montane, from Apennines to the High Tatra. In the Alps, from the Allgäu (location near Oberstdorf) and the province of Bergamo eastwards.

4 | Pinnate Bitter-cress
Cardamine heptaphylla – Brassicaceae

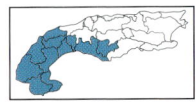

20–50cm tall, unbranched; stem hairless; leaves pinnate, mostly with 7 leaflets, the terminal leaflet about the same size as the lateral leaflets; petals white to pale lilac, 15–20mm long; sepals ⅓–½ as long as petals. Flowers April to June.
SIMILAR SPECIES: The form var. *intermedia*, with its rather palmate leaves, resembles Five-leaflet Bitter-cress, *C. pentaphyllos* (see p. 116), which however has a hairy lower stem.
HABITAT: Deciduous woods, especially beech woods; calcicole. To about 1,800m.
DISTRIBUTION: Southern European montane, from the Pyrenees to the Apennines.

5 | Kitaibel's Bitter-cress
Cardamine kitaibelii – Brassicaceae

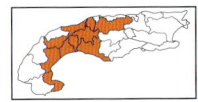

20–40cm tall, unbranched; lower stem hairy; stem leaves 2–3, in whorls; leaves pinnate, mostly with 7–9 narrowly lanceolate, pointed, toothed leaflets; raceme drooping before opening; petals pale yellow, 15–20mm long; sepals about half as long as petals. Flowers April to May.
SIMILAR SPECIES: Drooping Bitter-cress, *C. enneaphyllos*, which has stem leaves trifoliate, whorled, mostly in threes. Pinnate Bitter-cress, *C. heptaphylla*, after flowering, but in this species the entire stem is hairless.
HABITAT: Deciduous woods; calcicole. 400–1,660m.
DISTRIBUTION: Southern European montane, from the Alps and Apennines to the Klekovača Mountains, Bosnia.
NAME: In honour of Hungarian botanist, doctor and chemist Paul Kitaibel (1757–1817), who studied the flora of Hungary.

Brassicaceae

1 | Five-leaflet Bitter-cress
Cardamine pentaphyllos – Brassicaceae

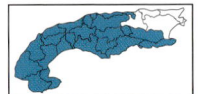

20–50cm tall, unbranched; lower stem densely hairy; leaves pinnate, mostly with 5 leaflets, upper leaves with mostly 3; petals purple-lilac, 15–20mm long; sepals ⅓–½ as long as petals. Flowers April to June.
SIMILAR SPECIES: Pinnate Bitter-cress, *C. heptaphylla*, (see p. 114).
HABITAT: Deciduous woods, wooded ravines; calcicole. To 1,700m, sometimes higher as on the Weissstein, Lienz Dolomites, Austria.
DISTRIBUTION: Southern European montane, from the Pyrenees to Macelj in the northern Dinaric Alps.

2 | Mignonette-leaved Bitter-cress
Cardamine resedifolia – Brassicaceae

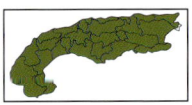

2–15cm tall; stem leaves pinnate with 2–3 pairs of lobes; leaf stalk with auricles at base; lower leaves undivided; petals white, 4–6mm long, twice as long as sepals. Flowers May to August.
SIMILAR SPECIES: Plumier's (Ivy-leaved) Bitter-cress, *C. plumieri*, from the western Alps, has ivy-like lower leaves with 3–5 blunt lobes, and trifoliate lower stem leaves with obovate lateral lobes.
HABITAT: Stony sites with soil, damp rocks, snow-melt hollows; calcifuge. 1,400–3,300m, occasionally lower, as at Köstland near Brixen (Bressanone), South Tyrol, Italy (700m), or higher, as on Monte Rosa, Switzerland (3,500m).
DISTRIBUTION: Southern European montane, from the Sierra Nevada to the eastern Carpathians.

3 | Stream Bitter-cress
Cardamine rivularis – Brassicaceae

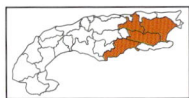

10–50cm tall, unbranched; basal leaves in a rosette, pinnate, with 3–15 pairs of lobes, terminal lobes equal or only slightly larger; petals deep pink, 4–10mm long. Flowers June to August.
SIMILAR SPECIES: Cuckooflower (Lady's-smock), *C. pratensis*, has pale pink or white flowers with 8–12mm long petals.
HABITAT: Wet flushes, stream sides, damp meadows; calcicole. About 1,400–2,200m.
DISTRIBUTION: Probably Southeast European montane, from the Alps to the Sudeten and Rhodope Mountains.
NOTE: It is an open question as to whether the alpine and Carpathian forms of *C. rivularis* should be separated.

4 | Trifoliate Bitter-cress
Cardamine trifolia – Brassicaceae

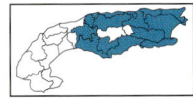

10–30cm tall, at most branching towards the top, hairless, with runners; basal leaves trifoliate, dark green, evergreen, undersides of previous year's leaves purple-violet; petals white, 8–11mm long; anthers yellow. Flowers April to June.
SIMILAR SPECIES: Hardly any.
HABITAT: Woods, especially Spruce-Fir-Beech woods; calcicole. To about 1,600m.
DISTRIBUTION: European montane, from the Jura and northern Apennines to the Sudeten Mountains, and Bosnia.

5 | Waldstein's Bitter-cress
Cardamine waldsteinii – Brassicaceae

10–40cm tall, unbranched; lower stem weakly hairy; stem leaves alternate, 3-lobed; leaflets lanceolate, toothed; inflorescence upright; petals white, 10–24mm long; sepals violet. Flowers April to June.
SIMILAR SPECIES: Large Bitter-cress, *C. amara* (see p. 112), has pinnate leaves with 5–19 leaflets.
HABITAT: Deciduous woods, especially beech, wooded ravines, riverine woods. 300–1,500m.
DISTRIBUTION: Eastern alpine–Illyrian, from Steiermark (Styria), Austria to Bosnia.
NAME: In honour of Austrian botanist and military strategist Franz Adam Norbert von Waldstein-Wartenberg (1759–1823).

Brassicaceae

1 | Alpine Scurvygrass
Cochlearia excelsa – Brassicaceae

3–10cm tall (often taller in fruit), hairless; basal leaf blades kidney-shaped, 0.5–1.4cm long, 0.5–1.9cm broad, heart-shaped at base; petals white to yellowish-white, 4–7mm long; fruit obovate, 3–5mm long; fruit stalk 1–2x as long as the fruit. Flowers July to August.
SIMILAR SPECIES: Pyrenean Scurvygrass, *C. pyrenaica*.
HABITAT: Wet, mossy rocks and rubble, wet flushes; calcifuge. 2000–2,360m.
DISTRIBUTION: Eastern alpine endemic. The species is a glacial relict, restricted to the Seckau Tauern and Gurktal Alps, though rare even there.
NOTE: Regarded by some authorities as a subspecies of Pyrenean Scurvygrass. The Scurvygrass genus contains some 25 species, of which 12 are European and 3(4) are found in the Alps. Bavarian Scurvygrass, *C. bavarica*, the status of which is still uncertain, is likely to be a hybrid between Common Scurvygrass, *C. officinalis* and Pyrenean Scurvygrass, *C. pyrenaica*; it is restricted to the Bavarian Alps and has intermediate characters.

2 | Pyrenean Scurvygrass
Cochlearia pyrenaica – Brassicaceae

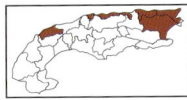

10–30cm tall, hairless; basal leaves long-stalked; leaf blades kidney-shaped, 1–3.8cm long, 1.2–4.5cm broad, with heart-shaped base; petals white, 4–7mm long; fruit oval, pointed on both sides, 4–6.5mm long; fruit stalk 0.5–1.5x as long as the fruit. Flowers May to July.
SIMILAR SPECIES: Alpine Scurvygrass, *C. excelsa*, is only 3–10cm tall at flowering and has smaller leaf blades, only 0.5–1.4cm long. Asarabacca-leaved Bitter-cress, *Cardamine asarifolia* (see p. 114).
HABITAT: In and around springs, only in very pure water; on carboniferous rocks. To about 1,300m.
DISTRIBUTION: European montane, from Northwest Spain and Scotland to the Carpathians.

3 | Mountain Wallflower Cabbage
Coincya cheiranthos subsp. *montana* – Brassicaceae
(Syn.: *Rhynchosinapsis cheiranthos* subsp. *montana*)

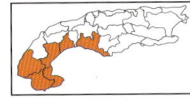

10–40cm tall; lower plant with bristly hairs; leaves pinnate, stalked, with 3–6 narrow, ± right-angled lobes; petals yellow, 12–20mm long; fruit 4–7cm long, 2mm broad, horizontal to upright. Flowers May to August.
SIMILAR SPECIES: Watercress-leaved Rocket, *Erucastrum nasturtiifolium*, has 5–10 leaf lobes on each side and 8–12mm long petals.
HABITAT: Rock debris, open grassland; calcifuge. 1,600–2,400m.
DISTRIBUTION: Southern European montane, from the French Massif Central to the southern and western Alps.
NOTE: The nominate form subsp. *cheiranthos* (30–60cm tall, petals 8–14mm long) is found at lower levels in the Alps.
NAME: The genus is in honour of French botanist Auguste de Coincy (1837–1903).

4 | Richer's Wallflower Cabbage
Coincya richeri – Brassicaceae
(Syn.: *Rhynchosinapsis richeri*)

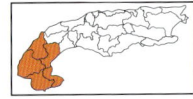

15–50cm tall; basal leaves hairless, narrowly ovate, stalked, entire to irregularly toothed, blades 40–70mm long, 10–30mm broad; petals pale yellow, 12–20mm long; fruit 30–60mm long, 3–6mm broad, hairless, on a stalk 8–15mm long. Flowers June to August.
SIMILAR SPECIES: Austrian Hare's-ear Mustard, *Conringia austriaca*, has 6–8mm long petals and in the Alps is only found in the lowlands of Lower Austria.
HABITAT: Rock crevices, rock debris, grassy habitats; calcifuge. 1,200–2,500m.
DISTRIBUTION: Southwest alpine endemic.
NAME: In honour of French botanist Pierre Richer de Belleval (1564–1632), who studied the flora of Languedoc.

Brassicaceae

1 | Yellow Whitlowgrass
Draba aizoides – Brassicaceae

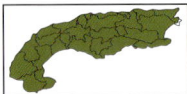

5–10cm tall; stem hairless and leafless; basal leaves narrowly lanceolate, stiff, leathery, 3–20mm long, with long ciliate hairs at the edges; petals yellow, 4–8mm long; anthers about the same length as the petals; fruit lanceolate, 4.5–13mm long, pointed at tip, usually hairless; fruit stalk 3–15mm long. Flowers February to June.

SIMILAR SPECIES: Hoppe's Whitlowgrass, *D. hoppeana*, which has 2.5–4mm long petals and 1.5–3.5mm long fruit stalk. Rough Whitlowgrass, *D. aspera* (see p. 123, **2B**), has a hairy stem and is only 1.5–3cm tall. Sauter's Whitlowgrass, *D. sauteri*, has anthers clearly shorter (0.5–0.8x as long) than the petals.
HABITAT: Rock crevices, rock debris, stony grassland; calcicole. To 3,400m.
DISTRIBUTION: Southern European montane, from the Pyrenees to the northern Carpathians.
NOTE: Two alpine subspecies are:
– subsp. *aizoides*: the nominate form, with 4–6mm long petals (**1A**) is widespread.
– subsp. *beckeri*: with 6–8mm long petals is restricted to the north-eastern Alps.
Hybrids are found in this genus and can be tricky to identify.

2 | Austrian Whitlowgrass
Draba dubia – Brassicaceae

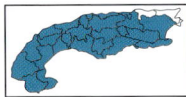

1–15cm tall; stem unbranched, 1–3 leaved, sparsely hairy; basal leaves in dense rosettes, with felty grey stellate hairs; petals white, 3–5.5mm long; fruit lanceolate, 5–13mm long, pointed above and below, usually hairless, often twisted; fruit style 0.1–0.4mm long; fruit stalk hairless or with sparse, stellate hairs. Flowers May to July.

SIMILAR SPECIES: Downy Whitlowgrass, *D. tomentosa* (see p. 122), has round, always hairy fruits and densely hairy fruit stalk.
HABITAT: Rock crevices, especially on intermediate rocks. 1,400–3,800m.
DISTRIBUTION: Southern European montane.

3 | Hoppe's Whitlowgrass
Draba hoppeana – Brassicaceae

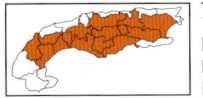

1–4cm tall; stem hairless and leafless; basal leaves narrowly lanceolate, keeled, stiff, leathery, 3–9mm long, with long ciliate hairs at edges; inflorescence compact, with 1–9 flowers; petals yellow, 2.5–4mm long; anthers about as long as petals; fruit 4–7mm long, blunt above and below, usually hairless; fruit stalk 1.5–3.5mm long. Flowers July to August.

SIMILAR SPECIES: Yellow Whitlowgrass, *D. aizoides*, and Sauter's Whitlowgrass, *D. sauteri* (see p. 122), the latter with anthers clearly shorter (0.5–0.8x as long) than the petals.
HABITAT: Rock debris, rocks, snow-melt hollows. 2,600–3,100m.
DISTRIBUTION: Alpine endemic.
NAME: In honour of German botanist and doctor David Heinrich Hoppe (1760–1846), who studied the flora of the eastern Alps.

4 | Engadine Whitlowgrass
Draba ladina – Brassicaceae

1–5cm tall; stem leafless and ± hairless; basal leaves lanceolate, fleshy, 5–8mm long, 1.5–2mm broad, hairy, with ciliate margins; petals pale yellow, 3.5–5mm long; fruit spindle-shaped, 5–9mm long, hairy; fruit style 0.7–1.2mm long; fruit stalk 2–4mm long. Flowers July to August.

SIMILAR SPECIES: Dolomite Whitlowgrass, *D. dolomitica*, which also has pale yellow petals, has hairless fruit 4–6.5mm long, and fruit style 0.4–0.8mm long.
HABITAT: Dolomite rocks and debris; calcicole. In Switzerland: 2,600m (Piz dal Fuorn) to 3,050m (Piz Foraz near Piz dal Botsch).
DISTRIBUTION: Endemic to Graubünden, Unterengadin (Switzerland). Also recorded from nearby Monte Pettini (Italy).
NOTE: Molecular genetic research has shown that *Draba ladina* is a species derived from a hybrid between *D. aizoides* (male) and *D. tomentosa* (female).

Brassicaceae

1 | Pacher's Whitlowgrass
Draba pacheri – Brassicaceae

4–20cm tall; stem unbranched or branched, hairy, with 0–7 leaves; basal leaves tongue-shaped to lanceolate, 10–30mm long, 3–8mm broad, hairy, entire; petals white, 2.8–4.2mm long; fruit hairless, 5–7.5mm long, 2–3.3mm broad; fruit style 0.2–0.6mm long. Flowers June to August.

SIMILAR SPECIES: Hoary Whitlowgrass, *D. incana*, has mostly toothed leaves. Starry Whitlowgrass, *D. stellata*, has 4.5–8mm long petals and a 0.7–1.2mm long fruit style.
HABITAT: Rock crevices, rock debris, grassy gaps, snow-melt hollows, pioneer vegetation. 1,850–2,650m.
DISTRIBUTION: Eastern alpine–Carpathian.
NAME: In honour of Austrian botanist and clergyman David Pacher (1816–1902), who studied the flora of Carinthia.
NOTE: There are some 300 species of whitlowgrass (including *Erophila*), with 42 in Europe and 21 in the Alps, of which 5 are restricted to the Alps (endemic): *Draba dolomitica*, *D. hoppeana*, *D. ladina*, *D. sauteri*, *D. stellata*.

2 | Sauter's Whitlowgrass
Draba sauteri – Brassicaceae

2–15cm tall; stem hairless and leafless; basal leaves lanceolate-spoon-shaped, 5–8mm long, 1.5–3.5mm broad, with comb-like ciliate hairs at margins; raceme with 2–5 flowers; petals (pale) yellow, 4–5.5mm long; anthers notably shorter (0.5–0.8x as long) than petals; fruit oval, 4–6mm long; fruit style 3–5mm long. Flowers May to July.

SIMILAR SPECIES: Yellow Whitlowgrass, *D. aizoides* (see p. 120), and Rough Whitlowgrass, *D. aspera* (**2B**), which has a hairy stem.
HABITAT: Flat or slightly sloping calcareous rocks and debris on exposed summits; calcicole. 1,850–2,900m.
DISTRIBUTION: Northern alpine endemic.
NAME: In honour of Austrian botanist and doctor Anton Sauter (1800–1881), who studied the flora of Salzburg, and whose favourite flower was Christmas Rose, *Helleborus niger*.

3 | Carinthian Whitlowgrass
Draba siliquosa – Brassicaceae

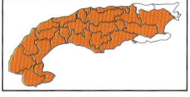

3–10cm tall; stem hairless or hairy towards base, with 0–4 leaves; basal leaves lanceolate, 0.5–1cm long, hairless or hairy, with ciliate margins; petals white, 2–3mm long; fruiting cluster at least half as long as the rest of the stem; fruits 3.5–9.5mm long, each with 10–14 seeds. Flowers June to July.

SIMILAR SPECIES: Flattnitz Whitlowgrass, *D. fladnizensis*, has a fruiting cluster less than half as long as the rest of the stem.
HABITAT: Base-rich rock crevices and debris, on ridges. 1,500–3,400m.
DISTRIBUTION: Southern European montane.

4 | Starry Whitlowgrass
Draba stellata – Brassicaceae

2–10cm tall; lower stem ciliate, upper stem hairless; basal leaves narrowly obovate, entire or with 1–2 teeth at the tip and covered with grey felty hairs; stem leaves 2–3; petals white, 4.5–8mm long; fruit 4–10mm long, 1.7–3.8mm broad, hairless, rarely weakly ciliate; fruit style 0.7–1.2mm long. Flowers June to July.

SIMILAR SPECIES: Norwegian Whitlowgrass, *D. norvegica*, has stem hairy down to the flower stalks and fruit style only 0.1–0.3mm long. In the Alps known only from the Rax region in Austria.
HABITAT: Rocky sites, snow-melt sites; calcicole. 1,800–2,400m.
DISTRIBUTION: Northeast alpine endemic.

5 | Downy Whitlowgrass
Draba tomentosa – Brassicaceae

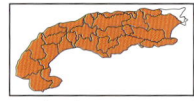

2–10cm tall; stem hairy, with 1–3 leaves; basal leaves elliptical to oval, with felty hairs; petals white, 3.5–6mm long; fruit elliptical, rounded above and below, 5–10mm long, 2–4mm broad, hairy; fruit style 0.2–0.7mm long. Flowers June to August.

SIMILAR SPECIES: Austrian Whitlowgrass, *D. dubia* (see p. 120) has lanceolate fruits that are pointed above and below and mostly hairless.
HABITAT: Rock crevices and rocky debris; calcicole. 1,900–3,400m.
DISTRIBUTION: Southern European montane.

Brassicaceae

1 | Orange Treacle-mustard
Erysimum aurantiacum – Brassicaceae

25–60cm tall, perennial; rosette leaves linear-lanceolate, toothed or entire, 5–12cm long, 3–7mm broad; stem leaves 2–10cm long, 1.5–7mm broad, toothed or rarely entire; inflorescence with 8–30 flowers; sepals 7–10mm long, 1.3–2mm broad; petals yellow-orange, 12–19mm long, 4.5–7mm broad; fruit style 0.5–1mm long. Flowers May to July.
SIMILAR SPECIES: Wood Treacle-mustard, *E. sylvestre*, has yellow petals.
HABITAT: Sunny, stony, warm poor meadows, cracks in rocks; calcicole. 500–800m.
DISTRIBUTION: Alpine endemic, to a small area of the southern Alps in Trentino, Italy: near Stenico, Molveno, Nembia, S. Lorenzo, and La Molina.

2 | Piedmont Treacle-mustard
Erysimum jugicola – Brassicaceae

5–25cm tall, perennial: leaves linear to narrowly spoon-shaped, entire or distantly toothed, 15–60mm long, 3–5mm broad; sepals lanceolate, greenish-yellow, 7–10mm long, 2–3mm broad; petals yellow, 14–20mm long; fruit 35–55mm long, 1–1.2mm broad. Flowers June to July.
SIMILAR SPECIES: Provence Treacle-mustard, *E. collisparsum*, is 60cm tall and has 13–16mm long petals. Mountain Treacle-mustard, *E. montosicola*, has fruits 60–90mm long and 1.3–2mm broad.
HABITAT: Rock debris, stony grassland; calcicole. 1,100–3,000m.
DISTRIBUTION: Western alpine endemic.

3 | Pale Yellow Treacle-mustard
Erysimum ochroleucum – Brassicaceae

10–50cm tall, perennial: stem ridged, branching; leaves linear-lanceolate, distantly toothed to almost entire; sepals 10–15mm long, yellow-green, edged pale; petals pale yellow, 15–20mm long. Fruit 4–9cm long, 1.5–2mm broad; fruit style 2.6–3.2mm long. Flowers May to June.
SIMILAR SPECIES: Italian Treacle-mustard, *E. rhaeticum*, has deep yellow petals and fruit 1–1.5mm broad.
HABITAT: Calcareous scree; calcicole. To about 2,100m.
DISTRIBUTION: Western alpine, from the south-western Alps to the Jura.

4 | Italian Treacle-mustard
Erysimum rhaeticum – Brassicaceae

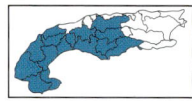

10–50cm tall, perennial; stem ridged; rosette leaves 5–15cm long, long-stalked, linear to linear-lanceolate; leaf margins distantly toothed or double-toothed; sepals 9–11mm long, 2 inner sepals inflated at base; petals yellow, 16–20mm long; fruit 4–9cm long, 1–1.5mm broad; fruit style 2.6–3.2mm long. Flowers June to July.
SIMILAR SPECIES: Wood Treacle-mustard, *E. sylvestre*. Also, Piedmont Treacle-mustard, *E. jugicola*, which has 1.5–6cm long leaves and 3.5–5.5cm long fruits.
HABITAT: Rocky slopes, poor grassland, rocks. To 2,700m, occasionally higher, as in the Aosta Valley, Italy (2,800m).
DISTRIBUTION: Alpine endemic. Reported finds from the Balkan Peninsula turned out to belong to other species, such as *E. drenowskii*.

5 | Wood Treacle-mustard
Erysimum sylvestre – Brassicaceae

8–40cm tall, perennial; stem ridged; rosette leaves 5–15cm long, long-stalked, linear-lanceolate; leaf margins entire, with just the lowest leaves distantly toothed; sepals 9–11mm long, with white membranous tips; petals yellow, 16–20mm long; fruit style 0.8–1.5mm long. Flowers May to July.
SIMILAR SPECIES: Italian Treacle-mustard, *E. rhaeticum*, has fruit style 2.6–3.2mm long and most leaves slightly toothed.
HABITAT: Stony slopes, sunny rocks, open pinewoods; calcicole. 500–2,600m, occasionally higher, as on the Rote Säule near Hinterbichl, Austria (2,700m).
DISTRIBUTION: Eastern alpine-Illyrian, south to the Albanian mountains.

Brassicaceae

1 | Rigid Treacle-mustard
Erysimum virgatum – Brassicaceae

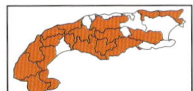

40–100cm tall, biennial; stem blunt-edged; leaves lanceolate, distantly toothed to entire; sepals 4–7mm long, with white membranous margins at tip; petals yellow, 9–12mm long, hairy on outside; fruit 30–60mm long, 4-angled, surface hairier than the ridges. Flowers May to June, often repeat-flowering into the autumn.
SIMILAR SPECIES: Hungarian Treacle-mustard, *E. hungaricum*, has 60–85mm long fruit and round stem with 2 weak ridges.
HABITAT: Track sides, clearings, ruderal sites. To about 2,300m.
DISTRIBUTION: European-Asiatic, from Iceland to Kamchatka.

2 | Few-flowered Rock-cress
Fourraea alpina – Brassicaceae
(Syn.: *Arabis pauciflora*)

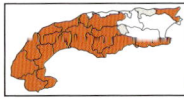

30–100cm tall; leaves and stem hairless, blue green; basal leaves undivided, elliptical-elongate to almost circular, narrowing towards long stalk, in rosette; stem leaves heart-shaped, clasping; flowers in dense raceme; petals white; fruits in a loose raceme, 3–8cm long, 1.5–2mm broad, upright. Flowers May to July.
SIMILAR SPECIES: Tower Mustard, *Turritis glabra*, has pinnate basal leaves and yellowish-white petals.
HABITAT: Open woods, stony sites, clearings; calcicole. To about 2,100m.
DISTRIBUTION: Southern European montane.
NOTE: Long known as *Arabis pauciflora*, but since 1984 it has been assigned to the monotypic genus *Fourraea*.

3 | Dame's Violet (Sweet Rocket)
Hesperis matronalis – Brassicaceae

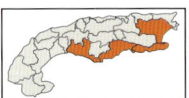

40–80cm tall; usually branched, with bristly hairs; basal leaves oval to lanceolate, short-stalked, to 15cm long; leaf margins finely toothed to almost entire; middle and upper stem leaves short-stalked, not clasping stem; petals 20–25mm long, white (subsp. *candida*) or pale lilac to purple (subsp. *matronalis*); fruit 3–10cm long, 1.5–3mm broad. Flowers May to August.
SIMILAR SPECIES: Scentless Dame's Violet, *H. inodora*, endemic to the Maritime Alps, has white flowers and middle and upper stem leaves clasping stem. Honesty, *Lunaria annua*, is similar in flower, but has heart-shaped leaves and flattened oval fruits.
HABITAT: Ravine woods, nitrate-rich tall herb vegetation, river valley woods, ruderal sites. To about 1,500m, occasionally higher, as at Wildfeld in the Eisenerz Alps, Austria (1,600m).
DISTRIBUTION: European-Asiatic, from the Apennines to Dzungaria, Central Asia. The subsp. *candida* (**3A**) is native to the south-eastern Alps, while subsp. *matronalis* (**3B**) is naturalised.

4 | Alpine Chamois Cress
Hornungia alpina – Brassicaceae
(Syn.: *Hutchinsia alpina*, *Pritzelago alpina*)

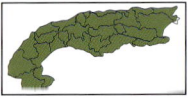

2–10cm tall; stem leafless; leaves clustered at base, pinnate; petals white, 1.5–5mm long; fruit 2.5–5.5mm long; fruit style 0.05–0.5mm long. Flowers May to August.
SIMILAR SPECIES: Mignonette-leaved Bitter-cress, *Cardamine resedifolia* (see p. 116), has 10–20mm long linear fruits.
HABITAT: Seeping wet stony debris, snow-melt hollows. 1,300–3,100m, sometimes lower, as on the banks of the Inn River near Brixlegg, Austria (530m).
DISTRIBUTION: Southern European montane, from the mountains of north-west Spain to the Korab Mountains, Albania.
NOTE: 3 subspecies in the Alps:
– subsp. *alpina*: calcicole, petals 3–5mm long, basal leaves with 2–4 pairs of lateral lobes (**4A**).
– subsp. *austroalpina*: calcicole, petals 2.5–3mm long; southern Alps (**4B**).
– subsp. *brevicaulis*: petals 1.5–2.6mm long, basal leaves with 1–2 pairs of lateral lobes (**4C**).
NAME: In honour of German pharmacist Ernst Gottfried Hornung (1795–1862), after whom the Carpathian species *Arabis hornungia* is also named.

Brassicaceae

1 | Few-flowered Chamois Cress
Hornungia pauciflora – Brassicaceae
(Syn.: *Hymenolobus pauciflorus*)

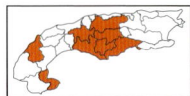

2–10cm tall, usually prostrate or ascending, delicate; leaves 1–2cm long, undivided, ovate-lanceolate, entire, narrowing towards the stalk; inflorescence with 2–6 flowers; petals 4, white, 0.6–2mm long; fruit broad oval, 2–5mm long, 1–1.5x as long as broad. Flowers May to June.
SIMILAR SPECIES: Vegetatively, chickweed and stitchwort species, genus *Stellaria*, but their flowers have 5 petals, divided almost to the base.
HABITAT: Fine sandy substrates, livestock resting sites under rocks; calcicole and nitrophilous. 600–2,300m, occasionally lower, as in Val Vestino, Italy (500m).
DISTRIBUTION: Southern European montane, from the Iberian Peninsula to Sicily.

2 | Tansy-leaved Rocket
Hugueninia tanacetifolia – Brassicaceae

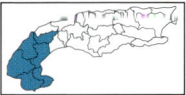

30–100cm tall; lower leaves very large, pinnate, with 8–12 pairs of narrowly-lanceolate, similarly sized, coarsely-toothed to feathery lobes, and a similarly sized terminal lobe; upper leaves smaller, sessile; inflorescence umbel-like; petals yellow, c. 4mm long. Flowers June to July.
SIMILAR SPECIES: Pale Rocket, *Sisymbrium pallescens*, has irregularly toothed leaf lobes and petals 5–6mm long.
HABITAT: Tall herb vegetation, rocky debris, damp slopes, livestock resting sites; nitrophilous. 1,700–2,500m.
DISTRIBUTION: Western alpine. A closely-related form is found in the mountains of the Iberian peninsula.
NAME: The generic name honours French botanist Auguste Huguenin (1780–1860).

3 | Mont Aurouze Candytuft
Iberis aurosica – Brassicaceae

4–15cm tall, perennial: leaves lanceolate, 6–20mm long and 1.5–2.5mm broad, with sunken central vein; inflorescence compact, 15–25mm in diameter; petals pale pink, 2 outer petals larger, 6–9mm long, 2–3mm broad; inner petals 4–6mm long, 1.5–2.5mm broad; sepals mostly absent at fruiting; fruit 4–5mm long, 3–3.5mm broad, with 3–5mm long stalk; fruit style 2–3mm long. Flowers June to August.
SIMILAR SPECIES: Dwarf Candytuft, *I. nana*, has spoon-shaped leaves 7–16mm long and 3–5mm broad, and is biennial. Candolle's Candytuft, *I. candolleana*, has spoon-shaped leaves 7–10mm long and 2–3mm broad, and is restricted to Mont Ventoux, France.
HABITAT: Scree, stony grassland; calcicole. 1,300–2,000m.
DISTRIBUTION: Endemic to the south-western French Alps.

4 | Rock Candytuft
Iberis saxatilis – Brassicaceae

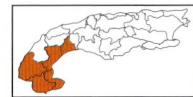

5–15cm tall, aromatic when crushed; stem woody, low-lying, branched; leaves linear, entire, evergreen, leathery, somewhat fleshy, and sharply pointed; outer petals 6–8mm long, about twice as long as the inner; fruit round, flat, broadly winged. Flowers April to July.
SIMILAR SPECIES: Evergreen Candytuft, *I. sempervirens* (**4B**), has 10–15mm long outer petals, and the leaves are not sharply pointed.
HABITAT: Stony grassland, rock crevices; calcicole. To about 2,200m.
DISTRIBUTION: Mediterranean-montane.

5 | Alpine Woad
Isatis alpina – Brassicaceae

10–30cm tall; leaves blue-green, spoon-shaped to lanceolate, hairless; petals 3–5mm long, yellow; fruit broadly elliptical to obovate, 15–22mm long, 8–13mm broad, narrowly winged. Flowers July to August.
SIMILAR SPECIES: Richer's Wallflower Cabbage, *Coincya richeri* (see p. 118), has fruit 30–60mm long and 3–6mm broad.
HABITAT: Rock debris; calcicole. 1,500–2,500m.
DISTRIBUTION: Western alpine–Apennine.

Brassicaceae

1 | Rock Kernera
Kernera saxatilis – Brassicaceae

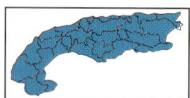

10–30cm tall; stem simple or branched, lower stem with appressed hairs; basal leaves entire or toothed to pinnate, in a rosette; stem leaves getting smaller up the stem; petals white, 3–4mm long; fruit almost spherical, 2–3mm in diameter. Flowers May to July.
SIMILAR SPECIES: Sand Rock-cress, *Arabidopsis arenaria*, and Haller's Rock-cress, *A. halleri*, which have linear fruits, 1–4cm long.
HABITAT: Rocks, rock debris; calcicole. To 2,700m.
DISTRIBUTION: Southern European montane, from the Corbières to Mount Olympus.
NAME: In honour of German botanist Johann Simon von Kerner (1755–1830), who wrote a flora of Stuttgart, one of the earliest German local floras.

2 | Perennial Honesty
Lunaria rediviva – Brassicaceae

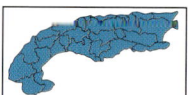

30–140cm tall, branched; especially lower stem with erect hairs; all leaves stalked, lower leaves large, heart-shaped, irregularly toothed; upper leaves lanceolate; petals pale lilac to almost white, 12–20mm long; fruit elongate-elliptical, pointed. Flowers May to July.
SIMILAR SPECIES: With its disc-shaped, silvery, shiny dry fruits, hard to mistake.
HABITAT: Wooded gorges, damp tall herb vegetation, Green Alder scrub; calcicole, moisture-loving. To 1,400m, occasionally higher, as at Formarinsee, Austria (1,500m).
DISTRIBUTION: European, from Portugal to Oberlausitz and to the southern Carpathians.
NOTE: Garden Honesty, *Lunaria annua*, is widely cultivated and naturalised. It differs in having purple flowers, and almost circular fruits that are often used by florists.

3 | East Alpine Penny-cress
Noccaea crantzii – Brassicaceae
(Syn.: *Thlaspi alpinum, T. alpestre*)

5–15cm tall, loosely hairy; rhizomes with terminal rosettes and short runners; basal leaves almost circular, 0.5–2.5cm long, shiny, narrowing abruptly into the stalk; stem leaves bluish-green, lanceolate, clasping; petals white, 5–7mm long; fruit elongate, wedge-shaped at base, 5–6.5mm long and 3–4mm broad, winged ± 0.5mm broad at tip; fruit style 1–2.2mm long. Flowers June to July.
SIMILAR SPECIES: Mountain Penny-cress, *N. montana*, has round fruits round at base with winged tip 1.5–2mm broad. Green Penny-cress, *N. virens* (Syn. *Thlaspi virens*), is found in the western Alps and has wing on fruit only 0.2mm broad.
HABITAT: Stony, snowy sites, snow-melt soils; calcicole. 600–2,300m.
DISTRIBUTION: Northeast alpine endemic.
NAME: In honour of Austrian botanist and doctor Heinrich Johann Edler von Crantz (1722–1797), whose name is given to several species and to the genus *Crantzia* (family Gesneriaceae). The generic name honours Italian botanist Domenico Nocca (1758–1841), who was Director of the Botanic Garden in Mantua.

4 | Kerner's Penny-cress
Noccaea minima – Brassicaceae
(Syn.: *Thlaspi minimum, T. kerneri*)

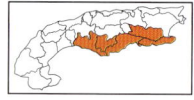

5–10cm tall, loosely hairy; runners with alternate leaves; leaves dull blue-green, fleshy; basal leaves almost circular, narrowing abruptly into the stalk; stem leaves lanceolate, sessile; petals white, 3.5–5.5mm long; fruit narrowly winged; fruit style 1–2.2mm long. Flowers May to July.
SIMILAR SPECIES: Matterhorn Penny-cress, *N. sylvia* (Syn. *Thlaspi sylvium*), from the western Alps, has fruit style 2.5–3mm long. Alpine Penny-cress, *N. caerulescens* (Syn. *Thlaspi caerulescens*, **4B**), has 0.8–4.2mm long petals and fruit style 0.3–1.6mm long.
HABITAT: Fine rock debris, stony poor grassland; calcicole. 1,600–2,400m.
DISTRIBUTION: Southeast alpine endemic.

Brassicaceae

1 | Round-leaved Penny-cress
Noccaea rotundifolia – Brassicaceae
(Syn.: *Thlaspi rotundifolium*)

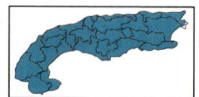

3–12cm tall; runner with opposite leaves; leaves thick, oval to round, blueish-green to bright green, hairless; petals lilac, 5.5–8mm long; fruit almost unwinged, keeled. Flowers April to August.
SIMILAR SPECIES: Burnt Candytuft, *Aethionema saxatile*, has 2–4mm long petals.
HABITAT: Rock debris. 1,400–3,400m, sometimes washed down to lower levels, as near Arnoldstein, Austria, subsp. *cepaeifolia* (600m), or higher, as on the Theodulhorn, Italy/Switzerland, subsp. *corymbosa* (3,450m).
DISTRIBUTION: Alpine endemic.
NOTE: Four subspecies in the Alps:
- subsp. *rotundifolia*: calcicole, basal leaves in rosette, leaf rounded, mostly entire.
- subsp. *cepaeifolia*: calcicole, basal leaves not in rosette, leaf rounded, toothed; south-eastern Alps.
- subsp. *corymbosa*: on gravel, basal leaves elongate, western Alps.
- subsp. *grignense*: calcicole, Grigna region, Italy.

2 | Garlic Cress
Peltaria alliacea – Brassicaceae

40–60cm tall, garlic-like smell when crushed; leaves hairless, blue-green; stem leaves ovate lanceolate, sharply heart-shaped at base and clasping; petals white, 3–4mm long, ±2x as long as sepals; fruit almost circular, 7–10mm in diameter. Flowers May to July.
SIMILAR SPECIES: Few-flowered Rock-cress, *Fourraea alpina* (see p. 126), has fruits 3–8cm long and 1–2mm broad.
HABITAT: Woodland edges, stony slopes, forest clearings; nutrient-rich soil, calcicole. To 1,400m.
DISTRIBUTION: Southeast European montane, from the eastern Alps to the Pindus Mountains.

3 | Pyrenean Whitlow-grass
Petrocallis pyrenaica – Brassicaceae

2–8cm tall, forms cushions; leaves in dense rosette, 3–5-lobed, hairy; petals pink-lilac, rarely white, 4–5mm long; fruit elliptical, 4–6mm long, hairless. Flowers May to July.
SIMILAR SPECIES: Hardly any.
HABITAT: Scree, rock crevices, exposed ridges; calcicole. 1,700–3,000m, occasionally higher, as on the Furggengrat near Zermatt, Switzerland (3,400m).
DISTRIBUTION: Southeast European montane, from the Pyrenees to the Tatras.

4 | Alpine Scurvygrass
Rhizobotrya alpina – Brassicaceae

1–4cm tall; leaves spoon-shaped, 10–20mm long, in rosettes; petals white, 2–2.5mm long, scarcely longer than sepals; fruit oval-spherical, 2–3mm in diameter; fruit stalk ± as long as the fruit. Flowers July to August.
SIMILAR SPECIES: Rock Kernera, *Kernera saxatilis* (see p. 130), is 10–30cm tall and the fruit stalk is 2–5x as long as the fruit.
HABITAT: Steep slopes with fine rock debris, especially in avalanche paths, rocky sites; calcicole. 1,900–2,800m.
DISTRIBUTION: Endemic to the Dolomites.

5 | Northern Yellow-cress
Rorippa islandica – Brassicaceae

3–20cm tall, prostrate to ascending, branched at base; stem hairless; leaves lyre-shaped, pinnate, with large terminal lobe; sepals 1–1.5mm long; petals pale yellow, 1.6–2.5mm long; fruit 5–12mm long, 2–3mm broad, fruit stalk ⅓–½ as long as fruit. Flowers June to September.
SIMILAR SPECIES: Marsh Yellow-cress, *R. palustris*, grows upright and is not branched at base, with sepals 1.6–2.5mm long and fruit stalk about as long as the fruit.
HABITAT: Lakesides, fens, alluvial soils, marshy sites. About 1,500–2,700m.
DISTRIBUTION: Arctic–alpine, south to the Pyrenees and Gramos Mountains, Albania/Greece.
NOTES: The species *Rorippa islandica* formerly included *R. palustris*. After the common *R. palustris* was separated, the original name remained with the rare *R. islandica*, which sometimes causes confusion.

Campanulaceae

1 | Large-flowered Bellflower
Campanula alpestris – Campanulaceae

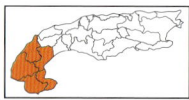

3–12cm tall; basal leaves linear-lanceolate, entire to weakly toothed; flowers violet-blue, 30–40mm long, solitary, upright or nodding; calyx lobes no more than ½ as long as corolla. Flowers June to August.
SIMILAR SPECIES: Stunted forms of Canterbury-bells, *C. medium*, which is multi-flowered, 30–80cm tall, and is a lowland species, reaching at most 1,300m.
HABITAT: Rock debris, stony grassland; calcicole. 1,400–2,800m.
DISTRIBUTION: West alpine endemic.

2 | Alpine Bellflower
Campanula alpina – Campanulaceae

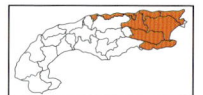

5–20cm tall; leaves narrowly lanceolate, entire to distantly small-toothed, shaggy hairy to almost hairless; calyx lobes longer than half the corolla, with 0.5–1mm long appendages between; flowers violet-blue to almost white, 10–20mm long. Flowers June to August.
SIMILAR SPECIES: Bearded Bellflower, *C. barbata*.
HABITAT: Pasture, acidic, poor grassland, dwarf shrub heath. 1,300–2,600m.
DISTRIBUTION: Southeast European montane.

3 | Bearded Bellflower
Campanula barbata – Campanulaceae

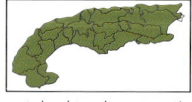

10–40cm tall, roughly hairy; basal leaves lanceolate to narrowly elliptical, shallowly notched to almost entire; calyx lobes about ⅓ as long as corolla, with 1.5–3mm long reflexed appendages between; flowers usually pale blue, 15–30mm long, with curly hairs inside. Flowers June to August.
SIMILAR SPECIES: Alpine Bellflower, *C. alpina*, has calyx lobes longer than half the corolla, and 0.5–1mm long appendages.
HABITAT: Pasture, meadows, open woods, dwarf shrub heath; calcifuge. 1,100–2,900m.
DISTRIBUTION: European montane.
NOTE: 2 varieties in the Alps:
– var. *barbata*: flowers nodding.
– var. *strictopedunculata*: flowers upright.

4 | Beck's Bellflower
Campanula beckiana – Campanulaceae

20–60cm tall; middle stem leaves large, 7–14mm broad, 3–10x as long as broad; inflorescence a many-flowered panicle; corolla 15–18mm long. Flowers June to September.
SIMILAR SPECIES: Paniculate Bellflower, *C. witasekiana* (see p. 142), has middle stem leaves 2–6mm broad and 15–40x as long as broad.
HABITAT: Woods, pasture, meadows, tall herb vegetation. 300–1,200m.
DISTRIBUTION: Northeast alpine endemic.
NAME: In honour of Austrian botanist Günther Beck, Knight of Mannagetta and Lerchenau (1856–1931), who wrote a flora of Lower Austria.

5 | Flax-leaved Bellflower
Campanula carnica – Campanulaceae

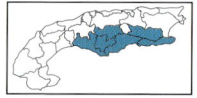

12–40cm tall; rosette leaves round heart-shaped, hairless, mostly present at flowering; stem leaves lanceolate to linear; flowers solitary or few, nodding in bud; calyx lobes protruding or reflexed, 0.5–1x as long as corolla; corolla 15–25mm long; fruit upright. Flowers June to August.
SIMILAR SPECIES: Rax Mountain Bellflower, *C. praesignis*, has upright flower buds and many-flowered inflorescence.
HABITAT: Rock crevices, rock debris; calcicole. To 2,200m.
DISTRIBUTION: Eastern alpine.
NOTE: 2 subspecies in the Alps:
– subsp. *carnica*: stem hairless; found throughout the range of the species.
– subsp. *puberula*: lower stem finely hairy. Restricted to the southern Italian Alps, especially the Bergamasque Alps.

Campanulaceae

1 | Mount Cenis Bellflower
Campanula cenicia – Campanulaceae

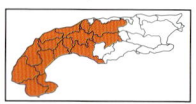

2–5cm tall, creeping, with sterile leaf rosettes; rosette leaves round to obovate, 5–8mm broad, entire; flowers solitary and terminal, lilac-blue, open bell-shaped, divided almost to the centre; petal lobes 4–6mm long, ± as long as corolla tube. Flowers July to August.
SIMILAR SPECIES: Rainer's Bellflower, *C. raineri* (see p. 138), has notched leaves and corolla only up to ⅓ divided.
HABITAT: Rock debris, moraines; calcicole. 2,200–3,600m.
DISTRIBUTION: Alpine endemic.

2 | Tufted Bellflower
Campanula cespitosa – Campanulaceae

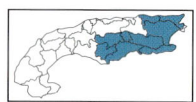

5–25cm tall, with sterile leaf rosettes; hairs on stem 0.03–0.15mm long; rosette leaves rounded-ovate to rhomboid, coarsely serrated; lower stem leaves lanceolate, clustered; flower buds and fruits nodding; flower 10–18mm long, narrowing a little under the corolla lobes. Flowers July to September.
SIMILAR SPECIES: Fairy's Thimble, *C. cochleariifolia*.
HABITAT: Rocks, rock debris, open pinewoods; calcicole. To about 2,200m.
DISTRIBUTION: Eastern alpine–Dinaric.

3 | Fairy's Thimble (Dwarf Bellflower)
Campanula cochleariifolia – Campanulaceae

4–15cm tall, loose-growing; flowering stems arching upwards from the ground; stem hairs 0.25–0.8mm long; basal leaves broadly ovate, narrowing towards the stalk, toothed, present at flowering; stem leaves elliptical to linear, increasingly small towards the top; inflorescence usually with 1–6 flowers; flower buds and fruits nodding; corolla 10–18mm long. Flowers June to September.
SIMILAR SPECIES: Tufted Bellflower, *C. cespitosa*, has flower narrowing a little under the corolla lobes.
HABITAT: Rocks, scree, river alluvium, walls; calcicole. To 3,100m.
DISTRIBUTION: Southern European montane.

4 | Lombardy Bellflower
Campanula elatinoides – Campanulaceae

10–30cm tall, with white felty hairs; stem to 60cm long; basal leaves in rosette, blades ovate, heart-shaped at base, serrated, teeth with cartilaginous tips; flowers in a tight panicle; corolla deeply 5-lobed, pale violet-blue. Flowers July to September.
SIMILAR SPECIES: Piedmont Bellflower, *C. elatines*, has leaves hairless above, dark blue-violet corolla and grows on siliceous soils.
HABITAT: Rocks; calcicole. To 1,900m.
DISTRIBUTION: Southern alpine endemic.

5 | Perforate Bellflower
Campanula excisa – Campanulaceae

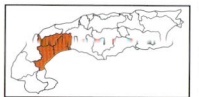

5–15cm tall; stem leaves narrowly lanceolate to linear; flowers mostly solitary, often nodding, narrow bell-shaped, 12–22mm long, divided almost to half; corolla lobes rounded and joined at base. Flowers July to August.
SIMILAR SPECIES: Hardly any.
HABITAT: Rock debris, stony sward, rock crevices; siliceous substrates. 1,200–3,000m.
DISTRIBUTION: Western alpine endemic.

6 | Large-rooted Bellflower
Campanula macrorhiza – Campanulaceae

15–40cm tall, hairless; base covered in leaves and remains of stems; basal leaves ovate-heart-shaped, toothed, present at flowering; stem leaves linear-lanceolate, untoothed; buds upright; calyx lobes linear, spreading; corolla 15–25mm long. Flowers May to September.
SIMILAR SPECIES: Fritsch's Bellflower, *C. fritschii*, has basal leaves withered by flowering, and toothed stem leaves.
HABITAT: Rock crevices; calcicole. To about 1,800m.
DISTRIBUTION: Western alpine–(Corsican?).

Campanulaceae

1 | Dolomite Bellflower
Campanula morettiana – Campanulaceae

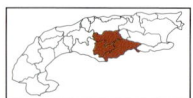

3–6cm tall, creeping, with sterile rosettes; basal leaves rounded-ovate to heart-shaped, toothed, with stiff hairs; sepals 4–6mm long, ± erect, shorter than ½ corolla tube; corolla violet-blue, 20–30mm long. Flowers July to August.
SIMILAR SPECIES: Rainer's Bellflower, *C. raineri*.
HABITAT: Rock crevices, stony sward; calcicole. 1,500–2,500m.
DISTRIBUTION: Dolomite endemic.
NAME: In honour of Italian botanist Guiseppe Moretti (1782–1853), Professor of Botany at the University of Pavia.

2 | Rock Bellflower
Campanula petraea – Campanulaceae

15–40cm tall, with stem arching upwards; leaves pale green, notched; flowers in dense, rounded, terminal inflorescence; calyx as long as corolla, toothed, with shaggy hairs; corolla pale yellow. Flowers July to September.
SIMILAR SPECIES: Whitish Bellflower, *C. albicans*, is very closely related and often indistinguishable. It has creamy-white flowers and is endemic to the French Maritime Alps.
HABITAT: Crevices on steep rocks at beech forest levels, cracks in walls; calcicole. To 1,300m.
DISTRIBUTION: Eastern alpine endemic.

3 | Solitary Harebell/Bellflower
Campanula pulla – Campanulaceae

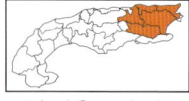

4–15cm tall; rosette leaves round, withered at flowering; stem leaves oval to elliptical, notched; flower buds and flowers nodding; sepals 7–12mm long, protruding only a little from corolla; corolla 15–25mm long, dark bluish-violet. Flowers June to August.
SIMILAR SPECIES: Hardly any.
HABITAT: Damp rocks and rocky sward, snow-melt ground; calcicole. 1,200–2,200m, occasionally lower, as near Gstatterboden, Enns Valley, Austria (570m).
DISTRIBUTION: Eastern alpine endemic.

4 | Rainer's Bellflower
Campanula raineri – Campanulaceae

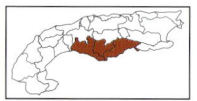

3–10cm tall; loose-growing, with stem arching upwards; leaves elliptical, bluntly notched, hairless to lightly hairy; flowers terminal and solitary; calyx lobes broadly lanceolate, clearly 3-veined, about ½ as long as corolla; corolla wide funnel-shaped, 30–40mm broad, lobes divided up to ⅓ the length of corolla. Flowers July to August.
SIMILAR SPECIES: Mount Cenis Bellflower, *C. cenicia* (see p. 136), and Dolomite Bellflower, *C. morettiana*, which has corolla 18–25mm broad and very hairy leaves.
HABITAT: Rocks, rock debris; calcicole. 1,300–2,400m.
DISTRIBUTION: South-eastern alpine endemic.
NAME: In honour of Archduke Rainer von Österreich (1783–1853), Viceroy of Lombardy and Veneto, who was passionate about flowers and maintained a botanical garden at his summer residence in Monza.

5 | Broad-leaved Harebell (Broad-leaved Bellflower)
Campanula rhomboidalis – Campanulaceae

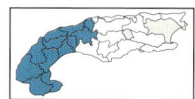

20–60cm tall; stem angular; rosette leaves rounded, withering by flowering; stem leaves many, sessile, oval, with coarsely serrated margins; middle stem leaves 1–2.5x as long as broad inflorescence of 4–5 flowers; flower buds ± upright; sepals narrowing towards tip; corolla 12–20mm long, wide bell-shaped. Flowers June to August.
SIMILAR SPECIES: Beck's Bellflower, *C. beckiana* (see p. 134), has narrowly-elliptical to narrowly-lanceolate middle stem leaves, 3–7x as long as broad.
HABITAT: Meadows, pasture, woodland edges. To 2,800m.
DISTRIBUTION: Southwest European montane, naturalised in some places in the eastern Alps.

Campanulaceae

1 | Scheuchzer's Bellflower
Campanula scheuchzeri – Campanulaceae

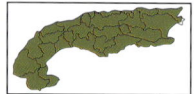

8–25cm tall; hairless, rarely hairy (**1B**); rosette leaves rounded to heart-shaped, notched, mostly withered by flowering; stem leaves linear-lanceolate; 1–5-flowered, usually in a nodding raceme; flower buds nodding; corolla deep violet-blue, 16–25mm long. Flowers June to August.
SIMILAR SPECIES: Harebell, *C. rotundifolia*, has erect flower buds and is usually many-flowered. Cottian Bellflower, *C. stenocodon*, has narrow funnel-shaped, long-stalked corolla.
HABITAT: Pasture, poor grassland, stony grassland; 1,400–3,100m.
DISTRIBUTION: Southern European montane.
NAME: In honour of Jakob Scheuchzer (1672–1733), Swiss naturalist and Chief Physician of Zurich.
NOTE: A range of insects specialise in visiting bellflowers, including the bees *Dufourea dentiventris* and *Melitta haemorrhoidalis*. Insects with long or short probosces are both able to reach the nectar.

2 | Spiked Bellflower
Campanula spicata – Campanulaceae

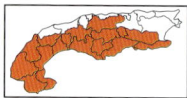

15–80cm tall; leaves lanceolate, often with wavy margins, stiffly hairy; basal leaves in rosette; stem leaves ovate-lanceolate, semi-clasping; flowers violet-blue, in an impressive spike. Flowers June to July.
SIMILAR SPECIES: The very variable Clustered Bellflower, *C. glomerata*, has flowers in terminal clusters and the basal leaves are not in rosettes.
HABITAT: Poor grassland, stony sward. To 2,200m.
DISTRIBUTION: Southern European montane.

3 | Clustered Yellow Bellflower
Campanula thyrsoides subsp. *thyrsoides* – Campanulaceae

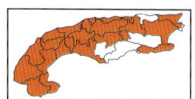

10–50cm tall, stiffly hairy; basal leaves elongate wedge-shaped, in rosette; stem leaves linear-lanceolate, broad-based and sessile; inflorescence oval to cylindrical, 8–20cm long, opening upwards from the base; corolla pale yellow. Flowers June to August.
SIMILAR SPECIES: Carniolic Yellow Bellflower, *C. thyrsoides* subsp. *carniolica*, has inflorescence 20–60cm long with creamy-white flowers, opening from the middle upwards and downwards.
HABITAT: Poor grassland, montane mat vegetation, rock debris; calcicole. 1,000–2,800m.
DISTRIBUTION: Southern European montane.

4 | Carniolic Yellow Bellflower
Campanula thyrsoides subsp. *carniolica* – Campanulaceae

40–120cm tall, stiffly hairy; basal leaves elongate wedge-shaped, in rosette; stem leaves linear, broad-based and sessile; inflorescence elongate, 20–60cm long, opening from the middle upwards and downwards; corolla creamy white. Flowers June to August.
SIMILAR SPECIES: Clustered Yellow Bellflower, *Campanula thyrsoides* subsp. *thyrsoides*.
HABITAT: Stony sward, open pinewoods, poor grassland; calcicole. To about 1,800m.
DISTRIBUTION: Eastern alpine–Illyrian.

5 | Nettle-leaved Bellflower
Campanula trachelium – Campanulaceae

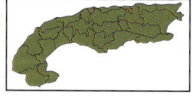

30–100cm tall, stiffly hairy; stem sharp-edged; lower leaves stalked, heart-shaped; upper leaves sessile, lanceolate; inflorescence usually branched; corolla 3–4cm long, violet-blue, occasionally pale lilac or white, divided less than to the middle. Flowers June to September.
SIMILAR SPECIES: Giant Bellflower, *C. latifolia*, has round grooved, almost hairless stem and 4–6cm long corolla. Peach-leaved Bellflower, *C. persicifolia*, is almost hairless, with linear-lanceolate leaves and broad bell-shaped corolla.
HABITAT: Woods, scrub. To about 1,800m.
DISTRIBUTION: European-Asiatic.

Campanulaceae

1 | Paniculate Bellflower (Witasek's Bellflower)
Campanula witasekiana – Campanulaceae

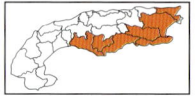

20–50cm tall; rhizome with root swellings 5–10mm thick; rosette leaves rounded to heart-shaped, notch-toothed, long-stalked, mostly withered by flowering; stem leaves linear-lanceolate, 2–6mm broad, 15–40x as long as broad; flowers in multi-flowered panicle; flower buds and fruits nodding; corolla blue, 12–15mm long. Flowers July to September.
SIMILAR SPECIES: Beck's Bellflower, *C. beckiana* (see p. 134), has 7–14mm broad stem leaves, 3–10x as long as broad. Scheuchzer's Bellflower, *C. scheuchzeri* (see p. 140), has few-flowered inflorescence and 16–25mm long corolla.
HABITAT: Meadows, pasture, Dwarf Mountain Pine scrub, open pinewoods. 600–2,100m.
DISTRIBUTION: Southeast European montane.
NAME: In honour of Austrian botanist Johanna Witasek (1865–1910), who published a revision of the bellflower section Heterophyllae.

2 | Crimped Bellflower (Zois's Bellflower)
Campanula zoysii – Campanulaceae (Syn.: *Favratia zoysii*)

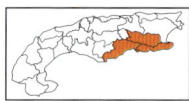

3–10cm tall; loose-growing, with sterile leaf rosettes; basal leaves round to oval; inflorescence with 1–4 flowers; corolla with dense white hairs inside, the lobes narrowing and crimped together, the tips forming a striking 5-rayed star. Flowers June to August.
SIMILAR SPECIES: None.
HABITAT: Calcareous rocks, scree; calcicole. 900–2,200m, descending occasionally to 550m on the Sava River.
DISTRIBUTION: Southeast alpine endemic.
NAME: In honour of Lower Styrian botanist Karl Freiherr von Zois (1756–1800), who discovered the species near Bohinj, Slovenia.

3 | Tufted Devil's Claw
Physoplexis comosa – Campanulaceae

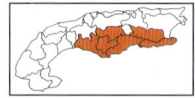

5–15cm tall; basal leaves long-stalked, coarsely toothed; bracts narrowly elliptical to lanceolate, mostly deeply serrated; inflorescence umbel-like, mostly with 8–20 flowers; corolla purple-lilac, dark purple towards the tip; 2 stigmas. Flowers June to July.
SIMILAR SPECIES: None.
HABITAT: Limestone and dolomite crevices. 900–2,000m, occasionally also lower, as on the banks of Lake Garda, Italy (60m).
DISTRIBUTION: Southeast alpine endemic.

4 | Betony-leaved Rampion
Phyteuma betonicifolium – Campanulaceae

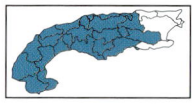

20–70cm tall; basal leaves ovate-lanceolate, heart-shaped at base, truncate or narrowing towards the stem, 3–5x as long as broad, present at flowering; inflorescence oval to cylindrical, 4–9cm long. Usually 3 stigmas. Flowers June to August.
SIMILAR SPECIES: Peach-leaved Rampion, *P. persicifolium*, usually has 2 stigmas, and is restricted to the eastern Alps.
HABITAT: Poor grassland, pasture, open woods; calcifuge. 600–2,700m.
DISTRIBUTION: Alpine endemic.
NOTE: The genus *Phyteuma* contains about 24 species, all native to central and southern Europe, with the Alps the most species-rich.

5 | Charmeil's Rampion
Phyteuma charmelii – Campanulaceae

5–25cm tall; leaves bright green; basal leaves long-stalked, narrowly heart-shaped to linear; stem leaves linear-lanceolate, distantly toothed; corolla curved before opening; 2 stigmas. Flowers June to August.
SIMILAR SPECIES: Scheuchzer's Bellflower, *C. scheuchzeri* (see p. 146), and the Provence and Maritime Alps endemic Villar's Rampion, *P. villarsii*, have grey-green, strongly-toothed leaves.
HABITAT: Rocks; calcicole. To about 2,200m.
DISTRIBUTION: Southwest European montane.
NAME: In honour of French botanist and doctor Joseph Pierre Charmeil (1781–1833), who made great contributions to the flora of the Dauphiné, in south-east France.

Campanulaceae

1 | Confused Rampion
Phyteuma confusum – Campanulaceae
(Syn.: Phyteuma nanum)

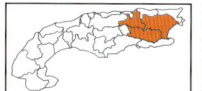

3–15cm tall; basal leaves 3–10cm long, narrowly lanceolate to tongue-shaped, mostly longer than broad, pointed; outer bracts inflorescence of 5–10 flowers. Flowers July to August.
SIMILAR SPECIES: Rosette-leaved Rampion, *P. globulariifolium*.
HABITAT: Rocky sward, Trailing Azalea scrub, scree; calcifuge. 1,700–2,700m.
DISTRIBUTION: Southeast European montane.
NOTE: The botanical generic name comes from the ancient Greek and means something like 'that which is planted'. Linnaeus treated the name as feminine, although it is actually neuter. At the 1987 Berlin Congress it was officially decided in the nomenclatural code that it should be treated as neuter.

2 | Rosette-leaved Rampion
Phyteuma globulariifolium – Campanulaceae

2–10cm tall; basal leaves 1–3cm long, spoon-shaped to obovate-lanceolate, broadest at or above the middle; inflorescence with 4–12 flowers; outer bracts about the same length as the inflorescence. Flowers July to August.
SIMILAR SPECIES: Confused Rampion, *P. confusum*, has 3–10cm long, narrowly-lanceolate to tongue-shaped basal leaves.
HABITAT: Stony grassland, rocky sward; on siliceous substrates. 1,800–3,200m, occasionally higher, as on the Matterhorn (3,600m).
DISTRIBUTION: Alpine–Pyrenean.
NOTE: 2 subspecies in the Alps:
– subsp. *globulariifolium*: outer bracts round, in the eastern Alps.
– subsp. *pedemontana*: outer bracts ovate-lanceolate, in the western Alps, east to the South Tyrol.

3 | Globe-headed Rampion
Phyteuma hemisphaericum – Campanulaceae

3–20cm tall; basal leaves linear, grass-like, 1–2mm broad, mostly entire; outer bracts oval to broadly ovate-lanceolate, pointed, 0.5–1.3x as long as the inflorescence, mostly entire; corolla curving inwards before opening. Flowers July to August.
SIMILAR SPECIES: Rhaetian Rampion, *P. hedraianthifolium*, has linear-lanceolate outer bracts, 1.5–2x as long as the inflorescence. Dwarf Rampion, *P. humile*, has 2–4mm broad basal leaves, and long pointed outer bracts 1–1.5x as long as the inflorescence.
HABITAT: Rocky grassland, pasture, dwarf shrub heath; calcifuge. 1,700–3,100m, sometimes lower, as in the Zillertal near Hippach, Austria (800m), or higher, as on the Weißtor in Wallis, Switzerland (3,600m).
DISTRIBUTION: Southern European montane.

4 | Micheli's Rampion
Phyteuma michelii – Campanulaceae

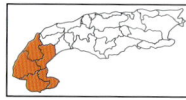

20–40cm tall; basal leaves linear-lanceolate, ciliate at base, mostly withered by flowering; stem leaves similar, linear; inflorescence short and cylindrical; 2 stigmas. Flowers June to August.
SIMILAR SPECIES: Scorzonera-leaved Rampion, *P. scorzonerifolium* (see p. 146), has hairless, unciliated basal leaves and a long cylindrical inflorescence.
HABITAT: Poor meadows, open woods, rocky grassland; calcifuge. 1,200–2,600m.
DISTRIBUTION: West alpine endemic.
NAME: In honour of Italian botanist and mycologist Pier Antonio Micheli (1679–1737), one of the fathers of mycology.

5 | Round-headed Rampion
Phyteuma orbiculare – Campanulaceae

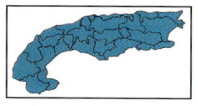

10–50cm tall; basal leaves oval to lanceolate, stalked, heart-shaped or round at the base; outer bracts ovate-lanceolate, usually clearly wider at the base, the longest 2–4x as long as broad; corolla curving strongly inwards before opening. Flowers May to July.
SIMILAR SPECIES: Horned Rampion (Scheuchzer's Rampion), *P. scheuchzeri*, has linear outer bracts, hardly broadening at base, 5–25x as long as broad.
HABITAT: Poor grassland, pasture, fen meadows, pinewoods; calcicole. To 2,600m.
DISTRIBUTION: European.

Campanulaceae

1 | Dark Rampion (Haller's Rampion)
Phyteuma ovatum – Campanulaceae

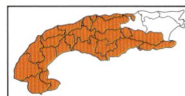

30–100cm tall; basal leaves heart-shaped, long-stalked; leaf margins coarsely double-toothed; lower stem leaves resembling basal leaves; corolla usually dark violet, very rarely white or steely blue, strongly curved before opening. Flowers May to August.
SIMILAR SPECIES: Spiked Rampion, *P. spicatum*.
HABITAT: Tall herb vegetation, meadows, woods. To 2,400m.
DISTRIBUTION: Southern European montane.

2 | Horned Rampion (Scheuchzer's Rampion)
Phyteuma scheuchzeri – Campanulaceae

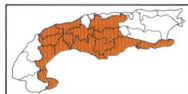

10–40cm tall; basal leaves heart-shaped-oval to lanceolate, long-stalked, mostly present at flowering; outer bracts linear, scarcely broadening at base, 5–25x as long as broad, entire, hairless; corolla only slightly curved before opening; 3 stigmas. Flowers June to August.
SIMILAR SPECIES: Round-headed Rampion, *P. orbiculare* (see p. 144) and Charmeil's Rampion, *P. charmelii* (see p. 142), have 2 stigmas and basal leaves withering by flowering.
HABITAT: Rocks, stony grassland. To about 2,100m.
DISTRIBUTION: Alpine–Illyrian.
NOTE: 2 subspecies in the Alps:
– subsp. *scheuchzeri*: leaf base wedge-shaped.
– subsp. *columnae*: leaf base heart-shaped.
NAME: In honour of Swiss naturalist Johann Jakob Scheuchzer (1672–1733), who carried out the first measurements of altitude using barometric pressure.

3 | Scorzonera-leaved Rampion
Phyteuma scorzonerifolium – Campanulaceae

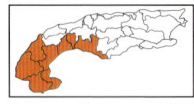

8–20x as long as broad, hairless, mostly withered by flowering; stem leaves similar; flower spike long and slender. Flowers June to July.

SIMILAR SPECIES: Micheli's Rampion, *P. michelii* (see p. 144) and Betony-leaved Rampion, *P. betonicifolium* (see p. 142), have heart-shaped basal leaves, still present at flowering.
HABITAT: Meadows, open woods, scrub; calcifuge. To about 2,200m.
DISTRIBUTION: Western alpine–Apennine.

4 | Sieber's Rampion
Phyteuma sieberi – Campanulaceae

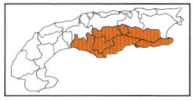

4–25cm tall; basal leaves ovate heart-shaped to lanceolate, 5–10mm broad, widest at or below the middle; stem leaves ovate lanceolate to oval, upper leaves broader than the middle leaves; outer bracts round, pointed, sharply toothed, densely ciliate; inflorescence usually with 5–15 flowers; corolla dark blue. Flowers June to August.
SIMILAR SPECIES: Maritime Rampion, *P. cordatum*, endemic to the Maritime Alps, has rhomboid to heart-shaped stem leaves, and pale blue flowers.
HABITAT: Rocks, scree, stony grassland, calcicole. 1,200–2,600m.
DISTRIBUTION: Southeast alpine endemic.
NAME: In honour of Austrian botanist Franz Wilhelm Sieber (1785–1844), who researched the flora of the Alps and the Orient.

5 | Spiked Rampion
Phyteuma spicatum – Campanulaceae

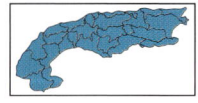

30–70cm tall; basal leaves heart-shaped, long-stalked, often dark-spotted, margins coarsely double-toothed; lower stem leaves resembling basal leaves; corolla yellowish to greenish-white or pale blue. Flowers May to June.
SIMILAR SPECIES: Dark Rampion (Haller's Rampion), *P. ovatum*, normally has dark violet flowers.
HABITAT: Deciduous woods, tall herb vegetation, montane meadows. To about 2,300m.
DISTRIBUTION: European.
NOTE: Two subspecies in the Alps:
– subsp. *spicatum*: corolla greenish to yellowish-white (**5A**).
– subsp. *coeruleum*: corolla pale blue, rarely deep blue (**5B**).

Caprifoliaceae, Caryophyllaceae

1 | Alpine Honeysuckle
Lonicera alpigena – Caprifoliaceae

50–200cm tall shrub; leaves c.1cm long, elliptical, stalked, hairless, shiny beneath; corolla yellowish to red; flowers paired, with ovary and fruit completely fused; fruit cherry red. Flowers May to July.
SIMILAR SPECIES: Blue-berried Honeysuckle, *L. caerulea*, has yellowish flowers, bluish-green leaves, and blue fruits. Fly Honeysuckle, *L. xylosteum*, has fruits paired, but not fused, and leaves hairy on both sides.
HABITAT: Wooded ravines, deciduous woods, to 2,200m.
DISTRIBUTION: Southern European montane.
NAME: In honour of German botanist and doctor Adam Lonitzer (1528–1586), author of a herbal that was published many times from 1557 until the end of the 18th century.

2 | Two-flowered Sandwort
Arenaria biflora – Caryophyllaceae

1–3cm tall, 10–30cm long; leaves elliptical to round, 2–5mm long, 1–2x as long as broad, hairless, with short, ciliate stem; flowers 2 or solitary, petals as long or slightly longer than calyx; sepals 4–4.5mm long, hairless. Flowers July to August.
SIMILAR SPECIES: Fringed Sandwort, *A. ciliata*, has leaves 2–4x as long as broad.
HABITAT: Damp rocky sward, snow-melt hollows; calcifuge. 1,600–3,000m, sometimes higher, as on Piz Linard, Unterengadin, Switzerland (3,100m).
DISTRIBUTION: Southeast European montane, from the Pyrenees to the Carpathians and the mountains of the Balkan Peninsula.

3 | Fringed Sandwort
Arenaria ciliata – Caryophyllaceae

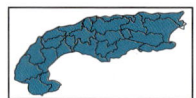

1–5cm tall; stem prostrate or ascending; leaves oval to lanceolate, 3–7mm long, ciliate at least on lower half; 1–2 flowers on each branch, 12–15mm in diameter; petals 1.25–2x as long as sepals. Flowers July to August.
SIMILAR SPECIES: Many-stemmed Sandwort, *A. multicaulis* (see p. 150), has 3–7 flowers per branch, and flowers 7–10mm in diameter.
HABITAT: Cushion Sedge (*Carex firma*) sward, Mouse-tail Bog Sedge (*Carex myosuroides*) vegetation, stabilised scree; calcicole. 1,800–3,100m.
DISTRIBUTION: Southeast European montane, (excluding the arctic *A. frigida*) from the western Alps to the Carpathians.

4 | Large-flowered Sandwort
Arenaria grandiflora – Caryophyllaceae

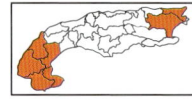

3–15cm tall; stem and calyx with short glandular hairs; leaves linear-lanceolate, 5–13mm long, 6–20x as long as broad, with awn-like tips; flowers solitary and long-stalked; petals 1.5–2.5x as long as sepals; sepals 4–6mm long, spiky, with glandular hairs. Flowers May to July.
SIMILAR SPECIES: Carpathian Sandwort, *Minuartia langii* (see p. 164), has petals lacking glandular hairs.
HABITAT: Rocks, scree; calcicole. About 1,200–1,900m.
DISTRIBUTION: Southern European montane, with 3 subspecies. The entire European range stretches from the Iberian Peninsula to Sicily and the Pöllau Mountains (Pálava), Czechia.

5 | Huter's Sandwort (Carnic Sandwort)
Arenaria huteri – Caryophyllaceae

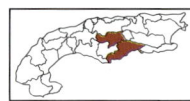

3–20cm tall, often drooping, forming loose, glandular-hairy cushions; stem thin, richly branching; leaves 5–13mm long, 2–3x as long as broad; sepals 4.5–6.5mm long, with glandular hairs on the outside; petals 1.75–2x as long as sepals, not notched. Flowers June to August.
SIMILAR SPECIES: Diels's Sandwort, *Moehringia dielsiana*, is hairless, and has petals 1.25–1.5x as long as sepals.
HABITAT: Dolomite rocks. 700–1,900m.
DISTRIBUTION: South Tyrol dolomite endemic. Also found in the adjacent Italian Carnic and Venetian Alps.
NAME: In honour of Tyrolean Rupert Huter (1834–1919), from Kals, Pastor in Ried near Sterzing (Vipiteno), who researched the flora of the eastern Alps.

Caryophyllaceae

1 | Marschlins's Sandwort
Arenaria marschlinsii – Caryophyllaceae

2–7cm tall, with bristly hairs; leaves oval, pointed, 2–5mm long, 1–2x as long as broad, with 0.2–0.5mm long hairs; flowers bunched, sepals pointed, 4–5mm long, hairy; petals about ⅓ shorter than calyx. Flowers July to August.
SIMILAR SPECIES: Thyme-leaved Sandwort, *A. serpyllifolia*, has hairs only 0.1–0.2mm long, smells like cucumber when crushed, and grows only to upper montane levels.
HABITAT: Siliceous rock debris, moraines, livestock resting sites. 1,900–3,200m.
DISTRIBUTION: Alpine–Pyrenean.
NAME: In honour of the Swiss Adalbert Ulysses von Salis-Marschlins (1795–1886), who studied the flora of Graubünden, southern France, and Corsica.

2 | Many-stemmed Sandwort
Arenaria multicaulis – Caryophyllaceae
(Syn.: *Arenaria ciliata* subsp. *moehringioides*)

5–10cm tall; stem prostrate to ascending; leaves elliptical, 3–7mm long, with at least the lower half ciliate; flowers 3–7 per branch, 7–10mm in diameter; petals 1.25–1.5x as long as sepals. Flowers July to August.
SIMILAR SPECIES: Fringed Sandwort, *A. ciliata* (see p. 148).
HABITAT: Patchy grassland, moraines; calcicole. 1,800–3,100m, sometimes swept downstream, as near Felsberg in the North Rhaetian Alps, Switzerland (600m).
DISTRIBUTION: Southwest European montane, from the Cantabrian Mountains to the Alps.

3 | Sweet William Catchfly
Atocion armeria – Caryophyllaceae
(Syn.: *Silene armeria*)

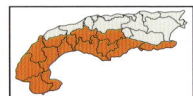

15–60cm tall; stem and leaves blue-green, hairless, sticky below nodes; leaves broadly lanceolate; inflorescence umbel-like, terminal; calyx 14–20mm long, hairless, narrowly club-shaped; petals purple-pink, 20–28mm long. Flowers June to September.
SIMILAR SPECIES: Rock Soapwort, *Saponaria ocymoides* (see p. 170), has a glandular-hairy calyx.
HABITAT: Rocky slopes, dry grassland, open scrub, chestnut woods, scree, stony steppe; calcifuge. To 1,200m.
DISTRIBUTION: Southern European, from France to Russia and Turkey.

4 | Rock Campion
Atocion rupestre – Caryophyllaceae
(Syn.: *Silene rupestris*)

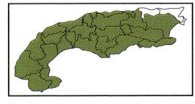

5–20cm tall, branched from the base, hairless, blue-green; leaves lanceolate; calyx 3–5mm long; petals white, rarely pale pink, 6–9mm long, deeply notched. Flowers July to August.
SIMILAR SPECIES: Species of *Heliosperma*, have grass-green leaves and toothed, not notched, petals.
HABITAT: Stony, sandy, open soils, rock crevices, rocky slopes; calcifuge. To 2,900m.
DISTRIBUTION: European montane, from the Sierra Nevada to the eastern Carpathians, and northern Europe.

5 | Field Mouse-ear
Cerastium arvense subsp. *strictum* – Caryophyllaceae

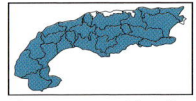

5–12cm tall; in loose cushions, the sterile shoots much shorter than the flowering shoots; stem with reflexed to upright hairs; leaves narrowly lanceolate, 6–15mm long and 1–4mm broad; bracts hairy to the tip; sepals 4–6mm long, petals 10–12mm long; fruit curved, as is the fruit stalk below the calyx. Flowers June to August.
SIMILAR SPECIES: Subspecies *C. arvense* subsp. *suffruticosum* (**5B**) has bracts hairy only in the lower third, and leaves 0.6–1.2mm broad. Julian Mouse-ear, *C. julicum*, has straight fruits, and straight fruit stalk below the calyx. Narrow-leaved Mouse-ear, *C. lineare*, has 20–35mm long narrow leaves and is found on limestone-poor soils in the western Alps.
HABITAT: Grassland, stony drifts; calcicole. 1,000–3,000m, occasionally lower, as in Misox near Lostallo, Switzerland (425m).
DISTRIBUTION: Montane species, from Spain to the Dinaric Alps.

Caryophyllaceae

1 | Carinthian Mouse-ear
Cerastium carinthiacum – Caryophyllaceae

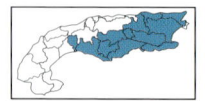

5–20cm tall; plant almost hairless (subsp. *carinthiacum*), or with dense glandular hairs, especially on upper stems (subsp. *austroalpinum*); leaves oval to lanceolate, 13–26mm long, 3–8mm broad; upper bracts lacking membranous margin (subsp. *austroalpinum*), or with broad membranous margin (subsp. *carinthiacum*); sepals 5–6mm long; petals 1.5–2.25x as long as sepals. Flowers June to September.
SIMILAR SPECIES: Alpine Mouse-ear, *C. alpinum*, has 7–10mm long sepals, and Broad-leaved Mouse-ear, *C. latifolium*, is mostly single-flowered (*C. carinthiacum* is many-flowered).
HABITAT: Scree, stony grassland, Dwarf Mountain One scrub; calcicole. 1,500–2,200m, sometimes washed down lower.
DISTRIBUTION: Eastern alpine, formerly divided into 2 subspecies (*carinthiacum*, *austroalpinum*).

2 | Starwort Mouse-ear
Cerastium cerastoides – Caryophyllaceae

5–15cm tall; prostrate, flowering stems upright, glandular-hairy; leaves elongate-lanceolate, c. 1cm long, hairless; sepals 4–7mm long; petals 1.5–2x as long as sepals. Stigmas 3(-5). Flowers July to August.
SIMILAR SPECIES: Differs from the other alpine mouse-ear species in the number of stigmas (the others have 5).
HABITAT: Damp stony sward, snow-melt hollows, wet flushes; calcifuge. 1,700–3,000m.
DISTRIBUTION: Arctic–alpine, from the Arctic and Subarctic south to Scotland and southern Scandinavia and all European mountains. Further to the mountains of Asia Minor and the Himalaya.

3 | Woolly Mouse-ear
Cerastium eriophorum – Caryophyllaceae

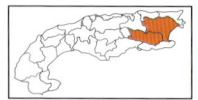

5–20cm tall; vegetative shoots in rosette, with white woolly tips; leaves ovate lanceolate, 0.5–2cm long, 1.5–4x as long as broad, the older leaves also hairy; sepals 7–9mm long; petals about 2x as long as sepals. Flowers July to August.
SIMILAR SPECIES: Alpine Mouse-ear, *C.alpinum*, has basal rosettes without white woolly tips, and the older leaves wither.
HABITAT: Rocky sward, poor grassland; calcicole. About 1,700–2,500m.
DISTRIBUTION: Southeast European montane, from the eastern Alps to the Carpathians and Balkan mountains.

4 | Pedunculate Mouse-ear (Bell-flowered Mouse-ear)
Cerastium pedunculatum – Caryophyllaceae

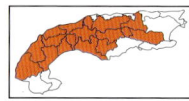

2–8cm tall with few sterile shoots; leaves lanceolate, broadest below the middle, hairy; bracts without membranous margin; sepals 5–7mm long, with narrow membranous margin; petals 6–9mm long, 1–1.3x as long as sepals. Flowers July to August.
SIMILAR SPECIES: Glacier Mouse-ear, *C. uniflorum* (see p. 154), has 10–15mm long petals, 1.5–2x as long as sepals.
HABITAT: Rock debris, moraines; calcifuge. 2,100–3,160m, occasionally washed down to lower levels, as in the Vennbach Valley near Brenner (1,600m).
DISTRIBUTION: Alpine endemic.

5 | Slovenian Mouse-ear
Cerastium subtriflorum – Caryophyllaceae

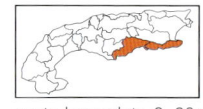

20–40cm tall; stem prostrate to ascending, glandular, with short erect hairs; leaves ovate-lanceolate, 8–20mm long, 5–10mm broad; inflorescence branched; flower stalks glandular; sepals 4–5mm long; petals 2–3x as long as sepals. Flowers April to July.
SIMILAR SPECIES: Wood Mouse-ear, *C. sylvaticum*, has leaves 2–5cm long, and Common Mouse-ear, *C. fontanum*, has corolla only 1–1.5x as long as sepals.
HABITAT: Calcareous scree, damp rocks, gravel, edges of beech forests; calcicole. To 2,000m.
DISTRIBUTION: Endemic to the Julian Alps.

Caryophyllaceae

1 | Glacier Mouse-ear
Cerastium uniflorum – Caryophyllaceae

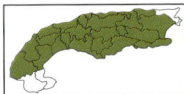

2–8cm tall, with shaggy and glandular hairs; hairs 0.5–1.5mm long; stem 1–3-flowered; leaves oval, broadest above the middle, 5–15mm long; bracts similar to the leaves, without membranous border; petals white, 10–25mm long, 1.5–2x as long as sepals. Flowers July to August.
SIMILAR SPECIES: Broad-leaved Mouse-ear, *C. latifolium* (**1B**), has leaves 12–30mm long, broadest below the middle. Alpine Mouse-ear, *C. alpinum*, has bracts with narrow membranous margin, and hairs 1.2–4.2mm long.
HABITAT: Slate debris, rock crevices, moraines; calcifuge (although also on limestone in the Dolomites). 1,700–3,400m.
DISTRIBUTION: Alpine–Carpathian; Alps and Tatra.

2 | Alpine Pink
Dianthus alpinus – Caryophyllaceae

5–10cm tall; leaves linear lanceolate, 15–35mm long, lower leaves 3–5mm broad; flowers bright pink, purplish-red at base, speckled white; petals 2x as long as calyx, flat surface of petal 15–18mm long. Flowers June to August.
SIMILAR SPECIES: Glacier Pink, *D. glacialis* (see p. 156), has flat surface of petal only 9–10mm long, and leaves just 1–2mm broad.
HABITAT: Stony grassland, calcicole. 1,000–2,250m, sometimes lower.
DISTRIBUTION: Northeast alpine endemic, in Austria from the Totes Gebirge (Dead Mountains) to the Sonnwendstein near Semmering, and to the Viennese Schneeberg. Also recorded at Seekar, Koralpe, but not yet confirmed.

3 | Sweet William (Bearded Pink)
Dianthus barbatus – Caryophyllaceae

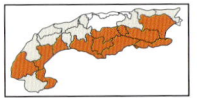

25–50cm tall, hairless; leaves lanceolate, 5–18mm broad; inflorescence dense, umbrella-shaped, with 12–40 flowers; petals purplish-red, with white and dark dots and stripes; calyx 15–18mm long. Flowers June to August.
SIMILAR SPECIES: The very variable Carthusian Pink, *D. carthusianorum*, and Deptford Pink, *D. armeria*, which has a 2–15-flowered inflorescence.
HABITAT: Montane meadows, woodland edges, scrub. To 2,500m.
DISTRIBUTION: Southeast European montane. Often cultivated and naturalised.

4 | Carthusian Pink
Dianthus carthusianorum – Caryophyllaceae

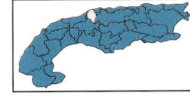

10–60cm tall, hairless, with many sterile shoots; leaves linear, 0.8–4mm broad; inflorescence with 2–15 flowers, surrounded by brown scaly bracts; calyx dark purple, 14–18mm long; petals purplish-pink, flat surface of petal 6–12mm long. Flowers June to September.
SIMILAR SPECIES: Blood-red Pink, *D. sanguineus*, has bright red petals, with flat surface only 3–4mm long, and is restricted to the lower altitudes in the south-eastern Alps.
HABITAT: Poor and semi-arid grassland, rocks, dry woodland. To 2,600m.
DISTRIBUTION: European, from Spain to Russia, and a site in northern Anatolia.
NOTE: There are 9 subspecies, of which 5 are found in the Alps:
– subsp. *carthusianorum*: scattered through the Alps.
– subsp. *atrorubens*: southern and western Alps.
– subsp. *capillifrons*: on serpentine in the eastern Alps.
– subsp. *latifolius*: eastern Alps.
– subsp. *vaginatus*: scattered through the Alps.

5 | Maiden Pink
Dianthus deltoides – Caryophyllaceae

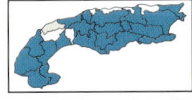

10–30cm tall, with fine downy hairs, mostly branching above, with sterile shoots; leaves narrowly lanceolate, 10–25mm long, 1–2mm broad; flowers long-stalked, terminal, solitary or 2–3; calyx 12–18mm long; petals deep pink, with white spots and a purple ring. Flowers June to September.
SIMILAR SPECIES: Seguier's Pink, *D. seguieri* (see p. 158), has 2–8 flowers, clustered.
HABITAT: Poor meadows, pasture, woodland edges; calcifuge. To 2,000m.
DISTRIBUTION: Eurosiberian, from Spain and Norway to the Yenisei region, Siberia.

Caryophyllaceae

1 | Painted Pink
Dianthus furcatus – Caryophyllaceae

3–35cm tall; leaves linear-lanceolate, 15–40mm long, 1–2mm broad; calyx 10–18mm long, epicalyx scales broadly lanceolate, pointed; flowers solitary, rarely paired; petals pink, petal blade slightly or irregularly toothed (subsp. *furcatus*, subsp. *dissimilis*) or deeply toothed or incised (subsp. *lereschii*). Flowers June to August.
SIMILAR SPECIES: Subspecies *furcatus* flowers resemble those of Short-stalked Pink, *D. subacaulis*, but the latter has calyx 6–10mm long and oval scales.
HABITAT: Stony grassland, dry rocky slopes. 900–2,200m.
DISTRIBUTION: Southern European montane, with 5 subspecies from the Pyrenees to Corsica and the western Alps.
NOTE: Variable species, with 3 subspecies in the western Alps (subsp. *furcatus*, subsp. *lereschii*, subsp. *dissimilis*).

2 | Glacier Pink
Dianthus glacialis – Caryophyllaceae

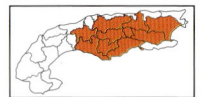

2–5cm tall; leaves linear, 20–50mm long, 1–2mm broad; flowers vivid pink, with 3 purple stripes above the throat; petals c.1.5x as long as calyx; petal blade 9–10mm long. Flowers July to August.
SIMILAR SPECIES: Alpine Pink, *D. alpinus* (see p. 154). Peacock-eye Pink, *D. pavonius*, restricted to the south-western Alps, has petals that are greenish underneath.
HABITAT: Stony grassland, wind-exposed ridges. 1,900–2,900m.
DISTRIBUTION: Eastern alpine–Carpathian. Eastern Alps, Tatra, and Romanian Carpathians.

3 | Fringed Pink
Dianthus hyssopifolius – Caryophyllaceae (Syn.: *Dianthus monspessulanus*)

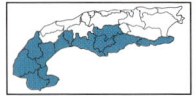

20–50cm tall; leaves linear-lanceolate, soft, 3–10cm long, 1–4mm broad, about as long or longer than internodes; flowers 2–5; calyx 20–25mm long; petals white with greenish base or pink with whitish base; petal blade 12–16mm long, split almost to the middle. Flowers June to August.
SIMILAR SPECIES: Sternberg's Pink, *D. sternbergii* (see p. 158), is usually single-flowered and has stiff leaves, shorter than internodes.
HABITAT: Rocky slopes, scrub, open woods, in warm sites; calcicole. To 2,100m.
DISTRIBUTION: Southeast European montane.

4 | Peacock-eye Pink
Dianthus pavonius – Caryophyllaceae
(Syn: *Dianthus neglectus*)

2–12cm tall, with grass-like leaves and many non-flowering rosettes; leaves (also upper stem leaves) linear, 10–35mm long, 1–2.5mm broad, hairless; calyx 12–16mm long; petals vivid pink, greenish beneath; petal blade 10–15mm long. Flowers July to August.
SIMILAR SPECIES: Glacier Pink, *D. glacialis*. Cheddar Pink, *D. gratianopolitanus*, has scale-like upper stem leaves.
HABITAT: Stony sward, scree, rocks; mainly on primary rocks. 1,200–3,000m.
DISTRIBUTION: Western alpine endemic, east to Aosta Valley, Italy.

5 | Common Pink
Dianthus plumarius – Caryophyllaceae

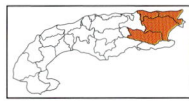

10–25cm tall; stem rectangular, with blue-green bloom, hairless; leaves linear-lanceolate, 1–3.5mm broad, upper stem leaves small and stiffly upright; 1–5-flowered; petals pink, petal blade 12–18mm long, cut to about a third. Flowers May to July.
SIMILAR SPECIES: Sternberg's Pink, *D. sternbergii* (see p. 158).
HABITAT: Rocky sward, dry grassland, rock debris, open pinewoods; calcicole. To 1,750m.
DISTRIBUTION: Eastern alpine–Carpathian. 3 subspecies (or possibly varieties?) in the area: subspp. *blandus*, *hoppei*, *neilreichii*. These are mainly differentiated geographically and have intermediates.
NAME: Subsp. *hoppei* is in honour of German doctor and botanist David Heinrich Hoppe (1760–1846), who contributed much to the study of the flora of the Alps. Subsp. *neilrechii* honours Austrian botanist August Neilreich (1803–1871), who mainly studied the flora of Lower Austria.

1 | Seguier's Pink
Dianthus seguieri – Caryophyllaceae

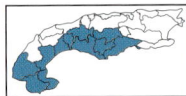

30–60cm tall, with individual sterile shoots, ± hairless; leaves narrowly lanceolate; flowers 2–8, in compact clusters, surrounded by green bracts; epicalyx lobes 0.5–0.8x as long as calyx, awned; petals deep pink, with purple dots. Flowers June to August.
SIMILAR SPECIES: Woodland Pink, *D. sylvaticus* (Syn.: *D. seguieri* subsp. *glaber*), has 1–3-flowered inflorescence and epicalyx lobes only 0.3–0.4x as long as calyx.
HABITAT: Scrub, open woods, rocky slopes. To 1,700m.
DISTRIBUTION: Alpine–Apennine. Southern and South-western Alps and northern Apennines.
NAME: In honour of Jean-François Séguier (1703–1784), French botanist and astronomer.

2 | Sternberg's Pink
Dianthus sternbergii – Caryophyllaceae

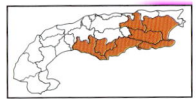

10–25cm tall; leaves linear, stiff, 1–2mm broad, mostly shorter than internodes; all stem leaves leafy; flowers mostly single; calyx 18–25mm long; petals pink, purple bearded at base; petal blade 15–20mm long, cut to about the middle. Flowers June to August.
SIMILAR SPECIES: Fringed Pink, *D. hyssopifolius* (see p. 156). Common Pink, *D. plumarius* (see p. 156), has scale-like upper stem leaves.
HABITAT: Rock debris, rough scree, stony meadows; only on limestone and dolomite. To 2,200m.
DISTRIBUTION: Eastern alpine, from the Veronese Alps, Italy to Steiermark, Austria.
NAME: In honour of Kaspar Maria von Sternberg (1761–1838), Bohemian theologian and botanist.

3 | Short-stalked Pink
Dianthus subacaulis – Caryophyllaceae

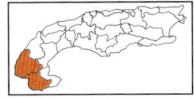

3–20cm tall; leaves linear, hairless, with obvious central vein, blue-green, 1–1.5mm broad; flowers mostly solitary, 6–12mm in diameter; calyx brownish-red, 6–12mm long, sepal tips oval, entire; petals pink, petal blade 4–5mm long. Flowers May to August.
SIMILAR SPECIES: Painted Pink, *D. furcatus* (see p. 156), is 20cm tall and has 10–18mm long calyx. Rough Pink, *D. scaber*, has hairy leaves.
HABITAT: Dry rocky slopes, rock debris; calcicole. 1,000–2,300m.
DISTRIBUTION: Southwest French alpine endemic.

4 | Alpine Fringed Pink
Dianthus superbus subsp. *alpestris* – Caryophyllaceae

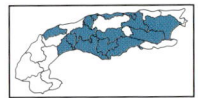

30–60cm tall, hairless; stem with bluish bloom, 1–5-flowered; leaves narrowly lanceolate, to 8cm long, 2–6mm broad; calyx brownish-red to violet; petals whitish to deep pink, cut to about the middle, towards the throat olive green or black with long purple hairs; petal blade about 30mm long. Flowers July to August.
SIMILAR SPECIES: Fringed Pink, *D. superbus* subsp. *superbus*, has grass-green, 5–10-flowered stems, and grows at lower levels.
HABITAT: Poor grassland, especially Mat Grass (*Nardus stricta*) vegetation, pasture. About 1,300–2,400m.
DISTRIBUTION: Southern European montane, from the Alps and Jura to the Tatra and eastern Carpathians.

5 | Wood Pink
Dianthus sylvestris – Caryophyllaceae

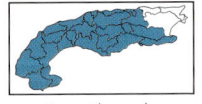

8–30cm tall, unbranched or upper stems branched, hairless; sterile leaf rosettes at base; leaves narrowly linear, 2–10cm long, 0.5–2mm broad; calyx 15–26mm long; epicalyx lobes 2–4, 0.25x as long as calyx, with short, pointed tips; petals pink, with unmarked throat. Flowers June to August.
SIMILAR SPECIES: Cheddar Pink, *D. gratianopolitanus*, has a bearded corolla throat and 4–6 epicalyx lobes.
HABITAT: Poor stony and dry grassland, rocks. To 2,800m.
DISTRIBUTION: Southern European montane, with several subspecies.

Caryophyllaceae

1 | Alpine Gypsophila
Gypsophila repens – Caryophyllaceae

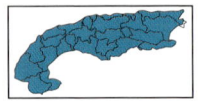

3–20cm tall, prostrate to creeping, blue-green; leaves linear, to 3cm long; sepals with white membranous stripes; petals pink or white, 6–10mm long, at least 2x as long as calyx; lacks scale-like secondary corolla at throat. Flowers May to September.
SIMILAR SPECIES: Rock Campion, *Atocion rupestre* (see p. 150), has scale-like secondary corolla at throat.
HABITAT: Rock debris, rocks, stony grassland; calcicole. 1,200–2,600m, sometimes higher, as near Zermatt (3,100m), or lower on river gravel.
DISTRIBUTION: Southern European montane, from the mountains of northern Spain to the northern Carpathians.

2 | Alpine Catchfly
Heliosperma alpestre – Caryophyllaceae (Syn.: *Silene alpestris*, *S. quadrifida*)

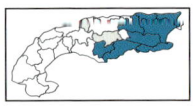

10–25cm tall; upper stem sticky, lower stem with 2 rows of hairs; leaves lanceolate, 3–6mm broad, clustered on lower stem; calyx 5–7mm long, with glandular hairs; petals white. Flowers June to August.
SIMILAR SPECIES: Small Alpine Catchfly, *H. pusillum* subsp. *pusillum*, has leaves 1–3mm broad, and hairless stems. Woolly Catchfly, *H. veselskyi*, differs in having woolly hair.
HABITAT: River gravel, rock debris, pinewoods; calcicole. 1,000–2,200m, often carried to lower levels by streams and rivers.
DISTRIBUTION: Eastern alpine–Illyrian, from the Dolomites to Mount Snežnik, Slovenia.

3 | Small Alpine Catchfly
Heliosperma pusillum subsp. *pusillum* – Caryophyllaceae (Syn.: *Silene pusilla*)

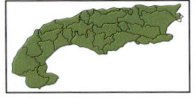

8–20cm tall; upper stem sticky, lower stem also hairless; leaves narrowly lanceolate, 1–3mm broad, ciliate at base; calyx 3.5–5.5mm long, hairless; petals white. Flowers June to September.

SIMILAR SPECIES: Alpine Catchfly, *Heliosperma alpestre*, Rock Campion, *Atocion rupestre* (see p. 150), and Pink Alpine Catchfly, *Heliosperma pusillum* subsp. *pudibundum*, the latter with pink petals and calyx 5.5–6.5mm long.
HABITAT: Damp, shady rocks and scree, springs; calcicole. 1,000–2,400m, often lower, as in the Garnitzenschlucht, Carinthia, Austria (500m).
DISTRIBUTION: Southern European montane, from northern Spain to the mountains of the Balkans.

4 | Pink Alpine Catchfly
Heliosperma pusillum subsp. *pudibundum* – Caryophyllaceae (Syn.: *Silene pudibunda*)

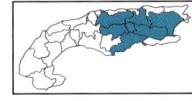

15–25cm tall; upper stem sticky, lower stem also hairless; leaves narrowly lanceolate, 1–3mm broad, leaf stalks hairless; calyx 5.5–6.5mm long, glandular-hairy; petals pink. Flowers July to September.
SIMILAR SPECIES: Wall Gypsophila, *Gypsophila muralis*, has striped petals, and is found in fields and forest clearings in the lowlands.
HABITAT: Springs, stream sides; calcifuge. 1,200–2,200m, occasionally lower, as in Austria at Grafendorfer Bach near Lienz, (800m), and Thurntaler Mountain, Sillian (2,300m).
DISTRIBUTION: Southeast European montane, from the Alps to the mountains of the Balkan Peninsula.

5 | Smooth Rupturewort
Herniaria glabra – Caryophyllaceae

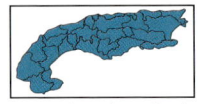

1–3cm tall, prostrate, branching and spreading at base, hairless or at most somewhat ciliate, fresh to yellow-green; stem sometimes reddish; leaves oval to lanceolate, 3–8mm long, sessile; flowers inconspicuous, in clusters along the stem; sepals greenish, about 0.5mm long; 5 petals, stunted, or absent. Flowers June to August.
SIMILAR SPECIES: Alpine Rupturewort, *H. alpina*, is grey-green and hairy.
HABITAT: Ruderal sites, river gravel and sand, dry, open sites; calcifuge. To 2,700m.
DISTRIBUTION: European–Western Asiatic.

Caryophyllaceae

1 | Ragged-robin
Lychnis flos-cuculi – Caryophyllaceae
(Syn.: *Silene flos-cuculi*)

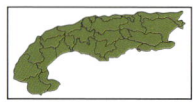

30–80cm tall, with scattered short hairs; sterile basal rosettes; leaves lanceolate; inflorescence paniculate; calyx 6–9mm long, hairless, with 10 grey-brown veins; petals deep pink, without olive green or black markings, 15–25mm long, deeply divided into 4 narrow lobes. Flowers May to July.
SIMILAR SPECIES: Fringed Pink, *D. superbus*, has olive green or black markings on the petals.
HABITAT: Damp meadows. To 1,900m.
DISTRIBUTION: European, north to Iceland.

2 | Flower of Jove
Lychnis flos-jovis – Caryophyllaceae
(Syn.: *Silene flos-jovis*)

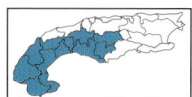

30–60cm tall, with dense white felty hairs; leaves broadly lanceolate; inflorescence compact, with 4–10 flowers; flower stalks 0.5–1cm long; petals deep pink, 2–3cm long, entire, or weakly 2-lobed. Flowers June to July.
SIMILAR SPECIES: Rose Campion, *L. coronaria*, has lilac-purple solitary flowers, with stalks 3–10cm long.
HABITAT: Rocky steppe, scrub, montane meadows and open woodland; calcifuge. 1,100–2,400m.
DISTRIBUTION: Western alpine–Apennine, from the Ligurian Alps to the South Tyrol.

3 | Austrian Sandwort
Minuartia austriaca – Caryophyllaceae

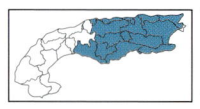

8–20cm tall, forming loose sward; leaves narrowly lanceolate, 2cm long and 1mm broad; stems mostly 2-flowered; flower stalk 4–8x as long as calyx; sepals 4–6mm long; petals almost 2x as long as calyx. Flowers June to August.
SIMILAR SPECIES: Villar's Sandwort, *M. villarii*, has stems with 3–7 flowers and grows in the western Alps. Bergamasque Sandwort, *M. grignensis*, has petals only 1.25–1.5x as long as sepals. Restricted to the Bergamasque Alps.
HABITAT: Rock debris; calcicole. 1,400–2,470m, sometimes washed downstream, as on the Mühlauer Bach, Tyrol (650m).
DISTRIBUTION: Eastern alpine endemic.

4 | Cushion Sandwort
Minuartia cherlerioides – Caryophyllaceae

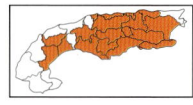

1–4cm tall, forming cushions, hairless; stem with dense, overlapping leaves; leaves elongate-ovate, very small and blunt, 1–3mm long, 3-veined; flowers 4-partite; sepals 2–4mm long, 3-veined; petals, if present, longer than sepals. Flowers July to August.
SIMILAR SPECIES: Rock Sandwort, *M. rupestris* (see p. 166), and Northern Sandwort, *M. biflora*, have 5-partite flowers.
HABITAT: Rocks, stable scree. 1,900–2,950m.
DISTRIBUTION: Alpine endemic.
NOTE: 2 subspecies:
– subsp. *cherlerioides*: eastern alpine, on limestone.
– subsp. *rionii*: central alpine, on siliceous substrates.

5 | Spring Sandwort (Gerard's Sandwort)
Minuartia gerardii – Caryophyllaceae
(Syn.: *Minuartia verna* p.p.)

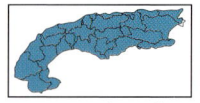

2–10cm tall; upper stem with glandular hairs; leaves 5–10mm long; flowers 5-partite, 1–6, terminal; sepals pointed, 3–4mm long, 3-veined, with narrow membranous margin; petals 4–5mm long. Flowers June to September.
SIMILAR SPECIES: Hill Sandwort, *M. glaucina*, has 10–20-flowered inflorescence and grows at lower altitudes. Recurved Sandwort, *M. recurva* (see p. 164).
HABITAT: Grassland, rock debris; calcicole. 1,500–3,300m.
DISTRIBUTION: European montane, from Spain and Ireland to Sicily and northern Russia.
NAME: In honour of French botanist and physicist Louis Gerard (1733–1819), author of *Flora Galloprovincialis*.

Caryophyllaceae

1 | Lang's Sandwort (Carpathian Sandwort)
Minuartia langii – Caryophyllaceae
(Syn.: *Minuartia laricifolia* subsp. *kitaibelii*)

5–25cm tall; leaves needle-like, 5–15mm long; sepals 6–7mm long, 3–5-veined, the lateral veins prominent along the full length; petals 1.5–2x as long as sepals; fruit 1.5–2x as long as sepals; seeds 1–1.3mm broad. Flowers June to July.

SIMILAR SPECIES: Larch-needled Sandwort, *M. laricifolia*, and Flax-flowered Sandwort, *M. capillacea*, sepals with veins only prominent on lower half. Grass-leaved Sandwort, *M. graminifolia*, has a branched inflorescence and lanceolate leaves 1–3cm long, and is restricted to the Italian provinces of Belluno and Pordenone.

HABITAT: Limestone and dolomite rocks, river gravel; calcicole. About 500–1,800m.

DISTRIBUTION: Eastern alpine–Carpathian.

NAME: The genus *Minuartia* is in honour of Juan Minuart (1693–1700), a pharmacist in Barcelona and Professor of Botany in Madrid.

NOTE: Sandwort species can be distinguished from similar, white-flowered members of the family by having 3 styles, dehiscent capsules with 3 blunt teeth, and kidney-shaped seeds without appendages.

2 | Larch-needled Sandwort
Minuartia laricifolia – Caryophyllaceae

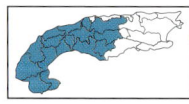

8–30cm tall; leaves needle-shaped, 5–15mm long; sepals 5–6mm long, 3–5-veined, lateral veins along the whole length; petals 1.5–2x as long as sepals; fruit 1–1.5x as long as sepals; seeds 0.8–1mm broad. Flowers July to August.

SIMILAR SPECIES: Lang's Sandwort, *Minuartia langii*, has 6–7mm long sepals and in the Alps is restricted to the north-eastern limestone Alps. Its fruit is 1.5–2x as long as sepals and the seed 1–1.3mm broad. Flax-flowered Sandwort, *M. capillacea*, has veins only obvious in the lower half of sepals.

HABITAT: Dry rocky sites, stony slopes, open pinewoods, dry river gravel; calcifuge. 600–2,000m, sometimes higher, as at Timmelsjoch in the Ötztaler Alps, Austria (2,500m).

DISTRIBUTION: Alpine–Pyrenean, from the mountains of central Spain to the eastern Alps.

3 | Changeable Sandwort
Minuartia mutabilis – Caryophyllaceae
(Syn.: *Minuartia rostrata*)

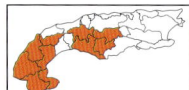

5–15cm tall, with leafy lower stems; leaves to 1cm long, 3-veined; flowers in loose, clustered inflorescence; sepals pointed, 3.5–5.5mm long, white with green stripes, 1–3-veined; petals 0.6–1x as long as sepals. Flowers June to August.

SIMILAR SPECIES: Tufted Sandwort, *M. rubra* (**3B**), has petals only 0.25–0.5x as long as sepals. At 10–30cm, it is generally taller than Changeable Sandwort. Tufted Sandwort is found on similar habitats but grows only up to subalpine levels.

HABITAT: Rocks, dry slopes, scree; on limestone and siliceous substrates. 600–2,800m.

DISTRIBUTION: Southern European montane, from the Pyrenees to Corsica and the Tyrol.

4 | Sickle-leaved Sandwort
Minuartia recurva – Caryophyllaceae

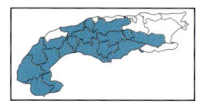

3–15cm tall, densely tufted, cushion-forming, often woody at base; leaves sickle-shaped; petals white, as long or longer than calyx; sepals 5-veined, often suffused purple. Flowers July to August.

SIMILAR SPECIES: Spring Sandwort, *Minuartia gerardii* (see p. 162), has 3-veined sepals and ± straight leaves. Rock Sandwort, *M. rupestris* (see p. 166), differs in having lanceolate leaves.

HABITAT: Curved Alpine Sedge (*Carex curvula*) sward, windswept crests; calcifuge. 1,800–3,000m, occasionally washed lower, as on the Möll near Sagritz, Austria (1,000m), or higher, as on the Hochwilde near Obergurgl, Austria (3,400m).

DISTRIBUTION: Southern European montane, from the Cévennes and Iberian mountains to the Rhodope and Carpathians.

Caryophyllaceae

1 | Rock Sandwort
Minuartia rupestris – Caryophyllaceae

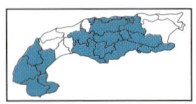

1–8cm tall; stem creeping, with loose leaf clusters; leaves 2–15mm long, broadly lanceolate, pointed, 3–7-veined; flowers terminal, solitary (subsp. *rupestris*), or 2–3 (subsp. *clementei*); flower stalks with dense glandular hairs; sepals pale green, 3.5–5mm long, 5-veined; petals a little longer than sepals. Flowers July to August.
SIMILAR SPECIES: Northern Sandwort, *M. biflora*, has 1-veined leaves and blunt sepals.
HABITAT: Exposed ridges, rocks, and scree. 1,900–3,100m.
DISTRIBUTION: Alpine endemic.
NOTE: 2 subspecies in the Alps:
– subsp. *rupestris*: Maritime Alps to south-eastern Alps.
– subsp. *clementei*: South-western Alps.

2 | Mossy Cyphel
Minuartia sedoides – Caryophyllaceae

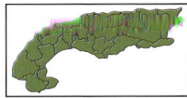

1–5cm tall, forming dense cushions; leaves lanceolate, 3–5mm long, fused in pairs at the base; flowers 5-partite, solitary, sessile or short-stalked; sepals 2–3mm long, pale green; petals absent or minimally developed. Flowers July to August.
SIMILAR SPECIES: The petal-less form of Cushion Sandwort, *M. cherlerioides* (see p. 162), has 5-partite flowers.
HABITAT: Rock debris, crevices, moraines, vegetation dominated by Cushion Sedge (*Carex firma*), Curved Alpine Sedge (*Carex curvula*) or Mouse-tail Bog Sedge (*Carex myosuroides*). 1,800–3,300m.
DISTRIBUTION: European montane.

3 | Narrow-leaved Sandwort
Moehringia bavarica – Caryophyllaceae

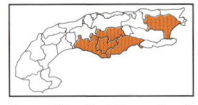

5–20cm tall; leaves fleshy, blue-green, 1–2cm long, 1–2.5mm broad; flowers 5-partite, 7–14mm in diameter; sepals 3–4mm long; petals barely longer (subsp. *insubrica*), or almost twice as long (subsp. *bavarica*) than sepals. Flowers June to August.
SIMILAR SPECIES: Grey-green Sandwort, *M. glaucovirens*, has delicate, barely fleshy leaves, 0.3–0.6mm broad, and sepals 2.5–3mm long.
HABITAT: Vertical or overhanging rock faces; calcicole. To about 1,200m.
DISTRIBUTION: Eastern alpine-Illyrian, with 2 subspecies (subspp. *bavarica* and *insubrica*).
NOTE: The specific name *bavarica* is misleading as the species is not found in Bavaria. It was first mentioned in 1601 by Veronese pharmacist Pona (1565–1630) as *Saxifraga bavarica jungermannia*, from Monte Baldo. This area belonged for a long time to the Earldom of Tyrol and was also temporarily part of Bavaria.

4 | Creeping Sandwort
Moehringia ciliata – Caryophyllaceae

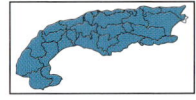

2–8cm tall; leaves linear, 3–10mm long, fleshy, blade hairless, with short ciliate hairs at base; flowers 5-partite, 6–10mm in diameter, 1–3, terminal; petals longer than sepals; sepals 3–4mm long, with narrow membranous margins. Flowers June to August.
SIMILAR SPECIES: Concarena Sandwort, *M. concarenae*, has non-ciliated leaves and flowers 5–6mm in diameter. Endemic to the southern Italian Alps.
HABITAT: Damp rocky sward, scree, snow-melt hollows, sparse grassland, rocks; calcicole. 1,600–3,100m, sometimes lower, as on the Tagliamento River near Venzone, Friuli, Italy (230m).
DISTRIBUTION: Southern European montane.

5 | South-east Alpine Sandwort
Moehringia diversifolia – Caryophyllaceae

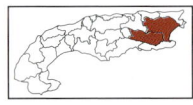

10–30cm long; upper leaves linear-lanceolate, lower leaves lanceolate, 1-veined; flowers 4–5mm in diameter, 5-partite; petals as long or somewhat longer than sepals. Flowers May to August.
SIMILAR SPECIES: Three-veined Sandwort, *M. trinervia*, has oval, 3–5-veined leaves.
HABITAT: Rock crevices, rock debris below cliffs; calcifuge. 400–1,800m.
DISTRIBUTION: Austrian endemic. West to Pöllinggraben in Lavanttal and near Eppenstein, northwards and eastwards to the Schwarzkogel near Bruck an der Mur and south to Krummbachgraben in the Koralpe.

Caryophyllaceae

1 | Mossy Sandwort
Moehringia muscosa – Caryophyllaceae

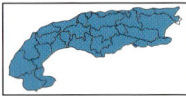

5–20cm tall/long, forming loose cover, much-branched, hairless; stems mostly 3–5-flowered; leaves narrowly linear, needle-shaped, 1–3cm long, fresh green; flowers 4-partite, with 8 stamens; petals 1–1.5x as long as sepals. Flowers May to September.
SIMILAR SPECIES: Markgraf's Sandwort, *M. markgrafii*, is nearly always single-flowered, and only occurs in the Brescia Prealps. Provence Sandwort, *M. intermedia*, has succulent leaves and is restricted to the French South-western Alps.
HABITAT: Shady damp rocks, scree, glaciated tall herb vegetation, Dwarf Mountain Pine scrub; calcicole. To 2,300m.
DISTRIBUTION: Southern European montane, from the mountains of Spain to the Carpathians.
NAME: The genus is named in honour of German doctor, botanist and ornithologist Paul Heinrich Moehring (1710–1792), from Jever, Oldenburg.
NOTE: Sandworts differ from similarly white-flowered members of the family in having 3 styles, dehiscent capsules with 3 blunt teeth, and kidney-shaped seeds without obvious appendages.

2 | Sedum-like Sandwort
Moehringia sedoides – Caryophyllaceae

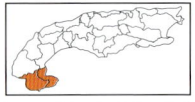

5–10cm tall, green; leaves linear, fleshy, 5–10mm long; flowers 2–3, 4-partite; sepals lanceolate, indistinctly 3-veined, about 4mm long; petals about 2x as long as sepals. Flowers May to June.
SIMILAR SPECIES: Presolana Sandwort, *M. dielsiana*, endemic to the Bergamasque Alps, has 5-partite flowers.
HABITAT: Rock faces; calcicole. To 1,500m.
DISTRIBUTION: Endemic to the Maritime Alps.

3 | Short-haired Sandwort
Moehringia villosa – Caryophyllaceae

5–15cm long, hairless or with short erect hairs; leaves linear, to 20mm long and 2mm broad; flowers 5-partite, 7–10mm in diameter; sepals lanceolate, pointed, inner sepals with broad membranous margins; petals about 1.25x as long as sepals. Flowers May to August.
SIMILAR SPECIES: Maritime Alps Sandwort, *M. lebrunii*, restricted to the Maritime Alps, has succulent leaves 2–3mm broad.
HABITAT: Rock faces, rock crevices and scree; calcicole. About 900–1,600m.
DISTRIBUTION: Endemic to the Bohinj region of the Julian Alps, Slovenia.

4 | Silver Nailwort
Paronychia kapela – Caryophyllaceae

2–8cm tall; grows in a dense sward; leaves crowded, oval, pointed, to 3.5mm long, ciliate, with narrowly-lanceolate shiny white stipules; flowers in terminal 7–15mm broad clusters; bracts silvery-white, much longer than the flowers; petals absent. Flowers May to July.
SIMILAR SPECIES: Knotgrass-leaved Nailwort, *P. polygonifolia*, has flower clusters up to 5mm broad, along the stems.
HABITAT: Rock crevices, scree; in the Alps to about 1,900m.
DISTRIBUTION: 4 subspecies across the entire Mediterranean, from Spain to Libya; 3 in the Alps:
– subsp. *kapela*: in the French and Italian south-western Alps.
– subsp. *serpyllifolia*: in the French and Italian south-western Alps.
– subsp. *galloprovincialis*: Provence.

5 | Tunic Flower (Saxifrage Childing Pink)
Petrorhagia saxifraga – Caryophyllaceae

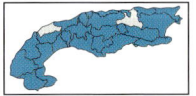

10–25cm tall, hairless or with very short hairs; Leaves narrowly linear, 5–15mm long, 0.5–1.5mm broad, blue-green; inflorescence loose, panicle-like; calyx bell-shaped, 4–6mm long; petals white to pink, with 3 darker veins. Flowers June to October.
SIMILAR SPECIES: Low Baby's-breath, *Gypsophila muralis*, has green leaves, 1.5–3mm broad.
HABITAT: Rocky sward, dry grassland; calcicole. To 1,650m.
DISTRIBUTION: Southern European, from Portugal to northern Anatolia and Iran.

Caryophyllaceae

1 | European False Stitchwort
Pseudostellaria europaea – Caryophyllaceae

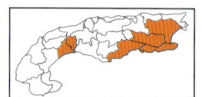

5–15cm tall, with thread-like rhizome and root nodules; stem round, upper stem with single row of hairs; leaf blades ovate-lanceolate, to 4cm long, hairless; flowers 1–3, on 2–3cm long stalks, 5-partite; petals 5–8mm long, deeply notched, about 1.5x as long as calyx. Flowers April to May.
SIMILAR SPECIES: Distinguished from all other similar members of the family by the presence of root nodules.
HABITAT: Damp, shady deciduous woods on streams and slopes with springs; calcifuge. To 700m.
DISTRIBUTION: Alpine–Illyrian, in south-eastern Alps, south to Karlovac, Croatia. Also recorded from Tessin, Switzerland, and southwest in the adjacent Italian provinces.

2 | Alpine Pearlwort
Sagina saginoides – Caryophyllaceae

1–7cm tall; loose to densely growing, hairless; stem low-lying or ascending; leaves linear, 5–15mm long, with 0.1–0.3mm long pointed tips; flowers 5-partite (sometimes 4-partite); sepals 2–3mm long; petals somewhat shorter than sepals. Flowers June to August.
SIMILAR SPECIES: Hairless Pearlwort, *S. glabra*, has petals longer than sepals.
HABITAT: Damp, poor, patchy grassland with long snow cover, wet flushes, snow-melt hollows; calcifuge. 1,500–2,900m, sometimes lower, as, in Switzerland, in Minox (Mesolcina) (300m), or higher, as near Zermatt (3,200m).
DISTRIBUTION: Arctic–alpine. Arctic regions of Eurasia and North America. South into the mountains.

3 | Yellow Soapwort
Saponaria lutea – Caryophyllaceae

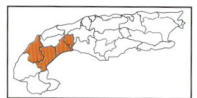

5–10cm tall with many sterile rosettes; leaves to 4cm long, narrowly lanceolate, ciliate; flowers terminal, in tight clusters; petals pale yellow, 10–15mm long; calyx 7–8mm long, with woolly hairs. Flowers July to August.
SIMILAR SPECIES: Hardly any.
HABITAT: Short, stony sward, patchy pasture. 1,500–2,600m.
DISTRIBUTION: Western alpine endemic.

4 | Rock Soapwort
Saponaria ocymoides – Caryophyllaceae

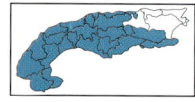

5–25cm tall, prostrate, ascending or drooping, with many patch-forming sterile shoots; leaves ovate to lanceolate, 2–3cm long, 0.5–1.3cm broad, hairy; inflorescence loosely forked, shaggy and sticky; calyx 6–8mm long, brownish-red, with glandular hairs; corolla purple-pink, 12–18mm long. Flowers April to October.
SIMILAR SPECIES: Sweet William Catchfly, *Atocion armeria* (Syn.: *Silene armeria*) (see p. 150), has a hairless calyx.
HABITAT: Dry slopes, stony sward, open pinewoods, riverbeds, open embankments; calcicole. To 2,300m.
DISTRIBUTION: Southern European montane, from the mountains of southern Spain to the eastern Alps and Abruzzi.

5 | Dwarf Soapwort
Saponaria pumila – Caryophyllaceae

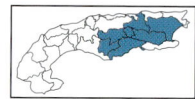

1–5cm tall, forming flat cushions; single-flowered; leaves evergreen, needle-shaped; corolla 20–25mm in diameter, petals purple-pink; calyx inflated, with short shaggy hairs, brownish-red to dark purple, with blunt teeth. Flowers June to September.
SIMILAR SPECIES: Large-flowered Catchfly, *Silene elisabethae* (see p. 172), has broadly lanceolate leaves and is a calcicole endemic of the Insubrian Alps.
HABITAT: High-altitude siliceous grassland, alpine to nival cushion vegetation, patchy grassland over silicate substrates, open wind-exposed sites, dwarf shrub heath and siliceous rock debris; calcifuge. 1,800–2,700m, occasionally lower, as in the Wölzer Tauern, (980m), Austria, or higher, as on the Schönleitenspitze, Austria (2,800m).
DISTRIBUTION: Eastern alpine–Carpathian. Eastern Alps and eastern south Carpathians. In the Alps from the Adamello group to the Stub- and Gleinalpe. In Romania, only known from the Fagaras Alps (Muntii Fagarasului), southern Carpathians.

Caryophyllaceae

1 | Moss Campion
Silene acaulis subsp. *longiscapa* – Caryophyllaceae (Syn.: *Silene acaulis* subsp. *acaulis*)

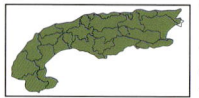

1–4cm tall, forming dense flat cushions; single-flowered; stems very leafy; leaves linear-lanceolate, 8–12mm long; flower stalk 10–30mm long; petals pink, 5–14mm long; calyx 5–8mm long, narrowed at base; capsule 3–13mm long. Flowers June to August.
SIMILAR SPECIES: Short-stemmed Moss campion, *S. acaulis* subsp. *exscapa*, has leaves 4–8mm long, flower stalk 1–5mm long and calyx 3.5–5mm long.
HABITAT: Stony poor grassland, rock crevices and debris; calcicole. 1,400–2,900m, sometimes lower, as washed down on the river Enns, Austria (500m), or higher, as in the Cottian Alps (3,500m).
DISTRIBUTION: Southern European montane, from the mountains of Spain to Romania.
NOTE: *Silene* species have a characteristic tube-like calyx without calyx scales at the base, petals with a flat surface, often notched or lobed, and dehiscent capsule with usually 6 teeth.

2 | Short-stemmed Moss Campion
Silene acaulis subsp. *exscapa* – Caryophyllaceae (Syn.: *Silene exscapa*)

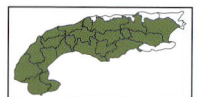

1–3cm tall, forming dense flat cushions; single-flowered, stems very leafy; leaves linear-lanceolate, 4–8mm long; flower stalk 1–5mm long; calyx 3.5–5mm long. Flowers June to August.
SIMILAR SPECIES: Moss Campion, *S. acaulis* subsp. *longiscapa*.
HABITAT: Siliceous rocky sward, Curved Alpine Sedge (*Carex curvula*) vegetation, ridges; calcifuge. 1,900–3,500m.
DISTRIBUTION: Southern European montane, from the Pyrenees to the eastern Carpathians.

3 | Heart-leaved Catchfly
Silene cordifolia – Caryophyllaceae

5–20cm tall, with glandular hairs, forming loose sward; basal leaves oval; stem leaves larger, pointed, upper stem leaves clasping; flowers 10–18mm in diameter, corolla white to pale pink; calyx 10–15mm long, with dense glandular hairs, lightly inflated, 10-veined. Flowers June to August.
SIMILAR SPECIES: Night-flowering Catchfly, *S. noctiflora*, has flowers 18–30mm in diameter.
HABITAT: Rock crevices, stabilised scree; calcifuge. 1,000–2,400m.
DISTRIBUTION: Maritime Alps endemic.

4 | Red Campion
Silene dioica – Caryophyllaceae

30–90cm tall; fairly densely hairy, hairs over 2mm long; basal leaves in rosette, stem leaves opposite, broadly lanceolate to oval; calyx 10–15mm long, green or reddish; petals deep pink, 18–25mm long. Flowers April to September.
SIMILAR SPECIES: Night-flowering Catchfly, *S. noctiflora*, has pale pink petals and calyx about 20mm long.
HABITAT: Tall herb vegetation, damp scrub, calcareous meadows. To 2,600m, sometimes higher, as on the Stelvio Pass, Italy/Switzerland.
DISTRIBUTION: European, from Portugal to North Cape, Norway.
NOTE: Where it occurs with White Campion, *S. latifolia*, hybrids (*Silene* x *hampeana*), with pink flowers and intermediate characters, are not uncommon.

5 | Large-flowered Catchfly
Silene elisabethae – Caryophyllaceae

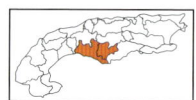

5–20cm tall; stem growing arched upwards from the side of basal leaf rosette; rosette leaves broadly lanceolate, 3–6cm long; stem leaves glandular; flowers 3–4cm in diameter, deep pink; calyx 18–24mm long, with glandular hairs. Flowers June to July.
SIMILAR SPECIES: Dwarf Soapwort, *Saponaria pumila* (see p. 170). Red Campion, *S. dioica*, which sometimes grows in stunted form, has an inflated calyx 10–15mm long.
HABITAT: Limestone and dolomite rock crevices, stabilised scree, patchy sward, especially Cushion Sedge (*Carex firma*) vegetation; calcicole. 1,400–2,450m.
DISTRIBUTION: Insubrian endemic, between lakes Como and Garda, Italy.
NAME: The species name honours Maria Elisabeth von Savoyen-Carignan (1800–1856), Princess of Savoy and aunt of Viktor Emanuel, the first king of united Italy.

Caryophyllaceae

1 | Hayek's Catchfly
Silene hayekiana – Caryophyllaceae

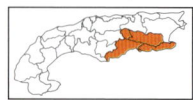

10–30cm tall, loose-growing; lower stem with short hairs, upper stem sticky; leaves narrowly linear, 0.5–2cm long; petals yellowish or reddish-white, greenish beneath; claw (base) of petals protruding far beyond calyx; entire fruit raised above calyx. Flowers June to August.
SIMILAR SPECIES: Tufted Catchfly, *S. saxifraga*.
HABITAT: Sunny rocks, stony slopes; calcicole. To about 1,900m.
DISTRIBUTION: Eastern alpine–Illyrian, from the south-eastern Alps to Klek Mountain, Croatia.
NAME: In honour of Austrian doctor and botanist August von Hayek (1871–1928), who studied the flora of Austria and the Balkan Peninsula.

2 | Insubrian Catchfly
Silene nutans subsp. *insubrica* – Caryophyllaceae

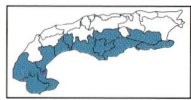

30–80cm tall, hairy, glandular and sticky above; long, thin vegetative shoots with rosette leaves, mostly with internodes 3–20x as long as broad; leaves lanceolate to spoon-shaped; inflorescence omnidirectional; petals olive green to dingy red on outside, yellowish-white to pale pink inside. Flowers May to August.
SIMILAR SPECIES: The Eurosiberian nominate form, subsp. *nutans*, has inflorescence nodding to one side, and short, thick vegetative shoots (most internodes 1–3x as long as broad).
HABITAT: Open woods, scrub, rocks; calcicole. To about 1,500m.
DISTRIBUTION: Southeast European montane, from the south-western Alps to the Carpathians and the mountains of northern Albania.

3 | Tufted Catchfly
Silene saxifraga – Caryophyllaceae

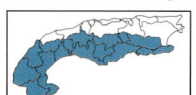

10–20cm tall, loose-growing; lower stem with short hairs, upper stem sticky; leaves narrowly linear, 0.5–2cm long; petals white inside, on outside reddish or yellow-green; claw (base) of petals protruding only a little beyond calyx; fruit remaining partly inside calyx. Flowers June to August.
SIMILAR SPECIES: Hayek's Catchfly, *S. hayekiana*, has claw of petals protruding far beyond calyx, and entire fruit raised above calyx. The western alpine Narrow-leaved Catchfly, *S. campanula*, is hairless.
HABITAT: Sunny rocks, stony slopes; calcicole. To about 2,100m.
DISTRIBUTION: Southern European montane, from the Iberian Peninsula to northern Greece.

4 | Valais Catchfly
Silene vallesia – Caryophyllaceae

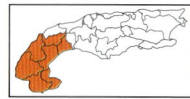

5–20cm tall, upright, glandular; 1–3-flowered; leaves lanceolate, 15–30mm long, 4–12mm broad; calyx 18–28mm long, broad-tubular, 10-veined; petals 25–35mm long, pale pink above, dull red beneath. Flowers June to July.
SIMILAR SPECIES: Petrarch's Catchfly, *S. petrarchae*, has 2–4mm broad leaves and is probably restricted to Mont Ventoux, France. Narrow-leaved Catchfly, *S. campanula*, is hairless, has 1–1.5mm broad leaves and a 7–10mm long calyx.
HABITAT: Rock debris, stony sward; calcifuge. 900–2,500m.
DISTRIBUTION: Western alpine endemic.

5 | Bladder Campion
Silene vulgaris – Caryophyllaceae

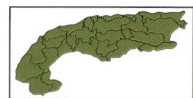

10–90cm tall, very variable, usually hairless; stem not sticky, with sterile shoots at base; leaves lanceolate to oval, pointed; calyx 12–18mm long, inflated, reticulately 20-veined; petals white, styles 3. Flowers June to September.
SIMILAR SPECIES: White Campion, *S. latifolia*, has 5 styles (not in every individual plant, as dioecious!).
HABITAT: Meadows, ecotones, stony sward, tall herb vegetation, dry walls. To 3,000m.
DISTRIBUTION: European-Asiatic, from the Azores and north Scandinavia to the Himalaya and lowlands of Siberia.
NOTE: 8 subspecies in Europe, of which 4 are found in the Alps:
– subsp. *vulgaris*: throughout the Alps (**5A**).
– subsp. *antelopum*: eastern Alps.
– subsp. *glareosa*: limestone alpine regions (**5B**).
– subsp. *prostrata*: western Alps.

Caryophyllaceae, Cistaceae

1 | Bog Stitchwort
Stellaria alsine – Caryophyllaceae
(Syn.: *Stellaria uliginosa*)

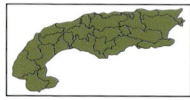

10–40 cm tall; stem smooth; leaves lanceolate to oval, pointed, to 2.5cm long, bluish-green, hairless, ciliate at base; petals divided almost to the base, shorter than the 2.5–3.5mm long sepals. Flowers May to July.
SIMILAR SPECIES: Long-leaved Stitchwort, *S. longifolia*, has petals somewhat longer than sepals, and rough-edged upper stem.
HABITAT: Stream sides, wet flushes, forest track hollows; calcifuge. To 2,200m.
DISTRIBUTION: Eurosiberian–North American, from Portugal, Ireland and Norway to Japan and North America.

2 | Alpine Catchfly
Viscaria alpina – Caryophyllaceae
(Syn.: *Silene suecica*)

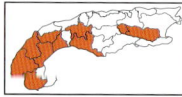

5–15cm tall, hairless, not sticky; leaves lanceolate; flowers in dense terminal raceme; petals 6–10mm long, bright pink, 2-lobed. Flowers July to August.
SIMILAR SPECIES: Sticky Catchfly, *V. vulgaris*, is 30–60cm tall, with sticky stem and grows in lowland sites.
HABITAT: Sunny, dry, wind-exposed, base-poor grassland, especially Curved Alpine Sedge (*Carex curvula*) and Mouse-tail Bog Sedge (*Carex myosuroides*) sward. 1,900–3,100m.
DISTRIBUTION: Arctic–alpine, northern Europe and North America. South into the mountains.

3 | Alpine Rock-rose
Helianthemum alpestre – Cistaceae

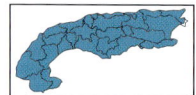

3–15cm tall, woody at base; leaves hairless to sparsely bristly-hairy beneath; stipules absent, leaves on flowering stems smaller than on vegetative stems, leaf blade obovate-lanceolate; inflorescence 2–7-flowered; sepals 5–7mm long, petals 6–10mm long. Flowers June to September.
SIMILAR SPECIES: Common Rock-rose, *H. nummularium*. Hoary Rock-rose, *H. canum*, has felty grey hairs on leaf undersides, and 3–5.5mm long sepals.
HABITAT: Rocky and poor grassland; calcicole. 900–2,700m, sometimes lower, as near Riva on Lake Garda, Italy (200m), or higher, as in the Bernina region, Switzerland (2,850m).
DISTRIBUTION: Southern European montane.

4 | Ligurian Rock-rose
Helianthemum lunulatum – Cistaceae

3–20cm tall, woody at base; lower stems often leafless and withered; leaf blades narrowly elliptical, 8–12mm long, 3–4mm broad, opposite, without stipules, sparsely hairy beneath; flowers mostly solitary; petals 5–10mm long, often with orange, crescent-shaped spots. Flowers June to July.
SIMILAR SPECIES: Italian Rock-rose, *H. italicum*, has 5–20-flowered inflorescence.
HABITAT: Rocks, sunny, open sward; calcicole. 1,700–2,300m.
DISTRIBUTION: Maritime and Ligurian alpine endemic.

5 | Common Rock-rose
Helianthemum nummularium – Cistaceae

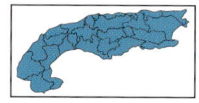

10–30cm tall, woody at base; upper stem hairy; leaf blades oval to lanceolate, margins usually recurved; stipules present; leaves of flowering stems at least as large as those of vegetative stems; petals yellow (also subspecies with pink petals in the western Alps); corolla 16–30mm in diameter. Flowers May to September.
SIMILAR SPECIES: Alpine Rock-rose, *H. alpestre*, has no stipules, and leaves of flowering stems smaller than those of vegetative stems.
HABITAT: Poor grassland, ecotones, stony montane grassland. To 2,800m.
DISTRIBUTION: As various subspecies, from the Atlas Mountains to Sweden and Armenia.
NOTE: 7 subspecies in the Alps:
– subsp. *nummularium*: widespread.
– subsp. *berteroanum*: south-western Alps (**5B**).
– subsp. *glabrum*: mainly in north-eastern Alps.
– subsp. *grandiflorum*: in most of the Alps.
– subsp. *obscurum*: lowland sites.
– subsp. *semiglabrum*: south-western Alps.
– subsp. *tomentosum*: southern and western Alps.

Celastraceae, Crassulaceae

1 | Alpine Spindle-tree
Euonymus latifolius – Celastraceae

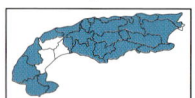

1–5 cm tall shrub; twigs round or slightly compressed; leaves elliptical, pointed, very finely and regularly toothed, hairless, 7–14cm long, 3–6cm broad, stalked; 3–15-flowered; petals inconspicuous, greenish-yellow, often suffused purple, oval, 2.5–3mm long, 4–5-lobed; fruit purple-pink, seed aril orange. Flowers May to June.
SIMILAR SPECIES: Common Spindle-tree, *E. europaeus*, has square twigs.
HABITAT: Wooded ravines, damp deciduous woods; calcicole. To 1,600m.
DISTRIBUTION: Southern European montane.

2 | Round-leaved Stonecrop (Reddish Stonecrop; Evergreen Orpine)
Hylotelephium anacampseros – Crassulaceae (Syn.: *Sedum anacampseros*)

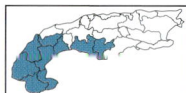

10–30cm tall, arched upwards, with sterile shoots densely leafy towards the top; leaves oval, entire, fleshy, sessile, 10–30mm long; flowers 5-partite; petals about 4.5mm long, dull dark purple. Flowers July to August.
SIMILAR SPECIES: Orpine, *H. telephium* (Syn.: *Sedum telephium*), lacks sterile shoots and has leaves 20–100mm long.
HABITAT: Rock debris, rocks; calcifuge. 1,300–2,500m.
DISTRIBUTION: Southwest European montane, from the Pyrenees to the Apennines and southern Alps.

3 | Hen-and-chickens Houseleek
Jovibarba globifera – Crassulaceae (Syn.: *Sempervivum globiferum*)

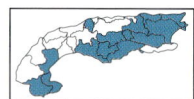

5–25cm tall; leaf rosettes 1–6cm in diameter; young rosettes easily detached from the parent plant; rosette leaves 8–20mm long, 5–7mm broad; leaves with glandular hairs at margin; petals 6, yellow, bell-shaped, leaning together, with fringed edges. Flowers July to September.
SIMILAR SPECIES: Yellow-flowered species of the houseleek genus (*Sempervivum*) have >10, unfringed petals.
HABITAT: Rocky sward, patchy dry grassland. To about 2,000m.
DISTRIBUTION: European, from the western Alps to the central Russian plains.
NOTE: 4 subspecies in the Alps:
– subsp. *allionii*: rosette leaves with short glandular hairs also on the surface (only this subspecies); western alpine endemic.
– subsp. *arenaria*: stem leaves narrower or as broad as rosette leaves, margins with hairs 0.2–0.35mm long; calcifuge; eastern alpine endemic.
– subsp. *hirta*: stem leaves as broad or broader than rosette leaves; calcicole; eastern Alps (**3B**).
– subsp. *pseudohirta*: stem leaves narrower than rosette leaves, margins with hairs 0.5–0.8mm long; calcifuge; endemic to the Tyrol?

4 | Roseroot
Rhodiola rosea – Crassulaceae (Syn.: *Sedum rosea*)

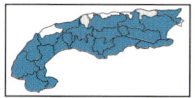

20–35cm tall; stem unbranched; leaves lanceolate, flat, dense, alternate, grey-green, increasing in size upwards; inflorescence an umbel-like many-flowered dense panicle; flowers 4-partite; petals yellow. Flowers June to August.
SIMILAR SPECIES: None.
HABITAT: Rocky sward, stony wet flushes, pasture, coarse rock debris; on limestone and siliceous substrates. (900)1,400–3,000m.
DISTRIBUTION: Arctic–alpine, circumpolar, widespread. Further south restricted to the high mountains of Europe, Asia and North America.

5 | White Stonecrop
Sedum album – Crassulaceae

5–20cm tall, hairless; richly branched towards base, with many prostrate sterile shoots; leaves linear-cylindrical, 5–15mm long, alternate; inflorescence axes hairless, many-flowered umbel-like panicle; petals white, sometimes pale pink. Flowers June to September.
SIMILAR SPECIES: Thick-leaved Stonecrop, *S. dasyphyllum*, has inflorescence axes with glandular hairs and 3–6mm long, mainly opposite leaves.
HABITAT: Stony sward, fine rock debris, walls, warm, dry patchy grassland, gravel banks; soil indifferent. To 2,500m.
DISTRIBUTION: Mediterranean-European.

Crassulaceae

1 | Alpine Stonecrop
Sedum alpestre – Crassulaceae

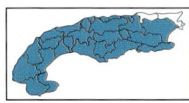

4–8cm tall, prostrate and upwardly arching, branched and often reddish at base, hairless, with densely leafy sterile shoots; leaves cylindrical-linear; petals yellow, about 1.5x as long as sepals. Flowers June to August.
SIMILAR SPECIES: Annual Stonecrop, *S. annuum*, lacks sterile shoots. Biting Stonecrop, *S. acre*, and Tasteless Stonecrop, *S. sexangulare*, have petals about 2x as long as sepals.
HABITAT: Rocks and stony sward, snow-melt hollows; calcifuge. 1,200–3,100m, sometimes lower, as near Arvigo in Tessin (750m), or higher, as on Monte Rosa (3,500m).
DISTRIBUTION: Southern European montane, from the Pyrenees to Sardinia and the Carpathians.

2 | Annual Stonecrop
Sedum annuum – Crassulaceae

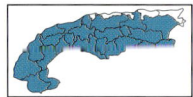

3–12cm tall, branched at base, hairless, lacking sterile shoots; leaves cylindrical-linear, blunt, 3–5mm long; flowers sessile; petals yellow, pointed; sepals blunt to rounded, as are the stem leaves. Flowers June to August.
SIMILAR SPECIES: Alpine Stonecrop, *S. alpestre*.
HABITAT: Rocks and stony sward; calcifuge. 1,200–2,800m, occasionally lower, as near Cannobio, Italy (250m).
DISTRIBUTION: Northern European-alpine, north to Iceland and Greenland, and east to the Caucasus.

3 | Dark Stonecrop
Sedum atratum – Crassulaceae

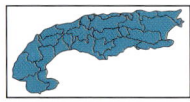

2–8cm tall, hairless, usually without sterile shoots; leaves club-shaped, 4–7mm long, mostly obviously thickened above the middle, brownish-red (subsp. *atratum*), or pale green (subsp. *carinthiacum*); petals yellowish-white, greenish or reddish, 1.25–2x as long as calyx. Flowers June to August.
SIMILAR SPECIES: Red Stonecrop, *S. rubens*, has leaves 10–25mm long, and in the Alps is only found in the lowlands.
HABITAT: Rocks and rock debris, stony sward; calcicole. 1,000–3,100m, sometimes lower, as near Salurn, South Tyrol (230m).
DISTRIBUTION: Southern European montane, from the Pyrenees to the mountains of the Balkan Peninsula.
NOTE: 2 subspecies in the Alps:
– subsp. *atratum*: vegetative parts brownish-red; petals only slightly extending beyond sepals (**3A**).
– subsp. *carinthiacum*: vegetative parts pale green; petals about 2x as long as sepals (**3B**).

4 | Thick-leaved Stonecrop
Sedum dasyphyllum – Crassulaceae

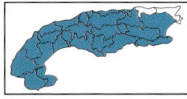

3–10cm tall, prostrate to ascending, richly branched, blue-green, often suffused reddish, upper plant glandular; leaves mainly opposite, 3–6mm long, ± flat above, strongly curved beneath; petals 5–6(7), white, often striped red, 2–3x as long as sepals. Flowers June to August.
SIMILAR SPECIES: White Stonecrop, *S. album* (see p. 178). Spanish Stonecrop, *S. hispanicum*, has leaves 7–15mm long, and petals about 4x as long as sepals.
HABITAT: Rock debris, stony sward, walls. To 2,500m.
DISTRIBUTION: Southern European–northwest African.

5 | Spanish Stonecrop
Sedum hispanicum – Crassulaceae

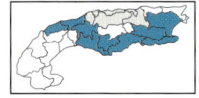

5–15cm tall, without creeping shoots, not patch-forming; stem often branched at base, with sterile side shoots; leaves elongate, 7–15mm long, ± blue-green, fleshy, hairless; petals usually 6, white, with reddish stripes on the back, pointed, about 4x as long as sepals. Flowers June to July.
SIMILAR SPECIES: Thick-leaved Stonecrop, *S. dasyphyllum*.
HABITAT: Rock debris, stony sward, railway gravel, walls; calcicole. To 1,900m.
DISTRIBUTION: South-eastern European–western Asiatic.
NAME: Both the botanical species name and the English common name are misleading, as the species is not native to Spain. Blue-green Stonecrop might be a better common name.

Crassulaceae

1 | Mountain Stonecrop
Sedum montanum – Crassulaceae

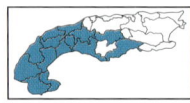

5–30cm tall, woody at base, with several upwardly arching stems and sterile shoots; leaves fleshy, linear to awl-shaped, spiny-tipped; inflorescence upright when in bud; umbel flat, not arching downwards; petals bright yellow. Flowers June to August.
SIMILAR SPECIES: Rock Stonecrop, *S. rupestre*, has inflorescence nodding when in bud. Pale Yellow Stonecrop, *S. anopetalum*, and Pale Stonecrop, *S. sediforme*, have pale yellow petals.
HABITAT: Rocky sward, Larch woods, scree, walls. To about 2,200m.
DISTRIBUTION: Alpine–Pyrenean.

2 | Hairy Stonecrop
Sedum villosum – Crassulaceae

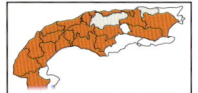

5–20cm tall, especially upper plant with glandular hairs; leaves linear to obovate, 4–9mm long, fleshy, yellow-green to red-brown; petals pink, 4–5mm long, about 2x as long as sepals. Flowers June to July.
SIMILAR SPECIES: Few.
HABITAT: Wet flushes, fens, wet rocky sites; calcifuge. From about 1,100–3,000m.
DISTRIBUTION: European montane.

3 | Cobweb Houseleek
Sempervivum arachnoideum subsp. *arachnoideum* – Crassulaceae

4–12cm tall; leaf rosettes small and round, 0.5–1.5cm in diameter, ± compact, loose to ± densely cobweb-hairy, sometimes balding; rosette leaves broadening only a little towards the tip; petals 8–10mm long, purple-red with dark central vein; stamen filaments purple. Flowers July to September.
SIMILAR SPECIES: Woolly Cobweb Houseleek, *S. arachnoideum* subsp. *tomentosum*, has leaf rosettes 1.5–2.5cm in diameter, with very dense cobweb hairs.
HABITAT: Mostly lime-poor stony sites. To 2,900m.
DISTRIBUTION: South European montane.

4 | Woolly Cobweb Houseleek
Sempervivum arachnoideum subsp. *tomentosum* – Crassulaceae

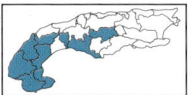

4–12cm tall; leaf rosettes 1.5–2.5cm in diameter, oval, rounded, ± closed, densely hairy, never balding; rosette leaves distinctly widening towards tip; petals 8–10, 8–10mm long, purplish-red with dark central vein; stamen filaments purple. Flowers July to September.
SIMILAR SPECIES: Cobweb Houseleek, *S. arachnoideum* subsp. *arachnoideum*.
HABITAT: Mostly lime-poor stony sites on hot, dry slopes. To about 2,000m.
DISTRIBUTION: Southwest European montane.

5 | Limestone Houseleek
Sempervivum calcareum – Crassulaceae

15–30cm tall; leaf rosettes 3–12cm in diameter, rather flat; rosette leaves blue-green to olive green, with clear reddish-brown tip, 8–12mm broad; corolla pink, petals 7–8mm long. Flowers June to September.
SIMILAR SPECIES: Common Houseleek, *S. tectorum* (see p. 184).
HABITAT: Rock crevices, stony sward; calcicole.
DISTRIBUTION: Southwest alpine endemic.

6 | Large-flowered Houseleek
Sempervivum grandiflorum – Crassulaceae

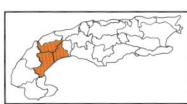

10–25cm tall; plant smells strongly of resin; rosettes star-shaped, spreading, 4–15cm in diameter; rosette leaves green, mostly purple towards tip, 8–15mm broad, covered in glandular hairs, without spiny tip; petals 11–15, pale yellow with purple base; stamen filaments purple. Flowers June to August.
SIMILAR SPECIES: Wulfen's Houseleek, *S. wulfenii* (see p. 184). Serpentine Houseleek, *S. pittonii* (see p. 184), has yellowish-white stamen filaments.
HABITAT: Siliceous rocks, stony sward; calcifuge. 1,700–3,000m.
DISTRIBUTION: West alpine endemic.

Crassulaceae

1 | Mountain Houseleek
Sempervivum montanum – Crassulaceae

5–15cm tall; leaf rosettes at first rounded, then spreading into a star shape, 1–8cm in diameter; rosette leaves abruptly pointed; marginal glandular hairs only a little longer than the hairs on the surface; 3–7-flowered; petals purple-red. Flowers July to September.
SIMILAR SPECIES: Styrian Houseleek, *S. stiriacum*, has rosette leaves with marginal hairs distinctly longer than the hairs on the surface.
HABITAT: Rocky sward, stony pasture, dwarf shrub heath; calcifuge. 300–3,400m.
DISTRIBUTION: Southern European montane, from the Pyrenees to the High Tatra.
NOTE: 2 subspecies in the Alps:
– subsp. *montanum* (**1A**): widespread; rosettes 1–2.5cm in diameter.
– subsp. *burnatii* (**1B**): restricted to the south-western Alps; rosettes 2.5–8cm in diameter.

2 | Serpentine Houseleek
Sempervivum pittonii – Crassulaceae

12–15cm tall; plant with dense glandular hairs; rosettes 2–4cm in diameter; rosette leaves 4–6mm broad; petals usually 12, pale yellow; stamen filaments yellowish-white. Flowers July to August.
SIMILAR SPECIES: Wulfen's Houseleek, *S. wulfenii*, has purple stamen filaments and hairless rosette leaf surfaces.
HABITAT: Steep serpentine rocky sward; on serpentine, dunite and magnesite. 650–800m.
DISTRIBUTION: Endemic to the central Mur Valley near Kraubath, Austria.
NAME: In honour of Josef Claudius Pittoni (1797–1878), Knight of Dannenfeld, and a zealous promoter of botany.

3 | Styrian Houseleek
Sempervivum stiriacum – Crassulaceae

5–15cm tall; rosettes round, later star-shaped, 2.5–4.5cm in diameter; rosette leaves ovate-lanceolate, abruptly pointed; with dense glandular hairs, marginal hairs distinctly longer than the hairs on the surface; petals purple-red. Flowers July to September.
SIMILAR SPECIES: Mountain Houseleek, *S. montanum*. Dolomite Houseleek, *S. dolomiticum*, has rosette leaves gradually coming to a point; restricted to the Dolomites.
HABITAT: Rocky sward, stony pasture, dwarf shrub heath; calcifuge. 1,700–2,600m.
DISTRIBUTION: Endemic to the central Alps, from the High Tauern to the Semmering region.

4 | Common Houseleek
Sempervivum tectorum – Crassulaceae

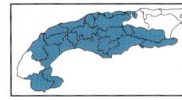

10–50cm tall; leaf rosettes 3–14cm in diameter; rosette leaves 10–15mm broad, stiff, hairless on the surface, with ciliate margins, usually with red, pointed tip; inflorescence with 20–100 flowers; corolla purple, petals mostly 12 or 13, 9–10mm long; Flowers June to September.
SIMILAR SPECIES: Limestone Houseleek, *S. calcareum* (see p. 182), has pink petals, 7–8mm long.
HABITAT: Rocks, rock debris sward, stony poor grassland, gravel. To 2,800m.
DISTRIBUTION: Southern European montane, from the Pyrenees to the mountains of the Balkan Peninsula.

5 | Wulfen's Houseleek
Sempervivum wulfenii – Crassulaceae

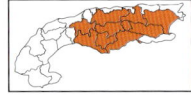

10–25cm tall; rosettes star-shaped, spreading, 4–8cm in diameter; rosette leaves blue-green, often reddish at base, 8–12mm broad, with marginal glandular hairs, hairless surfaces, pointed; petals 11–15, yellowish, with purple base. Flowers July to August.
SIMILAR SPECIES: Large-flowered Houseleek, *S. grandiflorum* (see p. 182), has green leaves covered in glandular hairs, without spiny tip.
HABITAT: Lime-poor rocky sward, stony poor grassland, 1,500–2,740m, sometimes lower, as on the Geierwand near Herberstein in eastern Styria, Austria (500m).
DISTRIBUTION: Eastern alpine endemic.
NAME: In honour of Carinthian clergyman and botanist Franz Xaver Freiherr von Wulfen (1728–1805), who studied the flora and minerals of the eastern Alps.

Dipsacaceae

1 | Long-leaved Scabious
Knautia longifolia – Dipsacaceae

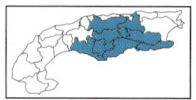

30–100cm tall; leaf rosettes next to the flowering stems few or absent; lower stems hairless or with short fluffy hairs (var. *brachytricha*); leaves undivided, lanceolate, entire, mostly hairless; flower head stems with fine downy, glandular and long upright hairs; corolla purple-pink. Flowers June to August.
SIMILAR SPECIES: Monte Baldo Scabious, *K. baldensis*, endemic to the south-eastern Alps, has base of stem with upright hairs and leaves shallowly toothed. West-alpine Scabious, *K. subcanescens*, endemic to the western Alps, has broadly lanceolate to oval leaves with serrated to toothed margins.
HABITAT: Montane meadows, tall herb vegetation; 1,400–2,200m.
DISTRIBUTION: Southeast European montane.
NAME: The generic name honours German doctor and botanist Christian Knaut (1656–1716), who classified flowering plants according to the arrangement of their petals.
NOTE: The genus *Knautia* differs from *Scabiosa* in having a 4-lobed corolla, an inconspicuous epicalyx at most 0.3mm high, and calyx with usually 8–10 bristles. There are some 17 alpine *Knautia* species, which are often hard to distinguish.

2 | Wood Scabious
Knautia maxima – Dipsacaceae
(Syn.: *Knautia dipsacifolia*)

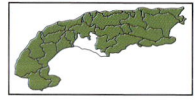

30–90cm tall; stem, especially lower, with bristly hairs (subsp. *maxima*), or shiny and hairless (subsp. *sixtina*); leaves undivided, broadly lanceolate, ± toothed; flower head 2.5–4cm in diameter; corolla blue-violet. Flowers June to September.
SIMILAR SPECIES: The variable Hungarian Scabious, *K. drymeia*, is uniformly finely hairy and has a purple-lilac corolla.
HABITAT: Woods, woodland margins, tall herb vegetation. To 2,300m.
DISTRIBUTION: Southern European montane.

3 | Soft Scabious
Knautia mollis – Dipsacaceae

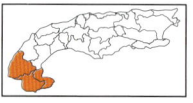

20–60cm tall, densely hairy; leaves covered in grey felty hairs, all pinnate, with 3–7 pairs of lobes; flower head 3–5cm in diameter; corolla pink. Flowers June to August.
SIMILAR SPECIES: Purple Scabious, *K. purpurea*, a western alpine species, has a purple-pink corolla and green, loosely hairy leaves.
HABITAT: Stony grassland, rock debris, scrub. To about 2,000m.
DISTRIBUTION: South-west alpine endemic.

4 | Ressmann's Scabious
Knautia ressmannii – Dipsacaceae

30–100cm tall; mostly with leaf rosettes next to flowering stems; lower stem hairless, upper stem sparsely hairy; leaves undivided, lanceolate, shallowly toothed; flower head stalk hairy, but not glandular; corolla purple-pink. Flowers June to August.
SIMILAR SPECIES: The western alpine Savoy Scabious, *K. maxima* subsp. *sixtina*, has glandular-hairy flower head stalk.
HABITAT: Meadows, woodland margins, pinewoods; calcicole. To about 1,500m.
DISTRIBUTION: Southeast alpine endemic.
NAME: In honour of Austrian lawyer and amateur botanist Franz Ressmann, who mapped plants in Carinthia and Friuli.

5 | South Alpine Scabious
Knautia transalpina – Dipsacaceae

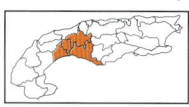

20–70cm tall; lower stem with loose long hairs, upper stem glandular, with shorter hairs; basal leaves undivided, obovate-lanceolate or with 1–5 pairs of lobes; corolla purple-pink. Flowers July to August.
SIMILAR SPECIES: Carinthian Scabious, *K. carinthiaca*, endemic to the Görschitztal, Carinthia, is 15–30cm tall, with pinnate stem leaves and pale lilac corolla.
HABITAT: Meadows, stony sward, scrub; calcicole. 700–2,000m.
DISTRIBUTION: Southern alpine endemic.

Dipsacaceae, Droseraceae

1 | Velvety Scabious
Knautia velutina – Dipsacaceae

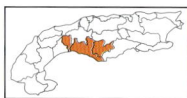

20–70cm tall; lower stem with shaggy hairs; basal leaves broadly lanceolate, lobed in lower half, softly hairy on both sides, grey-green; stem leaves pinnate with long terminal leaflet; flower stem hairy and glandular; corolla pink to purplish-pink. Flowers July to August.
SIMILAR SPECIES: Peach Scabious, *K. persicina*, has undivided stem leaves and flower stem not glandular.
HABITAT: Poor grassland, rocky sward; calcicole. 1,200–2,000m.
DISTRIBUTION: Southern alpine endemic.

2 | Grass-leaved Scabious
Lomelosia graminifolia – Dipsacaceae
(Syn.: *Scabiosa graminifolia*)

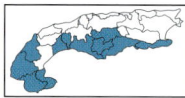

10–50cm tall; stem leaves ascending, unbranched, single-headed; leaves linear-lanceolate, entire, with silvery, silky hairs on both sides; flower heads 3–4.5cm in diameter; corolla pinkish-lilac. Flowers June to August.
SIMILAR SPECIES: Distinguished from all other alpine members of the teasel and scabious family (Dipsacaceae) by having linear-lanceolate leaves.
HABITAT: Rock debris, stony slopes; calcicole. To about 1,500m.
DISTRIBUTION: Southern European montane.

3 | Shiny Scabious
Scabiosa lucida – Dipsacaceae

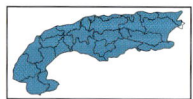

10–50cm tall; leaves mostly hairless, somewhat shiny above; basal leaves lower stem leaves mostly undivided, middle stem leaves 1-pinnate, the terminal lobe at least 2x as broad as the lateral lobes; flower head 2.5–4cm in diameter; calyx bristles 5–8mm long, 4–5x as long as the rim of the epicalyx. Flowers June to September.
SIMILAR SPECIES: Small Scabious, *S. columbaria*, has scattered hairs and calyx bristles 3–5mm long. The southwest alpine Silky Scabious, *S. holosericea*, has leaves with dense silky hairs.
HABITAT: Poor grassland, rocky slopes, pine-woods, rock debris; calcicole. To about 2,800m.
DISTRIBUTION: Southern European montane.

4 | Southern Scabious
Scabiosa triandra – Dipsacaceae

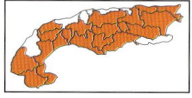

20–80cm tall; lower stem with recurved hairs; basal leaves and lower stem leaves 1-pinnate; middle stem leaves 2–3-pinnate; flower head 1.5–3cm in diameter; calyx bristles absent or 1–3mm long, 0–2x as long as the rim of the epicalyx. Flowers June to September.
SIMILAR SPECIES: Small Scabious, *S. columbaria*, has calyx bristles 3–5mm long and mostly undivided basal and lower stem leaves. The south alpine endemic Tyrolean Scabious, *S. vestina*, has undivided basal leaves and calyx bristles 4–5x as long as the rim of the epicalyx.
HABITAT: Poor meadows, dry grassland. To about 1,800m.
DISTRIBUTION: Southern European.
NOTE: The genus *Scabiosa* differs from often similar members of the genus *Knautia* in having a 5-lobed corolla, 4-lobed in *Knautia*.

5 | Round-leaved Sundew
Drosera rotundifolia – Droseraceae

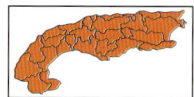

5–15cm tall; leaves basal, horizontally spread, with round blade about as long as broad; blade with long-stalked, sticky glands, that trap and digest small insects for their nitrogen (carnivorous); stem leafless, arising from the centre of the leaf rosette; petals white; flowers nodding to one side in a small cluster. Flowers July to August.
SIMILAR SPECIES: Oblong-leaved Sundew, *D. intermedia*, has leaf blades 2–3x as long as broad, and stem arising from the side of the leaf rosette. Great Sundew, *D. anglica*, has leaf blade 4–8x as long as broad.
HABITAT: Raised bogs, intermediate mires and peat-moss mounds in fens. To 1,800m, sometimes higher, as in the Gotthard region, Switzerland (1,920m).
DISTRIBUTION: Eurosiberian–North American.
NOTE: In addition to *D. intermedia*, a hybrid between *D. anglica* x *D. rotundifolia*, in the Alps there is also the primary hybrid *Drosera* x *obovata*. This differs from *D. intermedia* in having a flowering stem 2–3x as long as the leaves. In *D. intermedia*, the flowering stem is no longer or only a little longer than the leaves.

Ericaceae

1 | Heather (Ling)
Calluna vulgaris – Ericaceae

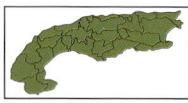

10–50cm tall evergreen dwarf shrub; leaves scale-like, 1–3mm long, about 0.5mm broad, in 4 rows, overlapping; petals about 2mm long, sepals about 4mm long, both purple-pink. Flowers July to September.
SIMILAR SPECIES: Few.
HABITAT: Nutrient-poor, acid woods, dwarf shrub heath, poor pasture, raised bogs; light-loving; calcifuge. To 2,500m, sometimes higher, as on Lenzerhorn in the Rhaetian Alps, Switzerland (2,680m).
DISTRIBUTION: European, from the Azores and Iceland to western Siberia.

2 | Spring Heath
Erica carnea – Ericaceae

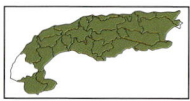

15–30cm tall dwarf shrub; leaves solitary, needle-like, hairless margins rolled under; flower stalks 2–3mm long; corolla and calyx purple-pink, corolla about 5mm long. Flowers February to May.
SIMILAR SPECIES: Bell Heather, *E. cinerea*, has clustered leaves. Heather, *Calluna vulgaris*, has scale-like, overlapping leaves, in 4 rows, and flowers from July to September.
HABITAT: Pinewoods and rocky sward on calcareous, more rarely siliceous, quartzite or serpentine substrates. To c. 2,300m, occasionally higher, as on the Rothorn in Graubünden, Switzerland (2,650m).
DISTRIBUTION: Southern European montane; Alps, Apennines, and Illyrian mountains.

3 | Trailing Azalea
Kalmia procumbens – Ericaceae (Syn.: *Loiseleuria procumbens*)

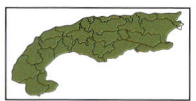

2–15cm tall richly branching carpet-forming dwarf shrub; leaves elliptical to lanceolate, 4–6mm long, leathery; terminal umbel-like raceme with 2–5 upright flowers; calyx dark red, corolla pink. Flowers May to July.
SIMILAR SPECIES: None.
HABITAT: Acidic, exposed dwarf shrub heath; calcifuge. 1,500–2,500m, sometimes higher, as on Gornergrat in Valais, Switzerland (2,950m), or lower, as by the Sihl River, Studen in Canton Schwyz, Switzerland (900m).
DISTRIBUTION: Eurosiberian–North American, from Iceland and the Pyrenees to Sakhalin and Kamchatka; northern North America.
NAME: In honour of Swedish-Finnish botanist Pehr Kalm (1716–1779), a student of Linnaeus. Kalm travelled in North America in the years 1748 to 1751 and brought the first American *Kalmia* plants to Europe. The earlier generic name, no longer valid, honours French doctor and botanist Jean-Louis-Auguste Loiseleur-Deslongchamps (1774–1849), who wrote *Flora Gallica*.

4 | One-flowered Wintergreen
Moneses uniflora – Ericaceae

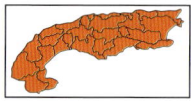

5–12cm tall; leaves in basal rosette; leaf blades round, 1–2cm in diameter, margins finely toothed; flowers solitary, fragrant, nodding; corolla white, spreading; style straight, as long or longer than ovary. Flowers May to July.
SIMILAR SPECIES: None.
HABITAT: Humus-rich, shady, damp woods, especially coniferous woods. To 2,000m, sometimes higher, as near the Thurntaler Rast, Innervillgraten, Austria (2,100m).
DISTRIBUTION: Eurosiberian–North American.

5 | Round-leaved Wintergreen
Pyrola rotundifolia – Ericaceae

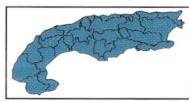

15–30cm tall; stem blunt-edged; leaves in basal rosette; leaf blade circular, 3–5cm in diameter; inflorescence drooping to all sides, 8–30-flowered; calyx lobes 3–4mm long, 2–3x as long as broad; petals white, often suffused pink; style 6–8mm long, curved. Flowers June to July.
SIMILAR SPECIES: Intermediate Wintergreen, *P. media*, has a straight style when in flower. Common Wintergreen, *P. minor* (**5B**), has a 1–2mm long style.
HABITAT: Woods, especially coniferous. To 2,200m, occasionally higher, as on Piz Alf, Engadin, Switzerland (2,300m).
DISTRIBUTION: Eurosiberian–North American.

Ericaceae, Euphorbiaceae

1 | Alpenrose
Rhododendron ferrugineum – Ericaceae

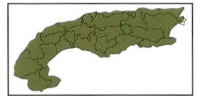

20–100cm tall shrub; leaves evergreen, oval to lanceolate, 1.5–4cm long, entire, not ciliate, with margins rolled under, rusty brown beneath; flowers 6–12, in umbel-like terminal raceme; corolla purplish-red. Flowers June to July, often flowering twice a year in the southern Insubrian Alps.
SIMILAR SPECIES: Hairy Alpenrose, *R. hirsutum*, has ciliate leaves green on both sides.
HABITAT: Moist, mainly acid dwarf shrub heath, open coniferous woods, subalpine low, woody scrub; calcifuge. 1,500–2,600m, sometimes higher, as on the Colle del Argentera in the Maritime Alps, Italy (3,200m), or lower, as near Nazzaro on Lake Maggiore, Italy (210m).
DISTRIBUTION: Southern European montane, from the Pyrenees to Illyria.

2 | Hairy Alpenrose
Rhododendron hirsutum – Ericaceae

20–100cm tall shrub; leaves evergreen, oval to lanceolate, 1.5–4cm long, entire to finely notched, not recurved, with ciliate hairs 1–3mm long remaining green and glandular on both sides; flowers 6–12, in terminal umbel-like raceme; corolla purplish-pink. Flowers May to July.
SIMILAR SPECIES: Alpenrose, *R. ferrugineum*.
HABITAT: Rocks, Dwarf Mountain Pine scrub, dwarf shrub heath; calcicole, needing snow cover. 1,200–2,500m, sometimes descending as near Dobovec, Slovenia (250m).
DISTRIBUTION: Alpine.
NOTE: Where Alpenrose, (*R. ferrugineum*) and Hairy Alpenrose (*R. hirsutum*) occur together, they often form the hybrid *Rhododendron* x *intermedium*.

3 | Dwarf Alpenrose
Rhodothamnus chamaecistus – Ericaceaee

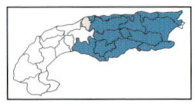

5–25cm tall dwarf shrub with prostrate to ascending shoots; leaves lanceolate to obovate, leathery, opposite; flowers 1–4, terminal, spreading, without corolla tube; flower stalk 10–15mm long, glandular; corolla bright pink. Flowers May to July.
SIMILAR SPECIES: Hairy Alpenrose, *R. hirsutum*, has an obvious corolla tube and alternate leaves.
HABITAT: Rock debris, stony sward, dwarf shrub heath and Dwarf Mountain Pine scrub; calcicole. 1,000–2,100m, sometimes higher, as at Nuvolau, Ampezzo, Italy (2,350m). Occasionally reaching lower levels in gorges.
DISTRIBUTION: Eastern alpine endemic.

4 | Wood Spurge
Euphorbia amygdaloides – Euphorbiaceae

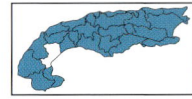

30–60cm tall, with many sterile shoots; leaves obovate-lanceolate, narrowing towards the short stalk; leaves at the middle of flowering stem in rosettes; terminal umbel-like inflorescence with 5–9 rays; bracts fused at base; nectar glands crescent-shaped, yellow or purple. Flowers April to June.
SIMILAR SPECIES: Sweet Spurge, *E. dulcis*, has unfused bracts, and terminal umbel-like inflorescence with 3–5 rays. Canut's Spurge, *E. hyberna* subsp. *canuti*, has no sterile shoots when flowering, and unstalked stem leaves.
HABITAT: Deciduous woods, calcicole. To 1,700m.
DISTRIBUTION: European–western Asiatic.
NOTE: Irish Spurge, *E. hyberna*, of western and southern Europe, is locally common in south-west Ireland, and very rare in south-west England.

5 | Variable Spurge
Euphorbia variabilis – Euphorbiaceae

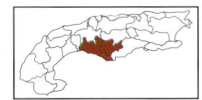

15–35cm tall, hairless; stems ascending to upright; leaves lanceolate, bluish-green, increasing in size up the stem; umbel terminal, usually with flowering secondary branches from leaf axils. Flowers April to July.
SIMILAR SPECIES: Vallino's Spurge, *E. valliniana*, is 6–15cm tall and has oval leaves.
HABITAT: Montane meadows, bushy slopes, woodland margins; calcicole. To 1,700m.
DISTRIBUTION: Southern alpine endemic.

Euphorbiaceae

1 | Austrian Spurge
Euphorbia austriaca – Euphorbiaceae

40–80cm tall; upper stem with scattered hairs; middle and upper stem leaves narrowly elliptical to obovate-lanceolate, 7–10cm long, 2–3.5cm broad, hairless above, softly hairy beneath; lateral flowering secondary branches not protruding beyond the main umbel; bracts of inflorescence rays oval, yellow-green. Flowers May to July.
SIMILAR SPECIES: Hairy Spurge, *E. villosa*, has hairless upper stem, and lateral flowering secondary branches clearly protruding beyond the main umbel, leaves 1–2cm broad.
HABITAT: Damp, calcareous, open woods, tall herb vegetation, rich pasture, streamsides and low woody scrub; calcicole. 800–2,100m, occasionally lower, as near Molln in the Sengsengebirge, Austria (490m).
DISTRIBUTION: North alpine endemic, west to Scharfberg, Austria.

2 | Carniolan Spurge
Euphorbia carniolica – Euphorbiaceae

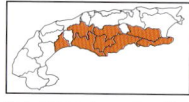

25–50cm tall; stem unbranched, arching upwards; leaves ovate-lanceolate 3–6cm long, 0.7–1.5cm broad, entire, ± hairy beneath, mostly hairless above; bracteoles elliptical to oval, almost entire; terminal inflorescence (cyathium) with 5–15mm long stalk. Flowers May to June.
SIMILAR SPECIES: Angular Spurge, *E. angularis*, has an angular stem and terminal inflorescence stalk 1–3mm long.
HABITAT: Open deciduous woods, damp edge habitats, pinewoods, montane meadows; calcifuge. To 1,900m.
DISTRIBUTION: Southern European montane, from the southern Alps to the eastern Carpathians.

3 | Cypress Spurge
Euphorbia cyparissias – Euphorbiaceae

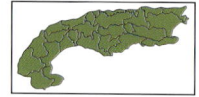

15–35cm tall, much-branched; non-flowering side branches beneath the inflorescence; leaves linear, 1.5–3cm long, 1–3mm broad, narrowing towards base; inflorescence with 10–20 rays; bracts greenish-yellow or red; fruit with hemispherical warts. Flowers April to June.
SIMILAR SPECIES: Siberian Spurge, *E. seguieriana*, has smooth fruits and leaves 3–7mm broad.
HABITAT: Poor grassland, pasture, rocky sward, open dry woods. To 2,700m.
DISTRIBUTION: European, east to Lake Baikal.
NOTE: Plants affected by pea rust fungus have orange pustules and look quite different.

4 | Rock Spurge
Euphorbia saxatilis – Euphorbiaceae

5–12cm tall; stem arching upwards from prostrate base; middle of flowering stems with dense almost rosette-like leaves; leaves bluish-green, lanceolate; umbels 3–5-rayed, terminal. Flowers May to June.
SIMILAR SPECIES: Kerner's Spurge, *E. triflora* subsp. *kerneri*.
HABITAT: Open Black Pine woods, stony poor grassland, dolomite rocks and stony sward. 360–1,100m.
DISTRIBUTION: Northern alpine endemic.

5 | Kerner's Spurge
Euphorbia triflora subsp. *kerneri* – Euphorbiaceae

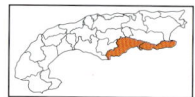

6–20cm tall; leaves of flowering stems 7–20mm long, 5–7mm broad; leaves of non-flowering stems 30–40mm long, 6–8mm broad; bracts roundish, bracteoles rhomboid, broader than long. Flowers April to June.
SIMILAR SPECIES: Rock Spurge, *E. saxatilis*, endemic to the north-eastern Alps, has middle of flowering stem densely leafy.
HABITAT: Calcareous rock debris, rocks, stony sward; calcicole. To 1,400m.
DISTRIBUTION: South-eastern alpine endemic.
NAME: The subspecies honours Austrian botanist Anton Joseph Kerner von Marilaun (1831–1898). Kerner established experimental gardens at different altitudes in the Tyrol to study the influence of climate on plants. These test sites were on the Nockspitze at 1,700m, on the Seegrubenspitze at around 2,000m and on the Patscherkofel at 2,300m.

Fabaceae

1 | Mountain Kidney Vetch
Anthyllis montana – Fabaceae

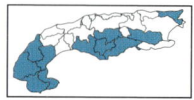

2–12cm tall; leaves pinnate, with 11–31 leaflets; leaflets lanceolate, terminal leaflet no larger than lateral leaflets. Corolla purplish-red (subsp. *montana*, **1A**) or pale pink with purple veins to almost white (subsp. *jacquinii*, **1B**). Flowers May to July.
SIMILAR SPECIES: Few.
HABITAT: Stony grassland, calcareous rocks, pinewoods, scree; calcicole. To about 2,300m.
DISTRIBUTION: Southern European montane.
NOTE: The nominate form subsp. *montana* is only in the western Alps; subsp. *jacquinii* only in the eastern Alps.

2 | Alpine Kidney Vetch
Anthyllis vulneraria subsp. *alpicola* – Fabaceae

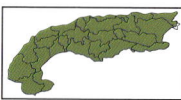

5–20cm tall; leaves pinnate, with larger terminal leaflet some 2x as long and 2–3x as broad as lateral leaflets; basal leaves of this subspecies sometimes with just the large terminal leaflet (**2B**); corolla golden yellow to pale yellow, in dense flower heads; calyx inflated, 13–15mm long, with white hairs. Flowers May to August.
SIMILAR SPECIES: The other subspecies have calyx only 8–13mm long and terminal leaflets the same size as or only slightly larger than lateral leaflets.
HABITAT: Rock debris, stony poor grassland; calcicole. 1,000–2,900m.
DISTRIBUTION: Southern European montane.
NOTE: One of Europe's most variable species. 8 subspecies in the Alps:
– subsp. *alpicola*: throughout the Alps.
– subsp. *carpatica*: scattered through the Alps, but absent from much of the south and south-western Alps.
– subsp. *forondae*: south-western Alps.
– subsp. *polyphylla*: scattered through the Alps, but absent from much of the northern Alps.
– subsp. *pseudovulneraria*: scattered throughout the Alps.
– subsp. *rubriflora*: south-western Alps and outer edges of the southern Alps.
– subsp. *valesiaca*: western alpine endemic.
– subsp. *vulnerarioides*: south-western Alps.

3 | Foxtail Milk-vetch
Astragalus alopecurus – Fabaceae
(Syn.: *Astragalus centralpinus*)

40–120cm tall with usually many branching, densely hairy stems to 1cm thick; leaves to 30cm long, usually with 41–53 leaflets; leaflets oval, hairless above, hairy beneath; inflorescence oval; corolla pale yellow; calyx with dense woolly hairs. Flowers June to August.
SIMILAR SPECIES: None.
HABITAT: Dry grassland, open montane woods. To about 1,900m.
DISTRIBUTION: European–western Asiatic.

4 | Alpine Milk-vetch
Astragalus alpinus – Fabaceae

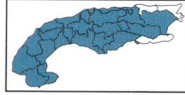

5–25cm tall; ascending; pinnate, with 15–25 leaflets; leaflets oval to broadly lanceolate, 5–20mm long; flowers 5–15 in a raceme; flower 10–12mm long; corolla white, standard and keel tipped violet. Flowers June to August.
SIMILAR SPECIES: Norwegian Milk-vetch, *A. norvegicus* (see p. 200), has uniformly violet-blue flowers and leaves with 13–15 leaflets. Southern Milk-vetch, *A. australis*, has whitish flowers with violet-tipped keel and leaves with 9–15 leaflets.
HABITAT: Poor meadows, pasture, open Larch woods; calcicole. 1,300–3,100m, sometimes lower, as on the Rhine near Rothenbrunnen, Switzerland (520m).
DISTRIBUTION: Arctic–alpine.

5 | Southern Milk-vetch
Astragalus australis – Fabaceae

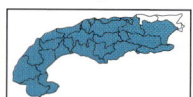

3–20cm tall, prostrate to ascending; leaves with 9–15 leaflets; leaflets lanceolate to elliptical, 6–16mm long, 2–5mm broad; inflorescence with 8–16 flowers; flowers yellowish-white to pinkish-white with violet-tipped keel. Flowers May to August.
SIMILAR SPECIES: Alpine Milk-vetch, *A. alpinus*.
HABITAT: Stony sward, coarse scree; calcicole. 1,600–3,100m, occasionally washed down lower, as on the river Kander near Thun, Switzerland (560m).
DISTRIBUTION: Eurosiberian, from the Pyrenees to the Altai.

Fabaceae

1 | Sprawling Milk-vetch
Astragalus depressus – Fabaceae

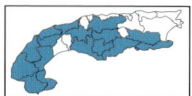

2–6cm tall, prostrate; leaves with appressed hairs on underside, hairless above, pinnate, with 17–25 leaflets, in rosette at stem base; leaflets broadly ovate, often shallowly notched, 5–12mm long; Inflorescence 6–14-flowered; corolla whitish to pale violet. Flowers May to July.
SIMILAR SPECIES: Alpine Milk-vetch, *A. alpinus* (see p. 196), has basal leaves not in rosette.
HABITAT: Rocky steppe, dry grassland; calcicole. To 2,700m.
DISTRIBUTION: Southern European–western Asiatic.

2 | Stemless Milk-vetch
Astragalus exscapus – Fabaceae

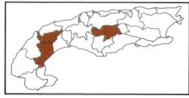

3–10cm tall, ± stemless, leaves and flowers basal; leaves pinnate with 25–39 leaflets; leaflets 10–20mm long, with upright hairs; inflorescence 3–9-flowered; corolla yellow. Flowers May to August.
SIMILAR SPECIES: None.
HABITAT: Dry grassland, pinewoods; calcicole. To 2,200m.
DISTRIBUTION: From the western Alps to Ukraine.

3 | Pallid Milk-vetch
Astragalus frigidus – Fabaceae

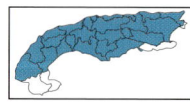

10–35cm tall; stem hairless; leaves pinnate with 7–17 leaflets; leaflets oval, 15–35mm long, 7–15mm broad, reticulate beneath; corolla 14–17mm long, yellowish-white. Flowers July to August.
SIMILAR SPECIES: Mountain Lentil, *A. penduliflorus* (see p. 200), has leaves with 15–31 leaflets, each 3–6mm broad.
HABITAT: Poor grassland, steep slopes and ridges; calcicole. 1,700–2,800m, sometimes lower, as swept downstream on the river Linth, Switzerland (780m).
DISTRIBUTION: Arctic–alpine.

4 | Purple Milk-vetch
Astragalus hypoglottis – Fabaceae

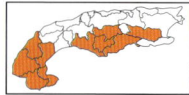

5–25cm tall; stem and leaves with dense white hairs; leaves with 15–25 leaflets; leaflets 8–20mm long and 3–5mm broad; stipules fused for about ⅓ of their length; flowers 1.2–1.4cm long, in clusters of 5–20; calyx with pale to blackish hairs; calyx teeth shorter than calyx tube; corolla purple; fruit 10–15mm long. Flowers May to July.
SIMILAR SPECIES: Danish Milk-vetch, *A. danicus*, has a 7–8mm long fruit and stipules fused to ½ their length.
HABITAT: Poor grassland, scree; calcicole. To about 1,900m.
DISTRIBUTION: Southern European montane.

5 | Tyrolean Milk-vetch
Astragalus leontinus – Fabaceae

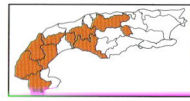

5–20cm tall; leaves with 13–21 leaflets; leaflets narrowly elliptical, 5–15mm long, 2–6mm broad; inflorescence dense, 10–20-flowered; corolla blue-violet to lilac, 12–15mm long; standard petal oval, projecting at most 3mm beyond wings. Flowers June to August.
SIMILAR SPECIES: Sainfoin Milk-vetch, *A. onobrychis* (see p. 200). Austrian Milk-vetch, *A. austriacus*, has 5–8mm long flowers and 1–2mm broad leaflets.
HABITAT: Dry grassland, scree, open pine and larch woods; calcicole. 1,000–2,600m.
DISTRIBUTION: Alpine–Illyrian.

6 | Montpellier Milk-vetch
Astragalus monspessulanus – Fabaceae

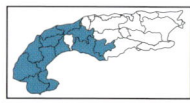

5–20cm tall, ± stemless, with leaves and flowering stalks therefore ± basal; leaves with 21–41 leaflets; leaflets oval to broadly lanceolate, 5–12mm long and 3–5mm broad; inflorescence 8–15-flowered; corolla purplish-red to pinkish-white, 2–3cm long; standard petal projecting beyond wings. Flowers April to July.
SIMILAR SPECIES: Sainfoin Milk-vetch, *A. onobrychis* (see p. 200).
HABITAT: Dry grassland, pinewoods, river debris; calcicole. To 2,600m.
DISTRIBUTION: Mediterranean.

Fabaceae

1 | Norwegian Milk-vetch
Astragalus norvegicus – Fabaceae

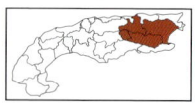

10–30cm tall; leaves pinnate, with 13–15 leaflets; leaflets oval-elliptical, 1–2.5cm long; flowers 10–12mm long, upright or nodding; corolla pale violet-blue. Flowers July to August.
SIMILAR SPECIES: Alpine Milk-vetch, *A. alpinus* (see p. 196).
HABITAT: Damp meadows and rocky sward. 1,700–2,500m.
DISTRIBUTION: Arctic–alpine, from the mountains of Scandinavia to southern Siberia, the Alps and central Carpathians.

2 | Sainfoin Milk-vetch
Astragalus onobrychis – Fabaceae

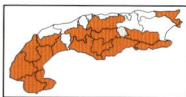

10–30cm tall, prostrate to ascending; leaves pinnate, with 17–27 appressed, hairy leaflets; leaflets lanceolate, 6–15mm long and 2–3mm broad; corolla bright purple to lilac-purple, 18–24mm long; standard petal almost linear, about 6–10mm longer than the wings. Flowers May to July.
SIMILAR SPECIES: Montpellier Milk-vetch, *A. monspessulanus* (see p. 198), has all leaves ± basal, and leaflets 3–5mm broad. Danish Milk-vetch, *A. danicus*, has lilac-violet flowers with yellowish base, and standard at most 1¼x as long as the wings. Tyrolean Milk-vetch, *A. leontinus* (see p. 198), has lilac corolla and an oval standard petal.
HABITAT: Dry grassland, pinewoods, calcareous rocky debris; calcicole. To 1,900m.
DISTRIBUTION: Eastern European–western Asiatic, from southern France to the Altai.

3 | Mountain Lentil
Astragalus penduliflorus – Fabaceae

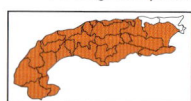

30–70cm tall, upright or ascending, branched, hairy; leaves pinnate with 15–31 leaflets; leaflets lanceolate, 3–6mm broad; corolla bright yellow, 9–13mm long; fruit very inflated. Flowers July to August.
SIMILAR SPECIES: Pallid Milk-vetch, *A. frigidus* (see p. 198).
HABITAT: Sunny, stony poor grassland, rocky debris. 1,300–2,850m, occasionally lower, as in the Traufbachtal Valley in the Allgäu near Spielmannsau, Germany (1,140m).
DISTRIBUTION: Southern European montane, from the Pyrenees to the Carpathians.

4 | Mountain Tragacanth
Astragalus sempervirens – Fabaceae

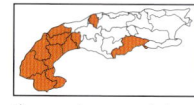

5–20cm tall, prostrate to ascending, woody, densely covered with the thorny midribs of the previous year's leaves; leaves with long hairs on both sides, pinnate, with 12–22 leaflets and a sharp thorn replacing the terminal leaflet; inflorescence 3–8-flowered; corolla white to pale pink. Flowers May to August.
SIMILAR SPECIES: The thorny leaves distinguish it from all the other *Astragalus* species.
HABITAT: Sony, south-facing slopes, calcareous rocks; calcicole. To 2,740m.
DISTRIBUTION: Western alpine, Pyrenees and Apennines.
NOTE: In the Alps there is the nominate form with upright hairs and larger flowers (15–118mm), and subsp. *alpinus* with more appressed hairs and smaller flowers (12–15mm).

5 | Inflated Milk-vetch
Astragalus vesicarius – Fabaceae

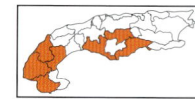

5–25cm tall; stem and leaves densely covered with silver-grey appressed hairs; leaves with 7–19 leaflets; leaflets ovate-lanceolate, 5–15mm long, 2–5mm broad; inflorescence 3–13-flowered; flowers 2–2.5cm long, corolla purple-violet or yellow; calyx with short black and long white hairs, inflated after flowering. Flowers May to July.
SIMILAR SPECIES: Distinguished from all the other alpine *Astragalus* species by the post-flowering inflated calyx.
HABITAT: Dry grassland, rocky sward, open pinewoods. To about 1,700m.
DISTRIBUTION: In the Alps there is the nominate form subsp. *vesicarius* with purple-violet flowers, and subsp. *pastellianus* with yellow flowers.

Fabaceae

1 | Hairy Broom
Chamaecytisus hirsutus – Fabaceae

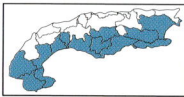

5–100cm tall shrub; new branches covered with shaggy hairs until 2nd year; leaves 3-partite, with 1–3cm long leaflets; flowers 1–4, on short lateral shoots, forming a raceme-like leafy inflorescence, without terminal flower heads. Flowers April to June.
SIMILAR SPECIES: Large-flowered Broom, *C. supinus*, has rather bare young branches, 1–3 flowers on the short lateral shoots, and 2–6 at the end of the long shoots.
HABITAT: Stony mat vegetation, oak-pine woods, rocky sward, poor meadows, rocks. To 2,200m.
DISTRIBUTION: Southern European–western Asiatic.
NOTE: 3 subspecies in the Alps:
– subsp. *hirsutus* (**1A**): to 100cm tall, calyx and fruit with long upright hairs; from the Maritime Alps to Burgenland.
– subsp. *ciliatus*: to 100cm tall, fruit hairless or ciliate; calcifuge; south-eastern Alps.
– subsp. *pumilus* (**1B**): to 25cm tall, calyx and fruit with long, upright hairs; calcicole; southwest alpine endemic.

2 | Purple Broom
Chamaecytisus purpureus – Fabaceae

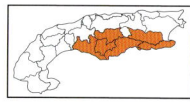

15–80cm tall shrub with prostrate to ascending branches; leaves 3-partite, leaflets obovate, with scattered hairs or hairless; flowers 1–3 on short shoots in the axils of the previous year's branches; corolla purple-pink. Flowers April to June.
SIMILAR SPECIES: None.
HABITAT: Pinewoods, rocky slopes, poor pasture; calcicole. To 1,500m.
DISTRIBUTION: Eastern alpine–Illyrian.

3 | Southern Broom
Cytisophyllum sessilifolium – Fabaceae (Syn.: *Cytisus sessilifolius*)

0.3–2m tall hairless shrub; leaves 3-partite, lower leaves short-stalked, upper leaves sessile; leaflets round to rhomboid, pointed, with bluish bloom; flowers 2–10, in terminal racemes. Flowers May to July.
SIMILAR SPECIES: Lugano Broom, *Cytisus emeriflorus*, has all leaves stalked, and 1–4 flowers in leaf ails. Black Broom, *Cytisus nigricans*, has a hairy calyx, stalked leaves and racemes with 20–80 flowers.
HABITAT: Rocky slopes, edges of scrub, open woods; calcicole. To 1,700m.
DISTRIBUTION: Mediterranean, from Spain to the South Tyrol.

4 | German Greenweed
Genista germanica – Fabaceae

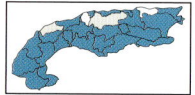

10–60cm tall hairy shrub; older branches thorny and leafless, younger growth leafy and thornless; leaves simple, entire, 1–1.5cm long; flowers 8–10mm long. Flowers May to June.
SIMILAR SPECIES: Dyer's Greenweed, *G. tinctoria*, is thornless and has 1.5–3.5cm long leaves.
HABITAT: Acid, dry woods, poor meadows, woodland margins; calcifuge, acid indicator. To 2,300m.
DISTRIBUTION: European, east to the Volga.

5 | Hairy Greenweed
Genista pilosa – Fabaceae

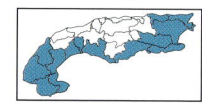

5–30cm tall thornless dwarf shrub; entire plant with appressed silky hairs; leaves 6–13mm long, narrowly elliptical to narrowly obovate, young leaves with silky hairs, mainly beneath; flowers 1–3, on short stalks 2–3mm long; flower wings arched upwards. Flowers April to June.
SIMILAR SPECIES: Silky Greenweed, *G. sericea* (see p. 204). Villars' Greenweed, *G. pulchella* subsp. *villarsiana*, restricted to the French Alps, has 2–9mm long leaves and solitary flowers.
HABITAT: Dry grassland, rocky steppe, woods, especially pinewoods, poor meadows. To about 1,800m.
DISTRIBUTION: European, from Portugal and the UK to Poland and the Balkan Peninsula.

Fabaceae

1 | Southern Greenweed
Genista radiata – Fabaceae

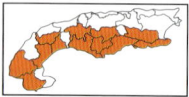

20–80cm tall, branched, sparsely spherical shrub with thornless stems and opposite to whorled green branches; leaves opposite, 3-lobed; leaflets linear, 1–2cm long and about 1mm broad; flowers in short racemes. Flowers May to July.
SIMILAR SPECIES: Differs from the other alpine *Genista* species in having linear leaflets.
HABITAT: Warm, dry rocky slopes, open woods of pine and Hop-hornbeam; calcicole. To 2,200m.
DISTRIBUTION: Southern European montane, from the western Alps to the Carpathians.
NOTE: The Broom Seed Beetle, *Bruchidius villosus*, is a specialist feeder on the seeds of greenweeds and relatives. Greenweed species are also important food plants for the larvae of the geometrid moths *Isturgia roraria*, and Broom-tip, *Chesias rufata*.

2 | Winged Greenweed
Genista sagittalis – Fabaceae

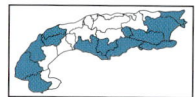

10–30cm tall sub-shrub with creeping, thornless stems and numerous upright, leafy branches; stems and branches with wide wings; leaves undivided, broadly lanceolate, 0.5–2cm long; flowers in short, dense, terminal racemes. Flowers May to July.
SIMILAR SPECIES: None: the wide-winged stem is distinctive.
HABITAT: Dry, acid, poor meadows, open pine and oak woods, woodland margins; calcifuge. To 1,960m.
DISTRIBUTION: Southern European, from Spain to Transylvania, Romania.
NOTE: The nominate form is widespread in the Alps; subsp. *delphinensis* is restricted to the Department of Drôme, France.

3 | Silky Greenweed
Genista sericea – Fabaceae

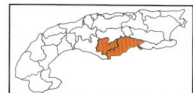

8–20cm tall dwarf shrub with thornless branches and short, silvery hairy twigs; leaves 10–25mm long and 2–4mm broad, hairless above, underside and margins with silky hairs; flowers 2–5, in compact terminal racemes. Flowers May to June.
SIMILAR SPECIES: Hairy Greenweed, *G. pilosa* (see p. 202), has 6–13mm long leaves.
HABITAT: Scrub, rocky sward, poor pasture; calcicole. To 1,100m.
DISTRIBUTION: Eastern alpine–Illyrian.

4 | Briançon Sainfoin
Hedysarum brigantiacum – Fabaceae

20–40cm tall, upright or ascending; leaves pinnate with 13–17 leaflets; leaflets elliptical to oval; stipules fused to about halfway; petals purple-red. Flowers June to August.
SIMILAR SPECIES: Alpine Sainfoin, *H. hedysaroides*. White Sainfoin, *H. boutignyanum*, a western alpine species, has white petals and glandular leaf stalks.
HABITAT: Stony meadows, rocky slopes. 1,600–2,800m.
DISTRIBUTION: Endemic to the Cottian Alps, France/Italy.

5 | Alpine Sainfoin
Hedysarum hedysaroides – Fabaceae

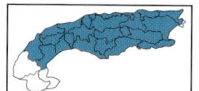

10–40cm tall, upright or ascending; leaves pinnate with 9–21 leaflets; leaflets elliptical to oval, unstalked; stipules fused for almost their entire length; petals purple; flowers 12–35, in ± one-sided racemes. Flowers June to August.
SIMILAR SPECIES: Briançon Sainfoin, *H. brigantiacum*, has stipules fused only to about halfway.
HABITAT: Poor grassland, meadows; calcicole. 1,400–2,900m, sometimes lower, as near Hätzingen in Glarus, Switzerland (600m).
DISTRIBUTION: Arctic–alpine: northern Eurasia and northern North America.
NOTE: 2 subspecies in the Alps:
- subsp. *hedysaroides* (**5A**): 5–20cm tall, 9–13 leaflets with tips up to 0.5mm long.
- subsp. *exaltatum* (**5B**): 30–40cm tall, 13–21 leaflets with tips 0.5–1mm long.

Fabaceae

1 | Horseshoe Vetch
Hippocrepis comosa – Fabaceae

2–5cm tall, prostrate, spreading; leaves pinnate, with 9–13 leaflets; leaflets 5–12mm long and 2–5mm broad, without cartilaginous margins; flowers 7–12mm long, fragrant, 5–12, in umbels; fruit pods pinched into horseshoe-shaped segments. Flowers May to June.
SIMILAR SPECIES: Small Scorpion-vetch, *Coronilla vaginalis*, has leaves with cartilaginous margins, and ± straight fruit pods.
HABITAT: Semi-arid grassland, poor meadows, rock debris, pinewoods; calcicole. To 2,800m.
DISTRIBUTION: European.
NOTE: Horseshoe Vetch is local in southern England, on unimproved calcareous grassland, north to north Yorkshire.

2 | Scorpion Senna
Hippocrepis emerus – Fabaceae

50–200cm tall shrub; leaves pinnate, with 5–9 leaflets; leaflets oval, 1–2cm long; flowers 1–3, 15–20mm long. Flowers April to June.
SIMILAR SPECIES: Lugano Broom, *Cytisus emeriflorus*, has 3-lobed leaves.
HABITAT: Warm, dry open deciduous woods, pinewoods; calcicole. To 1,800m.
DISTRIBUTION: Southern European–south-west Asiatic.

3 | Alpine Laburnum
Laburnum alpinum – Fabaceae

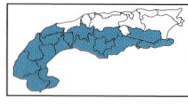

2–5cm tall shrub or small tree; 1st year branches and leaf stalks hairless; leaves 3-lobed, long-stalked; leaflets 8–13cm long, 3–6cm broad, hairy beneath when young, later becoming hairless; inflorescence a 20–40-flowered dense raceme, 15–30cm long; flowers 1.4–1.8cm long. Flowers May to July.
SIMILAR SPECIES: Laburnum, *L. anagyroides*, has 1st year branches, leaf stalks and leaf undersides with short, appressed grey hairs.
HABITAT: Rocky slopes in humid sites, pinewoods, beech woods on shallow soils. To 1,900m.
DISTRIBUTION: Southern European montane, from the southern Jura to the northern mountains of the Balkan Peninsula.

4 | Alpine Bird's-foot-trefoil
Lotus alpinus – Fabaceae

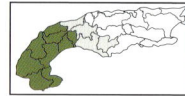

2–10cm cm tall, prostrate to ascending, mostly hairless; leaves 5-partite, the lowest 2 leaflets stipulate; leaflets 3–8mm long, 2–6mm broad; inflorescence 1–3-flowered; calyx lobes ± the same length as the calyx tube; petals yellow, often red in bud, and often orange after flowering; keel tip often purple. Flowers July to August.
SIMILAR SPECIES: East-alpine Bird's-foot-trefoil, *L. corniculatus* var. *alpicola*, has calyx lobes distinctly shorter than calyx tube, and is found in the eastern Alps. The exact borders of the ranges are unknown.
HABITAT: Pasture, grassland, alluvial soils. 1,900–3,300m.
DISTRIBUTION: Western alpine. It is not known how far east it extends in the Alps, because of confusion with East-alpine Bird's-foot-trefoil, *L. corniculatus* var. *alpicola*.
NOTE: The larvae of the Six-spot Burnet moth, *Zygaena filipendulae*, feed on Bird's-foot-trefoil, and are unharmed by the hydrogen cyanide that is released when the plant tissue is damaged. They store the harmful chemicals in their brightly-marked bodies as protection from predators.

5 | Large-leaved Lupin
Lupinus polyphyllus – Fabaceae

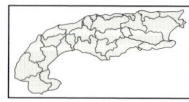

60–150cm tall; leaves palmate, with 9–17 leaflets; leaflets lanceolate, 4–15cm long, 1–3cm broad; inflorescence 50–80-flowered; corolla blue to purple, sometimes pink or white. Flowers June to September.
SIMILAR SPECIES: None.
HABITAT: Forest rides, clearings, embankments. To about 1,800m.
DISTRIBUTION: North American.
NOTE: Large-leaved Lupin is often used to stabilise embankments, as a food plant for game, as green manure, and as an ornamental garden plant, and is also widely naturalised.

Fabaceae

1 | Varied-leaved Everlasting-pea
Lathyrus heterophyllus – Fabaceae

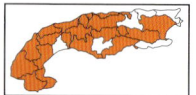

150–250cm long, prostrate or climbing; stem with 2–3.5mm broad wings; upper leaves with 4–6 leaflets, lower and middle leaves with 2 leaflets; leaf stalk wide-winged up to the first pair of leaflets; leaflets 5–10cm long, 1–3.5cm broad; inflorescence 3–12-flowered; flowers 1.5–2cm long; calyx teeth very unequal, the lower 2x as long as both upper teeth; corolla pale purple-pink. Flowers June to August.
SIMILAR SPECIES: Narrow-leaved Everlasting-pea, *L. sylvestris*, has upper leaves also with 2 leaflets. Broad-leaved Everlasting-pea, *L. latifolius*, has 2–3cm long, bright purple-pink corolla, and it too has all leaves with 2 leaflets. It is found in lower levels in the Alps, is often grown, and is occasionally naturalised.
HABITAT: Open scrub, rocky debris, rocks; calcicole. To 2,000m.
DISTRIBUTION: (Central-)European, centred on the Alps.
NOTE: Members of the genus *Vicia* and those of the genus *Lathyrus* are not always easy to distinguish. In *Vicia* species, the calyx tube is slanted at the front and the underside is longer. The leaflets usually have branching veins, the stamen tube ends obliquely at the front, the lower stamen filaments are fused to a greater length, and the style is hairy all round at the front or only on the underside.

2 | Yellow Pea
Lathyrus laevigatus – Fabaceae
(Syn.: *Lathyrus ochraceus*, *L. luteus*)

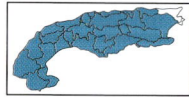

20–60cm tall; stem unwinged; leaves with 6–12 leaflets and awn-like tip without tendril; corolla pale yellow, fading to a pretty orange-brow; in 3–14-flowered raceme. Flowers June to July.
SIMILAR SPECIES: Pale Vetch, *Vicia oroboides* (see p. 220).
HABITAT: Tall herb vegetation, meadows, open woods; calcicole. To 2,000m.
DISTRIBUTION: European, from the Pyrenees to the Baltic.

NOTE: 2 subspecies in the Alps:
– subsp. *laevigatus*: leaves mostly completely hairless, lower calyx teeth less than half the length of calyx tube. South-eastern Alps, from the province of Brescia eastwards (**2A**).
– subsp. *occidentalis*: leaf underside and stalk hairy, lower calyx teeth half as long or as long as calyx tube. Most of the Alps (**2B**).

3 | Bitter Vetch
Lathyrus linifolius – Fabaceae

15–30cm tall; prostrate, ascending or upright; stem with 0.5–1.5mm broad wings; leaves pinnate with 4–8 leaflets and awn-like tip, without tendril; leaflets lanceolate to elliptical, 3–8mm broad, sharp-pointed; inflorescence 3–6-flowered; corolla pale purple, fading to blue-green. Flowers April to June.
SIMILAR SPECIES: Spring Pea, *L. vernus*. Slender Vetch, *L. filiformis*, has purple-violet corolla, and linear, 2–4mm broad leaves.
HABITAT: Poor, acidic grassland, open woods, woodland margins; calcifuge. To about 2,000m.
DISTRIBUTION: European, from Portugal and Norway to northern Russia.

4 | Spring Pea
Lathyrus vernus – Fabaceae

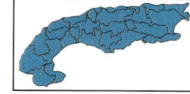

20–30cm tall; stem ridged, not winged; leaves pinnate with 4–8 leaflets; leaflets 4–14cm long, 2–30mm broad; inflorescence 3–8-flowered; corolla 15–20mm long, purple, fading to blue-violet to turquoise. Flowers April to June.
SIMILAR SPECIES: Venetian Vetchling (Venice Pea), *L. venetus*, has a 10–15mm long corolla and 8–20-flowered inflorescence. Bitter Vetch, *L. linifolius*, has winged stems.
HABITAT: Deciduous woods; calcicole. To 1,900m.
DISTRIBUTION: Eurosiberian, from Portugal and Norway to western Siberia.
NOTE: 2 subspecies in the Alps:
– subsp. *vernus*: leaflets oval, 20–30mm broad.
– subsp. *gracilis*: leaflets linear, 2–5mm broad.

Fabaceae

1 | Pirona's Medick
Medicago pironae – Fabaceae

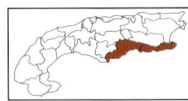

10–30cm tall, hairless; leaves trifoliate; leaflets obovate to rhomboid, 5–15mm long, 5–12mm broad, with finely toothed margins; inflorescence 2–8-flowered; corolla bright yellow, 5–7mm long; fruit almost spherical, spiralled into 3–4 turns, with glandular hairs and a single row of 1–2mm long spines. Flowers May to June.
SIMILAR SPECIES: Karst Medick, *M. carstiensis*, has hairless fruit spiralled into 5 turns.
HABITAT: Calcareous rocks, scree, roadside gravel; calcicole. To 1,800m.
DISTRIBUTION: South-east alpine endemic.
NAME: In honour of Italian botanist Giulio Andrea Pirona (1822–1895), who studied the flora of the Friuli region.

2 | Mountain Sainfoin
Onobrychis montana – Fabaceae

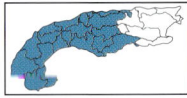

10–30cm tall, prostrate to ascending; leaves pinnate with 11–15 leaflets that are elongate-elliptical, 5–20mm long, and 3–6mm broad; inflorescence short and compact; petals bright purple; standard petal about 1–2mm shorter than keel. Flowers June to August.
SIMILAR SPECIES: Sainfoin, *O. viciifolia*, is 30–60cm tall and has standard petal roughly the same length as keel.
HABITAT: Sunny poor grassland, limestone slopes, rock debris; calcicole. To 2,700m.
DISTRIBUTION: Southern European montane.

3 | Mount Cenis Restharrow
Ononis cristata – Fabaceae

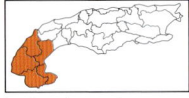

5–20cm tall, prostrate, thornless, slightly glandular-hairy, woody at base; leaves trifoliate, leaflets lanceolate to narrowly ovate, toothed at least at the top; flowers solitary, long-stalked, arising from the leaf axils; standard petal purple-pink, wings and keel whitish; calyx glandular and sticky. Flowers June to September.
SIMILAR SPECIES: None.
HABITAT: Rocky slopes, dry rock debris, open woods; calcicole. To 2,000m.
DISTRIBUTION: Southwest European montane.

4 | Shrubby Restharrow
Ononis fruticosa – Fabaceae

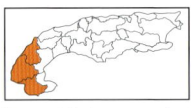

30–100cm tall, woody at base; stem glandular; leaves trifoliate; leaflets lanceolate to narrowly ovate, hairless, sessile, margins sharply toothed; flowers 2–4, in 5–20-flowered terminal inflorescence; standard and keel purple-pink, 1–2cm long, wings usually paler. Flowers June to September.
SIMILAR SPECIES: Round-leaved Restharrow, *O. rotundifolia*, has round or broadly ovate leaflets.
HABITAT: Scrub, stabilised calcareous rock debris, open oak and pine woods; calcicole. To about 1,600m.
DISTRIBUTION: West Mediterranean.

5 | Yellow Restharrow
Ononis natrix – Fabaceae

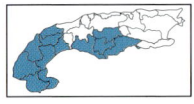

20–40cm tall, thornless, sticky, glandular, woody at base; leaves trifoliate; leaflets ovate to broadly lanceolate, 1–2cm long, toothed and stalked; Flowers long-stalked, in a raceme; calyx shorter than corolla; petals yellow, 1.5–2cm long, with purple veins. Flowers May to July.
SIMILAR SPECIES: Dwarf Restharrow, *O. pusilla*, has calyx as long or longer than corolla and almost unstalked flowers.
HABITAT: Dry poor meadows, stony slopes, pine and Downy Oak woods; calcicole. To 2,100m.
DISTRIBUTION: Mediterranean, east to Crimea.

6 | Round-leaved Restharrow
Ononis rotundifolia – Fabaceae

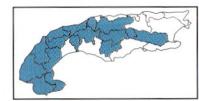

15–50cm tall, woody at base, thornless, densely glandular-hairy; leaves trifoliate; leaflets round to broadly ovate, 1–3cm long, toothed; flowers nodding, 1–3, long-stalked; standard and keel pink, wings usually paler. Flowers May to September.
SIMILAR SPECIES: Common Restharrow, *O. repens*, has unstalked, almost sessile flowers.
HABITAT: Pinewoods, scree, river gravel; calcicole. To 1,970m.
DISTRIBUTION: Southern European montane, from the Pyrenees to the Abruzzi and eastern Alps.

Fabaceae

1 | Meadow Milk-vetch
Oxytropis campestris – Fabaceae

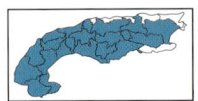

3–15cm tall, sparsely hairy to almost hairless; leaves in ± basal rosette, pinnate, with 21–31 leaflets; leaflets 5–15mm long and 2–4mm broad; inflorescence 8–18-flowered; calyx teeth only about ¼ as long as calyx tube; corolla yellowish-white (var. *campestris*, **1A**) or lilac (var. *tiroliensis*, **1B**). Flowers June to August.
SIMILAR SPECIES: The lilac-flowered var. *tiroliensis*. Swiss Milk-vetch, *O. helvetica*, has 3–7mm long leaflets, and calyx teeth at least half as long as calyx tube.
HABITAT: Poor grassland, rock debris, ridges; calcicole. 1,700–3,000m, sometimes lower, as by the Linth Canal near Weesen, Switzerland (430m).
DISTRIBUTION: Arctic–alpine.

2 | Stinking Milk-vetch
Oxytropis fetida – Fabaceae

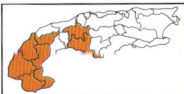

5–15cm tall, ± stemless, sticky, with tiny glands, unpleasant smelling; leaves pinnate, with 29–51 leaflets; leaflets somewhat fleshy, 3–8mm long, margins mostly rolled upwards; inflorescence 3–7-flowered; corolla white to dingy white, sometimes suffused violet, about 2cm long. Flowers July to August.
SIMILAR SPECIES: Meadow Milk-vetch, *O. campestris*, is not glandular and the inflorescence has 8–18 flowers.
HABITAT: Calcareous scree, stony slopes; calcicole. 1,800–3,000m.
DISTRIBUTION: Alpine endemic.

3 | Silky Milk-vetch
Oxytropis halleri – Fabaceae

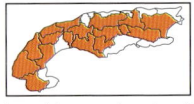

5–20cm tall; stem, leaves and calyx with dense silky hairs; leaves and flowering stalks ± basal; leaves pinnate, with 15–27 leaflets; inflorescence stalk 1–1.7mm in diameter, inflorescence 6–16-flowered; corolla intense purple, 1.5–2cm long. Flowers June to August.
SIMILAR SPECIES: Tyrolean (Vinschgau) Milk-vetch, *O. xerophylla* (Syn.: *O. halleri* subsp. *velutina*), has pale lilac flowers, inflorescence stalk 2–3mm in diameter, and leaves with 25–37 leaflets.

HABITAT: Dry poor grassland, rock debris. Mainly from 1,500–2,800m.
DISTRIBUTION: Southern European montane; Pyrenees, Alps and Carpathians.
NAME: In honour of Swiss polymath Albrecht von Haller (1708–1777). Haller was a physician, botanist, and poet. He published about 50,000 pages of high-quality scientific texts.

4 | Swiss Milk-vetch
Oxytropis helvetica – Fabaceae

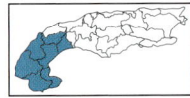

3–10cm tall, flat and spreading; leaves pinnate, with 15–29 leaflets; leaflets 3–7mm long, with dense grey silky hairs on both sides; inflorescence stalk thin, 0.5–0.7mm in diameter, with appressed hairs; calyx teeth at least half as long as calyx tube; corolla pale violet. Flowers July to August.
SIMILAR SPECIES: Amethyst Milk-vetch, *O. amethystea*, has leaves with 27–41 leaflets, and inflorescence stalk about 1mm in diameter. Mountain Milk-vetch, *O. montana* (see p. 214), has bright violet to purple flowers and 5–14mm long leaflets.
HABITAT: Calcareous sward, rock debris, calcicole. 1,400–3,100m.
DISTRIBUTION: Western alpine endemic.

5 | Northern Milk-vetch
Oxytropis lapponica – Fabaceae

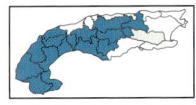

5–25cm tall, ascending; leaves pinnate, with 17–25 leaflets, with silky hairs on both sides; leaf stalk green; leaflets 5–11mm long, 1.5–3mm broad; inflorescence 6–12-flowered; corolla purple-violet; bracts extending over the middle of calyx tube; fruit pendent. Flowers June to July.
SIMILAR SPECIES: Mountain Milk-vetch, *O. montana* (see p. 214), usually has red leaf stalks, and bracts scarcely reaching to the middle of calyx tube.
HABITAT: Scree, poor grassland, alluvial substrates; calcicole. 1,500–2,700m, occasionally lower, as in Switzerland in Misox (1,200m), or higher, as on Piz Tasna in Graubünden (2,990m).
DISTRIBUTION: European-Asiatic.

Fabaceae

1 | Mountain Milk-vetch
Oxytropis montana – Fabaceae (Syn.: *Oxytropis jacquinii*)

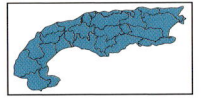

5–20cm tall; leaves pinnate, with 17–35 leaflets, mostly with reddish stalks; leaflets 5–14mm long; inflorescence 5–20-flowered, stalk with dark, appressed hairs; calyx teeth at most ⅓ as long as calyx tube; bracts reaching barely to the middle of calyx tube; corolla bright violet to purple; fruit upright or protruding. Flowers June to August.
SIMILAR SPECIES: Pyrenean Milk-vetch, *O. neglecta*, usually has green leaf stalks, and calyx teeth about half the length of calyx tube. Carinthian Milk-vetch, *O. x carinthiaca* (**1B**), is a hybrid between *O. montana* and *O. neglecta*, sometimes found without either parent, and has intermediate appearance.
HABITAT: Rock debris, dry, stony sward, rocks; limestone and dolomite. 1,700–2,900m, sometimes carried down on streams to lower levels, as at Frastanzer Au, Vorarlberg, Austria (470m).
DISTRIBUTION: Alpine. Alps and Jura.
NOTE: Milk-vetches (*Oxytropis*) differ from the similar members of the genus *Astragalus* in having flower keel with an obvious point just under the tip, a feature lacking in *Astragalus*.

2 | Pyrenean Milk-vetch
Oxytropis neglecta – Fabaceae (Syn.: *O. pyrenaica*)

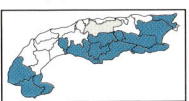

5–20cm tall, almost or completely stemless; leaves pinnate, with 15–41 leaflets and usually a green stem; inflorescence stalk with pale and dark appressed hairs; inflorescence 7–12-flowered; calyx teeth about half as long as calyx tube. Flowers June to August.
SIMILAR SPECIES: Mountain Milk-vetch, *O. montana*. Carinthian Milk-vetch, *O. x carinthiaca*, the hybrid between *O. montana* and *O. neglecta*, has intermediate appearance.
HABITAT: Poor grassland, rock debris; calcicole. 1,600–2,800m.
DISTRIBUTION: Southern European montane.

3 | Woolly Milk-vetch
Oxytropis pilosa – Fabaceae

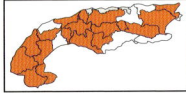

10–40cm tall, stem leafy, with shaggy hairs; leaves pinnate, with 19–27 leaflets, lanceolate, 1–2cm long; inflorescence 5–25-flowered; corolla pale yellow. Flowers May to August.
SIMILAR SPECIES: Meadow Milk-vetch, *O. campestris* (see p. 212), is loosely hairy to almost hairless, and stemless.
HABITAT: Dry grassland, rocky sward, sloping steppe; calcicole. To about 1,900m.
DISTRIBUTION: Eastern European–western Asiatic.

4 | Three-flowered Milk-vetch
Oxytropis triflora – Fabaceae

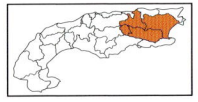

3–7cm tall; leaves pinnate, with 19–31 leaflets, 3–7mm long; inflorescence 3–5-flowered, stalk with appressed hairs; calyx teeth half as long to almost as long as calyx tube; corolla bright violet to purple. Flowers June to August.
SIMILAR SPECIES: Mountain Milk-vetch, *O. montana*, has 5–20-flowered inflorescence.
HABITAT: Poor grassland, cushion vegetation, rocky sites, especially over limestone slate. 2,000–2,700m, sometime lower, as at Nassfeld, near Böckstein, Austria (1,600m).
DISTRIBUTION: Eastern alpine endemic.

5 | Crown Vetch
Securigera varia – Fabaceae (Syn.: *Coronilla varia*)

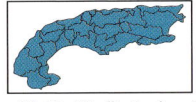

30–120cm long, prostrate or ascending; stem hairless or weakly hairy; leave spinate, with 11–25 elliptical, pointed leaflets; umbel with 10–15 fragrant flowers; corolla 2-coloured, standard pink, wings white and keel white with dark purple tip. Flowers May to September.
SIMILAR SPECIES: Few.
HABITAT: Alongside paths, poor grassland, gravelly sites; calcicole. To about 1,800m.
DISTRIBUTION: European–western Asiatic.

Fabaceae

1 | Alpine Zigzag Clover
Trifolium alpestre – Fabaceae

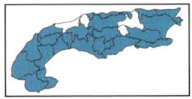

15–40cm tall; stem with dense, appressed hairs; leaflets elongate-oval, 2.5–8x as long as broad, appressed hairy beneath; flower heads paired at end of stalk, surrounded by the upper leaves; calyx tube hairy on outside, 20-veined; petals dark purple. Flowers May to July.
SIMILAR SPECIES: Zigzag Clover, *T. medium*, has a 10-veined calyx tube, hairless on the outside.
HABITAT: Open woods, edges of scrub, dry meadows. To 2,300m.
DISTRIBUTION: European, from Spain to the Urals.
NOTE: The genus *Trifolium* contains some 240 species, about 100 of which occur in Europe, with 36 in the alpine region. Only one species, namely Rock Clover, *T. saxatile*, is restricted to the Alps, and is thus an alpine endemic. Although many species show similarities, hybrids in the alpine region are not so far known.

2 | Alpine Clover
Trifolium alpinum – Fabaceae

5–20cm tall; all leaves basal; leaflets linear-lanceolate, 10–50mm long, 3–6mm broad, hairless almost entire; inflorescence 3–12-flowered; corolla purple, more rarely yellowish-white, 18–21mm long, with rather sickly-sweet scent. Flowers May to August.
SIMILAR SPECIES: Few.
HABITAT: Calcium-poor, acid sward; calcifuge. Commonest from 1,700–2,500m, but also lower, as in the Maiental, Canton Uri, Switzerland (980m), or higher, as at the Col du Géant in the Mont Blanc Massif (3,100m).
DISTRIBUTION: Southern European montane, from the mountains of Spain to the Apennines.

3 | Brown Clover
Trifolium badium – Fabaceae

8–25cm tall, upright or ascending; leaflets oval, finely toothed, all evenly short-stalked; inflorescence spherical to oval, 1–1.5x as long as broad; calyx teeth hairless to weakly ciliate; corolla golden yellow, fading to dark brown, 6–9mm long. Flowers June to August.
SIMILAR SPECIES: Large Brown Clover, *T. spadiceum*, has inflorescence about 2x as long as broad, and calyx teeth with cilia about 1mm long. Golden Clover, *T. aureum*, has flowers that fade to pale brown.
HABITAT: Rich and damp meadows, moraines, stream sides, pasture, wet flushes. 1,200–3,100m, occasionally lower, as near Bolzano, Italy (300m).
DISTRIBUTION: Southern European montane, from northern Spain to the mountains of the Balkan Peninsula.

4 | Rock Mountain Clover
Trifolium montanum subsp. *rupestre* – Fabaceae

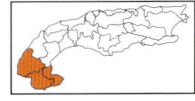

5–15cm tall, upright, hairy; leaflets oval to lanceolate, with finely sharp-toothed margins; inflorescence long-stalked in the axils of the upper leaves, usually broader than tall; corolla pink, 10–12mm long. Flowers May to July.
SIMILAR SPECIES: The nominate form, Mountain Clover, *T. montanum* subsp. *montanum*, has white corolla, and grows to 15–50cm tall (**4B**).
HABITAT: Poor grassland, rocky sward; calcifuge. About 1,200–1,900m.
DISTRIBUTION: Mediterranean-montane. South-western Alps and Apennines.

5 | Cream Clover
Trifolium noricum – Fabaceae

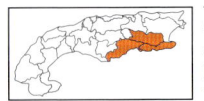

5–15cm tall; stem densely hairy; leaflets broadly lanceolate, 1–1.5cm long, 6–8mm broad, with shaggy hairs beneath; flower heads 2.5–4cm broad, solitary, nodding at first, projecting well above the upper leaves; corolla creamy-white. Flowers July to August.
SIMILAR SPECIES: The white-flowering subspecies (variety?) of Red Clover, *T. pratense* subsp. *nivale*, has flower heads mostly paired, and upright from the start.
HABITAT: Pasture, scree; calcicole. 1,900–2,600m.
DISTRIBUTION: Southern European montane, from the Apennines and south-eastern Alps to the Illyrian Mountains.

Fabaceae

1 | Ruddy Clover
Trifolium rubens – Fabaceae

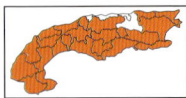

25–60cm tall; leaflets narrowly ovate, 4–7cm long, 0.8cm broad, 4–7x as long as broad; flower head 3–7cm long, 1–3cm broad; petals purplish-red. Flowers June to July.
SIMILAR SPECIES: Narrow-leaved Clover, *T. angustifolium*, has whitish-pink petals and leaflets 8–15x as long as broad.
HABITAT: Dry open deciduous and pine woods, transitional habitats (ecotones), warm slopes. To 2,050m.
DISTRIBUTION: European, from Spain to Ukraine.

2 | Rock Clover
Trifolium saxatile – Fabaceae

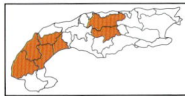

3–15cm long, prostrate to ascending; leaflets 4–6mm long, 2–3x as long as broad, hairy on both sides; flower head ± spherical, unstalked, surrounded by enlarged stipules; calyx teeth densely hairy; corolla white to pale pink, inconspicuous, shorter than calyx. Flowers July to August.
SIMILAR SPECIES: Hare's-foot Clover, *T. arvense*, has obviously stalked flower heads, not surrounded by stipules.
HABITAT: Dry scree, moraine debris, sandy alluvium, siliceous grit. 900–3,100m.
DISTRIBUTION: Alpine endemic.

3 | Thal's Clover
Trifolium thalii – Fabaceae

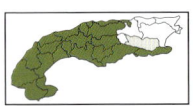

4–8cm tall, forming dense patches; stem almost absent, 0–3cm long, not rooting; leaflets obovate to elliptical; flowering stem 1–1.6mm long, shorter than calyx tube; corolla at first white, then bright pink, fading to pale brown; calyx 10-veined, the smaller calyx teeth shorter than calyx tube. Flowers July to August.
SIMILAR SPECIES: Pale Clover, *T. pallescens* (**3B**), is loose-growing, with creeping and ascending stems 5–15cm long. White Clover, *T. repens*, is creeping and rooted at the nodes.
HABITAT: Rich pasture, manured sites, snow-melt soils; calcicole. 1,400–3,000m.
DISTRIBUTION: Southern European montane.
NAME: In honour of German botanist and doctor Johannes Thal (1542–1583), known as the 'Father of Floristics'.

4 | Monte Cusna Vetch
Vicia cusnae – Fabaceae

20–50cm tall; leaves pinnate with 14–42 leaflets and terminal tendrils; leaflets linear, 10–35mm long; calyx, fruit and flowering stalks hairy; flower head 5–15-flowered; calyx teeth as long as or shorter than calyx tube; corolla lilac to pinkish-lilac. Flowers June to July.
SIMILAR SPECIES: Mountain Tufted Vetch, *V. oreophila* (Syn.: *V. cracca* susbsp. *oreophila*), has heads with 10–35 flowers.
HABITAT: Rock debris, rock crevices, stony sward; calcicole. About 1,400–2,000m.
DISTRIBUTION: Western alpine–Apennine.
NOTE: The vetch genus (*Vicia*) contains around 140 species, of which 54 are European, 27 in the alpine region. The Tufted Vetch group, *Vicia cracca*, is particularly variable, with 4 subspecies in the Alps (subsp. *cracca*, subsp. *incana*, subsp. *oreophila*, subsp. *tenuifolia*), considered by some to deserve species status.

5 | Sainfoin Vetch
Vicia onobrychioides – Fabaceae

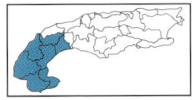

30–100cm long, ascending or weakly climbing; leaves pinnate with 10–18 leaflets and mostly with branched terminal tendril; leaflets lanceolate, 1–4mm broad, spiky; inflorescence 6–12-flowered, in one-sided racemes; corolla 18–25mm long; standard petal violet-blue, keel and wings usually paler. Flowers May to July.
SIMILAR SPECIES: Wood Vetch, *V. sylvatica* (see p. 220).
HABITAT: Dry meadows, open woods. To 1,700m.
DISTRIBUTION: Mediterranean, from Morocco and Portugal to Greece.

Fabaceae, Fumariaceae

1 | Pale Vetch
Vicia oroboides – Fabaceae

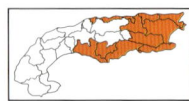

20–40cm tall; leaves pinnate, 2–6-lobed, without terminal tendril; leaflets pale green, oval, pointed, 4–8cm long, 3–4.5cm broad; flowers 2–8, in terminal raceme; corolla pale yellow, fading to orange-brown; calyx pale green, often with red markings. Flowers May to June.
SIMILAR SPECIES: Yellow Pea, *Lathyrus laevigatus* (see p. 208), has leaves with 6–12 leaflets, and a long-stalked inflorescence.
HABITAT: Deciduous woods, tall herb vegetation; calcicole. To 1,700m.
DISTRIBUTION: Eastern alpine–Illyrian.

2 | Pyrenean Vetch
Vicia pyrenaica – Fabaceae

5–20cm tall, prostrate to ascending, hairless or with short hairs; leaves pinnate, with 4–14 leaflets and terminal tendril; leaflets oval, pointed, 4–16mm long, 2–8mm broad; inflorescence 1–3-flowered; corolla purple-pink, 15–25mm long. Flowers June to August.
SIMILAR SPECIES: The purple subspecies of Pannonian Vetch, *V. pannonica* subsp. *striata*, has leaves with 14–18 leaflets.
HABITAT: Calcareous debris, open woods, poor grassland; calcicole. 900–2,400m.
DISTRIBUTION: Southwest European montane. Art.

3 | Wood Vetch
Vicia sylvatica – Fabaceae

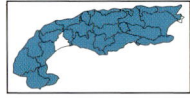

50–200cm long, prostrate or climbing; stem limp, square; leaves pinnate, with 12–18 leaflets and terminal tendril; leaflets oval to elliptical, 3–10mm broad; inflorescence 10–20-flowered, one-sided; corolla white, with violet veins and often violet tip to keel. Flowers June to August.
SIMILAR SPECIES: Alpine Milk-vetch, *Astragalus alpinus* (see p. 196) has unpaired pinnate leaves, and corolla lacking pronounced purple veins. Sainfoin Vetch, *V. onobrychioides* (see p. 218), has blue-violet corolla and lanceolate 1–4mm broad leaflets.
HABITAT: Damp woods, woodland margins, clearings, and tall herb vegetation. To 2,000m, sometimes higher, as on Falknis, Graubünden, Switzerland (2,150m).
DISTRIBUTION: Eurosiberian, from Provence and Norway to Siberia.

4 | Bulbous Corydalis (Hollowroot)
Corydalis cava – Fumariaceae

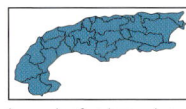

10–25cm tall; underground tuber hollow; stem unbranched, without lower leaf at base; leaves twice 3-pinnate, with incised segments; raceme 6–20-flowered; corolla purple or white; bracts entire. Flowers March to May.
SIMILAR SPECIES: Intermediate Corydalis, *C. intermedia*, has a scale-like bract at the leaf base, and a 1–6-flowered inflorescence. Solid-root Corydalis, *C. solida*, has palmately-split bracts.
HABITAT: Deciduous woods, riverine woods, alpine pasture. To about 1,700m.
DISTRIBUTION: European.

5 | Yellow Corydalis
Pseudofumaria lutea – Fumariaceae

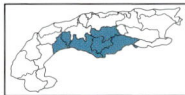

10–30cm tall, with many leafy stems; leaves 2–3-pinnate, bluish-green; flowers in terminal, 5–15-flowered raceme; corolla bright yellow. Flowers May to September.
SIMILAR SPECIES: White Corydalis, *P. alba*, has a whitish corolla with yellow tip.
HABITAT: Shady limestone and dolomite scree, humid walls; calcicole, but also on primary rock. To 1,700m.
DISTRIBUTION: Southern alpine, from the province of Novara to Belluno. Otherwise naturalised in large parts of central and western Europe.
NOTE: The genus *Pseudofumaria* contains only 2 species (*P. lutea* and *P. alba*), both formerly assigned to the genus *Corydalis*.

Gentianaceae

1 | Dwarf Gentian
Comastoma nanum – Gentianaceae
(Syn.: *Gentianella nana*)

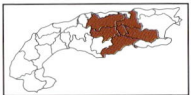

2–5cm tall, often branching at base; leaves obovate, 1.5–3x as long as broad; perianth usually 5-lobed; corolla violet-blue; corolla tube 3–7mm long, 1–2x as long as broad. Flowers July to September.
SIMILAR SPECIES: Slender Gentian, *C. tenellum*.
HABITAT: Damp, fine, usually non-calcareous soils, moraines, moss cushions. 2,200–2,900m.
DISTRIBUTION: Eastern alpine–central Asiatic.

2 | Slender Gentian
Comastoma tenellum – Gentianaceae
(Syn.: *Gentianella tenella*)

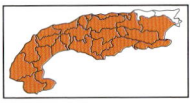

2–12cm tall, often branching at base; leaves lanceolate to spoon-shaped, 2–6x as long as broad; perianth usually 4-lobed; corolla pale lilac to sky blue; corolla tube 3–10mm long, 2–4x as long as broad. Flowers July to August.
SIMILAR SPECIES: Dwarf Gentian, *C. nanum*, has perianth usually 5-lobed, corolla tube 1–2x as long as broad, and leaves 1.5–3x as long as broad.
HABITAT: Patchy grassland, ridges, rock debris. 1,700–3,200m.
DISTRIBUTION: Arctic–alpine.
NOTE: Species of *Comastoma* differ from those of the closely-related genus *Gentianella* in having the calyx fused only at the base, and so lacking an obvious calyx tube. In *Gentianella*, the calyx is fused to at least ¼ of its length.

3 | Stemless Gentian (Trumpet Gentian)
Gentiana acaulis – Gentianaceae

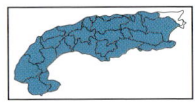

5–15cm tall; basal leaves 2–10cm long, in rosette; corolla 4–6cm long, trumpet-like, with olive green spots inside; calyx lobes slightly constricted at the base, and less than half the length of calyx tube. Flowers June to August.
SIMILAR SPECIES: Clusius's Gentian, *G. clusii* (see p. 224). Southern Gentian, *G. alpina*, has rosette leaves only 1–2cm long, and corolla 2–3.5cm long.
HABITAT: Meadows and pasture on acidic soil. 1,100–3,000m, sometimes lower in the valleys, as near Feldkirch, Austria (550m).
DISTRIBUTION: Southern European montane, from the mountains of northern Spain to the Carpathians.

4 | Narrow-leaved Gentian
Gentiana angustifolia – Gentianaceae

7–15cm tall; basal leaves lanceolate, 2–10cm long, 3–6x as long as broad, broadest above the centre; calyx teeth shorter than half of calyx tube, constricted at base and protruding from corolla; corolla 4–6cm long, with olive green spots on the inside. Flowers May to July.
SIMILAR SPECIES: Ligurian Gentian, *G. ligustica* (see p. 226). Clusius's Gentian, *G. clusii* (see p. 224) has calyx teeth at least half as long as calyx tube, and not constricted at base.
HABITAT: Poor meadows, stony sward; calcicole. To 2,900m.
DISTRIBUTION: Western alpine–Pyrenean.

5 | Willow Gentian
Gentiana asclepiadea – Gentianaceae

20–80cm tall; stem upright to arching, many-flowered; leaves opposite, ovate-lanceolate, pointed, 1–3cm broad; flowers 1–3 in upper leaf axils; corolla bright deep blue, 3.5–5cm long. Flowers August to October.
SIMILAR SPECIES: Few. Marsh Gentian, *G. pneumonanthe*, has narrowly-lanceolate leaves at most 1cm broad, and grows in wet and fen meadows.
HABITAT: Woods, clearings, pasture, tall herb vegetation. To 2,200m.
DISTRIBUTION: European montane, from France to north-west Ukraine.

Gentianaceae

1 | Bavarian Gentian
Gentiana bavarica – Gentianaceae

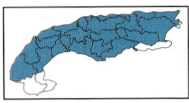

3–15cm tall, with sterile shoots; leaves obovate, broadest in upper third, most rounded, 5–13mm long, overlapping, also as rosettes in var. *subaulis* (**1B**); leaves in 2–4 pairs on flowering stalk, upper leaves as long as or shorter than the lower leaves; corolla tube 15–22mm long. Flowers July to September.
SIMILAR SPECIES: Rostan's Gentian, *G. rostanii* (see p. 230), restricted to the south-western Alps, has linear leaves, and upper stem leaves shorter than the lower leaves.
HABITAT: Wet meadows and pasture, rock debris, cushion vegetation. 1,800–3,600m, occasionally lower, as near Wildhaus, Switzerland (1,350m).
DISTRIBUTION: Alpine endemic.

2 | Short-leaved Gentian
Gentiana brachyphylla – Gentianaceae

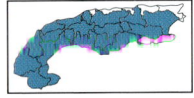

3–6cm tall; basal leaves 4–10mm long, ovate-lanceolate to rhomboid, in a rosette; corolla lobes greenish beneath; corolla tube very narrow, ± 3mm diameter; calyx with 0–0.3mm broad wings. Flowers June to August.
SIMILAR SPECIES: Spring Gentian, *G. verna* (see p. 232). Round-leaved Gentian. *G. orbicularis* (see p. 228), has calyx wings 0.5–1mm broad, and corolla lobes are not greenish beneath.
HABITAT: Poor grassland, rock debris, snow-melt hollows; calcifuge. 1,800–3,100m, sometimes higher, as on the Matterhorn (4,200m).
DISTRIBUTION: Alpine–Pyrenean.

3 | Clusius's Gentian
Gentiana clusii – Gentianaceae

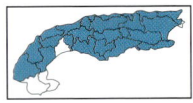

4–10cm tall; basal leaves broadly lanceolate, pointed, 2–5cm long, 2–5x as long as broad, in a rosette; stem leaves smaller, 0–3 pairs; flowers solitary on short stalks; corolla 4–6cm long, without olive green spots inside; calyx teeth at least half as long as calyx tube, not constricted at base, and lacking whitish connecting tissue. Flowers May to July.
SIMILAR SPECIES: All other species from the *Gentiana acaulis* group (*G. acaulis, G. alpina, G. angustifolia, G. ligustica*) have calyx teeth constricted at base, with whitish connecting tissue, and inside of corolla with olive green spots.
HABITAT: Poor, calcareous grassland, Blue Moor-grass (*Sesleria caerulea*) - Evergreen Sedge (*Carex sempervirens*) sward, rocky debris, scree, fens, open pinewoods; calcicole. 500–2,500m, sometimes lower, as in the southern Tessin, Switzerland (220m), or higher, as on Serles near Innsbruck, Austria (2,630m).
DISTRIBUTION: Southern European montane, from the Pyrenees to the eastern Carpathians.
NAME: In honour of Carolus Clusius (1526–1609), who studied the flora of the north-eastern Alps during his 14-year stay in Vienna. Clusius was one of the greatest botanists of the 16th century. His insight into recognising and distinguishing between related plant species was ground-breaking. With his 2 books, one on the plants of Spain and the other on the flora of eastern Austria, he laid the foundations for the creation of the first flora in the modern sense.

4 | Cross Gentian
Gentiana cruciata – Gentianaceae

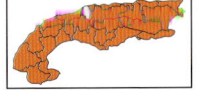

10–40cm tall, with densely leafy stem; leaves leathery and fleshy, crossed opposite; corolla 4-lobed, blue, 20–25mm long. Flowers July to September.
SIMILAR SPECIES: None.
HABITAT: Dry meadows and pasture, transitional habitats (ecotones); calcicole. To 2,200m.
DISTRIBUTION: European–western Asiatic.

5 | Tauern Gentian (Styrian Gentian)
Gentiana frigida – Gentianaceae

5–10cm tall; leaves lanceolate, with single vein; corolla bell-shaped, 20–35mm long, pale yellow to creamy-white, with greenish-violet longitudinal stripes, spots and dashes, rarely opening fully. Flowers July to August.
SIMILAR SPECIES: None.
HABITAT: Stony sward, rock debris. 1,900–2,500m.
DISTRIBUTION: Southern European montane, from the Lower Tauern and High Tatra to south-western Bulgaria.
NOTE: In the Alps, only in the Styrian Lower Tauern, Austria: Wölzer Tauern, Schladminger Tauern, and Seckauer Tauern.

Gentianaceae

1 | Karawanken Gentian
Gentiana froelichii – Gentianaceae

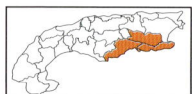

5–10cm tall; leaves lanceolate, often upwardly rolled at margin; corolla bright sky blue, 30–40mm long; stigma lobes unfringed. Flowers July to September.
SIMILAR SPECIES: Members of the stemless gentian group, *G. acaulis* agg., which flower in early summer, with the typical gentian blue flower, and which have fringed stigma lobes.
HABITAT: Rocks and rock debris, stony grassland; calcicole. 1,600–2,400m.
DISTRIBUTION: South-eastern alpine endemic.
NOTE: 2 subspecies:
– subsp. *froelichii* (**1A**): sepals straight or curved.
– subsp. *zenariae* (**1B**): sepals sickle-shaped.
NAME: In honour of German medic, botanist, naturalist and Court Doctor Josef Alois Frölich (1766–1841). In 1796 he completed his medical doctoral thesis on the gentian genus, an unusual topic for this faculty.

2 | Ligurian Gentian
Gentiana ligustica – Gentianaceae

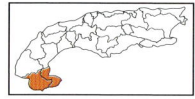

5–12cm tall; rosette leaves oval, ± 3x as long as broad; corolla with olive green spots inside; calyx teeth as long as or a little longer than broad, constricted at base, arched backwards, and less than half the length of calyx tube. Flowers May to July.
SIMILAR SPECIES: Stemless Gentian (Trumpet Gentian), *G. acaulis* (see p. 222) has calyx teeth ± 1.5x as long as broad, and is calcifuge. Narrow-leaved Gentian, *G. angustifolia* (see p. 222), has rosette leaves 3–6x as long as broad.
HABITAT: Stony sward, rock crevices, open woods, meadows; calcicole. 700–2,900m.
DISTRIBUTION: South-western alpine endemic

3 | Yellow Gentian
Gentiana lutea subsp. *lutea* – Gentianaceae

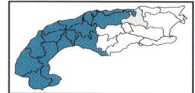

50–120cm tall; leaves blue-green, opposite, broadly lanceolate, with 5–7 curved and branched main veins; bracts of central clusters of inflorescence projecting only slightly or not at all beyond the clusters; anthers free; stigmas spiralling backwards after flowering. Flowers June to August.
SIMILAR SPECIES: The subspecies *symphandra* and *vardjanii*. White False Helleborine, *Veratrum album* (see p. 416), when not flowering, may resemble Yellow Gentian, but has alternate leaves.
HABITAT: Montane meadows, pasture, tall herb vegetation. To about 2,500m.
DISTRIBUTION: South-western European montane.

4 | Fused-anthered Yellow Gentian
Gentiana lutea subsp. *symphyandra* – Gentianaceae

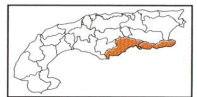

50–120cm tall; leaves blue-green, opposite, broadly lanceolate, with 5–7 curved and branched main veins; anthers fused into a tube, stigmas upright after flowering. Flowers June to August.
SIMILAR SPECIES: The nominate form, subsp. *lutea*, has anthers free, and stigmas spiralling backwards after flowering.
HABITAT: Montane meadows, pasture, tall herb vegetation. To about 2,200m.
DISTRIBUTION: South-eastern European montane.

5 | Vardjan's Yellow Gentian
Gentiana lutea subsp. *vardjanii* – Gentianaceae

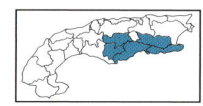

50–120cm tall; leaves blue-green, opposite, broadly lanceolate, with 5–7 curved and branched main veins; bracts of central clusters of inflorescence projecting well beyond the clusters; anthers free. Flowers June to August.
SIMILAR SPECIES: The nominate form, subsp. *lutea*, has bracts of central clusters of inflorescence projecting only slightly or not at all beyond the clusters.
HABITAT: Montane meadows, pasture, tall herb vegetation. Around 1,200–2,200m.
DISTRIBUTION: Alpine endemic.
NAME: In honour of Slovenian botanist Miran Vardjan (1919–2005).

Gentianaceae

1 | Snow Gentian
Gentiana nivalis – Gentianaceae

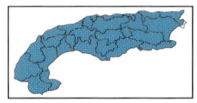

1–15cm tall, annual, without sterile shoots; leaves oval to lanceolate, in basal rosette; flowers solitary and terminal; corolla lobes 3–6mm long; calyx tube 2–4mm broad, not inflated, winged to 0.2–0.5mm along edges. Flowers June to August.
SIMILAR SPECIES: Bladder Gentian, *G. utriculosa* (see p. 230), has an inflated calyx with ridges winged to 2–3mm broad.
HABITAT: Stony sward, poor meadows, pasture. 1,300–3,000m.
DISTRIBUTION: Arctic–alpine.

2 | Round-leaved Gentian
Gentiana orbicularis – Gentianaceae
(Syn.: *Gentiana favrati*)

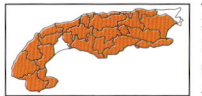

3–6cm tall; basal leaves in a rosette; rosette leaves 4–10mm long, round to obovate; calyx wings 0.5–1mm broad. Flowers July to August.
SIMILAR SPECIES: Spring Gentian, *G. verna* (see p. 232). Short-leaved Gentian, *G. brachyphylla* (see p. 224).
HABITAT: Poor grassland, rocky sward; calcicole. 2,000–3,500m.
DISTRIBUTION: Southern European montane, from the western Alps to the Carpathians.

3 | Hungarian Gentian (Brown Gentian)
Gentiana pannonica – Gentianaceae

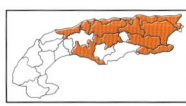

20–60cm tall; leaves ovate-lanceolate, shiny green; corolla 25–50mm long, purple-red-violet, with dark spots; calyx irregularly 5–8-partite to about the middle, with lanceolate, outwardly curving lobes. Flowers July to September.
SIMILAR SPECIES: Purple Gentian, *G. purpurea* (see p. 230), has a 2-lobed calyx, split almost the base on one side.
HABITAT: Grazed grassland, tall herb vegetation, limestone pavement. 1,000–2,300m, sometimes lower, as in the Ötschergräben (Ötscher Gorge), Austria (600m).
DISTRIBUTION: Eastern alpine.
NOTE: Very rarely in a pale yellow form, as on Stuhleck, Styria, Austria.

4 | Pygmy Gentian
Gentiana prostrata – Gentianaceae

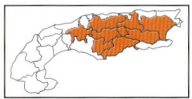

2–7cm tall, prostrate to ascending; leaves obovate, 6–9mm long; flowers solitary, sky blue, 10–20mm long, seemingly 10-lobed because of intermediate lobes of almost equal length. Flowers July to August.
SIMILAR SPECIES: None.
HABITAT: Stony sward; on intermediate substrates. 1,600–2,800m.
DISTRIBUTION: Arctic–alpine.

5 | Dwarf Gentian
Gentiana pumila – Gentianaceae

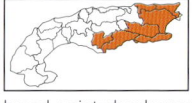

3–12cm tall; basal leaves in a rosette; rosette leaves linear-lanceolate, 1–3mm broad, pointed; calyx narrowly winged, 10–15mm long. Flowers June to August.
SIMILAR SPECIES: Dauphiné Gentian, *G. verna* subsp. *delphinensis*, a southwest alpine species, has a 15–20mm long calyx.
HABITAT: Damp poor grassland, snow-melt hollows; calcicole. 1,500–2,500m.
DISTRIBUTION: Eastern alpine endemic.

6 | Spotted Gentian
Gentiana punctata – Gentianaceae

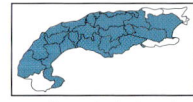

20–60cm tall; leaves shiny green, elliptical to oval, with 5–7 veins; corolla pale yellow, usually with dark violet spots, 25–35mm long; calyx split to about the middle into 5–8 lobes. Flowers June to August.
SIMILAR SPECIES: Villars's Gentian, *G. villarsii* (see p. 232), has fused sepals with 2 narrow outwardly-directed lobes.
HABITAT: Pasture, tall herb vegetation, dwarf shrub heath; calcifuge. 1,100–3,050m.
DISTRIBUTION: South-eastern European montane, from the western Alps to the mountains of the Balkan Peninsula.

Gentianaceae

1 | Purple Gentian
Gentiana purpurea – Gentianaceae

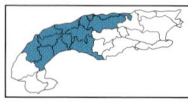

20–60cm tall; leaves ovate-lanceolate, shiny green; corolla 25–40mm long, purplish-red, yellowish inside; calyx 2-lobed, divided almost to the base on one side. Flowers July to September.

SIMILAR SPECIES: Hungarian Gentian (Brown Gentian), *G. pannonica* (see p. 228).
HABITAT: Pasture, tall herb vegetation, dwarf shrub heath, Green Alder scrub. 1,200–2,750m.
DISTRIBUTION: Alpine–Scandinavian. Alps, southern Norway.
NOTES: At some sites, such as in the Bergamasque Alps, Italy, there are plants with orange or yellow flowers (**1B**, **1C**). The tall, yellow- or purple-flowered alpine gentians (*Gentiana lutea*, *G. pannonica*, *G. punctata*, *G. purpurea*, and *G. villarsii*) occasionally hybridise, thereby increasing the splendour and diversity of this group of gentians.

2 | Rostan's Gentian
Gentiana rostanii – Gentianaceae

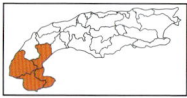

3–15cm tall, hairless; non-flowering stems densely leafy; leaves linear, 5–20mm long; stem leaves in 2–4 pairs; flowers solitary, terminal; calyx tube narrow, barely winged, usually suffused dark; calyx teeth shorter than calyx tube, with rounded gaps between. Flowers July to August.

SIMILAR SPECIES: Bavarian Gentian, *G. bavarica* (see p. 224).
HABITAT: Wet meadows. About 1,600–2,800m.
DISTRIBUTION: Western alpine endemic.
NAME: In honour of French botanist and physician Édouard Rostan (1826–1895), an outstanding expert on the flora of the Cottian Alps, France/Italy.

3 | Schleicher's Gentian
Gentiana schleicheri – Gentianaceae

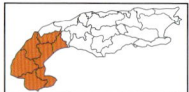

3–6cm tall; with sterile shoots; leaves 3–9mm long, oval to lanceolate, broadest at or below the middle, pointed, close together, lower leaves somewhat larger than the upper leaves; calyx 10–15mm long, with narrow wings. Flowers July to August.

SIMILAR SPECIES: Triglav Gentian, *G. terglouensis*. Bavarian Gentian, *G. bavarica* (see p. 224), has leaves that are widest in the upper third and usually rounded at the tip.
HABITAT: Stony sward, alpine mat vegetation. 2,000–3,100m.
DISTRIBUTION: Western alpine–Pyrenean.
NAME: In honour of German-Swiss pharmacist, botanist, and company owner Johann Christoph Schleicher (1768–1834), author of a 'Catalogus Plantarum Helvetia'.

4 | Triglav Gentian
Gentiana terglouensis – Gentianaceae

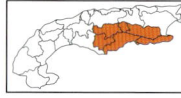

3–10cm tall, with sterile shoots; leaves 3–5mm long, oval to lanceolate, broadest at or below the middle, pointed, close together, all about the same size; calyx 8–13mm long, scarcely winged. Flowers June to August.

SIMILAR SPECIES: Schleicher's Gentian, *G. schleicheri*, restricted to the western Alps, has lower leaves somewhat larger than the upper leaves.
HABITAT: Stony poor grassland, rock debris; calcicole. 1,900–2,700m.
DISTRIBUTION: Eastern alpine endemic.

5 | Bladder Gentian
Gentiana utriculosa – Gentianaceae

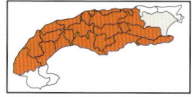

1–20cm tall, annual, without sterile shoots; leaves oval to lanceolate, in basal rosette; flowers solitary and terminal; corolla lobes 5–8mm long; calyx tube 4–8mm broad, inflated, winged 2–3mm broad at edges. Flowers May to August.

SIMILAR SPECIES: Snow Gentian, *G. nivalis* (see p. 228).
HABITAT: Wet meadows, fens, grazed grassland, open woods; calcicole. To 2,400m.
DISTRIBUTION: Southern European montane, from the western Alps to the Carpathians.

Gentianaceae

1 | Spring Gentian
Gentiana verna – Gentianaceae

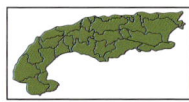

3–10cm tall; basal leaves in a rosette; rosette leaves 10–30mm long, lanceolate; calyx ridges with wings to 1–2mm broad; calyx tube 4–7mm broad. Flowers March to June.
SIMILAR SPECIES: Short-leaved Gentian, *G. brachyphylla* (see p. 224), has calyx with 0–0.3mm broad wings and rosette leaves only 4–10mm long. Round-leaved Gentian, *G. orbicularis* (see p. 228), has calyx with 0.5–1mm broad wings, and rounded obovate rosette leaves, 4–10mm long.
HABITAT: Poor grassland, pasture, fens, dwarf shrub heath. To 3,550m.
DISTRIBUTION: Southern European montane.
NOTE: 2 subspecies in the Alps:
- subsp. *verna*: rosette leaves broadly lanceolate, 4–9mm broad. Throughout the Alps.
- subsp. *delphinensis*: rosette leaves narrowly lanceolate, 2–4mm broad. South-western Alps.

2 | Villars's Gentian
Gentiana villarsii – Gentianaceae
(Syn.: *Gentiana burseri* subsp. *villarsii*)

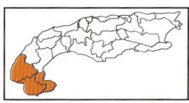

30–80cm tall; leaves elliptical to oval, 7–9 veined, shiny green; corolla pale yellow, usually with dark violet spots inside; sepals fused, with 2 narrow out-turned lobes. Flowers July to August.
SIMILAR SPECIES: Spotted Gentian, *G. punctata* (see p. 228).
HABITAT: Meadows, pasture, tall herb vegetation, dwarf shrub heath. 1,300–2,600m.
DISTRIBUTION: Southwest alpine endemic.
NAME: In honour of French botanist Dominique Villars (1745–1814), author of a fundamental work on the flora of the western Alps.

3 | Dolomites Gentian
Gentianella anisodonta – Gentianaceae

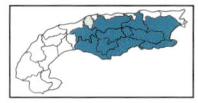

2–25cm tall; corolla 19–30mm long, blue-violet; calyx lobes differently shaped, 1–2.5x as long as calyx tube, margins clearly rolled downwards; ovary with 1–4mm long stalk. Flowers June to September.
SIMILAR SPECIES: Other *Gentianella* species, especially Engadin Gentian, *G. engadinensis*, which has margins of calyx lobes only slightly rolled downwards, red-violet corolla 17–25mm long, and is only 2–10cm tall.
HABITAT: Poor grassland, dwarf shrub heath, pasture. 900–2,600m.
DISTRIBUTION: South-eastern European montane.

4 | Rough Gentian
Gentianella aspera – Gentianaceae

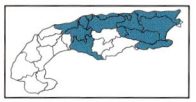

5–35cm tall; stem leaves rough-edged; corolla 30–39mm long, blue-violet; calyx lobes mostly broadly triangular, 1.2–2.3x as long as calyx tube, with sharp gaps between; calyx lobe margins mostly weakly rolled downwards, with papillae at least twice as long as broad (use hand lens); ovary with 1–5mm long stalk. Flowers May to September.
SIMILAR SPECIES: German Gentian, *G. germanica* (see p. 234), has smooth edges to stem leaves and papillae on calyx lobe margins ± as long as broad (hand lens).
HABITAT: Stony sward, semi-arid grassland; calcicole. 1,200–2,500m.
DISTRIBUTION: European montane.

5 | Austrian Gentian
Gentianella austriaca – Gentianaceae

5–30cm tall; stem leaves with smooth edges; corolla lilac to reddish-violet, 25–45mm long; calyx lobes narrow, linear, 1.5–2.5x as long as calyx tube, mostly similarly shaped, with U-shaped gaps between; calyx lobe margins only weakly rolled downwards, smooth; ovary with 2–7mm long stalk. Flowers June to October.
SIMILAR SPECIES: German Gentian, *G. germanica*, has broad, triangular calyx lobes, with sharp gaps between. Hairy Gentian, *G. pilosa*, is a strongly calcicole species of the south-eastern Alps, and has calyx lobes with papillose edges and with sharp gaps between lobes.
HABITAT: Poor grassland, pasture, rocky sward. To 2,400m.
DISTRIBUTION: South-east European.
NOTE: In Styria and Carinthia there are occasionally plants with characters intermediate between German Gentian, *G. germanica*, and Austrian Gentian, *G. austriaca*, which have been named Styrian Gentian, *G. styriaca*.

Gentianaceae

1 | Field Gentian
Gentianella campestris – Gentianaceae

5–20cm tall; branched; calyx and corolla 4-partite; calyx with 2 large oval and 2 small linear lobes, without rolled margins and with pointed gaps. Flowers June to October.
SIMILAR SPECIES: All the other alpine *Gentianella* species have 5-partite calyx and corolla.
HABITAT: Poor grassland, pasture. 1,000–2,800m.
DISTRIBUTION: European.

2 | German Gentian
Gentianella germanica – Gentianaceae (incl. *G. rhaetica*)

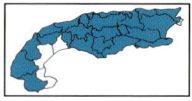

5–30cm tall; stem leaves smooth-edged; corolla lilac to reddish-violet, 23–35mm long; calyx lobes all similar, mostly broadly triangular, 1–2x as long as calyx tube, with pointed gaps; calyx lobe margins mostly only weakly rolled under, with papillae ± as long as broad (hand lens). Flowers May to October.
SIMILAR SPECIES: Difficult to distinguish from the other *Gentianella* species, especially Rough Gentian, *G. aspera* (see p. 232). Austrian Gentian, *G. austriaca* (see p. 232), has rounded gaps between calyx lobes. Dolomites Gentian, *G. anisodonta* (see p. 232), has strikingly unevenly shaped calyx lobes. Branched Gentian, *G. ramosa*, has smooth-edged calyx lobes 2–3x as long as calyx tube, is only 3–16cm tall, flowers from August to September, and is calcifuge.
HABITAT: Poor grassland, fens, pasture, rocky sward. To 2,700m.
DISTRIBUTION: European.

3 | Insubrian Gentian
Gentianella insubrica – Gentianaceae

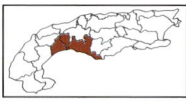

10–25cm tall; corolla lilac to reddish-violet, 18–28mm long; calyx lobes dissimilar, 1–3 of them significantly broader than the others, with papillose margins and pointed gaps between; ovary stalk 2–6mm long. Flowers June to October.
SIMILAR SPECIES: German Gentian, *G. germanica*, has calyx lobes all similar width. Autumn Gentian, *G. amarella*, has 14–18mm long corolla, and unstalked ovary.
HABITAT: Poor meadows, grassy woodland sites, stony sward; calcicole. From about 1,000–2,200m.
DISTRIBUTION: Southern alpine endemic.

4 | Fringed Gentian
Gentianopsis ciliata – Gentianaceae (Syn.: *Gentianella ciliata*)

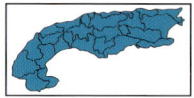

5–25cm tall; flowers solitary and terminal; leaves narrowly lanceolate, with single vein; no basal rosette; perianth 4-partite; corolla 30–50mm long, deep blue (gentian blue); corolla lobes with long fringes along the sides. Flowers August to November.
SIMILAR SPECIES: Species of *Gentianella*, have lilac or violet flowers, and corolla lobes without fringes.
HABITAT: Semi-arid grassland, stony sward, pasture; calcicole. To 2,500m.
DISTRIBUTION: European montane.

5 | Blue Felwort
Lomatogonium carinthiacum – Gentianaceae

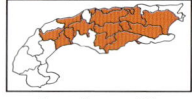

2–12cm tall; leaves oval to ovate-lanceolate; flowers solitary, on long, leafless stems; corolla pale grey-blue to whitish; calyx shorter than corolla. Flowers August to September.
SIMILAR SPECIES: None.
HABITAT: Short-grazed pasture, patchy grassland. 1,400–2,600m.
DISTRIBUTION: European-Asiatic.

6 | Marsh Felwort
Swertia perennis – Gentianaceae

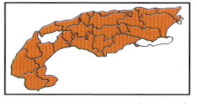

15–50cm tall; stem unbranched; lower leaves alternate, oval to elliptical, upper leaves opposite, narrowly oval to lanceolate; petals pointed, whitish, with violet markings to completely dark violet. Flowers June to August.
SIMILAR SPECIES: None.
HABITAT: Fens, marshy meadows, wet flushes. 600–2,300m.
DISTRIBUTION: Southern European montane.
NAME: In honour of Dutch gardener Emanual Swert (1552–1612).

Geraniaceae

1 | Rodie's Storksbill
Erodium rodiei – Geraniaceae

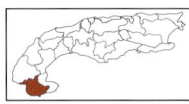

5–30cm tall; leaves all basal, deeply divided, with linear lobes; inflorescence 2–8-flowered, on 8–20mm long stalk; flowers 20–30mm in diameter; petals pink, with purple veins; ripe fruit beak 3–5cm long. Flowers May to June.
SIMILAR SPECIES: None.
HABITAT: Southerly exposed rocky scree; calcicole. 900–1,150m.
DISTRIBUTION: Endemic to the southern French Pre-Alps, around Grasse.
NAME: In honour of French botanist Joseph Rodie (1881–1973), who discovered the plant in 1932.

2 | Silvery Cranesbill
Geranium argenteum – Geraniaceae

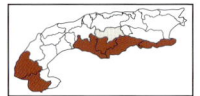

3–15cm tall; leaves silvery grey-green, shiny, deeply divided to the base into 5–7 lobes, with silvery, silky hairs on both sides; flowers 25–30mm broad, pale pink, with darker veins. Flowers June to July.
SIMILAR SPECIES: Bloody Cranesbill, *G. sanguineum*, has purple-pink flowers, and leaves without silky hairs.
HABITAT: Limestone and dolomite rocky sward. 1,690–2,200m.
DISTRIBUTION: Alpine–Apennine. Southern Alps, and Tuscan and Umbrian Apennines.
NOTE: The botanical generic name *Geranium* comes from the ancient Greek 'geranos' (= crane), alluding to the similarity of the fruit to the bill of a crane. Similarly, the genus *Pelargonium* derives from 'pelargos' (= stork). The German name Storckenschnabel was used as early as the 12th century by Hildegard of Bingen.

Carl von Linné (Linnaeus) included *Pelargonium* in the genus *Geranium* and it was French botanist Charles Louis L'Heritier who split *Pelargonium* from *Geranium*, in 1789. Nevertheless, the German name for *Geranium* remained Storchschnabel, although the English name is cranesbill, which is in line with the Greek origin. Storksbill in English is used for species of the genus *Erodium*.

There are about 430 cranesbill species worldwide, of which 38 are European, with 21 in the Alps. The sole species found only in the Alps is River Cranesbill, *Geranium rivulare* (see p. 238).

3 | Rock Cranesbill
Geranium macrorrhizum – Geraniaceae

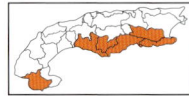

10–40cm tall, with aromatic scent; rhizome strikingly strong, almost on the surface; leaves palmately divided, lobes deeply notched to pinnate; inflorescence 3–9-flowered; petals purple-pink, 15–20mm long; filaments red, to 22mm long. Flowers May to July.
SIMILAR SPECIES: Few.
HABITAT: Rocky sward, stony tall herb vegetation; calcicole. To about 1,900m.
DISTRIBUTION: South-eastern European, north to the Plöcken Pass, Austria/Italy.

4 | Knotted Cranesbill
Geranium nodosum – Geraniaceae

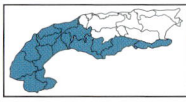

20–40cm tall; stem slightly thickened at branching points; leaves 3–5-divided, with oval, pointed, irregularly toothed lobes, hairless; petals 12–18mm long, pink to pale lilac, with purple veins, notched. Flowers May to August.
SIMILAR SPECIES: Bohemian Cranesbill, *G. bohemicum*, has 6–10mm long petals and leaves softly hairy on both sides.
HABITAT: Deciduous woods. To 1,600m.
DISTRIBUTION: Southern European montane, from the mountains of Spain to those of Greece.

5 | Lilac Dusky Cranesbill
Geranium phaeum subsp. *lividum* – Geraniaceae

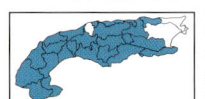

30–60cm tall; stem with erect hairs; leaf blades unspotted, 5–12cm in diameter, 7-divided to over the middle, with rhomboid lobes; petals pink, 10–13mm long, spreading to reflexed, not notched; filaments purple. Flowers June to July.
SIMILAR SPECIES: The nominate form, Dusky Cranesbill, *Geranium phaeum* subsp. *phaeum*, has dark purple petals and usually has spotted leaves. Pyrenean Cranesbill, *G. pyrenaicum*, has pale violet, deeply-notched petals 6–10mm long.
HABITAT: Montane meadows, tall herb vegetation, To about 2,400m.
DISTRIBUTION: Alpine subspecies.

Geraniaceae, Globulariaceae

1 | River Cranesbill
Geranium rivulare – Geraniaceae

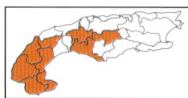

20–60cm tall; leaf blades divided almost to the base, with lobes 2–5x as long as broad; flower stalks without glandular hairs, upright after flowering; petals 10–15mm long, white, with violet veins. Flowers June to August.
SIMILAR SPECIES: White-flowered form of Meadow Cranesbill, *G. pratense*, has glandular-hairy flower stalk, drooping after flowering.
HABITAT: Open Larch and Arolla Pine woods, dwarf shrub heath; calcifuge. 1,400–2,300m.
DISTRIBUTION: Alpine. Mainly in western Alps.

2 | Herb Robert
Geranium robertianum – Geraniaceae

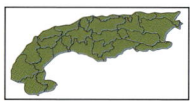

20–40cm tall, unpleasant smelling, ascending or upright; leaf blades deeply cut into 3–5 leaflets, each leaflet also deeply cut, with notched lobes; petals pink, 10–13mm long, with blade 5–8mm long. Flowers May to October.
SIMILAR SPECIES: Shining Cranesbill, *G. lucidum*, has shiny 3-lobed leaves.
HABITAT: Woods, gorges, rocky debris, clearings. To about 1,900m.
DISTRIBUTION: European-Asiatic–North American.

3 | Wood Cranesbill
Geranium sylvaticum – Geraniaceae

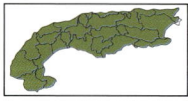

30–60cm tall; lower stem with short hairs; leaf blade 5–7-divided to over the middle; flower stalks with glandular hairs, upright after flowering; petals purple-violet, with white base; corolla spreading and slightly cup-shaped. Flowers June to August.
SIMILAR SPECIES: Meadow Cranesbill, *G. pratense*, has lilac-blue spreading corolla, flower stalk drooping after flowering, and leaf blades deeply divided, to at least ⅚ of the length of leaf.
HABITAT: Tall herb vegetation, montane meadows, woods, dwarf shrub heath. To 2,500m.
DISTRIBUTION: Eurosiberian.

4 | Heart-leaved Globe Daisy
Globularia cordifolia – Globulariaceae

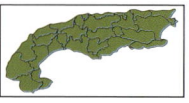

3–10cm tall; shoots much-branched, woody, forming carpet; leaves 1–3cm long, 0.3–1cm broad, blade spoon-shaped to narrowly obovate, rounded or notched at the tip; corolla 6–11mm long. Flowers May to July.
SIMILAR SPECIES: Creeping Globe Daisy, *G. repens*, is 1–3cm tall, with pointed leaves, 0.2–0.5cm broad.
HABITAT: Rock cervices, stony sward; calcicole. To about 2,800m.
DISTRIBUTION: Southern European montane.

5 | Leafless-stemmed Globe Daisy
Globularia nudicaulis – Globulariaceae

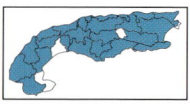

5–25cm tall; unbranched, without prostrate shoots; leaf blades 5–12cm long, 1–2.5cm broad, narrowing towards the stalk; corolla 10–12mm long. Flowers June to July.
SIMILAR SPECIES: Few.
HABITAT: Snowy poor grassland, Dwarf Mountain Pine scrub, dwarf shrub heath, open pinewoods; calcicole. 500–2,600m.
DISTRIBUTION: Southern European montane.

6 | Creeping Globe Daisy
Globularia repens – Globulariaceae

1–3cm tall; shoots much-branched, woody, forming carpet; leaves 1–2cm long, 0.2–0.5cm broad, blade lanceolate to oval, pointed at tip, folded upwards; corolla 6–10mm long. Flowers May to July.
SIMILAR SPECIES: Heart-leaved Globe Daisy, *G. cordifolia*.
HABITAT: Rock crevices; calcicole. To about 2,500m.
DISTRIBUTION: South-western European montane.

Grossulariaceae, Hypericaceae

1 | Alpine Currant
Ribes alpinum – Grossulariaceae

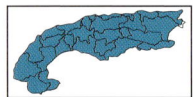

0.8–1.5m tall shrub; leaves including stalk 2–4cm long, leaf stalk less than half the length of blade, leaves 3-lobed, the central lobe longer than lateral lobes; bracts mostly longer than flower stalk; racemes upright, with short glandular hairs; berries ± round, red. Flowers April to June.
SIMILAR SPECIES: Rock Currant, *R. petraeum*, has larger leaves, up to 10cm diameter, drooping racemes and bracts shorter than flower stalk.
HABITAT: Rocky wooded ravines, deciduous woods, scrub; calcicole. To 2,000m.
DISTRIBUTION: European–South-western Asiatic.

2 | Imperforate St. John's-wort
Hypericum maculatum – Hypericaceae

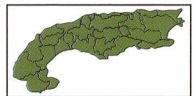

20–60cm tall; stems 4-ridged, not winged; leaves elongate-oval, 2–4cm long; sepal tips mostly blunt and entire; petals yellow, with black spots, mostly not spotted at margin, 2–3x as long as calyx. Flowers July to August.
SIMILAR SPECIES: Perforate St John's-wort, *H. perforatum*, has a round stem with 2 longitudinal ridges opposite each other. *H. maculatum* subsp. *obtusiusculum* (Syn.: *H. dubium*), has mostly pointed, irregularly toothed sepals, and petals with black spots also on margins.
HABITAT: Damp to alternately moist, lime-poor grassland and pasture, Mat Grass (*Nardus stricta*) sward, transitional vegetation, woodland clearings, tall herb vegetation and mires; calcifuge. To 2,300m, sometimes higher, as at Schanfigg, Graubünden, Switzerland (2,540m).
DISTRIBUTION: Eurosiberian, from Ireland to western Siberia.

3 | Pale St John's-wort (Mountain St John's-wort)
Hypericum montanum – Hypericaceae

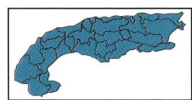

30–70cm tall; stem round, not ridged; leaves widely separated, broadly oval, sessile, bluish-green, with black glandular spots around the edges on both sides; upper stem internodes notably longer than the others; petals pale yellow, in short inflorescence. Flowers June to July.
SIMILAR SPECIES: Slender St John's-wort, *H. pulchrum*, has heart-shaped leaves, and leaf margins without glandular spots.
HABITAT: Woods. To 2,000m.
DISTRIBUTION: Eurosiberian.

4 | Round-leaved St John's-wort
Hypericum nummularium – Hypericaceae

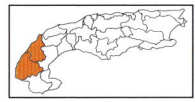

5–30cm tall, prostrate to ascending; leaves rounded, edged with pale glands; sepals 4–5mm long, oval, with stalked black glands at margin; flowers 18–25mm in diameter. Flowers July to September.
SIMILAR SPECIES: Trailing St John's-wort, *H. humifusum*, has lanceolate leaves and flowers 8–15mm in diameter.
HABITAT: Damp calcareous rocks; calcicole. About 700–2,100m.
DISTRIBUTION: Western alpine–Pyrenean.

5 | Alpine St John's-wort
Hypericum richeri – Hypericaceae

20–60cm tall, with several, upwardly arching, often 2-ridged stems; leaves oval, sessile, 2–4cm long, with black glands around margin on underside; sepals 6–8mm long, finely fringed at margin; petals 2–4x as long as sepals; flowers 25–30mm in diameter. Flowers June to August.
SIMILAR SPECIES: Pale St John's-wort, *H. montanum*, has flowers only 15–20mm in diameter.
HABITAT: Stony pasture, open scrub, rocky slopes, tall herb vegetation; calcicole. 1,100–2,400m.
DISTRIBUTION: Southern European montane. 2 subspecies in the Alps:
– subsp. *richeri*: western Alps.
– subsp. *grisebachii* (**5**): south-eastern Alps.
NAME: Species name in honour of French botanist and physician Pierre Richer de Belleval (1564–1632), who studied the flora of Languedoc.

Lamiaceae

1 | Pyramidal Bugle
Ajuga pyramidalis – Lamiaceae

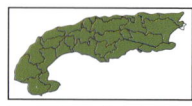

5–25cm tall; pyramid-shaped, without runners, strongly hairy; rosette leaves always larger than stem leaves; bracts usually purple, about twice as long as flowers; corolla blue with paler centre. Flowers May to August.
SIMILAR SPECIES: Common Bugle, *A. reptans*, has overground runners, and hairless or only sparsely hairy stem.
HABITAT: Poor meadows on acid soils, pasture, open montane woods; calcifuge. 800–2,700m.
DISTRIBUTION: European montane.

2 | Yellow Betony
Betonica alopecuros – Lamiaceae
(Syn.: *Stachys alopecuros*)

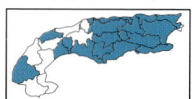

20–50cm tall; basal leaves heart-shaped, long-stalked, and coarsely toothed; flowers in dense whorls; corolla yellow. Flowers June to August.
SIMILAR SPECIES: Few.
HABITAT: Poor grassland, rocky sward, rock debris, avalanche affected sward; calcicole. To about 2,300m.
DISTRIBUTION: Southern European montane, from the Spanish to the Greek mountains.
NOTES: Two subspecies in the Alps:
– subsp. *alopecuros*: upper lip with 2 pointed teeth; in the Alps from Switzerland and Italy eastwards.
– subsp. *godronii*: upper lip with 2 round teeth; in the Alps only in France.

In 1753, Carl von Linné (Linnaeus) introduced the genus *Betonica*, which many botanists soon included in the genus *Stachys*. In terms of phylogenetic history, the independence of the genus has been repeatedly established, although even though the benchmark work *Flora Europaea* lists the betonies as a section within the genus *Stachys*, although molecular and chemotaxonomic features indicate that *Betonica* does not even belong to the tribe Stachydeae, but rather is more closely related to the genus *Galeopsis*.

The generic name *Betonica* goes back to the Celtic tribe the Vettones, who inhabited central Iberia.

3 | Alpine Betony
Betonica hirsuta – Lamiaceae (Syn.: *Stachys pradica*)

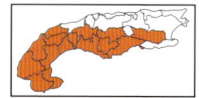

10–30cm tall; stem and leaves with dense woolly hairs, hairs on upper stem 1.5–3mm long; corolla purple-pink, 15–22mm long; calyx 12–15mm long. Flowers July to August.
SIMILAR SPECIES: Common Betony, *B. officinalis* (Syn.: *Stachys officinalis*), is 30–70cm tall, with hairs on upper stem 0.4–1.5mm long, and corolla 10–15mm long.
HABITAT: Poor meadows, dwarf shrub heath. 1,200–2,400m, also down to the lowlands in the Maritime Alps.
DISTRIBUTION: South-western European montane.

4 | Alpine Calamint
Clinopodium alpinum – Lamiaceae (Syn.: *Acinos alpinus*)

3–20cm tall; leaves oval, entire, or with 1–5 notches on each side, not rolled under at margin, and without prominent veins on underside; corolla violet, 15–20mm long; calyx opening at fruiting stage. Flowers May to September.
SIMILAR SPECIES: Basil Thyme, *C. acinos* (Syn.: *Acinos arvensis*), has lilac flowers, and corolla 7–10mm long. Calyx at fruiting stage closed by lobes arching together.
HABITAT: Stony poor grassland, pinewoods, rock debris, rocks; calcicole. To 2,900m.
DISTRIBUTION: Southern European montane.

5 | Large-flowered Calamint
Clinopodium grandiflorum – Lamiaceae (Syn.: *Calamintha grandiflora*)

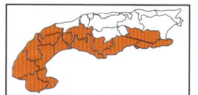

20–50cm tall, lemon-scented; leaves 3–7cm long, oval, coarsely serrated; corolla 20–40mm long, vivid pink; Calyx 10–13mm long, 11-veined, pale green. Flowers July to September.
SIMILAR SPECIES: Species in the Lesser Calamint group, *Clinopodium nepeta* agg. (Syn.: *Calamintha nepeta* agg.), have corolla 12–22mm long, and calyx 3–10mm long, often suffused purple, with 13 veins.
HABITAT: Damp deciduous woods, To 1,900m.
DISTRIBUTION: Mediterranean-montane.

Lamiaceae

1 | Northern Dragonhead
Dracocephalum ruyschiana – Lamiaceae

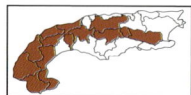

10–30cm tall; leaves linear, entire, 2–6mm broad; flower clusters 2–8-flowered; corolla 2.5–3cm long, upper lip curved like a helmet. Flowers June to August.
SIMILAR SPECIES: Austrian Dragonhead, *D. austriacum*, has partially-pinnate leaves and 3.5–4.5cm long corolla. Large Selfheal, *Prunella grandiflora*, has 10–40mm broad, ovate-lanceolate leaves.
HABITAT: Grassland, high-alpine poor meadows, warm, dry pine and Larch woods. 1,400–2,200m.
DISTRIBUTION: Eurosiberian.
NAME: In honour of Dutch botanist and anatomist Frederik Ruysch (1638–1731).

2 | Large-flowered Hemp-nettle
Galeopsis speciosa – Lamiaceae

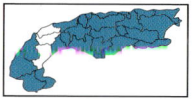

30–70cm tall; stem thickened and bristly below nodes; tips of glandular hairs on calyx and stem pale; leaves oval, coarsely toothed; corolla 20–35mm long, yellow, central lobes of lower lip violet. Flowers June to October.
SIMILAR SPECIES: Common Hemp-nettle, *G. tetrahit*, has purplish-red or white corolla, and dark-tipped glandular hairs on calyx and stem.
HABITAT: Woodland clearings, path sides, nutrient-rich scrub. To 2,000m.
DISTRIBUTION: Eastern European.

3 | Common Hemp-nettle
Galeopsis tetrahit – Lamiaceae

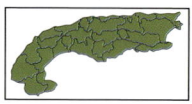

20–70cm tall; stem thickened and bristly below nodes; leaves oval to broadly lanceolate, toothed, stalked and hairy; flowers clustered in whorls; calyx with prickly awns, and dark-tipped glandular hairs; corolla 15–20mm long, purple to white, with yellow markings, about 1.5x as long as calyx. Flowers June to October.
SIMILAR SPECIES: Bifid Hemp-nettle, *G. bifida*, has a 10–15mm long corolla and pale-tipped glandular hairs on calyx. Hairy Hemp-nettle, *G. pubescens*, has corolla 2–3x as long as calyx.
HABITAT: Woodland clearings, path sides, nutrient-rich ruderal sward. To about 2,300m.
DISTRIBUTION: European.

4 | Dragonmouth
Horminum pyrenaicum – Lamiaceae

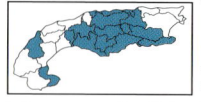

15–30cm tall; basal leaves long-stalked, oval, wrinkled, bluntly-toothed, and hairless; inflorescence ± unilaterally leaning; corolla violet, about 15–20mm long; upper lip notched. Flowers June to August.
SIMILAR SPECIES: Meadow Clary, *Salvia pratensis*, has a 15–20mm long corolla, and upper lip curved like a helmet.
HABITAT: Poor, calcareous grassland, rocky pasture. To about 2,500m.
DISTRIBUTION: South-western European montane.

5 | Gargano Dead-nettle
Lamium garganicum – Lamiaceae

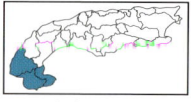

15–50cm tall; leaf blades heart-shaped to oval, 15–70mm long, 10–40mm broad, sparsely hairy, margins coarsely toothed; corolla pink, 25–40mm long. Flowers May to August.
SIMILAR SPECIES: Spotted Dead-nettle, *L. maculatum*, has corolla tube curved at base.
HABITAT: Rock crevices, rocky debris. To 1,900m.
DISTRIBUTION: Mediterranean-montane.

6 | Balm-leaved Red Dead-nettle
Lamium orvala – Lamiaceae

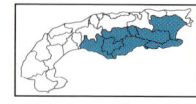

30–90cm tall; stem ridged; leaves opposite, blades 4–7cm broad, toothed at margin; corolla purplish-red, 30–40mm long. Flowers April to June.
SIMILAR SPECIES: Spotted Dead-nettle, *L. maculatum*, has 2–4cm broad leaves and 20–25mm long corolla.
HABITAT: Open deciduous woods, tall herb vegetation, transitional habitats, stream sides, scrub. To 1,600m.
DISTRIBUTION: Eastern alpine–Illyrian, from Valtellina, Italy, to Lake Balaton, Hungary, and to Transylvania, Romania.

Lamiaceae

1 | Yellow Archangel
Lamiastrum montanum – Lamiaceae
(Syn.: *Galeobdolon montanum*, *Lamium galeobdolon*)

20–50cm tall; with above-ground runners after flowering; base of stem with dense, erect hairs all around; whorls of 9–15 flowers; corolla golden yellow, 17–25mm long. Flowers April to June.
SIMILAR SPECIES: Pale Yellow Archangel, *L. flavidum*, does not produce runners, and has a pale yellow corolla, 14–17mm long. Variegated Yellow Archangel, *L. argentatum*, is often found as an escape or naturalised. The base of its stem is mostly only hairy on the ridges, and has whorls of 5–10 flowers.
HABITAT: Damp deciduous woods, wooded river valleys, hedges. To about 2,200m.
DISTRIBUTION: European.

2 | Lavender
Lavandula angustifolia – Lamiaceae

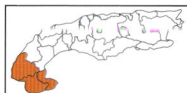

20–80cm tall, aromatic small shrub; leaves narrowly lanceolate, 2–5mm broad, rolled under at margins, softly grey hairy at first, later hairless; flowers in terminal whorled spikes; bracts in inflorescence 3–8mm long; corolla violet-blue. Flowers July to August.
SIMILAR SPECIES: Broad-leaved Lavender, *L. latifolia*, has 5–10mm broad leaves and 2–3mm long bracts.
HABITAT: Rocky sward, dry slopes. To 1,700m.
DISTRIBUTION: Mediterranean.

3 | Bastard Balm
Melittis melissophyllum – Lamiaceae

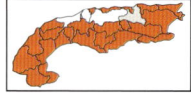

20–50cm tall; stem with erect hairs; leaves 3–9cm long, blade oval, regularly and coarsely toothed; corolla 30–45mm long, bicoloured purple-pink and white, sometimes entirely white or entirely purple-pink. Flowers May to June.
SIMILAR SPECIES: None.
HABITAT: Deciduous woods; calcicole. To 1,500m.
DISTRIBUTION: European.

NOTE: The variation in flower colour is striking. The pink and white form is found in most of the Alps, while in the south-eastern Alps, from Carniola to the Insubrian Alps, it is mostly the white form. In Drôme and Provence, however, it is mostly uniformly pink.
The generic name is from the ancient Greek meaning 'honeybee'. This makes little sense however, as Bastard Balm is mainly pollinated by bumblebees. The specific name refers to the fact that the leaves have a honey-like scent when crushed (*mellis* = honey).

4 | Horse Mint
Mentha longifolia – Lamiaceae

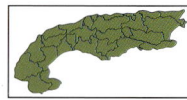

30–100cm tall, very aromatic; upper stem with white felty hairs; leaves elongate-lanceolate, pointed, grey-green above, with white felty hairs beneath; flowers in dense, spike-like clusters; corolla pale lilac, 3–4mm long. Flowers July to September.
SIMILAR SPECIES: Spear Mint, *M. spicata*, probably arose as a hybrid, *M. longifolia* x *M. suaveolens*. It is one of the parent species of Peppermint, *M. piperita*, and is occasionally naturalised in the Alps. It differs from Horse Mint in having leaves and stems either hairless or sparsely hairy only along the veins.
HABITAT: Banks, ditches, damp to wet pasture. To about 2,300m.
DISTRIBUTION: European-Asiatic.

5 | Wild Marjoram
Origanum vulgare – Lamiaceae

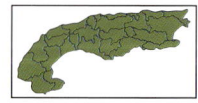

20–60cm tall, aromatic; leaf blades oval, entire or slightly toothed; flowers in dense terminal clusters; corolla pale pink, 4–7mm long, calyx green to purplish-red, hairless, or slightly hairy on outside. Flowers July to September.
SIMILAR SPECIES: Wild Basil, *Clinopodium vulgare*, has 10–15mm long corolla and calyx with erect hairs.
HABITAT: Woodland margins, dry grassland, transitional habitats, woodland clearings. To about 2,200m.
DISTRIBUTION: European-Asiatic.

Lamiaceae

1 | Large Selfheal
Prunella grandiflora – Lamiaceae

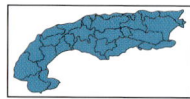

8–30cm tall; leaves ovate-lanceolate; uppermost pair of stem leaves not close to entire inflorescence; corolla 20–25mm long, violet. Flowers June to August.
SIMILAR SPECIES: Selfheal, *P. vulgaris*, has 10–15mm long flowers, and uppermost pair of stem leaves surrounding entire inflorescence. Hyssop-leaved Selfheal, *P. hyssopifolia*, found in the lowlands of the French Alps, has 15–18mm long flowers, and lanceolate leaves.
HABITAT: Semi-arid grassland, pinewoods, rocky sward, dry meadows, calcareous fens; calcicole. To 2,500m.
DISTRIBUTION: European–western Asiatic.

2 | Sticky Sage
Salvia glutinosa – Lamiaceae

40–90cm tall, glandular and sticky, especially in inflorescence; leaf blade heart-shaped, pointed; whorls 2–6-flowered; corolla 3–40mm long, pale yellow, lower lip with red-brown markings. Flowers July to September.
SIMILAR SPECIES: None.
HABITAT: Deciduous woods. To about 1,800m.
DISTRIBUTION: European-Asiatic, from northern Spain to the Himalaya.
NOTE: The wild alpine sage species are of great importance to animal life. The bug *Platyplax salviae* is a specialist on this genus. They are larval food plants for the noctuid moths Burnished Brass, *Diachrysia chrysitis*, and Scarce Burnished Brass, *Diachrysia chryson*, and a source of pollen for the Wool Carder Bee, *Anthidium manicatum*. Butterflies and moths with long proboscis visit them for nectar, including Swallowtail, Orange Tip, Pearl-bordered Fritillary, Clouded Yellow, Hummingbird Hawk-moth, Narrow-bordered and Broad-bordered Bee Hawk-moths, and Elephant Hawk-moth. Bumblebees are also often seen on their flowers.

3 | Saccardo's Sage
Salvia saccardiana – Lamiaceae (Syn.: *Salvia pratensis* subsp. *saccardiana*)

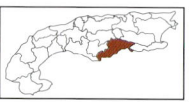

50–120cm tall, usually much-branched; leaf blade triangular to oval, irregularly toothed, with lobed margin; corolla violet-blue, 28–35mm long. Flowers May to July.
SIMILAR SPECIES: Meadow Clary, *S. pratensis*, with which it is included by some authors, is 60cm tall and has a 15–25mm long corolla.
HABITAT: Poor meadows, dry slopes, stony sward; calcicole. To about 1,300m.
DISTRIBUTION: Southeast alpine endemic.
NAME: In honour of Italian botanist Pier Andrea Saccardo (1845–1920), who mainly studied mycology.

4 | Whorled Clary
Salvia verticillata – Lamiaceae

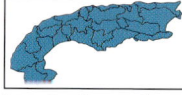

30–60cm tall; leaves irregularly bluntly-toothed, lower leaves often pinnate with 2–4 lateral leaflets and large terminal leaflets; stem leaves broadly heart-shaped; inflorescence whorls with 12–30 flowers; corolla 9–15mm long, pale violet to purple-lilac. Flowers June to September.
SIMILAR SPECIES: Balkan Clary, *S. nemorosa* (Syn.: *S. sylvestris*), has undivided leaves and 3–10-flowered whorls.
HABITAT: Stony poor grassland, rocky sward, dry ruderal sites; calcicole. To about 1,900m.
DISTRIBUTION: Mediterranean, widely naturalised elsewhere.

5 | Alpine Skullcap
Scutellaria alpina – Lamiaceae

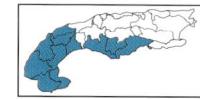

10–30cm tall, prostrate to ascending; leaf blade oval, blunt-toothed, with rounded or heart-shaped base; corolla 25–30mm long, blue-violet, lower lip and corolla tube partly white. Flowers June to August.
SIMILAR SPECIES: Large Selfheal, *Prunella grandiflora*, has uniformly blue corolla and leaf blades entire or at most shallowly notched.
HABITAT: Rocky sward, stony slopes; calcicole. To about 2,900m.
DISTRIBUTION: Southern European montane, from the Pyrenees to the mountains of the Balkan Peninsula.

1 | Alpine Woundwort (Limestone Woundwort)
Stachys alpina – Lamiaceae

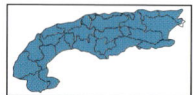

40–80cm tall; stem with erect hairs, upper stem glandular; leaves with short, appressed hairs, blade margin coarsely serrated; inflorescence of separated whorls, each of 8–18 flowers; corolla purple-pink, 15–18mm long, mostly with white centre. Flowers June to September.
SIMILAR SPECIES: Hedge Woundwort, *S. sylvatica*, usually has whorls of 6 flowers and dark purple corolla 12–15mm long.
HABITAT: Tall herb and nutrient-rich vegetation, open woods. To 2,100m.
DISTRIBUTION: European, from Spain and Wales to Turkey.

2 | Large-lipped Upright (Perennial Yellow) Woundwort
Stachys recta subsp. *labiosa* – Lamiaceae (Syn.: *Stachys labiosa*; *S. recta* subsp. *grandiflora*)

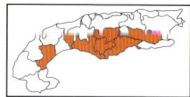

20–50cm tall; middle and upper stem leaves with blades 2.5–3x as long as broad, with more than 5 teeth on each side; lower whorls with 4–10 flowers; upper corolla lip ± ½ as long as lower lip. Flowers June to October.
SIMILAR SPECIES: The 2 other alpine subspecies:
– Upright (Perennial Yellow) Woundwort, *S. recta* subsp. *recta*, has lower whorls with 10–14 flowers, and upper corolla lip ± ⅔ as long as lower lip.
– Dalmatian Woundwort, *S. recta* subsp. *subcrenata*, has middle and upper stem leaves with blades 4x as long as broad, with at most 5 teeth on each side.
HABITAT: Scree, warmth-loving; calcicole. To 2,100m.
DISTRIBUTION: Alpine–Apennine.

3 | Wall Germander
Teucrium chamaedrys – Lamiaceae

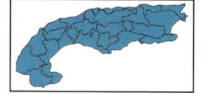

10–25cm tall; woody at base; leaves oval, rough, 1–2.5cm long, with coarsely-toothed margins; corolla pink, 10–15mm long, without upper lip. Flowers June to August.
SIMILAR SPECIES: Water Germander, *T. scordium*, grows in wet sites, has 0.6–1cm long flowers and the leaves smell of garlic.
HABITAT: Dry grassland, stony sward, open dry woods; calcicole. To 1,900m.
DISTRIBUTION: Mediterranean, north to France and Poland.

4 | Mountain Germander
Teucrium montanum – Lamiaceae

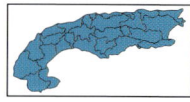

5–20cm tall; prostrate and spreading, with woody base; leaves narrowly lanceolate, 4–8x as long as broad, entire, with down-rolled margins, felty white beneath; corolla creamy-white. Flowers June to August.
SIMILAR SPECIES: Few.
HABITAT: Stony sward, dry, warm slopes, rocks, open pinewoods; calcicole. To 2,500m.
DISTRIBUTION: Southern European, north to the limestone regions of the lower Rhine.

5 | Pyrenean Germander
Teucrium pyrenaicum – Lamiaceae

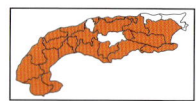

5–25cm tall; leaves oval to round, to 2.5cm long; inflorescence compact; corolla white, with purple markings; calyx 10–12mm long. Flowers June to July.
SIMILAR SPECIES: Few.
HABITAT: Stony sward, rocks, poor meadows; calcicole. 1,400–2,000m.
DISTRIBUTION: Pyrenean–western alpine.

6 | Wood Sage
Teucrium scorodonia – Lamiaceae

25–70cm tall, with runners; leaf blades oval to heart-shaped, 3–7cm long, 1.5–4.5cm broad, ± 1.5–2x as long as broad, with reticulate veins, wrinkled; inflorescence nodding unilaterally; corolla pale yellow, without upper lip. Flowers July to August.
SIMILAR SPECIES: Upright Woundwort, *Stachys recta*, has an upper lip, and leaves 2–4x as long as broad.
HABITAT: Open woods, transitional habitats, heaths; calcifuge. To 1,600m.
DISTRIBUTION: Western European.

Lamiaceae, Lentibulariaceae

1 | Hairy Wild Thyme
Thymus praecox subsp. *polytrichus*
– Lamiaceae

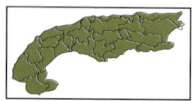

2–10cm tall, mat-forming, creeping; flowering stem rectangular to almost round, not furrowed, hairy or hairier on 2 sides only. Flowers May to September.
SIMILAR SPECIES: Early Wild Thyme, *T. praecox* subsp. *praecox*, has flowering stem hairy all round, although sometimes less hairy on 2 sides. Large Thyme, *T. pulegioides*, a widespread species, is distinguished by the stem under the flower head 4-ridged, with 2 narrower, clearly furrowed sides.
HABITAT: Stony sward, rock debris, poor meadows, To 3,400m.
DISTRIBUTION: Southern European montane.
NOTE: There are several forms of thyme in the Alps that are difficult to distinguish, being very variable and forming hybrids, often making identification problematic.

2 | Large Thyme
Thymus pulegioides – Lamiaceae

5–20cm tall; strongly aromatic, lacking creeping sterile shoots; stem beneath flower head sharply 4-ridged, with 2 narrower, clearly furrowed sides (**2B**), stem hairy only on the ridges or with much longer hairs on ridges than on narrower sides; leaves broadly lanceolate to oval; flower head cylindrical, terminal, on recent shoots. Flowers June to October.
SIMILAR SPECIES: The other common alpine thyme species do not have furrowed stems. Common Thyme, *T. vulgaris*, a Mediterranean species found in the southern and western Alps has shrub-like growth and has narrow leaves with down-rolled margins.
HABITAT: Semi-arid grassland, dwarf shrub heath. To about 2,800m.
DISTRIBUTION: European.

3 | Alpine Butterwort
Pinguicula alpina – Lentibulariaceae

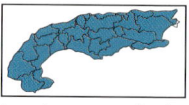

5–15cm tall; insectivorous, like all butterworts, snaring and digesting small insects as a supply of extra nitrogen; leaves in a basal rosette, oval, yellow-green, with edges upturned, the surface sticky and glandular; corolla white, with yellow throat spot; spur 2–4mm long; fruit ± 3x as long as broad. Flowers May to July.
SIMILAR SPECIES: None.
HABITAT: Wet rocks, damp stony grassland, fens; calcicole. To about 2,700m.
DISTRIBUTION: Arctic–alpine.

4 | Southern Butterwort
Pinguicula leptoceras – Lentibulariaceae

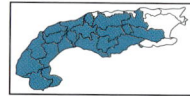

5–15cm tall; leaves in a basal rosette, oval, yellow-green, with edges upturned, the surface sticky and glandular; lower sepals divided to the base; corolla 20–30mm long, blue-violet, with white throat spot; lower lobe of corolla ± as long as broad; spur 4–6mm long; fruit almost spherical, 1.5–2x as long as broad. Flowers May to July.
SIMILAR SPECIES: Common Butterwort, *P. vulgaris*, has corolla 16–22mm long, lower corolla lobe longer than broad, and fruit 2–2.5x as long as broad. Large-flowered Butterwort, *P. grandiflora*, a western alpine species, has a 20–35mm long corolla with a 10–14mm long spur.
HABITAT: Spring mires, wet meadows, peat ridges. 1,200–3,000m, sometimes lower, as in the Mesolcina Valley (Misox), Switzerland (350m).
DISTRIBUTION: Alpine–Apennine.
NOTE: In addition to the 4 butterworts described above, there are 4 more species of limited distribution:
– *P. arvetii*: French western alpine endemic.
– *P. hirtiflora*: Mediterranean-montane, in the Alps only in the French Maritime Alps.
– *P. poldinii*: Endemic to the Italian province of Pordenone.
– *P. reichenbachiana*: Apennine–western alpine, in the south-western Alps.

Linaceae, Linnaeaceae, Menyanthaceae

1 | Alpine Flax
Linum alpinum – Linaceae

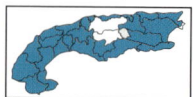

10–30cm tall; upright or ascending; stem densely leafy; leaves linear-lanceolate, to 2.5cm long and 1–2mm broad; stem usually with 1–8 flowers; flower buds nodding; petals blue, 12–18mm long; stigmas oval; fruit stalk upright and protruding. Flowers June to July.
SIMILAR SPECIES: Narbonne Flax, *L. narbonense*, has upright flower buds, 25–35mm long petals and narrow, club-shaped stigmas. Austrian Flax, *L. austriacum*, is 30–60cm tall, with downwardly curved fruit stalk.
HABITAT: Stony sward, rock debris, stony poor grassland; calcicole. 1,400–2,200m, occasionally lower, as near Hohenberg, Lower Austria (480m).
DISTRIBUTION: Southern European montane.
NOTE: In addition to the flax species described here there are also yellow-flowered species in the alpine lowlands:
- Bell-flowered Yellow Flax, *L. campanulatum*: Mediterranean species, north to the south-western Alps.
- Yellow Flax, *L. flavum*: South-eastern European species, west to the eastern Alps.
- Sea Flax, *L. maritimum*: Mediterranean species, also in lower regions of the French Alps.
- Upright Flax, *L. strictum*: Mediterranean species, also in lower regions of the south-western Alps.
- French Flax, *L. trigynum*: Mediterranean species, north to the southern Alps.

2 | White Flax (Pyrenean Flax)
Linum suffruticosum – Linaceae

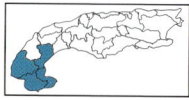

5–30cm tall, much-branched, with woody base and short sterile and longer flowering shoots; leaves linear, with rough edges with tiny bristles; sepals 3-veined; petals 15–25mm long, white, with pink or pale violet base. Flowers May to July.
SIMILAR SPECIES: Narrow-leaved Flax, *L. tenuifolium*, has single-veined sepals, and 10–15mm long petals.
HABITAT: Rock debris, stony dry grassland; calcicole. To about 1,900m.
DISTRIBUTION: Western Mediterranean.

3 | Sticky Flax
Linum viscosum – Linaceae

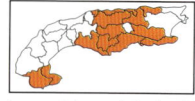

20–60cm tall; stem round, with erect shaggy white hairs; leaves broadly lanceolate, pointed, with 3–5 veins, with glandular ciliate hairs at margin; flowers clustered in racemes; sepals with glandular ciliate hairs; petals 17–22mm long, bright pink, with darker veins. Flowers May to July.
SIMILAR SPECIES: Hairy Flax, *L. hirsutum*, has lilac-blue flowers, and usually glandless sepals. White Flax, *L. suffruticosum*, has white petals with a lilac base, and in the Alps is restricted to the south-western Alps.
HABITAT: Calcareous meadows, transitional habitats, open pinewoods, and forest clearings; warmth-loving. To 1,900m.
DISTRIBUTION: Southern European montane, from the Iberian peninsula to Zala County, Hungary.

4 | Twinflower
Linnaea borealis – Linnaeaceae

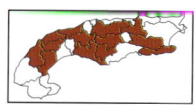

5–15cm tall; leaf stalks 1–3mm long; leaf blade round-ovate, notched in upper half; flowers nodding, mostly paired, sweet-smelling, white to pale pink. Flowers June to August.
SIMILAR SPECIES: None.
HABITAT: Mossy coniferous and rocky woods; calcifuge. 700–2,200m.
DISTRIBUTION: Eurosiberian–North American.

5 | Bogbean
Menyanthes trifoliata – Menyanthaceae

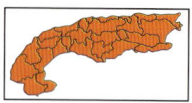

10–30cm tall (above water); rhizome creeping and branched; leaves trifoliate; inflorescence a raceme of 10–20 flowers; corolla white, inner surface of petals bearded. Flowers April to June.
SIMILAR SPECIES: None.
HABITAT: Calcium-poor spring mires and fens, marshy pool margins, raised bog pools. To 2,400m.
DISTRIBUTION: European-Asiatic–North American.

Myrsinaceae, Onagraceae

1 | Alpine Cyclamen
Cyclamen purpurascens – Myrsinaceae

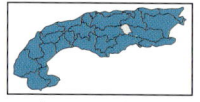

5–15cm tall; leaf blades kidney- to heart-shaped, dark green above, with pale green markings, purple beneath, long-stalked; petals purple, flowers fragrant. Flowers June to October.
SIMILAR SPECIES: When not flowering, may be confused with European Wild Ginger (Asarabacca), *Asarum europaeum*, which has unmarked leaves, green beneath.
HABITAT: Deciduous woods. To 1,800m, sometimes higher, as on Monte Conca, Italy (1,950m).
DISTRIBUTION: Southern European montane, from the Jura and Provence to the Carpathians.

2 | Yellow Pimpernel
Lysimachia nemorum – Myrsinaceae

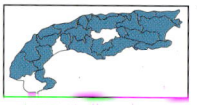

3–15cm tall; stem prostrate to ascending; leaves broadly lanceolate to oval, ± pointed, 1–3cm long, 1–2.5x as long as broad; flowers solitary in upper leaf axils; corolla yellow, sepals 4–5mm long and 1–2mm broad; corolla lobes 5–9mm long. Flowers May to August.
SIMILAR SPECIES: Creeping-Jenny, *L. nummularia*, has round, blunt leaves, and sepals 7–10mm long and 4–5mm broad.
HABITAT: Damp woods, scrub, forest clearings, stream sides. To 1,700m.
DISTRIBUTION: European, from the Azores and southern Sweden to the Caucasus.

3 | Chickweed-wintergreen
Trientalis europaea – Myrsinaceae

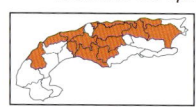

5–20cm tall; hairless; leaves broadly lanceolate, entire, 1.5–5cm long, mostly in terminal whorls; flowers solitary on long, thin stalks; corolla white, spreading, divided almost to the base into 7 pointed lobes. Flowers May to July.
SIMILAR SPECIES: None.
HABITAT: Margins of raised bogs, forested mires, humus-rich acid spruce woods; calcifuge. To 2,000m.
DISTRIBUTION: Eurosiberian–North American, rare, and very scattered in the Alps.

4 | Alpine Enchanter's-nightshade
Circaea alpina – Onagraceae

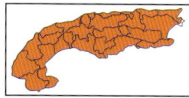

5–20cm tall; stem hairless; leaf blades oval, 1.5–6cm long, heart-shaped at base, margins sharply toothed; petals white, 0.6–1.5mm long; flower stalks with bristly bracts. Flowers June to August.
SIMILAR SPECIES: Enchanter's-nightshade, *C. lutetiana*, is 20–50cm tall and has 2–4mm long petals. Hybrids between both species, *C. x intermedia*, are not uncommon.
HABITAT: Shady, damp montane woods. To 2,150m.
DISTRIBUTION: Eurosiberian–North American.

5 | Whorled-leaved Willowherb
Epilobium alpestre – Onagraceae

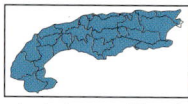

30–80cm tall; stem with 2 opposite lines of hairs; at least the lowest leaves 3(4), in whorls; leaves shiny above, sessile, partially clasping the stem; petals 8–12mm long, pink, with darker veins; stigmas fused into a club shape. Flowers June to August.
SIMILAR SPECIES: Broad-leaved Willowherb, *E. montanum*, has opposite leaves and spreading, star-shaped stigmas. Hill Willowherb, *E. collinum*, has opposite leaves and 4–6mm long petals.
HABITAT: Tall herb and nitrate-enriched vegetation, Green Alder scrub. To 2,400m.
DISTRIBUTION: Southern European montane, east to the Caucasus.
NOTE: Hybrids between willowherb species have often been described and are sometimes not that rare. These can be recognised, among other things, by their stunted seeds. The exceptions are those in the subgenus *Chamaenerion* (*E. angustifolium, E. dodonaei, E. fleischeri*), amongst which no natural hybrids are known to date.

Onagraceae

1 | Chickweed Willowherb
Epilobium alsinifolium – Onagraceae

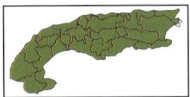

10–30cm tall, with underground stolons; leaves ovate-lanceolate, sessile or with stalks at most 4mm long, shallowly toothed, shiny; axils of inflorescence without glandular hairs; inflorescence 2–6-flowered; petals 8–12mm long; stigmas fused into a club shape; ripe fruit hairless. Flowers July to August.
SIMILAR SPECIES: Nodding Willowherb, *E. nutans*, has mainly entire leaves and densely hairy ripe fruit. Alpine Willowherb, *E. anagallidifolium*, is only 4–12cm tall, with 4–6mm long petals and almost hairless ripe fruit.
HABITAT: Wet patches around springs, tall herb vegetation, streams. 1,000–2,700m.
DISTRIBUTION: Arctic–alpine, from Iceland to northern Russia, and further south to the Pyrenees and the northern Balkans.
NOTE: Willowherbs are larval food plants for, among others, Dusky Hawk-moth, *Hyles vespertilio*, and Willowherb Hawk-moth, *Proserpinus proserpina*. Their flowers are regularly visited by leafcutter bees such as *Megachile willughbiella* and *M. lapponica*.

2 | Alpine Willowherb
Epilobium anagallidifolium – Onagraceae

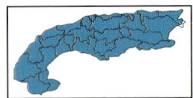

4–12cm tall, with above-ground stolons and unbranched stems, mostly patch-forming; hairless, just the upper stem with 2 or 4 longitudinal rows of hairs; leaves 1–2cm long, elliptical to elongate-lanceolate, opposite, with very short stalks (1–2mm); leaf margin entire or indistinctly toothed; inflorescence 1–6-flowered, ± nodding; petals pink, 4–6mm long, deeply notched; stigmas fused into a club shape; ovary and fruit very loosely glandular-hairy to almost hairless. Flowers June to August.
SIMILAR SPECIES: Nodding Willowherb, *E. nutans*, has mostly single shoots (not patch-forming) and ovary and fruit with dense non-glandular appressed hairs.
HABITAT: Wet patches around springs, damp rock debris; calcifuge. 1,300–3,100m.
DISTRIBUTION: Arctic–alpine, from Iceland to Siberia and the Altai region, and south to the Pyrenees and Caucasus; North America.

3 | Rosebay Willowherb
Epilobium angustifolium – Onagraceae

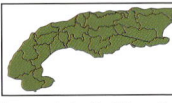

60–130cm tall, hairless; leaves alternate, sessile, or short-stalked, narrowly lanceolate, 8–15cm long, 1–2.5cm broad; raceme 20–50cm long. Flowers June to August.
SIMILAR SPECIES: None.
HABITAT: Forest clearings and margins, river sides, heaths. To 2,500m.
DISTRIBUTION: Eurosiberian–North American.

4 | Rosemary Willowherb
Epilobium dodonaei – Onagraceae

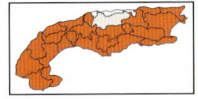

30–90cm tall, upright; leaves linear, 1–4mm broad, entire to distantly toothed, margins rolled under; calyx with dense appressed hairs. Flowers June to October.
SIMILAR SPECIES: Fleischer's Willowherb, *E. fleischeri*.
HABITAT: River gravel, quarries, lake shore gravel, gravel pits; calcicole. To 1,800m.
DISTRIBUTION: Southern European–western Asiatic.
NAME: After Flemish botanist and doctor Rembert Dodoens (1517–1585), in the Latin form Dodoneus. Dodoens was Court Physician to Emperor Maximilian II.

5 | Fleischer's Willowherb
Epilobium fleischeri – Onagraceae

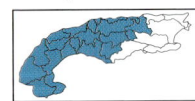

10–40cm tall; prostrate to ascending; leaves linear-lanceolate, 2–6mm broad, hairless, with small teeth, margins not rolled under; flowers purple, 4-partite; seeds with white silky plumes. Flowers June to August.
SIMILAR SPECIES: Rosemary Willowherb, *E. dodonaei*, has upright stem and leaves with down-rolled margins.
HABITAT: Intermittently dry stream and river gravel, gravel banks and moraine debris; calcifuge. 500–2,600m.
DISTRIBUTION: Alpine endemic.
NAME: In honour of German doctor Franz von Fleischer (1801–1878), who went on a botanical expedition through the Tyrol in 1825 and discovered the new species in the Sulden Valley, South Tyrol, Italy.

Orobanchaceae

1 | Carinthian Eyebright
Euphrasia cuspidata – Orobanchaceae

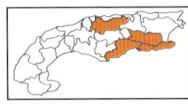

5–20cm tall; leaves narrow, 15–25mm long, 2–6mm broad, including the teeth; bracts, excluding teeth, 5–8x as long as broad; with 1–2 teeth on each side; corolla 8–10mm long. Flowers July to September.
SIMILAR SPECIES: Salzburg Eyebright, *E. salisburgensis*. Three-toothed Eyebright, *E. tricuspidata*, has bracts, excluding teeth, 6–15x as long as broad and only a single tooth on each side, immediately below the tip.
HABITAT: Calcareous rocky sward, stony grassland; calcicole. To about 1,800m.
DISTRIBUTION: Eastern alpine–Illyrian.
NOTE: Eyebright species are often hard to identify.

2 | Dwarf Eyebright
Euphrasia minima – Orobanchaceae

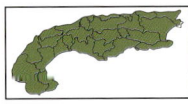

2–15cm tall; leaves with 1–4 unawned teeth on each side; corolla 5–7mm long, white or yellow, enlarging only slightly or not at all when flowering; style strongly curved from the start of flowering. Flowers July to September.
SIMILAR SPECIES: Christ's Eyebright, *E. christii*, has a yellow corolla 9–11mm long and bracts with awned teeth. Endemic to south Switzerland and adjacent Italy.
HABITAT: Curved Alpine Sedge (*Carex curvula*) vegetation, pasture; calcifuge. About 1,200–3,200m.
DISTRIBUTION: Southern European montane.

3 | Common Eyebright
Euphrasia officinalis – Orobanchaceae
(incl. *E. rostkoviana*)

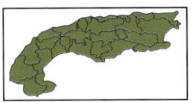

5–25cm tall; leaves oval, as long as broad or somewhat longer; bracts with 2–6 scarcely awned teeth on each side; corolla 8–14mm long, white, with yellow and violet markings, enlarging during flowering. Lower corolla lip at most 1½x as long as upper lip. Flowers May to October.
SIMILAR SPECIES: Alpine Speedwell, *Veronica alpina* (see p. 288), has a lilac lower lip to corolla, at least 1½x as long as upper lip, and bracts with 0.5–1.5mm long awns. Tessin Eyebright, *E. cisalpina*, has awns 1.5–3mm long on teeth of bracts.
HABITAT: Pasture, poor grassland. To about 2,800m.
DISTRIBUTION: European.
NOTE: 2 subspecies in the Alps:
– subsp. *rostkoviana*: leaves and bracts with glandular hairs.
– subsp. *picta*: leaves and bracts without glandular hairs, rarely with sessile glands.

4 | Salzburg Eyebright
Euphrasia salisburgensis – Orobanchaceae

4–20cm tall; internodes 2–3x as long as leaves; leaves with 2–5 teeth each side, those of basal leaves blunt, increasingly pointed towards the top, and awned; leaves often suffused purple; middle leaves 2–4x as long as broad; bracts with mostly 3 teeth on each side; corolla 5–7.5mm long. Flowers June to September.
SIMILAR SPECIES: South Tyrol Eyebright, *E. portae*, has a 7.5–9mm long corolla and internodes 1–2x as long as leaves. Carinthian Eyebright, *E. cuspidata*, has bracts with 1–2 teeth on each side, and corolla 8–10mm long.
HABITAT: Calcareous rocky sward, poor grassland; calcicole. To 3,300m.
DISTRIBUTION: Southern European montane.

5 | Short-haired Eyebright
Euphrasia stricta – Orobanchaceae
(incl. *E. pectinata*)

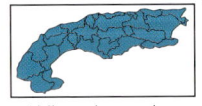

5–30cm tall, stem and leaves hairless or with short hairs, usually suffused purple; middle and upper leaves with 3–7 pointed teeth on each side, teeth of upper bracts noticeably awned; corolla 7–10mm long, usually with purple markings, not or only slightly enlarging during flowering; style curved during flowering. Flowers July to October.
SIMILAR SPECIES: Hairy Eyebright, *E. hirtella*, has a 4–7mm long corolla and style curved from the start of flowering.
HABITAT: Semi-arid grassland, poor pasture, prefers open, disturbed vegetation. To about 2,100m.
DISTRIBUTION: Eurosiberian.

Orobanchaceae

1 | Alpine Bartsia
Bartsia alpina – Orobanchaceae

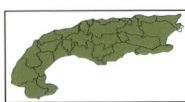

5–20cm tall; leaves opposite, oval, upper leaves suffused dark violet; corolla 15–22mm long, dark violet, as is calyx; lower lip 3-lobed, shorter than upper lip; calyx with glandular hairs. Flowers June to August.
SIMILAR SPECIES: None.
HABITAT: Pasture, stony sward, wet spring flushes, fens. 1,000–3,100m, often washed down to lowlands, as on the Isar, Lech and Ammer rivers.
DISTRIBUTION: Arctic–alpine.
NAME: In honour of German botanist and doctor Johann Bartsch (1709–1738), a close friend of Linné (Linnaeus), who died at an early age during an expedition to Suriname.

2 | Common Cow-wheat
Melampyrum pratense – Orobanchaceae

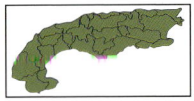

10–50cm tall; leaves lanceolate, entire, 20–100mm long and 2–20mm broad; bracts green, sometimes suffused dark purple; corolla 12–20mm long, pale yellow to rich yellow, often suffused purple, without nectar guides; corolla tube almost straight; calyx at most half as long as corolla tube. Flowers June to September.
SIMILAR SPECIES: Small Cow-wheat, *M. sylvaticum*.
HABITAT: Woods on acid soils, meadows, forest clearings, mires; calcifuge. To about 2,200m.
DISTRIBUTION: Eurosiberian.

3 | East-alpine Cow-wheat
Melampyrum subalpinum – Orobanchaceae (incl. *M. bohemicum* and *M. angustissimum*)

15–50cm tall; leaves lanceolate, 3–15mm broad; upper bracts at least violet; calyx with 0.5–2.5mm long hairs on the main veins and edges, with much shorter hairs between. Flowers June to September.
SIMILAR SPECIES: Wood Cow-wheat, *M. nemorosum*, has 15–35mm broad leaves and calyx with erect hairs also between the veins. Velebit Cow-wheat, *M. velebiticum*, has the longest hairs on the main veins and edges of calyx 0.5mm long.
HABITAT: Dry, open woods, To 1,200m.
DISTRIBUTION: Central European. Eastern edge of the Alps and Czechia.
NOTE: 2 subspecies in the eastern Alps:
– subsp. *subalpinum*: narrow leaves.
– subsp. *thermale*: broad leaves.

4 | Small Cow-wheat
Melampyrum sylvaticum – Orobanchaceae

5–20cm tall; leaves lanceolate, entire, 30–50mm long and 2–10mm broad; bracts green (in sunny sites may be suffused dark purple, (**4B**)); corolla 6–10mm long, usually dark yellow with orange-yellow lower lip and rusty-red nectar guides; corolla tube curved; calyx almost as long as corolla tube; calyx teeth spreading. Flowers June to September.
SIMILAR SPECIES: Common Cow-wheat, *M. pratense*, has a 12–20mm long white to yellow corolla, often suffused purple, an almost straight corolla tube, and calyx at most half as long as corolla tube.
HABITAT: Coniferous woods on acid soils, mires, pasture. To about 2,400m.
DISTRIBUTION: European, from Iceland and the Pyrenees to the Urals.

5 | Alpine Tozzia
Tozzia alpina – Orobanchaceae

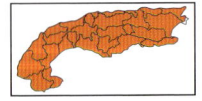

15–40cm tall; stem rectangular, with 2 rows of hairs; leaves oval, upper leaves with 1–3 coarse teeth; corolla 5–9mm long, yellow, with red spots. Flowers June to July.
SIMILAR SPECIES: Few.
HABITAT: Tall herb vegetation, Green Alder scrub. Mainly semi-parasitic on butterburs (*Petasites*), adenostyles (*Adenostyles*) and docks (*Rumex*). 800–2,400m.
DISTRIBUTION: Southern European montane.
NAME: In honour of Italian botanist and monk Bruno Tozzi (1656–1743), who published a work on Tuscan plants in 1703.

Orobanchaceae

1 | Thyme Broomrape
Orobanche alba – Orobanchaceae

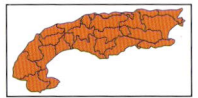

10–30cm tall; calyx lobes mostly simple; corolla pale yellowish-brown (never white, despite the species name), with violet veins, reddish towards the edge, with dark glandular hairs; stigma purple to reddish-brown; filaments inserted 1–2mm above base of corolla tube. Flowers May to July. Parasitic mainly on *Thymus*, but also on other labiates such as *Origanum* and *Clinopodium*.
SIMILAR SPECIES: Germander Broomrape, *O. teucrii*, has corolla with pale glandular hairs, and filaments inserted 3–5mm above base of corolla tube.
HABITAT: Dry grassland. To 2,200m.
DISTRIBUTION: European-Asiatic.
NOTE: The seeds of broomrapes are tiny, and contain an even tinier embryo and some nutrient tissue, sufficient for growing a few millimetres, after which a host must be found, since all broomrape species are parasitic. This explains the high seed production, with each fruit capsule able to produce thousands of seeds, which can remain in the soil for years or decades without losing their ability to germinate. Germination is triggered by inducers secreted by the roots of the host plants.

2 | Bedstraw Broomrape
Orobanche caryophyllacea – Orobanchaceae

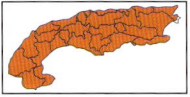

20–50cm tall, with scent of cloves; calyx 2-lobed; corolla pale yellow to pink or pale reddish-brown, with pale glandular hairs; stigma purple to reddish-brown; filaments inserted 1–2mm above base of corolla tube. Flowers May to July. Parasitic on *Galium* and *Asperula*.
SIMILAR SPECIES: Greater Broomrape, *O. rapum-genistae*, has a yellow stigma and is parasitic on *Cytisus* and other legumes.
HABITAT: Dry meadows. To about 2,000m.
DISTRIBUTION: European-Asiatic.

3 | Butterbur Broomrape
Orobanche flava – Orobanchaceae

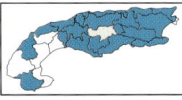

15–40cm tall; calyx undivided or very unevenly 2-lobed; corolla pale yellow to pale orange-brown, 15–22mm long, ± evenly curved; upper and lower lip with pale glandular hairs; stigma yellow; style hairless or sparsely glandular; filaments with glandular hairs towards the top, and inserted 4–6mm above base of corolla tube. Flowers June to July. Parasitic mainly on *Petasites*, especially Alpine Butterbur, *P. paradoxus* (see p. 86), but also on other composites such as *Adenostyles* and *Tussilago*.
SIMILAR SPECIES: Laserwort Broomrape, *O. laserpitii-sileris*, is parasitic only on Laserwort, *Laserpitium siler*, has a 22–30mm long corolla, and style with dense glandular hairs. Monk's-hood Broomrape, *O. lycoctoni* (see p. 266) is parasitic only on Wolfsbane, *Aconitum lycoctonum* agg., has a yellowish-white corolla with hairless upper and lower lips. Barberry Broomrape, *O. lucorum*, is mainly parasitic on *Berberis*, and more rarely on *Rubus*, and has filaments inserted 0–2mm above base of corolla tube.
HABITAT: Stony sward; calcicole. To about 2,000m.
DISTRIBUTION: Southern European montane.

4 | Slender Broomrape
Orobanche gracilis – Orobanchaceae

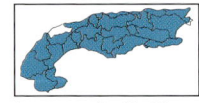

10–50cm tall; flowers with scent of cloves; calyx lobes free or somewhat fused at base; corolla 15–22mm long, shiny and dark red inside, yellow outside, edged reddish-brown; stigma yellow, edged purple; style glandular-hairy; filaments with glandular hairs towards the top, inserted 0–2mm above base of corolla tube. Flowers May to August. Parasitic on various legumes, Fabaceae.
SIMILAR SPECIES: Variegated Broomrape, *O. variegata*, has flowers with an unpleasant smell.
HABITAT: Semi-arid grassland. To about 1,900m.
DISTRIBUTION: Southern European.
NOTE: This species, as do a few other broomrape species, occasionally produces uniformly yellow plants.

Orobanchaceae

1 | Yellow Broomrape
Orobanche lutea – Orobanchaceae

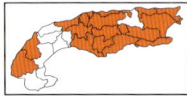

20–50cm tall; stem usually darker than corolla; calyx divided into 2 ± free halves; corolla 25–30mm long, light yellow to pale reddish-brown, fragrant, with pale glandular hairs; back of corolla tube straight, curving downwards along edges; stigma yellow; filaments inserted 3–6mm above base of corolla tube, with glandular hairs towards the top. Flowers May to June. Parasitic on legumes, Fabaceae, especially *Medicago*.
SIMILAR SPECIES: Germander Broomrape, *O. teuchrii*, has a brownish-red stigma and is parasitic on labiates, Lamiaceae.
HABITAT: Dry grassland; calcicole. To 1,600m.
DISTRIBUTION: European-Asiatic.
NOTE: Broomrapes are fully parasitic and lack features useful for separating species, such as normal leaves or true roots, making identification often difficult. Flower colour and also the colour of the entire plant can vary, as can the hairiness. Identifying the host plant is often a great help, as broomrapes are all more or less specialised on a particular host. Out of around 200 known species of broomrape, 27 (including the subgenus *Phelipanche*) are found in the Alps. The centre of distribution of the genus is in the warm temperate regions of the northern hemisphere.

2 | Monk's-hood Broomrape
Orobanche lycoctoni – Orobanchaceae

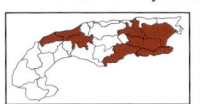

20–50cm tall; corolla pale yellow to whitish, abruptly curved distally; upper and lower lips hairless; stigma yellow. Flowers June to August. Parasitic only on Wolfsbane, *Aconitum lycoctonum* agg.
SIMILAR SPECIES: Butterbur Broomrape, *O. flava* (see p. 264).
HABITAT: Stabilised scree, tall herb vegetation, stony grassland; calcicole. To about 2,000m.
DISTRIBUTION: Southern European montane. Known from northern Spain and the Alps, but probably more widespread.
NOTE: The species was often confused with Butterbur Broomrape, *Orobanche flava*, or regarded as a variety of that species. The distribution map is therefore certainly incomplete, and new sites are being discovered, such as those in 2016 for the State of Salzburg.

3 | Thistle Broomrape
Orobanche reticulata – Orobanchaceae

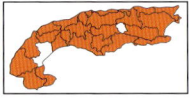

25–70cm tall; calyx simple; corolla pale yellow, purple at the front, with purple veins and dark glandular hairs; stigma purple to reddish-brown; lower styles with non-glandular hairs up to the middle. Flowers June to July. Parasitic on thistles (*Cirsium* and *Carduus*).
SIMILAR SPECIES: Scabious Broomrape, *O. pancicii*, has glandular-hairy upper styles, and is parasitic on members of the scabious family, especially Hungarian Widow-flower, *Knautia drymeia*.
HABITAT: Poor meadows, rocky slopes, riverine woods, warm ruderal sites. To about 2,400m.
DISTRIBUTION: Eurosiberian.
NOTE: 2 subspecies in the Alps:
– subsp. *reticulata*: corolla suffused purple, with dense dark glandular hairs, upper styles glandular; montane to subalpine.
– subsp. *pallidiflora*: corolla only slightly tinged purple, with sparse dark glandular hairs, upper styles almost hairless, foothills.

4 | Sage Broomrape
Orobanche salviae – Orobanchaceae

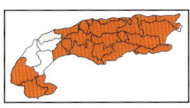

10–50cm tall; calyx with 2 free, undivided or unevenly 2-lobed halves; corolla 12–23mm long, yellow, later becoming brownish; stigma at first yellow, later brown; filaments inserted 0–2mm above base of corolla tube; style with glandular hairs. Flowers June to September. Parasitic on Sticky Sage, *Salvia glutinosa* (see p. 248).
SIMILAR SPECIES: Barberry Broomrape, *O. lucorum*, has a hairless stigma, and parasitises *Berberis* and *Rubus*.
HABITAT: Woods. To about 1,800m.
DISTRIBUTION: Southern European montane, from the western Alps and northern Apennines to the Illyrian mountains, with the Alps the centre of distribution.
NOTE: Sage Broomrape is almost exclusively parasitic on *Salvia glutinosa*, and very rarely also on *Salvia pratensis*. This close relationship with its host makes it relatively easy to identify, although the host plant may be some distance from the Sage Broomrape.

Orobanchaceae

1 | Ascending Lousewort
Pedicularis ascendens – Orobanchaceae

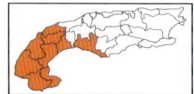

15–30cm tall, arched, ascending; leaves and leaf stalks hairless; leaves simply pinnate, with oval-lanceolate, deeply lobed segments; bracts ciliate, otherwise hairless; inflorescence elongate; outer calyx hairless, calyx lobes entire or weakly shallow-toothed, almost as long as calyx tube; corolla straw yellow, with beaked upper lip. Flowers June to August.
SIMILAR SPECIES: Long-beaked Yellow Lousewort, *P. tuberosa* (see p. 274), has a more compact inflorescence and hairy leaf stalks.
HABITAT: Montane meadows, pasture; calcicole. About 1,600–2,600m.
DISTRIBUTION: Western alpine–Apennine, east to the province of Brescia, Italy.
NOTE: Louseworts are semi-parasites that are able to rely on a wide variety of host species.

2 | Fern-leaved Lousewort
Pedicularis aspleniifolia – Orobanchaceae

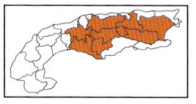

3–8cm tall, one flowering stem per leaf rosette; leaves 2–4cm long; inflorescence 2–5-flowered; calyx woolly, hairs 1–2mm long; corolla 13–17mm long, corolla tube as long as calyx; corolla upper lip with 4–6mm long beak, lower lip distinctly twisted. Flowers July to August.
SIMILAR SPECIES: Portenschlag's Lousewort, *P. portenschlagii* (see p. 272), and Kerner's Lousewort, *P. kerneri* (see p. 270).
HABITAT: Poor grassland, rocky sward. 1,900–2,800m.
DISTRIBUTION: Eastern alpine endemic.

3 | Crested Lousewort
Pedicularis comosa – Orobanchaceae

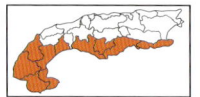

20–50cm tall; leaves 2-pinnate; inflorescence compact; calyx 5-lobed, toothed, hairy; corolla pale yellow, 20–25mm long, with short, 2-lobed beak. Flowers June to July.
SIMILAR SPECIES: Karst Lousewort, *P. hacquetii* (see p. 270), has a leathery calyx, divided down to the middle.
HABITAT: Montane meadows. 1,400–2,400m.
DISTRIBUTION: Southern European montane.

4 | Tall Lousewort
Pedicularis elongata – Orobanchaceae

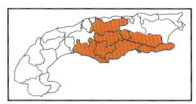

15–30cm tall; stem with 2–3 rows of hairs at base (**4B**); leaves simply pinnate, hairless, segments notched or almost entire; inflorescence notably longer than broad, even at start of flowering; bracts hairless or ciliate; calyx hairless on the outside, calyx lobes leaf-like, clearly toothed, with downy hairs inside; corolla 12–16mm long. Flowers June to August.
SIMILAR SPECIES: Julian Lousewort, *P. julica*, has bracts hairy on the outside, and outer calyx and leaf segments notched. Ascending Lousewort, *P. ascendens*, has entire to slightly undulate calyx lobes, as does Long-beaked Yellow Lousewort, *P. tuberosa* (see p. 274).
HABITAT: Poor grassland, open Dwarf Mountain Pine scrub; calcicole. About 1,300–2,600m.
DISTRIBUTION: Eastern alpine endemic.

5 | Leafy Lousewort
Pedicularis foliosa – Orobanchaceae

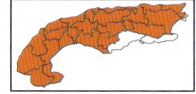

15–50cm tall; leaves 2–3-pinnate, 8–30cm long and 3–10cm broad; bracts longer than flowers, hairless or with short hairs at base, lower bracts resembling stem leaves; calyx membranous, not split, clearly 5-toothed; upper corolla lip with dense shaggy hairs. Flowers June to July.
SIMILAR SPECIES: Karst Lousewort, *P. hacquetii* (see p. 270), has a leathery calyx, divided to the middle, base of bracts with shaggy hairs, and upper corolla lip sparsely hairy or hairless. Hoermann's Lousewort, *P. hoermanniana* (see p. 270), is 40–90cm tall, with leathery calyx and upper corolla lip with short, downy hairs.
HABITAT: Rusty sedge (*Carex ferruginea*) sward, tall herb vegetation, Green Alder scrub; calcicole. 700–2,500m.
DISTRIBUTION: Southern European montane.

Orobanchaceae

1 | Tufted Lousewort
Pedicularis gyroflexa – Orobanchaceae

15–25cm tall, evenly and densely covered in short hairs; leaves 7–20cm long; inflorescence at first compact, later spike-like; bracts extending beyond calyx; calyx 10–15mm long, usually densely downy; calyx lobes ± as long as calyx tube, not reflexed; corolla 20–28mm long, upper lip with 2–3mm long beak. Flowers June to July.

SIMILAR SPECIES: Beaked Lousewort, *P. rostratocapitata* (see p. 274).
HABITAT: Stony slopes, pasture, rocky sward; calcicole. 1,300–2,800m.
DISTRIBUTION: Alpine endemic. Reported but not confirmed from the Pyrenees.
NOTE: Several lousewort species hybridise with other louseworts. Examples are: *Pedicularis x bohatschii* (= *P. elongata* x *P. rostratocapitata*), and *Pedicularis x erubescens* (= *P. rostratocapitata* x *P. tuberosa*). Very rare, and especially pretty, is *Pedicularis x pennina*, the hybrid of *P. recutita* x *P. rostratospicata*.

2 | Karst Lousewort
Pedicularis hacquetii – Orobanchaceae

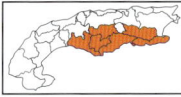

40–90cm tall; leaves 2–3-pinnate, 8–30cm long and 3–10cm broad; bracts with shaggy hairs at base, extending well beyond the flowers, lower bracts resembling stem leaves; calyx leathery, divided down to the middle; upper corolla lip hairless to sparsely hairy. Flowers June to July.

SIMILAR SPECIES: Leafy Lousewort, *P. foliosa* (see p. 268), Hoermann's Lousewort, *P. hoermanniana*.
HABITAT: Tall herb vegetation, meadows, coarse rocky sward; calcicole. About 1,100–1,900m.
DISTRIBUTION: Eastern alpine–Carpathian.
NAME: In honour of naturalist Balthasar Hacquet (1739–1815), who studied the flora and mineralogy of Carinthia and Carniola.

3 | Hoermann's Lousewort
Pedicularis hoermanniana – Orobanchaceae

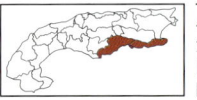

40–90cm tall; leaves 2–3-pinnate, 10–30cm long and 3–10cm broad; bracts extending well beyond flowers; calyx leathery, not divided, distinctly 5-lobed; corolla 18–25mm long, pale yellow; inflorescence axes with white woolly hairs; upper lip of corolla with short, downy hairs. Flowers June to July.

SIMILAR SPECIES: Leafy Lousewort, *P. foliosa* (see p. 268). Karst Lousewort, *P. hacquetii*, has calyx divided down to the middle.
HABITAT: Montane meadows, open scrub; calcicole. About 800–1,900m.
DISTRIBUTION: South-eastern European montane, from the south-eastern Alps to the mountains of south-western Bulgaria.
NAME: In honour of Bosnian scientist Kosta Hörmann (1850–1921), founder of the State Museum in Sarajevo.

4 | Kerner's Lousewort
Pedicularis kerneri – Orobanchaceae

3–10cm tall, prostrate to ascending, with 2–4 inflorescences per leaf rosette; leaves ± hairless, usually suffused dark purple; inflorescence 1–4-flowered; calyx evenly short and downy-hairy over entire surface, rarely hairless; corolla 17–20mm long; corolla tube about 1¼x as long as calyx. Flowers July to August.

SIMILAR SPECIES: Portenschlag's Lousewort, *P. portenschlagii* (see p. 272), has calyx with short ciliate hairs and downy hairs on the veins, but otherwise hairless, corolla 21–30mm long, and corolla tube 1½–2x as long as calyx. Fern-leaved Lousewort, *P. aspleniifolia* (see p. 268), has a shaggy woolly calyx, corolla tube as long as calyx, and a 2–6-flowered inflorescence.
HABITAT: Poor, acidic grassland, vegetated scree; calcifuge. 1,800–3,200m.
DISTRIBUTION: Alpine–Pyrenean.
NAME: In honour of Lower Austrian botanist Anton Joseph Kerner von Marilaun (1831–1898), who was greatly respected for his research into difficult genera such as *Rosa* and *Salix*, and their hybrids.

Orobanchaceae

1 | Oeder's Lousewort (Crimson-tipped Lousewort)
Pedicularis oederi – Orobanchaceae

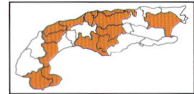

5–15cm tall; stem with 4 rows of hairs to hairless; leaves simply pinnate, lobes notched to serrated; bracts not extending beyond flowers; corolla yellow, upper lip with brown tip; fruit capsule about twice as long as calyx. Flowers June to August.

SIMILAR SPECIES: The other alpine, yellow-flowered louseworts lack the brown tip to the upper lip.
HABITAT: Stony sward. 1,600–2,600m.
DISTRIBUTION: Arctic–alpine. Arctic regions of Europe and America and the high mountains of the cool temperate zones.
NAME: In honour of German naturalist Georg Cristian von Oeder (1728–1791) who was Governor in Oldenburg, Schleswig-Holstein, and a contributor to *Flora Danica*.

2 | Marsh Lousewort (Red-rattle)
Pedicularis palustris – Orobanchaceae

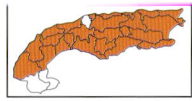

15–50cm tall, ± hairless, branching; lateral flowering stalks arching upwards; inflorescence 10–20-flowered; calyx deeply 2-lobed; corolla 18–25mm long, lower lip as long as upper lip; upper lip with a pointed tooth on each side. Flowers May to July.

SIMILAR SPECIES: Common Lousewort, *P. sylvatica*, is 5–15cm tall, with calyx unevenly 5-lobed, and inflorescence 3–10-flowered.
HABITAT: Fens and intermediate mires, marshy meadows. To 2,300m.
DISTRIBUTION: Eurosiberian–North American.

3 | Portenschlag's Lousewort (Tauern Lousewort)
Pedicularis portenschlagii – Orobanchaceae

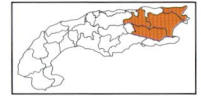

2–8cm tall, with a single inflorescence per leaf rosette; stem with 1–2 rows of hairs, otherwise hairless; inflorescence 1–3-flowered; calyx with short ciliate hairs, downy hairs along veins, otherwise hairless; corolla 21–30mm long, corolla tube longer than calyx. Flowers June to July.

SIMILAR SPECIES: Fern-leaved Lousewort, *P. aspleniifolia* (see p. 268), has a shaggy woolly calyx, corolla tube as long as calyx, and 2–6-flowered inflorescence. See also Kerner's Lousewort, *P. kerneri* (see p. 270).
HABITAT: Moderately acidic poor grassland and stony sward. 1,500–2,800m.
DISTRIBUTION: Eastern alpine endemic.
NAME: In honour of Viennese botanist Franz von Portenschlag-Ledermayer (1772–1822), who discovered the plant. His herbarium contained almost all the higher plants of Austria then known.

4 | Beakless Red Lousewort
Pedicularis recutita – Orobanchaceae

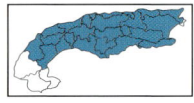

20–50cm tall, hairless; leaves pinnately divided, with toothed lobes, upper leaves often suffused dark purple; flowers in dense, terminal inflorescence; corolla 15–20mm long, yellowish-brownish-red to dark blood-red; Flowers June to July.

SIMILAR SPECIES: Few.
HABITAT: Tall herb vegetation, spring flushes, Green Alder scrub, wet meadows. 1,100–2,600m.
DISTRIBUTION: Alpine endemic.

5 | Pink Lousewort
Pedicularis rosea – Orobanchaceae

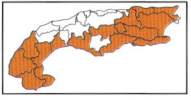

5–15cm tall; leaves elongate-lanceolate, simply pinnate, 5–8cm long, 0.6–1cm broad, often suffused dark purple; calyx woolly-white; corolla dark pink, 12–18mm long. Flowers June to August.

SIMILAR SPECIES: Stemless Lousewort, *P. acaulis*, lacks a stem and has basal flowers. Whorled Lousewort, *P. verticillata* (see p. 274), has stem leaves arranged in whorls.
HABITAT: Stony and rocky sward, Cushion Sedge (*Carex firma*) vegetation. 1,700–2,900m.
DISTRIBUTION: Alpine–Pyrenean.
NOTE: 2 subspecies in the Alps:
– subsp. *rosea* (**5A**): bracts no longer than flowers, 2 long filaments densely hairy. Eastern Alps.
– subsp. *allionii* (**5B**): bracts longer than flowers, filaments hairless or almost so. Western Alps.

Orobanchaceae

1 | Beaked Lousewort
Pedicularis rostratocapitata – Orobanchaceae

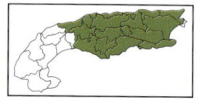

5–20cm tall; stem with 2 lines of hair; leaf blades hairless; inflorescence compact, 3–15-flowered, ± as long as broad; calyx 8–9mm long, usually ciliate and hairy along longitudinal veins, otherwise hairless; calyx lobes reflexed at tips, ± half as long as calyx tube; corolla 16–25mm long, upper lip with 3.5–5mm long beak, lower lip with short ciliate hairs. Flowers June to August.
SIMILAR SPECIES: Tufted Lousewort, *P. gyroflexa* (see p. 270), has a downy calyx, lobes not reflexed, and ± as long as calyx tube. Mount Cenis Lousewort, *P. cenisia* (**1B**), restricted in the Alps to the south-western Alps, has hairless lower corolla lip and hairy leaf blades.
HABITAT: Stony sward; calcicole. 1,300–2,800m.
DISTRIBUTION: South-eastern European montane, from the eastern Alps to the Carpathians and the mountains of the northern Balkan Peninsula.

2 | Flesh-pink Lousewort
Pedicularis rostratospicata – Orobanchaceae

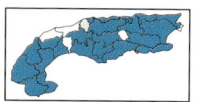

15–40cm tall; stem with 2 rows of hairs; leaves simply pinnate; inflorescence a spike, much longer than broad, with 8–15 flowers; calyx lobes of at least the upper flowers entire; corolla 11–16mm long, upper lip with distinct 4–5mm long beak. Flowers June to August.
SIMILAR SPECIES: Mount Cenis Lousewort, *P. cenisia* (**1B**), native to the south-western Alps, has an 18–25mm long corolla.
HABITAT: Poor grassland, pasture, stony sward; calcicole. About 1,500–2,700m.
DISTRIBUTION: Southern European montane, from the south-western Alps and Apennines to the Carpathians.
NOTE: 2 subspecies in the Alps:
– subsp. *rostratospicata* (**2A**): calyx lobes also of lower flowers entire, calyx and bracts with cobweb hairs.
– subsp. *helvetica* (**2B**): calyx lobes of lower flowers serrated, calyx and bracts with shaggy hairs.

3 | Moor-king Lousewort
Pedicularis sceptrum-carolinum – Orobanchaceae

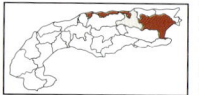

20–80cm tall; leaves 12–20cm long and 4cm broad; inflorescence 6–18-flowered; corolla yellow, 28–35mm long, lower lip edged red, upper lip not beaked; corolla throat almost closed by the adjacent lower lip. Flowers June to July.
SIMILAR SPECIES: Few.
HABITAT: Fens. 500–800m.
DISTRIBUTION: Eurosiberian, from Bavaria and Mecklenburg to Japan.

4 | Long-beaked Yellow Lousewort (Tuberous Lousewort)
Pedicularis tuberosa – Orobanchaceae

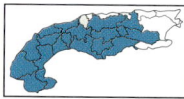

10–20cm tall; stem arching upwards, at base with woolly hairs on all sides; leaves hairless or sparsely hairy beneath; inflorescence at start of flowering ± as long as broad; calyx hairy on outside, lobes hairless inside, upper corolla lip extended into an obvious beak. Flowers June to July.
SIMILAR SPECIES: Tall Lousewort, *P. elongata* (see p. 268), has stem base also with 2–3 lines of hairs, insides of calyx lobes with downy hairs, and inflorescence longer than broad right from the start of flowering. Ascending Lousewort, *P. ascendens* (see p. 268), has hairless leaves and leaf stalks, and hairless outer calyx.
HABITAT: Poor acidic grassland, pasture. About 1,500–2,900m.
DISTRIBUTION: Southern European montane.

5 | Whorled Lousewort
Pedicularis verticillata – Orobanchaceae

5–20cm tall; leaves simply divided, basal and stem leaves mostly in whorls of 4; corolla 12–16mm long, upper lip blunt, not beaked. Flowers June to August.
SIMILAR SPECIES: Pink Lousewort, *P. rosea* (see p. 272). Beaked Lousewort, *P. rostratocapitata*, has beaked upper lip and stem leaves not whorled.
HABITAT: Poor grassland, pasture, spring flushes. 1,100–2,800m.
DISTRIBUTION: Arctic–alpine.

Orobanchaceae

1 | Greater Yellow-rattle
Rhinanthus alectorolophus – Orobanchaceae

10–60cm tall; bracts with teeth of almost equal length, not ciliate; calyx with dense non-glandular hairs; lobes of upper corolla lip usually bluish, 0.8–2.5mm long, distinctly longer than broad; corolla tube curved upwards. Flowers May to August.

SIMILAR SPECIES: Ancient Yellow-rattle, *R. antiquus*, has bract teeth with long ciliate hairs.
HABITAT: meadows; calcicole. To about 2,600m.
DISTRIBUTION: European.
NOTE: 3 subspecies in the Alps:
– subsp. *alectorolophus*: lower corolla lip close to upper lip, covering the throat, calyx with short, wavy hairs.
– subsp. *facchinii*: lower corolla lip spreading horizontally, leaving throat open, corolla tube curved sharply upwards, with teeth almost vertical.
– subsp. *freynii*: lower corolla lip close to upper lip, covering the throat, corolla tube curved weakly upwards, with teeth facing straight forward, calyx with short, unicellular hairs.

2 | Alpine Yellow-rattle
Rhinanthus alpinus – Orobanchaceae
(Syn.: *Rhinanthus pulcher*)

5–50cm tall; stem hairless or with 2 weak lines of hairs; teeth of lower sepals not ciliate, or with ciliate hairs at most 1mm long; calyx usually with blackish dots and scribbles; corolla yellow, often with violet markings; lower corolla lip spreading, leaving corolla tube entrance open. Flowers June to September.

SIMILAR SPECIES: Awned Yellow-rattle, *R. glacialis*.
HABITAT: Meadows, pasture, vegetation on glaciated sites, siliceous sward. To 2,300m, usually 1,200–2,000m.
DISTRIBUTION: South-eastern European montane.
NOTE: 2 subspecies in the Alps, connected by intermediate populations (e.g. on Zirbitzkogel in the Seetal Alps, Austria):
– subsp. *alpinus*: calyx hairless.
– subsp. *carinthiacus*: calyx with glandular hairs.

3 | Awned Yellow-rattle
Rhinanthus glacialis – Orobanchaceae
(Syn.: *Rhinanthus aristatus*)

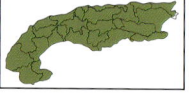

10–50cm tall, hairless or very sparsely hairy; lower teeth of bracts with 1–5mm long ciliate hairs; corolla 15–18mm long, often with violet markings; corolla tube curved upwards; teeth of corolla upper lip 0.8–2.5mm long, notably longer than broad, bluish. Flowers June to September.

SIMILAR SPECIES: Alpine Yellow-rattle, *R. alpinus*, has lower teeth of bracts without ciliate hairs or with hairs at most 1mm long. Pampanini's Lousewort, *R. pampaninii*, has sticky, fluffy stems.
HABITAT: Poor grassland, stony sward, open pinewoods. About 900–2,600m.
DISTRIBUTION: European.

4 | Yellow-rattle (Little Yellow-rattle)
Rhinanthus minor – Orobanchaceae

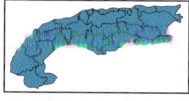

8–30cm tall; stem, leaves and calyx hairless or weakly hairy; teeth of bracts not ciliate; corolla 13–15mm long; upper lip teeth at most 0.7mm long, broader than long. Flowers May to August.

SIMILAR SPECIES: Ancient Yellow-rattle, *R. antiquus*, endemic to the central southern Alps, has upper corolla lip teeth ± as broad as long, and lower teeth of bracts with long ciliate hairs.
HABITAT: Poor meadows, pasture, fens. To about 2,200m.
DISTRIBUTION: Eurosiberian.

5 | Southern Yellow-rattle
Rhinanthus ovifugus – Orobanchaceae

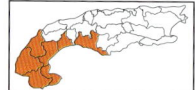

10–40cm tall; stem with 2 lines of hairs; lower teeth of bracts with ciliate hairs > 3mm long; calyx hairless; corolla 19–22mm long; lower corolla lip close to the upper lip, and so almost closing the corolla tube entrance. Flowers June to August.

SIMILAR SPECIES: Alpine Yellow-rattle, *R. alpinus*, has lower teeth of bracts not ciliate, or with ciliate hairs at most 1mm long.
HABITAT: Montane meadows. To 2,500m.
DISTRIBUTION: Southern European montane.

Oxalidaceae, Paeoniaceae, Papaveraceae

1 | Wood Sorrel
Oxalis acetosella – Oxalidaceae

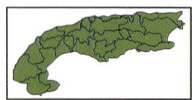

5–12cm tall; leaves and flowers basal; leaves trifoliate, the segments inverse heart-shaped; corolla white, with purple veins, 10–16mm long. Flowers April to June.
SIMILAR SPECIES: None.
HABITAT: Woods on rather acid soils, subalpine stunted woody scrub. To 2,200m.
DISTRIBUTION: Eurosiberian–North American.

2 | Common Peony
Paeonia officinalis – Paeoniaceae

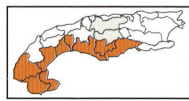

40–80cm tall; leaves large, leaflets mostly divided into 2–3 segments, lower leaves with 17–30 segments; sepals unequal, green or purple; petals purplish-red, 5–10; stamens numerous, fused at base into a nectar ring; 2–3 pistils. Flowers May to June.
SIMILAR SPECIES: Coral Peony, *P. mascula*, which is sometimes naturalised, has lower leaves with only 9–16 segments, and 3–5 pistils.
HABITAT: Calcareous substrates, Holm Oak and Downy Oak scrub, mountain slopes. To 1,700m.
DISTRIBUTION: Southern European montane, from Portugal to Albania and Romania. In the Alps only originally in the southern and south-western Alps.
NOTE: Common Peony is divided into 4 subspecies (subsp. *officinalis*, subsp. *banatica*, subsp. *microcarpa* and subsp. *villosa*), 2 of which are found in the Alps:
– subsp. *officinalis*: has hairless flower stalks; southern and western Alps.
– subsp. *villosa*: hairy flower stalks; French south-western Alps.

3 | North-eastern Alpine Poppy
Papaver alpinum subsp. *alpinum* – Papaveraceae

5–20cm tall; flower stem single-flowered, leafless, with white hairs; all leaves basal, grey-green, 2–3-pinnate, with 1–2mm narrow lobes; petals white, usually 4, sometimes 5, stigma rays. Flowers June to August.
SIMILAR SPECIES: Sendtner's Alpine Poppy, *P. alpinum* subsp. *sendtneri* (see p. 280), has simply pinnate leaves with 2–4mm broad lobes and usually 5 stigma rays.
HABITAT: Calcareous rocky sward; calcicole. 600–2,450m, sometimes lower, as at Steyr, Lower Austria (300m, formerly).
DISTRIBUTION: North-eastern alpine endemic. West in Austria to the Dead Mountains (Totes Gebirge) and to Grimming, and east to the Rax-Schneeberg Group, and south to the Eisenerzer Alps.
NOTE: North-eastern Alpine Poppy was discovered as long ago as 1616, on Schneeberg in the Viennese Alps by the doctor Joachim Burser (1583–1639) from Saxony.

According to recent molecular studies, the division of *Papaver alpinum* is no longer supported, but until we have better information, we are sticking with the long-established classification. Seven subspecies of *Papaver alpinum* are known in the alpine region. These can be distinguished according to flower colour, the arrangement of leaflets, the number of stigma rays, and by their distribution, although the characters are not always constant, partly because the species often has coarser first leaves, followed by more finely divided later leaves.

4 | Ernest Mayer's Alpine Poppy
Papaver alpinum subsp. *ernesti-mayeri* – Papaveraceae

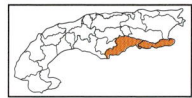

5–20cm tall; flower stem single-flowered, leafless, with white hairs; all leaves basal, grey-green, 2-pinnate, with 1–4mm broad, blunt lobes; petals white, stigma rays usually 5, running down $2/3$ the height of the ovary. Flowers July to August.
SIMILAR SPECIES: Western Alpine Poppy, *P. alpinum* subsp. *occidentale* (see p. 280), usually has only 4 stigma rays, running down to half the height of the ovary.
HABITAT: Calcareous rocky sward; calcicole. 1,700–2,400m, sometimes lower, as at Lake Predil, Italy (900m).
DISTRIBUTION: Eastern alpine–Apennine. In the Alps, only on the Julian Alps.
NAME: In honour of Slovenian botanist Ernest Mayer (1920–2009), an expert on the genera *Rhinanthus* and *Pedicularis*. Mayer described, sometimes in co-authorship, 25 new plant taxa, 11 of which are named after him, such as *Astragalus mayeri* from the Balkan mountains, and *Pedicularis ernesti-mayeri* from northern Albania.

Papaveraceae

1 | Kerner's Alpine Poppy
Papaver alpinum subsp. *kerneri* – Papaveraceae

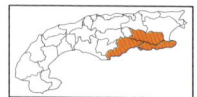

5–20cm tall; flowering stems single-flowered, leafless, with white hairs; all leaves basal, grey-green, 2–3-pinnate, with narrow 1–2mm broad leaflets; petals yellow; ovary 1.5–3x as long as broad usually 5 stigma rays. Flowers July to August.

SIMILAR SPECIES: Rhaetian Alpine Poppy, *P. alpinum* subsp. *rhaeticum*. Also, the relatively recently described subspecies *victoris*, which is restricted to the southern Julian Alps, and has ovary 3–4x as long as broad.

HABITAT: Calcareous rocky sward; calcicole. About 1,200–2,300m.

DISTRIBUTION: Eastern alpine–Illyrian, from the south-eastern Alps to Montenegro. In the Alps in the Karawanken, Julian and Steiner Alps.

NAME: In honour of Austrian botanist Anton Joseph Kerner von Marilaun (1831–1898). In the family album of one of his students, Ignaz Dörfler, he wrote: 'It is not easy to learn and understand the language spoken by plants. In the study one can only really learn how to spell. Reading and understanding can only be achieved in the great outdoors.' Kerner described 60 new plants, and about 120 taxa carry his name. He received several awards for his outstanding scientific work. In Vienna he was honoured by receiving the Austrian Decoration for Art and Science, the highest award for scientific achievement.

2 | Western Alpine Poppy
Papaver alpinum subsp. *occidentale* – Papaveraceae

5–20cm tall; flowering stem single-flowered, leafless, with white hairs; all leaves basal, grey-green, 1–2-pinnate, with leaflets 1–3mm broad, hairless on the blades, at most hairy on margins and stalk; petals white, usually 4 stigma rays. Flowers July to August.

SIMILAR SPECIES: Sendtner's Alpine Poppy, *P. alpinum* subsp. *sendtneri*.

HABITAT: Calcareous rocky sward; calcicole. About 2,000–2,500m.

DISTRIBUTION: Western alpine endemic.

3 | Rhaetian Alpine Poppy
Papaver alpinum subsp. *rhaeticum* – Papaveraceae

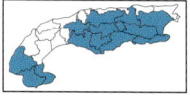

5–20cm tall; flowering stalk single-flowered, leafless, with white hairs; all leaves basal, grey-green, 1-pinnate, with blunt leaflets 2–4mm broad; petals yellow, stigma rays 5–7. Flowers July to August.

SIMILAR SPECIES: Kerner's Alpine Poppy, *P. alpinum* subsp. *kerneri*, has 2–3-pinnate leaves with narrow leaflets 1–2mm broad, and usually 5 stigma rays.

HABITAT: Stony sward, moraines, river gravel; calcicole. 1,800–2,700m, sometimes lower, as in Switzerland near Zernez (1,500m), or higher as on Piz Ftur in Unterengadin (3,070m).

DISTRIBUTION: Alpine–Illyrian, from the Maritime Alps to Montenegro.

4 | Sendtner's Alpine Poppy
Papaver alpinum subsp. *sendtneri* – Papaveraceae

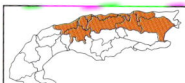

5–20cm tall; flowering stalk single-flowered, leafless, with white hairs; all leaves basal, grey-green, 1-pinnate, hairy, with pointed leaflets 2–4mm broad; petals white, usually 5 stigma rays. Flowers July to August.

SIMILAR SPECIES: Western Alpine Poppy, *P. alpinum* subsp. *occidentale*, has hairless leaf blades, and usually 4 stigma rays. Also, North-eastern Alpine Poppy, subspecies *alpinum* (see p. 278).

HABITAT: Calcareous rocky sward; calcicole. About 2,000–2,700m, on alluvial substrates occasionally down to 950m.

DISTRIBUTION: Eastern alpine endemic, from Unterwalden, Switzerland, and in Austria the Dachstein, and west to the Dead Mountains (Totes Gebirge).

NAME: In honour of German botanist Otto Sendtner (1813–1859), one of the founding fathers of phytogeography. In addition to the poppy, he is also honoured, among others, in the moss *Drepanocladus sendtneri* and in Sendtner's Hawkweed, *Hieracium caesium* subsp. *sendtneri*.

Parnassiaceae, Plantaginaceae

1 | Grass-of-Parnassus
Parnassia palustris – Parnassiaceae

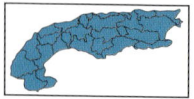

5–30cm tall; basal leaves long-stalked, with heart-shaped blade; flowering stem ridged, with a sessile heart-shaped leaf, single-flowered; flowers 1–3cm in diameter; petals white, with sunken veins; 5 stamens and 5 yellow-green glandular fringed nectar leaves. Flowers July to September.
SIMILAR SPECIES: None.
HABITAT: Marshy meadows, calcareous poor grassland, spring flush vegetation, fens. To 3,000m.
DISTRIBUTION: European-Asiatic–North American, from temperate to subarctic zones. South to the Atlas Mountains.

2 | Narrow-fruited Water-starwort
Callitriche palustris – Plantaginaceae

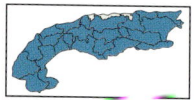

1cm (terrestrial form) – 30cm (aquatic form); small water plant with thread-like stem and terminal rosette; leaves spoon-shaped; flowers tiny, stigma 1–2mm long; flat side of fruit notably longer than broad. Flowers April to October.
SIMILAR SPECIES: All the other *Callitriche* species in the Alps. Blunt-fruited Water-starwort, *C. cophocarpa*, is relatively widespread and has flat side of fruit broader than long, or at least as long as broad.
HABITAT: Shallow, stagnant, nutrient-poor water, pools. To about 2,900m.
DISTRIBUTION: Eurosiberian–North American.
NOTE: All alpine water-starworts belong to the *Callitriche palustris* group. Ripe fruits are necessary for distinguishing the taxa. All the species have terrestrial and aquatic forms, the terrestrial forms looking noticeably different from the typical aquatic forms.

3 | Large Yellow Foxglove
Digitalis grandiflora – Plantaginaceae

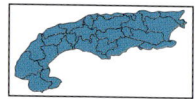

50–100cm tall; stem hairy; leaves ovate-lanceolate, to 25cm long, hairy beneath; corolla pale yellow, often spotted pale brown on the inside, 30–40mm long with a diameter of 15–20mm at the mouth; upper lip entire, blunt. Flowers June to August.
SIMILAR SPECIES: Small Yellow Foxglove, *D. lutea*, has corolla only 20–25mm long, with a diameter of 5–8mm at the mouth, and hairless stem.
HABITAT: Sunny slopes, woodland edges and clearings, rocky sites, scrub, tall herb vegetation. To 2,200m.
DISTRIBUTION: Eurosiberian, from France to the western Altai.
NOTE: Foxgloves are valuable bumblebee plants. The shape of the corolla tube matches precisely the size of the bumblebee. Hairs on the lower part of the flower deter access to the inside by smaller insects, as well as giving the bees a foothold. The pattern of spots inside the flower are perceived by the bumblebees as anthers, and act as an attractant.

4 | Small Yellow Foxglove (Straw Foxglove)
Digitalis lutea – Plantaginaceae

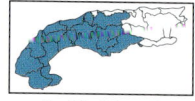

50–100cm tall; stem hairless; leaves lanceolate, up to 15cm long and 2–3cm broad; corolla 20–25mm long, with mouth diameter of 5–8mm; upper lip with 2 pointed lobes. Flowers June to August.
SIMILAR SPECIES: Large Yellow Foxglove, *D. grandiflora*.
HABITAT: Stony slopes, tall herb vegetation, open woods. To about 2,000m.
DISTRIBUTION: Southern European montane, from north-eastern Spain to south-western Germany and Calabria.

5 | Purple Foxglove
Digitalis purpurea – Plantaginaceae

50–150cm tall; leaves oval, with blunt teeth, wrinkled, grey felty hairs beneath; flowers in a long, unilaterally nodding raceme; corolla purplish-red or white, 3.5–6cm long, spotted inside. Flowers June to August.
SIMILAR SPECIES: None.
HABITAT: Forest clearings on acid soils, open woods. To about 1,600m.
DISTRIBUTION: Western European. Not native to the Alps, but often planted and naturalised.

Plantaginaceae

1 | Fairy Foxglove
Erinus alpinus – Plantaginaceae

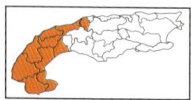

3–20cm tall; leaves spoon-shaped, toothed towards the tip, in a basal rosette and alternate on the stem; corolla purple-pink, 8–12mm in diameter, with notched corolla lobes. Flowers June to July.
SIMILAR SPECIES: Few.
HABITAT: Stony sward, rock debris and crevices; calcicole. To 2,400m.
DISTRIBUTION: Southern European montane. Mountains of western Mediterranean region, and also introduced and naturalised in the British Isles. The species has not been recorded in Austria for some time, although in 2013 G. Amann confirmed its presence in the Samina Valley in Vorarlberg.

2 | Alpine Toadflax
Linaria alpina – Plantaginaceae

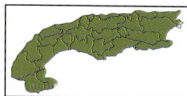

2–20cm tall, creeping in scree, hairless; leaves in whorls of 3–4, linear-lanceolate, with bluish bloom, fleshy; flowers in short terminal racemes; corolla blue-violet with yellow (or less often white) patch on the lower lip; spur 8–15mm long. Flowers June to August.
SIMILAR SPECIES: Few.
HABITAT: Rocks, screes. To 4,100m.
DISTRIBUTION: Southern European montane, from the mountains of the Iberian Peninsula to the Balkans and High Tatra.
NOTES: Two subspecies in the Alps:
– subsp. *alpina* (**2A**): 3–10cm tall, prostrate; calyx lobes obovate-lanceolate, lobes of upper corolla lip 1–2x as long as broad. In the Alps, to subalpine level.
– subsp. *petraea* (**2B**): 10–20cm tall, upwardly arching; calyx lobes semi-lanceolate, lobes of upper corolla lip 2–3x as long as broad. Montane level.
The toadflax genus (*Linaria*) contains about 150 species, of which 70 are European, 11 in the Alps. Only one, Tonzig's Toadflax, *Linaria tonzigii*, is restricted to the Alps.

3 | Striped Toadflax
Linaria repens – Plantaginaceae

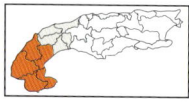

20–80cm tall; branching, hairless; leaves linear-lanceolate, 1.5–4cm long; corolla whitish to pale yellow or lilac, with violet stripes; spur 3–5mm long, entire corolla 8–15mm long. Flowers June to August.
SIMILAR SPECIES: Few.
HABITAT: Ruderal sites, edges of tracks and fields, woodland clearings, walls. To about 2,000m.
DISTRIBUTION: Western European. Native to the south-western Alps, naturalised further east.

4 | Prostrate Toadflax
Linaria supina – Plantaginaceae

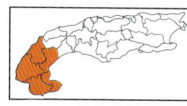

5–15cm tall, prostrate; leaves linear, fleshy, 0.5–2.5mm broad, 6–15x as long as broad; corolla 15–25mm long, yellow; spur 10–15mm long, yellow, often with purple or violet stripes. Flowers June to August.
SIMILAR SPECIES: Tonzig's Toadflax, *L. tonzigii*.
HABITAT: Stony sward, patchy dry meadows, stabilised scree. To about 2,200m.
DISTRIBUTION: South-western European, south to Morocco, and north to southern England and Sweden, where introduced and established.

5 | Tonzig's Toadflax
Linaria tonzigii – Plantaginaceae

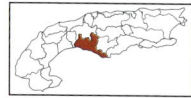

5–15cm tall; leaves broadly lanceolate, somewhat fleshy, grey-green, 8–25mm long, 5–8mm broad; corolla yellow, 21–27mm long; sepals broadly lanceolate, with dense woolly hairs. Flowers June to August.
SIMILAR SPECIES: Prostrate Toadflax, *L. supina*, has linear leaves, 0.5–2.5mm broad, and in the Alps is restricted to the South-western Alps.
HABITAT: Shifting scree; calcicole. 1,600–2,500m.
DISTRIBUTION: Endemic to the Bergamasque Alps.
NAME: In honour of Italian botanist Sergio Tonzig (1905–1998), who studied plant physiology and phytogeography.

Plantaginaceae

1 | Bluish Veronica (Bluish Paederota)
Paederota bonarota – Plantaginaceae

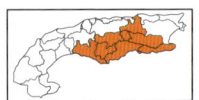

5–15cm tall; leaves 1.5–3cm long, 1–2.5cm broad, opposite, roundly ovate, with up to 9 coarse teeth on each side; inflorescence a dense many-flowered raceme; corolla deep violet-blue. Flowers June to July.
SIMILAR SPECIES: None.
HABITAT: Rock crevices; calcicole. To 2,500m.
DISTRIBUTION: Eastern alpine endemic.
NOTE: Where both *Paederota* species overlap they sometimes produce the hybrid *Paederota* x *churchilii*, distinguished by having a pink corolla (**1B**).

2 | Yellow Veronica (Yellow Paederota)
Paederota lutea – Plantaginaceae

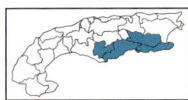

10–30cm tall; leaves ovate-lanceolate, 3–7cm long, 1.5–3cm broad, margins deeply serrated; corolla yellow, 10–13mm long, calyx 6–8mm long. Flowers May to June (July).
SIMILAR SPECIES: None.
HABITAT: Rock crevices and stony debris; calcicole. To 2,500m.
DISTRIBUTION: Eastern alpine–Illyrian, southeast to Herzegovina.

3 | Silver Plantain
Plantago argentea – Plantaginaceae

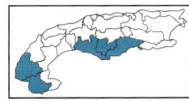

10–40cm tall; leaves basal, narrowly lanceolate, 10–30cm long, 0.4–1.5cm broad, hairy when young, later becoming hairless, 3–5-veined; flower spike stalk 10–40cm long, round, but longitudinally grooved, usually much longer than leaves; flower spike spherical to short-oval. Flowers June to August.
SIMILAR SPECIES: Hoary Plantain, *P. media*, has broadly lanceolate to narrowly oval leaves, 2–6cm broad, 5–7-veined. Ribwort Plantain, *P. lanceolata*, has flower spike stalk angular and longitudinally furrowed.
HABITAT: Dry slopes, stony pasture, karst; calcicole. To about 1,900m.
DISTRIBUTION: Southern European montane.

NOTE: In addition to the plantain species described, there are 7 more, mostly lowland alpine species:
– Narrow-leaved Plantain, *P. altissima*: South-eastern European.
– Sand Plantain, *P. arenaria*: European-Asiatic.
– Keeled Plantain, subsp. *holosteum*: Mediterranean.
– Hare's-foot Plantain, *P. lagopus*: Mediterranean.
– Greater Plantain, *P. major*: Eurosiberian-cosmopolitan.
– Sea Plantain, *P. maritima*: European.
– Shrubby Plantain (Evergreen Plantain), *P. sempervirens*: South-western European.

4 | Mountain Plantain (Dark Plantain)
Plantago atrata – Plantaginaceae

3–15cm tall; prostrate to obliquely upright; leaves narrowly lanceolate, 2.5–12mm broad, 3–5(7)-veined; flower spike spherical to oval, 0.5–2.5cm long; spike stalk 3–15cm long, as long as or longer than leaves. Flowers May to August.
SIMILAR SPECIES: Brownish Plantain, *P. fuscescens*, a species of the southern and south-western Alps, has 5–7-veined, shaggy silky hairs, and spike stalk 15–40cm tall.
HABITAT: Damp meadows and pasture, snow-melt soils. 1,200–2,800m, occasionally lower, as near Immenstadt, Germany (900m).
DISTRIBUTION: Southern European montane.

5 | Fleshy Plantain
Plantago strictissima – Plantaginaceae (Syn.: *Plantago serpentina*; *Plantago maritima* subsp. *serpentina*).

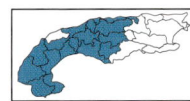

10–35cm tall; leaves linear, 20–50x as long as broad, hairless, 3-veined, the lateral leaf veins mid-way between the mid-vein and the leaf margin, or closer to the mid-vein; flower spike 3–12cm long. Flowers June to August.
SIMILAR SPECIES: Alpine Plantain, *P. alpina*, has a 1.5–3cm long flower spike, leaves 6–20x as long as broad, and lateral veins closer to the leaf margin than to the mid-vein.
HABITAT: Poor grassland, rocky sward, pasture, track sides. To about 2,600m.
DISTRIBUTION: South-western European montane.

Plantaginaceae

1 | Allioni's Speedwell
Veronica allionii – Plantaginaceae

5–12cm tall; stem prostrate, hairless; leaf blades 5–20mm long, hairless, indistinctly toothed; inflorescence upright, dense, with 30–60 flowers; 4 sepals; corolla violet-blue. Flowers July to August.
SIMILAR SPECIES: Heath Speedwell, *V. officinalis*.
HABITAT: Stony sward, montane pasture, open montane woods; calcifuge. 1,800–2,700m.
DISTRIBUTION: South-western alpine endemic.
NAME: In honour of Italian physician and scientist Carlo Allioni (1728–1804), who contributed greatly to the study of the flora of Piedmont.

2 | Alpine Speedwell
Veronica alpina – Plantaginaceae

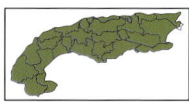

5–15cm tall, with erect hairs or almost hairless; stem not prostrate; lower leaves not in a rosette; stem with many leaves; leaf blades oval; inflorescence a terminal umbel-like raceme with 5–20 flowers; raceme and fruit without glandular hairs; fruit longer than broad. Flowers June to August.
SIMILAR SPECIES: Violet Speedwell, *V. bellidioides*. Thyme-leaved Speedwell, *V. serpyllifolia*, has above-ground creeping stems, and fruits broader than long.
HABITAT: Snow-melt hollows, animal resting sites, damp grassland, rocks, spring flush vegetation. 1,500–3,400m.
DISTRIBUTION: Arctic–alpine.

3 | Leafless-stemmed Speedwell
Veronica aphylla – Plantaginaceae

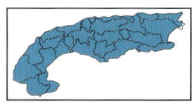

2–8cm tall; flowering stems upright, with leaves in a basal rosette; leaf blades oval, 8–15mm long; racemes 2–5-flowered, ± terminal; corolla lilac-blue, 6–8mm in diameter. Flowers June to August.
SIMILAR SPECIES: Few.
HABITAT: Stony calcareous sward, snow-melt soils; calcicole. 1,300–3,000m, sometimes lower, as near Haldenstein, Graubünden, Switzerland (650m).
DISTRIBUTION: Southern European montane.

4 | Water Speedwell (Brooklime)
Veronica beccabunga – Plantaginaceae

5–20cm tall, hairless; flowering stems creeping; leaves short-stalked; leaf blades oval to elongate-elliptical, fleshy, and shiny; flowers in opposite, stalked racemes; corolla 5–7mm in diameter. Flowers May to August.
SIMILAR SPECIES: Blue Water Speedwell, *V. anagallis-aquatica*, is not creeping, and 15–60cm tall, with sessile, unstalked middle stem leaves.
HABITAT: Spring flush vegetation, ditches, streams, banks. To about 2,400m.
DISTRIBUTION: European-Asiatic.

5 | Violet Speedwell
Veronica bellidioides – Plantaginaceae

5–20cm tall; stem not creeping; lower leaves 20–30mm long, in a rosette; stem with 2 (3) pairs of notably separated leaves; inflorescence a terminal 3–15-flowered umbel-like raceme; raceme and fruit with glandular hairs; fruit longer than broad. Flowers June to August.
SIMILAR SPECIES: Alpine Speedwell, *V. alpina*, has lower leaves not in rosette, and raceme and fruit without glandular hairs. Thyme-leaved Speedwell, *V. serpyllifolia*, has above-ground creeping stems and fruits broader than long.
HABITAT: Poor grassland on acid soils, dwarf shrub heath; calcifuge. 1,500–3,300m.
DISTRIBUTION: Southern European montane.

6 | Heath Speedwell
Veronica officinalis – Plantaginaceae

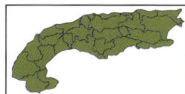

3–10cm tall; stem hairy, prostrate and rooting; leaf blades oval to elliptical, densely hairy; flowers almost sessile; 4 sepals, with glandular hairs; racemes ascending, 15–30-flowered; corolla light blue to pale purple, with darker veins. Flowers May to August.
SIMILAR SPECIES: Allioni's Speedwell, *V. allionii*, has hairless leaves and stems, and 30–60-flowered inflorescence.
HABITAT: Woods on acid soils, clearings, pasture; calcifuge. To about 2,300m.
DISTRIBUTION: Eurosiberian–North American

Plantaginaceae

1 | Germander Speedwell
Veronica chamaedrys – Plantaginaceae

10–30cm tall, with erect hairs, ascending; stem strongly hairy along 2 longitudinal lines, much more sparsely hairy between; leaf blades oval, 2–5cm long, 1.5–2.5cm broad; 10–20 flowers, in a loose raceme; corolla light to strong blue, 9–13mm in diameter; sepals loosely hairy. Flowers April to July.
SIMILAR SPECIES: Viennese Speedwell, *V. vindobonensis*, very similar, has leaf blades 1.1–2.2cm long and 0.7–1.5cm broad, light blue to whitish or pale pink corolla, and stem hairless between the longitudinal lines of hair. Mountain Speedwell (Wood Speedwell), *V. montana*, has a 2–8-flowered raceme, and stem evenly hairy all round.
HABITAT: Tall herb vegetation, meadows, open woods, animal resting sites, transitional vegetation. To about 2,300m.
DISTRIBUTION: European-Asiatic.
NOTE: 2 subspecies in the Alps:
– subsp. *chamaedrys*: stalks of upper leaves of flowering stems at most 2mm long, leaf blades at most 2x as long as broad.
– subsp. *micans*: stalks of upper leaves of flowering stems 2–4mm long, leaf blades 2–2.5x as long as broad; leaves often shiny.
NOTE: There are about 390 species of *Veronica* (including *Pseudolysimachion*), of which about 80 are found in Europe and 44 in the alpine region. One species, *Veronica allionii* (see p. 288), is restricted to the Alps.

2 | Rock Speedwell
Veronica fruticans – Plantaginaceae

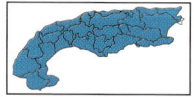

5–15cm tall; base of stem prostrate, branched and woody; flowering stem with 3–6 pairs of current year's leaves; leaf blades oval to spoon-shaped, ± hairless, ± as long as the stem internodes; raceme 3–7-flowered; corolla deep blue with purple ring at centre around white throat; calyx and flower stalk hairy, but not glandular. Flowers June to July.
SIMILAR SPECIES: Shrubby Speedwell, *V. fruticulosa*, has a pink corolla with purple veins, and glandular-hairy calyx and flower stalk.
HABITAT: Rocky sward, stony grassland. 1,200–3,100m.
DISTRIBUTION: Arctic–alpine.

3 | Shrubby Speedwell
Veronica fruticulosa – Plantaginaceae

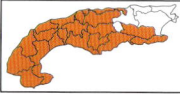

10–20cm tall; base of stem prostrate, branched and woody; leaves linear-lanceolate, at least 2x as long as the stem internodes; raceme 7–20-flowered; corolla pink, with purple veins; calyx and flower stalk with glandular hairs. Flowers June to July.
SIMILAR SPECIES: Rock Speedwell, *V. fruticans*.
HABITAT: Rock crevices, sunny stony sward; calcicole. 1,400–2,800m.
DISTRIBUTION: Southern European montane.

4 | Spiked Speedwell
Veronica spicata – Plantaginaceae
(Syn.: *Pseudolysimachion spicatum*)

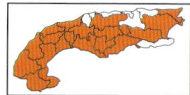

10–40cm tall; upper stem with horizontal to slightly downturned hairs; leaf blades elongate-lanceolate, finely toothed to entire; flowers scentless, in dense terminal raceme; sepals ciliate, with hairy surface. Flowers June to September.
SIMILAR SPECIES: Orchid Speedwell, *V. orchidea*, has upturned hairs on upper stem, and flowers that smell like burnt hair. Barrelier's Speedwell, *V. barrelieri* (**4B**), has ciliate sepals, hairless on the surface.
HABITAT: Dry grassland, rocky steppe country. To about 2,200m.
DISTRIBUTION: European-Asiatic.

5 | Nettle-leaved Speedwell
Veronica urticifolia – Plantaginaceae

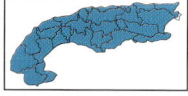

hairless; leaf blades ovate-lanceolate, 5–10cm long, with pointed teeth; corolla pale pink, with darker veins; fruit stalk at least 2x as long as its bract, curved noticeably upwards at the tip; fruit deeply notched, 2x as long as calyx. Flowers May to July.
SIMILAR SPECIES: Large Speedwell, *V. teucrium*, has a blue corolla and fruit weakly notched, 1.5x as long as calyx.
HABITAT: Wooded gorges, tall herb vegetation, stony woods. To about 2,000m.
DISTRIBUTION: Southern European montane.

Plantaginaceae, Plumbaginaceae, Polemoniaceae

1 | Carinthian Wulfenia (Wulfenia)
Wulfenia carinthiaca – Plantaginaceae

25–40cm tall; upper stem with sparse, almost scale-like leaves; basal leaves bright green, notched, 15–20cm long, elliptical to obverse-oval; corolla 12–15mm long, dark blue, 2-lipped. Flowers June to July.
SIMILAR SPECIES: None.
HABITAT: Tall herb vegetation and damp pasture. 1,000–1,900m.
DISTRIBUTION: Eastern alpine–Illyrian.
NOTE: The nominate subspecies is a local endemic to the Gartnerkofel mountain in Carinthia, Austria. A second subspecies, subsp. *blecicii*, is found in an area of around 400km² in the Albanian Alps (Prokletije Mountains). It is possible that the ancestor of the present European and Near Eastern species had a much wider distribution. The advent of a drier climate in the Early Tertiary Period could explain the reduction and fragmentation of the range. Gartnerkofel has a high annual rainfall – an average of 3,000mm.
NAME: In honour of Carinthian botanist Franz Xaver von Wulfen (1728–1805), who discovered the plant on Gartnerkofel on 12th July 1779.

A surviving letter from Wulfen to Alois Frölich from 1802 shows that the new genus was not quite so uncontroversial as today. Wulfen wrote: "Remember the improper conduct of Doctor Host towards me, for I have not insulted him with a single word." This followed the discovery by Wulfen and the subsequent description of *Wulfenia carinthiaca* by Jacquin. In 1802 Frölich wrote to Wulfen that Nicolaus Thomas Host, Imperial personal physician and teacher at the Vienna Collegium Theresianum, was loudly proclaiming everywhere that *Wulfenia carinthiaca* did not exist but was merely the species *Poderota* (= *Paederota*) *carniolica*. Other botanists did not follow Host, and so the genus *Wulfenia* remains valid to this day.

2 | Alpine Thrift
Armeria alpina – Plumbaginaceae

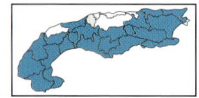

5–20cm tall; leaves linear, hairless, 2–5mm broad, with 1–3 veins, in a basal rosette; stem below inflorescence surrounded by a dry, membranous bract about 1cm long; flower head terminal on leafless stalk; corolla bright pink. Flowers June to August.
SIMILAR SPECIES: Plantain-leaved Thrift, *A. arenaria*, has leaves 3–7mm broad, with 3–7 veins, and pale pink flowers.
HABITAT: Poor alpine grassland, stony sward; pH indifferent. 1,500–2,700m, sometimes lower, as in the Styrian Schneealpe (1,100m), or higher, as on Roise des Banques (3,150m).
DISTRIBUTION: Central and Southern European montane, from Aragon to the eastern Carpathians.

3 | Plantain-leaved Thrift (Jersey Thrift)
Armeria arenaria – Plumbaginaceae

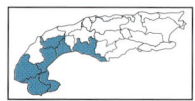

20–50cm tall; leaves in a basal rosette, hairless, linear-lanceolate, 3–7mm broad, with 3–7 veins; stem below inflorescence surrounded by a dry, membranous bract 2.5–4cm long; flower head terminal on leafless stalk; corolla pale pink. Flowers June to July.
SIMILAR SPECIES: Alpine Thrift, *A. alpina*. Sand Thrift, *A. elongata*, has ciliate leaves only 1.5–2.5mm broad.
HABITAT: Dry grassland. To about 2,000m.
DISTRIBUTION: South-western European.
NOTE: Variable species, with 3 subspecies in the Alps (subsp. *arenaria*, subsp. *bupleuroides*, and subsp. *praecox*).

4 | Jacob's Ladder
Polemonium caeruleum – Polemoniaceae

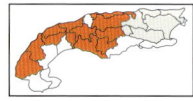

30–80cm tall; leaves alternate, unpaired and pinnate; corolla widely funnel-shaped to spreading, pale blue to violet-blue, sometimes white. Flowers June to August.
SIMILAR SPECIES: None.
HABITAT: Tall herb vegetation, damp meadows, bankside scrub, river gravel. To 2,400m.
DISTRIBUTION: Eurosiberian.
NOTE: Whether it is native to the eastern Alps or naturalised is open to question.

Polygalaceae

1 | Mountain Milkwort
Polygala alpestris – Polygalaceae

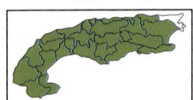

5–15cm tall; lower leaves not in rosette, and much shorter than the noticeably longer upper stem leaves, which are 10–15mm long; bracts oval, 0.7–2.6mm long; corolla blue, as long as or shorter than calyx wings. Flowers June to July.

SIMILAR SPECIES: Common Milkwort, *P. vulgaris*, has corolla longer than calyx wings, and 10–40mm long stem leaves. Nice Milkwort, *P. nicaeensis*, has linear-lanceolate bracts; there are 3 alpine subspecies with different flower colours (purple, violet, pink, blue or white).
HABITAT: Poor meadows, pasture, open woody alpine scrub, dwarf shrub heath; calcicole. 1,300–2,700m.
DISTRIBUTION: Southern European montane.

2 | Bitter Milkwort
Polygala amara – Polygalaceae

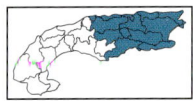

5–20cm tall; basal leaves longer than stem leaves, in a rosette; rosette leaves elliptical to obverse-ovate, upper stem leaves lanceolate; middle stem leaves the broadest; perianth usually bright blue; calyx wings longer than fruit, 4.8–8.5mm long, 2–5.5mm broad. Flowers May to July.

SIMILAR SPECIES: Dwarf Milkwort, *P. amarella*, has calyx wings 3.5–5.1mm long, 1.2–2.2mm broad, at most as long as fruit, and upper stem leaves the broadest.
HABITAT: Dry poor grassland, rocky sward, pinewoods; calcicole. To about 2,400m.
DISTRIBUTION: Eastern European.

3 | Chalk Milkwort
Polygala calcarea – Polygalaceae

5–15cm tall; shortly prostrate at base; lower leaves in a rosette or densely alternate, broadly spoon-shaped; upper leaves about the same length, but narrower; perianth bright pale blue, sometimes pink or white; calyx wings 5–7mm long, with reticulate veins; inflorescence 6–20-flowered. Flowers May to June.

SIMILAR SPECIES: Alpine Milkwort, *P. alpina*, is only 2–6cm tall, with pale blue perianth, 5–10-flowered raceme, and grows at higher levels in the Alps.
HABITAT: Dry meadows, rocky sward; calcicole. To about 2,200m.
DISTRIBUTION: Western European.

4 | Shrubby Milkwort
Polygala chamaebuxus – Polygalaceae

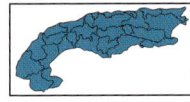

3–15cm tall dwarf shrub; leaves elliptical, evergreen, leathery, 1–1.5cm long; perianth yellow and white, purple and yellow in var. *grandiflora* (**4B**); flowers 1–3, in leaf axils; lower perianth segment (keel) is 4-lobed towards the tip. Flowers February to June.

SIMILAR SPECIES: None.
HABITAT: Open pine woods, dry poor meadows, wayside scrub, fens; calcicole. To 2,500m.
DISTRIBUTION: Southern European montane, from the eastern Pyrenees (possibly) to the Carpathians.

5 | Nice Milkwort
Polygala nicaeensis – Polygalaceae

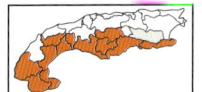

10–40cm tall; leaves alternate, lower leaves not in a rosette; upper leaves narrowly lanceolate, to 4cm long; bracts linear-lanceolate, longer than flower stalk; perianth pink, purple, violet, blue, white, or multicoloured; wings 7–10mm long, with branching lateral veins. Flowers April to July.

SIMILAR SPECIES: Tufted Milkwort, *P. comosa*, usually has purple flowers, with keel only 4.5–7mm long.
HABITAT: Dry grassland, stony sward. To about 2,000m.
DISTRIBUTION: Southern European montane/ Mediterranean.
NOTE: 3 subspecies in the Alps:
– subsp. *carniolica*: south-eastern European, in the southern Alps.
– subsp. *gariodiana*: western alpine, in the French Alps.
– subsp. *mediterranea*: Mediterranean, in the southern Alps.

Polygonaceae

1 | Mountain Sorrel
Oxyria digyna – Polygonaceae

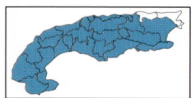

5–25cm tall; basal leaves long-stalked, with kidney-shaped blade, 1–3cm broad, hairless; stem mostly leafless; inflorescence simple or with upright branches; 4 tepals. Flowers July to August.
SIMILAR SPECIES: Snow Dock, *Rumex nivalis* (see p. 298), has oval or spear-shaped leaf blades, and 6 tepals.
HABITAT: Damp, gravelly scree, moraines, stony pasture; calcifuge. 1,700–2,800m, sometimes lower, as on the Isarco River (Eisack), South Tyrol, Italy (600m), or higher, as on the Mittagskogel, Austria (2,950m).
DISTRIBUTION: Arctic–alpine. Europe and North America, south to the mountains of Corsica and Lebanon.

2 | Alpine Knotgrass
Persicaria alpina – Polygonaceae
(Syn.: *Polygonum alpinum*)

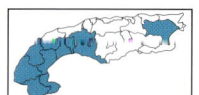

30–80cm tall, branched; leaf blades lanceolate, 3–15cm long, 1–3.5cm broad, sparsely hairy; lower leaves short-stalked; upper leaves sessile; flowers in loose panicles, forming a large inflorescence. Flowers June to August.
SIMILAR SPECIES: Himalayan Knotweed, *P. polystachya*, which is sometimes naturalised, is 80–180cm tall, with leaf blades 10–35cm long and 5–10cm broad.
HABITAT: Montane meadows, Green Alder and Alpenrose scrub, rocky sward, pine woods; calcifuge. 800–2,000m, sometimes lower, as in the Styrian serpentine region on Kirchkogel, Austria (680m), or higher, as in the Graubünden Alps, Switzerland (2,200m).
DISTRIBUTION: European-Asiatic, from central Spanish mountains to Russia and the mountains of south-west Asia.

3 | Common Bistort
Persicaria bistorta – Polygonaceae
(Syn.: *Polygonum bistorta*)

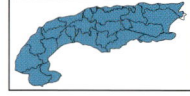

30–80cm tall, unbranched; lower leaves stalked, with elongate-oval blades, 10–22cm long and 1.5–5cm broad, truncate and winged at base; upper stem leaves lanceolate; flowers in dense, spike-like, 4–7cm long clusters. Flowers May to August.
SIMILAR SPECIES: Pale Persicaria, *P. lapathifolia*, has a branched stem.
HABITAT: Damp meadows. To 2,500m.
DISTRIBUTION: Eurosiberian, with a closely related form in Alaska.
NOTE: Larval food plant for, among others, the butterflies Bog Fritillary, *Boloria eunomia*, and Titania's Fritillary, *Boloria titania*.

4 | Alpine Bistort
Persicaria vivipara – Polygonaceae
(Syn.: *Polygonum viviparum*)

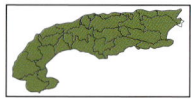

5–25cm tall; unbranched; leaves stalked, blade lanceolate, 1.5–7cm long, 0.5–2cm broad; spike-like inflorescence 3–5cm long, 0.4–0.8cm broad, with brown viviparous bulbils at the base that sometimes sprout small leaves while still on the parent plant (**4B**); flowers white. Flowers June to August.
SIMILAR SPECIES: The white-flowered form of Redshank, *P. maculosa*, has a branched stem.
HABITAT: Grassland, snow-melt hollows, stabilised stony sward. 1,100–3,000m, sometimes lower, as on the banks of the Inn near Telfs, Austria (625m).
DISTRIBUTION: Arctic–alpine. European and North American arctic, and further south into the mountains.

5 | Sheep's Sorrel
Rumex acetosella – Polygonaceae

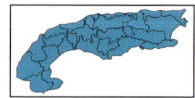

10–30cm tall; leaf blade 3–15x as long as broad, spear- to arrow-shaped, with narrow, spreading basal lobes; inflorescence loose, side branches upright, without bracts; flowers green to rusty-red, inner tepals not or barely extending beyond fruit. Flowers May to August.
SIMILAR SPECIES: Common Sorrel, *R. acetosa*, is 30–100cm tall, with inner perianth segments (tepals) at least 1.5x as long as fruit.
HABITAT: Sandy grassland, ruderal sites, woodland clearings, arable land; calcifuge. To about 2,700m.
DISTRIBUTION: Eurosiberian–North American.

Polygonaceae

1 | Mountain Dock
Rumex alpestris – Polygonaceae

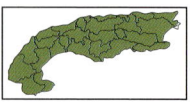

30–120cm tall; basal leaves about 2x as long as broad, spear-shaped, with blunt tips; stipule sheath of young leaves entire; leaf blade thin; inflorescence of loose, branched clusters; Flowers June to August.
SIMILAR SPECIES: Common Sorrel, *R. acetosa*, has stipule sheath of young leaves divided or toothed, and rather thicker leaf blades, 2–4x as long as broad.
HABITAT: Tall herb vegetation, animal resting sites, fertile meadows, grazed grassland. 1,400–2,600m, occasionally lower, as in the North Tyrol Alpbach, Austria (750m), or as on the Pischakopf, Switzerland (*c.* 2,500m).
DISTRIBUTION: Eurosiberian, from the mountains of northern Spain to Kamchatka.
NOTE: In addition to Common Sorrel, described above, there are other, very similar species:
– Intermediate Dock, *R. intermedius*: south-western alpine lowlands.
– Gussone's Dock, *R. nebroides*: south-western Alps.
– Compact Dock, *R. thyrsifolius*: alpine lowlands.
Members of the dock genus (those of the subgenus *Rumex*) tend to form hybrids. No natural hybrids from the *Rumex acetosa* group, such as Snow Dock and French Sorrel, have so far been recorded in the Alps.

Of the total of around 200 *Rumex* species, 44 are European, with 23 found in the Alps, although none is restricted to the Alps. Some species are difficult to separate. For precise determination, flowers, fruits, and basal leaves are necessary. Docks and sorrels, *Rumex*, differ from Mountain Sorrel, *Oxyria digyna* (see p. 296) in having 6 perianth segments (tepals) – Mountain Sorrel has 4.

2 | Alpine Dock (Monk's Rhubarb)
Rumex alpinus – Polygonaceae

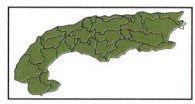

50–100cm tall; basal leaf blades oval to round, 1–1.5x as long as broad, round at the tip, with clearly heart-shaped base; leaf margin often undulate; inflorescence of crowded, upright, branching clusters. Flowers June to August.
SIMILAR SPECIES: Broad-leaved Dock, *R. obtusifolius*, has lower leaf blades *c.*2x as long as broad, and not as deeply heart-shaped at base.

HABITAT: Nitrogen-rich animal resting places, around alpine huts, tall herb vegetation; indicator of fertilised sites. 1,000–2,500m, sometimes washed down lower, as at the Rhine dam near Brugg, Switzerland (400m), or higher, as in the Bernina Range, Switzerland/Italy (2,640m).
DISTRIBUTION: Southern European montane, from the Pyrenees to Armenia.

3 | Snow Dock
Rumex nivalis – Polygonaceae

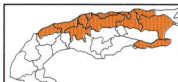

7–25cm tall; stem unbranched, leafless or with 1–2 leaves; basal leaf blades oval to spear-shaped; leaves rather thick, green, and almost without veins; inflorescence usually unbranched; inner tepals at least 1.5x as long as fruit; outer tepals fused at the base, bending backwards at fruiting stage. Flowers July to August.
SIMILAR SPECIES: Sheep's Sorrel, *R. acetosella* (see p. 296), has inner tepals not or barely extending beyond fruit. French Sorrel, *R. scutatus*.
HABITAT: Snow-melt hollows, rocky sward, stony poor grassland; calcicole. 1,600–2,700m, sometimes higher, as on Masnerkopf, Tyrol, Austria (2,800m).
DISTRIBUTION: Alpine–Illyrian, from the Bernese Oberland, Switzerland to the mountains of Montenegro.

4 | French Sorrel (Buckler-leaved Sorrel)
Rumex scutatus – Polygonaceae

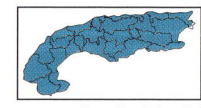

10–40cm tall, upright, often branching at base; leaves blue-green, rarely grass-green, all stalked; leaf blades spear-shaped; inflorescence with many upright branching stems; inner tepals at least 1.5x as long as fruit; outer tepals free (not fused) at base. Flowers May to August.
SIMILAR SPECIES: Snow Dock, *R. nivalis*, has outer tepals fused at the base. Sheep's Sorrel, *R. acetosella* (see p. 296), has inner tepals not or barely extending beyond fruit.
HABITAT: Coarse rocky sward, sunny, stony slopes, rocks, river deposits; calcicole. To 2,700m.
DISTRIBUTION: European–south-western Asiatic.

Primulaceae

1 | Pink Rock-jasmine
Androsace adfinis – Primulaceae
(Syn.: *Androsace carnea*)

2–10cm tall; leaves linear to narrowly lanceolate, 0.5–3cm long, 1–4mm broad, entire or sparsely toothed, pointed; inflorescence 2–10-flowered; petals white or pink, with yellow eye; flowers 5–9mm in diameter. Flowers June to August.

SIMILAR SPECIES: Chaix's Rock-jasmine, *A. chaixii*. Blunt-leaved Rock-jasmine, *A. obtusifolia* (see p. 302), has blunt-ended leaves.

HABITAT: Rocky debris, damp grassland, dwarf shrub heath. 2,000–3,300m.
DISTRIBUTION: Western alpine endemic.
NOTES: A variable species, with 3 subspecies in the Alps, considered by some authorities to have individual species status:
- subsp. *adfinis*: leaves toothed, ciliate only at margins, broadest in the middle.
- subsp. *brigantiaca* (**1A**): leaves partly toothed, weakly hairy, broadest in the middle.
- subsp. *puberula* (**1B**): leaves entire, hairy everywhere, broadest below the middle.

The rock-jasmine genus contains around 150 species, of which 24 are European, with 17 in the alpine region, and 6 of these are restricted to the Alps: *A. adfinis*, *A. alpina*, *A. brevis*, *A. hausmannii*, *A. pubescens*, and *A. wulfeniana*.

2 | Alpine Rock-jasmine
Androsace alpina – Primulaceae

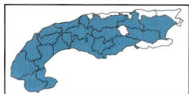

0.5–5cm tall, forming loose mats; leaves 3–6mm long, broadly lanceolate, not keeled, blunt, lacking red tip, in rosette-like clusters at ends of stems; flowers solitary, 5–9mm in diameter, pink or white, with yellow eye, barely protruding above the leaves; flower stalk at most twice as long as leaves. Flowers July to August.

SIMILAR SPECIES: Charpentier's Rock-jasmine, *A. brevis*, has clearly stalked flowers, with stalks twice as long or longer than leaves, raised well above the cushion. Wulfen's Rock-jasmine, *A. wulfeniana* (see p. 304), has keeled, red-tipped, pointed leaves.

HABITAT: Damp rocky sites and ridges; calcifuge. 2,000–4,000m, sometimes lower, as on the Berninabach in Graubünden, Switzerland (1,800m), or higher, as on the Matterhorn (4200m).
DISTRIBUTION: Alpine endemic.

3 | Chaix's Rock-jasmine
Androsace chaixii – Primulaceae

5–20cm tall; leaves 20–30mm long, 4–10mm broad, toothed, in basal rosettes; inflorescence 4–10-flowered; flower stalk 8–35mm long; calyx divided almost to the middle; petals pink, rarely white, longer than sepal lobes. Flowers April to June.

SIMILAR SPECIES: Pink Rock-jasmine, *A. adfinis*, is found at higher altitudes and has leaves 1–4mm broad.
HABITAT: Open woods, especially beechwoods, with patchy herb layer. To 1,900m.
DISTRIBUTION: Southwest alpine endemic.
NAME: In honour of French abbot and botanist Dominique Chaix (1730–1799).

4 | Ciliate Rock-jasmine
Androsace chamaejasme – Primulaceae

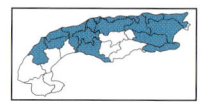

2–8cm tall; stem and flower stalks with hairs 0.5–2mm long, interspersed with glandular hairs; leaves lanceolate, 0.5–1.5cm long, entire, with marginal ciliate hairs, almost hairless above and below; lowest leaves of rosettes spreading horizontally; flowers 2–8, in umbel-like inflorescence, with 2–7mm long stalks; flowers white, with yellow eye. Flowers June to July.

SIMILAR SPECIES: Blunt-leaved Rock-jasmine, *A. obtusifolia* (see p. 302). Woolly Rock-jasmine, *A. villosa* (see p. 302), has leaves also hairy on underside, with hairs 1–2mm long.
HABITAT: Rocky grassland, stony sward; calcicole. 1,200–2,800m, sometimes lower, as on the Eisbach near the Königsee, Germany (610m), or higher, as on the Gornergrat, Valais, Switzerland (3,000m).
DISTRIBUTION: Arctic–alpine, from the Pyrenees to arctic east Siberia and North America.

Primulaceae

1 | Dwarf Rock-jasmine (Dolomite Rock-jasmine)
Androsace hausmannii – Primulaceae

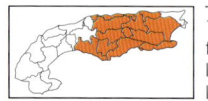

1–4cm tall, not mat-forming; leaves lanceolate, 5–10mm long, 1–2.5mm broad, hairy on both sides; hairs stellate, branching; flowers solitary, 3–6mm in diameter, white to pale pink, with yellow eye, barely protruding above the leaves; flower stalk 3–8mm long. Flowers June to July.
SIMILAR SPECIES: Hairy Rock-jasmine, *A. pubescens*, a western alpine species, has hairs with 1–2 strands.
HABITAT: Rock debris, dolomitic gravel, rock crevices; calcicole. 2,000–3,000m, sometimes lower, as at Passo Pampeago (Reiterjoch) in the Dolomites, Italy (1,900m), or higher, as on Cima Tosa in the Brenta Group, Italy (3,170m).
DISTRIBUTION: Eastern alpine endemic.
NAME: In honour of Austrian botanist Franz Freiherr von Hausmann (1810–1878), best known for researching the flora of the South Tyrol.

2 | Swiss Rock-jasmine
Androsace helvetica – Primulaceae

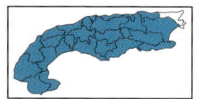

1–5cm tall, forming dense, rounded cushions; leaves 2–4mm long, elongate obverse oval, hairy; withered leaves from previous years retained; flowers solitary, white, with yellow eye, on stalks about 1mm long. Flowers May to July.
SIMILAR SPECIES: Vandelli's Rock-jasmine, *A. vandellii* (see p. 378), has 6mm long leaves with white felty hairs, 2–6mm long flower stalks, and is calcifuge.
HABITAT: Limestone rock crevices; calcicole. 1,600–3,500m, allegedly descending to 1,000m near Grindelwald, Switzerland.
DISTRIBUTION: Alpine endemic. There is also a reference to a record from the Pyrenees (Pic de Salettes).

3 | Milk-white Rock-jasmine
Androsace lactea – Primulaceae

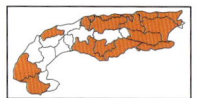

5–15cm tall; mostly hairless, with just a few ciliate hairs on leaf tips; leaves linear-lanceolate, entire, 1–2.5cm long, in loose rosettes; sterile rosettes present; corolla white, with yellow eye, on stalks of varied length; petals clearly notched. Flowers June to July.
SIMILAR SPECIES: Northern Rock-jasmine, *A. septentrionalis* (**3B**), has broadly lanceolate, toothed leaves, and is without sterile rosettes.
HABITAT: Rocky sward, stony grassland; calcicole. 1,000–2,300m, sometimes lower, as at the foot of the Rauschberg near Ruhpolding, Germany (750m).
DISTRIBUTION: Southern European montane, from the Jura to the eastern Carpathians.

4 | Blunt-leaved Rock-jasmine
Androsace obtusifolia – Primulaceae

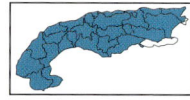

2–10cm tall; stem and flower stalks with 0.01–0.2mm long hairs, lacking glandular hairs; leaves 0.5–2.5cm long, 2–5mm broad, entire, lanceolate, rather blunt, broadest above the middle; flowers 1–8, on 2–12mm long stalks, in umbel-like inflorescence; corolla white, with yellow eye. Flowers June to August.
SIMILAR SPECIES: Ciliate Rock-jasmine, *A. chamaejasme* (see p. 300), has stem and flower stalks with hairs 0.5–2mm long, interspersed with glandular hairs.
HABITAT: Poor grassland; calcifuge. 1,600–3,100m, sometimes lower, as near Obernberg in the Tyrol, Austria (1,270m), or higher, as on Oberaarhorn in the Bernese Alps, Switzerland (3,400m).
DISTRIBUTION: Southern European montane, from the northern Apennines to Macedonia and the Carpathians.

5 | Woolly Rock-jasmine
Androsace villosa – Primulaceae

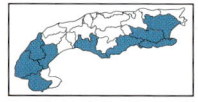

1–7cm tall; stem and flower stalk with 0.5–2mm long hairs, interspersed with glandular hairs; leaves lanceolate, 3–8mm long, 1–2mm broad, margins and undersides with 1–2mm long hairs; lower rosette leaves upright; flowers 2–8, with stalks 0–4mm long, in umbel-like inflorescence; corolla white to pale pink, with yellow, later purplish eye. Flowers June to July.
SIMILAR SPECIES: Ciliate Rock-jasmine, *A. chamaejasme* (see p. 300).
HABITAT: Stony, rocky sward; calcicole. 1,400–2,800m.
DISTRIBUTION: Southern European montane, from the Cantabrian mountains, to Mount Ossa.

Primulaceae

1 | Yellow Rock-jasmine
Androsace vitaliana – Primulaceae
(Syn.: *Vitaliana primuliflora*)

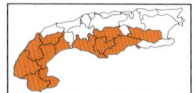

2–5cm tall; leaves in rosette, narrowly lanceolate, 3–15cm long, 0.8–2mm broad, hairiness varies with subspecies; flowers yellow, with a 10mm long corolla tube; flower stalk 1–5mm long. Flowers May to July.
SIMILAR SPECIES: None.
HABITAT: Damp stony debris, short sward on saturated soils, wet rocks. 1,700–3,100m.
DISTRIBUTION: Southern European montane, from the mountains of Spain to the Alps and Apennines.
NOTE: 3 subspecies in the Alps:
- subsp. *vitaliana*: leaves hairy beneath; scattered in western and southern Alps.
- subsp. *cinerea*: leaves with stellate hairs on both sides (**1**); south-western Alps.
- subsp. *sesleri*: leaves hairless, or ciliate at margins; south-eastern Alps.

2 | Wulfen's Rock-jasmine
Androsace wulfeniana – Primulaceae

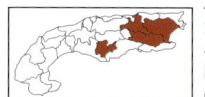

2–5cm tall; leaves 4–5mm long, 1–2mm broad, in dense half-open rosettes, ± keeled, pointed, with brownish-red tips; flower stalk 4–12mm long, extending above leaves; calyx narrowly bell-shaped, not divided to the middle; flowers 8–12mm in diameter, dark pink, with yellow eye. Flowers May to June.
SIMILAR SPECIES: Alpine Rock-jasmine, *A. alpina* (see p. 300), has blunt leaves, only 5–9mm in diameter, without brownish-red tips. Charpentier's Rock-jasmine, *A. brevis*, has calyx divided to the middle.
HABITAT: Windswept ridges and crests, dry rocky sites; calcifuge. 1,900–2,600m.
DISTRIBUTION: Eastern alpine endemic.
NAME: In honour of Austrian botanist, mineralogist and clergyman Franz Xaver von Wulfen (1728–1805), who, among other things, was part of the expedition to make the first ascent of the Grossglockner.

3 | Monte Alben Primrose
Primula albenensis – Primulaceae

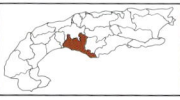

3–10cm tall; stem and leaves with dense covering of simple, glandular, and mealy hairs; leaf blades broadly oval, 1–7cm long, 1–3.5cm broad, lobed towards the tip; inflorescence 2–12-flowered; flower stalk 6–10mm long, glandular, mealy white; calyx 4–8mm long, mealy white, calyx lobes 1.5–3.5mm long, longer than broad; flowers pale violet to violet-pink, with white eye; corolla tube 10–15mm long. Flowers May to June.
SIMILAR SPECIES: Hairy Primrose, *P. hirsuta* (see p. 308), lacks the mealy hairiness.
HABITAT: Limestone rocks, cave entrances; calcicole, shade-loving. 1,150–2,000m.
DISTRIBUTION: Alpine endemic. So far, known only from Monte Alben in the Bergamasque Alps, Italy.

4 | Mountain Cowslip (Auricula, Bear's Ear)
Primula auricula – Primulaceae

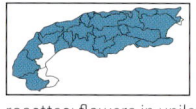

5–20cm tall; leaves obverse oval, blue-green, fleshy, often mealy, in basal rosettes; flowers in unilaterally nodding umbel; corolla bright yellow, with funnel-shaped, spreading lobes; fruit not much longer than calyx. Flowers April to June.
SIMILAR SPECIES: Cowslip, *P. veris* (see p. 312), and Oxlip, *P. elatior* (see p. 306), have wrinkled, not fleshy, leaves.
HABITAT: Rocks, stony sward, Cushion Sedge (*Carex firma*) vegetation; calcicole. 300–2,800m, sometimes lower, as in the Mödlinger Klause, Lower Austria (250m), or higher, as on the Rottal Ridge (Rottalgrat) of the Jungfrau, Switzerland (2,900m).
DISTRIBUTION: Southern European montane. Alps, Apennines, Black Forest, Jura, western Carpathians, and isolated in Banat and north Serbia.
NOTE: Mountain Cowslip is often split into 2 subspecies: subsp. *auricula* and subsp. *balbisii*. The distribution of these 2 taxa remains unclear, and where they overlap there are intermediate populations. Recent studies have contributed little to improving our knowledge, but rather have caused confusion through problematic nomenclatural changes.

Primulaceae

1 | Clusius's Primrose
Primula clusiana – Primulaceae

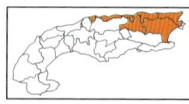

2–8cm tall; covered in short colourless glands; leaves elongate-lanceolate, 1.5–6cm long, shiny above, entire, with narrow white membranous margins; inflorescence 1–5-flowered; petals purplish-red; corolla tube 9–16mm long. Flowers May to June.

SIMILAR SPECIES: Wulfen's Primrose, *P. wulfeniana* (see p. 312). Entire-leaved Primrose, *P. integrifolia*, has a different distribution and lacks membranous margins to the leaves.

HABITAT: Damp stony sward, grassland, snow-melt soils; calcicole. 600–2,500m, occasionally lower, as on the Steyer near Klaus in Upper Austria (450m).

DISTRIBUTION: North-east alpine endemic.

NAME: In honour of the botanist Carolus Clusius (1526–1609), the first to climb the Ötscher to study its flora, and who is considered one to the earliest discoverers of the alpine flora.

2 | Val Daone Primrose
Primula daonensis – Primulaceae

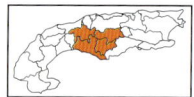

3–10cm tall, with 0.1–0.3mm long glandular hairs, mostly tipped reddish to blackish; leaves obovate to narrowly wedge-shaped, 1.5–7cm long, 0.6–1.7cm broad, shorter than the flower stem, undulate-toothed at the top; inflorescence 1–7-flowered; flowers purplish-pink, with white throat; calyx lobes 0.8–1.5mm long, ± triangular, as broad or broader than long. Flowers June to July.

SIMILAR SPECIES: Shaggy Primrose, *P. villosa* (see p. 312), has 0.8–1.5mm long glandular hairs, and 1–3.5cm broad leaves. Hairy Primrose, *P. hirsuta* (see p. 308).

HABITAT: Rocks, stony sward, Curved Alpine Sedge (*Carex curvula*) vegetation; calcifuge. 1,600–2,800m.

DISTRIBUTION: Alpine endemic.

3 | Oxlip
Primula elatior – Primulaceae

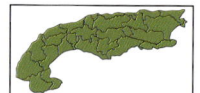

10–25cm tall; leaves in basal rosettes, elongate-lanceolate, wrinkled, with short hairs on both sides, irregularly finely toothed; flowering stalk about 10x as long as pedicels; petals pale yellow, only a little darker towards the throat; calyx ridged, not inflated; calyx lobes 3–7mm long, 2–2.5x as long as broad; fruit 10–15mm long, longer than calyx. Flowers March to May.

SIMILAR SPECIES: Southern Primrose, *P. intricata* (**3B**), has 2–3mm long calyx lobes, 1–1.7x as long as broad.

HABITAT: Deciduous woods, tall herb vegetation, damp meadows. To 2,400m, sometimes higher, as on the Weisshorn near Arosa, Switzerland (2,640m).

DISTRIBUTION: European, from England to Russia.

4 | Bird's-eye Primrose
Primula farinosa – Primulaceae

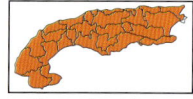

5–20cm tall; leaves in basal rosettes, elongate-obovate, narrowing to winged stalk, mealy white beneath; corolla purplish-pink, with yellow throat ring (eye); corolla tube 4–6mm long, about as long as calyx; calyx lobes about 2mm long. Flowers April to July.

SIMILAR SPECIES: Haller's Primrose (Long-flowered primrose), *P. halleri* (**4B**), has corolla tube 2–3.6x as long as calyx, and calyx lobes 3–4mm long.

HABITAT: Mires, poor grassland, fen meadows, seasonally wet meadows; calcicole. To 2,600, sometimes higher, as on Ewigschneehorn in Graubünden, Switzerland (2,750m).

DISTRIBUTION: Arctic–alpine, from Greenland and the Iberian mountains to Kamchatka; North and South America.

5 | Glaucous Primrose
Primula glaucescens – Primulaceae

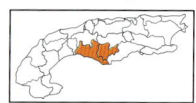

5–13cm tall, completely hairless; leaves basal, 3–5cm long, 0.7–2cm broad, pointed, with membranous, white margins; young leaves curling inwards; inflorescence 2–5-flowered; corolla purplish-red, funnel-shaped at base. Flowers May to June.

SIMILAR SPECIES: Splendid Primrose, *P. spectabilis* (see p. 312). Wulfen's Primrose, *P. wulfeniana* (see p. 312), has glandular leaf margins.

HABITAT: Rocks, stony grassland, damp, humus-rich, shady sites; calcicole. 600–2,400m, sometimes lower, as on Monte Alben, Italy (480m).

DISTRIBUTION: South-eastern alpine endemic.

Primulaceae

1 | Sticky Primrose
Primula glutinosa – Primulaceae

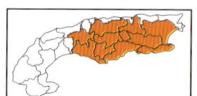

3–10cm tall, glandular, and sticky; leaf blades spoon-shaped, 1.5–6cm long, narrowing into a broadly winged stalk, upper blade finely toothed; flowers fragrant; petals blue-violet to reddish-violet; corolla tube 5–8mm long, about the same length as calyx; flower stalk 0.5–2mm long, much shorter than bracts. Flowers June to July.
SIMILAR SPECIES: Val Daone Primrose, *P. daonensis* (see p. 306), has purple-pink flowers and bracts shorter than flower stalks.
HABITAT: Damp stony sward, Curved Alpine Sedge (*Carex curvula*) vegetation; calcifuge. 1,700–3,000m, occasionally higher, as on Becher in Ridanna (Ridnaun), South Tyrol, Italy (3,100m).
DISTRIBUTION: Eastern alpine endemic.
NOTE: Primroses tend to produce hybrids, especially those in the same subgenus. For example, one often finds large patches of *Primula glutinosa* x *P. minima*. But those from different subgenera may also hybridise, such as natural hybrids in the Alps of *Primula auricula* x *P. minima*.

2 | Grigna Primrose
Primula grignensis – Primulaceae

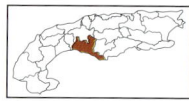

2–5cm tall; leaves oval to spoon-shaped, 15–20mm broad, with dense glandular hairs, margins often rolled upwards, with at most 6 notches; inflorescence 1–2-flowered; corolla purplish-pink, with white throat; corolla tube pale pink, about 15mm long; calyx lobes triangular, not protruding at flowering; fruit as long or longer than calyx. Flowers May to June.
SIMILAR SPECIES: Hairy Primrose, *P. hirsuta*, is calcifuge, has calyx lobes protruding at flowering, and fruit shorter than calyx.
HABITAT: Dolomite rocks, especially at humid sites; calcicole. 1,800–2,200m.
DISTRIBUTION: So far known only from the Mount Grigna (Grignetta) Group, Italy.
NOTE: First described in 1998, and previously assigned to Hairy Primrose, *P. hirsuta*.

3 | Hairy Primrose
Primula hirsuta – Primulaceae

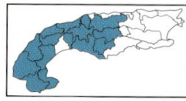

3–10cm tall; leaves round to oval, 1–9cm long, longer or as long as flower stalk, usually coarsely toothed, with colourless and reddish-tipped glandular hairs; corolla purple-pink, with white throat; calyx lobes protruding, 1.5–2.5mm long, ± triangular (see note), longer than broad. Flowers April to July.
SIMILAR SPECIES: Val Daone Primrose *P. daonensis* (see p. 306). Shaggy Primrose, *P. villosa* (see p. 312), has flower stalk longer than leaves, and calyx lobes not protruding. Both species have reddish- to blackish-tipped glandular hairs.
HABITAT: Rock crevices, stony sward, Curved Alpine Sedge (*Carex curvula*) vegetation; calcifuge. 600–3,300m, sometimes lower, as in Val Maggia near Locarno, Italy (220m), or higher, as on Monte Rosa, Switzerland/Italy (3,600m).
DISTRIBUTION: Alpine–Pyrenean.
NOTE: 2 subspecies:
- subsp. *hirsuta*: widespread; calyx lobes triangular, pointed.
- subsp. *valcuviancnsis*: known only from the mountains and valleys of Valcuvia in the north Italian province of Varese, on dolomite substrates; calyx lobes oval, blunt.

4 | Broad-leaved Primrose (Viscid Primrose)
Primula latifolia – Primulaceae

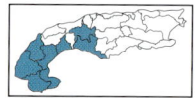

5–15cm tall, sticky with colourless glands, otherwise hairless; leaves 5–10cm long, 1–3cm broad, usually toothed from the middle upwards, with winged stalks; bracts 1–4mm long; inflorescence 5–15mm long; corolla tube 8–10mm long, 2–3x as long as calyx. Flowers June to July.
SIMILAR SPECIES: Hairy Primrose, *P. hirsuta*, has purple-pink corolla with white throat. Silver-edged Primrose, *P. marginata* (see p. 310), has mealy dusted leaves.
HABITAT: Rocks, scree; calcifuge. 1,800–2,800m, sometimes higher, as on Monte Vago, Italy (3,050m), or lower, as near San Dalmazzo in the Maritime Alps, Italy (650m).
DISTRIBUTION: Alpine–Pyrenean.

Primulaceae

1 | Silver-edged Primrose
Primula marginata – Primulaceae

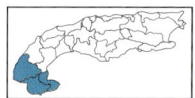

2–12cm tall; leaves obovate, 2–10cm long, mealy dusted, with curved teeth; bracts broadly ovate; flowers on 3–20mm long, mealy dusted stalk; corolla lilac to pinkish-violet, with a pale eye at the throat; corolla tube 5–15mm long, about 3x as long as the mealy calyx. Flowers May to July.

SIMILAR SPECIES: Broad-leaved Primrose, *P. latifolia* (see p. 308).

HABITAT: Rock crevices; calcicole. 500–2,700m.

DISTRIBUTION: Southwest alpine endemic.

2 | Alpine Bells
Primula matthioli – Primulaceae (Syn.: *Cortusa matthioli*)

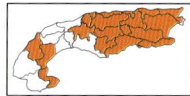

20–40cm tall, with glandular and non-glandular hairs; leaves basal, long-staked, blade round, square-lobed, with 7–13 coarse, sharp-toothed segments; flowers in 5–14-flowered, long-stalked umbel; petals purple-pink, 7–12mm long, tapering together into a bell shape. Flowers June to July.

SIMILAR SPECIES: None.

HABITAT: Green Alder scrub, tall herb vegetation, open, rocky and damp coniferous woods; calcicole. 1,100–2,100m, sometimes lower, as on the Mixnitzbach, Styria, Austria (900m).

DISTRIBUTION: South-eastern European montane/north-eastern European.

NAME: In honour of Italian botanist and medic Pietro Andrea Mattioli (1501–1577), personal physician to Archduke Ferdinand II.

NOTE: For a long time *Cortusa* was considered an independent genus within the primrose family, until recent molecular phylogenetic research showed that it should be included within the genus *Primula*.

3 | Fairy Primrose (Least Primrose)
Primula minima – Primulaceae

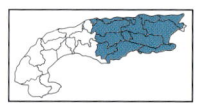

1–3cm tall; apparently hairless, though with tiny glandular hairs on the leaf blades and calyx; leaves obverse-triangular, 0.5–1.5cm long, lateral margins entire, 3–9 coarse teeth at the top; petals purple-pink, deeply incised; corolla tube 5–11mm long, longer than calyx. Flowers June to July.

SIMILAR SPECIES: Few.

HABITAT: Curved Alpine Sedge (*Carex curvula*) vegetation, snow-melt soils, damp poor grassland; calcifuge. 1,600–2,800m, occasionally lower, as on Breitlahner, Austria (1,250m), or higher, as on Kraxentrager, Austria/Italy (almost 3,000m).

DISTRIBUTION: Southern European montane, from the eastern Alps to the southern Carpathians and Pirin mountains, Bulgaria.

4 | Piedmont Primrose
Primula pedemontana – Primulaceae

7–15cm tall; leaves basal, 1–5cm long, 0.7–3cm broad, gradually tapering into the winged stalk, mostly toothed at the top, with reddish glandular hairs at margins; flower stalks with glandular hairs; corolla purple-pink, with white throat; corolla tube with glandular hairs on outside; calyx 4–6mm long, calyx lobes much shorter than calyx tube. Flowers June to July.

SIMILAR SPECIES: Shaggy Primrose, *P. villosa* (see p. 312), has calyx lobes about the same length as calyx tube.

HABITAT: Rock crevices, rocky debris, patchy grassland; calcifuge. 1,300–3,000m.

DISTRIBUTION: Southern European montane, from northern Spain to the western Alps.

5 | Recoaro Primrose
Primula recubariensis – Primulaceae

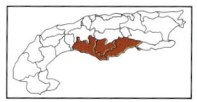

2–3cm tall, all green parts of the plant with 4–5-celled glandular hairs; leaves oval, 1–6cm long, 0.7–3.5cm broad, mostly lobed to toothed at the top; flower stalk always shorter than the leaves, 6–15mm long at flowering; calyx 2–5mm long; corolla pink-lilac to blue-lilac, with white throat; corolla tube 6–10mm long. Flowers May to June.

SIMILAR SPECIES: Hairy Primrose, *P. hirsuta* (see p. 308), is calcifuge, and has purple-pink petals.

HABITAT: Dolomite rocks, especially north exposed; calcicole. 1,400–2,030m.

DISTRIBUTION: Up to now known only from Lissini mountains, Italy.

Primulaceae

1 | Splendid Primrose
Primula spectabilis – Primulaceae

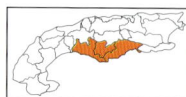

5–15cm tall, apparently hairless, but leaves and calyx have small, colourless glands; leaves ovate-lanceolate, 3–9cm long, 1–4cm broad, entire, young leaves rolled inwards; bracts mostly membranous, suffused red; calyx tubular, often reddish; corolla purple-red, broad funnel-shaped to spreading. Flowers May to June.
SIMILAR SPECIES: Glaucous Primrose, *P. glaucescens* (see p. 306), has completely hairless leaves.
HABITAT: Rocks, stony sward; calcicole. 500–2,500m.
DISTRIBUTION: South-east alpine endemic.

2 | Dolomites Primrose (Tyrolean Primrose)
Primula tyrolensis – Primulaceae

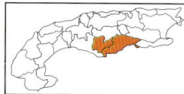

1–4cm tall; with dense up to 0.4mm long sticky glandular hairs; leaf blades 0.8–2cm long, round to oval, narrowing abruptly into the short stalk, finely toothed towards the tip; bracts somewhat fleshy, 4–8mm long; corolla pink, with white glandular-hairy throat; corolla tube 7–10mm long. Flowers May to July.
SIMILAR SPECIES: Allioni's Primrose, *P. allionii*, restricted to the south-western Alps, has leaves narrowing gradually into the stalk, and dry-skinned bracts. Entire-leaved Primrose, *P. integrifolia*, found from Bern to the North Tyrol, has entire leaves.
HABITAT: Steep rocks, humus-rich, damp rock crevices; calcicole. 1,000–2,300m.
DISTRIBUTION: Endemic to the southern Dolomites.

3 | Cowslip
Primula veris – Primulaceae

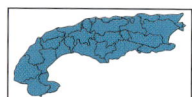

10–30cm tall; leaves elongate-oval, wrinkled, in a basal rosette; inflorescence a one-sided 5–20-flowered umbel; calyx inflated; petals bright yellow, with orange spots towards base; fruit 5–10mm long, shorter than calyx. Flowers April to June.
SIMILAR SPECIES: Oxlip, *P. elatior* (see p. 306), has calyx not inflated, and pale yellow petals.

HABITAT: Dry meadows, open woods. To 2,200m.
DISTRIBUTION: European-Asiatic.

4 | Shaggy Primrose
Primula villosa – Primulaceae (incl. *P. cottia*)

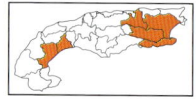

3–15cm tall, glandular-hairy, glandular hairs 0.3–0.75mm long, almost all tipped reddish to blackish; leaves obovate, 2–15cm long, 1–3.5cm broad, shorter than flower stalk, usually coarsely toothed towards the tip; inflorescence 2–8-flowered; petals purple-pink, throat white; calyx lobes close together. Flowers April to June.
SIMILAR SPECIES: Val Daone Primrose, *P. daonensis* (see p. 306), and Hairy Primrose, *P. hirsuta* (see p. 308).
HABITAT: Rock crevices, Curved Alpine Sedge (*Carex curvula*) vegetation; calcifuge. 1,000–2,400m, sometimes lower.
DISTRIBUTION: Alpine endemic.
NOTE: Some authorities separate *Primula cottia*, from the Pennine (Valais) Alps, from *P. villosa*.

5 | Wulfen's Primrose
Primula wulfeniana – Primulaceae

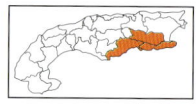

2–8cm tall; apparently hairless, but leaf margins and calyx covered with small, colourless sessile glands; leaves ovate-lanceolate, stiff, shiny, 1.5–4cm long, entire; bracts linear, 4–9mm long, not enclosing calyx; petals purple-pink; corolla tube 7–14mm long, not extending above calyx. Flowers May to July.
SIMILAR SPECIES: Glaucous Primrose, *P. glaucescens* (see p. 306), and Clusius's Primrose, *P. clusiana* (see p. 306), which has a different distribution, and glands on leaf margins with stalks 0.1–0.75mm long.
HABITAT: Rock crevices, damp rocky sward, short grassland, snow-melt soils; calcicole. 1,200–2,100m, sometimes lower, as in the Trögener Klamm, Austria (800m).
DISTRIBUTION: South-eastern alpine–Carpathian. In the southern Carpathians as the subsp. *baumgarteniana*.
NAME: In honour of Carinthian botanist, mineralogist and clergyman Franz Xaver von Wulfen (1728–1805), who, among other things, first described some members of the primrose family (*Androsace chamaejasme*, *Primula glutinosa*, *Primula villosa*).

Primulaceae

1 | Alpine Snowbell
Soldanella alpina – Primulaceae

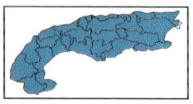

5–15cm tall; leaf blades thick, round to kidney-shaped, 1–3cm in diameter, entire to very shallowly notched; mostly 2–3-flowered; corolla violet, funnel-shaped, divided and ciliate to beyond the centre, ciliate hairs of ± equal length. Flowers April to July.
SIMILAR SPECIES: Dwarf Snowbell, *S. pusilla*, Mountain Snowbell, *S. montana*, and Large Snowbell, *S. major*, differ in having thin, clearly notched leaf blades, and ciliate hairs on corolla of unequal length.
HABITAT: Moist, snowy poor grassland, and margins of snow-melt soils. 800–2,800m. Commoner in the limestone Alps than on primary rocks.
DISTRIBUTION: Southern European montane, from the Pyrenees to the mountains of the Balkan Peninsula.

2 | Austrian Snowbell
Soldanella austriaca – Primulaceae

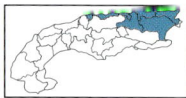

2–10cm tall; leaf blades thick, round, 4–10mm in diameter, very shallowly notched or not notched at base; flower stalk with loose cover of 0.05–0.1mm long glandular hairs; single-flowered; corolla whitish to pale lilac, divided to ¼–⅓ of length. Flowers May to July.
SIMILAR SPECIES: Least Snowbell, *S. minima*, and Dwarf Snowbell, *S. pusilla*.
HABITAT: Snow-melt soils; calcicole. 1,500–2,300m, often lower, as in the Erlauf gorge near Purgstall, Austria (300m).
DISTRIBUTION: North-eastern alpine endemic, in Austria from the Totes Gebirge to the Schneeberg, and an isolated western population on Sonntagshorn, Chiemgau Alps, Germany.

3 | Large Snowbell (Hungarian Snowbell)
Soldanella major – Primulaceae (Syn.: *Soldanella hungarica*)

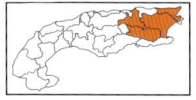

10–20cm tall; leaf blades thin, round to kidney-shaped, 2–4cm in diameter, clearly notched, also at base; leaf stalks with 0.2–0.4mm long glands with stalks 2–5x as long as head; mostly 3–8-flowered; corolla violet, funnel-shaped, ciliate and divided beyond middle, ciliate hairs of unequal length. Flowers May to June.
SIMILAR SPECIES: Mountain Snowbell, *S. montana*, has leaf stalks with 0.4–0.8mm long glands with stalks 8–10x as long as head.
HABITAT: Shady damp woods on acid soils, glacier scrub; calcifuge. 800–1,800m.
DISTRIBUTION: Eastern alpine endemic.

4 | Least Snowbell
Soldanella minima – Primulaceae

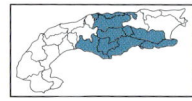

2–10cm tall; leaf blades 4–10mm in diameter, usually without basal notch; flower stalk densely covered in 0.15–0.2mm long glandular hairs, single-flowered; corolla whitish to pale lilac, divided to ¼–⅓ of its length. Flowers May to July.
SIMILAR SPECIES: Austrian Snowbell, *S. austriaca*, has flower stalk with loose cover of 0.05–0.1mm long glandular hairs. Dwarf Snowbell, *S. pusilla*,
HABITAT: 1,600–2,500m, often lower, as near Moggio in Friuli, Italy (300m).
DISTRIBUTION: Eastern alpine endemic, from Valtellina (Veltlin), Italy to the Ammergauer Alps, Germany, and the Julian Alps, Italy/Slovenia.

5 | Dwarf Snowbell
Soldanella pusilla – Primulaceae

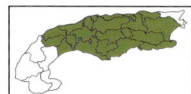

2–10cm tall; leaf blades thin, round to kidney-shaped, *c.* 10mm in diameter, with obvious basal notch; young flower stalks with scattered sessile glands, later becoming hairless, single-flowered; corolla narrowly bell-shaped, lilac, divided to about ¼ of its length; fruit capsule opening with 5 lobes. Flowers May to August.
SIMILAR SPECIES: Least Snowbell, *S. minima*, and Austrian Snowbell, *S. austriaca*, which have young flower stalk densely covered in stalked glandular hairs, and leaves only 4–10mm in diameter. Alpine Snowbell, *S. alpina*, is usually 2–8-flowered, with corolla divided to about half.
HABITAT: Snow-melt hollows; calcifuge. 1,800–3,100m, sometimes lower, as in the Zemmgrund valley near Ginzling, North Tyrol, Austria (900m).
DISTRIBUTION: Southeast European montane.

Ranunculaceae

1 | Narrow-leaved Monk's-hood
Aconitum angustifolium – Ranunculaceae

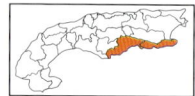

50–130cm tall; leaf blades divided into 1–2.5mm narrow segments; inflorescence unbranched to branched, hairless; flowers whitish to violet-blue, usually pale blue, hairless on outside; stamens hairless. Flowers June to September.

SIMILAR SPECIES: Other species in the *A. napellus* group. These however have less finely divided leaves with segments more than 2.5mm broad.
HABITAT: Calcareous tall herb vegetation, pasture, patchy grassland and limestone scree. 750–1,700m.
DISTRIBUTION: Endemic to the Julian Alps.
NOTE: The number of species in the genus *Aconitum* recognised by different authorities varies considerably. Götz (1967) recognises 70 species, Zander (2003), and Mabberley (2008) c. 100, Ramura in Kubitzki (1993) around 300, and Starmühler/Rottensteiner in Fischer et al. (2008) about 400 species.

2 | Yellow Monk's-hood
Aconitum anthora – Ranunculaceae

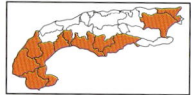

30–100cm tall, hairy; leaf blades divided to base in 5–7 narrowly linear lobes at most 2mm broad; flowers yellow, upper segment forming a helmet about as tall as broad; pistils 5. Flowers August to September.

SIMILAR SPECIES: The Wolf's-bane, *A. lycoctonum* group, have leaf lobes broader than 2mm, and helmet much taller than broad.
HABITAT: Stony slopes, scrub margins; calcicole. To 2,000m.
DISTRIBUTION: Southern European montane.

3 | Branched Monk's-hood
Aconitum degenii – Ranunculaceae
(Syn.: *Aconitum paniculatum*)

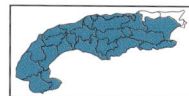

50–200cm tall; stem arched, often overhanging; leaf blades 5–7-palmate, twice divided, with network of veins; flowers violet-blue, helmet as tall or sightly taller than broad. Flowers July to September.

SIMILAR SPECIES: Variegated Monk's-hood, *A. variegatum* (see p. 318), and Common Monk's-hood, *A. napellus* (see p. 318).
HABITAT: Tall herb vegetation, wooded ravines, stream sides, damp meadows. From about 500–2,500m.
DISTRIBUTION: Alpine–Carpathian, from the western Alps to the Carpathians.
NAME: In honour of Hungarian doctor and botanist Árpád von Degen (1866–1934), who made outstanding contributions to research into the flora of Hungary and the Balkan Peninsula.

4 | South Alpine Wolf's-bane
Aconitum lycoctonum subsp. *ranunculifolium* – Ranunculaceae

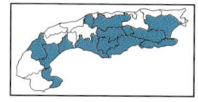

60–200cm tall; leaf blades 7–9-divided, cut almost to the base, connected for less than 1cm, segments narrowly lanceolate; inflorescence dense, usually branching upwards; flowers pale yellow. Flowers June to September.

SIMILAR SPECIES: Wolf's-bane, subspecies *vulparia*.
HABITAT: Tall herb vegetation, open woods, stony sites, pasture. To about 2,400m.
DISTRIBUTION: Southern European montane, from the mountains of Spain to Romania.
NOTE: Now regarded as the species Northern Wolf's-bane, *A. lamarckii*. The *A. lycoctonum* group is taxonomically rather complex, with several species and subspecies having been described, along with hybrids.

5 | Wolf's-bane
Aconitum lycoctonum subsp. *vulparia* – Ranunculaceae

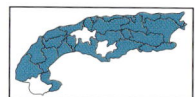

40–150cm tall; leaf blades 5–7-palmately divided, cut at most to 80% of their length, segments broadly lanceolate; flowers pale yellow; inflorescence loose, usually branching horizontally. Flowers May to August.

SIMILAR SPECIES: South Alpine Wolf's-bane, subspecies *ranunculifolium*, has 7–9 segments, cut almost to the base, connected for less than 1cm.
HABITAT: Woods, transitional sites, tall herb vegetation, stream sides, floodplains. To 2,400m.
DISTRIBUTION: European, from the Pyrenees and Netherlands to the Carpathians.
NOTE: Now regarded as the species *A. vulparia*.

Ranunculaceae

1 | Common Monk's-hood
Aconitum napellus – Ranunculaceae

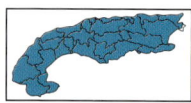

20–200cm tall; stem sturdy, stiff, upright; leaf blades 5–7 palmately divided to the base, segments lobed, hairless above; flowers violet-blue, helmet broader than tall. Flowers June to October.
SIMILAR SPECIES: Branched Monk's-hood, *A. degenii* (see p. 316). Variegated Monk's-hood *A. variegatum*. Burnat's Monk's-hood, *A. burnatii*, is hairy on upper leaf surfaces, and is restricted to the Maritime and Cottian Alps.
HABITAT: Tall herb vegetation, animal resting sites, stream sides, willow scrub, woodland edges. To 3,000m.
DISTRIBUTION: European montane, from Portugal and Sweden to the Carpathians.
NOTE: Very variable species, with 4 subspecies (species) in the Alps:
- subsp. *neomontanum*: scattered throughout the Alps.
- subsp. *vulgare*: scattered throughout the Alps.
- subsp. *hians*: Eastern Alps.
- subsp. *tauricum*: Eastern Alps

Monk's-hoods are perfectly adapted to pollination by bumblebees, and so *Aconitum* species are only found where these large bees also occur. Gerstaecker's Bumblebee, *Bombus gerstaeckeri* relies mainly on Monk's-hood, as do the larvae of the noctuid moth Golden Plusia, *Polychrysia moneta*.

2 | Variegated Monk's-hood (Manchurian Monk's-hood)
Aconitum variegatum – Ranunculaceae

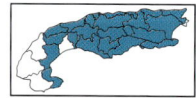

30–250cm tall; stem arching, often overhanging; leaf blades 5–7-palmately divided, segments deeply lobed, with network of veins; flowers violet-blue, helmet notably taller than broad. Flowers July to September.
SIMILAR SPECIES: Branched Monk's-hood, *A. degenii* (see p. 316), has helmet as tall or only slightly taller than broad. The *A. napellus* group differs in having helmet broader than tall, and a stiffly upright stem.
HABITAT: Tall herb vegetation, woodland edges, stream sides. To 2,300m.
DISTRIBUTION: European montane.

3 | Narcissus Anemone
Anemonastrum narcissiflorum – Ranunculaceae (Syn.: *Anemone narcissiflora*)

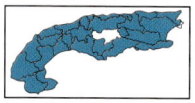

20–40cm tall; blades of basal leaves 3–5-palmately divided; 3–8 flowers, in an umbel; flowers white often flushed pink, with 5–6 hairless petal-like sepals. Flowers May to July.
SIMILAR SPECIES: None.
HABITAT: Damp, fine-soiled grassland; calcicole. 1,000–2,400m, sometimes lower, as in Austria near Bürs, Vorarlberg (570m), or higher, as in the Tilisunaalpe near Tschagguns (2,500m).
DISTRIBUTION: European-Asiatic–North American, from the Pyrenees to Kamchatka; North America.

4 | Monte Baldo Anemone
Anemone baldensis – Ranunculaceae

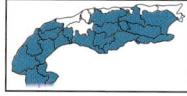

5–15cm tall; basal leaves twice trifoliate, lower stem leaves similar, in whorls; flowers solitary, with 7–10 petal-like sepals, 2.5–4cm in diameter. Flowers June to August.
SIMILAR SPECIES: Alpine Pasqueflower, *Pulsatilla alpina* (see p. 328), is 15–40cm tall, with whorled leaves in upper stem, and has 6–9 petal-like sepals.
HABITAT: Poor stony sward, fine limestone debris; calcicole. 1,700–3,050m.
DISTRIBUTION: Southern European montane, from the Maritime Alps to the mountains of Montenegro.

5 | Three-leaved Anemone
Anemone trifolia – Ranunculaceae

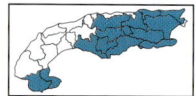

10–30cm tall; upper third of stem with 3 long-stalked trifoliate leaves with regularly toothed margins; petal-like sepals white, 10–23mm long, stamens bluish to white. Flowers May to June.
SIMILAR SPECIES: Wood Anemone, *A. nemorosa*, has pinnate leaves and yellow stamens.
HABITAT: Mixed deciduous woods, stony sites, scrub, meadows. To 1,860m.
DISTRIBUTION: Southern European, from Portugal to Croatia and Lower Austria. Also a record from Finland.

Ranunculaceae

1 | Baneberry
Actaea spicata – Ranunculaceae

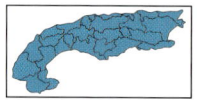

30–60cm tall; leaves mostly trifoliate, with roughly equal segments; flowers small, white, in dense racemes; fruit a black, many-seeded berry. Flowers May to July.
SIMILAR SPECIES: None.
HABITAT: Deciduous woods. To 1,900m.
DISTRIBUTION: European-Asiatic.

2 | Pyrenean Pheasant's-eye
Adonis pyrenaica – Ranunculaceae

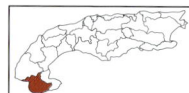

20–40cm tall; leaves 3-or-more-pinnate, with linear segments; flowers yellow, 4–8cm in diameter; sepals hairless. Flowers June to July.
SIMILAR SPECIES: Spring Pheasant's-eye, *A. vernalis*, has softly hairy sepals, and is only found in the lowlands.
HABITAT: Calcareous rocky sward, stony grassland; calcicole. About 1,400–2,200m.
DISTRIBUTION: Pyrenean–western alpine.

3 | Alpine Columbine
Aquilegia alpina – Ranunculaceae

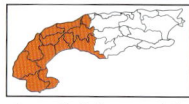

20–70cm tall; leaves twice trifoliate; stem with non-glandular downy hairs; flower stems 1–3-flowered; flowers violet-blue, 5–8cm in diameter; spur with straight or only slightly curved tip. Flowers June to August.
SIMILAR SPECIES: Common Columbine, *A. vulgaris* (see p. 322), has 3–12-flowered stems, and spur curving strongly inwards.
HABITAT: Stony, calcareous grassland, scrub. 950–2,400m, sometimes higher, as in the Bernina Heutal, Switzerland (2,500m).
DISTRIBUTION: Western alpine–Apennine.

4 | Dark Columbine
Aquilegia atrata – Ranunculaceae

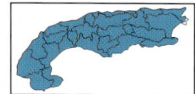

20–60cm tall; leaves twice trifoliate; flowers dark violet to brownish-purple, 3–4cm in diameter; tip of spur hooked; stamens protruding about 5–10mm beyond spurred petals. Flowers May to July.
SIMILAR SPECIES: Bulgarian Columbine, *A. nigricans* (see p. 322), has stamens protruding only about 2–5mm beyond spurred petals.
HABITAT: Woods, especially Scots Pine woods, transitional habitats, fen meadows, montane meadows; calcicole. To about 2,200m.
DISTRIBUTION: Southern European montane.

5 | Bertoloni's Columbine
Aquilegia bertolonii – Ranunculaceae

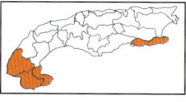

10–30cm tall; lower stem hairless, upper stem with glandular hairs; basal leaves long-stalked, twice trifoliate; flowers blue-violet, 4–4.5cm in diameter; tip of spur slightly curved. Flowers June to July.
SIMILAR SPECIES: Einsele's Columbine, *A. einseleana*, has smaller flowers, about 3cm broad.
HABITAT: Stony slopes, scrub, open woods, rocky debris. To about 1,800m.
DISTRIBUTION: Southern European montane.
NAME: In honour of Italian botanist Antonio Bertoloni (1775–1868), who was Director of the Botanical Garden of the University of Bologna.

6 | Einsele's Columbine
Aquilegia einseleana – Ranunculaceae

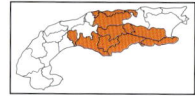

15–40cm tall; 1–3-flowered; upper stem with glandular downy hairs; leaves twice trifoliate, blue-green; leaf blades hairless beneath; flowers violet-blue, about 3cm in diameter; tip of spur straight or only slightly curved inwards. Flowers June to July.
SIMILAR SPECIES: Val Vestino Columbine, *A. vestinae* (see p. 322).
HABITAT: Open scrub, stony sward; calcicole. 600–1,900m, sometimes lower, as near Gemona, Friuli, Italy (250m).
DISTRIBUTION: Eastern alpine.
NAME: In honour of German doctor and botanist August Max Einsele (1803–1870), who studied the alpine flora of Bavaria, and discovered this species in the Berchtesgaden region in 1847.

Ranunculaceae

1 | Bulgarian Columbine
Aquilegia nigricans – Ranunculaceae

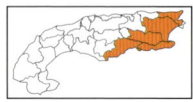

20–60cm tall; leaves twice trifoliate; flowers dark violet to purple-violet, 4–5cm in diameter; tip of spur hooked; stamens protruding about 2–5mm beyond spurred petals. Flowers May to July.
SIMILAR SPECIES: Dark Columbine, *A. atrata* (see p. 320), has stamens protruding about 5–10mm beyond spurred petals.
HABITAT: Woodland margins, stony slopes, meadows, rocks; calcicole. To about 2,000m.
DISTRIBUTION: South-eastern European montane, from the eastern Alps to the eastern Carpathians and to northern Greece.
NOTE: The botanical generic name is a Latinisation of the earlier German name 'Agleya', the earliest reference of which is found in the works of Hildegard von Bingen in the 12th century. Of the 80 columbine species, 19 are found in Europe, with 8 in the Alps. Three of these, *Aquilegia einseleana*, *A. vestinae*, and *A. thalictrifolia*, are restricted to the Alps.

2 | Meadow-rue-leaved Columbine
Aquilegia thalictrifolia – Ranunculaceae

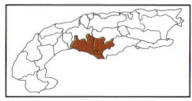

20–60cm tall, with glandular hairs; lower leaves twice trifoliate, with stalked segments divided almost to the middle; leaf blades hairy on both sides; flowers 3.5–4.5cm in diameter, violet-blue; tip of spur curved slightly inwards. Flowers June.
SIMILAR SPECIES: Einsele's Columbine, *A. einseleana* (see p. 320), has leaf undersides hairless.
HABITAT: Calcareous mulch beneath dripping overhanging limestone rocks; calcicole. To about 1,600m.
DISTRIBUTION: Alpine endemic.

3 | Val Vestino Columbine
Aquilegia vestinae – Ranunculaceae

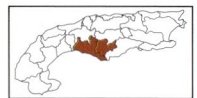

15–40cm tall, 1–3-flowered; stem with glandular hairs; leaves blue-green, blades with violet veins; flowers violet, about 3cm in diameter; tip of spur straight or only slightly curved inwards. Flowers June.
SIMILAR SPECIES: It remains to be decided whether this species should indeed be separated from the very similar Einsele's Columbine, *A. einseleana* (see p. 320). It differs in having violet leaf veins, which are lacking in *A. einseleana*.
HABITAT: Stony debris, rocky transitional habitats, and open scrub; calcicole. About 500–600m.
DISTRIBUTION: So far known only from the Italian provinces of Brescia and Trento, with the centre of distribution in the Alps between Lake Garda and Lake Idro.

4 | Common Columbine
Aquilegia vulgaris – Ranunculaceae

30–60cm tall; leaves twice trifoliate; stems 3–12-flowered; flowers violet-blue, 4–5cm in diameter; tip of spur hooked; stamens protruding only up to 2mm or not at all beyond spurred petals. Flowers May to July.
SIMILAR SPECIES: Bulgarian Columbine, *A. nigricans*, has stamens protruding about 2–5mm beyond spurred petals.
HABITAT: Open woods, meadows, scrub; calcicole. To 2,000m, occasionally higher, as in the Lower Engadine, Switzerland (2,150m).
DISTRIBUTION: European-Asiatic, from the Iberian Peninsula and British Isles to Asia with an uncertain eastern range (related taxa), and North Africa. Occasionally naturalised from gardens.

5 | Marsh Marigold (Kingcup)
Caltha palustris – Ranunculaceae

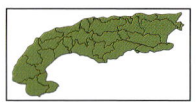

10–40cm tall; leaf blades shiny, heart- or kidney-shaped; flowers bright yellow, with usually 5 petal-like sepals; fruit follicles 3–8, curved outwards. Flowers March to May.
SIMILAR SPECIES: None.
HABITAT: Marshy meadows, ditches, Common Alder woods, stream sides, spring-fed flushes. To 2,530m.
DISTRIBUTION: Eurosiberian–North American, from Iceland, British Isles, and Portugal to China and Irkutsk; North America.

Ranunculaceae

1 | Anemone Crowfoot
Callianthemum anemonoides – Ranunculaceae

5–22cm tall; stem hairless, unbranched; leaves pinnate, basal leaves not fully developed at flowering; 10–18 petals white to pale pink, twice as long as sepals. Flowers March to May.
SIMILAR SPECIES: Coriander-leaved Crowfoot, *C. coriandrifolium*, has 6–13 petals, only 1.5x as long as sepals.
HABITAT: Pinewoods, damp, shady rocks, dolomite scree; calcicole. 450–1,700m.
DISTRIBUTION: Endemic to the north-eastern limestone Alps.
NOTE: Usually on dolomite, but on limestone in the Bärenschützklamm near Mixnitz, Austria. The botanical generic name comes from the ancient Greek words 'kalli' (= beautiful) and 'anthemon' (= flower).

2 | Coriander-leaved Crowfoot
Callianthemum coriandrifolium – Ranunculaceae

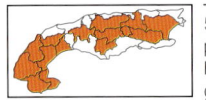

5–20cm tall, hairless, prostrate to ascending; leaves pinnate, blue-green, fully developed at flowering; flowers 2–3cm in diameter, with 6–13 white petals about 1.5x as long as sepals. Flowers May to July.
SIMILAR SPECIES: Kerner's Crowfoot, *C. kernerianum*.
HABITAT: Damp compact and stony grassland, around subalpine twisted woody scrub. 1,260–2,800m.
DISTRIBUTION: Southern European montane, from Asturias to the Carpathians and Bosnia.

3 | Kerner's Crowfoot
Callianthemum kernerianum – Ranunculaceae

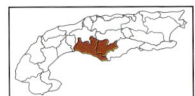

3–10cm tall, compact; stem blue-green to reddish, hairless, single-flowered, with 1–2 stem leaves; leaves pinnate, basal leaves not fully developed at flowering; flower about 3cm in diameter; petals 9–15 petals sometimes reddish. Flowers May to June.
SIMILAR SPECIES: Coriander-leaved Crowfoot, *C. coriandrifolium*, has basal leaves fully developed at flowering.
HABITAT: Stony grassland and Blue Moor-grass (*Sesleria caerulea*) vegetation on exposed mountain crests; calcicole. 1,500–2,200m.
DISTRIBUTION: Endemic to the southern Alps, on either side of Lake Garda: Monte Baldo, Scannuppia group, Monte Bondone, Monte Pizzoccolo, Monte Tremalzo.
NAME: In honour of Austrian botanist Anton Joseph Kerner von Marilaun (1831–1898). Kerner considered this plant from Monte Baldo, which was later named after him, to be conspecific with Coriander-leaved Crowfoot.

4 | Alpine Clematis
Clematis alpina – Ranunculaceae

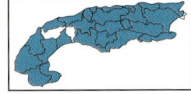

100–200cm tall clambering shrub; leaves twice trifoliate; flowers bright blue, nodding, with 10–12 staminodes and inner nectar-bearing stamens. Flowers May to July.
SIMILAR SPECIES: None.
HABITAT: Open rocky woods, Alpenrose and Dwarf Mountain Pine scrub, alpine coniferous woods. 1,200–2,200m, sometimes lower, as at Auer, near Bolzano, Italy (300m), or higher, as on the Rosengarten Massif, South Tyrol, Italy (2,400m).
DISTRIBUTION: Southern European montane, from the Maritime Alps to the Carpathians and Rhodope Mountains. There is a closely-related species (*C. sibirica*) in northern Europe and Siberia.

5 | Upright Clematis
Clematis recta – Ranunculaceae

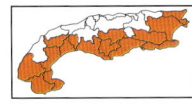

100–150cm tall; stem upright, not woody, not clambering; leaves blue-green, simply pinnate, with up to 9 stalked, entire leaflets; flowers many, in terminal panicles; tepals milk-white, hairless, felty only at the edge. Flowers June.
SIMILAR SPECIES: Traveller's Joy, *C. vitalba*, is woody and clambering. Fragrant Virgin's Bower, *C. flammula*, is also clambering, and has twice-pinnate leaves.
HABITAT: Dry transitional habitats, forest clearings, scrub. To about 1,700m.
DISTRIBUTION: European.

Ranunculaceae

1 | Dauphiné Larkspur
Delphinium dubium – Ranunculaceae

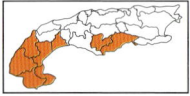

40–90cm tall, with smooth, shiny hairs that are appressed to slightly upright; leaf blades palmate; flowers dark blue to blue-violet, spur 11–20mm long. Flowers June to July.
SIMILAR SPECIES: Tall Larkspur, *D. elatum*, has rough, dull hairs, interspersed with flask-shaped hairs.
HABITAT: Tall herb vegetation, Green Alder scrub, forest clearings, stream sides. 1,150–2,400m.
DISTRIBUTION: Alpine endemic.
NOTE: Of the roughly 380 larkspur species, 30 are European, with 3 in the Alps. The centre of distribution of this predominantly northern temperate zone genus is in Asia. The botanical generic name is from the ancient Greek 'delphinion' (= dolphin) and relates to the dolphin-like shape of the nectaries in the spur. Recent molecular genetic research has shown that the genus *Consolida*, previously considered a separate genus, is actually within the phylogenetic tree of *Delphinium*. The question remains open as to whether *Consolida* species should be included in *Delphinium*, or whether *Delphinium* should be divided into a number of smaller genera.

2 | Tall Larkspur
Delphinium elatum subsp. *elatum* – Ranunculaceae

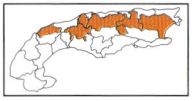

60–180cm tall; leaf blades palmate, with 5–7 lobes; flowers bright blue, in branching racemes; lower petal-like sepals 1.5–2.5x as long as broad; upper petal-like sepal with a long spur curving downwards at the tip; nectar-secreting petals brownish-black. Flowers July to September.
SIMILAR SPECIES: Dauphiné Larkspur, *D. dubium*. Austrian Larkspur, *D. elatum* subsp. *austriacum*, has blue or yellowish-white nectar-secreting petals. Swiss Larkspur, *D. elatum* subsp. *helveticum*, has petal-like sepals 2.5–3.5x as long as broad.
HABITAT: Tall herb vegetation, rocky debris, Green Alder scrub, stream sides, woodland margins. 1,000–2,200m.
DISTRIBUTION: Eurosiberian, from the French Alps to Mongolia.

3 | Austrian Larkspur
Delphinium elatum subsp. *austriacum* – Ranunculaceae

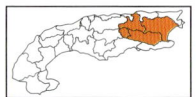

80–200cm tall; leaf blades palmate, 5–7-lobed; flowers bright violet-blue; nectar-secreting petals blue or yellowish-white. Flowers July to September.
SIMILAR SPECIES: Differs from all the other subspecies of *D. elatum* in having blue or yellowish-white nectar-secreting petals (brownish-black in the other subspecies).
HABITAT: Tall herb vegetation, woodland margins, open Larch woods, Green Alder scrub. About 800–2,100m.
DISTRIBUTION: Eastern alpine endemic.
NOTE: East Tyrol Larkspur, often considered as another subspecies, *D. elatum* subsp. *apolanum*, differs, among other ways, in having a white surface to the nectar-secreting petals.

4 | Swiss Larkspur
Delphinium elatum subsp. *helveticum* – Ranunculaceae

60–180cm tall; leaf blades palmate, 5–7-lobed; lower petal-like sepals 2.5–3.5x as long as broad; flowers bright violet-blue; nectar-secreting petals brownish-black. Flowers July to September.
SIMILAR SPECIES: Tall Larkspur, *D. elatum* subsp. *elatum*. Austrian Larkspur, *D. elatum* subsp. *austriacum*.
HABITAT: Tall herb vegetation, rocky debris, open woods, stream sides. About 1,300–2,100m.
DISTRIBUTION: Alpine endemic.

5 | Liverleaf (Liverwort)
Hepatica nobilis – Ranunculaceae

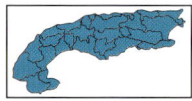

5–15cm tall; lower leaf blades with 3 heart-shaped lobes, often purple beneath, overwintering; flowers bright blue, more rarely white or pink, with 6–10 petal-like sepals. Flowers March to May.
SIMILAR SPECIES: None.
HABITAT: Deciduous woods; calcicole. To 2,200m.
DISTRIBUTION: European, from Spain and Norway to the Volga and Black Sea. Closely-related species in eastern Asia and North America.

Ranunculaceae

1 | Stinking Hellebore
Helleborus foetidus – Ranunculaceae

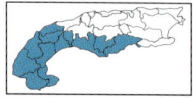

30–60cm tall, with leafy stem, many-flowered; leaf blades palmate with 7–9 lobes, evergreen, hairless; flowers drooping, petals absent, sepals green, mostly edged purple. Flowers March to April.
SIMILAR SPECIES: None.
HABITAT: Herb-rich beech and oak woods, transitional habitats and scrub in regions with mild winters. To 1,980m.
DISTRIBUTION: Southwest European, from southern Spain to Wales, Germany, and Apulia.
NOTE: Hellebores contain a substance in their rhizomes that induces sneezing. The German name for hellebores is 'Neiswurz' (meaning sneeze-root).

2 | Christmas Rose (Black Hellebore)
Helleborus niger – Ranunculaceae

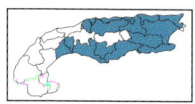

15–30cm tall; stem without true leaves, just with 1–2 pale green bracts; leaves dark green, evergreen, leathery, with wedge-shaped leaflets; flowers 6–10cm in diameter; perianth white, fading later to greenish or reddish; nectar-secreting petals cup-shaped, yellowish-green. Flowers (December) February to May.
SIMILAR SPECIES: Plants with perianth fading to greenish after flowering can be confused with Green Hellebore, *H. viridis*, but the latter has deciduous, pale green leaves.
HABITAT: Damp deciduous woods, especially Spruce-Fir-Beech woods, as well as Scots Pine woods, and Dwarf Mountain Pine scrub, calcareous rocky debris. To about 1,800m.
DISTRIBUTION: South-eastern European. Alps, northern Apennines and mountains of the northern Balkans.

3 | Green Hellebore
Helleborus viridis – Ranunculaceae

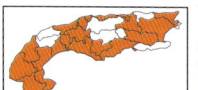

15–40cm tall; stems 2–3-flowered, leafy at branching points; sepals 2.5–3cm long, green, clearly overlapping at the margins. Flowers March to April.

SIMILAR SPECIES: Green-flowered Hellebore, *H. dumetorum*, is 10–15-flowered, and sepals overlapping at most at the base.
HABITAT: Deciduous woods, especially riverine woods and beech woods, clearings. To 1,600m.
DISTRIBUTION: European, from northern Spain and England to Austria and Poland. Very scattered in the Alps, in some places naturalised from cultivation (veterinary medicinal plant).

4 | Northern Alpine Pasqueflower
Pulsatilla alpina subsp. *alpina* – Ranunculaceae

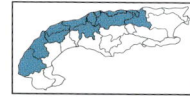

20–50cm tall; single basal leaf; leaf lobes 500–800 in total; leaf margins hairless at fruiting stage; flowers white, 4–5.5cm in diameter, usually with 7 petal-like sepals. Flowers May to July.
SIMILAR SPECIES: Schneeberg Alpine Pasqueflower, *P. alpina* subsp. *schneebergensis* (see p. 330) and Southern Alpine Pasqueflower, *P. alpina* subsp. *austroalpina* (see p. 330), have hairy leaf margins at fruiting stage.
HABITAT: Stony grassland, pasture, grassy slopes; calcicole. 1,200–2,500m, occasionally lower, as in Unterautal, Tyrol, Austria (980m).
DISTRIBUTION: Alpine. Jura and northern limestone Alps.

5 | Austrian Alpine Pasqueflower
Pulsatilla alpina subsp. *alba* – Ranunculaceae

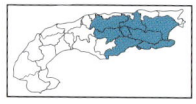

15–30cm tall; basal leaves 2–3; leaf blades clearly angled towards the stem; leaf margins hairless at fruiting stage; flowers white, 3–4.5cm in diameter. Flowers May to July.
SIMILAR SPECIES: Northern Alpine Pasqueflower, *P. alpina* subsp. *alpina*, has leaf blades not angled towards the stem, is clearly hairy, has flowers 4–5.5cm across, and is only found on limestone.
HABITAT: Poor grassland on acid soils, especially Mat Grass (*Nardus stricta*); calcifuge. 1,500–2,500m.
DISTRIBUTION: European montane, from the Cantabrian Mountains to the Carpathians.

Ranunculaceae

1 | Yellow Alpine Pasqueflower
Pulsatilla alpina subsp. *apiifolia* – Ranunculaceae

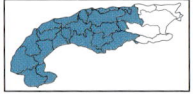

20–50cm tall; single basal leaf; leaf margins hairy at fruiting stage; flowers 5–6.5cm in diameter, sulphur yellow; usually 6 petal-like sepals. Flowers May to July.
SIMILAR SPECIES: None.
HABITAT: Stony grassland, Mat Grass (*Nardus stricta*) and Curved Alpine Sedge (*Carex curvula*) vegetation; calcifuge. 1,400–2,700m, sometimes higher, as on Faselfadspitze, Tyrol, Austria (2,990m), or lower, as near Orsière, Valais, Switzerland (1,090m).
DISTRIBUTION: South-western European montane, from the Spanish mountains to the Alps.
NOTE: Alpine Pasqueflower was previously split into 3 subspecies in the Alps, until recent research resulted in further division. There are now considered to be 7 subspecies in the alpine region. Even after flowering, pasqueflowers continue to look decorative in montane meadows because of their striking fruiting heads, resulting in their being given fanciful local folk names such as 'Almtreapale', 'Strubebube', 'Grantiger Jager' and 'Teufelsbart', which are also used for completely different plants with similarly shaggy fruiting heads.

2 | Southern Alpine Pasqueflower
Pulsatilla alpina subsp. *australpina* – Ranunculaceae

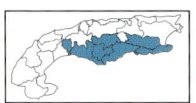

20–40cm tall; basal leaves 1–2; leaf lobes 700–900 in total; leaf margins hairy at fruiting stage; flowers white, 5.5–6.5cm in diameter; usually 7 petal-like sepals. Flowers May to July.
SIMILAR SPECIES: Northern Alpine Pasqueflower, *P. alpina* subsp. *alpina* (see p. 328), has leaf margins hairless at fruiting.
HABITAT: Dry grassland and rocky sward; calcicole. About 1,100–2,100m, in Insubria often lower.
DISTRIBUTION: Eastern alpine–Illyrian. Southern Alps from Ticino (Tessin), Switzerland to Croatia.

3 | Cottian Alpine Pasqueflower
Pulsatilla alpina subsp. *cottianaea* – Ranunculaceae

20–50cm tall; basal leaves 1–2; leaf lobes 500–900 in total; leaf margins hairy at fruiting stage; flowers white, 7–9cm in diameter; usually 8 petal-like sepals. Flowers May to July.
SIMILAR SPECIES: Many-lobed Alpine Pasqueflower, *P. alpina* subsp. *millefoliata*, has 3–5 basal leaves, and finely divided leaves with a total of 1,200–1,400 lobes.
HABITAT: Alpine grassland, open Larch woods, meadows; calcifuge. 1,200–2,000m.
DISTRIBUTION: Endemic to the Cottian Alps.

4 | Many-lobed Alpine Pasqueflower
Pulsatilla alpina subsp. *millefoliata* – Ranunculaceae

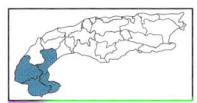

10–30cm tall; basal leaves 3–5; leaf lobes 1,200–1,400 in total; leaf margins hairless at fruiting stage; flowers white, 5–6cm in diameter; petal-like sepals usually 6–8. Flowers May to July.
SIMILAR SPECIES: The other white-flowered subspecies, which have less finely divided leaves with a total of at most 900 lobes.
HABITAT: Alpine grassland, open Larch woods, meadows; calcicole. 1,200–2,400m.
DISTRIBUTION: Western alpine–Apennine.

5 | Schneeberg Alpine Pasqueflower
Pulsatilla alpina subsp. *schneebergensis* – Ranunculaceae

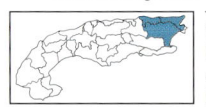

20–40cm tall; basal leaves 1–2, not developed by flowering; leaf lobes 150–200 in total; leaf margins hairy at fruiting stage; flowers white, 4–5.5cm in diameter; 6–7 petal-like sepals. Flowers May to July.
SIMILAR SPECIES: Northern Alpine Pasqueflower, *P. alpina* subsp. *alpina* (see p. 328), has finely divided leaves with a total of 500–800 lobes, and leaf margins hairless at fruiting stage.
HABITAT: Stony grassland, rocky sward, montane meadows; calcicole. 1,100–2,000m, sometimes lower, as in the Weizklamm gorge, Styria, Austria (800m).
DISTRIBUTION: North-eastern alpine endemic.

Ranunculaceae

1 | Haller's Pasqueflower
Pulsatilla halleri – Ranunculaceae

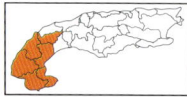

5–20cm tall; lobes of basal leaves 2–5mm broad, with 2–4mm long silky shiny hairs; petal-like sepals 2–3cm long, pale violet. Flowers May to July.
SIMILAR SPECIES: Common Pasqueflower, *P. vulgaris*, has leaf lobes at most 2mm broad.
HABITAT: Rocky grassland and poor meadows; calcicole. About 1,300–2,500m.
DISTRIBUTION: Western alpine endemic.
NAME: In honour of Swiss polymath Albrecht von Haller (1708–1777), who contributed significantly especially to medicine, botany, and literature.

2 | Mountain Pasqueflower
Pulsatilla montana – Ranunculaceae

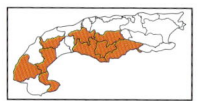

8–20cm tall; basal leaves 4-pinnate, with narrowly linear and very hairy lobes; basal leaves first emerging at flowering; stem very hairy, with terminal, nodding flowers; petal-like sepals dark violet, at least 2x as long as stamens, barely curving outwards at tip. Flowers March to May.
SIMILAR SPECIES: Black Pasqueflower, *P. pratensis* subsp. *nigricans*, has petal-like sepals only 1.25–1.5x as long as stamens, clearly curving outwards at tip.
HABITAT: Patchy dry grassland, Downy Oak woods; calcicole. To about 2,000m.
DISTRIBUTION: Southern European montane, from Piedmont to the Black Sea.

3 | Styrian Pasqueflower
Pulsatilla styriaca – Ranunculaceae

5–20cm tall; basal leaves simply pinnate, only slightly developed at flowering, lobes 2–5mm broad, with 4–5mm long silky shiny hairs; petal-like sepals pale violet, 3–4cm long. Flowers February to April.
SIMILAR SPECIES: Greater Pasqueflower, *P. grandis*, has 2-pinnate leaves.
HABITAT: Rocky dry grassland, warm woodland margins, pioneer dry gassland, Scots Pine woods; calcicole. 380–1,500m.
DISTRIBUTION: South-eastern European, from Styria to the Rila Mountains of Bulgaria.

4 | Spring Pasqueflower
Pulsatilla vernalis – Ranunculaceae

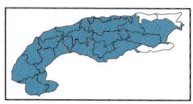

5–15cm tall; basal leaves evergreen, simply pinnate, with 2–3 pairs of leaflets; flowers on short, shaggy stems, at first upright, later nodding; petal-like sepals white to pale lilac inside, tinged violet and shaggily hairy on outside. Flowers March to June.
SIMILAR SPECIES: Few.
HABITAT: Siliceous poor grassland on acid soils. 1,500–2,600m, sometimes as high as 3,100m (Schwarzhorn, Valais, Switzerland) and down to lower levels.
DISTRIBUTION: European montane, from the Cantabrian Mountains to the Rila Mountains in Bulgaria, and southern Scandinavia.

5 | Globeflower
Trollius europaeus – Ranunculaceae

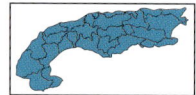

30–60cm tall; mostly single-flowered, hairless; leaf blades palmate; flowers yellow, cup-shaped, with 10–15 overarching round petal-like sepals. Flowers May to July.
SIMILAR SPECIES: None.
HABITAT: Wet meadows, tall herb vegetation, herb-rich damp grassland, open Larch woods. To 3000m.
DISTRIBUTION: Eurosiberian, from central Spain, Northern Ireland, and the North Cape to the Ob region of Russia.
NOTE: Globeflower and flies of the genus *Chiastocheta* are mutually dependent. The flies force their way into the flower through the sepals and in doing so transfer pollen from their bodies to the stigmas. They feed and mate within the protection of the flower cup and also lay their eggs there. When the larvae hatch, they feed on the seeds, but a sufficient number of seeds remain viable, thus ensuring the continued existence of both species.

Ranunculaceae

1 | Aconite-leaved Buttercup
Ranunculus aconitifolius – Ranunculaceae

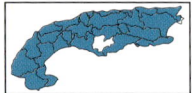

20–50cm tall; upright and branching; basal leaves 3–5-lobed, divided to the base; flower stalk 1–3x as long as its bracts, with short hairs below the flower; petals white; flowers about 1–2cm in diameter. Flowers May to July.
SIMILAR SPECIES: Large White Buttercup, *R. platanifolius* (see p. 338), has flower stalk 4–5x as long as bracts, and leaf lobes not divided to the base.
HABITAT: Woods with a rich herb layer, tall herb vegetation, stream sides, spring-fed flushes, gravelly sites. 900–2,200m, sometimes lower, as at Deutschlandsberger Klause, Austria (390m), or higher as on Mattlishorn, Graubünden, Switzerland (2,350m).
DISTRIBUTION: Southern European montane, from the Sierra Guadarrama, Spain to Westphalia and to the Vranica Mountains, Bosnia.

2 | Alpine Buttercup
Ranunculus alpestris – Ranunculaceae

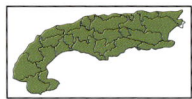

5–15cm tall; plant hairless, single-flowered; blades of basal leaves shiny, round to kidney-shaped, 3–5-lobed, with unevenly blunt-toothed lobes; central lobe of blade broader than 2mm at base; petals white; flower 2–2.5cm in diameter. Flowers May to August.
SIMILAR SPECIES: Traunfellner's Buttercup, *R. traunfellneri* (see p. 338), has central lobe of blade at most 2mm broad at base.
HABITAT: Stony sward, fine rocky debris, snow-melt hollows; calcicole. 1,200–2,800m, sometimes lower, as at Sparchenmühle near Kufstein Tyrol, Austria (500m), or higher as on Piz Beverin, Graubünden, Switzerland (2,940m).
DISTRIBUTION: Southern European montane, from northern Spain to the Carpathians.

3 | Two-lobed Buttercup
Ranunculus bilobus – Ranunculaceae

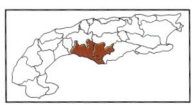

5–10cm tall; stem hairless, with 1–2 leaves, 1–3-flowered; blades of basal leaves kidney-shaped to almost round, notched, heart-shaped at base, 5-veined; flower about 2cm in diameter; petals white, heart-shaped. Flowers June to July.
SIMILAR SPECIES: Alpine Buttercup, *R. alpestris*, has 3–5-lobed basal leaf blades. Notched Buttercup, *R. crenatus*.
HABITAT: Damp fine stony debris, rocky outcrops, open grassland; calcicole. 1,400–2,000m.
DISTRIBUTION: Alpine endemic. In the southern Alps from the Bergamasque Alps to the Judicarian Alps. Monte Alben, Corna Blanca, Monte Tombea, Val Concei, Monte Tremalzo, Val di Ledro.

4 | Mountain Thread-leaved Water-crowfoot
Ranunculus confervoides – Ranunculaceae (Syn.: *Ranunculus trichophyllus* subsp. *eradicatus*)

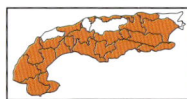

To 100cm long, delicate water plant without floating leaves; rooting at most nodes; often flowering underwater; achenes 5–15, round, with small, pointed tips. Flowers May to August.
SIMILAR SPECIES: Thread-leaved Water-crowfoot, *R. trichophyllus*, only roots at lower nodes, and has 15–30 achenes.
HABITAT: Nutrient-rich mountain lakes. 1,170–2,600m, sometimes higher, as in the Riffelsee near Zermatt, Switzerland (2,750m).
DISTRIBUTION: Arctic–alpine, from Greenland to Central Asia and Alaska.

5 | Notched Buttercup
Ranunculus crenatus – Ranunculaceae

4–10cm tall; stem hairless, with 1–2 leaves, 1–2-flowered; basal leaf blades almost round, notched all round, clearly 5-veined; flowers 2–2.5cm in diameter; petals round-oval. Flowers June to July.
SIMILAR SPECIES: Two-lobed Buttercup, *R. bilobus*, has heart-shaped petals, and is calcicole.
HABITAT: Damp grassland, lake margins, around melting snow; calcifuge. 1,750–2,350m.
DISTRIBUTION: South-eastern European montane. Eastern Alps, Carpathians and mountains of the Balkan Peninsula. In the Alps only in the Rottenmann and Wölz Tauern, Austria.

1 | Glacier Buttercup (Glacier Crowfoot)
Ranunculus glacialis – Ranunculaceae

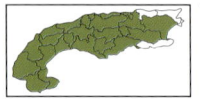

5–20cm tall, hairless; stem prostrate to ascending, 1–5-flowered; blades of basal leaves fleshy, 3-lobed, lobes short-stalked and divided; petals white, later pink; corolla 1.5–3cm in diameter; sepals with reddish-brown hairs. Flowers July to August.
SIMILAR SPECIES: Seguier's Buttercup, *R. seguieri* (see p. 338), has shaggy hairs when young.
HABITAT: Nutrient-poor stony sward, often with Mountain Sorrel, moraines; calcifuge. 1,900–4,000m, sometimes lower, as at Simplon, Valais, Switzerland (1,620m), or higher, as on Finsteraarhorn, Switzerland (4,274m).
DISTRIBUTION: Arctic–alpine. Scandinavia, Iceland, Greenland, Spitzbergen, and other arctic sites. Further south in the mountains.

2 | Hybrid Buttercup
Ranunculus hybridus – Ranunculaceae

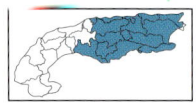

8–15cm tall; leaf blades broadly kidney-shaped, 3–5-lobed to deeply incised-serrated towards the top; lowest stem leaf usually below the middle of stem; basal leaves present at flowering. Flowers May to June.
SIMILAR SPECIES: Shield-leaved Buttercup, *R. thora* (see p. 338).
HABITAT: Rocky sward, stony grassland, alpine meadows; calcicole. 1,500–2,400m, sometimes lower, as in Achental near Seemahd, Austria (930m), or higher, as in the Pala Dolomites, Italy (2,500m).
DISTRIBUTION: Eastern alpine–Illyrian. Eastern Alps, High Karst and western Bosnia.

3 | Küpfer's Buttercup (Pyrenean Buttercup)
Ranunculus kuepferi – Ranunculaceae
(Syn.: *Ranunculus pyrenaeus*)

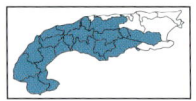

5–20cm tall; basal leaves narrowly lanceolate, hairless, entire, with parallel main veins; corolla 2–3cm in diameter. Flowers May to July.
SIMILAR SPECIES: None.
HABITAT: Damp poor grassland, snow-melt hollows. 1,660–2,900m, sometimes higher.
DISTRIBUTION: Southern European montane, from the Sierra Nevada to the Alps.

4 | Mountain Buttercup
Ranunculus montanus – Ranunculaceae

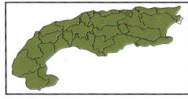

7–30cm tall; basal leaves shiny, hairless, or sparsely hairy, lateral lobes not deeply divided; lobes of stem leaves 2–7x as long as broad; flower stalk round, not furrowed; corolla yellow, 2–3cm in diameter. Flowers May to August.
SIMILAR SPECIES: Other species from the *montanus* group have dull, hairy basal leaves, or if hairless (Carinthian Buttercup, *R. carinthiacus*), have lobes of stem leaves 6–15x as long as broad.
HABITAT: Pasture, open woods, snow-melt hollows, fen meadows; calcicole. 1,000–2,700m, sometimes lower, as on the banks of the River Lech, Austria/Germany (400m), or higher, as near the Great St Bernard Pass, Valais, Switzerland (2,950m).
DISTRIBUTION: Alpine. Alps, alpine foothills, Swiss and German Jura, and Black Forest, Germany.
NOTE: The Mountain Buttercup (*R. montanus*) group consists of 5, very similar alpine subspecies:
– subsp. *aduncus*: western Alps.
– subsp. *breyninus*: most of the Alps.
– subsp. *carinthiacus*: scattered through the Alps.
– subsp. *venetus*: south-eastern Alps.
– subsp. *villarsii*: western Alps to the East Tyrol.

5 | Parnassus-leaved Buttercup
Ranunculus parnassifolius – Ranunculaceae

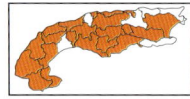

4–12cm tall; arching upwards, many-flowered; blades of basal leaves heart-shaped, entire, with curving main veins, shaggy hairy at margins and at base; corolla 2–2.5cm in diameter; sepals shaggy hairy. Flowers June to July.
SIMILAR SPECIES: None.
HABITAT: Damp, stony slopes, rocky sward; calcicole. 1,700–2,900m.
DISTRIBUTION: Alpine–Pyrenean, from the Cantabrian Mountains to the Eisenerz Alps, Styria, Austria.

Ranunculaceae

1 | Large White Buttercup
Ranunculus platanifolius – Ranunculaceae

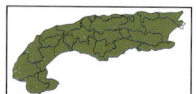

40–120cm tall, upright, branching; blades of basal leaves 3–5-lobed, fused at base; flower stalks 4–5x as long as their bracts, hairless beneath flower; corolla 1.2–2.5cm in diameter. Flowers June to July.
SIMILAR SPECIES: Aconite-leaved Buttercup, *R. aconitifolius* (see p. 334).
HABITAT: Tall herb vegetation, montane meadows, wooded ravines. 1,100–2,100m, occasionally higher, as on Mooser Berg, East Tyrol, Austria (2,200m).
DISTRIBUTION: European montane, from the Iberian Peninsula to Norway and Greece.

2 | Pygmy Buttercup
Ranunculus pygmaeus – Ranunculaceae

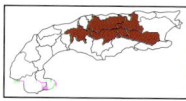

1–5cm tall, upright or arching upwards; blades of basal leaves 3–5-divided beyond the middle, hairless; corolla 0.5–1cm in diameter, petals yellow. Achenes 0.8–1.4mm in diameter. Flowers July to August.
SIMILAR SPECIES: Poor specimens of the Mountain Buttercup, *R. montanus* group (see p. 336) may look similar, but they have flowers more than 1cm diameter, and achenes more than 1.5mm diameter.
HABITAT: Snow-melt hollows, edges of glaciers, moraine slopes, damp rocks; calcifuge. 1,800–2,800m, sometimes higher, as on Eisjöchl near Lazins, South Tyrol, Italy (2,840 m).
DISTRIBUTION: Arctic–alpine, from Iceland and Spitzbergen, circumpolar to Greenland. Further south in the mountains, in Europe in the Alps and Tatra.

3 | Seguier's Buttercup
Ranunculus seguieri – Ranunculaceae

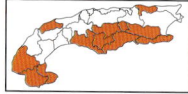

5–15cm tall; entire young plant covered in white shaggy hairs, later becoming hairless; blades of basal leaves palmately divided, many-lobed, split to the base; flower stalk round; corolla 2–2.5cm in diameter. Flowers May to July.
SIMILAR SPECIES: Alpine Buttercup, *R. alpestris* (see p. 334), is hairless, also when young.
HABITAT: Damp rocky sward; calcicole. 1,800–2,570m.
DISTRIBUTION: Alpine–Apennine. Alps and central Apennines. Closely-related species in the Cantabrian Mountains and in the Balkan Peninsula.
NAME: In honour of French botanist and archaeologist Jean-François Séguier (1703–1784), whose name has also been given to several species as well as the genus *Seguieria*, in the family Petiveriaceae.

4 | Shield-leaved Buttercup
Ranunculus thora – Ranunculaceae

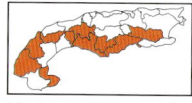

5–30cm tall; upper stem has leaf with a large round or kidney-shaped, finely toothed blade; basal leaves absent at flowering stage; corolla 1–2cm in diameter. Flowers May to July.
SIMILAR SPECIES: Hybrid Buttercup, *R. hybridus*, retains basal leaves at flowering stage.
HABITAT: Rocky sward, Dwarf Mountain Pine scrub, rock bands, Blue Moor-grass (*Sesleria caerulea*) and Evergreen Sedge (*Carex sempervirens*) sward; calcicole. 1,200–2,300m, sometimes lower, as in Carniola (650m), or higher, as in Val Cluozza, Unterengadin, Switzerland (2,400m).
DISTRIBUTION: Southern European montane, from the Cantabrian Mountains to the Carpathians, and Albanian Alps.

5 | Traunfellner's Buttercup
Ranunculus traunfellneri – Ranunculaceae

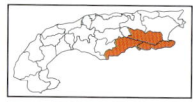

5–10cm tall; blades of basal leaves 3-lobed, central lobe about 2mm broad at base, lateral lobes deeply cut; petals white; corolla about 2cm in diameter. Flowers May to August.
SIMILAR SPECIES: Alpine Buttercup, *R. alpestris* (see p. 334).
HABITAT: Fine rocky debris, snow-melt hollows; calcicole. 1,500–2,500m.
DISTRIBUTION: Eastern alpine. South-eastern Alps to Snežnik (Schneeberg), High Karst, Slovenia.
NAME: In honour of Austrian pharmacist and botanist Alois Traunfellner (1782–1840), who discovered the species during his many botanical excursions.

Ranunculaceae, Rhamnaceae

1 | Alpine Meadow-rue
Thalictrum alpinum – Ranunculaceae

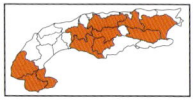

5–15cm tall, hairless; all leaves in basal rosettes, leaflets round, 2–4mm long; flowers in terminal raceme, later nodding; petals pale brownish-red, to 2mm long. Flowers June to July.

SIMILAR SPECIES: Lesser Meadow-rue, *T. minus*, has 5–30mm long leaflets and 4–5mm long petals.

HABITAT: Poor grassland, Mouse-tail Bog Sedge (*Carex myosuroides*) vegetation, Mat Grass (*Nardus stricta*) sward, fens. 1,800–2,600m, sometimes higher, as on Martrel-Grat, Graubünden, Switzerland (2,700m).

DISTRIBUTION: Arctic–alpine. Scattered across the Alps and other European high mountains (Sierra Nevada, Pyrenees, Carpathians, Šar Planina). Widespread in the arctic region.

2 | Greater Meadow-rue (French Meadow-rue)
Thalictrum acquilegiifolium – Ranunculaceae

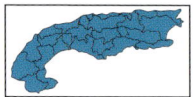

40–120cm tall; entire length of stem leafy; leaves blue-green, 1–3-pinnate, with round to oval, coarsely- and bluntly-toothed leaflets; inflorescence a much-branched panicle; stamens lilac to white, rarely pale yellow, thickened below the anthers. Flowers May to July.

SIMILAR SPECIES: Rare yellow form of Common Meadow-rue, *T. flavum*, has stamens not thickened below the anthers.

HABITAT: Tall herb vegetation, damp deciduous woods, riverine woods, and transitional vegetation. To about 2,400m, sometimes higher, as in Val da Fain, Switzerland (2,500m).

DISTRIBUTION: European, from northern Spain to the middle Volga and northern Russia.

NOTE: Greater Meadow-rue has tiny, inconspicuous petals that fall early, the flowers being dominated by numerous, colourful stamens, a feature unique in the native flora. It is also seen in some exotic plants such as myrtles, eucalypts or African acacias. The flowers offer pollen instead of nectar and the attractive display ensures insect pollination.

3 | Lesser Meadow-rue
Thalictrum minus – Ranunculaceae

20–150cm tall, hairless and scentless; stem furrowed to ridged; leaves 2–4-pinnate; leaflets 5–30mm long, about as long as broad; sepals 4–5mm long, like the stamens greenish to yellowish or pale purple-brown. Flowers May to August.

SIMILAR SPECIES: Stinking Meadow-rue, *T. foetidum*, has stem and leaves with short, glandular hairs, and leaflets 2–4mm long.

HABITAT: Warm, dry hillsides and rocks, scrub, open woods, semi-arid grassland. To 2,000m.

DISTRIBUTION: European-Asiatic with 4 subspecies in the Alps: subsp. *minus*, subsp. *majus*, subsp. *pratense*, and subsp. *saxatile*.

4 | Illyrian Buckthorn
Rhamnus fallax – Rhamnaceae

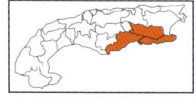

1–3m tall shrub; branches hairless, leaves 7–12cm long; blade elliptical to elongate-elliptical, notably shiny above, with 14–18 pairs of lateral veins; corolla yellow-green, 4-lobed. Flowers May to June.

SIMILAR SPECIES: Alpine Buckthorn, *R. alpina*, has ± hairy branches, and leaves with 9–12 pairs of lateral veins.

HABITAT: Rock debris, deciduous woods; calcicole. To about 1,900m.

DISTRIBUTION: South-eastern European montane, south to Greece.

5 | Dwarf Buckthorn
Rhamnus pumila – Rhamnaceae

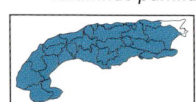

3–20cm tall prostrate, gnarled dwarf shrub, growing close on rocks; leaves 2–5cm long, alternate; blade obovate to elliptical, with 6–9 pairs of lateral veins. Flowers May to July.

SIMILAR SPECIES: Non-flowering specimens of creeping willows, such as Dwarf Willow, *Salix herbacea* (see p. 358), but these have leaves only 0.5–3cm long, and woody branches that are mostly underground.

HABITAT: Rock crevices, stony sward; calcicole. To 3,050m.

DISTRIBUTION: Southern European montane, from the Pyrenees to the central Apennines.

Rosaceae

1 | Alpine Lady's-mantle
Alchemilla alpina – Rosaceae (sect. *Alpinae*)

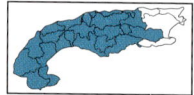

5–25cm tall, upright, with low-lying sterile side shoots; leaves palmately divided to base, silvery and silky beneath; 5–7 lanceolate leaf lobes, 2.5–4.5x as long as broad; teeth 0.5–1mm long, about as long as broad; flowering shoot 1–3x as long as longest leaf stalk. Flowers July to August.
SIMILAR SPECIES: Rock Lady's-mantle, *A. saxatilis*, always has 5 leaf lobes, and flowering shoot 3–7x as long as longest leaf stalk.
HABITAT: Mat Grass (*Nardus stricta*) sward, siliceous rock crevices, rocky sward dwarf shrub heath; calcifuge. 1,500–2,600m.
DISTRIBUTION: Arctic–alpine.
NOTE: There are about 200 lady's-mantle species in the Alps. *Alchemilla* species are mostly very similar as they are to a large extent the result of hybridisation, followed by genetic isolation, and then being recognised as separate species.

2 | Enns Valley Lady's-mantle
Alchemilla anisiaca – Rosaceae

5–20 cm tall; leaf blades kidney-shaped, divided to 75–85% of their length, up to 10cm in diameter, hairless to silky-hairy above, usually densely silky below, with 7(9) lobes, 3–5x as long as broad, serrated in upper third; teeth 1–3mm long. Flowers July to August.
SIMILAR SPECIES: Silky-shiny Lady's-mantle, *A. amphisericea*, has round leaf blades, and leaf lobes fused at base. In the Alps, almost entirely restricted to Switzerland.
HABITAT: Scree, rock bands, stony pasture, snow-melt soils; calcicole. 1,200–2,200m, sometimes washed down to lower levels, as near Steyr in Upper Austria.
DISTRIBUTION: North-eastern alpine endemic.

3 | Silver Lady's-mantle
Alchemilla conjuncta – Rosaceae

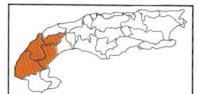

5–30cm tall, forming dense carpets; basal leaves bright green above, somewhat shiny, silvery-white and silky beneath; leaf blades divided to 50–90% of radius into 7(9) lobes; lobes lanceolate to obovate, 1.5–3x as long as broad, with 11–19 teeth; teeth 0.3–2.5mm long, not curved; partial inflorescences about 1cm in diameter. Flowers June to September.
SIMILAR SPECIES: Shiny Lady's-mantle, *A. nitida*, has leaf blades divided to 80–100% of radius into 7–9 lobes, with curved teeth.
HABITAT: Rock crevices; calcicole. 1,200–2,200m.
DISTRIBUTION: Western alpine.

4 | Smooth Lady's-mantle
Alchemilla glabra – Rosaceae

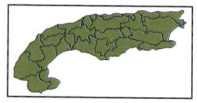

5–40cm tall; blades of basal leaves 9-lobed, blue-green to grass-green above, hairless below with appressed hairs along veins; teeth curving somewhat towards tips. Flowers June to August.
SIMILAR SPECIES: Velvet Lady's-mantle, *A. monticola*, has leaves densely hairy on both surfaces.
HABITAT: Damp rich meadows, spring flushes, tall herb vegetation, open woods. To 2,900m.
DISTRIBUTION: European.
NOTE: There are dozens of very similar species in the Alps that can often only be separated by specialists.

5 | Hoppe's Lady's-mantle
Alchemilla hoppeana – Rosaceae

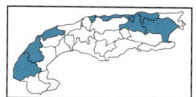

5–20cm tall; leaf blades divided to 80–95% of their length, with 7–9 lobes, dull blue-green to grey-green above, silky grey beneath; leaves circular; lobes fused at base, and only serrated at the top; teeth 0.3–1.6mm long. Flowers June to August.
SIMILAR SPECIES: Limestone Alp Lady's-mantle, *A. alpigena*, has leaf undersides with snow-white silky hairs, and leaf lobes serrated to almost half their length.
HABITAT: Stony grassland, rock crevices, rocky sward; calcicole. 1,100–2,200m.
DISTRIBUTION: European montane. Alps, Vosges, Jura, and Black Forest.
NAME: In honour of German botanist David Heinrich Hoppe (1760–1846), who collected the species on the Untersberg near Salzburg, Austria.

Rosaceae

1 | Goat's Beard
Aruncus dioicus – Rosaceae

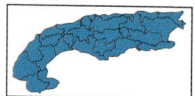

100–180cm tall; leaves 2–3-pinnate, without stipules; leaflets 5–8cm long, oval; flowers very small and very numerous, in dense, branching spikes; flowers of male plants pure white, those of female plants creamy-white; petals 1–2mm long. Flowers June to July.
SIMILAR SPECIES: Meadowsweet, *Filipendula ulmaria*, has stipules, and petals 2–5mm long.
HABITAT: Humid, shady sites on deep humus-rich soils, mainly in wooded ravines, by mountain streams, and in tall herb vegetation.
DISTRIBUTION: European-Asiatic, from Belgium and the Pyrenees to the Carpathians and Caucasus. There are closely-related species in central and eastern Asia, and in North America.

2 | Marsh Cinquefoil
Comarum palustre – Rosaceae (Syn. *Potentilla palustris*)

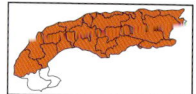

30–70cm tall, prostrate to ascending; lower leaves pinnate, upper leaves 3-lobed; leaflets elongate, sharply serrated, undersides bluish-green and hairy; flowers dark purple; outer sepals narrowly-lanceolate, about half as long as the broadly lanceolate, pointed inner sepals; petals 3–8mm long, about half as long as the inner sepals. Flowers June to July.
SIMILAR SPECIES: None.
HABITAT: Mires, marshes, banks; calcifuge. To 2,100m.
DISTRIBUTION: Eurosiberian–North American.

3 | Alpine Avens
Geum montanum – Rosaceae

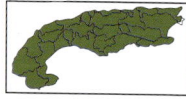

5–30cm tall, without runners; leaves in a basal rosette; basal leaves simply pinnate, terminal leaflet much larger than lateral leaflets; corolla yellow, with 5–6 petals. Flowers June to July.
SIMILAR SPECIES: Creeping Avens, *G. reptans*.
HABITAT: Pasture, dwarf shrub heath, tall herb vegetation; acid indicator. 1,400–3,100m, sometimes lower, as in Centovalli, Switzerland (700m), or higher, as on Monte Rosa, Switzerland/Italy (3,400m).
DISTRIBUTION: Southern European montane, from the Pyrenees to the mountains of the Balkan Peninsula.
NOTE: The German name for species in the genus *Geum* is Nelkenwurz (clove-root). Wood Avens, *Geum urbanum*, was (is) sometimes used as a substitute for cloves. It contains a compound also found in cloves and is used for example as a spice for flavouring soups.

4 | Creeping Avens
Geum reptans – Rosaceae

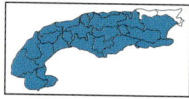

3–20cm tall, with long above-ground runners; leaves in a basal rosette; rosette leaves simply pinnate, deeply cut, with 3–5 leaflets; corolla yellow, solitary, 3–5cm in diameter, with 6–8 petals; the feathery, hairy styles form a tuft after flowering (**4B**). Flowers July to August
SIMILAR SPECIES: Alpine Avens, *G. montanum*, does not produce runners, and has leaves with much larger terminal lobes.
HABITAT: Rocky sward, moraines, streamside debris, rocks; calcifuge. 1,700–3,400m, occasionally lower, as on the Hüfi Glacier, Switzerland (1,450m), or higher, as on Grivola, Italy (3,800m).
DISTRIBUTION: Southern European montane, from the Alps to the Carpathians and the mountains of the Balkan Peninsula.

5 | Water Avens
Geum rivale – Rosaceae

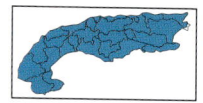

30–60cm tall; basal leaves long-stalked, interrupted unpaired pinnate, with 2–4 pairs of lateral leaflets and a larger terminal leaflet; flowers nodding, not upright until fruiting; calyx purple-brown; petals pale yellow on inside, orange-brown outside. Flowers April to July.
SIMILAR SPECIES: None.
HABITAT: Stream sides, tall herb vegetation, damp meadows, riverine woods. To 2,400m.
DISTRIBUTION: European-Asiatic–North American.
NOTE: The hybrid with Alpine Avens, *Geum* x *sudeticum* (**5B**), is occasional in the Alps.

Rosaceae

1 | Mountain Avens
Dryas octopetala – Rosaceae

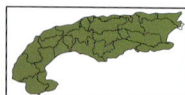

2–8cm tall dwarf shrub, with 50cm long branches; leaves evergreen, stalked, undivided; blade 1–2.5cm long, oval to ovate-lanceolate, deeply notched, mostly hairless above, undersides with dense white felty hairs; flowers solitary; petals white, usually 8. Flowers May to July.
SIMILAR SPECIES: None.
HABITAT: Cushion Sedge (*Carex firma*) vegetation, limestone sward, rocky debris; calcicole. To 2,900m, sometimes higher, as on Piz Tavrü, Switzerland (3,100m).
DISTRIBUTION: Arctic–alpine, with a circumpolar distribution, and further south in the mountains.

2 | Golden Cinquefoil
Potentilla aurea – Rosaceae

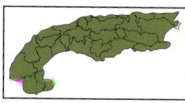

5–20cm tall; basal leaves 5-lobed; lobes lanceolate, wedge-shaped at base, with 2–4 forwardly-curved teeth, the terminal tooth notably smaller than adjacent teeth; leaflet margins with shiny silvery hairs; flowers 1.5–2.5cm in diameter; petals often with a dark spot at the base. Flowers June to September.
SIMILAR SPECIES: Alpine Cinquefoil, *P. crantzii* (see p. 348).
HABITAT: Pasture, meadows, open, grassy montane woods, stony debris; predominantly calcifuge. 1,100–3,000m, sometimes lower, as near Bolzano, Italy (300m), or higher, as on Piz Languard near Pontresina, Switzerland (3,250m).
DISTRIBUTION: Southern European montane.

3 | Dwarf Cinquefoil
Potentilla brauneana – Rosaceae

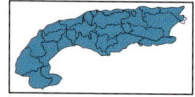

1–5cm tall; basal leaves 3-lobed, hairless or slightly hairy above, loosely hairy beneath; central leaf lobes with 7–9 teeth; leaf stalks 7–14mm long; flowers mostly solitary, about 1cm in diameter; petals about 4mm long, 1–1.5x as long as sepals. Flowers June to August.
SIMILAR SPECIES: Glacier Cinquefoil, *P. frigida* (see p. 348), has leaves also hairy on the upper surface, and is covered in yellowish glands.
HABITAT: Snow-melt soils, hollows with long-lasting snow cover, damp rocky sward; calcicole. 1,800–3,000m, sometimes lower, as near Admont, Styria, Austria (1,100m), or higher, as on Monte Antelao, Dolomites, Italy (3,160m).
DISTRIBUTION: Southern European montane, from the Pyrenees to the Dinaric Alps.

4 | Short-stemmed Cinquefoil (Limestone Cinquefoil)
Potentilla caulescens – Rosaceae

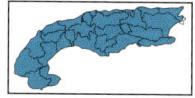

10–30cm long, mainly drooping; basal leaves 5-lobed, long-stalked; leaflets elongate-ovate, with a small number of teeth arching towards each other at the tip; inflorescence 5–20-flowered; flowers 1.5–2.5cm in diameter; filaments mostly densely hairy at base. Flowers July to September.
SIMILAR SPECIES: Clusius's Cinquefoil, *P. clusiana*, has 1–3-flowered inflorescence, and hairless filaments.
HABITAT: Limestone and dolomite rocks; calcicole. To 2,700m.
DISTRIBUTION: Southern European montane, from the Atlas Mountains to the Dinaric Alps.

5 | Clusius's Cinquefoil (Eastern Cinquefoil)
Potentilla clusiana – Rosaceae

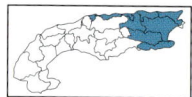

1–10cm tall, forming loose, densely silky-hairy, flat cushions; basal leaves 5-lobed; leaflets lanceolate, with 3–5 teeth towards the tip; inflorescence 1–3-flowered; calyx often tinged red; filaments hairless; style tinged red, especially after flowering. Flowers June to August.
SIMILAR SPECIES: Short-stemmed Cinquefoil, *P. caulescens*. Also, white-flowered forms of Pink Cinquefoil, *P. nitida* (see p. 350), which have 3-lobed leaves.
HABITAT: Limestone rocks, rocky debris, Cushion Sedge (*Carex firma*) vegetation; calcicole. 1,200–2,400m, sometimes lower, as on Balberstein near Miesenbach, Lower Austria (600m).
DISTRIBUTION: Eastern alpine–Illyrian, south to the Albanian Alps.
NAME: In honour of Flemish botanist Carolus Clusius (1526–1609), one of the greatest botanists of the 16th century. His insight into recognising related plant species was ground-breaking.

Rosaceae

1 | Alpine Cinquefoil
Potentilla crantzii – Rosaceae

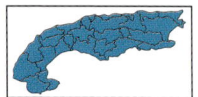

3–15cm tall; fairly densely hairy; sterile shoots with 2 rows of leaves at base; basal leaves 5-lobed, with broadly oval, 7–11-toothed leaflets, the terminal tooth hardly smaller than adjacent teeth; petals about 10mm long, 1–2x as long as sepals. Flowers May to September.
SIMILAR SPECIES: Golden Cinquefoil, *P. aurea* (see p. 346), has silvery shiny hairs at margins of leaflets, and terminal tooth of leaflets markedly smaller than adjacent teeth.
HABITAT: Poor grassland, stony sward, rocks; calcicole. 1,600–3,600m, sometimes lower, as on serpentine substrates near Redlschlag, Burgenland, Austria (700m).
DISTRIBUTION: Arctic–alpine.
NAME: In honour of Austrian botanist and doctor Heinrich Johann von Crantz (1772–1797), who first described the species in the genus *Fragaria*.
NOTE: There are some 500 species of *Potentilla*, with 75 in Europe and 38 (excluding the subspecies of the *collina* group) native to the Alps. The breadth of the genus is rather controversial. It is currently common for some species that were previously included in *Potentilla* to be assigned to other genera. For example, in the alpine region: *Drymocallis rupestris*, Rock Cinquefoil (formerly *P. rupestris*); *Dasiphora fruticosa*, Shrubby Cinquefoil (formerly *P. fruticosa*); *Comarum palustre*, Marsh Cinquefoil (formerly *P. palustris*); *Argentina anserina*, Silverweed (formerly *P. anserina*).

2 | Dauphiné Cinquefoil
Potentilla delphinensis – Rosaceae

20–40cm tall; with appressed hairs, upper plant much-branched; leaves 5-lobed; stalks of basal leaves 10–20cm long; leaflets narrowly oval, 3–6cm long and 1–2.5cm broad, mostly with 8–11 teeth on each side; petals 8–12mm long, longer than the calyx. Flowers June to August.
SIMILAR SPECIES: Large-flowered Cinquefoil, *P. grandiflora*. Also, Thuringian Cinquefoil, *P. thuringiaca*, which has 7(9)-lobed leaves, and tends to be found at lower levels in the Alps.
HABITAT: Alpine mat vegetation, poor grassland, tall herb vegetation; calcicole. 1,500–2,800m.
DISTRIBUTION: Endemic to the French western Alps.

3 | Tormentil
Potentilla erecta – Rosaceae

5–30cm tall; prostrate to ascending; eaves 3–5-lobed, with obovate, coarsely-toothed leaflets; flowers 4-partite, 7–11mm in diameter; pistils 4–8. Flowers May to September.
SIMILAR SPECIES: Notably *P.* x *italica*, the hybrid between Tormentil, *P. erecta* and Creeping Cinquefoil, *P. reptans*, which has flowers 14–18mm in diameter, of which about ¾ are 4-partite, and ¼ 5-partite. The hybrid has 20–50 pistils and is sterile.
HABITAT: Mires, poor meadows, pasture, woodland edges; indicator of poor soils. To 2,540m.
DISTRIBUTION: Eurosiberian, from north-west Africa to the Altai Mountains.

4 | Glacier Cinquefoil
Potentilla frigida – Rosaceae

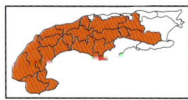

2–10cm tall, entire plant covered in shaggy hairs, with yellowish glands between hairs; basal leaves 3-lobed; leaflets oval, 0.5–1cm long; inflorescence 1–3-flowered; flowers about 10mm in diameter; petals about as long as sepals. Flowers July to August.
SIMILAR SPECIES: Dwarf Cinquefoil, *P. brauneana* (see p. 346).
HABITAT: Poor, acid grassland, especially Curved Alpine Sedge (*Carex curvula*) vegetation, rocky sward, wind-exposed crests and ridges; calcifuge. 2,100–3,500m.
DISTRIBUTION: Alpine–Pyrenean.

5 | Large-flowered Cinquefoil
Potentilla grandiflora – Rosaceae

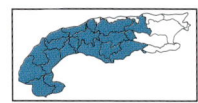

10–40cm tall, branching and many-flowered; leaves 3-lobed, basal leaves long-stalked, with obovate leaflets, 2–3cm long, with 3–8 large, blunt teeth on each side; petals 8–12mm long, 1.5–2x as long as sepals. Flowers June to August.
SIMILAR SPECIES: Dauphiné Cinquefoil, *P. delphinensis*, has 5-lobed leaves, and leaflets usually with 8–11 teeth on each side.
HABITAT: Poor grassland, stony sward, tall herb vegetation, sunny, rocky slopes; calcifuge. 1,800–3,000m.
DISTRIBUTION: Alpine–Pyrenean.

Rosaceae

1 | Pink Cinquefoil (Dolomite Cinquefoil)
Potentilla nitida – Rosaceae

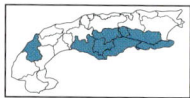

2–5cm tall, entire plant covered in silvery shiny hairs; leaves 3-lobed; petals purplish-pink, rarely white; filaments and styles purplish-red. Flowers June to August.
SIMILAR SPECIES: Clusius's Cinquefoil, *P. clusiana* (see p.346).
HABITAT: Limestone and dolomite rocks, exposed sward, screes; calcicole. 1,600–2,500m, sometimes down to 1,200m or up to 3,160m.
DISTRIBUTION: Alpine endemic. Unconfirmed reports also from the Tuscan Apennines and Istria.
NOTE: The generic name of cinquefoils comes from the Latin 'potentia' (= power, effectiveness) and refers to the healing power of certain species. According to another theory, the name is said to come from the Medieval Latin 'tomentilla', Tormentil.

2 | Snowy Cinquefoil
Potentilla nivea – Rosaceae

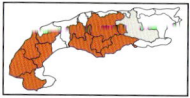

5–20cm tall, arching upwards, variably branching; basal leaves 3-lobed; leaflets 1–1.5cm long, densely white felty hairs beneath, with 2–7 long teeth on each side; stem 1–4-flowered; petals yellow, much longer than calyx. Flowers July to August.
SIMILAR SPECIES: Cut-leaved Cinquefoil, *P. multifida*, has pinnate leaves with linear lobes.
HABITAT: Sunny, wind-exposed slopes and stony sward with short period of snow cover; calcicole. 2,000–3,100m, sometimes lower, as on the Geisstein, North Tyrol, Austria (1,600m).
DISTRIBUTION: Arctic–alpine.

3 | Valdieri Cinquefoil
Potentilla valderia – Rosaceae

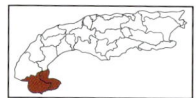

10–40cm tall; basal leaves stalked, mostly 7-lobed; leaflets tithed, grey-green above, undersides with grey felty hairs; petals dingy white, about 7mm long, shorter than calyx; epicalyx lobes as long as inner sepals, but narrower. Flowers June to August.
SIMILAR SPECIES: Snow Cinquefoil, *P. nivalis*, has leaflets with just a few teeth only at the tip, and epicalyx lobes longer than inner sepals. Saxifrage Cinquefoil, *P. saxifraga*, has 3–5-lobed basal leaves.
HABITAT: Rocky grassland, rocks; calcifuge. 1,200–2,500m.
DISTRIBUTION: Endemic to the Maritime Alps.

4 | Italian Burnet
Sanguisorba dodecandra – Rosaceae

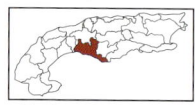

40–100cm tall, hairless or sparsely hairy, aromatic; leaves pinnate, with 3–8 pairs of leaflets; leaflet margins densely and sharply toothed, with 15–26 teeth on each side; flower spikes 5–8cm long; sepals pale green, stamens drooping, white, later yellow and rusty-red. Flowers July to September.
SIMILAR SPECIES: None.
HABITAT: Damp meadows, stony and gravelly stream banks; calcifuge. 700–2,300m.
DISTRIBUTION: Endemic to the southern Alps (Bergamasque and Rhaetian Alps).

5 | Sibbaldia
Sibbaldia procumbens – Rosaceae

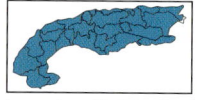

1–5cm tall; prostrate; leaves 3-lobed, bluish-green, long-stalked; leaflets obovate, truncate, with 3 teeth, almost hairless above, hairy beneath; inflorescence 3–10-flowered; petals pale yellow to yellowish-green, narrowly oval, shorter than the blue-green sepals. Flowers June to August.
SIMILAR SPECIES: Few.
HABITAT: Snowy hollows on acid soils; calcifuge. 1,900–3,300m, sometimes lower, as washed down near the Rhine, almost to Lake Constance/Bodensee (400m).
DISTRIBUTION: Arctic–alpine, with circumpolar distribution: Greenland, Iceland, Spitzbergen, North America, northern Europe, Scotland, northern Russia, central Asia, Kamchatka, Bering Straits. Many disjunct occurrences to the south, such as in the Alps, Vosges, Pyrenees, Tatra, and Caucasus.
NAME: In honour of Scottish doctor and botanist Robert Sibbald (1641–1722), who was one of the first to study the flora of Scotland.

Rosaceae

1 | Red-leaved Rose
Rosa glauca – Rosaceae

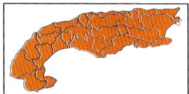

1–3m tall; leaves strikingly frosted blueish, or often purplish; leaflets oval, 1.5–4.5cm long and 1–2.5cm broad, simply serrated, non-glandular; stem and branches with similar, upright or curving thorns; sepals entire, rarely slightly divided; petals purplish-pink; fruit brick red to reddish-brown, hairless. Flowers June to July.

SIMILAR SPECIES: Red-leaved Rose, *R. glauca*, is relatively easy to distinguish from other species in what is a difficult genus, by the blue frosting on its leaves. Mountain Rose, *R. montana*, however may have similar blue frosting on the upper surface of its leaves, but differs in having fruits covered in stalked glandular hairs.

HABITAT: Scrub, woodland margins, stony sites. To 2,070m.

DISTRIBUTION: Southern European montane, from the Pyrenees to the Black Forest and Carpathians.

NOTE: There are about 35 rose species in the alpine region. Wild roses are taxonomically difficult as they tend to form hybrids, some of which behave like species, due to special cytogenetic mechanisms.

2 | Alpine Rose
Rosa pendulina – Rosaceae

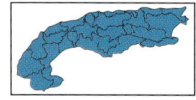

0.5–2m tall, forming colonial patches via runners; leaves with 7–11 oval, hairless, doubly-serrated leaflets; thorns absent, or thin and straight; flowering shoots mostly thornless; sepals undivided, hairless, upright after flowering; petals purplish-red; fruit drooping, oval to elongate flask-shaped, red, with stalked glands and spiny bristles. Flowers May to July.

SIMILAR SPECIES: The flask-shaped fruits (hips) make it relatively easy to distinguish from other rose species. However, Alpine Rose, and also French Rose, *R. gallica*, are the native species that are most likely to form hybrids with other wild roses.

HABITAT: Subalpine dwarf scrub, tall herb vegetation, montane woods, rocky slopes. To 2,600m.

DISTRIBUTION: Southern European montane, from north Spain to the Thuringian Forest and Pirin Mountains.

3 | Apple Rose
Rosa villosa – Rosaceae

0.5–1.5m tall, with short runners; leaves mostly 7-lobed, grey-green to blue-green; leaflets usually noticeably large, to 7cm long and 3cm broad, glandular, with serrated margins; thorns straight; sepals thickened at base, undivided or pinnate; petals pink, with dense glandular ciliate hairs at upper margin (hand lens); fruit round, 15–30mm in diameter, usually with stalked glandular chairs and glandular bristles, drooping when ripe. Flowers June to July.

SIMILAR SPECIES: This species is very variable, especially in the Alps, and most similar to Soft Downy Rose, *R. mollis*. The latter however has upper margins of petals only sparsely and patchily ciliate and glandular (hand lens).

HABITAT: Sunny, dry, stony slopes. To 2,500m.

DISTRIBUTION: Southern European montane–south-western Asiatic, from the Pyrenees to Iran.

NOTE: There are about 35 rose species native to the Alps, most of which are very similar. Certain identification requires intensive study of the genus.

4 | Friuli Spiraea
Spiraea decumbens – Rosaceae

10–25cm tall shrub with prostrate branches up to 50cm long; leaves hairless (subsp. *decumbens*) or with dense grey felty hairs on both sides (subsp. *tomentosa*), narrowly-elliptical to elongate-ovate, rounded or pointed at the tips, serrated, 1–3cm long, 1–1.5cm broad; flower stalk and inflorescence hairless (subsp. *decumbens*) or densely hairy (subsp. *tomentosa*); petals white to yellowish-white, almost round, about 2.5mm long. Flowers May to June.

SIMILAR SPECIES: Elm-leaved Spiraea, *S. chamaedryfolia*, is 1–2m tall and has 5–7mm long petals.

HABITAT: Sunny limestone sward, rock debris, streamside deposits, walls; on limestone and dolomite. To 2,000m.

DISTRIBUTION: Endemic to the south-eastern Alps.

NOTE: Subspecies: subsp. *decumbens* (**4A**), and subsp. *tomentosa* (**4B**).

1 | Rowan (Mountain Ash)
Sorbus aucuparia – Rosaceae

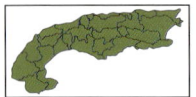

To 15m tall tree or shrub; leaves unpaired pinnate, with 5–9 pairs of leaflets; leaflets ovate-lanceolate, 4–6cm long, sharply toothed; 200–300 flowers, in umbel-like racemes; petals white, 4–5mm long, usually 2–4 styles. Flowers May to June.
SIMILAR SPECIES: Service Tree, *S. domestica*, has umbel-like racemes of 30–60 flowers, and petals 6–8mm long.
HABITAT: Open woods, rocky slopes, scrub, clearings. To 2,400m.
DISTRIBUTION: Eurosiberian, north to the North Cape and east to the River Ob region.
NOTE: 2 subspecies in the Alps:
– subsp. *aucuparia*: young branches and undersides of leaves hairy.
– subsp. *glabrata*: young branches and undersides of leaves almost hairless.

2 | Dwarf Whitebeam (False Medlar)
Sorbus chamaemespilus – Rosaceae

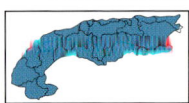

0.6–2m tall shrub; leaves undivided, blade oval, 5–10cm long, usually hairless, almost leathery, dark green above, often shiny, blue-green beneath; leaf margins serrated; flowers in umbel-like panicles; petals pink; fruit oval to round, red or brownish-red. Flowers June to July.
SIMILAR SPECIES: Whitebeam, *S. aria*, has creamy-white petals and grows to 15m tall.
HABITAT: Subalpine woody scrub, bushes, open montane woods; calcicole. 1,300–2,400m, sometimes lower, as near Feldkirch, Vorarlberg, Austria (520m).
DISTRIBUTION: Southern European montane, from the Pyrenees to the Balkan mountains, and north to the Riesengebirge/Krkonoše (Czechia, Poland).

3 | Neilreich's Woodruff (East Alpine Woodruff)
Asperula neilreichii – Rubiaceae

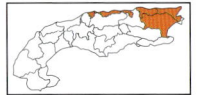

2–12cm tall, densely growing; leaves opposite; lower stem leaves reflexed, present at flowering; middle and upper stem leaves linear, 0.5–1mm broad; flowers pink to white, corolla tube 1.5–2.5mm long, 1–1.5x as long as corolla lobes. Flowers June to September.
SIMILAR SPECIES: Bristly Woodruff, *A. aristata*, has a 2.5–4mm long corolla tube, 2–3x as long as corolla lobes. Six-leaved Woodruff, *A. hexaphylla*, has leaves in whorls of 6, and a 5–7mm long corolla tube.
HABITAT: Rocky debris, rock crevices; calcicole. 400–1,900m.
DISTRIBUTION: Eastern alpine–Carpathian.
NAME: In honour of Austrian lawyer August Neilreich (1803–1871), who wrote a Flora of Vienna and a Flora of Lower Austria.

4 | Southern Woodruff
Asperula taurina – Rubiaceae

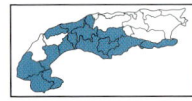

20–40cm tall; middle and upper leaves in whorls of 4, 3–6cm long, elliptical, with 3 longitudinal veins; flowers white, in dense clusters; involucral bracts broadly lanceolate to oval; corolla tube 6–8mm long. Flowers May to June.
SIMILAR SPECIES: Round-leaved Bedstraw, *Galium rotundifolium*, has 0.5–2cm long leaves, and small flowers only about 3mm in diameter.
HABITAT: Beechwoods, and other deciduous woods. To about 1,300m.
DISTRIBUTION: Southern European.

5 | Alpine Bedstraw
Galium anisophyllon – Rubiaceae

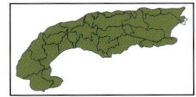

5–15cm tall, densely growing, with many sterile shoots; leaves linear, gradually widening towards the front and abruptly pointed, with a sharp tip; middle leaves in whorls of 7–9; leaf margins rough, with backwardly-directed bristles; flowers white to yellowish-white; fruit stalk straight. Flowers June to September.
SIMILAR SPECIES: Swiss Bedstraw, *G. megalospermum* (see p. 356), has pale greenish-yellow flowers and leaves mostly in whorls of 6–7.
HABITAT: Pasture, stony sward, snow-melt soils, meadows. 1,300–3,000m, sometimes washed down to lower levels.
DISTRIBUTION: Southern European montane.
NOTE: The bedstraw genus contains about 400 species, of which 46 are native to the Alps, with 9 restricted to the Alps.

Rubiaceae

1 | Swiss Bedstraw
Galium megalospermum – Rubiaceae

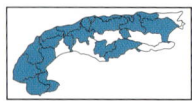

2–8cm tall, densely growing, widely creeping stems; leaves 3.5–5x as long as broad; leaves, prickly, rough-edged, in whorls mostly of 6–7; flowers greenish-cream-coloured; fruit stalk curved downwards. Flowers June to September.
SIMILAR SPECIES: Alpine Bedstraw, *G. anisophyllon* (see p. 354). West Alpine Bedstraw, *G. pseudohelveticum*, is very similar, but has leaf whorls of 7–8, and leaves 5–6x as long as broad. It is endemic to the French and Italian western Alps.
HABITAT: Rock debris; calcicole. 1,800–3,200m, often washed down to lower levels.
DISTRIBUTION: Alpine endemic.

2 | Honey Bedstraw
Galium meliodorum – Rubiaceae

15–40cm tall, with short runners; stem hairless, ascending, green at base; leaves thick, narrowly lanceolate, 10–20mm long, 0.5–2.1mm broad; leaf margins smooth, without prickles; flowers smell like honey; flowers yellowish- to greenish-white. Flowers June to August.
SIMILAR SPECIES: Traunsee Bedstraw, *G. truniacum*. Monte Arera Bedstraw, *G. montis-arerae* (**2B**), endemic to the Bergamasque Alps, has 5–12mm long leaves.
HABITAT: Rocky and stony sward; calcicole. 1,300–1,800m.
DISTRIBUTION: Endemic to the north-eastern Alps.

3 | Norican Bedstraw
Galium noricum – Rubiaceae

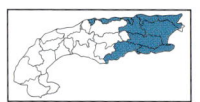

2–10cm tall; leaves thick, very shiny, linear-lanceolate, 5–8mm long, with sharply pointed tip 0.1mm long, most leaves broader than 1mm; flowers yellowish-greenish-white, 3.5–5mm in diameter. Flowers July to September.
SIMILAR SPECIES: Monte Baldo Bedstraw, *G. baldense*, has even the largest leaves less than 1mm broad, and flowers 3–3.5mm in diameter.
HABITAT: Stony poor grassland, rocky sward; calcicole. 1,400–2,500m.
DISTRIBUTION: Eastern alpine endemic.

4 | Col de Tende Bedstraw
Galium tendae – Rubiaceae

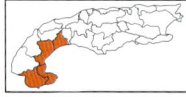

3–15cm tall, densely growing, with short runners; leaves 6–10mm long, 1–2mm broad, in whorls of 6–8; lower and upper leaves similar; flowers yellowish-greenish-white, 2.5–3mm in diameter. Flowers June to August.
SIMILAR SPECIES: String-of-pearls Bedstraw, *G. margaritaceum*, has very variably-shaped leaves: lower leaves oval, upper leaves linear-lanceolate.
HABITAT: Rocky debris, rock crevices; calcifuge. 1,500–2,900m.
DISTRIBUTION: Western alpine endemic

5 | Three-petaled Bedstraw
Galium trifidum – Rubiaceae

5–15cm tall; stem very delicate, prostrate, ascending or upright; leaves in whorls of 4, without sharply pointed tips; flowers about 1mm in diameter, in 2–3-flowered umbels; flowers mostly 3 lobed. Flowers June to July.
SIMILAR SPECIES: Easily distinguished from the other bedstraws by its 3-lobed flowers.
HABITAT: Margins of small mountain lakes. 1,700–1,800m.
DISTRIBUTION: Eurosiberian–North American. In the Alps only in the Seetaler and Gurktaler Alps, Austria.
NOTE: Alpine glacial relict.

6 | Traunsee Bedstraw
Galium truniacum – Rubiaceae

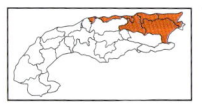

25–40cm tall, without runners; stem hairless, upright, with reddish base; leaves thin, narrowly lanceolate, 0.5–2.1mm broad; leaf margins smooth, without prickles; flowers pale yellow to creamy-white. Flowers June to August.
SIMILAR SPECIES: Shiny Bedstraw, *G. lucidum*, has underground runners, and green base to stem. Honey Bedstraw, *G. meliodorum*, has ascending stems, thick leaves, and green base to stem.
HABITAT: Stony sward; calcicole. 450–2,000m.
DISTRIBUTION: North-eastern alpine endemic.

Salicaceae

1 | Alpine Willow
Salix alpina – Salicaceae

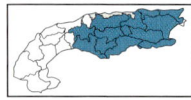

5–30cm tall, prostrate shrub; leaf blades broadly lanceolate to obovate, 1.5–3cm long, similarly green on both sides, hairless, with silky hairs when young; network of obvious leaf veins; leaf margins entire; flowers appearing with leaves. Flowers June to July.
SIMILAR SPECIES: Short-toothed Willow, *S. breviserrata*. Blunt-leaved Willow, *S. retusa* (see p. 360), has very inconspicuous connecting veins.
HABITAT: Rock debris and stony sward, dwarf shrub heath, pioneer grassland; calcicole. 1,400–2,400m.
DISTRIBUTION: Eastern alpine–Carpathian. Isolated in Macedonia.

2 | Short-toothed Willow
Salix breviserrata – Salicaceae

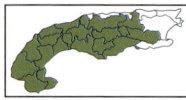

5–50cm tall, prostrate shrub; leaf blades broadly lanceolate to obovate, 1.5–3cm long, similarly green on both sides, leaf margins serrated to toothed; flowers appearing with leaves; fruits with dense curly hairs. Flowers June to July.
SIMILAR SPECIES: Alpine Willow, *S. alpina*, has entire leaf margins. Stinking Willow, *S. foetida*, has leaf undersides with bluish frosting.
HABITAT: Dwarf shrub heath, willow scrub, grassland, stony sward. 1,700–2,600m, also lower, as in the Vennbachtal, near Brenner (1,450m), or higher, as at the Gandegghütte above Zermatt, Switzerland (3,000m).
DISTRIBUTION: South-western European montane.
NOTE: Where the species overlap, there are often intermediate hybrid swarms with Alpine Willow, *S. alpina*.

3 | Smooth Willow
Salix glabra – Salicaceae

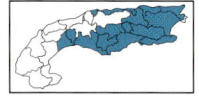

0.3–1.5m tall shrub; leaves hairless, leaf blades elliptical to obovate, notably shiny above, with bluish-green frosting on underside; flowers before the leaves appear; ovary hairless. Flowers May to June.
SIMILAR SPECIES: Waldstein's Willow, *S. waldsteiniana* (see p. 360), has leaf undersides weakly hairy only towards the tip, and ovary always hairy.
HABITAT: Stony sward, Dwarf Mountain Pine scrub, Scots Pine woods, sunny sites; calcicole. 1,400–2,100m, often lower, as in Nesselgraben near Reichenhall, Germany (580m).
DISTRIBUTION: Eastern alpine–Illyrian, from the eastern Alps to the Dinaric Alps.

4 | Swiss Willow
Salix helvetica – Salicaceae

0.3–1.5m tall shrub; twigs at first grey-brown, becoming brown and smooth; leaf blades elliptical to oval, 5–8cm long, dark green and sparsely hairy above, woolly-white beneath; leaf margins rolled under, entire to toothed; flowers opening a little before the leaves. Flowers June to August.
SIMILAR SPECIES: Silky Willow, *S. glaucosericea*, has leaves bluish-green above, silky-hairy beneath. Spear-leaved Willow, *S. hastata*, has undersides of leaves hairless.
HABITAT: Siliceous rocky sward, dwarf shrub heath, stream sides; calcifuge. 1,600–2,500m, sometimes lower, as at Schwarzsteingrund near Mayerhofen, Austria (1,400m), or higher, as on the Kesselspitze in the Stubaier Alps, Austria (2,700m).
DISTRIBUTION: Alpine–Carpathian.

5 | Dwarf Willow
Salix herbacea – Salicaceae

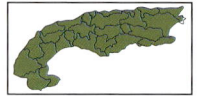

2–5cm tall, prostrate shrub, with underground woody rhizomes; leaf blades round to oval, 0.5–3cm long, 1–1.5x as long as broad, green on both sides, shiny, hairless or sparsely hairy beneath; leaf margins finely toothed; flowers opening with or just after the leaves; anthers purple, turning yellow; catkins at first green, then brownish-red. Flowers July to August.
SIMILAR SPECIES: Blunt-leaved Willow, *S. retusa* (see p. 360), has above-ground woody shoots, and leaves 1.5–3x as long as broad.
HABITAT: Snow-melt hollows, damp rocky debris, damp grassland; calcifuge. 1,800–3,300m.
DISTRIBUTION: Arctic–alpine.

Salicaceae

1 | Tauern Willow
Salix mielichhoferi – Salicaceae

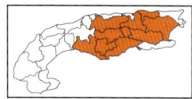

1–4m tall, upright shrub/tree with rounded crown; branches bare and shiny; leaves with 0.5–1cm long stalks, blade 3–10cm long, elliptical to ovate-lanceolate, hairless, similarly green on both sides, not frosted; vein network protruding on leaf undersides; flowers before leaves appear. Flowers May to June.
SIMILAR SPECIES: Dark-leaved Willow, *S. myrsinifolia*, has hairy leaf undersides, usually frosted bluish.
HABITAT: Damp alpine soils, Green Alder scrub, banks; calcicole. 1,300–1,900m.
DISTRIBUTION: Alpine endemic.
NAME: In honour of Salzburg botanist Mathias Mielichhofer (1772–1847), who discovered this willow species. He campaigned for improvements to working conditions in the Salzburg mines. The moss genus *Mielichhoferia* and the hybrid orchid *Dactylorhiza* x *mielichhoferi* (= *D. majalis* subsp. *alpestris* x *D. traunsteineri*) are also named after him.
NOTE: There are many willow species in the Alps.

2 | Net-leaved Willow
Salix reticulata – Salicaceae

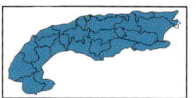

1–10cm tall, prostrate shrub; leaf blades round to broadly oval, 1–4cm long, with sunken network of veins, wrinkled, dark green above, greyish-white below; flowers opening with the leaves. Flowers June to August.
SIMILAR SPECIES: Dwarf Buckthorn, *Rhamnus pumila*, when not flowering may look similar, but lacks reticulate network of veins, having 4–9 parallel veins on both sides.
HABITAT: Calcareous snow-melt soils, rocky sites, damp stony sward; calcicole. 1,400–2,700m, sometimes higher, as on Monte Rosa, Switzerland/Italy (3,000m).
DISTRIBUTION: Arctic–alpine, from Scotland and Spitzbergen to the Altai Mountains. Arctic North America. In central and southern Europe, from the Pyrenees to the Pirin Mountains of Bulgaria.

3 | Blunt-leaved Willow
Salix retusa – Salicaceae

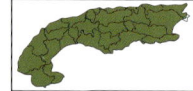

1–10cm tall, prostrate shrub; leaf blades obovate, 1–3cm long, 0.5–1.2cm broad, 1.5–3x as long as broad, with 4–6 lateral veins on each side, often notched at the top, entire, or finely toothed at base, green on both sides, hairless and shiny; flowers opening with the leaves. Flowers June to August.
SIMILAR SPECIES: Thyme-leaved Willow, *S. serpyllifolia*, has leaves just 0.3–1cm long and 0.2–0.4cm broad, with 2–4 pairs of lateral veins.
HABITAT: Snow-melt soils, stony grassland, damp rocky sward, dwarf shrub heath. 1,400–2,600m.
DISTRIBUTION: Southern European montane, from the Pyrenees to the Carpathians and mountains of the north and central Balkan Peninsula.

4 | Waldstein's Willow
Salix waldsteiniana – Salicaceae

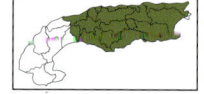

0.3–2m tall shrub; leaf blades elliptical to obovate, 2–5cm long, shiny above, frosted beneath, weakly hairy towards the tip (hand lens); leaf margins shallowly serrated to notched; flowers opening with the leaves; ovary hairy. Flowers June to July.
SIMILAR SPECIES: Smooth Willow, *S. glabra* (see p. 358). Tea-leaved Willow, *S. bicolor* (Syn.: *S. phylicifolia*), has entire leaf margins. Stinking Willow, *S. foetida*, has leaf margins densely and sharply serrated to toothed.
HABITAT: Dwarf Mountain Pine, willow and Green Alder scrub, damp rocky sites, dwarf shrub heath; calcicole. 1,200–2,200m, sometimes lower, as in Kundler Klamm gorge, Austria (650m), or higher, as on Kaserer Schartl in the Tux Alps (Tuxer Alpen), Austria (2,450m).
DISTRIBUTION: Eastern alpine–Illyrian, from the eastern Alps to the Korab Massif, Albania/North Macedonia.
NAME: In honour of Austrian military man and botanist Franz de Paula Adam Norbert Wenzel Ludwig Valentin von Waldstein (1759–1823), Franz Adam von Waldstein for short. He travelled in Hungary with Paul Kitaibel and together they wrote several botanical works. The bellflower *Campanula waldsteiniana* and the genus *Waldsteinia* (Rosaceae) are also named after him.

Sambucaceae, Santalaceae, Saxifragaceae

1 | Red-berried Elder
Sambucus racemosa – Sambucaceae

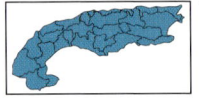

1–4m tall shrub; leaves unpaired pinnate with 5 leaflets; pith of branches ochre-coloured; corolla greenish-pale yellow, in pyramidal clusters; fruits red. Flowers April to May.
SIMILAR SPECIES: Few.
HABITAT: Woodland clearings, montane woods, coarse rock debris. To 2,300m.
DISTRIBUTION: European.

2 | Alpine Bastard-toadflax
Thesium alpinum – Santalaceae

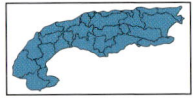

5–25cm tall; stems prostrate to ascending; leaves linear, 0.7–3mm broad, mostly 1-veined; inflorescence unbranched and unilaterally nodding; flowers mostly 4-lobed; each flower supported by 3 bracts. Flowers June to July.
SIMILAR SPECIES: Pyrenean Bastard-toadflax, *T. pyrenaicum*, usually has 5-lobed flowers and two-sided flower spikes.
HABITAT: Stony poor grassland, open pine woods, bushy slopes. To 2,700m.
DISTRIBUTION: European montane, from the Spanish mountains to southwest Sweden and Russia.

3 | Pyrenean Bastard-toadflax
Thesium pyrenaicum – Santalaceae

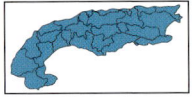

10–40cm tall; leaves linear, 0.5–2mm broad, 1–3-veined; flower spikes two-sided; flowers mostly 5-lobed, each flower supported by 3 bracts; flowers fragrant. Flowers May to July.
SIMILAR SPECIES: Bavarian Bastard-toadflax, *T. bavarum*, has 3–7mm broad leaves with 3–5 veins. Beaked Bastard-toadflax, *T. rostratum*, has only one bract per flower, and a tuft of leaves without flowers at the tip of the inflorescence.
HABITAT: Poor meadows, stony sward. To 2,500m.
DISTRIBUTION: European montane.
NOTE: 2 subspecies in the Alps:
– subsp. *pyrenaicum*: flowers 3–5mm long, ± as long as fruit.
– subsp. *alpestre*: flowers 6–8mm long, 1.5–2x as long as fruit.

4 | Ascending Saxifrage (Wedge-leaved Saxifrage)
Saxifraga adscendens – Saxifragaceae

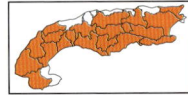

2–25cm tall, biennial, entire plant with sticky glandular hairs; basal leaves wedge- or spoon-shaped, 3–25mm long, with 2–7 teeth at the top; stem leaves numerous; inflorescence with stiff, upright, few-flowered branches; flower stalks 0.5–1.5x as long as the flowers; petals 3–5mm long, milky white, usually notched at tip; sepals oval, 1–2.5mm long. Flowers June to August.
SIMILAR SPECIES: Rue-leaved Saxifrage, *S. tridactylites*, grows at lower levels and has flower stalks 2–5x as long as the flowers. Scree Saxifrage, *S. androsacea* (see p. 364), has very few or no stem leaves.
HABITAT: Moderately damp, short, open pasture and sheep resting sites, damp calcareous debris. 1,800–3,480m.
DISTRIBUTION: Arctic–alpine.

5 | Yellow Saxifrage
Saxifraga aizoides – Saxifragaceae

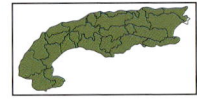

5–20cm tall, patch-forming; stem prostrate, arching upwards, densely leafy, with many sterile shoots; leaves fleshy, linear-lanceolate, ciliate; flowering stems 3–10-flowered, hairless; petals lemon yellow, orange or red. Flowers June to September.
SIMILAR SPECIES: None.
HABITAT: Spring-fed flushes, stony stream sides, damp rocky sward, snow-melt soils, alpine grassland; calcicole. To 3,000m.
DISTRIBUTION: Arctic–alpine. Widespread in the Arctic, further south restricted to the mountains, in Europe south to the mountains of Bulgaria.
NOTE: Yellow Saxifrage is very variable, especially with respect to flower colour. There are also very rare hybrids with *Saxifraga caesia* (= *S.* x *patens*) and *Saxifraga mutata* (= *S.* x *hausmannii*).

Saxifragaceae

1 | Scree Saxifrage
Saxifraga androsacea – Saxifragaceae

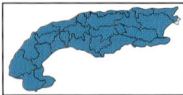

2–8cm tall; rosette leaves lanceolate to spoon-shaped, 5–25mm long, 2–6mm broad, entire or 3–5-lobed towards tip, and with erect glandular hairs at margins; flowering stems also with erect glandular hairs, 1–3-flowered; petals white, elliptical, touching each other, 2–3x as long as sepals. Flowers May to August.
SIMILAR SPECIES: Fassa Saxifrage, *S. depressa*, has 3-lobed leaves 6–9mm broad, and flowering stems 3–7-flowered.
HABITAT: Snow-melt soils, damp meadows, stony sward; somewhat calcicole. 1,450–3,125m.
DISTRIBUTION: European-Asiatic, from the Pyrenees to the Sayan Mountains of southern Siberia.

2 | Leafless Saxifrage
Saxifraga aphylla – Saxifragaceae

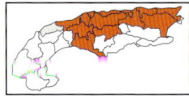

1–4cm tall, forming loose cushions; rosette leaves spoon-shaped to lanceolate, 3-lobed towards tip, rarely entire or 5-lobed, 7–15mm long; stem leafless, usually single-flowered; petals pale yellow, 2–2.5mm long, 0.3–0.5mm broad, as long or a little longer than sepals. Flowers July to September.
SIMILAR SPECIES: Styrian Saxifrage, *S. styriaca* (see p. 378). Seguier's Saxifrage, *S. seguieri* (see p. 376), has 1–3-flowered stems with usually one leaf.
HABITAT: Rock debris with long snow cover, damp rock crevices; calcicole. 1,730–3,200m.
DISTRIBUTION: Eastern alpine endemic, with distribution centred in the northern calcareous Alps.

3 | Cobweb Saxifrage
Saxifraga arachnoidea – Saxifragaceae

10–30cm long, forming loose mats, and covered in cobweb-like sticky glandular hairs; stems fragile, prostrate to ascending; lower leaf blades round, 3–5-lobed; petals pale yellow, 2–3mm long, longer than the greenish sepals. Flowers May to August.
SIMILAR SPECIES: Few.
HABITAT: Beneath overhanging rocks, caves, in damp calcareous soil. 600–1,850m.
DISTRIBUTION: Endemic to the Insubrian Alps.
NOTE: Molecular genetic studies have confirmed the close relationship between Cobweb Saxifrage and Fragile Saxifrage (*Saxifraga paradoxa*). Both species are considered to be Tertiary relicts which probably survived the cold periods not far from their present localities.

4 | Rough Saxifrage
Saxifraga aspera – Saxifragaceae

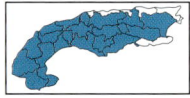

5–20cm tall, forming loose mats; leaves not in rosettes, 5–20mm long, linear-lanceolate, pointed, with bristly margins; inflorescence 1–10-flowered; petals 5–8mm long, broadest above the middle. Flowers July to August.
SIMILAR SPECIES: Moss Saxifrage, *S. bryoides* (see p. 366), has denser growth, and is only 2–5cm tall, with leaves 2–6mm long.
HABITAT: Shady rocks, rock debris, dry walls, stony slopes; calcifuge. 1,500–2,400m, sometimes lower, as in Valle Maggia, Tessin, Switzerland (400m), or higher, as on the Gornergrat, Valais, Switzerland (2,800m).
DISTRIBUTION: South-west European montane, from the central Pyrenees to the Tuscan Apennines and eastern Alps.

5 | Colli Berici Saxifrage
Saxifraga berica – Saxifragaceae

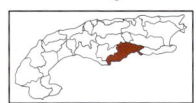

10–20cm tall, without sterile lateral shoots; flowering shoots richly branched, mostly interwoven; blades of basal leaves kidney-shaped, up to one third deeply incised and multi-lobed, with long glandular hairs; petals white, 5–8mm long, asymmetrical, varying in size within the flower. Flowers April to May.
SIMILAR SPECIES: Karst Saxifrage, *S. petraea* (see p. 374).
HABITAT: Shady rocks, caves, beneath overhanging rock ledges; calcicole. 200–300m.
DISTRIBUTION: Endemic to Monte Berici, Italy, in the foothills of the southern Alps.

Saxifragaceae

1 | Two-flowered Saxifrage
Saxifraga biflora – Saxifragaceae

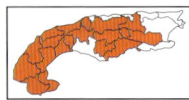

1–5cm tall, with prostrate shoots, producing fairly open patches; leaves obovate to almost round, blunt, often suffused reddish, with a spot at the tip; inflorescence 2–7-flowered; petals purplish-red, elliptical, 1–2mm broad, 3-veined. Flowers July to August.
SIMILAR SPECIES: The hybrid *S.* x *kochii* (= *S. biflora* x *S. oppositifolia*), which is not uncommon, has characters of both parent species, and petals usually more than 2mm broad.
HABITAT: Damp rocky sward and rocks; on intermediate rocks, especially calcareous mica schist. 2,000–3,000m, occasionally higher, as on the Matterhorn (4,200m).
DISTRIBUTION: Alpine endemic.
NOTE: Some authors recognise the hybrid *S. biflora* x *S. oppositifolia* as the subspecies *macropetala*.

2 | Ciliate Saxifrage
Saxifraga blepharophylla – Saxifragaceae

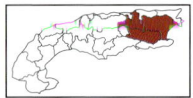

1–5cm tall, with prostrate shoots, producing fairly open patches; leaves spoon-shaped or blunt, with a usually inconspicuous whitish, non-calcareous spot, somewhat thickened at the top, 3–4mm long, the margins with long ciliate hairs; flowers solitary; petals purple, 5–8mm long, 2–3x as long as the sepals; sepals with non-glandular ciliate hairs. Flowers April to July.
SIMILAR SPECIES: Purple Saxifrage, *S. oppositifolia* (see p. 372), which is closely related. Rudolphi's Saxifrage, *S. rudolphiana* (see p. 376).
HABITAT: Rocks, stony sward; calcifuge. 2,100–3,240m.
DISTRIBUTION: Eastern alpine endemic.

3 | Moss Saxifrage
Saxifraga bryoides – Saxifragaceae

2–5cm tall, forming dense cushions; leaves in basal rosettes, 2–6mm long, covered in stiff ciliate hairs, bending inwards; mostly single-flowered; petals broadest in the middle, sometimes spotted red. Flowers July to August.
SIMILAR SPECIES: Rough Saxifrage, *S. aspera* (see p. 364).
HABITAT: Exposed rocky sward, rocks; calcifuge. 1,800–4,050m.
DISTRIBUTION: European montane, from the Pyrenees to the Riesengebirge/Karkonosze (Czechia, Poland) and the mountains of Bulgaria.

4 | Burser's Saxifrage
Saxifraga burseriana – Saxifragaceae

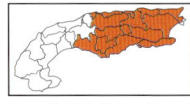

3–10cm tall; basal leaves awl-like to lanceolate, with long, sharp tips, 4–14mm long, 0.8–1.3mm broad, with pale grey coating on both sides; single-flowered; petals white, 7–15mm long. Flowers March to June.
SIMILAR SPECIES: Vandelli's Saxifrage, *S. vandellii* (see p. 378), has inflorescence with 2–6 flowers.
HABITAT: Rock crevices, rocky debris; calcicole. To 2,200m, sometimes higher, as on the Hochstadel near Lienz, Austria (2,500m).
DISTRIBUTION: Eastern alpine endemic.
NAME: In honour of German physician and botanist Joachim Burser (1583–1649). Burser discovered this saxifrage species in 1620 in the Radstadt Tauern, Austria.

5 | Blue-green Saxifrage
Saxifraga caesia – Saxifragaceae

3–12cm tall, forming fairly thick, firm cushions; rosette leaves blue-green, curved strongly backwards from the base, blunt, 2–5mm long, 0.7–1.5mm broad, with lime-encrusted spots around margins; stems bare or with few about 0.1mm long glandular hairs, with alternate leaves and 2–6 flowers; petals 3–4mm long. Flowers June to September.
SIMILAR SPECIES: Dolomites Saxifrage, *S. squarrosa* (see p. 376), has smaller leaves, 2.5–3mm long and 0.5–0.9mm broad, pointed at the tip and only slightly curved. Columnar Saxifrage, *S. diapensioides* (see p. 370), has 6–9mm long petals. Waldensian Saxifrage, *S. valdensis*, has stems with dense, 0.2–0.5mm long glandular hairs.
HABITAT: Rocky sward, stony grassland; calcicole. 1,500–2,900m, sometimes lower, as on the Isar River near Ebenhausen, Germany (550m).
DISTRIBUTION: Southern European montane, from the Pyrenees to the Tatra and the mountains of Montenegro.

Saxifragaceae

1 | Thick-leaved Saxifrage (Limestone Saxifrage)
Saxifraga callosa – Saxifragaceae

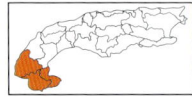

15–60cm tall, with many non-flowering rosettes; rosette leaves linear, to 10cm long and 0.6cm broad, entire, or slightly notched, blue-green, fleshy, lime-encrusted, often reddish at base; inflorescence hairless, arching over; petals white, often with red spots, 6–9mm long. Flowers May to July.

SIMILAR SPECIES: Pyramidal Saxifrage, *S. cotyledon* has leaves 0.9–1.5cm broad, and is calcifuge. Stunted forms of *S. callosa* may be confused with Paniculate Saxifrage, *S. paniculata* (see p.374), but the latter has leaves with serrated margins and a glandular inflorescence.
HABITAT: Rock crevices; calcicole. To 1,900m.
DISTRIBUTION: Western alpine–Apennine.
NOTE: The names saxifrage and *Saxifraga* come from the Latin words 'saxum' (= stone) and 'frangere' (= to break), derived from the belief that the plants cause the cracks in the rock.

2 | Nodding Saxifrage
Saxifraga cernua – Saxifragaceae

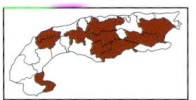

5–30cm tall; basal leaves (3)5(7)-lobed, with stems with curly hairs; basal and stem leaves with vegetative bulbils in axils; stem unbranched, single-flowered, or flowerless, often nodding towards the top; petals white, 5–9mm long. Flowers July.

SIMILAR SPECIES: Carpathian Saxifrage, *S. carpatica*, is many-flowered and has vegetative bulbils only in the axils of basal leaves. In the Alps known only from the Seckauer Tauern in Styria.
HABITAT: Damp and wet rocks in shady gorges, caves, and tall herb vegetation at animal resting sites. 1,500–2,830m.
DISTRIBUTION: Arctic–alpine. Widespread in the Arctic, further south in the mountains.

3 | Pyramidal Saxifrage
Saxifraga cotyledon – Saxifragaceae

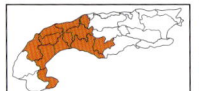

15–75cm tall (long), with many non-flowering rosettes; rosette leaves broadly linear, broader towards the tip, 2–8cm long, 9–15mm broad; leaf margins finely toothed; stem branching from at or near the base; panicle usually drooping; petals white, 5–10mm long. Flowers June to August.
SIMILAR SPECIES: Thick-leaved Saxifrage, *S. callosa*.
HABITAT: Warm, damp, siliceous rock crevices; calcifuge. To 2,600m.
DISTRIBUTION: Arctic–alpine. Pyrenees, Alps, Scandinavia, and Iceland.

4 | Encrusted Saxifrage
Saxifraga crustata – Saxifragaceae

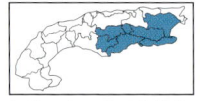

10–30cm tall, with many non-flowering rosettes; rosette leaves linear-lanceolate, 1–5cm long and 1.5–4mm broad, arching outwards (downwards), pointed, entire to very shallowly notched, with many spot-like depressions covered by lime encrustations; inflorescence with 1–3-flowered branches; petals white, ± 5mm long. Flowers June to August.
SIMILAR SPECIES: Paniculate Saxifrage, *S. paniculata* (see p. 374), has blunt, inwardly-curving rosette leaves 4–7mm broad.
HABITAT: Calcareous rocks, stony slopes, rock debris; calcicole. To 2,500m.
DISTRIBUTION: Eastern alpine–Illyrian, from the Adige River, Italy to western Serbia.

5 | Wedge-leaved Saxifrage (Spoon-leaved Saxifrage)
Saxifraga cuneifolia – Saxifragaceae

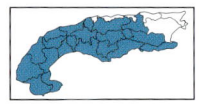

10–20cm tall, with many leaf rosettes, forming loose patches; leaf blades obovate to spoon-shaped, hairless, with a few blunt teeth and cartilaginous margins; flowering stems leafless; inflorescence usually downy and glandular; petals white, 2.5–4mm long, often with an orange-red spot. Flowers May to August.
SIMILAR SPECIES: Starry Saxifrage, *S. stellaris* (see p. 378).
HABITAT: Damp, shady rocks, and woodland boulders. To 2,200m.
DISTRIBUTION: Southern European montane, from northwest Spain to the eastern Carpathians.
NOTE: 2 subspecies in the Alps:
– subsp. *cuneifolia*: inflorescence with fewer than 10 flowers; only in the western Alps and northern Apennines.
– subsp. *robusta*: inflorescence usually with more than 10 flowers; found throughout the range of the species.

Saxifragaceae

1 | Columnar Saxifrage
Saxifraga diapensioides – Saxifragaceae

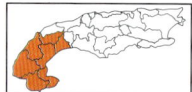

3–8cm tall; forming dense cushions; basal leaves 3–6mm long, 1–2mm broad, triangular to oval, blunt, tightly overlapping, with lime-exuding pits; inflorescence 1–6(9)-flowered, densely glandular; petals white to cream, 6–9mm long, 2–3x as long as sepals. Flowers April to July.
SIMILAR SPECIES: Tombea Saxifrage, *S. tombeanensis* (see p. 378), has spiny-tipped basal leaves.
HABITAT: Limestone and dolomite rocks. 850–2,800m.
DISTRIBUTION: Western alpine endemic.

2 | Furrowed Saxifrage
Saxifraga exarata – Saxifragaceae

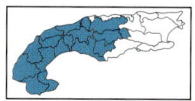

1–12cm tall; basal leaves elongate-wedge-shaped, 3–7-lobed at the top, sticky, glandular and with resinous scent, notably grooved above; stems with 2–4 leaves; inflorescence 2–12-flowered; petals white to creamy-yellow, 4–6mm long, 1.5–3x as long and about 2x broad as sepals. Flowers June to August.
SIMILAR SPECIES: Musky Saxifrage, *S. moschata* (see p. 372), has greenish-yellow to reddish petals, roughly as broad as and only a little longer than sepals.
HABITAT: Rock debris, rock crevices, ridges; calcifuge. 1,800–3,380m, sometimes lower.
DISTRIBUTION: Mountains of Europe and Asia Minor, from the western Alps to the Caucasus.

3 | Facchini's Saxifrage
Saxifraga facchinii – Saxifragaceae

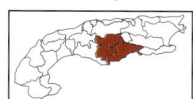

1–5cm tall; basal leaves elongate-lanceolate, rounded, 7–10mm long and 1–2mm broad, with glandular hairs; inflorescence 1–4-flowered; petals pale yellow to greenish-yellow or purple, 1.5–2mm long, barely extending beyond sepals. Flowers July to August.
SIMILAR SPECIES: Flat-leaved Saxifrage, *S. muscoides* (see p. 372), has petals 1.5–2x as long as sepals.
HABITAT: Cracks in rock, rock debris; calcicole. 1,800–3,360m.
DISTRIBUTION: Endemic to the Dolomites.
NAME: In honour of Italian botanist and physician Francesco Facchini (1788–1852). Facchini lived for a while in the Fassa Valley, working as a general practitioner. He wrote a flora of South Tyrol which was published 3 years after his death.

4 | Mercantour Saxifrage (The Ancient King)
Saxifraga florulenta – Saxifragaceae

15–40cm tall; rosette leaves 2–10cm long, dark bluish-green and shiny, pointed, with ciliate margins; flowers small and compact, in a long, pointed spike-like raceme; petals 5, white to pale pink, about 6mm long; top flower with 6–8 petals. Flowers July to August.
SIMILAR SPECIES: None.
HABITAT: Steep, silicate, often north-exposed rocks; calcifuge. 2,000–3,000m.
DISTRIBUTION: Endemic to the Maritime Alps.

5 | Hawkweed-leaved Saxifrage
Saxifraga hieraciifolia – Saxifragaceae

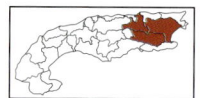

10–40cm tall; stem sturdy, leafless except for the leaves in the inflorescence, densely covered in long glandular hairs; leaves almost sessile, 3–7cm long, elliptical, finely toothed or almost entire, ciliate; flowers 15–30, in a dense slender spike; corolla yellowish-green to brownish-red. Flowers July to August.
SIMILAR SPECIES: None.
HABITAT: Damp stony sward, ravines; calcifuge. 1,600–2,500m.
DISTRIBUTION: Arctic–eastern alpine–Carpathian–central Asiatic. Glacial relict.
NOTE: Hawkweed-leaved Saxifrage is inconspicuous and very rare in the Alps, and so finding it requires an element of luck. In the region of Schießeck in the Styrian Wölzer Tauern, Austria, it grows alongside several other interesting alpine plants such as Styrian (Tauern) Gentian, *Gentiana frigida*, Three-flowered Milk-vetch, *Oxytropis triflora*, Alpine Meadow-rue, *Thalictrum alpinum*, Crimson-tipped (Oeder's) Lousewort, *Pedicularis oederi*, and Capitate Field Fleawort, *Tephroseris integrifolia* subsp. *capitata*.

Saxifragaceae

1 | Host's Saxifrage
Saxifraga hostii – Saxifragaceae

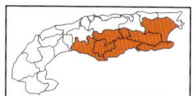

15–60cm tall, with many non-flowering rosettes; rosette leaves tongue-shaped to linear, 2–10cm long and 4–9mm broad, margins notched to serrated, ciliate at base, with lime-exuding pits on upper surface; inflorescence a panicle with 5–12 flowering branches; petals 4–8mm long, white with purple spots. Flowers May to July.
SIMILAR SPECIES: Pyramidal Saxifrage, *S. cotyledon* (see p. 368), has 9–15mm broad leaves, and is calcifuge.
HABITAT: Rock crevices, rocky grassland; calcicole. 900–2,500m, sometimes lower.
DISTRIBUTION: Eastern alpine. Also in Slovenia in the Trnovo Forest Plateau (Trnovski gozd), and on the Snežnik Plateau.
NOTE: 2 subspecies in the Alps:
– subsp. *hostii* (**1B**): rosette leaves broadening towards the top and rounded.
– subsp. *rhaetica* (**1C**): rosette leaves almost parallel-sided, with pointed triangular tips.
NAME: In honour of the Imperial personal physician Nicolaus Thomas Host (1761–1834), the author of *Flora Austriaca*.

2 | Musky Saxifrage
Saxifraga moschata – Saxifragaceae

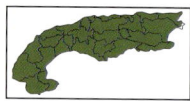

1–12cm tall, variable; basal leaves linear, entire or 3-lobed, weakly glandular, not furrowed above, or only faintly so; stem with 2–5 leaves, these undivided or more rarely 2–3-lobed; inflorescence 2–5-flowered; petals greenish-yellow to reddish, 4–6mm long, about the same width as and only a little longer than the sepals. Flowers June to August.
SIMILAR SPECIES: Furrowed Saxifrage, *S. exarata* (see p. 370).
HABITAT: Rock debris, stony pasture, snow-melt soils; alkaline-loving. 1,450–4,000m.
DISTRIBUTION: Mountains of Europe and Asia Minor, from the Pyrenees to the Caucasus.

3 | Flat-leaved Saxifrage
Saxifraga muscoides – Saxifragaceae

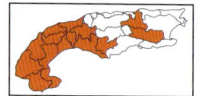

1–5cm tall, forming firm cushions, resin-scented; basal leaves lanceolate, 3–8mm long and 1–3mm broad, with glandular ciliate hairs at margins; flowering shoots densely glandular-hairy, and leafy; petals pale yellow to pale lemon yellow, blunt to notched, 1.5–2x as long as the sepals. Flowers June to August.
SIMILAR SPECIES: Facchini's Saxifrage, *S. facchinii* (see p. 370).
HABITAT: Cushion vegetation, rocky debris, especially on ridges. 1,800–4,200m, occasionally lower, as at the foot of the Hüfi Glacier, Switzerland (1,450m).
DISTRIBUTION: Alpine endemic, from the Cottian Alps to Lungau, Austria.

4 | Orange Saxifrage
Saxifraga mutata – Saxifragaceae

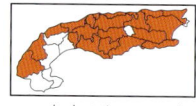

15–50cm tall; rosette leaves 3–7cm long, elongate-spoon-shaped to obovate, rounded at tips, margins fringed and notched; flowering stalks upright, mostly pyramidally branched, with dense glandular hairs; petals yellow, orange or red. Flowers June to July.
SIMILAR SPECIES: When in flower, none.
HABITAT: Damp rocks, rocky debris, river gravel, alpine grassland; calcicole. To 1,900m, sometimes higher, as on the Frau Hitt, Tyrol, Austria (2,200m).
DISTRIBUTION: Alpine–southern Carpathian.

5 | Purple Saxifrage
Saxifraga oppositifolia – Saxifragaceae

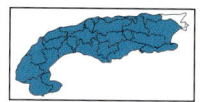

1–5cm tall, with prostrate shoots, loose-growing; leaves 2–4mm long, oval to lanceolate, blunt, broadest towards the tip, with 1(3) white lime spots; flowers solitary; petals purple, 7–10mm long, 2–3x as long as the sepals; sepals ciliate. Flowers April to July.
SIMILAR SPECIES: Ciliate Saxifrage, *S. blepharophylla* (see p. 366), has spoon-shaped leaves with a usually inconspicuous, not lime-encrusted spot near the tip. Rudolphi's Saxifrage, *S. rudolphiana* (see p. 376), is densely growing with compact cushions, and has leaves 1–2mm long. Wulfen's Saxifrage, *S. retusa* (see p. 374), has hairless sepals, 2–5-flowered inflorescence, and leaves with 3–5 spots near the tip.
HABITAT: Rocks, rock debris, glacier moraines, scree, stony sward; ± calcareous silicate soils. 1,700–3,800m, sometimes lower, as near Landquart, Switzerland (580m).
DISTRIBUTION: Arctic–alpine.

Saxifragaceae

1 | Paniculate Saxifrage
Saxifraga paniculata – Saxifragaceae

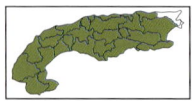

5–40cm tall, with many non-flowering rosettes; rosette leaves obovate-linear, 1–3cm long, 4–7mm broad, widening markedly towards the tip, blunt, grey-green, curving inwards and upwards at the tip; leaf margins finely toothed, with lime-encrusted spots; Flowers in loose, branching glandular panicles, branches 1–5-flowered. Flowers May to August.
SIMILAR SPECIES: Encrusted Saxifrage, *S. crustata* (see p. 368). Thick-leaved Saxifrage, *S. callosa* (see p. 368). Host's Saxifrage, *S. hostii* (see p. 372). Spoon-leaved Saxifrage, *S. cochlearis*, has spoon-shaped rosette leaves.
HABITAT: Rocks, stony sward; calcicole. To 3,400m.
DISTRIBUTION: European–North American.

2 | Fragile Saxifrage
Saxifraga paradoxa – Saxifragaceae

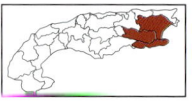

5–20cm tall, almost hairless; stems prostrate to ascending, fragile, basal leaf blades palmate with 5–7 entire lobes; petals green, 1.5–2.5mm long ± as long as the green sepals. Flowers June to August.
SIMILAR SPECIES: Alternate-leaved Golden Saxifrage, *Chrysosplenium alternifolium*, when not flowering, which has kidney-shaped leaf blades with more than 12 blunt notches.
HABITAT: Open caves, and silicate rock walls, sites with some protection from rain, but also with high humidity; mica schist, and also rarely on hard gneiss. 400–1,580m.
DISTRIBUTION: Endemic to the central Alps, from the Stubalpe and Packalpe in the north, to the Koralpe and Saualpe in the east, and to the Pohorje Mountains (Bachergebirge), Slovenia in the south. In Slovenia, it is found south to the Hudinja Gorge near Vitanje.

3 | Piedmont Saxifrage
Saxifraga pedemontana – Saxifragaceae

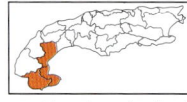

3–20cm tall, forming cushions, with non-flowering shoots; leaves in basal rosettes, densely glandular, palmate, wedge-shaped at base, divided almost to the centre into 3–7 lobes; inflorescence 3–10-flowered; petals white, 10–15mm long, 3-veined; sepals half as long as petals. Flowers June to August.
SIMILAR SPECIES: Furrowed Saxifrage, *S. exarata* (see p. 370), has 4–6mm long petals.
HABITAT: Shady rock walls, rock debris; calcifuge. 1,500–2,800m.
DISTRIBUTION: Several subspecies from Morocco to Romania. The subsp. *pedemontana* is endemic to the western Alps.

4 | Karst Saxifrage
Saxifraga petraea – Saxifragaceae

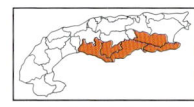

10–20cm tall, biennial, lacking sterile site shoots, flowering shoots richly branched, mostly intertwined; blades of basal leaves 3-palmate with toothed lobes and with long glandular hairs; petals white, 7–11mm long, symmetrical, similarly sized. Flowers April to July.
SIMILAR SPECIES: Colli Berici Saxifrage, *S. berica* (see p. 364), is perennial, and has unequally sized petals.
HABITAT: Shady, damp calcareous rocks, grotto-like depressions, beneath projecting walls. To 2,000m.
DISTRIBUTION: Eastern alpine–Illyrian, from Lake Como, Italy, to the Croatian karst region.

5 | Wulfen's Saxifrage
Saxifraga retusa – Saxifragaceae

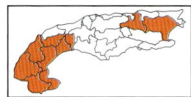

1–5cm tall, with prostrate shoots, forming compact cushions; leaves elongate-lanceolate to ovate-lanceolate, pointed, 2–4mm long, with 3–5 spots at the tip; inflorescence 2–5-flowered; petals purple, about 4mm long, 2x as long as sepals. Flowers May to August.
SIMILAR SPECIES: Purple Saxifrage, *S. oppositifolia* (see p. 372).
HABITAT: Wind-exposed ridges that are often snow free in winter; calcifuge. 2,100–3,400m.
DISTRIBUTION: Southern European montane, from the Pyrenees to the Rila Mountains, Bulgaria.
NOTE: 2 subspecies in the Alps:
– subsp. *retusa* (**5A**): sepals not glandular; western and eastern Alps.
– subsp. *augustana* (**5B**): sepals glandular; western Alps.

Saxifragaceae

1 | Round-leaved Saxifrage
Saxifraga rotundifolia – Saxifragaceae

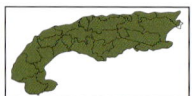

20–50cm tall, branching, many-flowered; basal leaf blades round to kidney-shaped, deeply notched to palmate, lobes pointed; leaf stalks 2–7x as long as blade; leaves getting increasingly small towards top of stem; petals 6–11mm long, white, with pretty yellow and red spots. Flowers June to September.
SIMILAR SPECIES: Alternate-leaved Golden Saxifrage, *Chrysosplenium alternifolium*, when not flowering, but this has blunt leaf lobes.
HABITAT: Shady, damp woods, tall herb and glaciated vegetation, Green Alder scrub. To 2,400m.
DISTRIBUTION: Southern European montane, from the Pyrenees to the Caucasus. In the Alps, occasionally into the northern alpine foothills.

2 | Rudolphi's Saxifrage
Saxifraga rudolphiana – Saxifragaceae

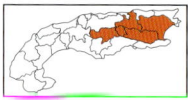

1–5cm tall, forming compact cushions; leaves obovate to tongue-shaped, pointed, 1.5–2mm long, curving backwards at the tip, with obvious lime encrustations; flowers solitary; petals purple; sepals glandular and ciliate. Flowers April to July.
SIMILAR SPECIES: Ciliate Saxifrage, *S. blepharophylla* (see p. 366), and Purple Saxifrage, *S. oppositifolia* (see p. 372), are looser-growing, have sepals with non-glandular ciliate hairs, and leaves 2–4mm long.
HABITAT: Rock debris, shady rocks; on intermediate substrates. 2,300–3,000m, sometimes higher, as on the Kitzsteinhorn, Austria (3,200m).
DISTRIBUTION: Eastern alpine endemic.
NAME: In honour of German botanist and zoologist of Swedish descent Karl Asmund Rudolphi (1771–1832). Rudolphi was Professor of Anatomy and Physiology in Greifswald from 1797, and in Berlin from 1810.

3 | Eastern Saxifrage
Saxifraga sedoides – Saxifragaceae

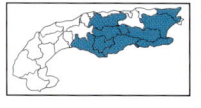

1–6cm tall, forming loose or dense patches; basal leaves lanceolate, almost always undivided, entire and pointed, 3–12mm long, 1–3mm broad, pale green with short glandular hairs; mostly 1–2-flowered; petals pale yellowish-green to yellow, narrowly triangular to oval, shorter than sepals; anthers yellow. Flowers June to September.
SIMILAR SPECIES: Hohenwart's Saxifrage, *S. hohenwartii*, has linear petals at least as long as sepals, and orange anthers. Bergamasque Saxifrage, *S. presolanensis* (**3B**), has 8–12cm long flowering stalks, and petals 2–2.5x as long as sepals: endemic to the Bergamasque Alps.
HABITAT: Damp stony and rocky sward; calcicole. 1,600–3,200m.
DISTRIBUTION: Eastern alpine–Apennine.

4 | Seguier's Saxifrage
Saxifraga seguieri – Saxifragaceae

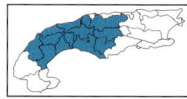

2–8cm tall, forming dense, flat patches; basal leaves spoon-shaped to lanceolate, 6–35mm long, 1–3.5mm broad, with short glandular hairs at margins; flower stalks 1–3-flowered, with 0–2 leaves; petals pale greenish-yellow, not overlapping, about as long as sepals. Flowers July to August.
SIMILAR SPECIES: Scree Saxifrage, *S. androsacea* (see p. 364), when not flowering, but this has long glandular hairs.
HABITAT: Rocky sward, rock crevices; calcifuge. 1,900–3,700m.
DISTRIBUTION: Alpine endemic.
NAME: In honour of French Jesuit and naturalist Jean-François Séguier (1703–1784). Séguier wrote a flora of Verona and described this species as *S. alpina minima*.

5 | Dolomites Saxifrage
Saxifraga squarrosa – Saxifragaceae

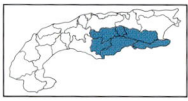

3–5cm tall; forming very dense and compact cushions; rosette leaves grey-green, pointed, curving slightly from the base, 2.5–3mm long, 0.5–0.9mm broad, with lime-exuding pits at margins; stem leaves alternate; stems 2–6-flowered; petals round. Flowers July to August.
SIMILAR SPECIES: Blue-green Saxifrage, *S. caesia* (see p. 366).
HABITAT: Rock crevices, rock debris; calcicole. 1,200–2,800m.
DISTRIBUTION: Southern alpine endemic.

Saxifragaceae

1 | Starry Saxifrage
Saxifraga stellaris subsp. *robusta* – Saxifragaceae

5–20cm tall, with stolons, forming loose patches; leaves in basal rosettes, shiny, obovate, coarsely toothed, unstalked; stems leafless up to the bracts, 3–15-flowered; inflorescence without bulbils; petals white, with 2 yellow spots. Flowers June to August.
SIMILAR SPECIES: Budding Starry Saxifrage, *S. stellaris* subsp. *prolifera* (**1B**), has inflorescence with many bulbils, few or no petals; endemic to the central eastern Alps. Wedge-leaved Saxifrage, *S. cuneifolia*, differs in having leaf stalks.
HABITAT: Spring-fed flushes, stream sides, snow-melt hollows. 1,400–3,000m, often lower, as near Grono, in Valle Mesolcina (Misox), Switzerland (300m), sometimes higher, as on Monte Rosa, Switzerland/Italy (3,100m).
DISTRIBUTION: Southern European montane subspecies, from Portugal to the Rhodope Mountains.
NOTE: The nominate subspecies, subsp. *stellaris*, is found in the arctic region.

2 | Styrian Saxifrage
Saxifraga styriaca – Saxifragaceae

1–6cm tall; patch-forming, with all shoots potentially flowering; rosette leaves fleshy, 10–25mm long, 3-lobed; stem leaves 0–1, elongate, mostly undivided; inflorescence single-flowered; petals yellowish-green, 0.3–0.7mm broad; sepals green, bluntly triangular, much broader than petals. Flowers May.
SIMILAR SPECIES: Leafless Saxifrage, *S. aphylla* (see p. 364), usually has many sterile shoots, and does not flower until high summer.
HABITAT: Wind-exposed, flat, damp sward and snow-melt hollows. 1,860–2,400m.
DISTRIBUTION: Eastern alpine endemic. First discovered in 1996.

3 | Slender Saxifrage (Awl-leaved Saxifrage)
Saxifraga tenella – Saxifragaceae

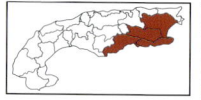

5–12cm tall, forming loose patches, with leafy creeping shoots; basal leaves linear-lanceolate, 8–12mm long, stiff, pointed, shiny, ciliate at base; stem leaves usually 4–6; inflorescence 2–9-flowered; petals yellowish-white, 2.5–3mm long, about 1.5x as long as sepals. Flowers June to July.
SIMILAR SPECIES: Rough Saxifrage, *S. aspera* (see p. 364), has leaves with stiff ciliate hairs, and 5–8mm long petals.
HABITAT: Shady, damp rocks, and rock debris; calcicole. 700–2,000m.
DISTRIBUTION: South-eastern alpine endemic.

4 | Tombea Saxifrage
Saxifraga tombeanensis – Saxifragaceae

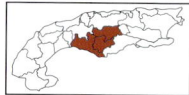

3–8cm tall, forming dense, compact cushions; basal leaves 2–5mm long, 1–1.5mm broad, overlapping, ovate-lanceolate, with incurved, pointed tips; stem leaves numerous, stem leaves and stem with glandular hairs; inflorescence usually 1–4-flowered; petals white, 9–12mm long. Flowers May to June.
SIMILAR SPECIES: Columnar Saxifrage, *S. diapensioides* (see p. 370).
HABITAT: Rock crevices; calcicole. 1,100–2,300m.
DISTRIBUTION: Endemic to the eastern southern Alps, in Italy from the Judicarian Alps (Giudicarie) to the Mendel Pass.

5 | Vandelli's Saxifrage
Saxifraga vandellii – Saxifragaceae

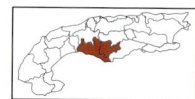

3–7cm tall; basal leaves 6–10mm long, 1.5–2.3mm broad, green, lanceolate to ovate-lanceolate, narrowing to a long, sharply pointed tip; inflorescence 2–6-flowered; petals white, 7–9mm long. Flowers May to June.
SIMILAR SPECIES: Burser's Saxifrage, *S. burseriana* (see p. 366).
HABITAT: Rock crevices; calcicole. 1,000–2,600m.
DISTRIBUTION: Endemic to the Italian southern Alps, from Lake Como to the Lombardy side of the Ortler Massif.
NAME: In honour of Domenico Vandelli (1735–1816), Italian mathematician and naturalist, who studied the flora of the south-eastern Alps and discovered this species.

Scrophulariaceae

1 | Jura Figwort (Hoppe's Figwort)
Scrophularia juratensis – Scrophulariaceae (Syn.: *Scrophularia canina* subsp. *hoppei*)

20–60cm tall, with glandular hairs when flowering, otherwise hairless; leaves pinnate; corolla reddish-brown, edged white, upper lip more than half as long as corolla tube. Flowers June to August.
SIMILAR SPECIES: French Figwort, *S. canina*, has corolla upper lip less than half as long as corolla tube, and inflorescence with almost sessile glands.
HABITAT: Stream side substrates, gravel, and rock debris; calcicole. To about 2,500m.
DISTRIBUTION: Southern European montane.

2 | Yellow Figwort
Scrophularia vernalis – Scrophulariaceae

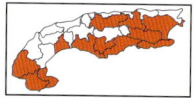

20–80cm tall, with loose woolly hairs, glandular; stems square; leaves undivided, heart-shaped, with glandular hairs; corolla yellow. Flowers April to June.
SIMILAR SPECIES: None.
HABITAT: Damp deciduous woods, clearings, animal resting sites, scrub. To about 1,800m.
DISTRIBUTION: Southern European, from the Iberian Peninsula to Iran. Naturalised in some places due to its earlier cultivation as a pasture nectar plant for bees.

3 | Alpine Mullein
Verbascum alpinum – Scrophulariaceae

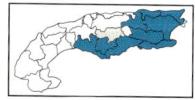

50–120cm tall; lower stem with dense woolly hairs; basal leaves heart-shaped at base; undersides of leaves felty and woolly-white, weakly hairy to hairless above; inflorescence spike unbranched or with a few side branches at the base; calyx with loose stellate hairs; corolla almost hairless; stamen filaments bearded purple-violet. Flowers May to July.
SIMILAR SPECIES: Dark Mullein, *V. nigrum*, has lower stem with sparse fluffy stellate hairs, and outer calyx and corolla covered with dense stellate hairs.
HABITAT: Woodland clearings, rocky grassland, vegetated scree. To about 2,000m.
DISTRIBUTION: Southern European montane.

4 | Annual Mullein (Boerhaave's Mullein)
Verbascum boerhavii – Scrophulariaceae

40–120cm tall, with woolly, fluffy white hairs; basal leaf blades oval to elliptical, 10–30cm long, 4–12cm broad; leaf margins toothed to notched; inflorescence simple; corolla 22–32mm in diameter; stamen filaments purple-violet and woolly. Flowers April to July.
SIMILAR SPECIES: Orange Mullein, *V. phlomoides*, has yellow stamen filaments.
HABITAT: Stony sward, dry ruderal sites. To about 1,900m.
DISTRIBUTION: Western Mediterranean.
NAME: In honour of Dutch physician, botanist and chemist Herman Boerhaave (1668–1738), who made outstanding contributions to the field of medicine. The genus *Boerhavia* in the family Nyctaginaceae is also named after him. His bust is displayed in the Walhalla hall of fame in Bavaria.

5 | Nettle-leaved Mullein (Chaix's Mullein)
Verbascum chaixii – Scrophulariaceae

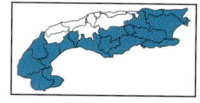

50–90cm tall; basal leaves wedge-shaped at base; inflorescence formed of several spike-like branched racemes; corolla 15–22mm in diameter; stamen filaments bearded purple-violet. Flowers July to October.
SIMILAR SPECIES: Dark Mullein, *V. nigrum*, has inflorescence unbranched or with just a few lateral racemes towards the base.
HABITAT: Poor meadows, rocky sward, margins of oak woods. To about 1,400m.
DISTRIBUTION: Southern European–Asiatic, east to western China.
NOTE: 2 subspecies in the Alps:
– subsp. *chaixii*: basal leaf blades with pointed serrations; grey felty-hairy beneath.
– subsp. *austriacum*: basal leaf blades with rounded serrations; hairy beneath, but green.
NAME: In honour of French botanist and clergyman Dominique Chaix (1730–1799), who studied the flora of the Dauphiné.

Scrophulariaceae, Solanaceae, Tamaricaceae

1 | Mountain Mullein
Verbascum crassifolium – Scrophulariaceae (Syn.: *Verbascum thapsus* subsp. *montanum*)

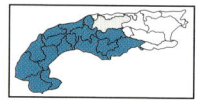

30–150cm tall; leaves with yellowish to reddish-brown hairs; basal leaf blades long and distinctly stalked; upper stem leaves sessile, not or only slightly running down stem at base; corolla broadly funnel-shaped, 15–30mm in diameter; lower stamen filaments only bare in upper part, otherwise with woolly hairs; stigma kidney-shaped. Flowers June to September.
SIMILAR SPECIES: Great Mullein, *V. thapsus*, has very short and indistinctly-stalked basal leaf blades, stem leaves with edges that run right down to the next lower leaf, and lower stamen filaments completely bare. Dense-flowered Mullein, *V. densiflorum*, has flatter flowers, 30–50mm in diameter, and a club-shaped stigma.
HABITAT: Sunny rocky slopes, margins of scrub. To about 2,300m.
DISTRIBUTION: South-western European montane.
NOTE: Carder bees of the genus *Anthidium* use the hairs of mulleins as nesting material. They scrape off hairs from the leaves and stems and carry it to their nesting holes. Other wild bees, such as mason bees, club-horned bees, masked bees and leafcutter bees sometimes use dead, pith-filled mullein stems as nest sites.

2 | White Mullein
Verbascum lychnitis – Scrophulariaceae

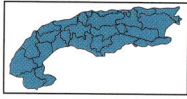

50–150cm tall; stems angular; upper sides of leaves with short, loose hairs or almost hairless, white felty hairs beneath; basal leaves wedge-shaped at base; corolla 12–18mm in diameter; Stamen filaments bearded whitish. Flowers June to July.
SIMILAR SPECIES: Hoary Mullein, *V. pulverulentum*, has round stems, and leaves white felty hairs on both sides.
HABITAT: Semi-arid grassland, transitional vegetation, clearings in warm oakwoods, semi-ruderal sites, embankments. To 1,800m.
DISTRIBUTION: European, east to the Caucasus and Siberia.

3 | Henbane Bell (European Scopolia)
Scopolia carniolica – Solanaceae

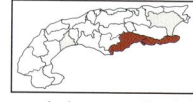

20–40cm tall, hairless; leaf blades elliptical to obovate, mostly entire; outer corolla shiny purple-brown, yellowish inside. Flowers March to April.
SIMILAR SPECIES: None.
HABITAT: Grey Alder (*Alnus incana*) woods and other deciduous woods. To 1,000m.
DISTRIBUTION: South-eastern European.
NAME: The generic name honours Austrian physician and naturalist Johann Anton Scopoli (1723–1788), who worked for 16 years as a doctor in a mine at Idrija in Carniola (now west Slovenia). He described 56 new plant species from this region.

4 | Woody Nightshade (Bittersweet)
Solanum dulcamara – Solanaceae

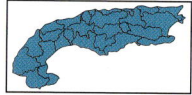

30–250cm tall, ± climbing; leaves stalked, simple or with 1–2 leaflets at base; corolla violet; fruit oval, shiny, bright red when ripe. Flowers June to August.
SIMILAR SPECIES: None.
HABITAT: Wet alder woods, riparian scrub, river valley woods, reedbeds, damp clearings and ruderal sward. To 1,700m.
DISTRIBUTION: Eurosiberian.

5 | German Tamarisk (German False Tamarisk)
Myricaria germanica – Tamaricaceae

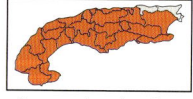

To 2m tall shrub with rod-like stems; leaves linear-lanceolate, blue-green, 2–5mm long, often overlapping; flowers in dense racemes; usually 5 petals, pale pink to white. Flowers June to July.
SIMILAR SPECIES: None.
HABITAT: Gravelly banks of fast-flowing rivers, gravel and sand pits. To 2,000m, sometimes higher, as on the Findel Glacier, Valais, Switzerland (2,350m).
DISTRIBUTION: European-Asiatic, from the Pyrenees and Norway to Afghanistan and Armenia.

Thymelaeaceae

1 | Alpine Daphne
Daphne alpina – Thymelaeaceae

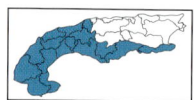

20–80cm tall, deciduous shrub; leaves ovate-lanceolate, 1–4cm long, hairy on both sides, at least when young, developed by flowering time; petals milky white, hairy; fruit orange-red. Flowers April to June.
SIMILAR SPECIES: Mezereon, *D. mezereum*.
HABITAT: Sunny, rocky sward, rocky slopes, open pine woods; calcicole. To 1,900m.
DISTRIBUTION: Southern European montane.
NOTE: The name Daphne was used by the Ancient Greeks for the Bay Tree (Bay Laurel), *Laurus nobilis*. The transfer of the name from Bay Tree involves the Spurge-laurel (*Daphne laureola*) which, with its green flowers, shiny, evergreen leaves and black fruits somewhat resembles the Bay Tree (Bay Laurel).

2 | Spurge-laurel
Daphne laureola – Thymelaeaceae

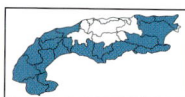

40–100cm tall, evergreen shrub; leaves broadly lanceolate, leathery; petals yellowish-green, hairless, faintly fragrant; fruit black. Flowers February to April.
SIMILAR SPECIES: None.
HABITAT: Warm, deciduous woods with mild winters, especially beechwoods; calcicole. To 1,200m.
DISTRIBUTION: Western European–Mediterranean.

3 | Mezereon (February Daphne)
Daphne mezereum – Thymelaeaceae

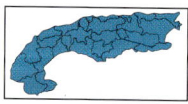

30–100cm tall, deciduous shrub; twigs only leafy towards the top; leaves lanceolate, 3–12cm long, hairless; flowers opening before leaves; petals purple-pink, with appressed hairs; flowers strongly fragrant; fruit bright red. Flowers February to May.
SIMILAR SPECIES: White-flowered forms may be confused with Alpine Daphne, *D. alpina*, but the latter has 1–4cm long leaves hairy on both sides, at least when young, and developed at flowering.
HABITAT: Deciduous woods, tall herb vegetation, rocky debris. To 2,600m.
DISTRIBUTION: European–western Asiatic.

4 | Rock Daphne
Daphne petraea – Thymelaeaceae

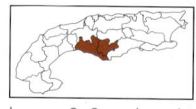

Low-growing 2–8cm tall, much-branched trailing shrub; leaves lanceolate, 0.8–1.2cm long, c. 2–3mm broad; inflorescence 3–5-flowered; petals pink, with fluffy hairs. Flowers June.
SIMILAR SPECIES: Striped Daphne, *D. striata*, has 10–25mm long leaves.
HABITAT: Crevices, usually on vertical, sunny dolomite rocks, rock debris; limestone and dolomite substrates. 700–2,000m.
DISTRIBUTION: Southern alpine endemic, from the mountain ranges of Lakes Ledro and Idro, to the northern side of Lake Garda.
NOTE: Rock Daphne forms (very rare) natural hybrids with Alpine Daphne, *Daphne alpina*. These pale pink-flowered plants, so far found west of Lake Garda, are named *Daphne* x *reichstenii*.

5 | Striped Daphne
Daphne striata – Thymelaeaceae

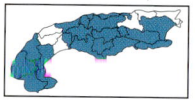

5–30cm tall, sparsely-branched evergreen dwarf shrub; leaves hairless, leathery, 10–25, long, about 5–6x as long as broad, clustered at tips of branches; flowers fragrant; petals purple-pink, with hairless tube. Flowers May to July.
SIMILAR SPECIES: Rose Daphne (Garland Flower), *D. cneorum*, has corolla tube and leaves densely covered in appressed hairs, and leaves 3–4x as long as broad.
HABITAT: Dwarf shrub heath, dry, stony poor grassland, rocky sward, Dwarf Mountain Pine scrub and open coniferous woods; calcicole. 1,200–2,600m, occasionally lower, as near Völs in the South Tyrol, Italy (900m), or higher, as on Sass Corviglia in Graubünden, Switzerland (2,860m).
DISTRIBUTION: Alpine endemic.
NOTE: In 2015 this species was found in the Styrian Kemet Mountains in the Dachstein Group, Austria, a good 100km from its centre of distribution.

Valerianaceae

1 | Celtic Valerian
Valeriana celtica – Valerianaceae

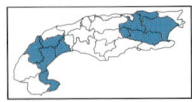

5–15cm tall, hairless; basal leaves obovate to lanceolate, narrowing into the stalk, entire; stem leaves linear-wedge-shaped, entire; corolla creamy-white to greenish-yellow or dull red; fruit with 4–6mm long feathery pappus hairs (**1B**). Flowers June to August.
SIMILAR SPECIES: Elongated Valerian, *V. elongata*, has oval to triangular stem leaves.
HABITAT: Acid pastures, Curved Alpine Sedge (*Carex curvula*) vegetation, rocky sward; calcifuge. 1,700–2,800m.
DISTRIBUTION: Alpine endemic.
NOTE: 2 subspecies in the Alps:
– subsp. *celtica*: leaves 3-veined; western Alps.
– subsp. *norica*: leaves 5-veined; eastern Alps.

2 | Elongated Valerian
Valeriana elongata – Valerianaceae

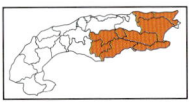

5–25cm tall; leaves shiny above; leaf blades oval to triangular, notched to coarsely toothed; flowers fragrant; corolla greenish to brownish. Flowers June to August.
SIMILAR SPECIES: Celtic Valerian, *V. celtica*.
HABITAT: Rock crevices, scree; calcicole. 1,400–2,300m.
DISTRIBUTION: Eastern alpine endemic.

3 | Mountain Valerian
Valeriana montana – Valerianaceae

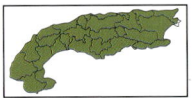

15–50cm tall; blades of basal leaves oval, wedge-shaped or blunt at base, rarely slightly heart-shaped; stem with 3–8 pairs of leaves; stem leaves all undivided, ovate-lanceolate; corolla pale pink, rarely white. Flowers May to July.
SIMILAR SPECIES: Three-lobed Valerian, *V. tripteris*. Round-leaved Valerian, *V. rotundifolia*, which is found only in the westernmost Alps, and is regarded as a variety of *V. montana*, has round basal leaf blades, and broadly oval stem leaves.
HABITAT: Stony slopes, rocky sward; calcicole. 700–2,700m, sometimes lower.
DISTRIBUTION: Southern European montane.

4 | Rock Valerian
Valeriana saxatilis – Valerianaceae

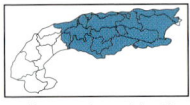

10–25cm tall; basal leaves narrowly obovate to lanceolate, narrowing into the stalk, ± entire, with ciliate margins; stem leaves linear; inflorescence a loose raceme or panicle; corolla white. Flowers June to July.
SIMILAR SPECIES: Few.
HABITAT: Limestone and dolomite rock crevices; calcicole. To 2,800m.
DISTRIBUTION: Eastern alpine–Apennine.

5 | Dwarf Valerian
Valeriana supina – Valerianaceae

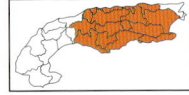

2–12cm tall, with creeping shoots, forming loose mats; stems with short hairs; leaves ciliate, blades obovate, ± entire; inflorescence compact, supported by bracts; corolla pale pink. Flowers June to August.
SIMILAR SPECIES: Willow-leaved Valerian, *V. saliunca*, has hairless stem and leaves, and narrowly spoon-shaped, often toothed leaf blades.
HABITAT: Fine rocky sward, snow-melt hollows; calcicole. 1,800–2,900m, sometimes washed down lower, as in the Oy Valley, Allgäu, Germany (1,000m).
DISTRIBUTION: Eastern alpine–Apennine.

6 | Three-lobed Valerian
Valeriana tripteris – Valerianaceae

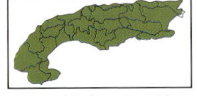

20–60cm tall; blades of basal leaves clearly heart-shaped, shallowly toothed; stem with 3 pairs of leaves; upper stem leaves 3-lobed, more rarely 5-lobed, or undivided; corolla white, rarely pale pink. Flowers April to July.
SIMILAR SPECIES: Mountain Valerian, *V. montana*, has basal leaves wedge-shaped or blunt at base, and stem leaves all undivided.
HABITAT: Damp, shady rocky slopes, woodland boulders; calcicole. To 2,700m.
DISTRIBUTION: Southern European montane.

Violaceae

1 | Alpine Violet (Alpine Pansy)
Viola alpina – Violaceae

3–10cm tall, stemless; leaves oval, slightly heart-shaped at base; stipules on leaf stalks; flowers blue-violet, 2–3cm in diameter; spur 3–4mm long. Flowers May to June.
SIMILAR SPECIES: Long-spurred Violet, *V. calcarata* (see p. 390), has a stem, though sometimes rather short.
HABITAT: Stony sward, rock crevices, poor grassland; calcicole. 1,500–2,250m.
DISTRIBUTION: Eastern alpine–Carpathian.
NOTE: The genus Viola contains about 500(620) species, mostly north temperate or South American montane. Europe has 90, with 32 in the Alps. Research suggests a South American origin, spreading to the northern hemisphere.

2 | Argentera Violet (Argentera Pansy)
Viola argenteria – Violaceae (Syn.: *V. nummulariifolia*)

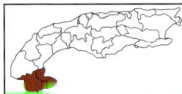

3–5cm tall, hairless, with low-growing, short stems; leaves broadly oval to heart-shaped, 0.5–2cm long, entire; leaf stalks about the same length as the blade; stipules lanceolate; flowers pale violet-blue, about 1cm in diameter; spur 1.5–3mm long, purple-violet, blunt. Flowers July to September.
SIMILAR SPECIES: Sand Violet, *V. rupestris*, is hairy, and has a pale violet spur.
HABITAT: Rocky sward with long snow cover, snow-melt hollows; calcifuge. About 1,500–2,700m.
DISTRIBUTION: Western alpine–Corsican.
NOTE: Sand Violet, *Viola rupestris*, is known as the Teesdale Violet in Britain, where it is very rare and most famously found on sugar limestone in upper Teesdale.

3 | Twin-flowered Violet (Yellow Wood Violet)
Viola biflora – Violaceae

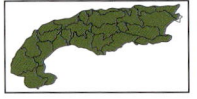

5–15cm tall; stem hairless, unbranched, 1–2-flowered; leaves kidney-shaped, broader than long; petals bright yellow, with dark veins; lateral petals pointing obliquely upwards. Flowers May to August.
SIMILAR SPECIES: None.
HABITAT: Shady, damp stony sward, tall herb vegetation, stunted woody subalpine scrub, woods. 400–2,800m, sometimes lower, as near Margreid, South Tyrol, Italy (260m), or higher, as on the Gornergrat, Valais, Switzerland (3,000m).
DISTRIBUTION: Arctic–alpine; Eurasia and North America. In the mountains of Europe, from the Catalonian Mountains to the Rhodope Mountains.

4 | Heath Dog-violet
Viola canina – Violaceae

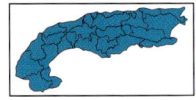

5–30cm tall, without basal leaves; 3–6 stem leaves, these broadly lanceolate, with heart-shaped base; stipules narrowly lanceolate, toothed to distantly fringed; flowers pale violet-blue, with whitish centre; spur 4–7mm long, white to yellowish-white. Flowers April to June.
SIMILAR SPECIES: Common Dog-violet, *V. riviniana*, has basal leaves, and lilac flowers.
HABITAT: Lime-poor meadows, heaths, open woods. To 2,300m.
DISTRIBUTION: European-Asiatic, from Iceland to Japan.
NOTE: 3 hard to separate subspecies in the Alps: subsp. *canina*, subsp. *ruppii* and subsp. *schultzii*.

5 | Mount Cenis Violet (Mount Cenis Pansy)
Viola cenisia – Violaceae

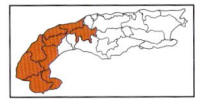

3–10cm tall, with very short, upright stems; leaf blades small, round to oval, entire; upper stipules stalked, mostly undivided and entire, more than half as long as the leaves; corolla 2–2.5cm in diameter, violet, mostly with yellow centre; spur 5–8mm long. Flowers June to August.
SIMILAR SPECIES: Long-spurred Violet, *V. calcarata* (see p. 390), has flowers 2.5–4cm, and leaves with 1–5 teeth on each side.
HABITAT: Limestone and dolomite scree. 2,000–2,900m, sometimes lower, as on the Lizerne River, Valais, Switzerland (1,200m), or higher, as on Rocciamelone near Susa, Italy (3,300m).
DISTRIBUTION: Alpine endemic.

Violaceae

1 | Long-spurred Violet (Long-spurred Pansy)
Viola calcarata subsp. *calcarata* – Violaceae

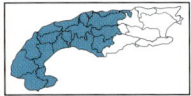

3–10cm tall, with very short, ascending stems; leaves all ± basal, oval to lanceolate, mostly distinctly longer than broad, with 1–5 teeth on each side; stipules linear to spoon-shaped, no longer than leaf stalks, usually with 1–2 coarse teeth at base; flowers blue-violet, purple, yellow, white, or multicoloured, 2.5–4cm in diameter; spur as long as petals. Flowers May to July.

SIMILAR SPECIES: The other subspecies have entire stipules (subsp. *zoysii*), pinnate stipules (subsp. *cavillieri*), or stipules with 2–4 narrow lateral lobes (subsp. *villarsiana*).

HABITAT: Poor meadows, rock debris, pasture. 1,500–3,000m, sometimes washed down, as on the Rhine near Fläsch, Switzerland (520m).

DISTRIBUTION: Alpine. Western Alps and southern Jura.

2 | Cavillier's Violet (Cavillier's Pansy)
Viola calcarata subsp. *cavillieri* – Violaceae

3–15cm tall, with very short, ascending stems; leaves all ± basal, lanceolate, distinctly longer than broad, with 1–5 teeth on each side; stipules pinnate, with lateral lobes, considerably narrower than the linear-lanceolate terminal lobe; flowers blue-violet, purple, yellow, white, or multicoloured, 2.5–4cm in diameter; spur as long as petals. Flowers May to July.

SIMILAR SPECIES: Long-spurred Violet, *V. calcarata* subsp. *calcarata*, and Villars's Violet, *V. calcarata* subsp. *villarsiana*.

HABITAT: Poor meadows, rock debris, pasture. 1,500–2,900m.

DISTRIBUTION: Western alpine–Apennine.

NAME: In honour of Swiss botanist François Georges Cavillier (1868–1953), who studied the flora of the Maritime Alps.

3 | Villars's Violet (Villars's Pansy)
Viola calcarata subsp. *villarsiana* – Violaceae

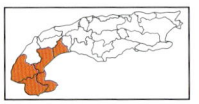

3–15cm tall, with very short, ascending stems; leaves all ± basal, oval to lanceolate, distinctly longer than broad, with 1–5 teeth on each side; stipules with 2–4 narrow lateral lobes that are only a little narrower than the lanceolate terminal lobe; flowers blue-violet, purple, yellow, white, or multicoloured, 2.5–4cm in diameter; spur as long as petals. Flowers May to July.

SIMILAR SPECIES: Long-spurred Violet, *V. calcarata* subsp. *calcarata*. Cavillier's Violet, *V. calcarata* subsp. *cavillieri*, has pinnate stipules with lateral lobes that are considerably narrower than the linear-lanceolate terminal lobe.

HABITAT: Poor meadows, rock debris, pasture. 1,500–3,000m.

DISTRIBUTION: South-western alpine endemic.

NAME: In honour of French botanist Dominique Villars (1745–1814), whose name is also honoured in the genus *Villarsia*, in the Bogbean family, Menyanthaceae.

4 | Karawanken Violet (Karawanken Pansy)
Viola calcarata subsp. *zoysii* – Violaceae

3–8cm tall, with very short, ascending stems; leaves all ± basal; blades almost circular; stipules undivided and entire; flowers always yellow, 2.5–4cm in diameter; spur as long as petals. Flowers May to June.

SIMILAR SPECIES: Long-spurred Violet, *V. calcarata* subsp. *calcarata*.

HABITAT: Poor meadows, rock crevices; calcicole. 1,600–2,300m.

DISTRIBUTION: Eastern alpine–Illyrian. South-eastern Alps and Dinaric Alps.

NAME: In honour of Carniolan botanist Karl von Zois (1756–1799), whose name is also honoured in the grass genus *Zoysia*.

Violaceae

1 | Comolli's Violet (Comolli's Pansy)
Viola comollia – Violaceae

3–8cm tall, with prostrate stem; leaves oval to round, entire; bracts similar, but smaller; flowers 20–25mm long, violet-pink, paler beneath; lowest petal with yellow throat spot; spur 2–4mm long. Flowers July to August.
SIMILAR SPECIES: Mount Cenis Violet, *V. cenisia* (see p. 388), has violet flowers, a 5–8mm long spur, and is calcicole.
HABITAT: Stable rocky debris; calcifuge. 1,500–2,500m.
DISTRIBUTION: Endemic to the Bergamasque Alps, from Val Barbellino to Monte Legnone.
NAME: In honour of Giuseppe Comolli (1780–1849), the author of a *Flora of Lake Como and the Valtellina Plateau*.

2 | Duby's Violet (Duby's Pansy)
Viola dubyana – Violaceae

8–25cm tall, multi-stemmed, hairless or with short hairs; leaves stalked, blades of lower leaves oval, middle and upper leaves narrowly lanceolate to linear, narrowing into the stalk; bracts with 5–7 linear lobes, almost as long as the leaves; flowers 20–25mm long, deep violet; spur about 5mm long, and straight. Flowers May to July.
SIMILAR SPECIES: Monte Guglielmo Violet, *V. culminis*, has a 10mm long spur, and flowers of varying colour (violet, yellow, white, multicoloured).
HABITAT: Calcareous rocky sward, rock cervices, patchy grassland; calcicole. 900–2,100m, sometimes lower, as washed down near Turano, Italy (670m).
DISTRIBUTION: Endemic to the southern calcareous Alps, from Grigna to Monte Baldo.
NAME: In honour of Swiss botanist and clergyman Jean Étienne Duby (1798–1885), who made a special study of the genus Primula and found the species in 1817 on the Corni di Canzo in the Bergamasque Alps.

3 | Mountain Pansy
Viola lutea – Violaceae

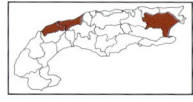

8–20cm tall, with prostrate stem; lower leaves almost round, upper leaves linear-lanceolate; upper bracts pinnately divided, with entire terminal lobe; flowers 2–4cm long, yellow, rarely bicoloured violet-yellow (**3B**). Flowers June to August.
SIMILAR SPECIES: Wild Pansy, *V. tricolor* (see p. 394), has bracts with notched terminal lobe.
HABITAT: Poor meadows, pasture; 1,000–2,100m.
DISTRIBUTION: European montane, from Britain and southern France to the Sudeten Mountains.
2 subspecies in the Alps:
– subsp. *lutea*: western Switzerland; calcicole.
– subsp. *sudetica*: Upper Styria, Austria; calcifuge.

4 | Marsh Violet
Viola palustris – Violaceae

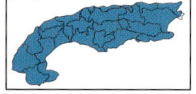

4–10cm tall, stemless; leaf blades round to kidney-shaped, somewhat broader than long, hairless; flowers lilac, lower petal with violet veins. Flowers April to July.
SIMILAR SPECIES: Almost unmistakable, from habitat and leaf shape.
HABITAT: Acid bogs, marshy woods, alder scrub, peaty meadows; calcifuge. To 2,300m, sometimes higher, as at the Schwarzsee near Zermatt, Switzerland (2,550m).
DISTRIBUTION: European–North American, north to Iceland and the North Cape, and south to the Sierra Nevada.

5 | Pinnate Violet
Viola pinnata – Violaceae

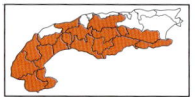

3–8cm tall, stemless; leaves basal, divided almost to the base, with several lobes; flowers pale violet, fragrant, with straight or slightly upcurved spur. Flowers May to July.
SIMILAR SPECIES: None.
HABITAT: Calcareous rock debris, pine woods, patchy meadows; calcicole. 900–2,400m, occasionally lower, as near Felsberg, Graubünden, Switzerland (610m).
DISTRIBUTION: Alpine, from the western Alps to the northern Dinaric Alps.

Violaceae

1 | Pyrenean Violet
Viola pyrenaica – Violaceae

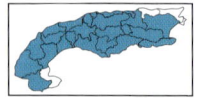

6–10cm tall, stemless and without stolons; summer leaf blades weakly hairy to hairless, heart-shaped at base, about as long as broad; sepals hairless; flowers pale blue-violet, with white throat, fragrant. Flowers April to June.
SIMILAR SPECIES: Hairy Violet, *V. hirta*, has a hairy calyx and is not fragrant.
HABITAT: Rocky sward, open woods, tall herb vegetation, rock crevices; shade-loving, calcicole. 1,000–2,200m, sometimes lower in stream gravel and avalanche gullies.
DISTRIBUTION: Southern European montane, from Cantabrian Mountains to the Caucasus region.
NOTE: Violet species tend to hybridise, and some 40 such hybrids have been described in the alpine region, mainly or even entirely from the section *Viola*.

Viola species are larval foodplants for a range of fritillary butterflies, such as Pearl-bordered Fritillary, *Boloria euphrosyne*, High Brown Fritillary, *Argynnis adippe*, Dark Green Fritillary, *Argynnis aglaja*, Niobe Fritillary, *Argynnis niobe*, and Silver-washed Fritillary, *Argynnis paphia*.

2 | Thomas's Violet
Viola thomasiana – Violaceae

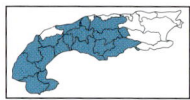

5–12cm tall, stemless and without stolons; leaf blades elongate-ovate to heart-shaped, c. 1.5x as long as broad, hairy, with blunt-angled incisions; bracts below the middle of the flower stalk; flowers violet to pale pink, fragrant; spur 10–15mm long, slender and thin, the same colour as the rest of the flower. Flowers April to July.
SIMILAR SPECIES: Hill Violet, *V. collina*, has a whitish spur, and bracts at or above the middle of flower stalk.
HABITAT: Rock crevices, poor grassland, pasture, open woods; calcifuge. 1,500–2,300m, sometimes lower, as at Lake Lugarno, Switzerland/Italy (300m).
DISTRIBUTION: Alpine endemic.
NAME: In honour of the Thomas family from Bex in the Rhone Valley, forest rangers who had expert knowledge of the alpine flora of western Switzerland and travelled widely through their Valais homeland: notably Abraham Thomas (1740–1824), his son Louis Thomas (1784–1823), and the plant collector Emanuel Thomas (1788–1859).

3 | Wild Pansy
Viola tricolor – Violaceae

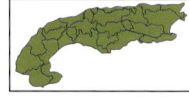

10–30cm tall, with well-developed, often branching stems; leaf blades round to lanceolate, with 1–5 teeth; bracts ½–1x as long as leaves; flowers 1.5–3.5cm long, yellow, violet, white or mostly multicoloured; spur 1–2x as long as sepal appendages. Flowers April to October.
SIMILAR SPECIES: Field Pansy, *V. arvensis*, has flowers only 1–1.5cm long. Mountain Pansy, *V. lutea* (see p. 392).
HABITAT: Poor meadows, rocky sward, embankments, stony slopes. To 2,500m, sometimes higher, as on the Riffelberg, Zermatt, Switzerland (2,700m).
DISTRIBUTION: Eurasian, from Iceland to the Altai region.
NOTE: Some authorities split the species into 2 subspecies:
– subsp. *tricolor*: petals all violet to lilac, or lower petal yellow to white, spur 3–5mm long.
– subsp. *saxatilis*: petals all yellow, the upper 2 sometimes lilac, spur 5–6mm long.

4 | Valdieri Violet (Valdieri Pansy)
Viola valderia – Violaceae

5–15cm tall, lower stems densely leafy; leaf blades 10–25mm long, ± entire, lower leaves almost round, upper leaves lanceolate to club-shaped; bracts resembling leaves, but smaller, with several unequal segments; flowers 2–2.5cm long, reddish-violet; spur 8–10mm long, straight. Flowers June to July.
SIMILAR SPECIES: Long-spurred Violet, *V. calcarata* (see p. 390), has 2.5–4cm long flowers, and leaf blades with 1–5 teeth on each side. Duby's Violet, *V. dubyana* (see p. 392), differs, among other things, in having a 4–6mm long spur.
HABITAT: Rock debris, stony sward, rocks, gravel. 1,200–1,900m.
DISTRIBUTION: Endemic to the Maritime Alps.

Flowering plants: monocotyledons

Alliaceae

1 | Keeled Garlic
Allium carinatum – Alliaceae

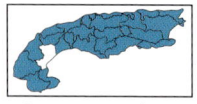

20–60cm tall; leaves flat or grooved, 2–4mm broad, green; bracts extending beyond inflorescence; inflorescence with or without bulbils; flowers 5–8mm long, purple-pink; stamens much longer than perianth. Flowers June to August.
SIMILAR SPECIES: Sand Leek, *A. scorodoprasum*, has stamens shorter than perianth.
HABITAT: Poor and dry grassland, scrub, path sides. To 2,000m.
DISTRIBUTION: European.
NOTE: 2 subspecies in the Alps:
– subsp. *carinatum* (**1A**): inflorescence with bulbils; most of the Alps, though rare in the south-western Alps.
– subsp. *pulchellum* (**1B**): inflorescence without bulbils; mainly southern and south-western Alps.

2 | Yellow-flowered Garlic
Allium flavum – Alliaceae

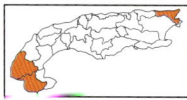

25–60cm tall; leaves blue-green, to 2mm broad; involucre formed of 2 separate bracts; inflorescence without bulbils; flowers yellow; stamens longer than perianth. Flowers June to August.
SIMILAR SPECIES: None.
HABITAT: Dry grassland and meadows. To 1,500m.
DISTRIBUTION: Mediterranean, from Spain to the Caucasus and western Asia.

3 | Lombardy Garlic
Allium insubricum – Alliaceae

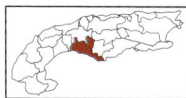

10–30cm tall; stem sharply triangular; leaves basal, sheathing the stem, 2–6mm broad; inflorescence 3–6-flowered, drooping, with membranous bracts; flowers purple. Flowers July to August.
SIMILAR SPECIES: Narcissus-flowered Garlic, *A. narcissiflorum*.
HABITAT: Scree slopes, rocky sward; calcicole. 1,400–2,100m.
DISTRIBUTION: Southern alpine endemic.

4 | Mountain Garlic
Allium lusitanicum – Alliaceae

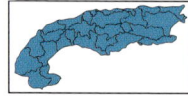

10–40cm tall; stem angular, leafless or leafy at base; leaves ± flat, not keeled, 2–4mm broad; inflorescence compact, 2–4cm in diameter, without bulbils; bracts not extending beyond inflorescence; flower stalk longer than perianth; stamens extending beyond perianth. Flowers July to September.
SIMILAR SPECIES: Upright Garlic, *A. strictum* (Syn.: *A. lineare*), has a round stem, and flower stalk about the same length as the perianth. Crimson Leek, *A. kermesinum*, endemic to Carinthia and Slovenia, has bright purple flowers, and inflorescence 1.5–2cm in diameter.
HABITAT: Sunny rocky sward, pine woods, rock crevices. To 2,300m.
DISTRIBUTION: European-Asiatic.

5 | Narcissus-flowered Garlic
Allium narcissiflorum – Alliaceae

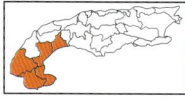

10–40cm tall; stem round, leafy, upper stem compressed and 2-edged; leaves linear; inflorescence 3–10-flowered, at first drooping, later upright; flowers purplish-pink, bell-shaped. Flowers July to August.
SIMILAR SPECIES: Lombardy Garlic, *A. insubricum*, has a triangular stem and inflorescence always drooping.
HABITAT: Scree slopes, rocks; calcicole. 1,300–2,400m.
DISTRIBUTION: Western alpine endemic.

6 | Yellow-white Garlic
Allium ochroleucum – Alliaceae (Syn.: *Allium ericetorum*)

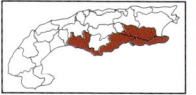

10–40cm tall; stem round, leafy only towards base; leaves flat, 2–5mm broad; flower stalk 4–10mm long; flowers yellowish-white, sometimes suffused pink. Flowers July to August.
SIMILAR SPECIES: Alpine Leek, *A. victorialis* (see p. 400), has similar flowers, but has 3–6cm broad leaves.
HABITAT: Rocky sward, rocks; calcicole. To about 2,000m.
DISTRIBUTION: Southern European montane.

Alliaceae

1 | Field Garlic
Allium oleraceum – Alliaceae

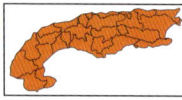

30–80cm tall; lower stem leafy; leaves flat or grooved, 2–4mm broad, hairless; inflorescence with purplish-brown bulbils; flowers broad bell-shaped, greenish-white to dull purple, with darker central and marginal lines; stamens about the same length as perianth. Flowers July to August.
SIMILAR SPECIES: Pale Garlic, *A. paniculatum*, has hairy leaves.
HABITAT: Meadows, scrub, path sides. To 2,100m.
DISTRIBUTION: European.

2 | Chives
Allium schoenoprasum – Alliaceae

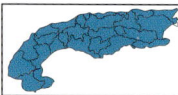

15–50cm tall, forming clumps; leaves tubular, round, hairless; inflorescence spherical, compact, without bulbils; flowers purplish-pink, 8–15mm long; flower stalk shorter than flower. Flowers June to August.
SIMILAR SPECIES: Upright Garlic, *A. strictum*, has flat, not tubular leaves.
HABITAT: Damp meadows, fens, spring-fed flushes. To 2,700m.
DISTRIBUTION: Eurosiberian–North American.

3 | Round-headed Leek
Allium sphaerocephalon – Alliaceae

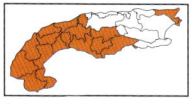

20–80cm tall; leaves semi-circular in cross section, grooved white; bracts 2, persisting at flowering; inflorescence without bulbils; flower stalk at most twice as long as flower; flowers 3.5–6mm long, dark purple or whitish with green veins. Flowers June to July.
SIMILAR SPECIES: Round Leek, *A. rotundum*, has flat leaves, hooded at the tip. Sand Leek, *A. scorodoprasum*, has bulbils in the inflorescence, as does Crow Garlic, *A. vineale*.
HABITAT: Rocky slopes, dry meadows, scrub. To 2,200m.
DISTRIBUTION: Mediterranean.

4 | Wild Garlic (Ramsons)
Allium ursinum – Alliaceae

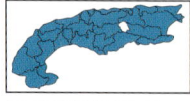

15–40cm tall, strongly garlic-scented when crushed; leaves basal, stalked, ovate-lanceolate, 3–6cm broad; inflorescence a loose umbel of 6–20 flowers; flowers white, tepals 7–12mm long. Flowers May.
SIMILAR SPECIES: Naples Garlic, *A. neapolitanum*, found in western and southern alpine lowlands, has 0.5–2cm broad leaves.
HABITAT: Deciduous and riverine woods. To 2,000m.
DISTRIBUTION: European.

5 | Alpine Leek (Victory Onion)
Allium victorialis – Alliaceae

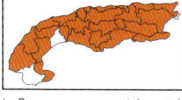

30–60cm tall; stem leaves broadly lanceolate, 10–30cm long, 3–6cm broad; inflorescence without bulbils, with more than 30 flowers, bracts not extending beyond; flowers pale greenish-yellow. Flowers June to August.
SIMILAR SPECIES: Few.
HABITAT: Montane meadows, hay fields, tall herb vegetation. 1,400–2,700m.
DISTRIBUTION: European-Asiatic.

6 | Crow Garlic (Wild Onion)
Allium vineale – Alliaceae

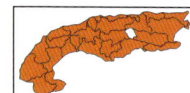

30–80cm tall; leaves 2–4, cylindrical and hollow; inflorescence spherical, often consisting only of bulbils, which often sprout green while still on the parent plant; single bract, extending beyond inflorescence; flowers, if present, pale green to purple. Flowers June to August.
SIMILAR SPECIES: Sand Leek, *A. scorodoprasum*, has flat leaves, and 2 bracts, shorter than inflorescence.
HABITAT: Dry grassland, scrub, field margins, vineyards. To 1,800m.
DISTRIBUTION: European.

1 | Spring Snowflake
Leucojum vernum – Amaryllidaceae

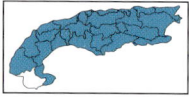

10–30cm tall; single-flowered; leaves fleshy, dark green, linear; flowers fragrant; tepals pressed together forming a bell, white, with green tips. Flowers February to April.
SIMILAR SPECIES: Summer Snowflake, *L. aestivum*, has 2–6-flowered stems. Winter Snowflake, *Acis nicaeensis*, lacks the green tips to the tepals.
HABITAT: Riverine woods, marshy meadows, woodland clearings, orchards. To about 1,800m.
DISTRIBUTION: Southern European.

2 | Wild Daffodil (Lent Lily)
Narcissus pseudonarcissus – Amaryllidaceae

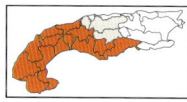

15–50cm tall; stem single-flowered; leaves linear, 7–15mm broad, fleshy; tepals pale yellow, corona (trumpet) egg-yolk yellow, the same length as tepals. Flowers March to June.
SIMILAR SPECIES: None.
HABITAT: Montane meadows, woodland clearings. To about 2,000m.
DISTRIBUTION: Western European.

3 | Narrow-leaved Daffodil
Narcissus radiiflorus – Amaryllidaceae

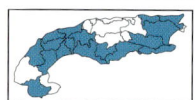

20–40cm tall; stem single-flowered; leaves linear, 5–8mm broad; tepals narrowly obovate, tapering at base, 22–30mm long, not overlapping at base; corona cup-shaped, 8–10mm in diameter. Flowers April to June.
SIMILAR SPECIES: Poet's Daffodil, *N. poeticus*, has tepals narrowing only slightly at base and overlapping, and corona 12–15mm in diameter.
HABITAT: Montane meadows, damp grassland. To about 2,100m.
DISTRIBUTION: Southern European montane.

4 | St. Bernard's Lily
Anthericum liliago – Anthericaceae

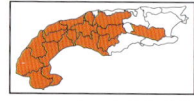

30–70cm tall; leaves basal, linear, to 40cm long, 3–7mm broad; inflorescence a loose raceme; tepals 1.6–2.2cm long, 2–4mm broad, all the same width, extending beyond the stamens. Flowers May to June.
SIMILAR SPECIES: Branched St. Bernard's Lily, *A. ramosum*, has 1–1.4cm long tepals, the inner broader than the outer. St. Bruno's Lily, *Paradisea liliastrum*, has tepals 3–6cm long and 8–16mm broad.
HABITAT: Dry grassland, rocky slopes, pine woods. To 1,900m.
DISTRIBUTION: European.

5 | Branched St. Bernard's Lily
Anthericum ramosum – Anthericaceae

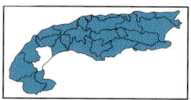

30–80cm tall; leaves basal; inflorescence a raceme; tepals 1–1.4cm long, 2–6mm broad, the inner distinctly broader than the outer, projecting 0.1–0.2cm beyond the stamens. Flowers July to August.
SIMILAR SPECIES: St. Bernard's Lily, *A. liliago*.
HABITAT: Dry grassland, pine woods, vegetated river gravel; calcicole. To 1,900m.
DISTRIBUTION: European.

6 | St. Bruno's Lily
Paradisea liliastrum – Anthericaceae

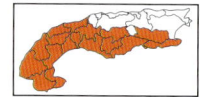

30–50cm tall; all leaves basal, 20–40cm long, 2–8mm broad; inflorescence a one-sided, 2–15-flowered raceme; tepals 3–6cm long and 8–16mm broad. Flowers June to July.
SIMILAR SPECIES: St. Bernard's Lily, *Anthericum liliago*.
HABITAT: Montane meadows. To 2,500m.
DISTRIBUTION: Southern European montane.
NAME: The generic name is in honour of Italian count and enthusiastic gardener Giovanni Paradisi (1760–1826). The botanist Giovanni Mazzucato discovered St. Bruno's Lily in the Julian Alps in 1811 and named it after his patron.

Aphyllanthaceae, Asparagaceae, Asphodelaceae, Colchicaceae, Cyperaceae

1 | Blue Grass Lily
Aphyllanthes monspeliensis – Aphyllanthaceae

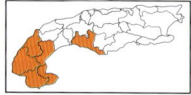

10–40cm tall, forming tufts; stems rush-like, blue-green, ribbed; basal leaves reduced to reddish-brown 3–8mm long sheaths; 6 tepals, pale blue, with darker veins. Flowers April to May.
SIMILAR SPECIES: None.
HABITAT: Dry scrub, garrigue, open woods; calcicole. To about 800m.
DISTRIBUTION: Mediterranean, from Morocco and Portugal to the southern Alps.

2 | Narrow-leaved Asparagus
Asparagus tenuifolius – Asparagaceae

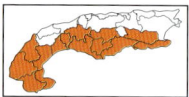

30–80cm tall; stem branched; 'leaves' fine and hair-like (cladodes), 10–25, clustered in the axils of true leaves which are reduced to chaff-like scales; flowers 6.5–8mm long; flower stalk jointed immediately beneath the flower; fruit red, 12–16mm in diameter. Flowers May to June.
SIMILAR SPECIES: Garden Asparagus, *A. officinalis*, has cladodes in clusters of 3–8, and fruit about 8mm in diameter.
HABITAT: Scrub on sunny southern slopes, warm rock walls, open woods. To about 1,100m.
DISTRIBUTION: Southern European, from southern France to Ukraine and Anatolia.

3 | White Asphodel
Asphodelus macrocarpus – Asphodelaceae (Syn.: *Asphodelus albus*, p. p.)

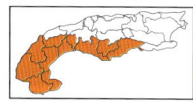

60–120cm tall; all leaves basal, linear, fleshy, grooved, 30–70cm long; inflorescence a dense terminal spike-like raceme; bracts dark brown; petals white, with brownish-purple central vein. Flowers May to July.
SIMILAR SPECIES: None.
HABITAT: Montane meadows, rocky sward, pasture. 800–2,200m.
DISTRIBUTION: Mediterranean-montane, from Morocco to Bulgaria.

4 | Spring Meadow Saffron
Colchicum vernum – Colchicaceae (Syn.: *Bulbocodium vernum*)

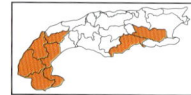

5–20cm tall; leaves up to 15cm long, to 1.5cm broad, with hooded tips, appearing at flowering; flowers pink, more rarely white, spreading open to 4–5cm, base of petals with one tooth at each side; one style in each flower. Flowers February to March.
SIMILAR SPECIES: Meadow Saffron, *C. autumnale*, flowers in the autumn, and has 3 styles per flower. Alpine Meadow Saffron, *C. alpinum*, flowers in late summer, and has flowers spreading to 2–3cm.
HABITAT: Snow-melt soils that dry out in the summer, dry rocks. To 2,100m.
DISTRIBUTION: Southern European–Caucasian, from the Pyrenees to western Asia.

5 | Black Alpine Sedge
Carex atrata – Cyperaceae

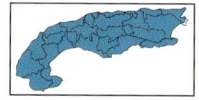

15–30cm tall; stem hairless; leaves 3–5mm broad; inflorescence ± upright, 2–4cm long, with 3–5 cylindrical, 1–2cm long spikes with 0.5–2cm long stalks; glumes blackish. Flowers June to August.
SIMILAR SPECIES: Coal Black Sedge, *C. aterrima*, is 30–60cm tall, with leaves 5–9mm broad, and nodding inflorescence.
HABITAT: Stony poor grassland, rocky sward; calcicole. 1,700–3,000m.
DISTRIBUTION: Arctic-alpine, from Greenland to Japan and Taiwan.

6 | Monte Baldo Sedge
Carex baldensis – Cyperaceae

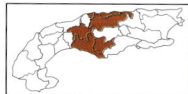

10–30cm tall; stem furrowed; leaves flat, 2–3mm broad; bracts leaf-like, 2–10cm long; spikes white; inflorescence terminal, compact, with tightly clustered spikelets. Flowers June to July.
SIMILAR SPECIES: With its white spikes, unmistakable.
HABITAT: Stony sward, rock debris; calcicole. To 2,400m.
DISTRIBUTION: Eastern alpine endemic.

Cyperaceae

1 | Curved Alpine Sedge
Carex curvula – Cyperaceae

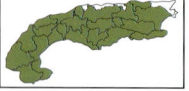

5–25cm tall; stem hairless; leaves 1–2mm broad, often dying early in the top third because of regular fungal infections; flowering heads dense, longer than broad; lateral spikes almost sessile, upright; bracts 5–15mm long; 3 stigmas; fruit covers (glumes) 3-angled. Flowers July to August.
SIMILAR SPECIES: The many other alpine sedge species, such as Hare's-foot Sedge, *C. lachenalii*, which has 2 stigmas.
HABITAT: Nutrient-poor soils with short snow cover, often dominant in vegetation. 1,800–3,400m.
DISTRIBUTION: South-eastern European montane, from the eastern Pyrenees to the Carpathians and the mountains of the Balkan Peninsula.
NOTE: In the Alps, the nominate form subsp. *curvula* is calcifuge, and the subsp. *rosae* is calcicole.
The sedge genus *Carex* is the most species-rich in the alpine region. There are about 2,000 species throughout the world, but it is absent from the lowlands of the tropics, where it is only represented by a few species in south-east Asia. There are some 100 species in Europe, 108 of which are found in the Alps. Monte Baldo Sedge (see p. 404) is restricted to the Alps.

2 | Cushion Sedge
Carex firma – Cyperaceae

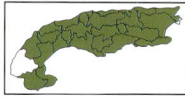

5–20cm tall, rosettes forming dense cushions; leaves 2–3mm broad, dark green, most less than 7cm long, often spreading horizontally on the ground; stems raised well above the leaves; inflorescence with 1–3 female spikes and a terminal male spike. Flowers June to August.
SIMILAR SPECIES: Few. The characteristic growth is distinctive.
HABITAT: Forms a highly characteristic plant community on wind-exposed sites; calcicole. 1,600–2,900m, sometimes at lower sites such as in Austria in the Ötschergräben in Lower Austria or near Kufstein (490m).
DISTRIBUTION: South-eastern European montane. Alps, Carpathians, Dinaric Alps, and Apennines.

3 | Large Yellow Sedge
Carex flava – Cyperaceae

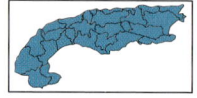

10–50cm tall; stem hairless, 3-angled; leaves flat, 3–5mm broad; inflorescence with 2–4 compact female spikes, 1–1.5cm long and ± 1cm broad; male spikes short-stalked. Flowers May to July.
SIMILAR SPECIES: Other species of the *Carex flava* group, such as Oeder's Sedge, *C. oederi*, which is 5–20cm tall, with finely folded leaves and has 3–6 compact female spikes 0.5–1cm long and ± 0.5cm broad.
HABITAT: Fens, reedbeds, wet meadows; calcicole. To about 2,500m.
DISTRIBUTION: European-Asiatic–North American.

4 | Few-flowered Sedge
Carex pauciflora – Cyperaceae

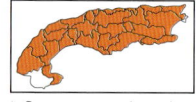

5–20cm tall, loose-growing; stem 3-angled, rough above; leaves flat, about 1mm broad; inflorescence a long, loose terminal spike; glumes 5–8mm long, straw yellow, bending backwards when fruits ripen. Flowers May to July.
SIMILAR SPECIES: The few-flowered inflorescence makes this one of the (few) easily identified sedge species.
HABITAT: Acid mires and bogs; calcifuge. To 2,200m.
DISTRIBUTION: Eurosiberian–North American.

5 | Cotton Deergrass (Alpine Bulrush)
Trichophorum alpinum – Cyperaceae

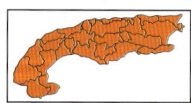

10–30cm tall, with underground creeping rhizomes; stem 3-angled, rough; spikelets 8–12-flowered; perianth bristles white, crinkled, 1.5–2.5cm long at fruiting, forming a curly tuft. Flowers April to June.
SIMILAR SPECIES: Deergrass (Tufted Bulrush), *T. cespitosum* (**5B**), has a round, furrowed stem, 3–6-flowered spikelets, and perianth bristles at most 3mm long.
HABITAT: Raised bogs and intermediate mires; calcifuge. To about 2,200m.
DISTRIBUTION: Eurosiberian–North American.

1 | Common Cottongrass
Eriophorum angustifolium – Cyperaceae

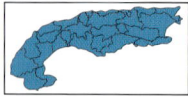

20–50cm tall, rhizome with 5–20cm long runners; stem round or bluntly 3-angled in upper stem; leaves 3–6mm broad, extended into a long, 3-angled tip; spikelets 3–5, 10–22mm long; spikelet stalks hairless. Flowers April to May.
SIMILAR SPECIES: Broad-leaved Cottongrass, *E. latifolium*, does not produce runners, and has 5–12, 6–10mm long spikelets.
HABITAT: Acid bogs and mires. To 2,600m.
DISTRIBUTION: Eurosiberian–North American.

2 | Scheuchzer's Cottongrass (White Cottongrass)
Eriophorum scheuchzeri – Cyperaceae

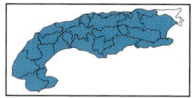

10–35cm tall, with runners; stem round, with a single upright terminal compact spikelet; leaf sheaths not obviously inflated. Flowers June to September.
SIMILAR SPECIES: Hare's-tail Cottongrass, *E. vaginatum*, does not produce runners, has inflated upper stem leaf sheaths, and 3-angled upper stem.
HABITAT: Vegetated margins of ponds, wet meadows, mires; calcifuge. 1,500–2,700m.
DISTRIBUTION: Arctic–alpine.
NAME: In honour of Swiss doctor and naturalist Johann Jakob Scheuchzer (1672–1733), after whom the prehistoric giant salamander *Andrias scheuchzeri* is named.

3 | Yellow Daylily
Hemerocallis lilioasphodelus – Hemerocallidaceae

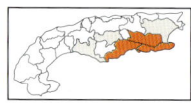

50–100cm tall; leaves 40–60cm long, 0.6–1.5cm broad; flowers fragrant; tepals yellow, 5–8cm long, with hairless margins. Flowers May to June.
SIMILAR SPECIES: None.
HABITAT: Damp meadows, moist open woods, also sunny, fairly dry slopes. To about 1,600m.
DISTRIBUTION: Eastern alpine endemic?
NOTE: Native to the south-eastern Alps. The generic name comes from the ancient Greek words 'hemera' (= day) and 'kallos' (= beauty), reflecting the fact that the individual flowers last just one day.

4 | Spiked Star-of-Bethlehem (Pyrenean Star-of-Bethlehem)
Loncomelos pyrenaicus – Hyacinthaceae (Syn.: *Ornithogalum pyrenaicum*)

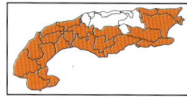

30–80cm tall; leaves basal, linear, 5–15mm broad, grooved, withering at flowering; inflorescence a 30–50-flowered spike-like raceme; flowers white to greenish-yellow; style 3mm long; ovary green at flowering. Flowers May to June.
SIMILAR SPECIES: Short-styled Star-of-Bethlehem, *L. brevistylus*, has pure white tepals except for a green dorsal stripe, style 2mm long, and ovary yellow at flowering.
HABITAT: Meadows, stream sides, scrub, beechwoods. To about 1,300m.
DISTRIBUTION: Southern European–Mediterranean.
NOTE: 2 subspecies in the Alps.

5 | Alpine Squill
Scilla bifolia s. lat. – Hyacinthaceae

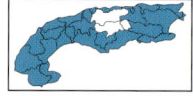

10–25cm tall, with 2 linear-lanceolate, 3–15mm broad stem leaves, curving inwards hood-like towards the top; inflorescence 2–9-flowered; tepals 6, blue, 6–12mm long, spreading star-like. Flowers March to May.
SIMILAR SPECIES: Siberian Squill, *Othocallis siberica* (Syn.: *Scilla siberica*), which is often naturalised, has drooping flowers, and 12–15mm long tepals.
HABITAT: Deciduous woods, valley meadows, orchards. To about 1,600m.
DISTRIBUTION: Southern European.
NOTE: *Scilla bifolia* s. lat. is a group encompassing many taxa, especially in southeast Europe and the eastern Mediterranean, including, in addition to *S. bifolia* s. str., *S. drunensis* and *S. vindobonensis*.

Iridaceae

1 | White Crocus
Crocus albiflorus – Iridaceae

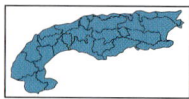

4–15cm tall; single-flowered; leaves basal, linear, with white central vein and margins rolled under, only partly developed at flowering; flowers white or violet; tepals 15–40mm long, 5–10mm broad; style shorter than stamens. Flowers March to June.
SIMILAR SPECIES: Illyrian Crocus, *C. exiguus*, has style at least as long as stamens.
HABITAT: Montane meadows, pasture. To 2,600m.
DISTRIBUTION: Southern European montane.

2 | Illyrian Crocus
Crocus exiguus – Iridaceae (Syn.: *Crocus vittatus*, *Crocus vernus* p.p.)

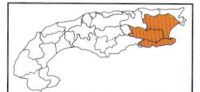

5–15cm tall; single-flowered; leaves basal, linear, with white central vein, at most 7mm broad at flowering; Flowers violet; tepals 20–50mm long, usually with a V-shaped mark towards the tip; style at least as long as stamens. Flowers February to June.
SIMILAR SPECIES: White Crocus, *C. albiflorus*.
HABITAT: Meadows, pasture, valley woods, orchards, deciduous woods. To 2,200m, as in the Koralpe, Austria.
DISTRIBUTION: South-eastern European, from Styria and Carinthia eastwards to Romania.

3 | Grass-leaved Iris
Iris graminea – Iridaceae

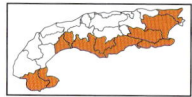

15–30cm tall; stem flattened and 2-winged; leaves 5–15mm broad, shiny, green, spreading flat on the ground after flowering; flowers with fruity scent. Flowers May.
SIMILAR SPECIES: None.
HABITAT: Semi-arid and poor grassland, scrub, open woods; calcicole. To about 1,500m.
DISTRIBUTION: Southern European, from northern Spain to Ukraine and the Balkan Peninsula.

4 | Cengio Alto Iris
Iris pallida subsp. *cengialti* – Iridaceae

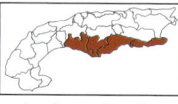

20–70cm tall; stem 2–3-flowered, longer than leaves; leaves with bluish bloom and protruding veins; flower spathes yellowish-white, papery at flowering; flowers fragrant; tepals blue-violet, with orange-yellow beard. Flowers April to May.
SIMILAR SPECIES: The nominate from Dalmatian Iris, *I. pallida* subsp. *pallida*, from south-eastern Europe is often grown and sometimes naturalised. It lacks the protruding leaf venation.
HABITAT: Stony sward, rock niches; calcicole. 300–1,000m.
DISTRIBUTION: South-eastern alpine endemic.
NOTE: Named after the village of Cengio Alto, Liguria, Italy.

5 | Dwarf Iris
Iris pumila – Iridaceae

8–15cm tall; stem 1–7cm long; leaves grey-green, 6–17mm broad, not evergreen; flowers blue, violet, purple, yellow, white, or multicoloured, corolla tube 25–90mm long, the outer tepals (falls) drooping. Flowers April.
SIMILAR SPECIES: Crimean Iris, *I. lutescens*, is similarly multicoloured, but has evergreen leaves. It is found in the lowlands of the south-western Alps.
HABITAT: Rocky steppe, patchy dry grassland. To 700m.
DISTRIBUTION: South-eastern European–western Asiatic.

6 | Siberian Iris
Iris sibirica – Iridaceae

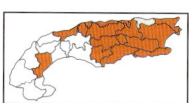

40–80cm tall; leaves 4–8mm broad; outer tepals (falls) whitish with violet-blue veins, yellow towards the base, inner tepals violet-blue. Flowers May to June.
SIMILAR SPECIES: None.
HABITAT: Marshy and wet meadows. To about 1,300m.
DISTRIBUTION: Eurosiberian.

Iridaceae, Juncaceae, Liliaceae

1 Marsh Gladiolus
Gladiolus palustris – Iridaceae

30–50cm tall; stem leafy; leaves linear-lanceolate, lowest stem leaf blade also pointed; inflorescence one-sided, 3–8-flowered; tepals 6, purple; each flower with a bracteole. Flowers June to July.
SIMILAR SPECIES: Illyrian Gladiolus, *G. illyricus*, has flowers ± in 2 rows. Meadow Gladiolus, *G. imbricatus*, has a blunt lowest stem leaf blade.
HABITAT: Marshy meadows, fens. To about 1,400m.
DISTRIBUTION: European.

2 Jacquin's Rush
Juncus jacquinii – Juncaceae

10–30cm tall; stem with a leaf in the upper third extending well above the inflorescence; basal leaves narrow, taller than stems; inflorescence compact, terminal, 5–12-flowered; stigma pink, corkscrew-like. Flowers June to August.
SIMILAR SPECIES: There are 26 other *Juncus* species in the Alps.
HABITAT: Damp grassland, spring-fed flushes; calcifuge. 1,600–3,000m.
DISTRIBUTION: Alpine–Apennine.
NAME: In honour of Austrian botanist Nikolaus Joseph von Jacquin (1727–1817).

3 Alpine Wood-rush
Luzula alpinopilosa – Juncaceae

10–30cm tall; lower stem leaves 1–4mm broad, sparsely hairy; bract shorter than inflorescence; inflorescence loose, upright to nodding, with protruding branches and 2–5-flowered heads; tepals brownish, c. 2mm long, with awned tips; ripe fruit dark brown, almost spherical. Flowers June to August.
SIMILAR SPECIES: Hairy Wood-rush, *L. pilosa*, has 5–10mm broad leaves.
HABITAT: Rock debris, snow-melt hollows; calcifuge. 1,600–3,300m, sometimes lower, as at Sellrain, Tyrol, Austria (1,250m).
DISTRIBUTION: South-western European montane.

4 Yellow Wood-rush
Luzula lutea – Juncaceae

10–25cm tall; leaves 3–6mm broad, sparsely hairy only at sheath opening, otherwise hairless; leaf sheath reddish-brown; inflorescence consisting of 6–10-flowered nodding clusters; flowers long-stalked; tepals yellowish. Flowers June to August.
SIMILAR SPECIES: Yellowish Wood-rush, *L. luzulina*, has solitary, upright flowers and hairy leaves only 2–3mm broad.
HABITAT: Rocky grassland, rock debris; calcifuge. 1,500–3,400m.
DISTRIBUTION: South-western European montane.

5 Snowy Wood-rush
Luzula nivea – Juncaceae

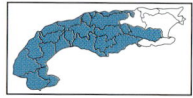

40–70cm tall; runners 5–10cm long; basal leaves 3–6mm broad, with appressed ciliate hairs; flower clusters 6–20-flowered; tepals pure white, 5mm long, twice as long as fruits. Flowers June to August.
SIMILAR SPECIES: White Wood-rush, *L. luzuloides*, has whitish, but not pure white tepals c. 3mm long, about as long as fruits.
HABITAT: Woods; calcifuge. To about 2,200m.
DISTRIBUTION: Southern European montane.

6 Dog's Tooth Violet
Erythronium dens-canis – Liliaceae

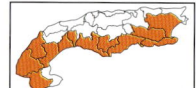

8–20cm tall; lower stem with 2 opposite, broadly lanceolate, to 10cm long, brown-mottled leaves; Flowers March to May.
SIMILAR SPECIES: None.
HABITAT: Deciduous woods, damp meadows. To about 1,800m.
DISTRIBUTION: European-Asiatic.
NOTE: The generic name comes from the ancient Greek 'erythros' (= red). The specific epithet is Latin, meaning 'dog's tooth' and refers to the narrow, pointed corm.

Liliaceae

1 | Alpine Fritillary
Fritillaria tubaeformis subsp. *tubaeformis* – Liliaceae

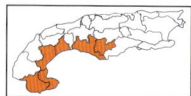

10–30cm tall; hairless; stem upright, leafy down almost to the lower third; flowers drooping; leaves usually 6, alternate, 4–9cm long, 6–12mm broad, blue-green; corolla lantern-shaped, purplish-red, with bluish sheen, and dark purple spots inside; tepals 4–5cm long, all blunt. Flowers May to June.
SIMILAR SPECIES: Piedmont Fritillary, *F. involucrata*, endemic to the south-western Alps, has upper stem leaves 3 to a whorl.
HABITAT: Montane meadows, stony grassland; calcicole. 1,000–2,100m.
DISTRIBUTION: Alpine endemic.

2 | Moggridge's Alpine Fritillary
Fritillaria tubaeformis subsp. *moggridgei* – Liliaceae

8–20cm tall, hairless; leaves usually 5, alternate, 6–12mm broad, bluish-green; corolla lantern-shaped; tepals yellow, with obvious purple chequering, about 4cm long. Flowers May to June, usually 2–3 weeks after the snow melts.
SIMILAR SPECIES: None.
HABITAT: Damp montane meadows; calcicole. About 1,000–2,000m.
DISTRIBUTION: Endemic to the Maritime Alps.
NAME: In honour of English botanist John Traherne Moggridge (1842–1874). Due to illness, Moggridge recuperated on the Riviera and, with the help of his father, wrote *Flora of Mentone*.

3 | Tubular Gagea
Gagea liotardii – Liliaceae (Syn.: *Gagea fistulosa*, *Gagea fragifera*)

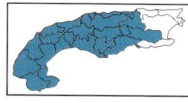

5–20cm tall; basal leaves 1–2, hollow, semi-circular to round, 2–3mm broad, narrower than bracts; stem leaves 2, bract-like; flower stalk hairy; tepals blunt. Flowers May to July.
SIMILAR SPECIES: The tube-like basal leaves distinguish it from all the other alpine *Gagea* species.
HABITAT: Nutrient-rich meadows, livestock resting sites, often around alpine huts; calcifuge. 1,200–2,500m.
DISTRIBUTION: Southern European montane.
NAME: The specific epithet honours French botanist Pierre Liotard (1729–1796). Liotard was the son of a worker, could barely read or write, yet familiarised himself with Linnaeus's system of plant classification.

4 | Late Alplily (Snowdon Lily)
Gagea serotina – Liliaceae
(Syn.: *Lloydia serotina*)

5–15cm tall; basal leaves usually 2, linear, thread-like; stem leaves linear-lanceolate; flowers upright and funnel-shaped; tepals white with reddish-brown markings. Flowers June to August.
SIMILAR SPECIES: None.
HABITAT: Wind-exposed grassland, stony sward, rock crevices. 1,600–3,100m.
DISTRIBUTION: Arctic–alpine.
NAME: The generic name *Lloydia* honours British-French botanist James Lloyd (1810–1896), who studied the flora of France. The usual English name of the species is Snowdon Lily, reflecting its distribution in Britain where it is very rare and restricted to Snowdonia in North Wales.
NOTE: The species is now usually re-assigned to the genus *Gagea* in which it was included as long ago as 1816. The specific epithet means 'late' and is misleading as the plant often flowers quite early in the short mountain summer.

5 | Wild Tulip
Tulipa sylvestris – Liliaceae

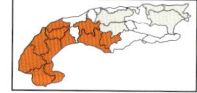

20–40cm tall; leaves narrowly lanceolate, 8–20cm long, 0.8–2cm broad; flowers solitary and upright; 6 pointed tepals. Flowers April to June.
SIMILAR SPECIES: None.
HABITAT: Montane and riverine meadows, rocky slopes, scrub, old parks. To 2,100m.
DISTRIBUTION: Mediterranean.
NOTE: 2 subspecies in the Alps:
– subsp. *sylvestris*: tepals yellow on both sides, sometimes greenish on outsides; flowers nodding before opening.
– subsp. *australis*: tepals yellow, suffused red on outsides; flowers upright before opening.

Liliaceae, Melanthiaceae

1 | Fire Lily (Orange Lily)
Lilium bulbiferum – Liliaceae

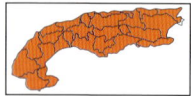

30–100cm tall; stem densely leafy, with or without bulbils; leaves narrowly lanceolate, alternate, sessile; flowers terminal, upright, solitary or 2–5 in an umbel-like inflorescence; tepals bright orange; sometimes without flowers and reproducing vegetatively. Flowers June to July.
SIMILAR SPECIES: None.
HABITAT: Montane meadows, stony sward, dry banks, forest margins, rocky heath, alluvial woods. To about 2,400m.
DISTRIBUTION: Southern European montane.
NOTE: 2 subspecies in the Alps:
– subsp. *bulbiferum*: bulbils in upper leaf axils, tepals mostly unspotted.
– subsp. *croceum*: without bulbils in leaf axils, tepals with blackish spots.

Lilies are valuable nectar plants for butterflies and moths with long proboscoes. The flowers of Martagon Lily give off a heavy, sweet scent, especially in the evening and at night, which is attractive to moths, especially hawkmoths, including Hummingbird Hawk-moth. The flowers of this species droop and also have an oily coating, making it difficult for insects that cannot hover to get a firm grip. Noctuid moths such as the Silver Y manage this feat by anchoring themselves firmly with their front legs, effecting pollination by fluttering.

Fire Lily on the other hand has nectaries on the tips of the leaves and buds which attract various ant species of the genera *Formica*, *Lasius* and *Myrmica*, which help protect the plant from being eaten.

2 | Carniolan Lily (Golden Apple)
Lilium carniolicum – Liliaceae

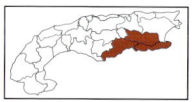

30–80cm tall; stem upright, hairless, densely leafy; leaves alternate, linear-lanceolate, 5–18mm broad; inflorescence 1–3-flowered; tepals strongly decurved, bright orange, with dark spots towards the base; anthers orange. Flowers June.
SIMILAR SPECIES: Red Lily, *L. pomponium*.
HABITAT: Tall herb vegetation, rock debris, montane meadows, open scrub; calcicole. To 2,300m.
DISTRIBUTION: Southern-European montane.

3 | Martagon Lily
Lilium martagon – Liliaceae

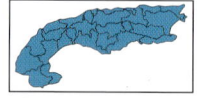

40–90cm tall; stem densely leafy; leaves broadly lanceolate, middle stem leaves in whorls of 4–8; flowers drooping; tepals strongly decurved, purple, with dark spots. Flowers June to July.
SIMILAR SPECIES: None.
HABITAT: Woods, montane meadows, woodland clearings, banks; calcicole. To about 2,300m.
DISTRIBUTION: European-Asiatic.

4 | Red Lily
Lilium pomponium – Liliaceae

30–90cm tall; stem upright, hairless, densely leafy; leaves narrowly lanceolate, 3–5mm broad; inflorescence 1–9-flowered; tepals strongly decurved, bright scarlet; anthers orange-red. Flowers June to July.
SIMILAR SPECIES: *L. carniolicum*, has 5–18mm broad leaves.
HABITAT: Rock debris, stony sward, rocks, poor grassland; calcicole. About 800–2,400m.
DISTRIBUTION: Western alpine endemic.

5 | White False Helleborine
Veratrum album – Melanthiaceae

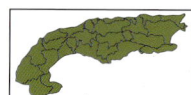

50–150cm tall; leaves arranged spirally on the stem, to 20cm long, with fluffy hairs beneath, deeply pleated lengthwise; inflorescence 20–60cm long; flowers white to green, more rarely yellowish. Flowers June to August.
SIMILAR SPECIES: When not flowering can be confused with Yellow Gentian, *Gentiana lutea* (see p. 226), which however has opposite, hairless, blue-green leaves.
HABITAT: Pasture, meadows, tall herb vegetation, livestock resting sites. To about 2,700m.
DISTRIBUTION: Eurosiberian.
NOTE: 2 subspecies in the Alps:
– subsp. *album* (**5A**): tepals white inside, greenish-white outside.
– subsp. *lobelianum* (**5B**): tepals green on both sides.

Orchidaceae

1 | Pyramidal Orchid
Anacamptis pyramidalis – Orchidaceae

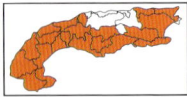

20–50cm tall; leaves 4–10, unspotted, narrowly lanceolate, 8–25cm long and 0.7–2cm broad; inflorescence pyramidal to cylindrical, densely flowered; flowers purplish-pink; lip deeply 3-lobed, 6–9mm long and broad, with 2 vertical ridges ('guide-plates') on upper surface; spur narrow, 10–15mm long, curved downwards. Flowers May to July.
SIMILAR SPECIES: None.
HABITAT: Dry to occasionally damp poor meadows, scrub and open woods; calcicole. To about 1,700m.
DISTRIBUTION: Western European–Mediterranean, from Morocco and Ireland to Estonia and Turkmenistan.

2 | Narrow-leaved Helleborine
Cephalanthera longifolia – Orchidaceae

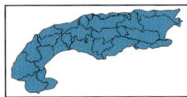

15–50cm tall; stem hairless, with 4–14 leaves in 2 rows; leaves lanceolate, to 18cm long, 4–6x as long as broad, somewhat folded; inflorescence of up to 40 flowers; flowers white; lip with orange-yellow longitudinal stripes and golden yellow tip. Flowers April to June.
SIMILAR SPECIES: White Helleborine, *C. damasonium*, has leaves only 2–3x as long as broad. The white form of Red Helleborine, *C. rubra*, has a glandular upper stem.
HABITAT: Woods, poor meadows, scrub; calcicole. To 1,800m.
DISTRIBUTION: European-Asiatic, from British Isles, Scandinavia, north-west Africa, to the Pamirs.

3 | Red Helleborine
Cephalanthera rubra – Orchidaceae

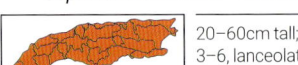

20–60cm tall; leaves 3–6, lanceolate, bluish-green, somewhat folded, 5–10cm long and 1–3cm broad; inflorescence loose, with 4–15 purplish-pink flowers; tepals forming a canopy-like hood; lip down-curved, with yellowish-brown longitudinal stripes and pink tip. Flowers May to July.
SIMILAR SPECIES: Pink forms of Narrow-leaved Helleborine, *C. longifolia*.
HABITAT: Open woods, mainly pine, oak, beech, and mixed deciduous, woodland clearings, shady meadows; calcicole. To 2,100m.
DISTRIBUTION: European–western Asiatic, from North Africa, Spain, England (very rare!), and southern Scandinavia to the Urals and northern Iran.

4 | Alpine Dwarf Orchid
Chamorchis alpina – Orchidaceae

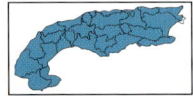

5–15cm tall, small and easily overlooked; stem pale green, angular; leaves linear-lanceolate, grass-like, 4–10, in basal rosette; inflorescence dense, with 5–15 small flowers; lip yellow with a green centre, tongue-like, entire, or weakly 3-lobed, with decurved edges. Flowers June to August.
SIMILAR SPECIES: Frog Orchid, *Dactylorhiza viridis* (see p. 422), has oval-lanceolate leaves and a leafy stem.
HABITAT: Cushion Sedge (*Carex firma*) vegetation, montane dry poor grassland, wind-exposed ridges with little winter snow cover; calcicole. 1,400–2,900m.
DISTRIBUTION: Arctic–alpine, Scandinavia, Alps, and Carpathians.
NOTE: Alpine Dwarf Orchid is the only European orchid that is pollinated by ants, and its specialised growth form and flower structure can be seen as adaptations to this relationship. The size and shape of the flowers match the dimensions of the head, body and legs of the ant species *Formica lemani*.

5 | Coralroot Orchid
Corallorhiza trifida – Orchidaceae

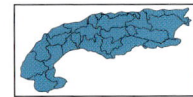

7–25cm tall; delicate, unobtrusive plant with a branching, coral-like rhizome; stem thin, yellowish-green to brownish-purple; stem leaves absent; inflorescence loose, with 3–10 small, greenish flowers; lip white, with a few red spots at base, blunt, tongue-shaped, with wavy edge, strongly decurved; spur absent. Flowers May to July.
SIMILAR SPECIES: None.
HABITAT: Shady, humus-rich coniferous and deciduous woods and forests, more rarely in montane meadows or on rotting tree stumps. To 2,550m.
DISTRIBUTION: Eurosiberian–North American, from the Pyrenees and Iceland, to Siberia, northern China, and North America.

Orchidaceae

1 | Lady's-slipper
Cypripedium calceolus – Orchidaceae

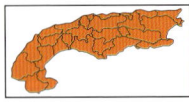

25–60cm tall; leaves 3–5, large, broadly elliptical to oval, strongly ribbed; inflorescence 1–2-flowered; flower large, with slipper-shaped, pouched, yellow lip; tepals dark maroon, spirally twisted, 3.5–5cm long. Flowers May to July.
SIMILAR SPECIES: None.
HABITAT: Open deciduous and pine woods, wooded ravines, scrub, semi-arid grassland, Dwarf Mountain Pine scrub; calcicole. To 2,200m.
DISTRIBUTION: European-Asiatic, from Spain, England (extremely rare) and northern Scandinavia to Sakhalin and Korea.
NOTE: Lady's-slipper is a trap-pollinator. Insects (mainly small bees and flies) are attracted to the contrasting colours of the flowers, especially by the sweet scent. When the insect lands on the inside of the lip, it often slips down inside due to the slippery inner surface, where it is trapped. Colourless bright 'windows' at the back of the 'slipper' signal an exit. The only way out is up a 'ladder' formed by hairs at the back of the lip, which takes the insect past the fertile anthers from which pollinia (masses of pollen grains) stick to its body. Pollination is achieved when an insect with pollen visits another flower and crawls out past the stigma. After pollination, the flower soon wilts, while unpollinated flowers last longer.

2 | Flecked Marsh-orchid
Dactylorhiza cruenta – Orchidaceae

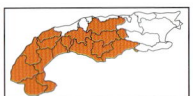

15–35cm tall, short, but sturdy; stem thick, hollow; leaves 3–5, oval to lanceolate, with purplish-brown spots on both sides, protruding from stem, not reaching the inflorescence; inflorescence cylindrical, dense and compact, with 10–30 flowers; flowers small, tepals pink to purple; lip entire to weakly 3-lobed, marked with looping lines and circles. Flowers June to July.
SIMILAR SPECIES: Early Marsh-orchid, *D. incarnata*, especially the variety *hyphaematodes*, which is spotted on both sides. *D. incarnata* differs in having leaves that are slightly hooded towards the tip, and which usually reach the inflorescence.
HABITAT: Fens, bogs, marshy meadows. To 2,600m.
DISTRIBUTION: Eurosiberian, from the Alps and Scandinavia to Siberia.

NOTE: The genus *Dactylorhiza* forms hybrids, such as when 2 or more species occur together. Hybrid swarms are not unusual.

3 | Common Spotted-orchid
Dactylorhiza fuchsii – Orchidaceae

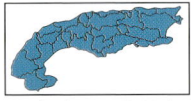

15–70cm tall, very variable; stem pith-filled, angular at the top, often tinged purple; leaves 5–10, lanceolate, usually spotted above, 5–20cm long, 1.2–3cm broad, upper leaves bract-like; inflorescence conical, densely flowered; tepals pink to purple or white; lip deeply 3-lobed, with looping markings, dots and lines; spur long and cylindrical, 6–12mm long and 1.4–2.5mm broad. Flowers May to August.
SIMILAR SPECIES: Broad-leaved Marsh-orchid, *D. majalis* (see p. 422), has a hollow stem.
HABITAT: Very adaptable. Meadows, pasture, semi-arid grassland, Mat Grass (*Nardus stricta*) vegetation, woods, marshes, roadsides, fen and spring-fed mires, woodland clearings. To 2,500m.
DISTRIBUTION: Eurosiberian, from Spain, Ireland, and Scandinavia to Siberia.
NAME: In honour of Leonhard Fuchs (1501–1566), Professor of Medicine at Tübingen, who published an illustration of this species in his herbal book *De Historia Stirpium*. Fuchs is regarded as one of the 'founding fathers' of botany.

4 | Lapland Marsh-orchid
Dactylorhiza lapponica – Orchidaceae

10–30cm tall; stem hollow, upper stem tinged violet-brown; leaves 2–5, lanceolate, 2.5–8cm long and 0.8–2cm broad, spotted above, increasingly spotted towards the outside, with the density of spots increasing from about the middle of the leaf; lowest leaf characteristically small and short-ovate; inflorescence short, loose and few-flowered, with 3–20 flowers; tepals dark pink to purple. Flowers June to July.
SIMILAR SPECIES: Broad-leaved Marsh-orchid, *D. majalis* (see p. 422), has 4–6 leaves, and a 15–50-flowered inflorescence.
HABITAT: Calcareous and spring-fed mires and fens; calcicole. 500–2,000m.
DISTRIBUTION: Northern European-alpine. Scandinavia and Alps.

Orchidaceae

1 | Broad-leaved Marsh-orchid
Dactylorhiza majalis – Orchidaceae

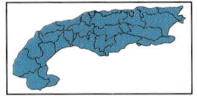

15–40cm tall; stem thick, hollow, upper stem angular and tinged purple; leaves 4–6, spotted on upper surface, oval to broadly lanceolate, 2–4x as long as broad; bracts broad, longer than flowers, purple or at least tinged purple; inflorescence dense, with 15–50 flowers; flowers dark pink to purple; lip 3-lobed, with blunt central lobe, or entire with projecting tip (subsp. *alpestris*), attractively patterned; spur conical, directed slightly downwards. Flowers April to July.
SIMILAR SPECIES: Narrow-leaved Marsh-orchid, *D. traunsteineri*, has leaves 6–10x as long as broad. Common Spotted-orchid, *D. fuchsii* (see p. 420), has a pith-filled stem.
HABITAT: Damp to wet poor meadows, damp spots on hay meadows and pasture, fens and spring-fed mires. To 2,500m.
DISTRIBUTION: European, from northern Spain and the north-western Balkans to southern Scandinavia, and east to the Urals.

2 | Elder-flowered Orchid
Dactylorhiza sambucina – Orchidaceae

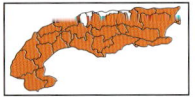

10–30cm tall, with hollow stem and 4–7 leaves; leaves lanceolate, 5–12cm long, 1–3cm broad, green, shiny, unspotted; bracts large, as long as or longer than flowers; flowers yellow or purplish-red; lip 7–12mm long, 9–17mm broad, with looping patterns consisting of purple dots, base of lip yellowish, even in red-flowered plants; spur thick, cylindrical-conical, curved downwards, 10–18mm long and 2.5–4.5mm across. Flowers April to June.
SIMILAR SPECIES: Yellow form of Pale-flowered Orchid, *Orchis pallens* (see p. 434), has an unmarked lip.
HABITAT: Damp to moderately-dry poor grassland, edges of scrub, poor pasture, dwarf shrub heath, flower-rich hay meadows. To 2,400m.
DISTRIBUTION: European, from Spain and southern Scandinavia to the Carpathians and Ukraine.
NOTE: Elder-flowered Orchid belongs to a group that uses deceptive pollination, only pretending to reward visiting insects. Occurring in forms with differing flower colour helps counteract the learning ability of the pollinators.

3 | Narrow-leaved Marsh-orchid
Dactylorhiza traunsteineri – Orchidaceae

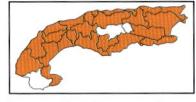

15–40cm tall, slender plant; stem thin, green, upper stem angular and often purple; leaves 3–5, protruding obliquely or upright, narrowly lanceolate, 5–18cm long and 0.5–1.8cm broad, 5–10x as long as broad, spotted or unspotted, furrowed to keeled; inflorescence cylindrical, loose, 3–8cm long, with 5–15 flowers; flowers relatively large, dark pink to purple. Flowers May to July.
SIMILAR SPECIES: Broad-leaved Marsh-orchid, *D. majalis*. Lapland Marsh-orchid, *D. lapponica* (see p. 420), has ovate-lanceolate leaves that are 2–4x as long as broad.
HABITAT: Damp to wet meadows, fens and spring-fed mires; base-rich, mainly calcareous soils. To 2,150m.
DISTRIBUTION: European.
NAME: In honour of Austrian botanist Joseph Traunsteiner (1798–1850), who discovered the species near Kitzbühel in 1830.

4 | Frog Orchid
Dactylorhiza viridis – Orchidaceae
(Syn.: *Coeloglossum viride*)

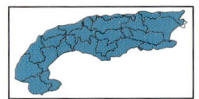

5–25cm tall, small plant; stem angular, pale green; leaves 3–7, clustered at stem base, 2.5–10cm long and 1.5–7cm broad, ovate-lanceolate, pointed; inflorescence cylindrical, with 5–25 green, yellowish-green or brownish-red flowers; lip tongue-shaped, 3-lobed, drooping to slightly curved, broadening towards the tip, the central lobe distinctly shorter; spur sack-like. Flowers May to August.
SIMILAR SPECIES: Alpine Dwarf Orchid, *Chamorchis alpina* (see p. 418), has narrow, grass-like leaves, and lacks a spur.
HABITAT: Poor grassland on acid soils, pasture and poor meadows, but also on nutrient-poor calcareous soils; dwarf shrub heath, woodland clearings, open pine woods. To 2,800m.
DISTRIBUTION: Eurosiberian–North American, from southern Spain and Iceland to Siberia and North America.

1 | Dark-red Helleborine
Epipactis atrorubens – Orchidaceae

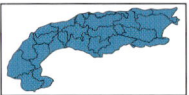

15–60cm tall; upper stem with dense fluffy hairs, and usually tinged purple; leaves 5–11, narrowly to broadly ovate, 4–8cm long and 1–4cm broad, pointed; inflorescence with 10–40 vanilla-scented flowers; tepals purplish-red, 5–8mm long; lip 5–6mm long, front lobe with 2 lateral wrinkled ridges, notched at the edge; ovary hairy. Flowers June to July.
SIMILAR SPECIES: Broad-leaved Helleborine, *E. helleborine*, sometimes has reddish flowers, but lacks the wrinkled ridges on the lip, and has a hairless ovary.
HABITAT: Pinewoods, poor grassland, calcareous scree, embankments, open deciduous woods, rocks; calcareous soils in warm sites. To 2,400m.
DISTRIBUTION: European-Asiatic, from Spain and British Isles to Siberia and the Caucasus.

2 | Broad-leaved Helleborine
Epipactis helleborine – Orchidaceae

25–80cm tall; lower stem hairless, upper stem with short, whitish downy hairs; leaves 4–12, with prominent veins, oval to lanceolate, protruding, 6–17cm long, getting smaller up the stem; flower stalks with purple base; tepals greenish, often suffused purple; front lobe of lip with 2 smooth to furrowed wart-like tubercles at the base, tip reflexed; ovary hairless. Flowers June to August.
SIMILAR SPECIES: In the Alps there are at least 11 further orchids in the *Epipactis helleborine* group, which are difficult to separate, except by experts.
HABITAT: Woods, scrub, track sides, calcareous rock debris, also meadows. To 2,300m.
DISTRIBUTION: European-Asiatic, from Spain, British Isles and Scandinavia to Siberia and the Himalaya.

3 | Marsh Helleborine
Epipactis palustris – Orchidaceae

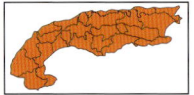

20–60cm tall; leaves 4–8, elongate-lanceolate, 7–18cm long and 1.5–4cm broad; inflorescence loose, 5–15cm long, with 6–20 flowers; inner tepals white, with purple markings, outer tepals brownish or purplish-green; lip to 12mm long, with a large round white front lobe, wavy and notched at the edge, with 2 yellow bulges at the base. Flowers June to August.
SIMILAR SPECIES: None.
HABITAT: Calcareous fens and damp meadows, lake margins; calcicole. To 2,200m.
DISTRIBUTION: European-Asiatic, from Spain and British Isles to Siberia and Iran.
NOTE: Darwin discovered the hinge mechanism on the lip of Marsh Helleborine in 1877. Small insects land on the front of the lip, causing it to bend downwards. When the insect moves to the back of the lip to reach the nectar, the front lip snaps back up, pushing the insect upwards and backwards into the flower, past the sticky gland and pollen masses.

4 | Ghost Orchid
Epipogium aphyllum – Orchidaceae

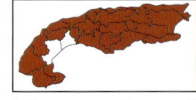

10–25 cm tall, pale, alien-looking plant without chlorophyll; stem leafless; inflorescence loose, with 1–8 drooping flowers; lip arched upwards, whitish, with 4–6 lines of reddish-purple spots; bracts narrow, pale yellow to delicate pink, pointing downwards. Flowers June to August.
SIMILAR SPECIES: None, although Yellow Bird's-nest, *Hypopitys monotropa* agg., is superficially similar and may confuse the non-expert, but its stem is covered in scale-like leaves.
HABITAT: Shady, damp deciduous and spruce woods, especially montane beechwoods and spruce forests. To 1,900m.
DISTRIBUTION: Eurosiberian, from Spain and Scandinavia to Kamchatka and Japan.
NOTE: Although the distribution range of Ghost Orchid is extensive, it is often rather rare, and if the conditions are not right may stop flowering for years. In Britain it was rediscovered in 1986, having been lost for 23 years, after which it disappeared again, only to be re-found in 2009. In 2001 it was first recorded in Taiwan, and in 2011 in Croatia.

Orchidaceae

1 | Creeping Lady's-tresses
Goodyera repens – Orchidaceae

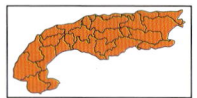

7–25cm tall; leaves heart-shaped to oval and pointed, 1.5–3.5cm long and 1–2cm broad, short-stalked, net-veined; inflorescence of 5–15 flowers in a one-sided weak spiral; flowers small; tepals white, arching hood-like together; sepals conspicuously glandular-hairy on outside. Flowers June to August.
SIMILAR SPECIES: *Spiranthes* spp., but these lack the net-veined leaves.
HABITAT: Coniferous woods, especially moss-rich pine and spruce woods. Shallow-rooted and rather uncompetitive, they prefer to grow on moss cushions above a layer of needle leaves.
DISTRIBUTION: Eurosiberian–North American, from Portugal and Norway to Japan, Kamchatka and North America.

2 | Chalk Fragrant Orchid
Gymnadenia conopsea – Orchidaceae

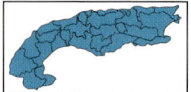

15–80cm tall; leaves 3–10, to 25cm long and 4cm broad, linear-lanceolate, upper leaves much smaller; inflorescence 5–30cm long with up to 50 flowers; flowers pale pink to intense lilac-pink, more rarely white, usually fragrant; lip 3-lobed, the central lobe somewhat longer than the lateral lobes; spur 1–2cm long, much longer than the ovary, thin, down-curved, with visible nectar. Flowers June to August.
SIMILAR SPECIES: Short-spurred Fragrant Orchid, *G. odoratissima*, has a 0.4–0.7cm long spur, shorter than the ovary.
HABITAT: Poor meadows, semi-arid grassland, variably wet meadows, fens and spring-fed mires, Mat Grass (*Nardus stricta*) and alpine cushion vegetation, open oak and pine woods. To 2,800m.
DISTRIBUTION: Eurosiberian, from Portugal and northern Scandinavia to Japan and southern China.

3 | Short-spurred Fragrant Orchid
Gymnadenia odoratissima – Orchidaceae

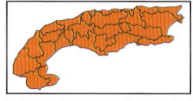

10–30cm tall, slender; leaves 6–10, narrow towards base of stem, to 12cm long and 0.8cm broad, slightly folded, grass-like, and therefore seeming even narrower; flowers small, variably coloured from white and pale yellow to pink and purple, with intense vanilla scent; lip to 5mm long with significantly longer central lobe; spur 4–7mm long, shorter than the ovary, slightly decurved. Flowers June to August.
SIMILAR SPECIES: Chalk Fragrant Orchid, *G. conopsea*.
HABITAT: Alpine mat vegetation on limestone, poor grassland, open pine woods, damp and wet meadows, fens and spring-fed mires; calcicole. To 2,600m.
DISTRIBUTION: European, from north-eastern Spain and southern Sweden to the Carpathians.

4 | White Adder's-mouth
Malaxis monophyllos – Orchidaceae

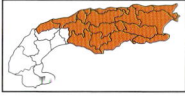

7–30cm tall; stem thin, hairless, pale green, upper stem angular; usually a single leaf, more rarely 2–3, pale green elliptical-ovate, 3–10cm long, 1.5–4.5cm broad; inflorescence long and cylindrical, with 40–100 flowers; flowers very small, pale green, with upturned lip; lip 1.5–2.5cm long, oval, with triangular tip. Flowers June to July.
SIMILAR SPECIES: Other greenish-flowered orchids. White Adder's-mouth is distinguished by its single basal leaf, and elongated, fishbone-like inflorescence.
HABITAT: Damp, mossy woods, herb-rich montane meadows; prefers calcareous substrates and high humidity. To 1,960m.
DISTRIBUTION: Eurosiberian, from the Alps and central Scandinavian mountains to Japan and southern China.
NOTE: The genus *Malaxis* contains several hundred species, mostly in the tropics and subtropics, centred in south-east Asia. There are only a few in temperate regions, with this the only one native to the Alps. Bog Orchid, *Hammarbya paludosa*, is closely related and was formerly named *Malaxis paludosa*. It is also found in Europe, including in the Alps.

Orchidaceae

1 | Burnt Orchid
Neotinea ustulata – Orchidaceae

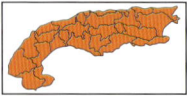

10–50cm tall; leaves 5–9, lower leaves in a near rosette, pale green to bluish-green; inflorescence many-flowered, at first conical, later cylindrical; flowers small, smelling of honey; tepals (except the lip) forming a dark red hood; lip 5–8mm long, white with purple spots; spur 1–2mm long, cylindrical, decurved. Flowers April to September (subsp. *aestivalis*).
SIMILAR SPECIES: None.
HABITAT: Semi-arid grassland, dry to occasionally damp poor grassland, moor grass meadows, marshy meadows, open scrub; calcicole. To 2,400m.
DISTRIBUTION: European–western Asiatic, from Spain and southern Scandinavian to the Urals and Caucasus.
NAME: The generic name honours Italian botanist Vincenzo Tineo (1791–1856), who was a Professor in Palermo.

2 | Lesser Twayblade
Neottia cordata – Orchidaceae
(Syn.: *Listera cordata*)

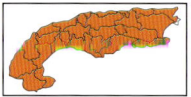

5–20 cm tall, inconspicuous; stem thin; leaves 2, small, heart-shaped to triangular, opposite, 1–3cm long and broad, shiny above; inflorescence 5–15-flowered; flowers green, often suffused brownish-red; fruits usually ripening before the flowers have wilted. Flowers June to August.
SIMILAR SPECIES: None.
HABITAT: Damp, mossy, acid coniferous woods, Dwarf Mountain Pine scrub, Spring Heath (*Erica carnea*) pine woods, mossy tree stumps, tundra-like dwarf shrub heath. Often in association with Wood Sorrel (*Oxalis acetosella*) and Bilberry (*Vaccinium myrtillus*). To 2,300m.
DISTRIBUTION: Eurosiberian–North American.
NOTES: Not very variable. There may be 3 or 4 stem leaves, and flowers may lack the purplish colour.

Neottia (incl. *Listera*) contains some 40 species, of which 3 are native to the Alps. The centre of diversity is in eastern Asia, and in recent decades more species have been described in that region. There are 17 species in the Himalaya.

3 | Bird's-nest Orchid
Neottia nidus-avis – Orchidaceae

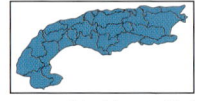

10–40cm tall, almost without chlorophyll; brown, leafless; stem thick and sturdy, grooved, hairless, with brownish scales; inflorescence many-flowered; tepals brown, forming a loose hood; lip with nectar-bearing cup-like depression at the base. Flowers May to July.
SIMILAR SPECIES: Broomrapes such as Sage Broomrape, *Orobanche salviae*, which is hairy. Bird's-nests, *Monotropa* spp., have bell-shaped flowers, which are initially nodding.
HABITAT: Shady, humus-, nutrient- and base-rich deciduous and coniferous woods and edge habitats, especially limestone beechwoods. To 2,050m.
DISTRIBUTION: Eurosiberian, from Portugal and Scandinavia to southern Siberia and Iran.
NOTE: Out of the roughly 22,000 orchid species worldwide, only about 200 lack chlorophyll and so cannot photosynthesise. In the Alps, the commonest of these is Bird's-nest Orchid.

4 | Common Twayblade
Neottia ovata – Orchidaceae
(Syn.: *Listera ovata*)

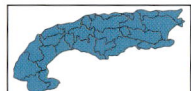

20–60cm tall; stem green, upper stem hairy, 2–3 scale leaves towards the base; true leaves 2, broadly oval, with prominent veins, 4–12cm long, 3–8cm broad; inflorescence with 10–60 green flowers; lip deeply 2-lobed, with a nectar-bearing longitudinal furrow; spur absent. Flowers May to July.
SIMILAR SPECIES: None.
HABITAT: Meadows, woods, fens, track sides, pasture. To 2,500m.
DISTRIBUTION: European-Asiatic, from Spain and Iceland to the Himalaya.
NOTE: The flowers produce a rich supply of nectar and are therefore visited by many insects. When an insect disturbs the gland at the edge of the stigma, this triggers an explosive reaction. A sticky drop of pollen is ejected, with the pollinia deposited onto the head of the insect.

Orchidaceae

1 | Archduke Johann's Vanilla Orchid
Nigritella archiducis-joannis – Orchidaceae (Syn.: *Gymnadenia archiducis-joannis*)

5–20cm tall; many leaves, the lower in basal rosettes, linear, grass-like, grooved; inflorescence hemi-spherical to spherical; flower buds pink to flesh-coloured, only slightly darker than the fully developed flower; central sepal and petals pointing straight forwards and forming a tube with the lip, so that the flower looks almost closed. Flowers June to July.
SIMILAR SPECIES: Other pale-flowered vanilla orchids. Distinguished by the rolled-up front part of the lip and the adjacent petals and lip making the flowers seem almost closed.
HABITAT: Calcareous poor grassland; calcicole. 1,540–2,150m.
DISTRIBUTION: Eastern alpine.
NAME: Honours Archduke Johann of Austria, who was an enthusiastic mountaineer and amateur botanist.
NOTE: Previously thought to be endemic to Styria. In 1996 it was found in the region of the Leckkogel in the Gosau Range near Salzburg, and later, on Hochobir, Carinthia, and on Triglav in the Julian Alps.

2 | Austrian Vanilla Orchid
Nigritella austriaca – Orchidaceae (Syn.: *Gymnadenia austriaca*)

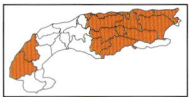

8–20cm tall; stem angular, light green; leaves linear, grass-like, clustered at the base, grooved; inflorescence hemi-spherical to spherical, usually broader than tall; perianth dark red; flowers fragrant, though not as pleasantly scented as *N. rhellicani*; bracts spreading; petals about half as broad as the lanceolate sepals; lip triangular and pointed, 6.8–10mm long. Flowers June to July.
SIMILAR SPECIES: Rhellicanus's Vanilla Orchid, *N. rhellicani* (see p. 432).
HABITAT: Calcareous poor grassland. 1,080–2,400m.
DISTRIBUTION: South-western European montane, from the Pyrenees to the eastern Alps.
NOTE: In the Alps, the nominate form, subsp. *austriaca*, widespread in the eastern Alps, is separated from subsp. *iberica* which is found in the French Alps.

3 | Bicoloured Vanilla Orchid
Nigritella bicolor – Orchidaceae (Syn.: *Gymnadenia bicolor*)

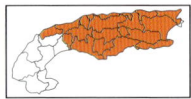

7–25cm tall; leaves linear, grass-like, grooved, in a basal rosette, 5–11cm long; inflorescence large (compared to the other *Nigritella* species); bracts green with reddish edges to completely brownish-red; perianth pinkish-red, with paler base; sepals spreading, 5.1–7.5mm long, 1.5–2.6mm broad; petals 4.4–6.4mm long and 1–1.5mm broad; lip 6.2–7.6mm long and 4–5mm broad. Flowers June to July.
SIMILAR SPECIES: The other pale-flowered vanilla orchids, especially Red Vanilla Orchid, *N. miniata*, which however has a uniformly red inflorescence and a 2.6–4.1mm broad lip. It is not always possible to make a clear distinction between these 2 species.
HABITAT: Alpine calcareous poor grassland; calcicole. 1,000–2,130m.
DISTRIBUTION: Southern European montane. Eastern Alps, Dinaric Alps, and Carpathians.
NOTE: *Nigritella bicolor* was first separated from *N. miniata* in 2010. This separation revealed that far more of the specimens of the former species *N. rubra* belong to *N. bicolor* that to *N. miniata*.

4 | West-alpine Vanilla Orchid
Nigritella corneliana – Orchidaceae (Syn.: *Gymnadenia corneliana*)

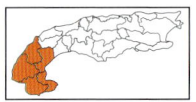

10–30cm tall; stems angular, leafy to the top; leaves grass-like, linear, to 10cm long; inflorescence dense, ovate-cylindrical; perianth pale pink to bright red or vermilion; sepals 6–8mm long and about 2mm broad; lip upwardly-directed, narrowing to a saddle shape above the base, 7–10mm long; spur 1mm long, blunt. Flowers July.
SIMILAR SPECIES: The red-flowered form of Rhellicanus's Vanilla Orchid, *N. rhellicani* (see p. 432), which however has a 5.5–7mm long lip.
HABITAT: Calcareous poor grassland. 1,900–2,500m, sometimes lower, as on Mt. Mounier, France (1,750m), or higher, as near Sestriere, Italy (2,600m).
DISTRIBUTION: South-west alpine endemic, from the Maritime Alps to the Cottian Alps.
NAME: In honour of Geneva botanist Cornelia Rudio, who found the species at the beginning of the 20th century at the Col du Lautaret at 2,300m.

Orchidaceae

1 | Kamnik Alps Vanilla Orchid
Nigritella lithopolitanica – Orchidaceae

8–22cm tall; leaves linear, grass-like, grooved, lower leaves in a basal rosette, upper leaves bract-like; inflorescence at first hemi-spherical to spherical, later blunt-conical; flowers opening wide, pale pink to dark pink, the buds more intensely coloured than the open flowers; bulbous base of lip about 2mm broad. Flowers June to July.
SIMILAR SPECIES: Widder's Vanilla Orchid, *N. widderi*, has bulbous base of lip about 3mm broad.
HABITAT: Calcareous poor grassland; calcicole. 1,500–2,100m.
DISTRIBUTION: Eastern alpine.
NOTE: Of the 16 known species of *Nigritella*, 13 are native to the Alps, mostly in the eastern Alps. Some authorities place the vanilla orchids in the genus *Gymnadenia*. However, the unique appearance of these orchids alone justifies their separation from this genus.

2 | Rhellicanus's Vanilla Orchid
Nigritella rhellicani – Orchidaceae
(Syn.: *Gymnadenia rhellicani*)

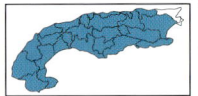

5–20cm tall; stem angular and leafy; leaves 10–25, linear, grass-like, grooved, lower leaves in a basal rosette; bracts narrowly lanceolate, pointed, about the same length as the flowers, lower bracts with a papillary margin, at least at the front half (strong hand lens); inflorescence with 20–75 flowers, at first conical, later cylindrical to spherical, mostly taller than broad; flowers dark red, strongly fragrant; lip 5–7mm long; spur 1.1–1.5mm long. Flowers June to August.
SIMILAR SPECIES: Austrian Vanilla Orchid, *N. austriaca* (see p. 430), has an inflorescence that is usually broader than tall, and lips 6.8–10mm long. Mount Cenis Vanilla Orchid, *N. cenisia*, found in the western Alps around Mont Cenis, has large, numerous flowers. It is endemic to the French and Italian south-western Alps from Col du Galibier to Col du Petit Saint Bernard.
HABITAT: Alpine and subalpine grassy vegetation on calcareous and non-calcareous substrates. 1,050–2,800m.
DISTRIBUTION: Southern European montane, from the mountains of northern Spain to the Carpathians and the mountains of the Balkan Peninsula.
NAME: In honour of Swiss clergyman and botanist Johannes Müller from Rellikon on Greifensee, known by the Latin form Johannes Rellicanus (1478/88–1542), noted for his work in early modern botany, and who first mentioned this species in 1536.

3 | Styrian Vanilla Orchid
Nigritella stiriaca – Orchidaceae
(Syn.: *Gymnadenia stiriaca*)

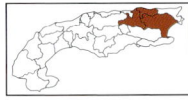

7–20cm tall; leaves linear, grass-like, grooved, lower leaves in a basal rosette; bracts red-edged or red; flowers bicoloured, dark pink, white towards the tip; sepals 6–7.3mm long and 1.6–2.8mm broad; petals 5.2–6.7mm long and 1.3–1.8mm broad; lip 7.8–8.2mm long, spreading to 5.6–5.8mm broad, rolled pouch-like. Flowers June to July.
SIMILAR SPECIES: The bicoloured flowers of Styrian Vanilla Orchid are distinctive; pink inside and whitish outside.
HABITAT: Calcareous poor grassland; calcicole. 1,250–1,900m.
DISTRIBUTION: Eastern alpine.

4 | Widder's Vanilla Orchid
Nigritella widderi – Orchidaceae

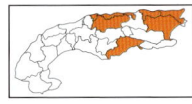

5–17cm tall; leaves linear, grass-like, clustered in a basal rosette; inflorescence hemispherical to oval; flowers pale pink, darker in bud, lower flowers paler (often almost white) than the upper; sepals 6.5–8mm long and 2.2–2.5mm broad; petals 5.7–6.3mm long and 1.5–2mm broad; lip 6.7–8mm long and 4.5–5.7mm broad, bulbous at base. Flowers June to July.
SIMILAR SPECIES: Kamnik Alps Vanilla Orchid, *N. lithopolitanica*.
HABITAT: Alpine calcareous poor grassland. 1,400–2,050m.
DISTRIBUTION: Eastern alpine–Apennine. Eastern limestone Alps and central Apennines.
NAME: In honour of Styrian botanist Felix Josef Widder (1892–1974), who started studying vanilla orchid species in the middle of the last century.

Orchidaceae

1 | Lake Garda Orchid
Ophrys benacensis – Orchidaceae

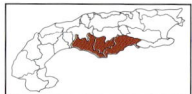

10–30cm tall; stem pale green; leaves lanceolate, pale green to bluish-green, in a rosette; inflorescence 3–6-flowered; lip dark purple, with short brown hairs at margin, 13–19mm long and broad; lip patch large, shiny, brownish-violet, often with pale edge; cavity of stigma somewhat broader than tall. Flowers April to May.
SIMILAR SPECIES: Drôme Orchid, *O. drumana*, has a lip 8–13mm long, flowers later, and is restricted to the south-western Alps.
HABITAT: Poor meadows, rocky dry grassland, edges of olive groves, abandoned vineyards. To 850m.
DISTRIBUTION: Southern alpine endemic.

2 | Fly Orchid
Ophrys insectifera – Orchidaceae

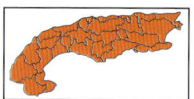

15–40cm tall; stem pale green; leaves lanceolate, pale green to bluish-green, basal; inflorescence a loose, slender spike with 2–10 flowers; inner tepals narrow 'antennae'; lip resembles an insect, reddish-brown to dark brown, rather narrow, with 2 shiny black 'eye spots' at the base, deeply lobed, the central lobe deeply notched; central spot of lip blue-grey. Flowers May to July.
SIMILAR SPECIES: None.
HABITAT: Poor and semi-arid grassland, open pine woods, Dwarf Mountain Pine vegetation, stabilised river gravel, fens; calcicole. To 2,000m.
DISTRIBUTION: European, from northern Spain and Greece to British Isles and western Russia.

3 | Early Purple Orchid
Orchis mascula – Orchidaceae

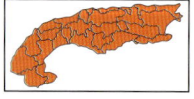

20–60cm tall; upper stem tinged purple; leaves lanceolate, 4–17cm long and 1–3.5cm broad, spotted or unspotted; inflorescence 8–50-flowered; bracts purple, membranous; flowers pink to purple; lip 3-lobed, 7–14mm long and 7.5–18mm broad; spur cylindrical, blunt, directed upwards. Flowers April to July.
SIMILAR SPECIES: Green-winged Orchid, *Anacamptis morio*, has greenish or greyish veins on the outer tepals.
HABITAT: Poor meadows, open woods, montane pasture. To 2,600m.
DISTRIBUTION: European, from the Canaries, Morocco and Norway, scattered to the Urals and northern Iran.
NOTE: 2 subspecies in the Alps:
– subsp. *mascula* (**3A**): lateral sepals 7–10mm long.
– subsp. *speciosa* (**3B**): lateral sepals 12–15mm long.

4 | Pale-flowered Orchid
Orchis pallens – Orchidaceae

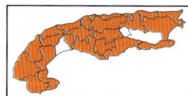

15–40cm tall; stem sturdy, pale green; leaves 4–6, unspotted, shiny, 6–12cm long and 1.5–4cm broad, in a basal rosette; flowers pale yellow, with scent of elderflowers; lip almost flat to slightly arched, shallowly 3-lobed, without markings; spur cylindrical, 7–14mm long, blunt, horizontal to upcurved. Flowers April to June.
SIMILAR SPECIES: Yellow forms of Elder-flowered Orchid, *Dactylorhiza sambucina* (see p. 422), but this always has purple markings on the lip, and the spur curves downwards.
HABITAT: Open woods, montane meadows, poor grassland; calcicole. To 1,900m.
DISTRIBUTION: Southern European, from northern Spain to the Caucasus.

5 | Spitzel's Orchid
Orchis spitzelii – Orchidaceae

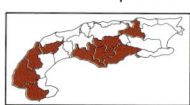

20–35cm tall; stem pale green, upper stem tinged purple; leaves 2–7, basal, unspotted, shiny; inflorescence cylindrical, with 10–20 flowers; flowers olive green, with purple markings; lip 8–15mm long and 9–18mm broad, deeply 3-lobed, purple-pink with purple spots; spur conical, thick, curved downwards. Flowers June to July.
SIMILAR SPECIES: Early Purple Orchid, *O. mascula*, has no olive green in the flowers.
HABITAT: Pasture, dwarf montane scrub, open montane woods. 700–2,000m.
DISTRIBUTION: Mediterranean and scattered from Morocco to Iran.
NAME: In honour of Munich forester and plant collector Anton von Spitzel (1807–1853), who first discovered the species near Saalfelden when he was a forester in Reichenhall.

Orchidaceae

1 | Lesser Butterfly-orchid
Platanthera bifolia – Orchidaceae

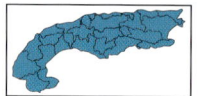

15–50cm tall; usually 2 leaves close to the base, rarely more, oval to broadly lanceolate, 7–20cm long, unspotted, shiny; upper half of stem with 3–5 small, bract-like leaves; inflorescence cylindrical; flowers white to pale greenish-white, pleasantly scented, especially in the evening; lip tongue-shaped, white, narrowing and greenish towards tip; pollinia parallel, about 1mm apart; spur thread-like, not thickened, 15–32mm long, curved downwards. Flowers May to July.
SIMILAR SPECIES: Greater Butterfly-orchid, *P. chlorantha*, has pollinia widely diverging below, and spur flattened and widening at the tip.
HABITAT: Woods, poor grassland, fen meadows, mires, dwarf shrub heath. To 2,500m.
DISTRIBUTION: European-Asiatic, from northern Spain and northern Scandinavia to Siberia and the Himalaya.

2 | Greater Butterfly-orchid
Platanthera chlorantha – Orchidaceae

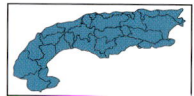

20–50cm tall; 2 large leaves near the ground, oval to broadly lanceolate, shiny; upper stem with 3–5 small bract-like leaves; flowers greenish-white, pleasantly scented, especially in the evening; lip tongue-shaped, greenish, narrowing towards tip; pollinia widely diverging, 2mm apart at the top and about 4mm apart at the bottom; spur narrow, to 4.5cm long, flatter and broader towards the tip. Flowers May to July.
SIMILAR SPECIES: Lesser Butterfly-orchid, *P. bifolia*.
HABITAT: Open pine woods and beech woods, poor meadows, mires; calcifuge. To 2,100m.
DISTRIBUTION: European, from northern Spain and central Scandinavia to Ukraine and the Caucasus.
NOTE: Most of the plants earlier thought to be hybrids between *P. bifolia* and *P. chlorantha*, such as Müllers Butterfly-orchid, *P. muelleri*, have, following recent research, been given species status.

3 | Small White Orchid
Pseudorchis albida – Orchidaceae

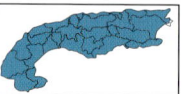

10–30cm tall; leaves 4–8, lower leaves 2–8cm long and 1–2.5cm broad, unspotted; inflorescence 2–12cm long with 20–100 flowers; flowers small, white, yellowish-white or greenish-white; tepals converging hood-like; lip 3-lobed, middle lobe tongue-shaped, blunt, all lobes of almost equal length or the middle lobe protruding; spur 2–3mm long, directed downwards. Flowers June to July.
SIMILAR SPECIES: Musk Orchid, *Herminium monorchis*, has only 2 leaves, and flowers smelling of honey. Calyculate Asphodel, *Tofieldia calyculata* (see p. 440), has narrow, grass-like leaves.
HABITAT: Poor meadows, pasture, open dwarf shrub stands, mires, Cushion Sedge (*Carex firma*) vegetation. 600–2,500m.
DISTRIBUTION: European-Asiatic, from Spain and Scandinavia to Kamchatka.
NOTE: 2 subspecies in the Alps:
– subsp. *albida*: inflorescence with 30–100 flowers; calcifuge.
– subsp. *tricuspis*: inflorescence with 20–30 flowers; calcicole.

4 | Globe Orchid (Round-headed Orchid)
Traunsteinera globosa – Orchidaceae

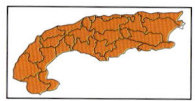

30–60cm tall, slender; green to blue-green, hairless; leaves 4–6, elongate-lanceolate, 5.5–13cm long and 1–3cm broad, distributed along the stem; inflorescence dense and many-flowered, pyramidal in flower, later spherical; flowers pink; lip pink with purple spots, deeply 3-lobed; spur thin, 2.5–3mm long, curved downwards. Flowers June to July.
SIMILAR SPECIES: Three-toothed Orchid, *Neotinea tridentata*, is only 10–30cm tall, has a 5–10mm long spur, and flowers from the end of April to the beginning of June.
HABITAT: Damp poor grassland, calcareous montane meadows, species-rich montane meadows, between loose stands of Dwarf Mountain Pine; calcicole. 300–2,600m.
DISTRIBUTION: Southern European montane. Mountains of north-east Spain to the Crimea.
NAME: Honours Austrian pharmacist Joseph Traunsteiner (1798–1850) from Kitzbühel, who studied the flora of the Tyrol and Vorarlberg.

1 | Mat Grass
Nardus stricta – Poaceae

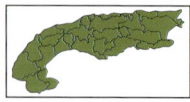

10–30cm tall, forming dense mats; leaves bristly, stiff, grey-green; inflorescence a 3–10cm long, very slender, 1-sided spike; spikelets single-flowered, 7–15mm long, purple. Flowers May to July.
SIMILAR SPECIES: Few.
HABITAT: Acid, poor grassland and pasture, character species of Mat Grass associations; calcifuge. To about 2,900m.
DISTRIBUTION: Eurosiberian.

2 | Alpine Meadow Grass
Poa alpina – Poaceae

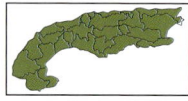

15–40cm tall; base of stem thickened by leaf sheaths; leaves 2–5mm broad, upper leaves with split ligules 2.5–4mm long; flowers consisting of bulbils (pseudovivipary); panicle ± pyramidal, the lower branches spreading; spikelets 5–10-flowered. Flowers June to August.
SIMILAR SPECIES: Mount Cenis Meadow Grass, *P. cenisia*, has 3–5-flowered spikelets, and rounded ligules.
HABITAT: Fertile pasture, livestock resting sites, meadows, stony sward. To 3,600m.
DISTRIBUTION: Eurosiberian–North American.

3 | Round-headed Moor Grass
Sesleria sphaerocephala – Poaceae

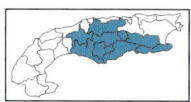

5–20cm tall; leaf blades folded together and bristly; inflorescence spherical, 0.5–1.3cm in diameter, yellowish-white to grey-blue; lemmas without awns, or awns at most 0.5mm long. Flowers July to August.
SIMILAR SPECIES: Oval Moor Grass, *S. ovata*, has lemmas with 5 distinct awns.
HABITAT: Stony grassland, rock debris, rock crevices; calcicole. 1,500–2,800m.
DISTRIBUTION: Eastern alpine endemic.
NAME: In honour of Italian botanist and physician Lionardo Sesler (†1785), who among other things studied the primrose family.

4 | Angular Solomon's-seal
Polygonatum odoratum – Ruscaceae

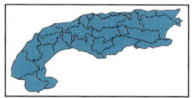

15–50cm tall; stems sharp-edged, unbranched, with leaves in 2 rows to the top; leaves blue-green, ovate-lanceolate, 2–5cm broad; flowers mostly solitary in leaf axils, more rarely 2–3, fragrant; filaments hairless; fruit blue-black. Flowers April to June.
SIMILAR SPECIES: (Eurasian) Solomon's-seal, *P. multiflorum*, has a round stem and is unscented; flowers hanging in groups of 2–5 from leaf axils.
HABITAT: Dry grassland, scrub, scree, open pine woods; calcicole. To about 2,000m.
DISTRIBUTION: European-Asiatic.
NOTE: In some, especially older, floras the lily family was treated more broadly, and also included families such as the Ruscaceae. This was mainly due to the similarity of the flowers, but is not supported by recent phylogenetic findings. The amaryllis and iris families have long been considered as separate families, mainly because of the external features of their inferior ovaries. Extensive research, especially on seeds, embryology, phytochemistry, DNA, etc. has shown that the 'old' lily family included groups that are not that closely related.

5 | Whorled Solomon's-seal
Polygonatum verticillatum – Ruscaceae

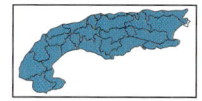

30–100cm tall, unbranched; stem angular; leaves linear-lanceolate, in even whorls; flowers unscented, 2–7, in axils; fruit red, later often blue-black. Flowers May to July.
SIMILAR SPECIES: None.
HABITAT: Woods, tall herb vegetation, spruce forests. To about 2,400m.
DISTRIBUTION: European-Asiatic, from the Arctic Circle in Norway and the Iberian Peninsula to central Europe, Asia Minor, the Caucasus, and Afghanistan.
NOTE: Solomon's-seals are pollinated by bumblebees. The entrance to the flower is closed by the stigma and the closely surrounding anthers so the nectar stored in the base of the flower can only be reached by insects with long proboscids.

Ruscaceae, Tofieldiaceae, Trilliaceae, Uvulariaceae

1 | Lily-of-the-valley
Convallaria majalis – Ruscaceae

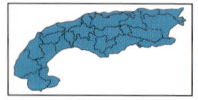

10–25cm tall; leaves 2, one above the other, broadly lanceolate to elliptical, shiny beneath; inflorescence one-sided, with 5–10 flowers; fruit a red berry. Flowers May to June.
SIMILAR SPECIES: The leaves of the (poisonous) Lily-of-the-valley may be confused with those of (edible) Wild Garlic, *Allium ursinum*, but the latter has, among other things, leaves shiny also above, and a strong smell of garlic.
HABITAT: Woods, montane meadows, scree. To about 2,400m.
DISTRIBUTION: European-Asiatic.

2 | May Lily
Maianthemum bifolium – Ruscaceae

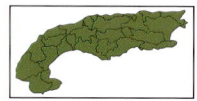

5–15cm tall; stem leaves 2, close together, sessile, heart-shaped; non-flowering plants with only 1 leaf; inflorescence 10–15-flowered; flowers upright; tepals bending backwards; fruit red with purple speckles. Flowers May to June.
SIMILAR SPECIES: None.
HABITAT: Acid woods. To about 2,100m.
DISTRIBUTION: Eurosiberian.

3 | Calyculate Asphodel
Tofieldia calyculata – Tofieldiaceae

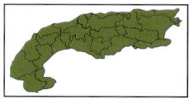

10–30cm tall; leaves 5–10cm long, 4–8mm broad; inflorescence 2–6cm long, 15–40-flowered; bracts entire; flower stalk with 3-partite bract directly beneath the flower; tepals pale greenish-yellow. Flowers June to August.
SIMILAR SPECIES: Dwarf Asphodel, *T. pusilla*.
HABITAT: Spring-fed flushes, damp rocks, fens, wet meadows; calcicole. To about 2,600m.
DISTRIBUTION: European.
NAME: The generic name honours English botanist and hydraulic engineer Thomas Tofield (1730–1779), a contributor to *Flora Anglica*.

4 | Dwarf Asphodel (Scottish Asphodel)
Tofieldia pusilla – Tofieldiaceae

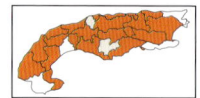

5–10cm tall; leaves 1–5cm long; inflorescence dense, 0.5–1.5cm long, 5–10-flowered; bracts 3-lobed; flower stalk without bract; tepals greenish-white. Flowers July to August.
SIMILAR SPECIES: Calyculate Asphodel, *T. calyculata*, has 5–10cm long leaves, entire bracts and pale greenish-yellow flowers.
HABITAT: Spring-fed mires, snow-melt hollows, rocky sward. 1,800–2,700m.
DISTRIBUTION: Arctic–alpine.

5 | Herb Paris
Paris quadrifolia – Trilliaceae

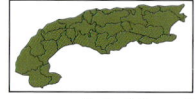

10–30cm tall; stem unbranched, single-flowered; leaves pointed, usually 4, more rarely 5–6, in a whorl high on upper stem; flowers green, with 8 free tepals; fruit a blue-black berry. Flowers April to June.
SIMILAR SPECIES: None.
HABITAT: Riverine and wet woods. To about 1,900m.
DISTRIBUTION: European-Asiatic.

6 | Clasping Twistedstalk
Streptopus amplexifolius – Uvulariaceae

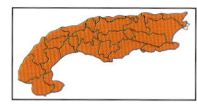

30–100cm tall; stems bending back and forth, often branched; leaves ovate-lanceolate, alternate, clasping the stem; flowers greenish-white, usually solitary, on strikingly-thin, bendy stalks; fruit oval, bright red. Flowers June to July.
SIMILAR SPECIES: Solomon's-seals, *Polygonatum* spp. (see p. 438), have leaves that do not clasp the stem.
HABITAT: Wooded ravines, tall herb vegetation, damp, shady rocky slopes. 800–2,300m.
DISTRIBUTION: European–North American.

Acknowledgements

PHOTO CREDITS

Photos by A. Axmann p. 207 (5B), p. 235 (1), p. 275 (1B); W. Baier p. 29 (2A), p. 41 (4), p. 59 (1B), p. 67 (5), p. 71 (1), p. 73 (3B), p. 179 (2B), p. 211 (5), p. 289 (3), p. 367 (4); Botanik im Bild/H. Wagner p. 379 (5); F. Dunkel p. 39 (2), p. 57 (4), p. 97 (3), p. 121 (4), p. 133 (4), p. 149 (5), p. 169 (3), p. 219 (2/4), p. 227 (1B), p. 237 (1), p. 303 (2), p. 309 (2), p. 365 (5), p. 391 (1), p. 395 (4); W. Franz p. 261 (1), p. 361 (1); M. Futterknecht p. 51 (4A); O. Gerbaud p. 93 (3), p. 227 (1A); M. Grabler p. 55 (4), p. 121 (3); L. Griebl p. 145 (3); G. Gübitz p. 205 (1B), p. 297 (2); P. Hubert p. 23 (5B) , p. 25 (1), p. 69 (1), p. 91 (3B), p. 155 (1A/3/5), p. 183 (4), p. 185 (1A), p. 201 (2A), p. 225 (1B), p. 233 (4), p. 263 (1), p. 269 (2), p. 293 (2), p. 309 (1A/1B), p. 329 (2B), p. 359 (1A), p. 367 (5A), p. 373 (3), p. 389 (1), p. 401 (2/3), p. 411 (5), p. 415 (4), p. 441 (2); D. Jakely p. 59 (1A), p.101 (3), p. 195 (3B), p. 204 (2B), p. 417 (5A), p. 427 (4), p. 437 (1B); F. Kummert p. 305 (3B), p. 311 (5); W. Kussegg p. 29 (4B), p. 33 (1), p. 51 (6A/6B), p. 87 (1A), p. 135 (1/3A), p. 141 (1A), p. 143 (4A), p. 149 (4), p. 151 (2), p. 157 (2), p. 167 (4), p. 181 (4), p. 183 (3B), p. 191 (4B), p. 193 (1A), p. 205 (1), p. 207 (4), p. 211 (3), p. 223 (3), p. 231 (2), p. 239 (2B), p. 275 (3), p. 315 (3), p. 321 (5), p. 327 (1), p. 333 (3), p. 343 (1), p. 351 (3B), p. 363 (5B), p. 367 (2/3B/5B), p. 369 (1), p. 379 (1A), p. 387 (1B), p. 389 (2), p. 393 (3A), p. 399 (5), p. 407 (4), p. 417 (4), p. 425 (3); F. Le Driant p. 39 (5), p. 51 (2), p. 55 (5), p. 213 (4/5), p. 221 (2), p. 349 (4); MarikaStoun/Shutterstock p. 462; mindscapephotos/Shutterstock pp. 443–44; P. Nachbaur p. 105 (2); B. Ocepek p. 119 (1A), p. 339 (2), p. 393 (3B); A. Pleschberger p.137 (1/4/5), p. 139 (2), p. 223 (1/2), p. 225 (5B), p. 231 (1A/3), p. 235 (3), p. 389 (5), p. 395 (2); H. Salzburger p. 83 (4A); K. Schebesta p. 59 (3), p. 101 (4), p. 419 (2), p. 425 (2), p. 435 (2); H. Schön p. 103 (4), p. 119 (2), p. 185 (2A), p. 199 (2), p. 405 (4/5), p. 425 (1); W.Seiche p. 87 (3), p. 115 (5), p. 413 (1); B. Schubert p. 419 (1), p. 423 (2A), p. 435 (3A), p. 437 (2); U. Tinner/FloraFoto p. 371 (4); F. Tod p. 195 (4); G. Tritt-hart p. 25 (4/5B), p. 35 (4), p. 37 (5B), p. 39 (1B), p. 47 (5A), p. 51 (1), p. 57 (1/3), p. 61 (5A), p. 63 (2), p. 75 (3), p. 79 (1/6), p. 81 (2C), p. 87 (4), p. 89 (2), p. 91 (3A/3C), p. 99 (1B), p. 101 (2B/5), p. 113 (3), p. 127 (4C), p. 135 (2A/5), p. 141 (1B), p. 143 (2/4B), p. 149 (1A), S 159 (4B), p. 161 (5), p. 169 (1), p. 179 (2), p. 189 (5A), p. 197 (4), p. 205 (4), p. 211 (6), p. 219 (3B), p. 225 (2), p. 229 (4/6), p. 233 (2), p. 235 (4/5/6B), p. 245 (3), p. 249 (5), p. 251 (4), p. 253 (5), p. 255 (1), p. 259 (3B), p. 265 (1/3), p. 285 (4), p. 289 (2/4), p. 293 (1A/1B), p. 299 (4), p. 301 (2), p. 305 (2A/2B), p. 307 (1), p. 309 (3), p. 333 (2), p. 345 (2), p. 349 (5), p. 351 (5), p. 355 (4), p. 359 (5), p. 361 (2A/2B), p. 367 (1), p. 369 (2), p. 377 (2/4), p. 383 (3), p. 385 (5), p. 387 (1A/2), p. 391 (1B/4), p. 393 (4), p. 403 (6A), p. 407 (1/2/5B), p. 409 (1), p. 411 (1A/2/6), p. 413 (2), p. 427 (1B), p. 429 (2A), p. 433 (1A/3), p. 439 (3); J. Weinzettl p. 77 (1), p. 193 (1B), p. 217 (2), p. 243 (2B), p. 255 (5B), p. 267 (1A), p. 387 (4).

All other photos by Norbert Griebl

THANKS

My sincere thanks go to the many contributors to this book who have helped to make it a success by providing photos and sharing their findings or other information: Andreas Axmann, Dr. Wilhelm Baier, Christina Dombrowski, Dr. Franz-Georg Dunkel, Gerlinde Fischer, Prof. Dr. Manfred A. Fischer, Franz Fohringer, Dr. Wilfried Robert Franz, Albert Fröhlich, Dr. Olivier Gerbaud, Markus Grabler, Lilly Griebl, Prof. Dr. Gerald Gübitz, Ulrich Heidtke, Peter Hubert, Dietmar Jakely, Siegfried Kanitsch, Helene and Rudolf Khun, Fritz Kummert, Walter Kussegg, Peter Nachbaur, Bernhard Ocepek†, Armin Plesch berger, Hubert Salzburger, Karl Schebesta, Hans Schön, Fritz Schreiber, Bernhard Schubert, Lucia Schubert, Werner Seiche, Elfriede Stopper, Josef Stopper†, Franz Tod, Gertrud Tritthart and Josef Weinzettl.

Selected reading

Booker, C. and Charlton, D. 2012. *Mountain Flowers: The Dolomites*. Collett's Mountain Holidays, Saffron Walden.

Booker, C. & Charlton, D. 2017. *Mountain Flowers: Pyrenees and Picos*. Collett's Mountain Holidays, Saffron Walden

Gretler, T. 2023. *Field Guide to Alpine Wildlife*. Bloomsbury Publishing, London.

Hoppe, A. 2013. *A Field Guide to the Flowers of the Alps*. Pelagic Publishing, London.

Kühn, R., Pedersen, H., and Cribb, P. 2024. *Field Guide to the Orchids of Europe and the Mediterranean*. Kew Publishing, London.

Langley, J. and Gannon, P. 2022. *The Alps: A Natural Companion*; Oxford Alpine Club Publishing, Oxford.

Thorogood, C. 2021. *Field Guide to the Wild Flowers of the Western Mediterranean*, 2nd edition. Kew Publishing, London.

ABOUT THE AUTHOR

Norbert Griebl, born in 1969, is a passionate gardener and a 'plant fanatic' since childhood. He has searched tirelessly for the most beautiful flowers of the world – whether on the heights of his local mountains around Stainz, Austria, or in Tierra del Fuego, Patagonia. This love of plants is mirrored in his books, excursions and lectures. Alpine plants fascinate almost all naturalists. The barren, often hostile environment in which they occur, coupled with their frequently bright colours, arouse interest and admiration. On countless mountain visits, Norbert Griebl has captured the flora of the Alps in photographs, and with this book enables the reader to appreciate the diversity of alpine plants, and to identify them correctly.

ABOUT THE TRANSLATOR

Martin Walters is a writer and editor with a particular interest in natural history. He studied zoology at the University of Oxford and was a biology editor at Cambridge University Press. He first encountered German when working as a student gardener in the Munich Botanic Garden, and has travelled to the Alps many times, especially to the alpine foothills of Bavaria. His first publication (with Oleg Polunin) was *A Guide to the Vegetation of Britain and Europe* (Oxford University Press, 1985), since when he has published many books on natural history, and has translated several from German, including *Flowers of the Alps* (Pelagic Publishing, 2013), and most recently *Field Guide to Alpine Wildlife* (Bloomsbury, 2023), and *Owls of Europe* (Bloomsbury, 2024). A keen birdwatcher and botanist, he has travelled widely, in Europe and beyond, watching and studying wildlife.

Index of common names

A
Adenostyles, Alpine 50
  Hedge-leaved 50
  White-leaved 50
Alison, Alpine 108
  Ligurian 108
  Obir 108
  Wulfen's 108
Alkanet, False 100
Alpenrose 192
  Dwarf 192
  Hairy 192
Alplily, Late 414
Ancient King 370
Anemone, Monte Boldo 318
  Narcissus 318
Angelica, Wild 32
Aposeris 52
Archangel, Yellow 246
Arnica 52
Ash, Mountain 354
Asparagus, Narrow-leaved 404
Asphodel, Calyculate 440
  Dwarf 440
  Scottish 440
  White 404
Aster, Alpine 56
  Star 56
Auricula 304
Avens, Alpine 344
  Creeping 344
  Mountain 346
  Water 344

B
Baneberry 320
Barrelier's Bugloss 100
Barrenwort, Alpine 100
Bartsia, Alpine 262
Bastard Balm 246
Bastard-toadflax, Alpine 362
  Pyrenean 362
Bear's Ear 304
Bedstraw Alpine 354
  Col de Tende 356
  Honey 356
  Norican 356
  Swiss 356
  Three-petaled 356
  Traunsee 356

Bellflower, Alpine 134
  Bearded 134
  Beck's 134
  Carniolic Yellow 140
  Clustered Yellow 140
  Crimped 142
  Dolomite 138
  Flax-leaved 134
  Large-flowered 134
  Large-rooted 136
  Lombardy 136
  Mount Cenis 136
  Nettle-leaved 140
  Paniculate 142
  Perforate 136
  Rainer's 138
  Rock 138
  Scheuchzer's 140
  Spiked 140
  Tufted 136
  Witasek's 142
  Zois's 142
Bellflower, Broad-leaved 138
  Solitary 138
Bellflower, Dwarf 136
Bells, Alpine 310
Berardia 56
Betony, Alpine 242
  Yellow 242
Birch, Dwarf 100
Bird's-foot-trefoil, Alpine 206
Bistort, Alpine 296
  Common 296
Bitter-cress, Alpine 112
  Asarabacca-leaved 114
  Coralroot 114
  Drooping 114
  Five-leaflet 116
  Kitaibel's 114
  Large 112
  Mignonette 116
  Pinnate 114
  Stream 116
  Trifoliate 116
  Waldstein's 116
Bittersweet 382
Blue-eyed Mary 104
Bog Stitchwort 176
Bogbean 254
Boomrape Bedstraw 264
  Butterbur 264

  Slender 264
  Thyme 264
Bracken 20
Braya, Alpine 112
Brittle Bladder-fern 20
Brooklime 288
Broom, Hairy 202
  Purple 202
  Southern 202
Broomrape, Monk's-hood 266
  Sage 266
  Thistle 266
  Yellow 266
Buckler-fern, Rigid 22
  Villars' 22
Buckler Mustard, Smooth 112
Buckthorn, Dwarf 340
  Illyrian 340
Bulbous Corydalis 220
Bulrush, Alpine 406
Burnet, Italian 350
Burr-grass, Fine-leaved 34
  South-Tyrol 34
Butterbur, Alpine 86
Buttercup, Aconite-leaved 334
  Alpine 334
  Glacier 336
  Hybrid 336
  Küpfer's 336
  Large White 338
  Mountain 336
  Notched 334
  Parnassus-leaved 336
  Pygmy 338
  Pyrenean 336
  Seguier's 338
  Shield-leaved 338
  Traunfellner's 338
  Two-lobed 334
Butterfly-orchid, Greater 436
  Lesser 436
Butterwort, Alpine 252
  Southern 252

C
Cabbage, Mountain
  Wallflower 118
  Richer's Wallflower 118
Calamint, Alpine 242
  Large-flowered 242

Campion, Betony-leaved 142
   Bladder 174
   Moss 172
   Red 172
   Rock 150
   Short-stemmed Moss 172
Candy Carrot 34
Candytuft, Mont Aurouze 128
   Rock 128
Catchfly, Alpine 160, 176
   Halek's 174
   Heart-leaved 172
   Insubrian 174
   Lower-flowered 172
   Pink-alpine 160
   Small-alpine 160
   Tufted 174
   Valais 174
Cat's-ear, Giant 80
Cat's-foot 52
   Carpathian 52
Chervil, Hairy 36
   Villars' 36
Chickweed-wintergreen 256
Chives 400
Cinquefoil, Alpine 348
   Clusius's 346
   Dauphiné 348
   Dolomite 350
   Dwarf 346
   Eastern 346
   Glacier 348
   Golden 346
   Large-flowered 348
   Limestone 346
   Marsh 344
   Pink 350
   Short-stemmed 346
   Snowy 350
   Valdieri 350
Clasping Twistedstalk 440
Clematis, Alpine 324
   Upright 324
Clover, Alpine 216
   Alpine Zigzag 216
   Brown 216
   Cream 216
   Rock 218
   Rock Mountain 216
   Ruddy 218
   Thal's 218

Clubmoss, Alpine 22
   Fir 24
   Interrupted 24
   Swiss 24
Colt's-foot, Alpine 80
   Purple 80
Columbine, Alpine 320
   Bertolini's 320
   Bulgarian 322
   Common 322
   Dark 320
   Einsele's 320
   Meadow-rue-leaved 322
   Val Vestino 322
Cornflower, Mountain 70
Corydalis, Yellow 220
Cotton Deergrass 406
Cottongrass, Common 408
   Scheuchzer's 408
   White 408
Cow-wheat, Common 262
   East-alpine 262
   Small 262
Cowslip 312
   Mountain 304
Cranesbill, Knotted 236
   Lilac Dusky 236
   River 238
   Rock 236
   Silvery 236
   Wood 238
Creeping Lady's-tresses 426
Cress, Alpine Chamois 126
   Few-flowered Chamois 128
   Garlic 132
Crocus, Illyrian 410
   White 410
Crowfoot, Anemone 324
   Coriander-leaved 324
   Kerner's 324
Crowfoot, Glacier 336
Cudweed, Dwarf 74
   Hoppe's 74
   Norwegian 74
Currant, Alpine 240
Cyclamen, Alpine 256

D

Daffodil, Narrow-leaved 402
   Wild 402
Dandelion, Alpine 96

   Handel's 96
   Hooded 96
Daphne, Alpine 384
   February 384
   Rock 384
   Striped 384
Daylily, Yellow 408
Dead-nettle, Balm-leaved Red 244
   Gargano 244
Devil's Claw, Tufted 142
Dock, Alpine 298
   Snow 298
Dock, Mountain 298
Dog-daisy, Carpathian 52
Dog-violet, Heath 388
Dragonhead, Northern 244
Dragonmouth 244

E

Edelweiss 82
Elder, Red-berried 362
Enchanter's-nightshade, Alpine 256
Eryngo, Alpine 38
   Silver 38
Evergreen Orpine 178
Eyebright, Carinthian 260
   Common 260
   Dwarf 260
   Salzburg 260
   Short-haired 260

F

Fairy's Thimble 136
Felwort, Blue 234
   Marsh 234
Fennel, Giant Hog 46
Fern, Beech 24
   Holly 22
   Oak 22
   Parsley 24
Feverfew, Scentless 94
Figwort, Jura 380
   Hoppe's 380
   Yellow 380
Flax, Alpine 254
   Pyrenean 254
   Sticky 254
   White 254
Fleabane, Alpine 76

Index of common names

Greek 76
One-flowered 76
Schleicher's 76
Variable 76
Fleawort, Brook 96
Capitate Field 96
Long-leaved 98
Southern Alpine 98
Swiss 98
Flowers of Jove 162
Forget-me-not, Alpine 104
Lake Constance 104
Water 104
Wood 104
Fox-and-cubs 84
Glaucous 84
Foxglove, Fairy 284
Large Yellow 282
Purple 282
Small Yellow 282
Straw 282
Fritillary, Alpine 414
Moggridge's Alpine 414
Friuli Spiraea 352

G

Garlic, Crow 400
Field 400
Keeled 398
Lombardy 398
Narcissus-flowered 398
Wild 400
Yellow-flowered 398
Yellow-white 398
Gentian, Austrian 232
Bavarian 224
Bladder 230
Brown 228
Clusius's 224
Cross 224
Dolomites 232
Dwarf 222, 228
Field 234
Fringed 234
Fused-anthered Yellow 226
German 234
Hungarian 228
Isubrian 234
Karawanken 226
Ligurian 226
Narrow-leaved 222

Purple 230
Pygmy 228
Rostan's 230
Rough 232
Round-leaved 228
Schleicher's 230
Short-leaved 224
Slender 222
Snow 228
Spotted 228
Spring 232
Stemless 222
Styrian 224
Tauern 224
Triglav 230
Trumpet 222
Vardjan's Yellow 226
Villar's 232
Willow 222
Yellow 226
Germander, Mountain 250
Pyrenean 250
Wall 250
Gladiolus, Marsh 412
Globe Daisy, Creeping 238
Heart-leaved 238
Leafless-stemmed 238
Globeflower 332
Goat's Beard 344
Golden Apple 416
Golden-drop, Swiss 102
Goldenrod 94
Good-King-Henry 32
Grafia 38
Grass, Alpine Meadow 438
Mat 438
Round-headed Moor 438
Grass-of-Parnassus 282
Green Alder 100
Greenweed, German 202
Hairy 202
Silky 204
Southern 204
Winged 204
Gypsophila, Alpine 160

H

Hard-fern 20
Harebell, Broad-leaved 138
Solitary 138
Hare's-ear, Rock 34

Starry 36
Three-veined 36
Hart's-tongue 20
Hawkbit, Rough 82
Mountain 88
Saffron 88
Swiss 88
Hawk's-beard, Alpine 66
Frölich's 68
Golden 68
Jacquin 68
Mountain 68
Northern 68
Pygmy 70
Pyrenean 66, 70
Triglav 70
Hawkweed, Alpine 78
Endive 78
Glaucous 78
Moris's 78
Rough-leaved 78
Shaggy 80
Whitish 78
Woolly 78
Heather 190
Hellebore, Black 328
Green 328
Stinking 328
Helleborine, Broad-leaved 424
Dark-red 424
Marsh 424
Narrow-leaved 418
Red 418
White False 416
Hemlock, Striped 42
Hemp Nettle, Common 244
Large-flowered 244
Henbane Bell 382
Herb Paris 440
Herb Robert 238
Hogweed, Dwarf 38
Mountain 40
Pink Austrian 40
White Austrian 40
Hollowroot 220
Honeysuckle, Alpine 148
Honeywort, Smooth 100
Horse Mint 246
Hound's-tongue, Common 102
Houseleek, Cobweb 182

Common 184
Hen-and-chickens 178
Large-flowered 182
Limestone 182
Mountain 184
Serpentine 184
Styrian 184
Woolly Cobweb 182
Wulfen's 184

I
Iris, Cento Alto 410
  Dwarf 410
  Grass-leaved 410
  Siberian 410

J
Jacob's Ladder 292
Jacquin's Rush 412
Juniper, Common 28

K
King-of-the-Alps 102
Kingcup 412
Knapweed, Greater 60
  Plume 60
  Short-fringed 60
  Singleflower 60
  Squarrose 70
  Wig 60
Knotgrass, Alpine 296

L
Laburnum, Alpine 206
Lady's-mantle, Alpine 342
  Enns Valley 342
  Hoppe's 342
  Silver 342
  Smooth 342
Lady's-slipper 420
Larch, European 28
Larkspur, Austrian 326
  Dauphiné 326
  Swiss 326
  Tall 326
Lavendar 246
Leafy Goosefoot 32
Leek, Alpine 400
  Round-headed 400
Lentil, Mountain 200
Leopard's-bane, Austrian 70

Clusius's 72
Glacier 72
Great 74
Heart-leaved 72
Large-flowered 72
Torrent 72
Tufted 72
Lettuce, Mountain 80
  Blue 80
  Purple 86
Lily
  -of-the-Valley 440
  Blue Grass 404
  Branched St Bernard's 402
  Carniolan 416
  Fire 416
  Lent 402
  Martagon 416
  May 440
  Orange 416
  Red 416
  Snowdon 414
  St Bernard's 402
  St Bruno's 402
Ling 190
Liverleaf 326
Liverwort 326
Lousewort, Ascending 268
  Beaked 274
  Beakless Red 272
  Crested 268
  Crimson-tipped 272
  Ferb-leaved 268
  Flesh-pink 274
  Hoermann's 270
  Karst 270
  Kerner's 270
  Leafy 268
  Long-beaked Yellow 274
  Marsh 272
  Moor-king 274
  Oeder's 272
  Pink 272
  Portenschlag's 272
  Tall 260
  Tauren 272
  Tuberous 274
  Tufted 270
  Whorled 274
Lovage, Alpine 44
Lungwort, Carnic 106

Hairy 106
Southern 106
Styrian 106
Lupin, Large-leaved 206

M
Marguerite, Black-edged 82
  Mountain 82
  Varied-leaved 82
Marigold, Marsh 322
Marjoram, Wild 246
Marsh-orchid, Flecked 420
  Broad-leaved 422
  Lapland 420
  Narrow-leaved 422
Masterwort 44
  Bavarian 32
  Great 34
  Raibl 44
Meadow-rue, Alpine 340
  French 340
  Greater 340
  Lesser 340
Mezereon 384
Milfoil, Dwarf 50
  Musk 50
Milfoil, Silvery 48
Milk-vetch, Alpine 196
  Foxtail 196
  Inflated 200
  Meadow 212
  Montpellier 198
  Mountain 214
  Northern 212
  Norwegian 200
  Pallid 198
  Purple 198
  Pyrenean 214
  Sainfoin 200
  Silky 212
  Southern 196
  Sprawling 198
  Stemless 198
  Stinking 212
  Swiss 212
  Three-flowered 214
  Tyrolean 198
  Woolly 214
Milkwort, Bitter 294
  Chalk 294
  Mountain 294

Index of common names

Nice 294
Shrubby 294
Monk's-hood, Branched 316
   Common 318
   Manchurian 318
   Narrow-leaved 316
   Three-leaved 318
   Variegated 318
   Yellow 316
Monk's Rhubarb 298
Moon Carrot 46
Moon-daisy, Alpine 84
   Saw-leaved 82
Moonwort 24
Mossy cyphel 166
Mouse-ear, Carinthian 152
   Bell-flowered 152
   Field 150
   Glacier 154
   Pendunculate 152
   Slovenian 156
   Starwort 152
   Woolly 152
Mouse-ear-hawkweed,
   Glacier 84
   Hoppe's 84
Mullein, Alpine 380
   Annual 380
   Boerhaave's 380
   Chaix's 380
   Mountain 382
   Nettle-leaved 380
   White 382

N

Nailwort, Silver 168

O

Onion
   Victory 400
   Wild 400
Orchid, Alpine Dwarf 418
   Archduke Johann's Vanilla 430
   Austrian Vanilla 430
   Bicoloured Vanilla 430
   Bird's-nest 428
   Burnt 428
   Chalk Fragrant 426
   Coralroot 418
   Early Purple 434
   Elder-flowered 422
   Fly 434
   Frog 422
   Ghost 4242
   Globe 436
   Kamnik Alps Vanilla 432
   Lake Garda 434
   Pale-flowered 434
   Pyramidal 418
   Rhellicanus's Vanilla 432
   Round-headed 436
   Short-spurred Fragrant 426
   Small White 436
   Spitzel's 434
   Styrian Vanilla 432
   West-alpine Vanilla 430
   Widder's Vanilla 432
Ox-eye, Showy 94
   Dwarf 94
   Yellow 56
Oxlip 306

P

Paederota, Bluish 286
   Yellow 286
Pansy, Alpine 388
   Argentera 388
   Cavillier's 390
   Comolli's 392
   Duby's 392
   Karawanken 390
   Long-spurred 390
   Mount Cenis 388
   Mountain 392
   Twin-flowered 388
   Valdieri 394
   Villar's 390
   Wild 394
Pasqueflower, Austrian Alpine 328
   Cottian Alpine 330
   Haller's 332
   Many-lobed Alpine 330
   Mountain 332
   Northern Alpine 328
   Schneeberg Alpine 330
   Southern Alpine 330
   Spring 332
   Styrian 332
   Yellow Alpine 330
Pea, Spring 208
   Yellow 208
Pearlwort, Alpine 170
Penny-cress, East Alpine 130
   Kerner's 130
   Round-leaved 132
Peony, Common 278
Perennial Honesty 130
Pimpernel, Yellow 256
Pine, Arolla 28
   Dwarf Mountain 28
Pink, Alpine 154
   Alpine-fringed 158
   Bearded 154
   Carthusian 154
   Common 156
   Fringed 156
   Glacier 156
   Maidan 154
   Painted 156
   Peacock-eye 156
   Seguier's 158
   Short-stalked 158
   Sternberg's 158
   Wood 156
Pirona's Medick 210
Plantain, Fleshy 286
   Dark 286
   Mountain 286
   Silver 286
Pleurospermum, Austrian 46
Poppy, Ernest Mayer's Alpine 278
   Kerner's Alpine 280
   North-eastern Alpine 278
   Rhaetian Alpine 280
   Sendtner's Alpine 280
   Western Alpine 280
Primrose, Bird's-eye 306
   Broad-leaved 308
   Clusis's 306
   Dolomite 312
   Fairy 310
   Glaucous 306
   Grigna 308
   Hairy 308
   Least 310
   Mount Alben 304
   Piedmont 310
   Recoaro 310
   Shaggy 312
   Silver-edged 310

Splendid 312
Sticky 308
Tyrolean 312
Val Daone 306
Viscid 308
Wulfen's 312
Pyramidal Bugle 242
Pyranean Pheasant's-eye 320

R
Ragged-robin 162
Ragwort, Alpine 90
  Carniolan 90
  Chamois 92
  Haller's 92
  Marjoram-leaved 90
  Mountain 94
  Pinnate-leaved 90
  Rock 92
  Spring 92
  Wood 92
Rampion, Chamiel's 142
  Confused 144
  Dark 146
  Globe-headed 144
  Haller's 146
  Horned 146
  Micheli's 144
  Rosette-leaved 144
  Round-headed 144
  Scheuchzer's 146
  Scorzonera-leaved 146
  Sieber's 146
  Spiked 146
Ramsons 400
Red-rattle 272
Restharrow, Mount Cenis 210
  Round-leaved 210
  Shrubby 210
  Yellow 210
Rock-cress, Allioni's 108
Rock-cress, Alpine 110
  Blue 110
  Bohinj 110
  Dwarf 110
  Few-flowered 126
  Soyer's 110
Rock-jasmine, Alpine 300
  Blunt-leaved 302
  Chaix's 300
  Ciliate 300

Dolomite 302
Dwarf 302
Milk-white 302
Pink 300
Swiss 302
Woolly 302
Wulfen's 304
Yellow 304
Rock Kernera 130
Rock-rose, Alpine 176
  Common 176
  Ligurian 176
Rocket, Tansy-leaved 128
Rose, Alpine 352
  Apple 352
  Christmas 328
  Red-leaved 352
Roseroot 178
Rowan 354
Rupturewort, Smooth 160

S
Saffron, Spring Meadow 404
Sage, Saccardo's 248
  Sticky 248
  Wood 250
Sainfoin, Alpine 204
  Briançon 204
  Mountain 210
Saint John's-wort, Alpine 240
  Imperforate 240
  Mountain 240
  Pale 240
  Round-leaved 240
Sandwort, Austrian 162
  Carnic 148
  Carpathian 164
  Changeable 164
  Creeping 166
  Cushion 162
  Fringed 148
  Gerard's 162
  Huter's 148
  Lang's 164
  Larch needled 164
  Large-flowered 148
  Many-stemmed 150
  Marschlins's 150
  Mossy 168
  Narrow-leaved 166
  Rock 166

Sedum-like 168
Short-haired 168
Sickle-leaved 164
South-east Alpine 166
Spring 162
Two-flowered 148
Sanicle, Broad-leaved 38
Saw-wort, Alpine 86
  Dwarf 86
  Heart-leaved 86
  Large-headed 94
Saxifrage, Ascending 362
  Awl-leaved 378
  Blue-green 366
  Burser's 366
  Ciliate 366
  Cobweb 364
  Colli Berici 364
  Columnar 370
  Dolomites 376
  Eastern 376
  Encrusted 368
  Facchini's 370
  Flat-leaved 372
  Fragile 374
  Furrowed 370
  Greater Burnet 46
  Hawk-leaved 370
  Host's 372
  Karst 374
  Leafless 364
  Limestone 368
  Mercantour 370
  Moss 366
  Musky 372
  Nodding 368
  Orange 372
  Paniculate 374
  Piedmont 374
  Purple 372
  Pyramidal 368
  Rough 364
  Round-leaved 376
  Rudolphi's 376
  Scree 364
  Seguier's 376
  Slender 378
  Spoon-leaved 368
  Starry 378
  Styrian 378
  Thick-leaved 368

Index of common names

Tombea 378
Two-flowered 366
Vandelli's 378
Wedge-leaved 362, 368
Wulfen's 374
Yellow 362
Saxifrage Childing Pink 168
Scabiosa, Giant 86
Scabious, Grass-leaved 188
   Long-leaved 186
   Ressman's 186
   Shiny 188
   Soft 186
   South Alpine 186
   Southern 188
   Velvety 188
   Wood 186
Scopolia, European 382
Scurvygrass, Alpine 118, 132
   Pyrenean 118
Sedge, Black Alpine 404
   Curved Alpine 406
   Cushion 406
   Few-flowered 406
   Large Yellow 406
   Monte Baldo 404
Selfheal, Large 248
Senna, Scorpion 206
Seseli, Austrian 46
Shining Lovage 36
Shiny Chervil 32
Shrubby Moltkia 102
Sibbaldia 350
Singleflower Knapweed 60
Skullcap, Alpine 248
Sneezewort, Alpine 50
   Dark-stemmed 48
   Large-leaved 48
Snowbell, Alpine 314
   Austrian 314
   Dwarf 314
   Hungarian 314
   Large 314
   Least 314
Soapwort, Dwarf 170
   Rock 170
   Yellow 170
Solomon's-seal, Angular 438
   Whorled 438
Sorrel, French 298
   Buckler-leaved 298

   Mountain 296
   Sheep's 296
   Wood 278
Sow-thistle, Alpine 80
Speedwell, Alicia's 288
   Alpine 288
   Germander 290
   Heath 288
   Leafless-stemmed 288
   Nettle-leaved 290
   Rock 290
   Shrubby 290
   Spiked 290
   Violet 288
   Water 288
Spignel 42
Spindle-tree, Alpine 178
Spleenwort, Forked 20
   Green 20
Spotted-orchid, Common 420
Spring Heath 190
Spring Snowflake 402
Spurge, Austrian 194
   Carniolan 194
   Cypress 194
   Kerner's 194
   Rock 194
   Variable 192
   Wood 192
Spurge-laurel 384
Squill, Alpine 408
Stalked Willemetia 98
Star-of-Bethlehem, Spiked 408
   Pyrenean 408
Stitchwort, European False 170
Stonecrop, Alpine 180
   Annual 180
   Dark 180
   Hairy 182
   Mountain 182
   Reddish Stonecrop 178
   Round-leaved 178
   Spanish 180
   Thick-leaved 180
Storksbill, Rodie's 236
Sundew, Round-leaved 188
Surmountain, Broad-leaved 42
   French 40

   Gaudin's 42
   Haller's 40
   Hog's Fennel 42
   Narrow-leaved 42
Swallow-wort 48
Sweet Cicely 44
Sweet Rocket 126
Sweet William 154
Sweet William Catchfly 150

T

Tamarisk, German 382
   German False 382
Thistle, Acanthus-leaved
   Carline 62
   Alpine 58
   Carniolic 62
   Dwarf 62
   Great Marsh 58
   Greimler's 66
   Italian 58
   Marsh 66
   Melancholy 64
   Montpellier 64
   Mountain 64
   Musk 58
   South-eastern 56
   Southern Globe 74
   Spiniest 66
   Stemless 62
   Stemless Carline 62
   Tuberos 66
   Woolly 64
   Yellow Melancholy 64
Thread-leaved Water-crowfoot, Mountain 334
Thrift, Alpine 292
   Jersey 292
   Plantain-leaved 292
Thyme, Hairy Wild 252
   Large 252
Toadflax, Alpine 284
   Prostrate 284
   Striped 284
   Tonzig's 284
Tolpis 62
Tormentil 348
Torrent Nakedweed 62
Touch-me-not Balsam 98
Tozzia, Alpine 262
Tragacanth, Mountain 200

Trailing Azalea 190
Treacle-mustard, Italian 124
   Orange 124
   Pale Yellow 124
   Piedmont 124
   Rigid 126
   Wood 124
Tuberous Comfrey 102
Tubular Gagea 414
Tulip, Wild 414
Tunic Flower 168
Twayblade, Common 428
   Lesser 428
Twinflower 254

U
Unbranched Lovage 44

V
Valerian, Celtic 386
   Dwarf 386
   Elongated 386
   Mountain 386
   Rock 386
   Three-lobed 386
Varied-leaved Everlasting-pea 208
Veronica, Bluish 286
   Yellow 286
Vetch, Alpine Kidney 196
   Bitter 208
   Crown 214
   Horseshoe 206
   Monte Cusna 218
   Mountain Kidney 196
   Pale 220
   Pyrenean 220
   Sainfoin 218
   Wood 220
Violet, Alpine 388
   Argentera 388
   Cavillier's 390
   Comolli's 392
   Dame's 126
   Duby's 392
   Karawanken 390
   Long-spurred 390
   Marsh 392
   Mount Cenis 388
   Pinnate 392
   Pyrenean 394
   Thomas's 394
   Twin-flowered 388
   Valdieri 394
   Villar's 390
   Yellow Wood 388
Viper's-grass, Bearded 88
   Rosy 88

W
Water-starwort, Narrow-fruited 282
White Adder's-mouth 426
White Stonecrop 178
Whitebeam, Dwarf 354
Whitlowgrass, Austrian 120
   Carinthian 122
   Downy 122
   Engadine 120
   Hoppe's 120
   Pacher's 122
   Sauter's 122
   Starry 122
   Yellow 120
Whorled Clary 248
Willow, Alpine 358
   Blunt-leaved 360
   Dwarf 358
   Net-leaved 360
   Short-toothed 358
   Smooth 358
   Swiss 358
   Tauern 360
   Waldstein's 360
Willowherb, Alpine 258
   Chickweed 258
   Fleischer's 258
   Rosebay 258
   Rosemary 258
   Whorled-leaved 256
Winter-cress, Pale-yellow 112
Wintergreen, One-flowered 190
   Round-leaved 190
Woad, Alpine 128
Wolf's-bane 316
   South Alpine 316
Wood Horsetail 22
Wood-rush, Alpine 412
   Yellow 412
Woodruff, Neilreich's
   East Alpine 354
   Southern 354
Woody Nightshade 382
Wormwood, Alpine 56
   Chamomile 54
   Common 54
   Dark Alpine 54
   Glacier 54
   Spiked 54
Woundwort, Alpine 250
   Large-lipped-Upright 250
   Limestone 250
   Perennial Yellow 250
Wulfenia 292
   Carinthian 292

Y
Yarrow, Black 48
   Large-leaved 48
   Silvery 48
   Sudetan 48
Yellow-cress, Northern 132
Yellow-rattle
   Alpine 276
   Awned 276
   Greater 276
   Little 276
   Southern 276

Index of scientific names

A

Achillea atrata 48
 clavennae 48
 macrophylla 48
 millefolium subsp. sudetica 48
 moschata 50
 nana 50
 oxyloba 50
Aconitum angustifolium 316
 anthora 316
 degenii 316
 lycoctonum subsp. ranunculifolium 316
 lycoctonum subsp. vulparia 316
 napellus 318
 variegatum 318
Actaea spicata 320
Adenostyles alliariae 50
 alpina 50
 leucophylla 50
Adonis pyrenaica 320
Ajuga pyramidalis 242
Alchemilla alpina 342
 anisiaca 342
 conjuncta 342
 glabra 342
 hoppeana 342
Alliaceae 398–400
Allium carinatum 398
 flavum 398
 insubricum 398
 lusitanicum 398
 narcissiflorum 398
 ochroleucum 398
 oleraceum 400
 schoenoprasum 400
 sphaerocephalon 400
 ursinum 400
 victorialis 400
 vineale 400
Alnus alnobetula 100
Alyssum alpestre 108
 ligusticum 108
 ovirense 108
 wulfenianum 108
Amaranthaceae 32
Amaryllidaceae 402
Anacamptis pyramidalis 418
Anchusa barrelieri 100

Androsace adfinis 300
 alpina 300
 chaixii 300
 chamaejasme 300
 hausmannii 302
 helvetica 302
 lactea 302
 obtusifolia 302
 villosa 302
 vitaliana 304
 wulfeniana 304
Anemonastrum narcissiflorum 318
Anemone baldensis 318
 trifolia 318
Angelica sylvestris 32
Antennaria carpatica 52
 dioica 52
Anthemis carpatica 52
Anthericaceae 402
Anthericum liliago 402
 ramosum 402
Anthriscus nitidus 32
Anthyllis montana 196
 vulneraria subsp. alpicola 196
Aphyllanthaceae 404
Aphyllanthes monspeliensis 404
Apiaceae 32–46
Aposeris foetida 52
Aquilegia alpina 320
 atrata 320
 bertolonii 320
 einseleana 320
 nigricans 322
 thalictrifolia 322
 vestinae 322
 vulgaris 322
Arabis allionii 108
 alpina 110
 caerulea 110
 pumila 110
 soyeri 110
 vochinensis 110
Arenaria biflora 148
 ciliata 148
 grandiflora 148
 huteri 148
 marschlinsii 150
 multicaulis 150

Armeria alpina 292
 arenaria 292
Arnica montana 52
Artemisia absinthium 54
 atrata 54
 chamaemelifolia 54
 genipi 54
 glacialis 54
 mutellina 56
Aruncus dioicus 344
Asclepiadaceae 48
Asparagaceae 404
Asparagus tenuifolius 404
Asperula neilreichii 354
 taurina 354
Asphodelaceae 404
Asphodelus macrocarpus 404
Aspleniaceae 20
Asplenium scolopendrium 20
 septentrionale 20
 viride 20
Aster alpinus 56
Asteraceae 48–98
Astragalus alopecurus 196
 alpinus 196
 australis 196
 depressus 198
 exscapus 198
 frigidus 198
 hypoglottis 198
 leontinus 198
 monspessulanus 198
 norvegicus 200
 onobrychis 200
 penduliflorus 200
 sempervirens 200
 vesicarius 200
Astrantia bavarica 32
 major 34
Athamanta cretensis 34
 turbith 34
 vestina 34
Atocion armeria 150
 rupestre 150

B

Balsaminaceae 98
Barbarea bracteosa 112
Bartsia alpina 262
Bellidiastrum michelii 56
Berardia subacaulis 56

Berberidaceae 98
Betonica alopecuros 242
  hirsuta 242
Betula nana 100
Betulaceae 100
Biscutella laevigata 112
Blechnaceae 20
Blechnum spicant 20
Boraginaceae 100-2
Botrychium lunaria 24
Brassicaceae 108-32
Braya alpina 112
Buphthalmum salicifolium 56
Bupleurum petraeum 34
  ranunculoides 36
  stellatum 36

C

Callianthemum anemonoides 324
  coriandrifolium 324
  kernerianum 324
Callitriche palustris 282
Calluna vulgaris 190
Caltha palustris 322
Campanula alpestris 134
  alpina 134
  barbata 134
  beckiana 134
  carnica 134
  cenicia 136
  cespitosa 136
  cochleariifolia 136
  elatinoides 136
  excisa 136
  macrorhiza 136
  morettiana 138
  petraea 138
  pulla 138
  raineri 138
  rhomboidalis 138
  scheuchzeri 140
  spicata 140
  thyrsoides subsp. *carniolica* 140
  thyrsoides subsp. *thyrsoides* 140
  trachelium 140
  witasekiana 142
  zoysii 142
Campanulaceae 134-46

Caprifoliaceae 148
Cardamine alpina 112
  amara 112
  asarifolia 114
  bulbifera 114
  enneaphyllos 114
  heptaphylla 114
  kitaibelii 114
  pentaphyllos 116
  resedifolia 116
  rivularis 116
  trifolia 116
  waldsteinii 116
Carduus carduelis 56
  defloratus 58
  litigiosus 58
  nutans 58
  personata 58
Carex atrata 404
  baldensis 404
Carlina acanthifolia 62
  acaulis 62
Caryophyllaceae 148-76
Centaurea nervosa 60
  nigrescens 60
  pseudophrygia 60
  scabiosa 60
  uniflora 60
Cephalanthera longifolia 418
  rubra 418
Cerastium arvense subsp. *strictum* 150
  carinthiacum 152
  cerastoides 152
  eriophorum 152
  pedunculatum 152
  subtriflorum 152
  uniflorum 154
Cerinthe alpina 100
Chaerophyllum hirsutum 36
  villarsii 36
Chamaecytisus hirsutus 202
  purpureus 202
Chamorchis alpina 418
Chenopodium bonus-henricus 32
  foliosum 32
Chondrilla chondrilloides 62
Circaea alpina 256
Cirsium acaule 62
  carniolicum 62

  eriophorum 64
  erisithales 64
  greimleri 66
  heterophyllum 64
  monspessulanum 64
  montanum 64
  palustre 64
  spinosissimum 66
  tuberosum 66
Cistaceae 176
Clematis alpina 324
  recta 324
Clinopodium alpinum 242
  grandiflorum 242
Cochlearia excelsa 118
  pyrenaica 118
Coincya cheiranthos subsp. *montana* 118
  richeri 118
Colchicaceae 404
Colchicum vernum 404
Comarum palustre 344
Comastoma nanum 222
  tenellum 222
Convallaria majalis 440
Corallorhiza trifida 418
Coristospermum lucidum sub sp. *seguieri* 36
Corydalis cava 220
Crassulaceae 178-84
Crepis albida 66
  alpestris 66
  aurea 68
  froelichiana 68
  jacquinii 68
  mollis 68
  pontana 68
  pygmaea 70
  pyrenaica 70
  terglouensis 70
Crocus albiflorus 410
  exiguus 410
Cryptogramma crispa 24
Cupressaceae 28
Cyanus montanus 70
  triumfettii 70
Cyclamen purpurascens 256
Cynoglossum officinale 102
Cyperaceae 404-8
Cypripedium calceolus 420
Cystopteris fragilis 20

Index of scientific names

Cytisophyllum sessilifolium 202

D

Dactylorhiza cruenta 420
   fuchsii 420
   lapponica 420
   majalis 422
   sambucina 422
   traunsteineri 422
   viridis 422
Daphne alpina 384
   laureola 384
   mezereum 384
   petraea 384
   striata 384
Delphinium dubium 326
   elatum subsp. *austriacum* 326
   elatum subsp. *elatum* 326
   elatum subsp. *helveticum* 326
Dennstaedtiaceae 20
Dianthus alpinus 154
   barbatus 154
   carthusianorum 154
   deltoides 154
   furcatus 156
   glacialis 156
   hyssopifolius 156
   pavonius 156
   plumarius 156
   seguieri 158
   sternbergii 158
   subacaulis 158
   superbus subsp. *alpestris* 158
   sylvestris 156
Digitalis grandiflora 282
   lutea 282
   purpurea 282
Diphasiastrum alpinum 22
Dipsacaceae 186–8
Doronicum austriacum 70
   cataractarum 72
   clusii 72
   columnae 72
   glaciale 72
   grandiflorum 72
   pardalianches 74
Draba aizoides 120
   dubia 120
   hoppeana 120
   ladina 120
   pacheri 122
   sauteri 122
   siliquosa 122
   stellata 122
   tomentosa 122
Dracocephalum ruyschiana 244
Drosera rotundifolia 188
Droseraceae 188
Dryas octopetala 346
Dryopteridaceae 20–2
Dryopteris villarii 22

E

Echinops ritro 74
Epilobium alpestre 256
   alsinifolium 258
   anagallidifolium 258
   angustifolium 258
   dodonaei 258
   fleischeri 258
Epimedium alpinum 100
Epipactis atrorubens 424
   helleborine 424
   palustris 424
Epipogium aphyllum 424
Equisetaceae 22
Equisetum sylvaticum 22
Erica carnea 190
Ericaceae 190–2
Erigeron alpinus 76
   atticus 76
   glabratus 76
   schleicheri 76
   uniflorus 76
Erinus alpinus 284
Eriophorum angustifolium 408
   scheuchzeri 408
Eritrichium nanum 102
Erodium rodiei 236
Eryngium alpinum 38
   spinalba 38
Erysimum aurantiacum 124
   jugicola 124
   ochroleucum 124
   rhaeticum 124
   sylvestre 124
   virgatum 126
Erythronium dens-canis 412
Euonymus latifolius 178
Euphorbia amygdaloides 192
   austriaca 194
   carniolica 194
   cyparissias 194
   saxatilis 194
   triflora subsp. *kerneri* 194
   variabilis 192
Euphorbiaceae 192–4
Euphrasia cuspidata 260
   minima 260
   officinalis 260
   salisburgensis 260
   stricta 260

F

Fabaceae 196–220
Fourraea alpina 126
Fritillaria tubaeformis subsp. *moggridgei* 414
   tubaeformis subsp. *tubaeformis* 414
Fumariaceae 220

G

Gagea liotardii 414
   serotina 414
Galeopsis speciosa 244
   tetrahit 244
Galium anisophyllon 354
   megalospermum 356
   meliodorum 356
   noricum 356
   tendae 356
   trifidum 356
   truniacum 356
Genista germanica 202
   pilosa 202
   radiata 204
   sagittalis 204
   sericea 204
Gentiana acaulis 222
   angustifolia 222
   asclepiadea 222
   bavarica 224
   brachyphylla 224
   clusii 224
   cruciata 224
   frigida 224
   froelichii 226

ligustica 226
lutea subsp. lutea 226
lutea subsp. symphyandra 226
lutea subsp. vardjanii 226
nivalis 228
orbicularis 228
pannonica 228
prostrata 228
pumila 228
punctata 228
purpurea 230
rostanii 230
schleicheri 230
terglouensis 230
utriculosa 230
verna 232
villarsii 232
Gentianaceae 222–34
Gentianella anisodonta 232
aspera 232
austriaca 232
campestris 234
germanica 234
insubrica 234
Gentianopsis ciliata 234
Geraniaceae 236–8
Geranium argenteum 236
macrorrhizum 236
nodosum 236
phaeum subsp. lividum 236
rivulare 238
robertianum 238
sylvaticum 238
Geum montanum 344
reptans 344
rivale 344
Gladiolus palustris 412
Globularia cordifolia 238
nudicaulis 238
repens 238
Globulariaceae 238
Gnaphalium hoppeanum 74
norvegicum 74
supinum 74
Goodyera repens 426
Grafia golaka 38
Grossulariaceae 240
Gymnadenia conopsea 426
odoratissima 426
Gymnocarpium dryopteris 22

Gypsophila, repens 160

H

Hacquetia epipactis 38
Hedysarum brigantiacum 204
hedysaroides 204
Helianthemum alpestre 176
lunulatum 176
nummularium 176
Heliosperma alpestre 160
pusillum subsp. pudibundum 160
pusillum subsp. pusillum 160
Helleborus foetidus 328
niger 328
viridis 328
Hemerocallidaceae 408
Hemerocallis lilioasphodelus 408
Hepatica nobilis 326
Heracleum austriacum subsp. austriacum 40
austriacum subsp. siifolium 40
pumilum 38
sphondylium subsp. elegans 40
Herniaria glabra 160
Hesperis matronalis 126
Hieracium alpinum 78
glaucum 78
intybaceum 78
pilosum 78
prenanthoides 78
tomentosum 78
villosum 78
Hippocrepis comosa 206
emerus 206
Homogyne alpina 80
Horminum pyrenaicum 244
Hornungia alpina 126
pauciflora 128
Hugueninia tanacetifolia 128
Huperzia selago 24
Hyacinthaceae 408
Hylotelephium anacampseros 178
Hypericaceae 240
Hypericum maculatum 240
montanum 240

nummularium 240
richeri 240
Hypochaeris uniflora 80

I

Iberis aurosica 128
saxatilis 128
Impatiens noli-tangere 98
Iridaceae 410–12
Iris graminea 410
pallida subsp. cengialti 410
pumila 410
sibirica 410
Isatis alpina 128

J

Jovibarba globifera 178
Juncaceae 412
Juncus jacquinii 412
Juniperus communis 28

K

Kalmia procumbens 190
Kernera saxatilis 130
Knautia longifolia 186
maxima 186
mollis 186
ressmannii 186
transalpina 186
velutina 188

L

Laburnum alpinum 206
Lactuca alpina 80
perennis 80
Lamiaceae 242–52
Lamiastrum montanum 246
Lamium garganicum 244
orvala 244
Larix decidua 28
Laserpitium gallicum 40
halleri 40
krapfii subsp. gaudinii 42
latifolium 42
peucedanoides 42
siler 42
Lathyrus heterophyllus 208
laevigatus 208
linifolius 208
vernus 208
Lavandula angustifolia 246

Index of scientific names

Lentibulariaceae 252
Leontodon hispidus 82
Leontopodium alpinum 82
Leucanthemopsis alpina 84
Leucanthemum adustum 82
   atratum 82
   heterophyllum 82
Leucojum vernum 402
Liliaceae 412–16
Lilium bulbiferum 416
   carniolicum 416
   martagon 416
   pomponium 416
Linaceae 254
Linaria alpina 284
   repens 284
   supina 284
   tonzigii 284
Linnaea borealis 254
Linnaeaceae 254
Linum alpinum 254
   suffruticosum 254
   viscosum 254
Lomatogonium carinthiacum 234
Lomelosia graminifolia 188
Loncomelos pyrenaicus 408
Lonicera alpigena 148
Lotus alpinus 206
Lunaria rediviva 130
Lupinus polyphyllus 206
Luzula alpinopilosa 412
   lutea 412
   nivea 412
Lychnis flos-cuculi 162
   flos-jovis 162
Lycopodiaceae 22–4
Lycopodium annotinum 24
Lysimachia nemorum 256

M

Maianthemum bifolium 440
Malaxis monophyllos 426
Medicago pironae 210
Melampyrum pratense 262
   subalpinum 262
   sylvaticum 262
Melanthiaceae 416
Melittis melissophyllum 246
Mentha longifolia 246
Menyanthaceae 254

Menyanthes trifoliata 254
Meum athamanticum 42
Minuartia austriaca 162
   cherlerioides 162
   gerardii 162
   langii 164
   laricifolia 164
   mutabilis 164
   recurva 164
   rupestris 166
   sedoides 166
Moehringia bavarica 166
   ciliata 166
   diversifolia 166
   muscosa 168
   sedoides 168
   villosa 168
Molopospermum peloponnesiacum 42
Moltkia suffruticosa 102
Moneses uniflora 190
Mutellina adonidifolia 44
Myosotis alpestris 104
   rehsteineri 104
   scorpioides 104
   sylvatica 104
Myricaria germanica 382
Myrrhis odorata 44
Myrsinaceae 256

N

Narcissus pseudonarcissus 402
   radiiflorus 402
Nardus stricta 438
Nigritella archiducis-joannis 430
   austriaca 430
   bicolor 430
   corneliana 430
   lithopolitanica 432
   rhellicani 432
   stiriaca 432
   widderi 432
Noccaea crantzii 130
   minima 130
   rotundifolia 132

O

Omphalodes verna 104
Onagraceae 256

Onobrychis montana 210
Ononis cristata 210
   fruticosa 210
   natrix 210
   rotundifolia 210
Onosma helvetica 102
Ophioglossaceae 24
Ophrys benacensis 434
   insectifera 434
Orchidaceae 418–36
Orchis mascula 434
   pallens 434
   spitzelii 434
Origanum vulgare 246
Orobanchaceae 260–76
Orobanche alba 264
   caryophyllacea 264
   flava 264
   gracilis 264
   lutea 266
   lycoctoni 266
   reticulata 266
   salviae 266
Oxalidaceae 278
Oxalis acetosella 278
Oxyria digyna 296
Oxytropis campestris 212
   fetida 212
   halleri 212
   helvetica 212
   lapponica 212
   montana 214
   neglecta 214
   pilosa 214
   triflora 214

P

Pachypleurum mutellinoides 44
Paederota bonarota 286
   lutea 286
Paeonia officinalis 278
Paeoniaceae 278
Papaver alpinum subsp. alpinum 278
   alpinum subsp. *ernesti-mayeri* 278
   alpinum subsp. *kerneri* 280
   alpinum subsp. *occidentale* 280

alpinum subsp. *rhaeticum* 280
alpinum subsp. *sendtneri* 280
Papaveraceae 278–80
Paradisea liliastrum 402
Paris quadrifolia 440
Parnassia palustris 282
Parnassiaceae 282
Paronychia kapela 168
Pedicularis ascendens 268
  aspleniifolia 268
  comosa 268
  elongata 268
  foliosa 268
  gyroflexa 270
  hacquetii 270
  hoermanniana 270
  kerneri 270
  oederi 272
  palustris 272
  portenschlagii 272
  recutita 272
  rosea 272
  rostratocapitata 274
  rostratospicata 274
  sceptrum-carolinum 274
  tuberosa 274
  verticillata 274
Peltaria alliacea 132
Persicaria alpina 296
  bistorta 296
  vivipara 296
Petasites paradoxus 86
Petrorhagia saxifraga 168
Peucedanum ostruthium 44
  rablense 44
  verticillare 46
Phegopteris connectilis 24
Physoplexis comosa 142
Phyteuma betonicifolium 142
  charmelii 142
  confusum 144
  globulariifolium 144
  hemisphaericum 144
  michelii 144
  orbiculare 144
  ovatum 146
  scheuchzeri 146
  scorzonerifolium 146
  sieberi 146
  spicatum 146
Pilosella angustifolia 84
  aurantiaca 84
  hoppeana 84
  lactucella 84
Pimpinella major 46
Pinaceae 28
Pinguicula alpina 252
  leptoceras 252
Pinus cembra 28
  mugo 28
Plantaginaceae 282–92
Plantago argentea 286
  atrata 286
  strictissima 286
Platanthera bifolia 436
  chlorantha 436
Pleurospermum austriacum 46
Plumbaginaceae 292
Poa alpina 438
Poaceae 438
Polemoniaceae 292–8
Polemonium caeruleum 292
Polygala alpestris 294
  amara 294
  calcarea 294
  chamaebuxus 294
  nicaeensis 294
Polygonatum odoratum 438
  verticillatum 438
Polystichum lonchitis 22
Potentilla aurea 346
  brauneana 346
  caulescens 346
  clusiana 346
  crantzii 348
  delphinensis 348
  erecta 348
  frigida 348
  grandiflora 348
  nitida 350
  nivea 350
  valderia 350
Prenanthes purpurea 86
Primula albenensis 304
  auricula 304
  clusiana 306
  daonensis 306
  elatior 306
  farinosa 306
  glaucescens 306
  glutinosa 308
  grignensis 308
  hirsuta 308
  latifolia 308
  marginata 310
  matthioli 310
  minima 310
  pedemontana 310
  recubariensis 310
  spectabilis 312
  tyrolensis 312
  veris 312
  villosa 312
  wulfeniana 312
Primulaceae 300–14
Prunella grandiflora 248
Pseudofumaria lutea 220
Pseudorchis albida 436
Pseudostellaria europaea 170
Pteridaceae 24
Pteridium aquilinum 20
Pulmonaria australis 106
  carnica 106
  mollis 106
  stiriaca 106
Pulsatilla alpina subsp. *alba* 328
  alpina subsp. *alpina* 328
  alpina subsp. *apiifolia* 330
  alpina subsp. *austroalpina* 330
  alpina subsp. *cottianaea* 330
  alpina subsp. *millefoliata* 330
  alpina subsp. *schneebergensis* 330
  halleri 332
  montana 332
  styriaca 332
  vernalis 332
Pyrola rotundifolia 190

R

Ranunculaceae 316–40
Ranunculus aconitifolius 334
  alpestris 334
  bilobus 334
  confervoides 334
  crenatus 334

Index of scientific names

glacialis 336
hybridus 336
kuepferi 336
montanus 336
parnassifolius 336
platanifolius 338
pygmaeus 338
seguieri 338
thora 338
traunfellneri 338
Rhamnaceae 340
Rhamnus fallax 340
pumila 340
Rhaponticum scariosum 86
Rhinanthus alectorolophus 276
alpinus 276
glacialis 276
minor 276
ovifugus 276
Rhizobotrya alpina 132
Rhodiola rosea 178
Rhododendron ferrugineum 192
hirsutum 192
Rhodothamnus chamaecistus 192
Ribes alpinum 240
Rorippa islandica 132
Rosa glauca 352
pendulina 352
villosa 352
Rosaceae 342–54
Rubiaceae 354–6
Rumex acetosella 296
alpestris 298
alpinus 298
nivalis 298
scutatus 298
Ruscaceae 438–40

S

Sagina saginoides 170
Salicaceae 358–60
Salix alpina 358
breviserrata 358
glabra 358
helvetica 358
herbacea 358
mielichhoferi 360
reticulata 360

retusa 360
waldsteiniana 360
Salvia glutinosa 248
saccardiana 248
verticillata 248
Sambucaceae 362
Sambucus racemosa 362
Sanguisorba dodecandra 350
Santalaceae 362
Saponaria lutea 170
ocymoides 170
pumila 170
Saussurea alpina 86
discolor 86
pygmaea 86
Saxifraga adscendens 362
aizoides 362
androsacea 364
aphylla 364
arachnoidea 364
aspera 364
berica 364
biflora 366
blepharophylla 366
bryoides 366
burseriana 366
caesia 366
callosa 368
cernua 368
cotyledon 368
crustata 368
cuneifolia 368
diapensioides 370
exarata 370
facchinii 370
florulenta 370
hieraciifolia 370
hostii 372
moschata 372
muscoides 372
mutata 372
oppositifolia 372
paniculata 374
paradoxa 374
pedemontana 374
petraea 374
retusa 374
rotundifolia 376
rudolphiana 376
sedoides 376
seguieri 376

squarrosa 376
stellaris subsp. robusta 378
styriaca 378
tenella 378
tombeanensis 378
vandellii 378
Saxifragaceae 362–78
Scabiosa lucida 188
triandra 188
Scilla bifolia s. lat. 408
Scopolia carniolica 382
Scorzonera aristata 88
rosea 88
Scorzoneroides crocea 88
helvetica 88
montana 88
Scrophularia juratensis 380
vernalis 380
Scrophulariaceae 380–2
Scutellaria alpina 248
Securigera varia 214
Sedum album 178
alpestre 180
annuum 180
atratum 180
dasyphyllum 180
hispanicum 180
montanum 182
villosum 182
Selaginella helvetica 24
Selaginellaceae 24
Sempervivum arachnoideum subsp. *arachnoideum* 182
arachnoideum subsp. tomentosum 182
calcareum 182
grandiflorum 182
montanum 184
pittonii 184
stiriacum 184
tectorum 184
wulfenii 184
Senecio abrotanifolius 90
cacaliaster 90
carniolicus 90
cordatus 90
doronicum 92
fontanicola 92
halleri 92
ovatus 92
rupestris 92

subalpinus 94
Serratula macrocephala 94
Seseli austriacum 46
   libanotis 46
Sesleria sphaerocephala 438
Sibbaldia procumbens 350
Silene acaulis subsp. exscapa 172
   acaulis subsp. longiscapa 172
   cordifolia 172
   dioica 172
   elisabethae 172
   hayekiana 174
   nutans subsp. insubrica 174
   saxifraga 174
   vallesia 174
   vulgaris 174
Solanaceae 382
Solanum dulcamara 382
Soldanella alpina 314
   austriaca 314
   major 314
   minima 314
   pusilla 314
Solidago virgaurea 94
Sorbus aucuparia 354
   chamaemespilus 354
Spiraea decumbens 352
Stachys alpina 250
Stachys recta subsp. labiosa 250
Stellaria alsine 176
Streptopus amplexifolius 440
Swertia perennis 234
Symphytum tuberosum 102

T

Tamaricaceae 382
Tanacetum corymbosum subsp. subcorymbosum 94
Taraxacum handelii 96
   sect. Alpina 96
   sect. Cucullata 96
Telekia speciosissima 94
Tephroseris crispa 96
   integrifolia subsp. capitata 96
   longifolia 98
   pseudocrispa 98
   tenuifolia 98

Teucrium chamaedrys 250
   montanum 250
   pyrenaicum 250
   scorodonia 250
Thalictrum acquilegiifolium 340
   alpinum 340
   minus 340
Thelypteridaceae 24
Thesium alpinum 362
   pyrenaicum 362
Thymelaeaceae 384
Thymus praecox subsp. polytrichus 252
   pulegioides 252
Tofieldia calyculata 440
   pusilla 440
Tofieldiaceae 440
Tolpis staticifolia 62
Tozzia alpina 262
Traunsteinera globosa 436
Trientalis europaea 256
Trifolium alpestre 216
   alpinum 216
   badium 216
   montanum subsp. rupestre 216
   noricum 216
   rubens 218
   saxatile 218
   thalii 218
Trilliaceae 440
Trochiscanthes 48
Trochiscanthes nodiflora 48
Trollius europaeus 332
Tulipa sylvestris 414

U

Uvulariaceae 440

V

Valeriana celtica 386
   elongata 386
   montana 386
   saxatilis 386
   supina 386
   tripteris 386
Valerianaceae 386
Veratrum album 416
Verbascum alpinum 380
   boerhavii 380

   chaixii 380
   crassifolium 382
   lychnitis 382
Veronica allionii 288
   alpina 288
   aphylla 288
   beccabunga 288
   bellidioides 288
   chamaedrys 290
   fruticans 290
   fruticulosa 290
   officinalis 288
   spicata 290
   urticifolia 290
Vicia cusnae 218
   onobrychioides 218
   oroboides 220
   pyrenaica 220
   sylvatica 220
Vincetoxicum hirundinaria 48
Viola alpina 388
   argenteria 388
   biflora 388
   calcarata subsp. calcarata 390
   calcarata subsp. cavillieri 390
   calcarata subsp. villarsiana 390
   calcarata subsp. zoysii 390
   canina 388
   cenisia 388
   comollia 392
   dubyana 392
   lutea 392
   palustris 392
   pinnata 392
   pyrenaica 394
   thomasiana 394
   tricolor 394
   valderia 394
Violaceae 388–94
Viscaria alpina 176

W

Willemetia stipitata 98
Wulfenia carinthiaca 292

BLOOMSBURY WILDLIFE

Bloomsbury Publishing Plc

50 Bedford Square, London, WC1B 3DP, UK

Bloomsbury Publishing Ireland Limited

29 Earlsfort Terrace, Dublin 2, D02 AY28, Ireland

BLOOMSBURY, BLOOMSBURY WILDLIFE and the Diana logo are trademarks of Bloomsbury Publishing Plc

First published in the United Kingdom by Bloomsbury Publishing, 2025

This edition published by arrangement with Franckh-Kosmos Verlags-GmbH & Co. KG, Stuttgart, Germany

First published in 2022 in Germany as *Alpen Flora* by Franckh-Kosmos Verlags-GmbH & Co. KG © Franckh-Kosmos Verlags-GmbH & Co. KG, Stuttgart, Germany, 2022

Translation © Martin Walters, 2025

Cover image © Scisetti Alfio and Shutterstock

Norbert Griebl has asserted his right under the Copyright, Designs and Patents Act, 1988, to be identified as Author of this work

All rights reserved. No part of this publication may be: i) reproduced or transmitted in any form, electronic or mechanical, including photocopying, recording or by means of any information storage or retrieval system without prior permission in writing from the publishers; or ii) used or reproduced in any way for the training, development or operation of artificial intelligence (AI) technologies, including generative AI technologies. The rights holders expressly reserve this publication from the text and data mining exception as per Article 4(3) of the Digital Single Market Directive (EU) 2019/790.

A catalogue record for this book is available from the British Library

ISBN: PB: 978-1-3994-1988-8; ePub: 978-1-3994-1986-4;
ePDF: 978-1-3994-1989-5

Layout for this edition by Rod Teasdale

Bloomsbury Publishing Plc makes every effort to ensure that the papers used in the manufacture of our books are natural, recyclable products made from wood grown in well-managed forests. Our manufacturing processes conform to the environmental regulations of the country of origin.

To find out more about our authors and books visit www.bloomsbury.com and sign up for our newsletters. For product safety related questions contact productsafety@bloomsbury.com